AF473784

# THE WORLD IN THE EYE OF A FANTASY ARTIST

## Live from Weiye Yin's Scene Creation

By Weiye Yin

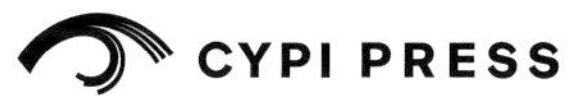

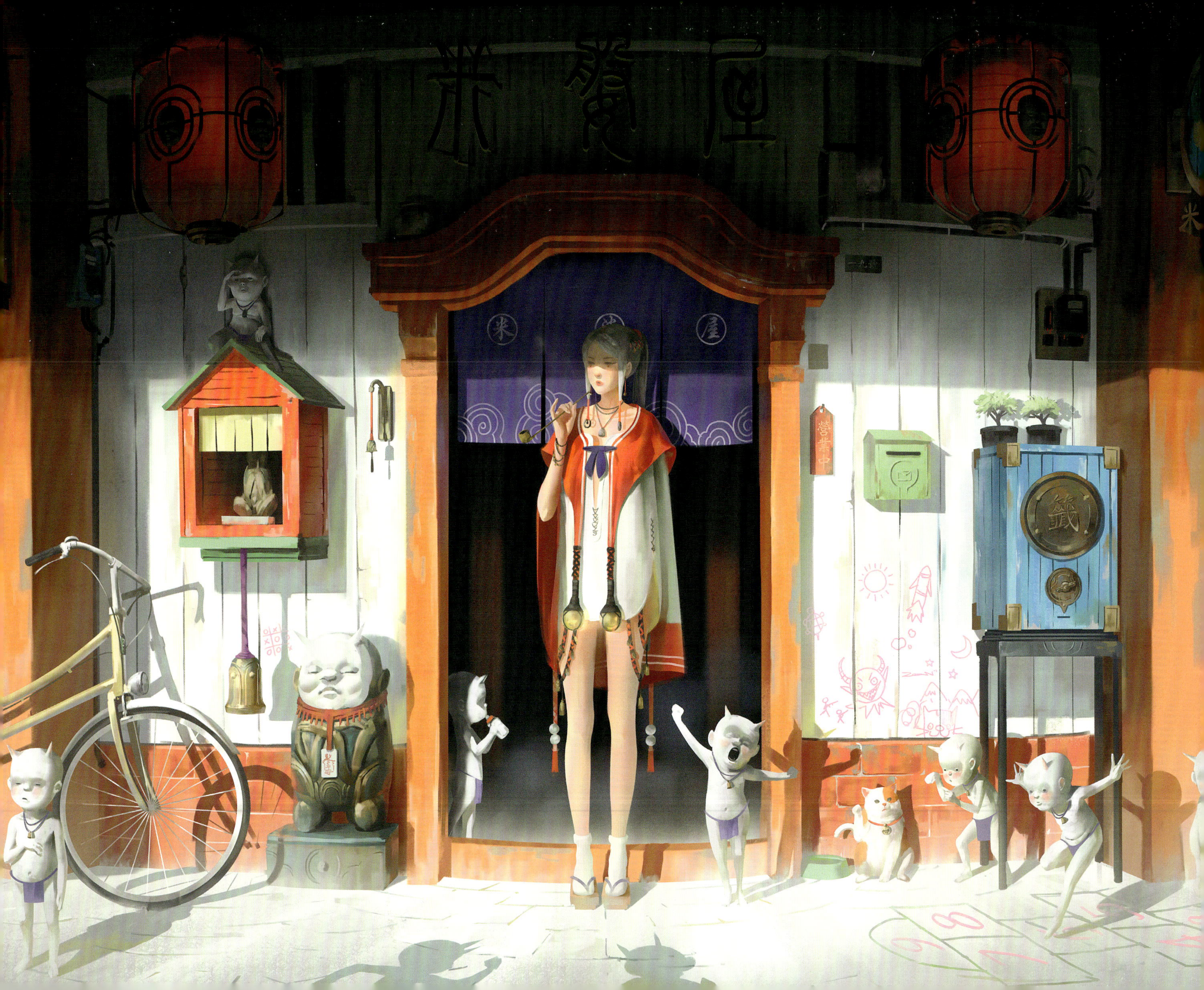
営業中

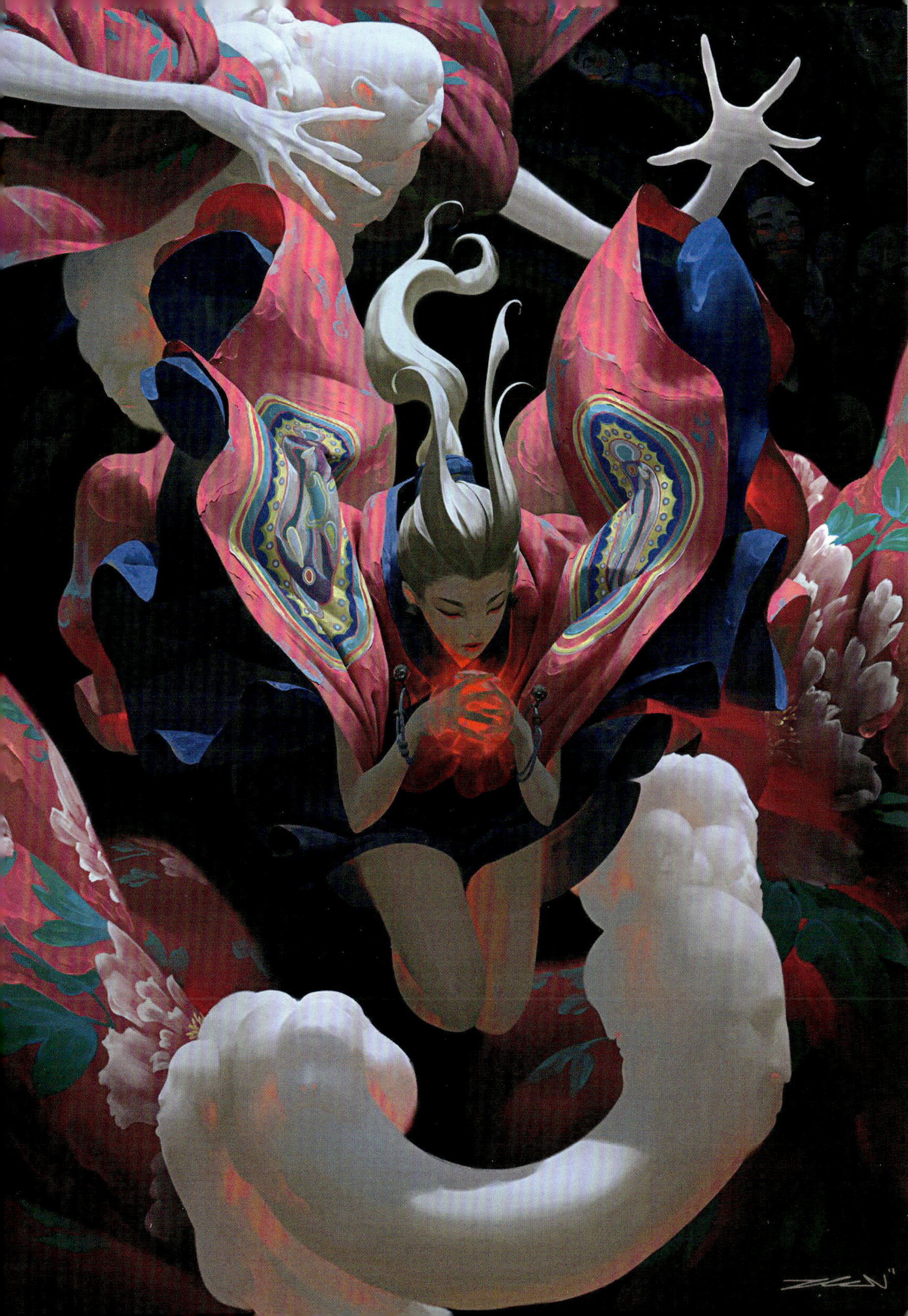

# PREFACE

First of all, I must admit that I am not an artist who likes scene sketching. That does not mean I hate scene sketching but that it is too difficult, so I always admire artists who excel at this kind of art. Most people consider sketched scenes lacking in content. But that is not at all the case. In fact, I highly recommend this collection of scene sketches exactly because the efforts of the artist Weiye Yin to consider and research each and every last detail are so apparent in how the pieces look and feel. I hope everyone gets the chance to enjoy his designs in this book and be transported to a wholly new art world.

Zeen Chin
Freelance Illustrator
Malaysia

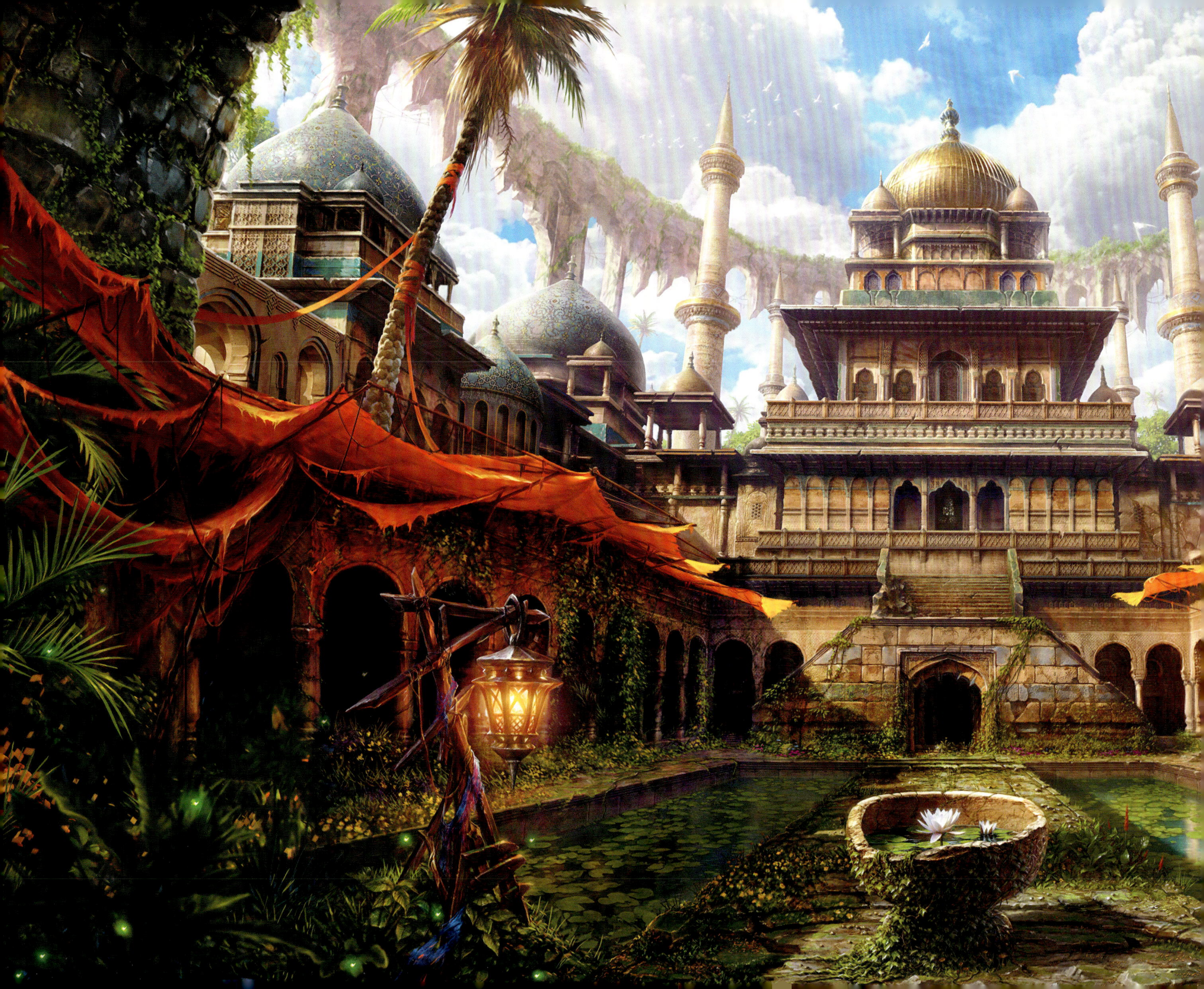

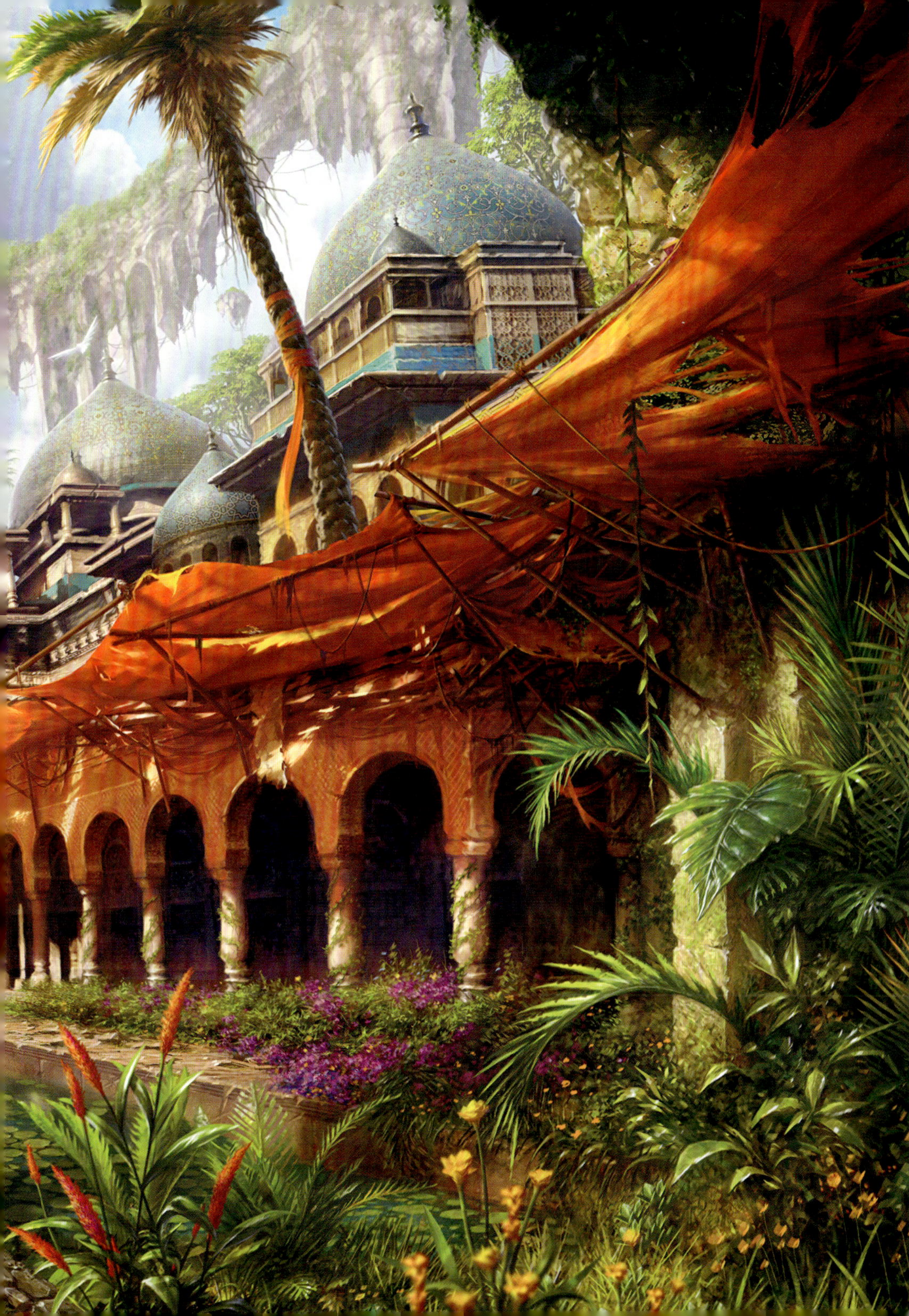

# OVERVIEW

This is not simply a book of illustrations or a collection of scenes. Besides design techniques and all kinds of landscape depictions, these pages are informed by what I saw and heard on my travels with a view to providing some wider cultural experience to you – the readers and artists. This innovative method of instruction aims to take you on an extraordinary journey where you can see this world from a different perspective.

From "Beijing" to "Dubai" and then "Maldives", the book presents and analyses three entirely different landscapes, namely an "ancient city", a "desert", and finally, a "sea island", each with distinct climate conditions and historical and cultural tales. In this series of paintings, I have put down what I encountered during my travels. In the fantasy elements, I have injected my own feelings and inspirations. Through colour schemes and playing with light and shade, I have attempted to capture the most impressive aspects of my memories.

Franc

Weiye Yin
Senior Concept Designer
CG Artist and Illustrator

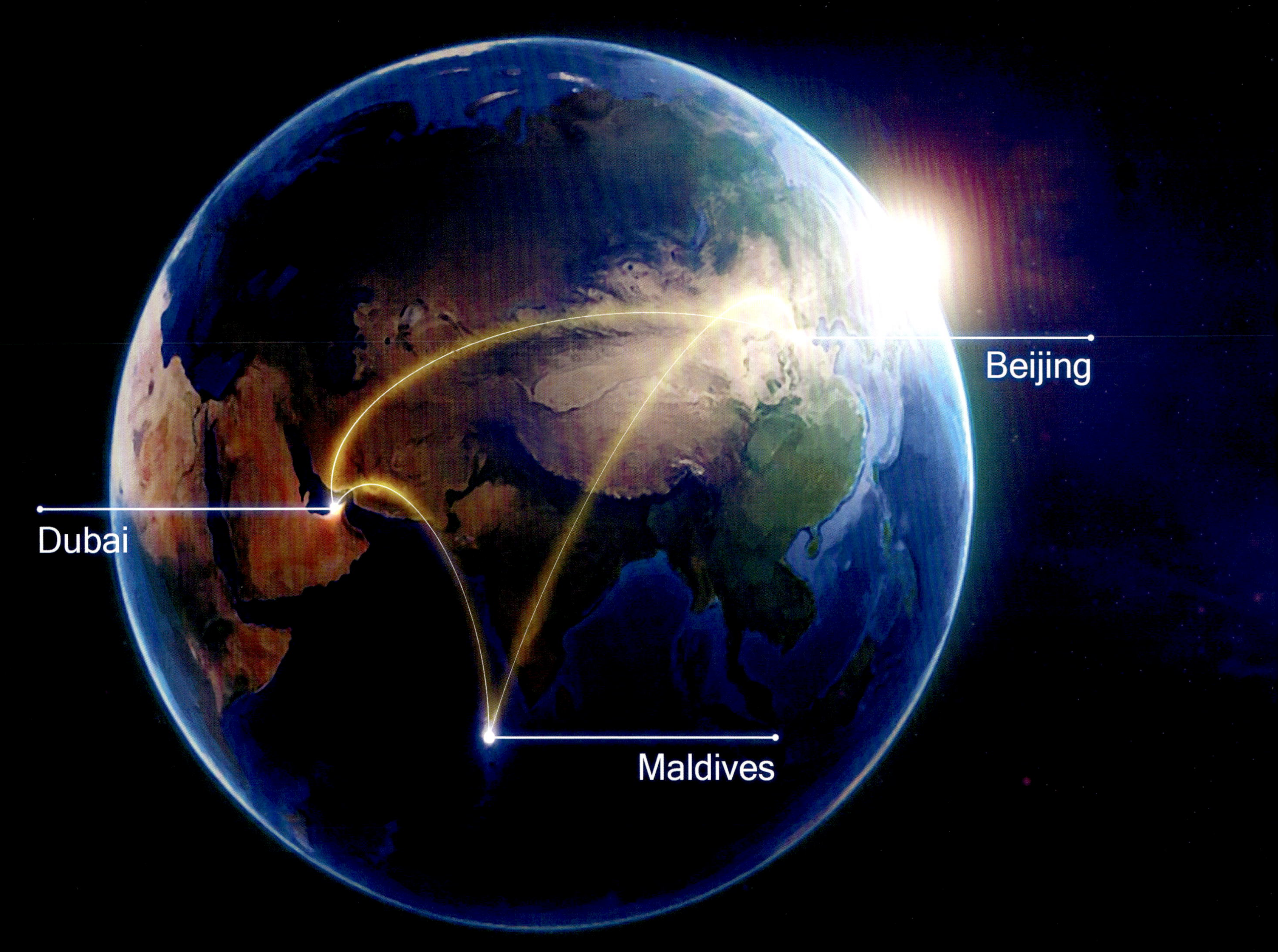
Beijing
Dubai
Maldives

# CONTENTS

As a well-preserved ancient capital that boasts a history of more than three thousand years and has undergone the vicissitudes of several dynasties, Beijing is undoubtedly the crossroads of Chinese and even Asian cultures and has logically become a hub for cultural tourism. The city's rich cultural and historical vein runs through every one of its innumerable ancient temples, over the towering mountains where the Great Wall snakes, along each street and alley lined with antique stores and calligraphy and painting stalls, and, of course, out of the Forbidden City, Summer Palace, and many magnificent palaces and imperial gardens for which it's renowned.

In stark contrast to its antiquity is Beijing's status as a metropolis of rapid urban development, endless ranks of imposing buildings, intertwining networks of overpasses, and unending streams of traffic. Now, it is also the nation's heart of political governance and military deployment.

All in all, Beijing integrates recreational tourism, cultural transmission, historical experience, political governance, military deployment, finance, trade, communication, and academia. No city is lucky enough to possess one or two of these features, but in Beijing, they all stand together on equal ground. There lies the city's exceptional uniqueness.

Even with such diversity and potential to explore on this fantasy art tour, my pen is drawn to describe the history and culture of little-known corners that pulse to a rhythm all of their own.

CHAPTER 1

# BEIJING

## The Ancient Oriental Capital — North Temperate Zone, Monsoon Climate

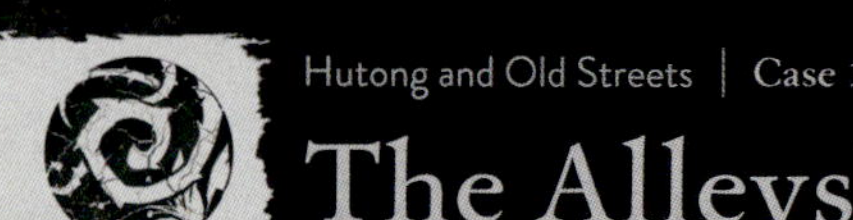



# The Alleys and Streets of the Past

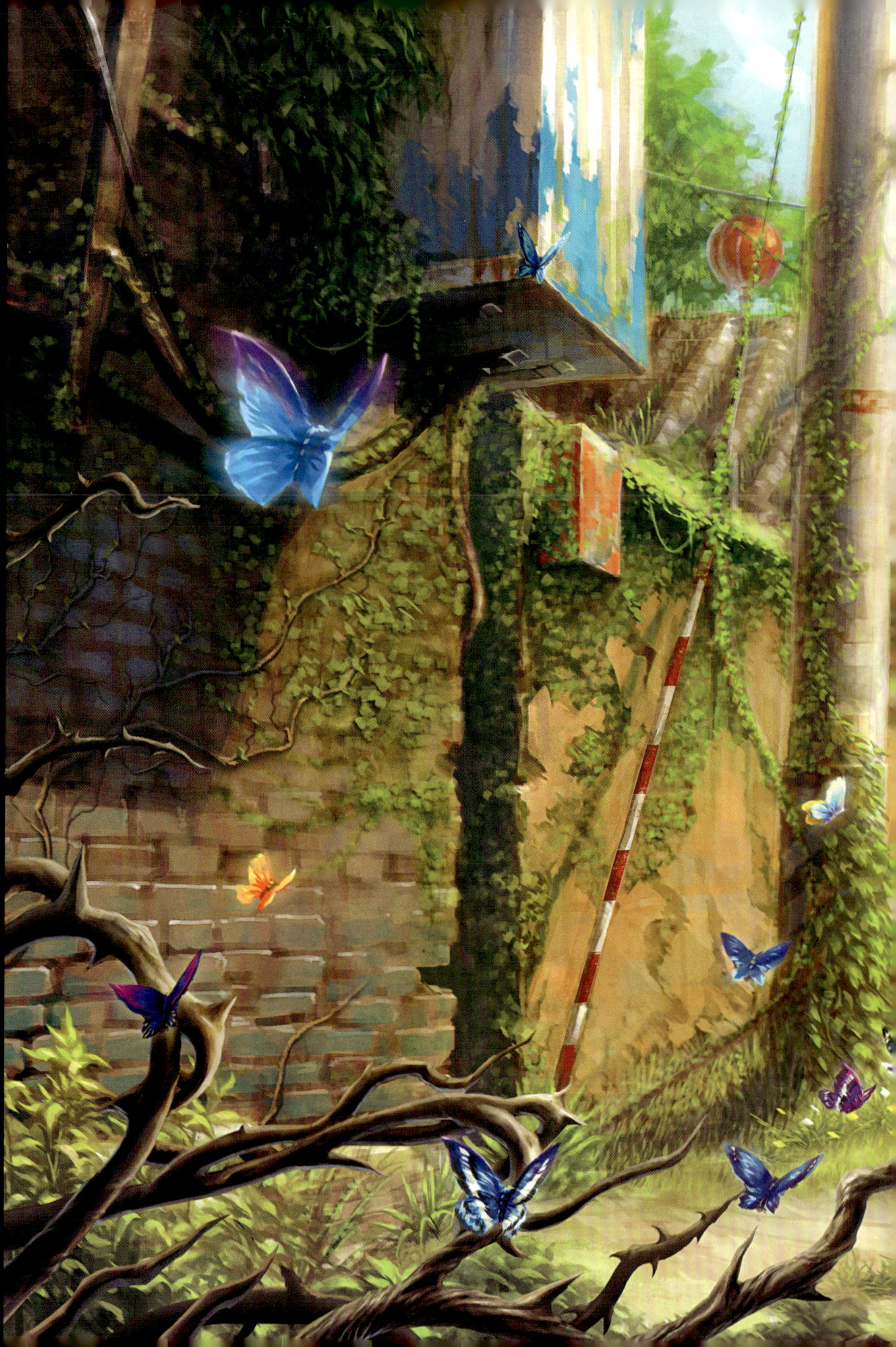

An excellent scene design needs fantastical elements, but most importantly, it must project the spirit you've imagined for the scene onto the viewer. This is an achievement far beyond that of a realist sketch. Likewise, to accurately express your desired emotion requires sophisticated painting skills that encompass the creation and application of objects, light, shade, and colours. A balanced combination of these will allow you to weave the visual story you wish. To build an immersive fantasy, you need to first capture reality in a convincing manner before incorporating elements of fantasy to enchant your viewers.

*The Alleys and Streets of the Past* is a work of art with the end of the world as its theme. The work's emphasis, however, is not pessimism in the face of destruction but the vigor inherent in new life. Though any worldview can be expressed in fantasy art, you need to remember that "it is simply a tool, not a guide". Many people are reminded of death and ruin by the mention of "the end of the world". Such a reaction is conditioned by perspective biases. But what about if we changed our stance for just a second? All destruction is followed by a new beginning and thus new possibilities for expression.

Of course, a work can represent whatever a creator wishes it to. It can comfort viewers or shock them. For a non-commercial piece or a work without clear expressive intentions, I personally look for a greater focus on things of beauty. I believe that is the responsibility of fantasy artists: to envision promising futures for people. Once an artist has attained sufficient mastery of their pen to successfully convey particular emotions, then they will find that "hope" and "beauty" wield greater power than criticizing the darkness of reality.

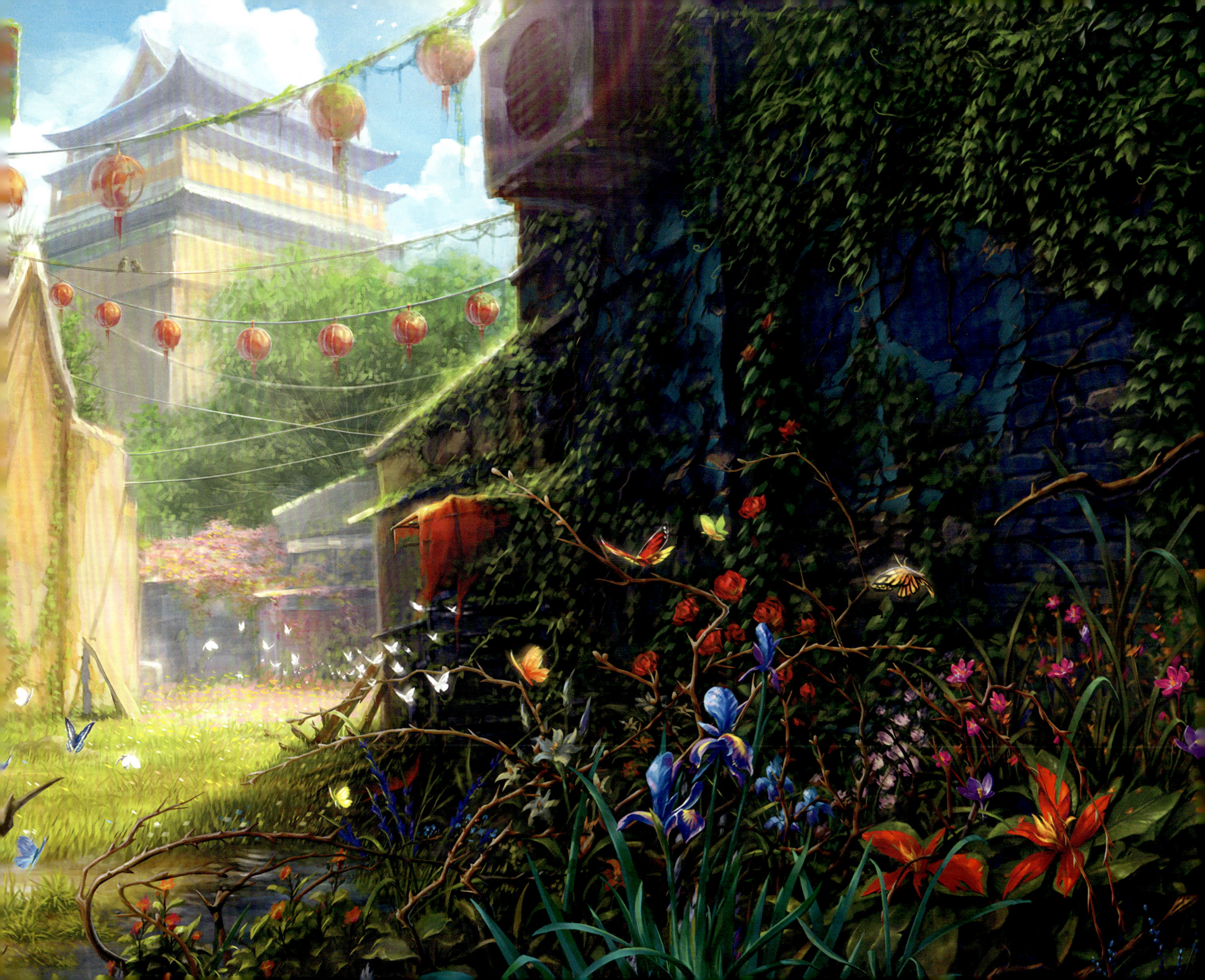

# THOUGHTS ON CREATION

*Before creating a piece of work, we need to collect folklore, legends, and other relevant information. Collecting folklore promotes empathy with a cultural environment so as when it comes to creation, our memories can guide us to capture the nuanced emotions and rhythm of the scene, thus making our work more vivid and resonant. However, given costs and time restraints, we often do not have the chance to perform this invaluable practice (for every creation). It is such instances that we artists must be active and conscientious in accumulating life experiences and points of reference and inspiration (to remedy our inability to research).*

*To this, some people might respond, "I always think up my paintings at home, and without going out, I can still create a lot of fantastic scenes". Of course, this is entirely possible. Just as a young child, uninitiated in the world and naïve to much of its contents, can dream of many things they have never experienced before either. But one thing is for sure: even their most fantastical dreams are derived from scenery they have already perceived in real life. On this account, the wider your scope of experience, the greater the scope of your creations. Why let your actions restrain your ideas?*

*Others, however, might ask, "With how advanced the accessibility and connectivity of the Internet is now, what's the point of leaving the house in search of inspiration when everything I need is right there online?" My response is that though picture resources are readily available and require no first-hand (cultural) experience to access, scouring the videos and pictures online for instances which align with your direction your focus is no mean feat. What you'll find instead are reflections of another perspective, a perspective which is likely entirely different from yours even if you intend to produce a work of a similar kind.*

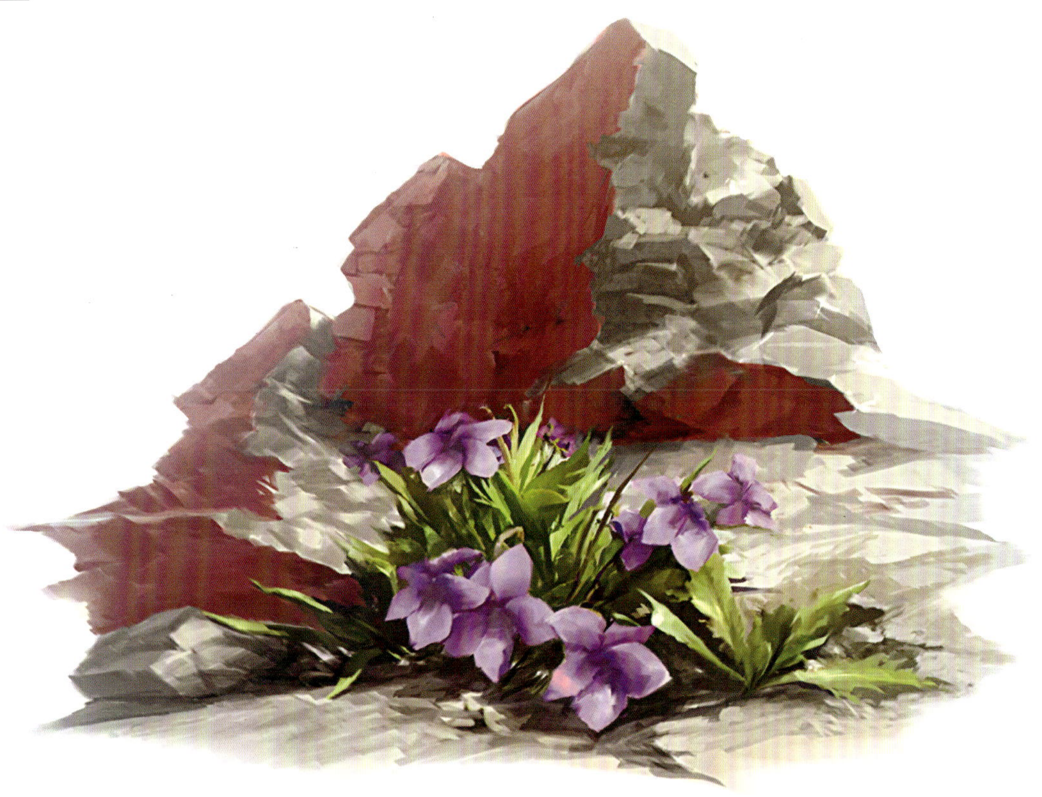

*I once saw a technically and figuratively excellent artwork by a Western artist which depicted the ancient oriental capital. In the center of the painting is a Chinese-style palace gate and passers-by in traditional oriental clothes toing and froing before it. The whole scene was gorgeous and vibrant. In this fantasy world as constructed by the artist, you cannot tell which dynasty the architecture belongs to nor whether the costume of the passers-by are historically accurate and consistent. Nevertheless, the blending of elements of ancient China make the whole scene seem congruent and harmonious while the personal touches of creativity convincingly bring it to life. I'd thus say that is a fine fantasy work. Unfortunately, at the same time it's clear that the creator has only made a perfunctory effort to compose a full piece since much of it is a blatant copy of "materials" from the Internet found with a simple search for a few key*

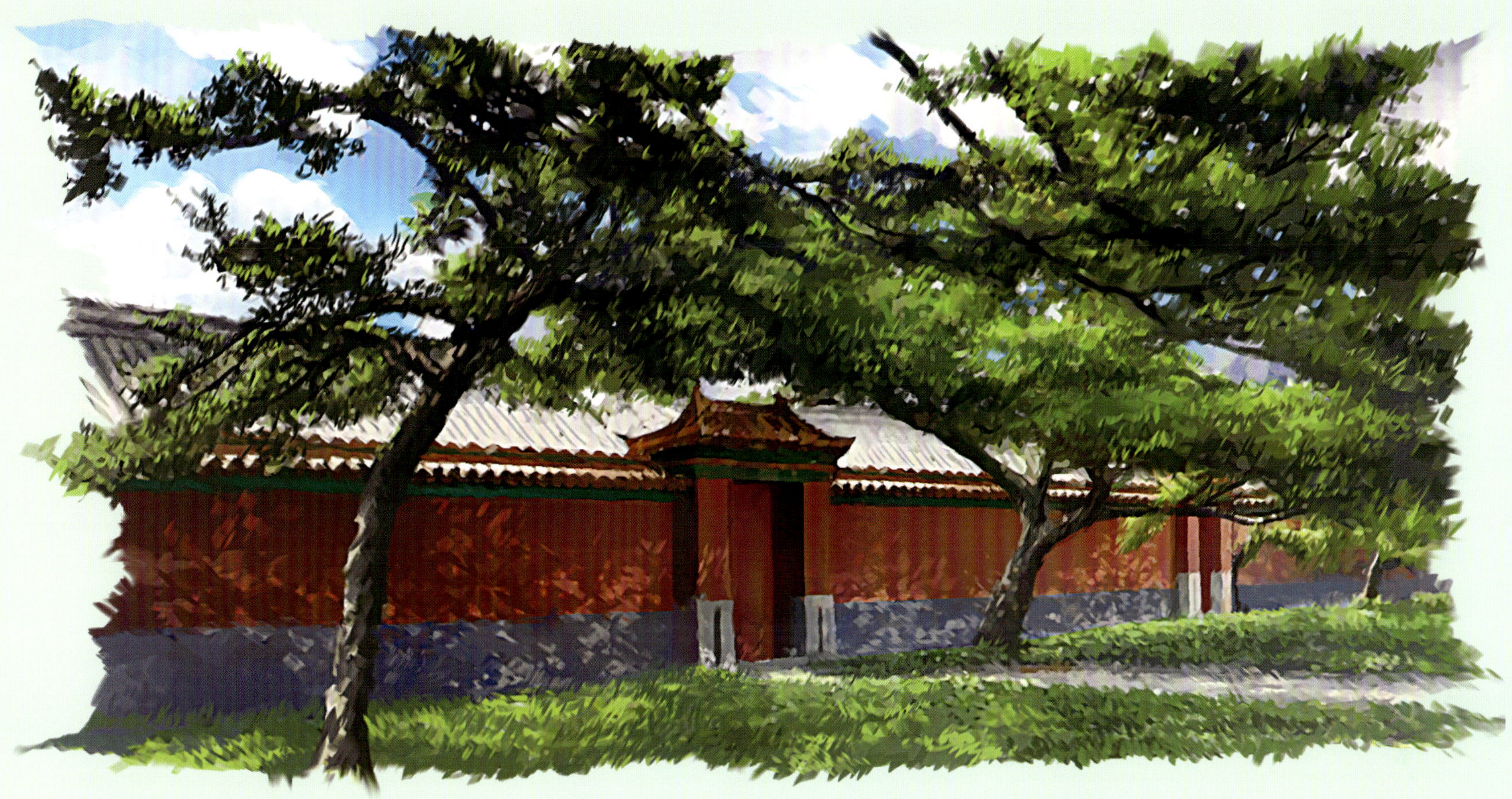

*words. The plaque from the Forbidden City reading "Palace Museum" is clearly visible above the gate. Conversely, there is no protective moat in front of the magnificent palace and it seems like any ordinary citizen could just wander in when and how they wish. It's these such ill-conceived elements that have deprived the scene of its immersive power.*

*Whereas if the artist had visited the site himself, the result would have been totally different. He would have observed a distance between China's imperial palaces and the common people on the street. He would have seen and felt the significant hierarchy in ancient China. He would have understood that the grandeur of the palace lies behind its sheer majesty. And he would have known that "Palace Museum" is a name given by later generations to refer to museums, not the palace's original title. If the work was re-created, I think its expressiveness and resonance with viewers would be greater.*

*Back on the theme of "streets", let's now turn to the preliminary preparations for a work of this kind. Since any idea or scene has multiple ways of being expressed, we need to first decide what kind of a feeling we want to depict so as to be able to choose the most suitable objects to represent it.*

*When it comes to Beijing, we must talk about its hutongs and siheyuan, the earliest residences for Beijing citizens. Those preserved to date serve as records of the vicissitudes of history and trivialities of common people's lives.*

*Hutongs in Beijing date back to the 13th century in the Yuan Dynasty and their story spans hundreds of years. Usually stretching east-west, they are formed by lines of different-sized siheyuan or courtyard residences (see the right image) arranged side-by-side. The passage running between these rows of siheyuan is known as a hutong.*

*A siheyuan is a quadrangle with buildings symmetrically laid out on all sides. The arrangement generally symbolizes interpersonal harmony and reunion, and each hutong or siheyuan has its own legends and tales to tell.*

*Compared with the avenues and roads lined with modern skyscrapers and jammed with traffic, hutongs embody more distinct regional, historical, and cultural characteristics. Hence why I've chosen them as the model for illustrating the creative process.*

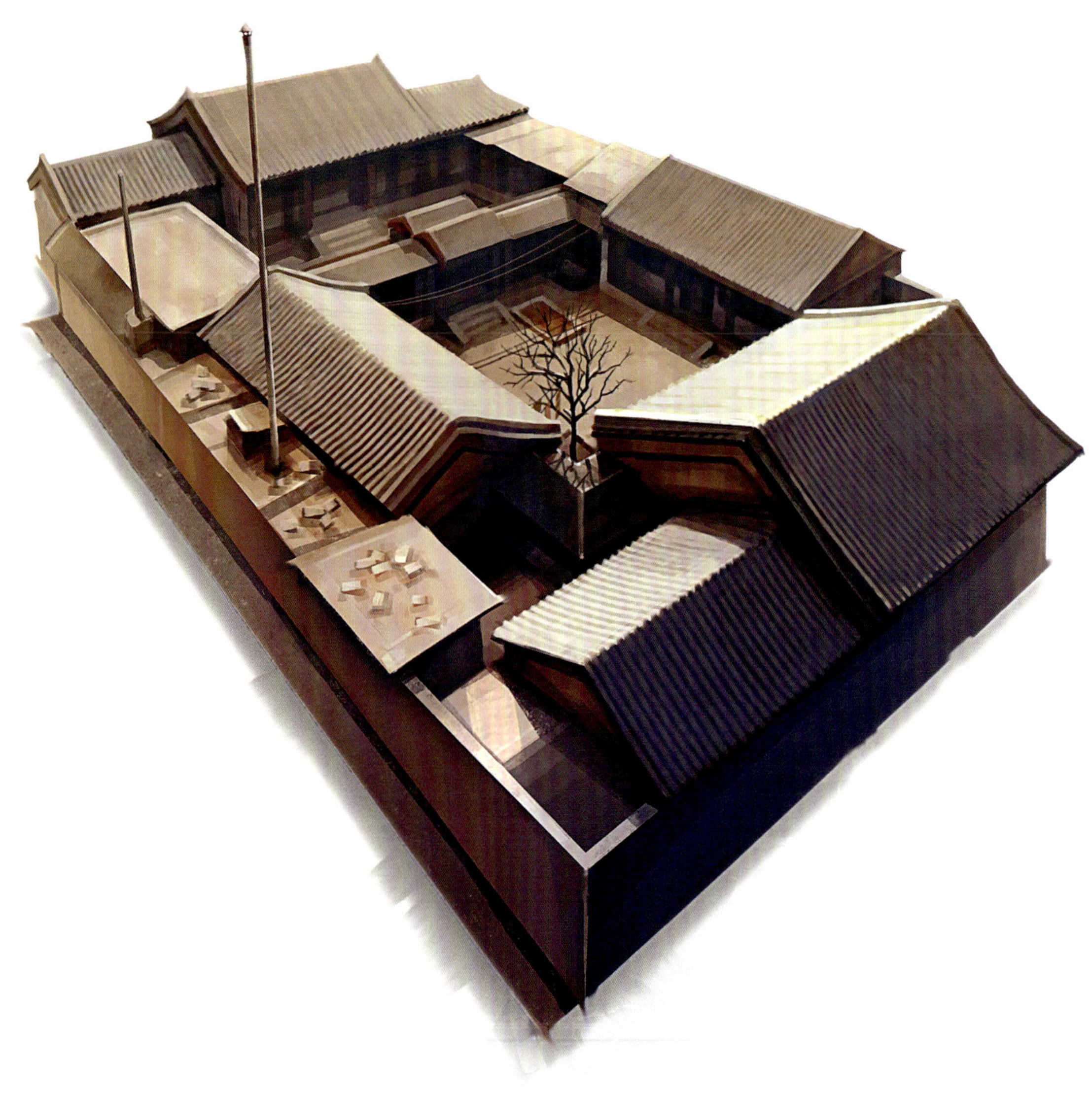

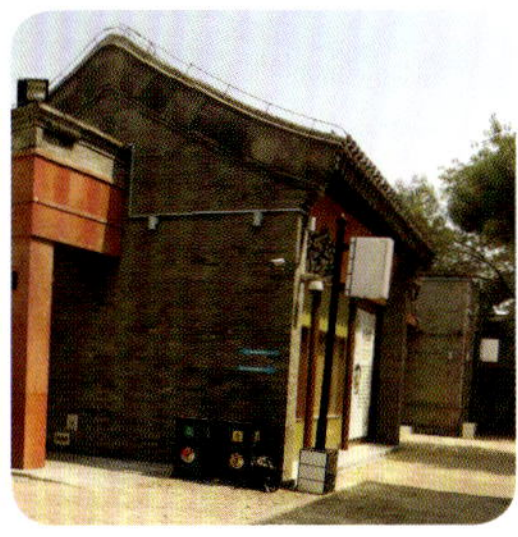
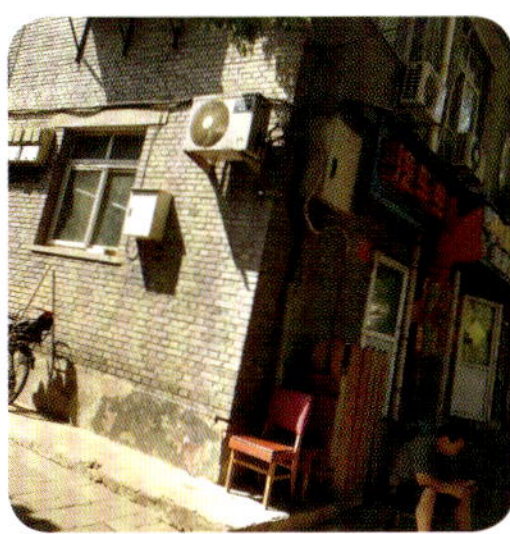
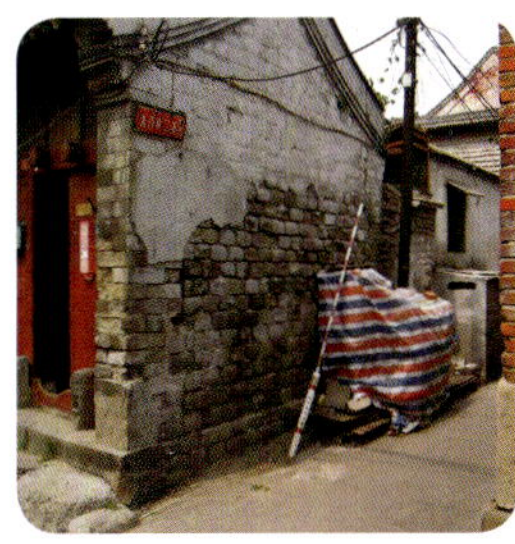

## ▲ SIHEYUAN

Beside such relics of history and folklore, we also need to collect elements of the modern era. After *siheyuans* are renovated, you can see utility poles, electric transformer boxes, and A/C units attached to walls everywhere. This combination of traditional residences with modern life needs has become the new narrative of *siheyuans*.

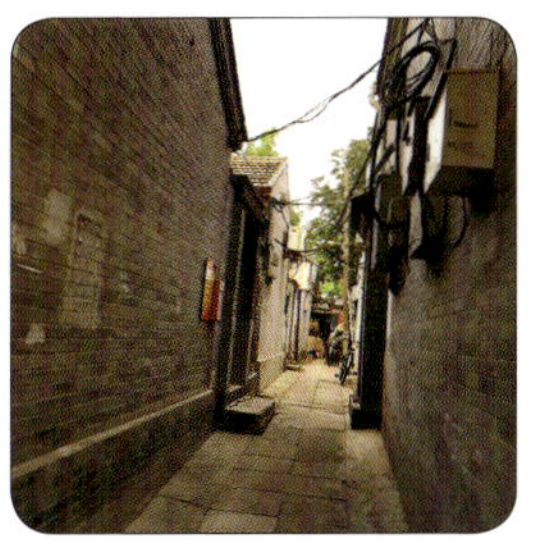
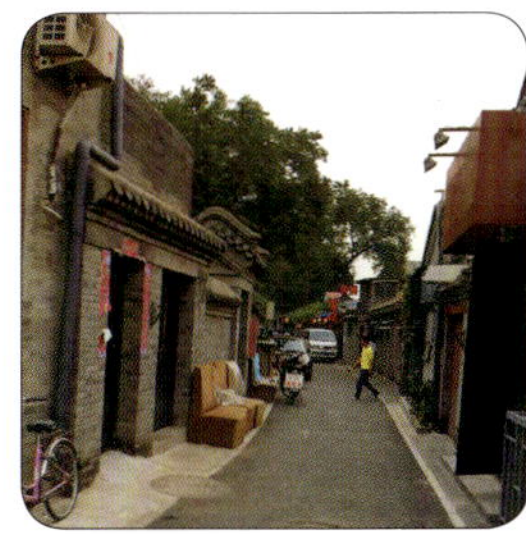
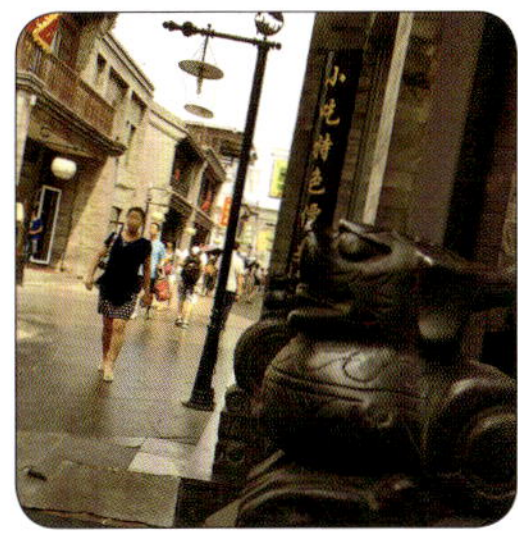

## ▲ HUTONG

There are generally three types of *hutong*: small *hutongs* which are too narrow for anything but people to pass through, medium-sized *hutongs* wide enough for a car, and large *hutongs* flanked by shops and residences. Composing a too narrow layout will make for a cramped and oppressive space while a too wide layout will rob a quiet residence of its intimacy and life pulse. For this reason, I went with a *hutong* of a moderate size for the purpose of this model theme.

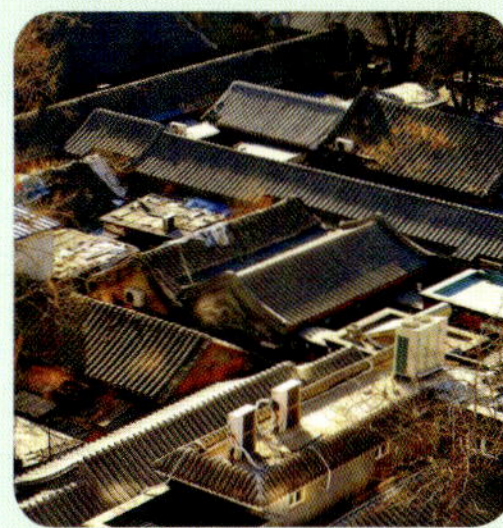
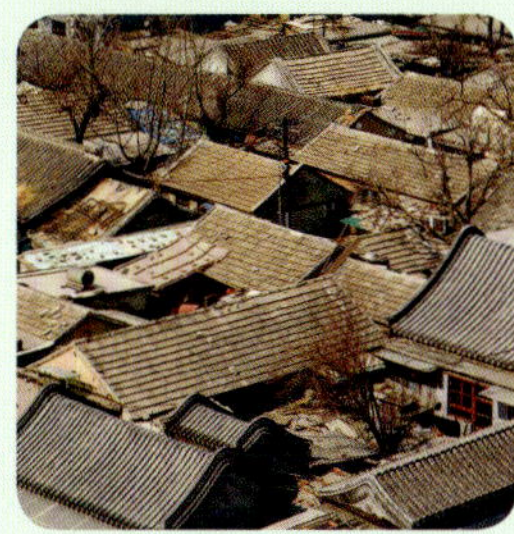

## ▲ TRADITIONAL RESIDENCE

From a different perspective, you may realize that Beijing is not what it used to be. Time have gradually transformed classical spaces like *siheyuans* and *hutongs*.

Once a residence for the whole extended family to live, the *siheyuan* is now a shared space where many different families dwell, with neighbours being close or amicable or sometimes at odds. The quadrangle is often split into different areas with a variety of purposes and in some instances even the rooftop is dragged into the renovations. Complex arrays of "pigeonhole" mini studios, solar panels, and self-made shelters or attics produce multiplex intersections of architectural style and meetings of life.

Originally constructed according to design blueprints out of bricks, beams, pillars, and tiles, the residences are methodically arranged. They are worlds apart from many of the self-built houses or shanty areas across the world. Crowded but orderly, or organised chaos, is a feature unique to the modern state of Beijing's traditional housing.

Next, I picked out the most relevant elements from the plenty source materials and began to sketch. Key words for this particular piece included "serenity", "after the end of the world", "nostalgic old residences of historical flavor", and the "vitality of new life".

In this first series of photos, I was attracted to the perspective. It's a perspective familiar to viewers, that which takes the street and its contents as the main focus of the scene's composition. This allowed me to better grasp the basic effects and interplays of light, shade, form, and shape. That said, crucially, the more common something is, the more likely it is to move viewers. For a creation aimed at narrating a story or manifesting some idiosyncrasy or essential concept, oblique and grandiose perspective may fail to express the finer and more nuanced emotional layers.

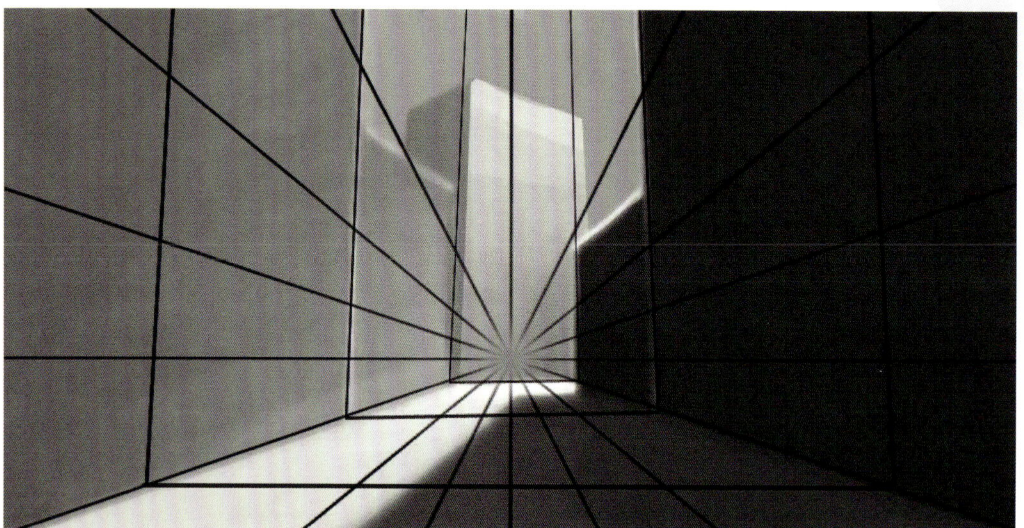

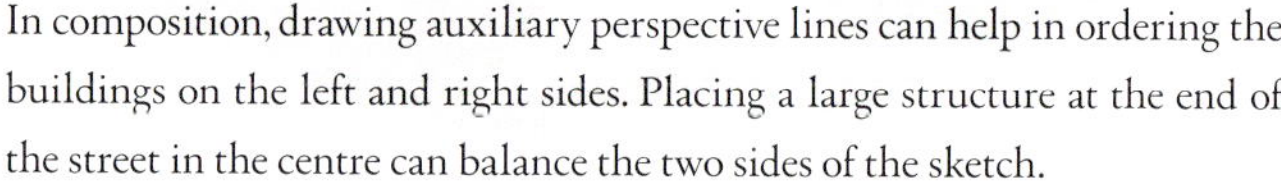

In composition, drawing auxiliary perspective lines can help in ordering the buildings on the left and right sides. Placing a large structure at the end of the street in the centre can balance the two sides of the sketch.

In order to bestow the scene with a stereoscopic effect and eliminate the sense of flatness caused by balanced composition, we can insert an imagined source of light off to one side of the frame, whose rays enhance the contrast of light and shade. As the work is intended to portray an afternoon, the sun's light should cast down and into the scene from a diagonal angle without losing its intensity. In this way, the darker part could perhaps brighten over time with the slow, changing reflection of light.

Another technique for illustrating the shift from bright to dark, besides relying on impressions of depth, is to warm colors in the lit areas and cool colors in the dark area. This results in a more vibrant, lively scene.

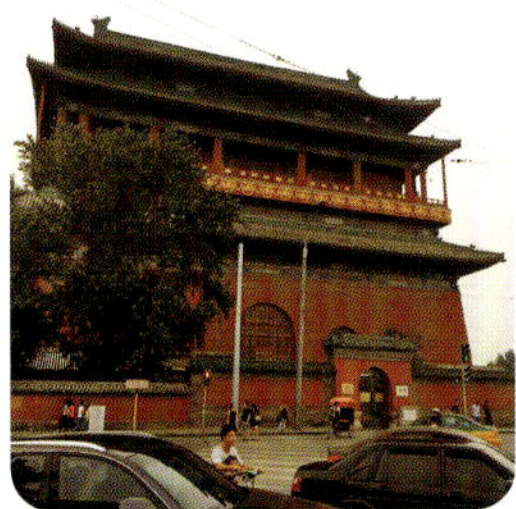

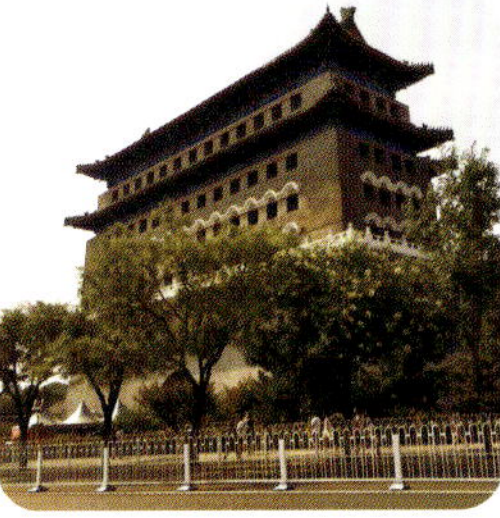

## ▲ ANCIENT CITY GATE TOWERS

As an ancient capital of China, Beijing preserves many historical buildings, among which there are multi-story city walls and gate towers which once served as the most effective fortifications at safeguarding imperial families and palaces. During urban development, however, these walls were found to significantly imped the construction and extension of public transport routes, which led to many of them being demolished. Several extant city gate towers still stand as embodiments of the nostalgia felt for old Beijing.

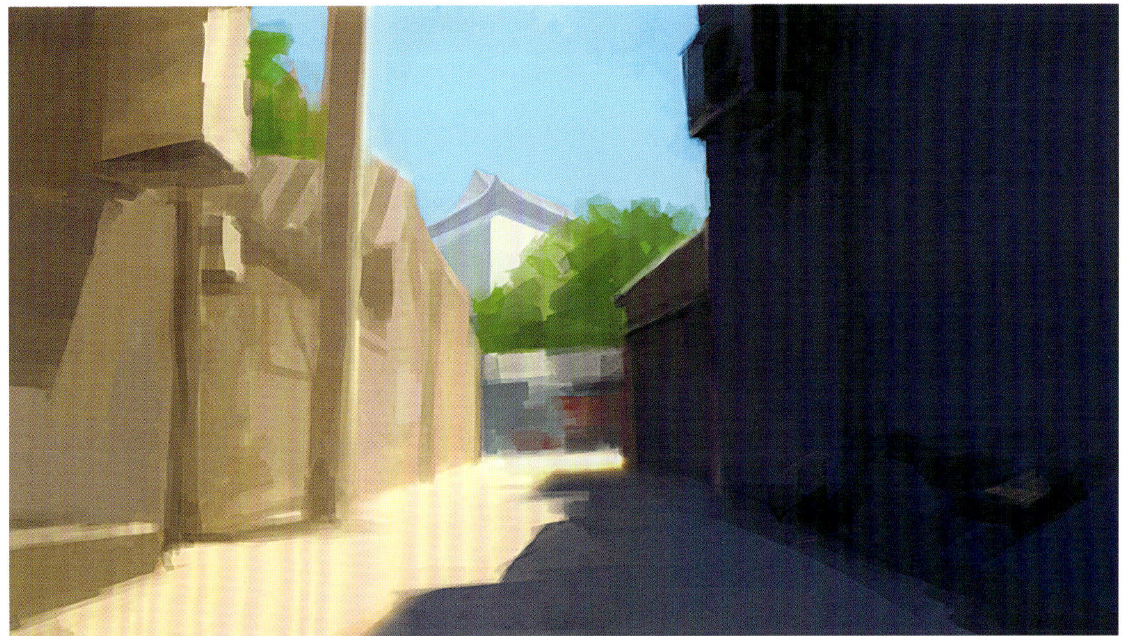

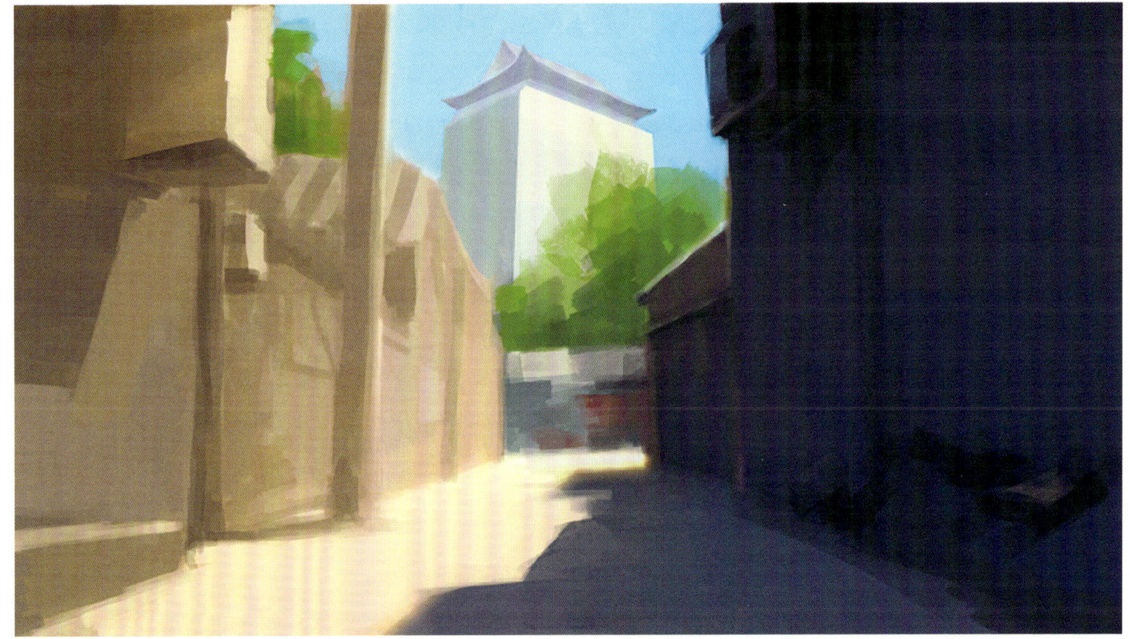

To complement the classic stature of the *siheyuan*, such structures as these "ancient city gate towers" are an optimal choice as the background anchor.

People who have visited Beijing may find a scene such as above quite ordinary. In cultural conservation areas, ancient city structures, like the gates and towers, usually exist alongside residences and no matter how big or small these structures might seem, their height always represented the apex of the ancient city skyline; they were the highest an ancient building in China would reach. Naturally, compared with modern highrises, they appear relatively small. Moreover, considering the law of perspective that an object appears smaller at a distance and bigger when it is moved closer, a city gate tower, as shown above, might no longer seem so magnificent to onlookers. In an art piece, however, we of course have free reign to exaggerate the size of objects to give expression to a certain feeling and strength.

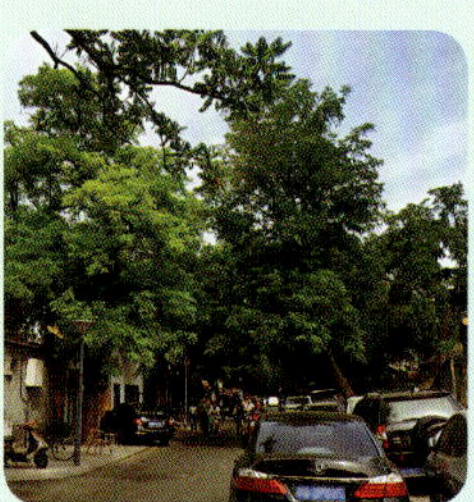

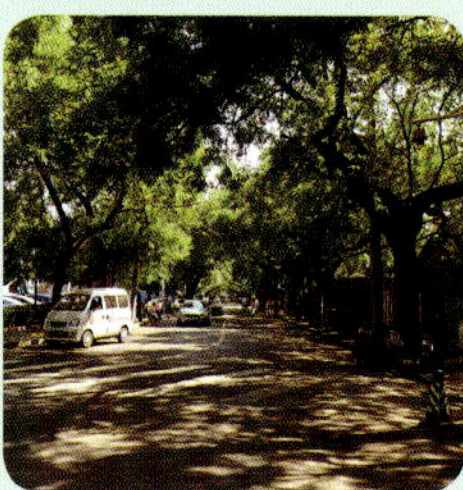

## ◀ OLD TREES

Old trees are ubiquitous in *hutongs*. Not only do they create a greener environment and add a sense of serenity and peace to the atmosphere, but they can also provide shade for residents to enjoy the cool and have a rest. Some trees may be as old as the *siheyuan* they stand by and, similarly, are evocative of a bygone era.

As such, a picture like this might remind residents pining for old Beijing of "the cicadas' chirping" from luxuriant trees in midsummer.

Then, we should further define the various elements of the picture. It's important here to concentrate on the details which convey and accentuate the desired emotional space.

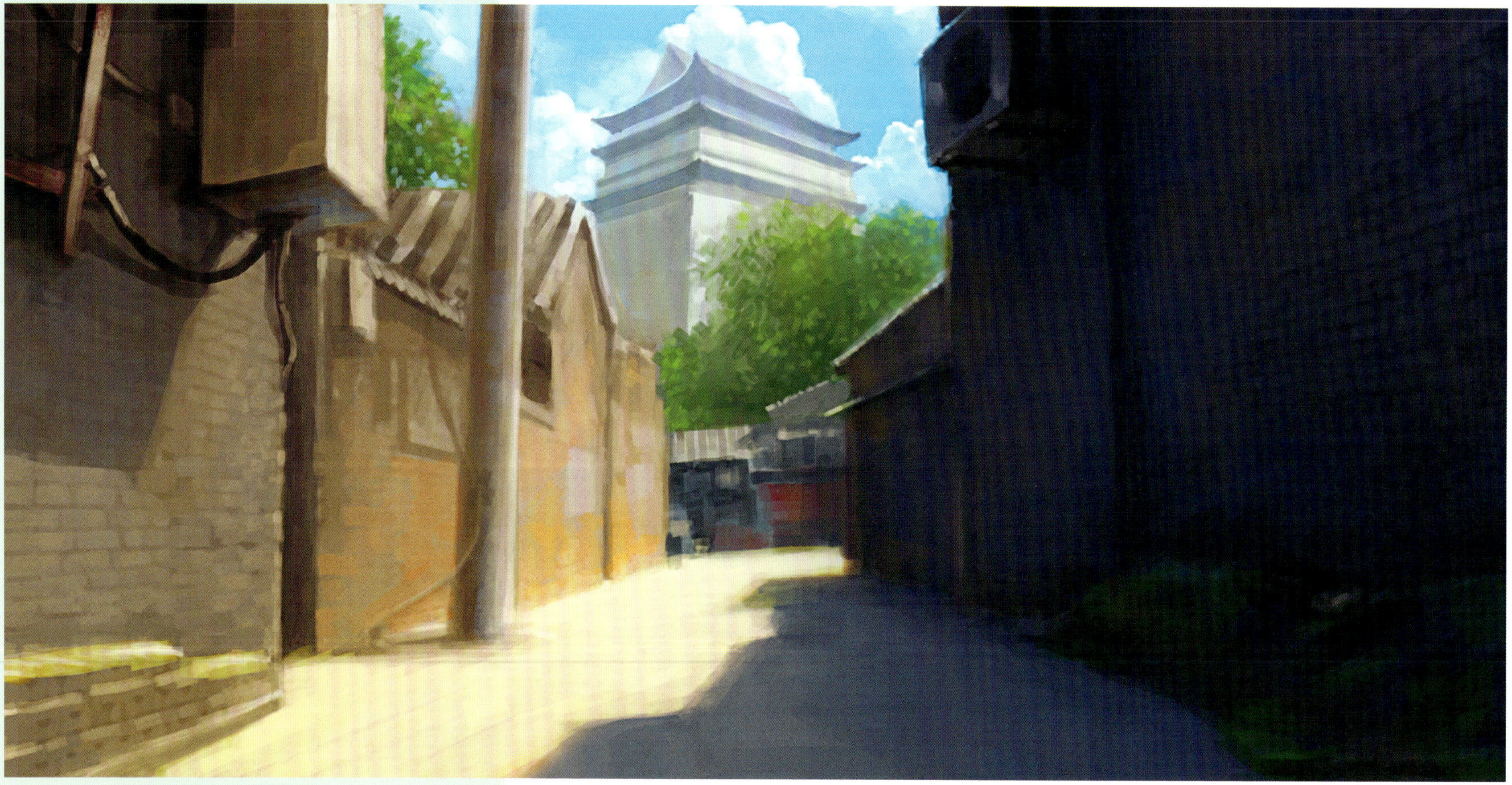

When drawing the tree in the distance, there's no need to painstakingly depict its every detail. That would consume so much time for so little added value that the progress would be unnecessarily slowed. We only need to imbue the form with an impression of lighting, adding brighter colors to the well-lit areas and loosely sketching form to simulate the effect of leaves receiving light, while in the dark parts drawing some branches and trunks that grow in a similar direction.

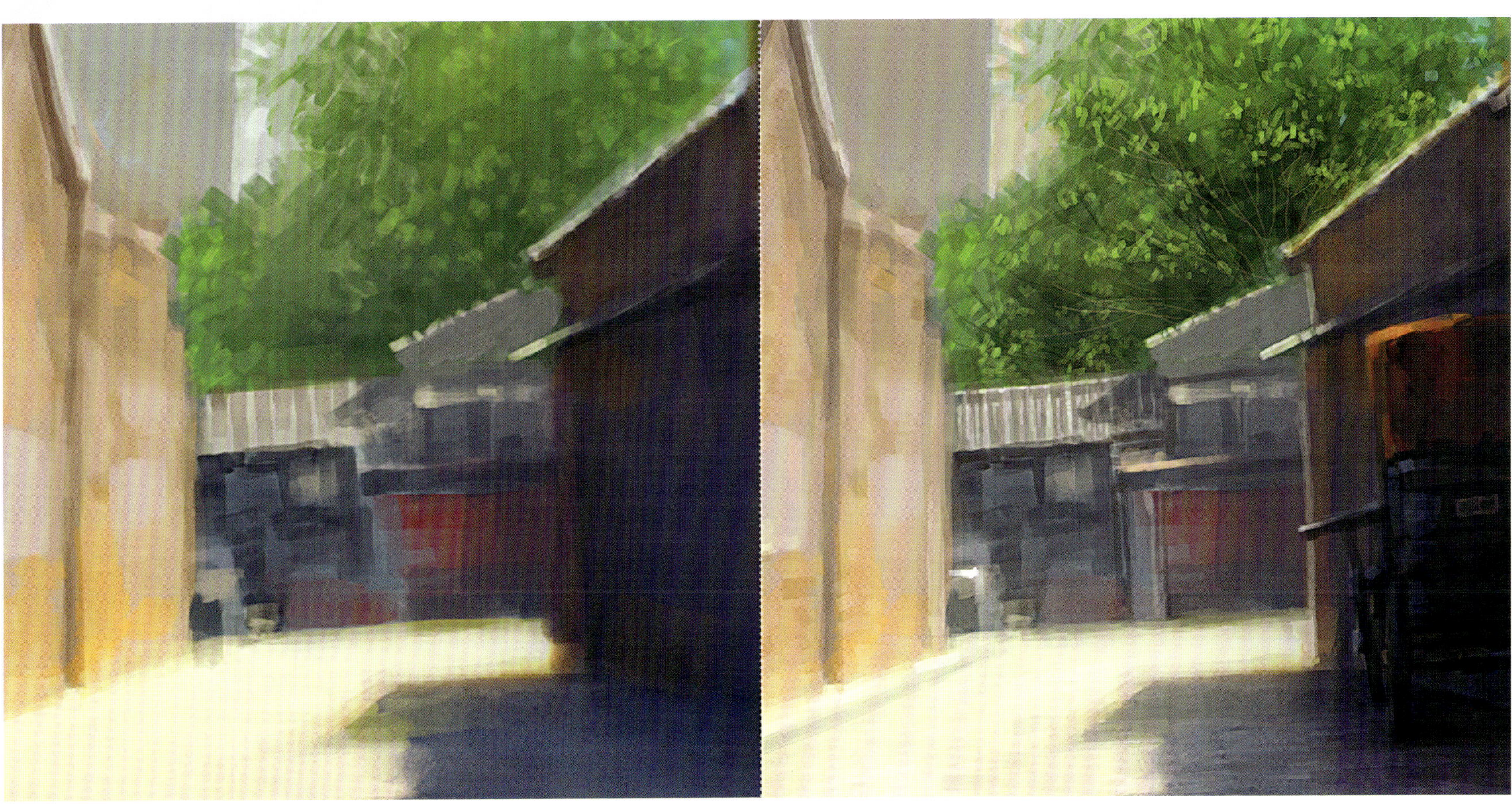

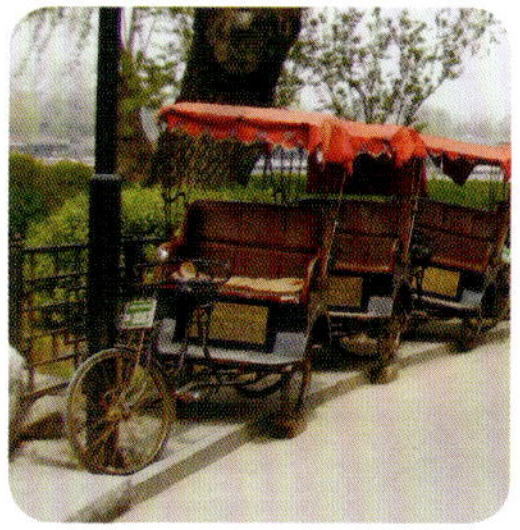

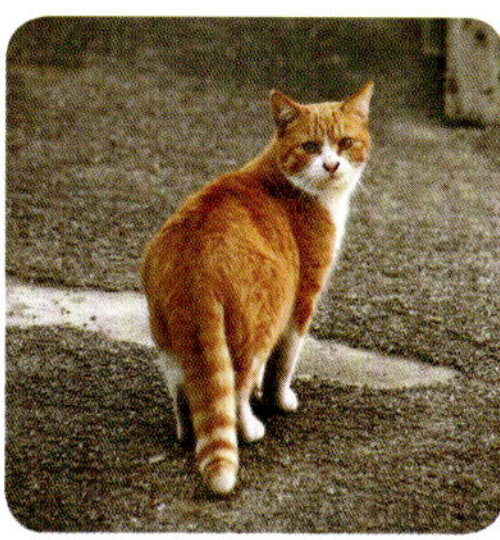

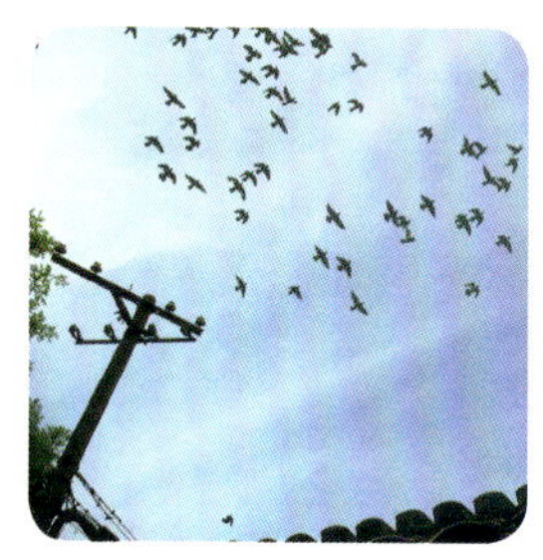

## ◀ SIGHTSEEING CART, CATS AND PIGEON

In Beijing *hutongs*, you may see such scenes as sightseeing carts with red covers randomly lining the streets, pet cats roaming freely around streets and alleys, and sometimes, a flocks of humming pigeons arcing overhead. These elements bestow the otherwise clean and quiet alleys with a touch of color and vitality. Integrating such features into your picture will imbue it with that same spark of life.

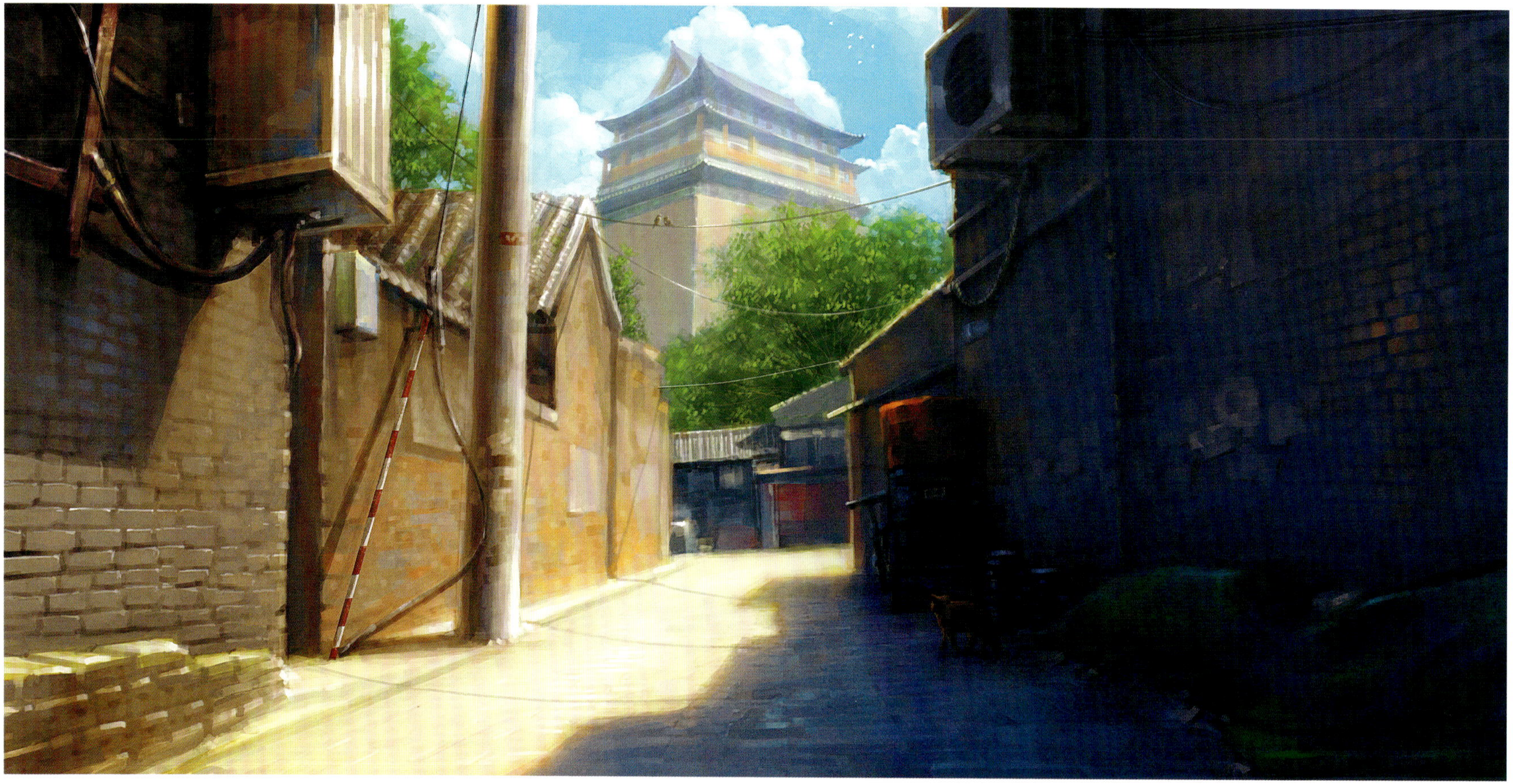

The next step is to further adjust the light and shading by aligning the color and contrast with the intended mood or feeling: a greyish color [low saturation] and a weak contrast may make people feel "depressed", while brighter colors and a stronger contrast provide people with a sense of "brightness"; beyond a certain level of intensity, the image may have an "irritant" or "agitation" effect on people. Any judgment of "appropriateness" is of course subjective to the creator, and so if used effectively, a scene will manage to express a variety of feelings at once through its coloring and contrast.

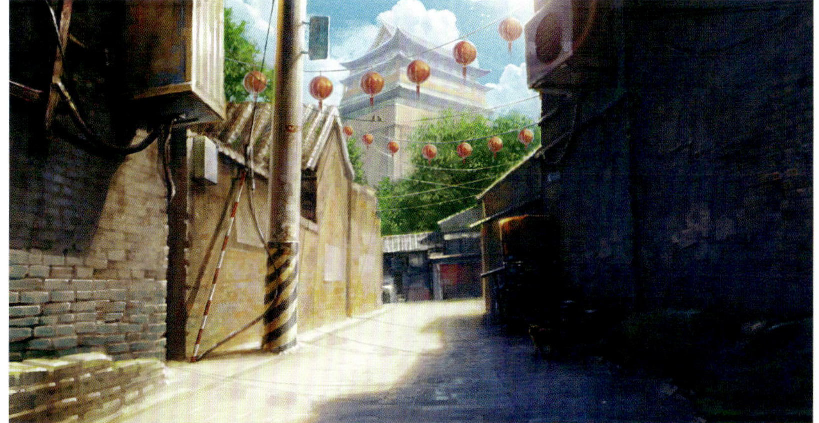

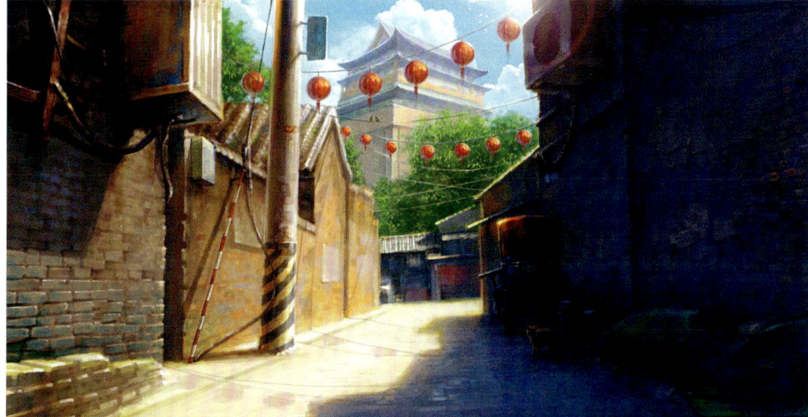

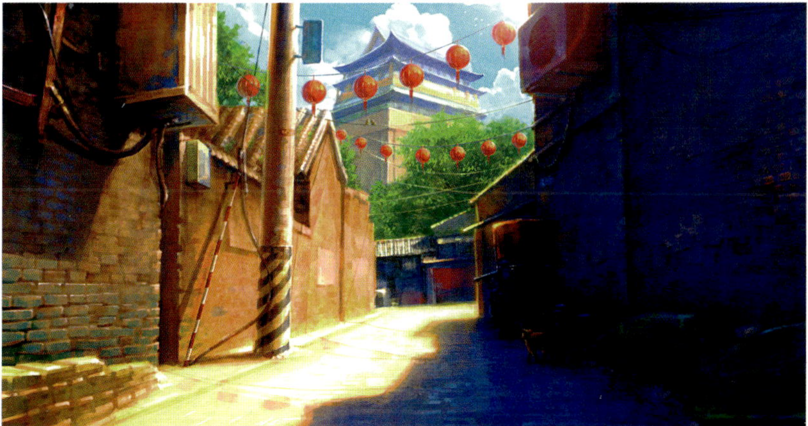

## ► STONE DRUMS

In practice, once you've selected a model scene you wish to portray, it's time to search for specific elements to shape it.

Stone drums are common in *hutongs*. As its name suggests, a stone drum is a drum-shaped ornament made of stone. Set in front of a *siheyuan*, it can be used to support a doorframe, decorate a gate, or ward off ill fortune and evil spirits. It can also serve as a symbol of the identity and status of a house owner as represented by the complexity of its shaping and patterns of its carving.

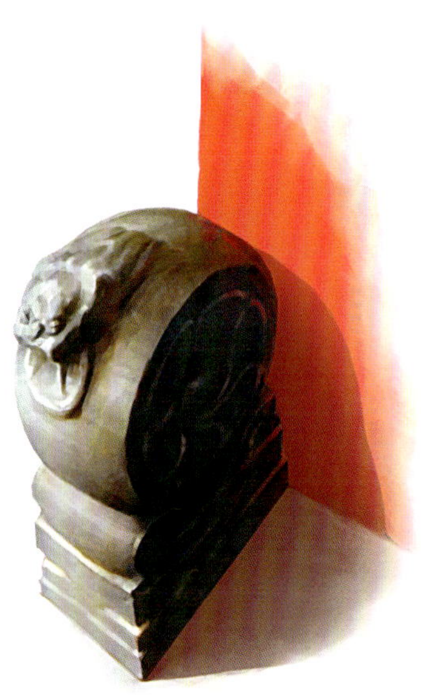

## ◄ LANTERNS

Lanterns are also common in old *hutongs*. Sometimes known as "coloured lanterns", these lanterns were the earliest lighting equipment used in China, yet with the development of spiritual culture, their symbolic significance has far surpassed their practicality. Over 1,800 years ago in the Western Han Dynasty, people would hang up these lanterns during the Lantern Festival on the fifteenth day of the first lunar month to symbolize reunion and create a festive atmosphere.

Adjusting the overall color and contrast of an image is achieved via modern Computer Graphic (CG) programs. These software programs also provide a range functions which make it possible to realize more diverse filter effects. Such versatility of course makes means that digital paintings are more readily editable than traditional handworks, however, in order to ensure consistency of creation when working with digital technology, I suggest that adjustment be limited to the draft phase when a piece first begins to take shape. Subsequent adjustments should be kept to as few as possible.

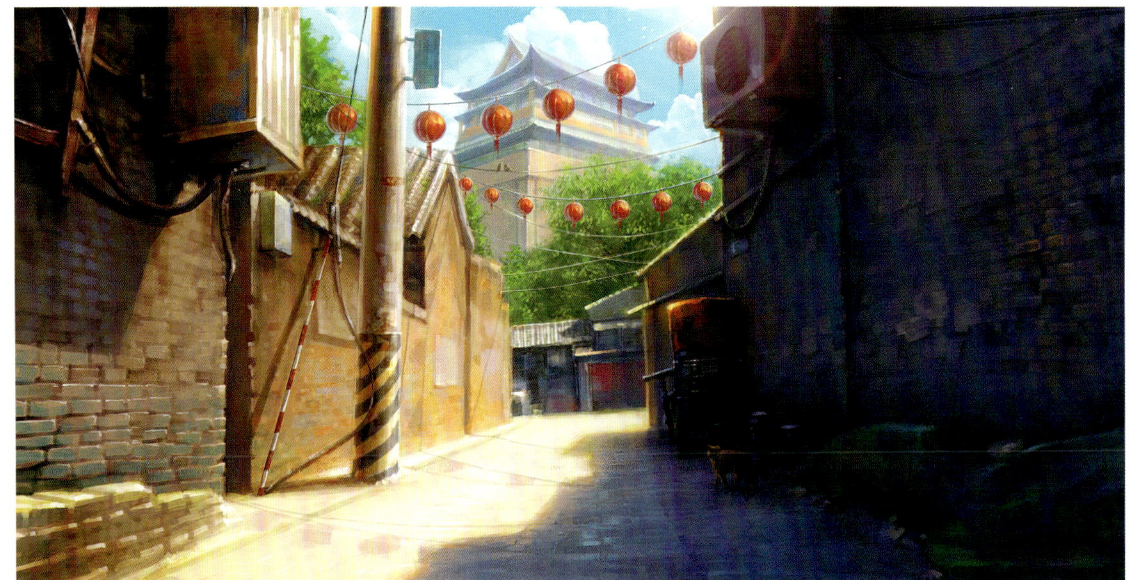

More details and relevant contents can be added to fill out the scene once the foundational color, contrast, and form have been established. Here I only added some "lanterns" as extra references to China's history and culture. By this point in the creation process, I felt that they would serve a harmonizing function within the composition, for example, the frame contains too many objects in a vertical arrangement, leaving it monotonous and dull. The horizontal strings of lanterns, naturally then, enrich the scene by breaking up such "regularity". Their warm red color, moreover, balances the large area of cool colors, such as the blue of the sky and green of the trees, which dominate the upper middle part of the painting.

At this point we must remember to modify other parts in the scene that would be influenced by any newly added elements. Using the lanterns still as our example, it's important we add their shadows upon the ground.

Now, as this is a "fantasy work", we first need to step into the realms of fantasy and imagine: suppose it is a quiet and peaceful street anyway, come the end of the world, it would most likely remain as quiet before, and as we do not want to represent a scene of ruin and destruction, we can leave the buildings intact. How, then, should we represent the end of the world and birth of new life in its wake? Here I chose plants. Plants growing rampant and unchecked over everything work to show the desolation and untrodden state of the scene.

Even though we are not including any damage to the buildings, in order to capture the effects of the lapse of time, we need to depict the lanterns and red car covers as if they have been exposed to, and subsequently worn at by, the wind and elements.

In the distance, we can add a vine-color to create an uneven fog effect which will exaggerate the sense of depth and tie together the overall atmosphere of the piece.

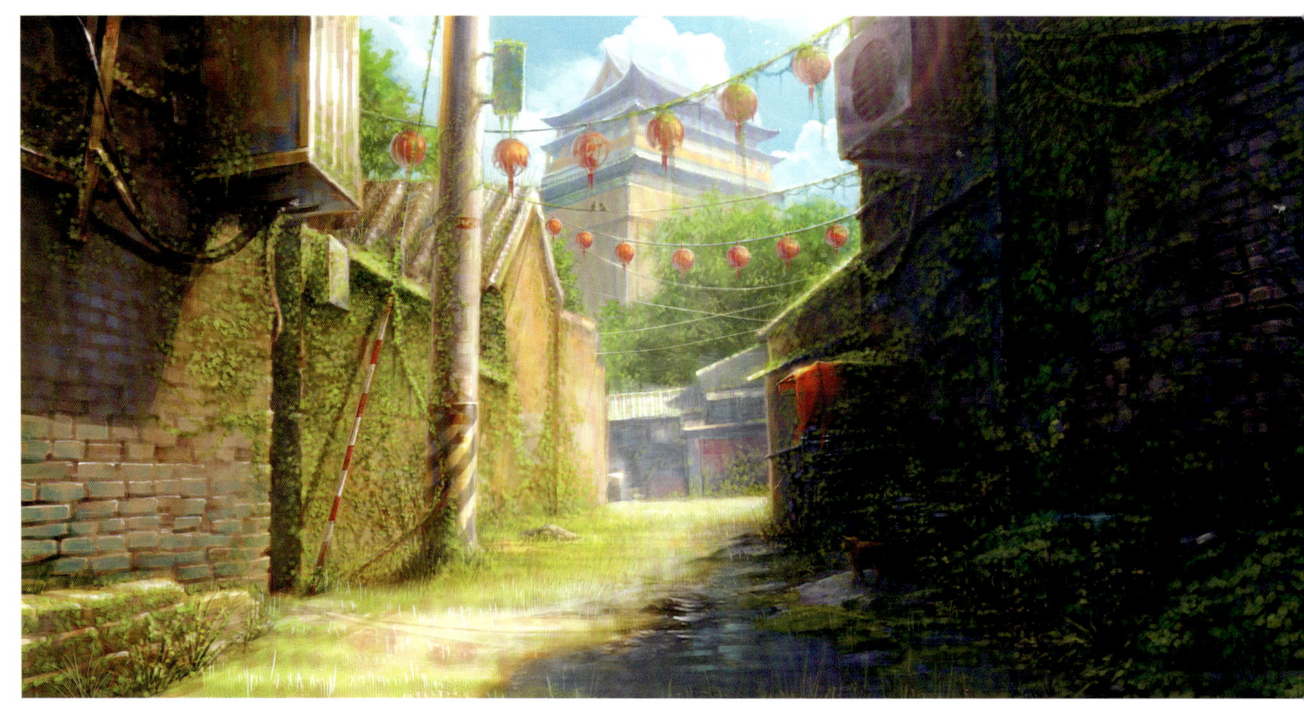

Considering the fact that plants in the wild grow in a disorderly way, we can add more types of flowers and grass in an uneven distribution throughout the scene, rendering it more abundant and natural in appearance and richer in color and form.

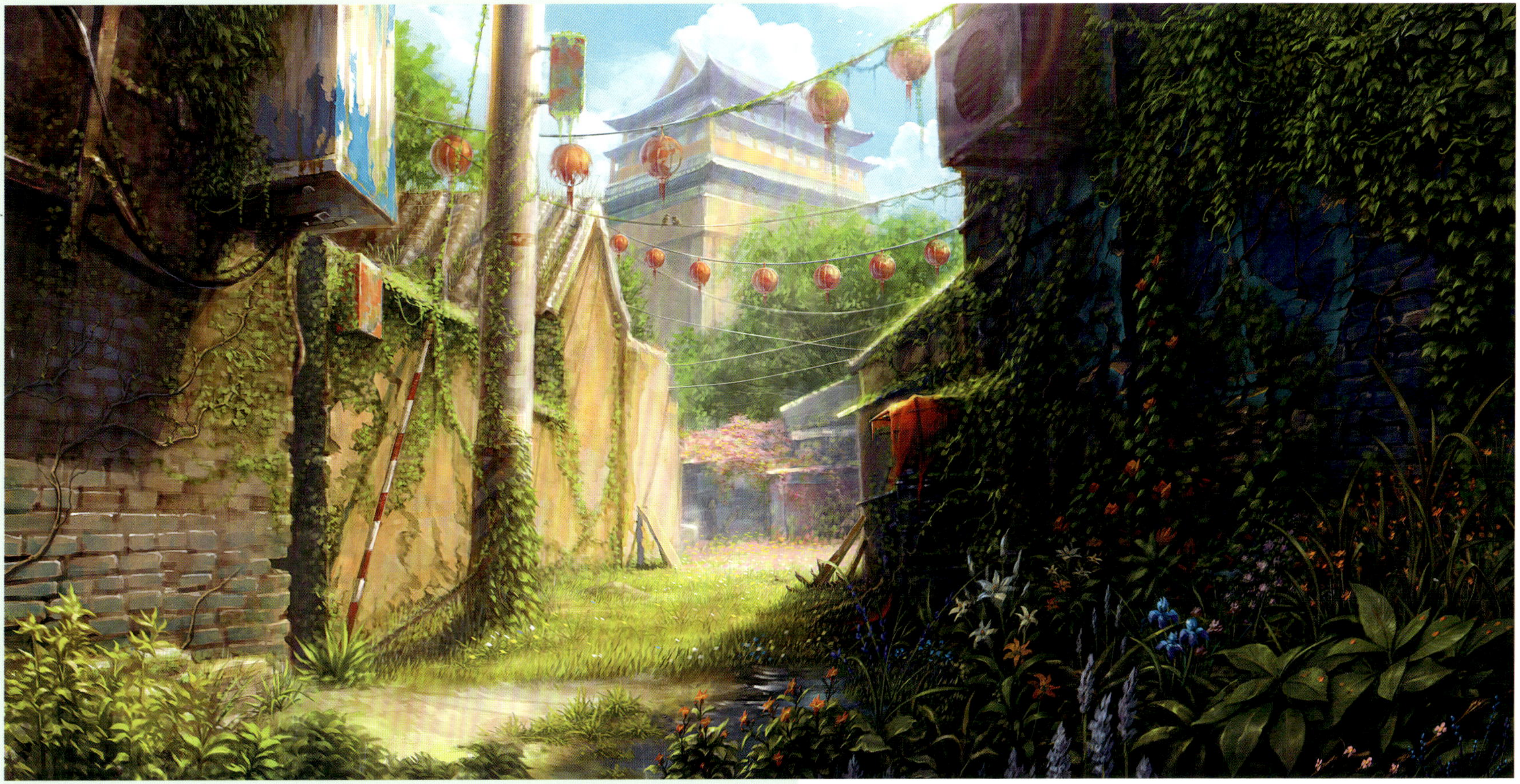

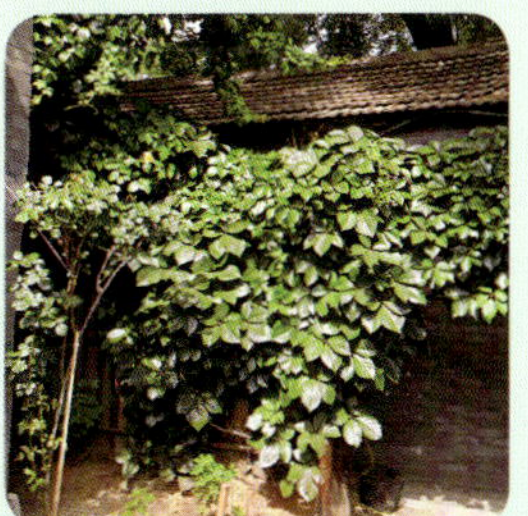

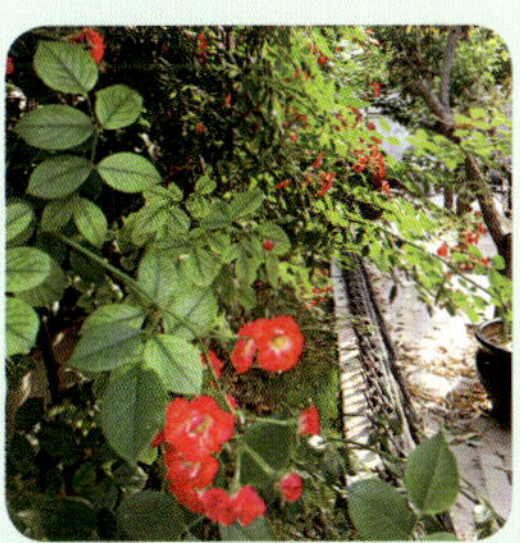

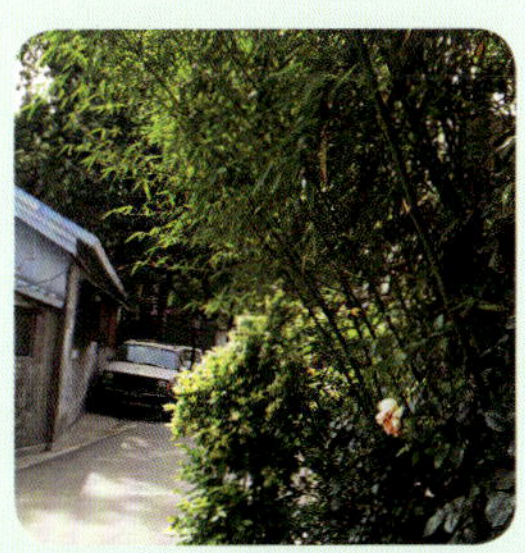

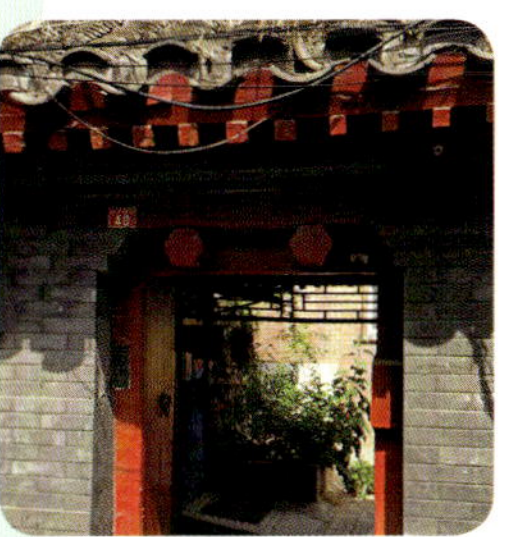

## ◀ PLANTS AND FLOWERS

Plants hold great importance for many residents in Beijing. People of refined taste and elegance appreciate "the plum blossom, the orchid, the bamboo, and the chrysanthemum" because these plants add refinement to their life while the majority of citizens decorate their courtyards with green plants to break to some degree with the flatness of life.

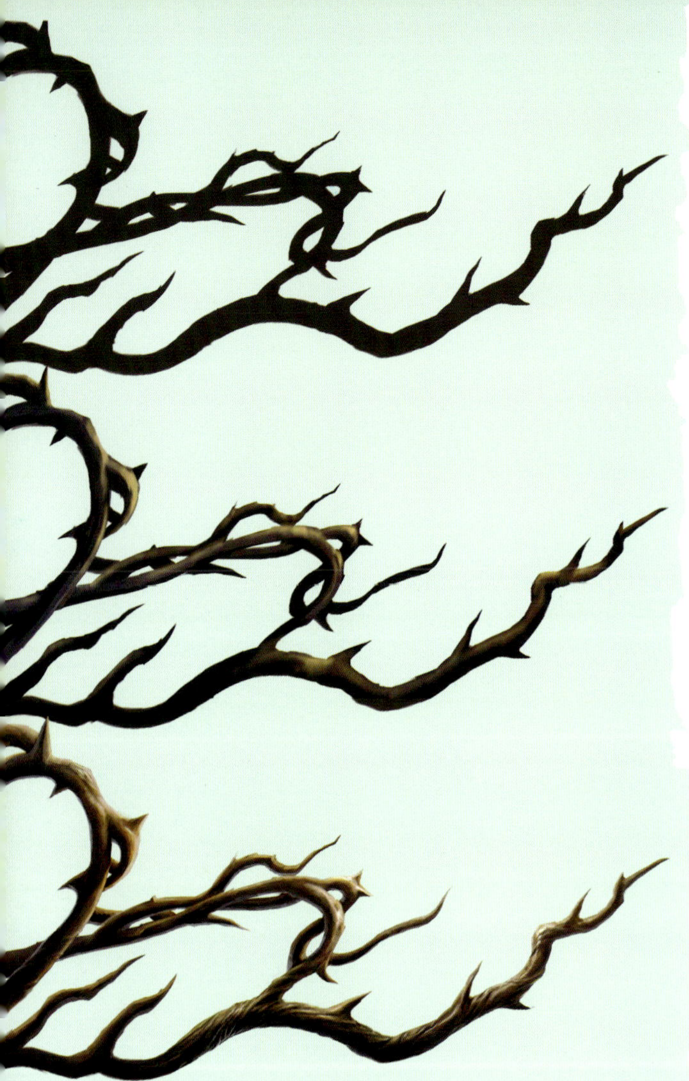

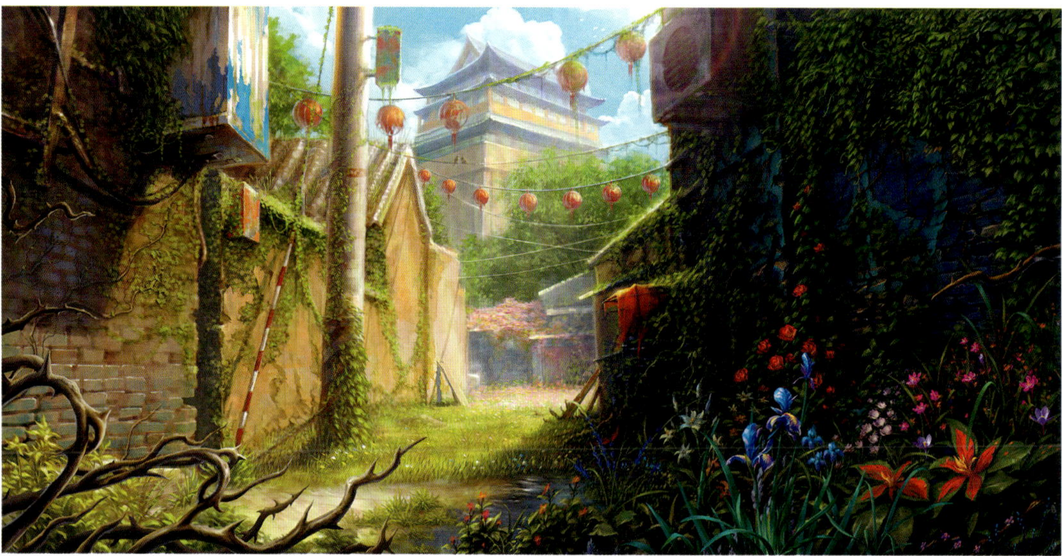

Although we are portraying verdant, disorderly masses of plants, we need to take care to accurately represent the characteristics of each plant. "Shade-loving plants" should not be put in the well-lit areas and "climbing plants" should be twined around other present objects. Also, we need to adjust the density of plants according to the overall composition of the scene. For example, if the creepers on the well-lit wall are so many as they are affecting those creepers in the dark part, then we should reduce their density.

As the density of green upon the canvas increases, we need to add more contrasting colors or complementary colors so as to avoid a largely monochromatic scene. In this instance, I've added blue to the electric transformer box, orange to the switch box and the road sign, and pink to the cluster of flowers on the rooftop in the distance.

In addition, we need to shape plants according to their actual patterns of growth. Different types of plants should not solely occupy allocated "areas". Both creepers and flowering plants grow out in all directions and twist themselves around each other, this should be taken into account when attempting to represent a natural scene.

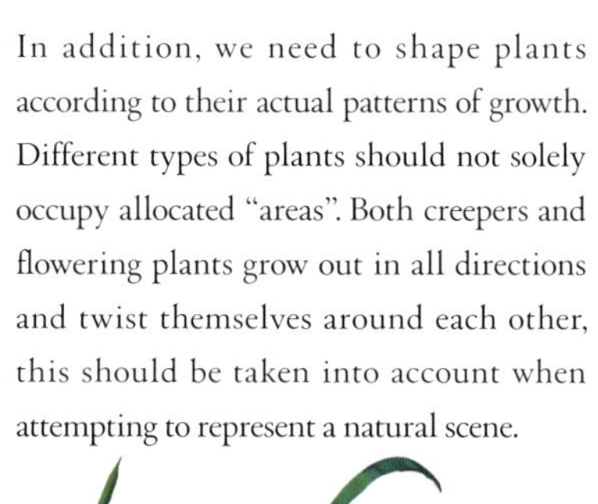

Plant content has been made as diverse as possible yet predominantly includes "flowers, grass, creepers, and thorns" that are short and dense so as to fill the foreground with activity without obstructing objects in the distance. In order to make the plants stand out, we can adopt a silhouetting method, which is best employed during the early stages of creation. Silhouetting can make the direction of plants' growth clear, thus helping us to adapt the position of other objects along that course. Once the plant outlines are established, it becomes much easier to refine the details.

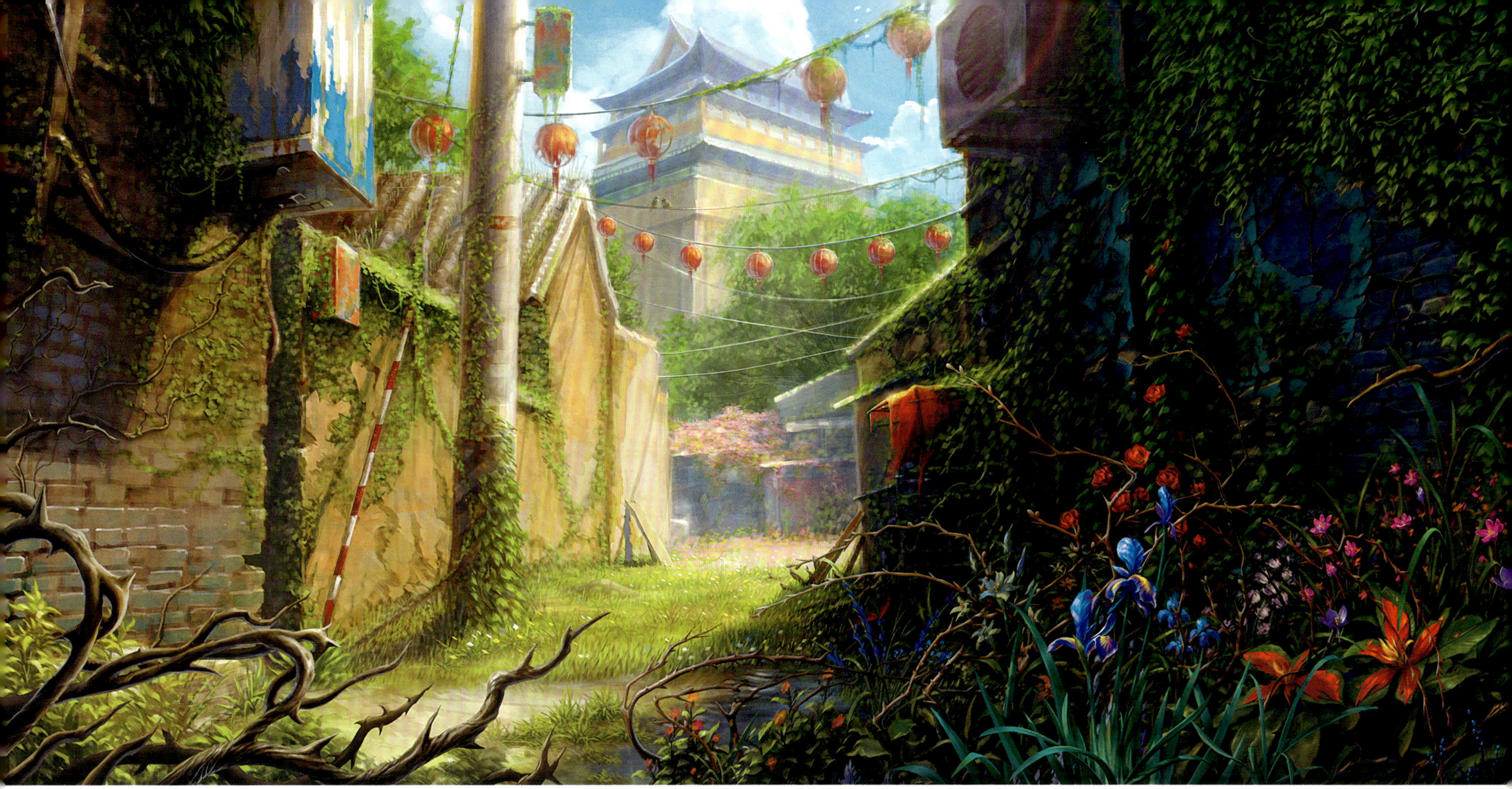

I then touched up the plants and added thorns to diversify the color and form within the frame. At the same time, irregular lines are used to mix up the mainly vertical direction of plant and flower growth. They serve the same function as the lanterns.

## ▼ BUTTERFLIES

Butterflies of different colors are also painted in as the last major decorative elements.

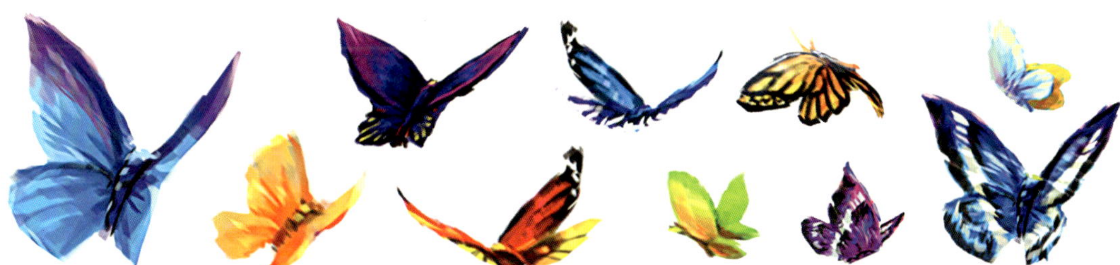

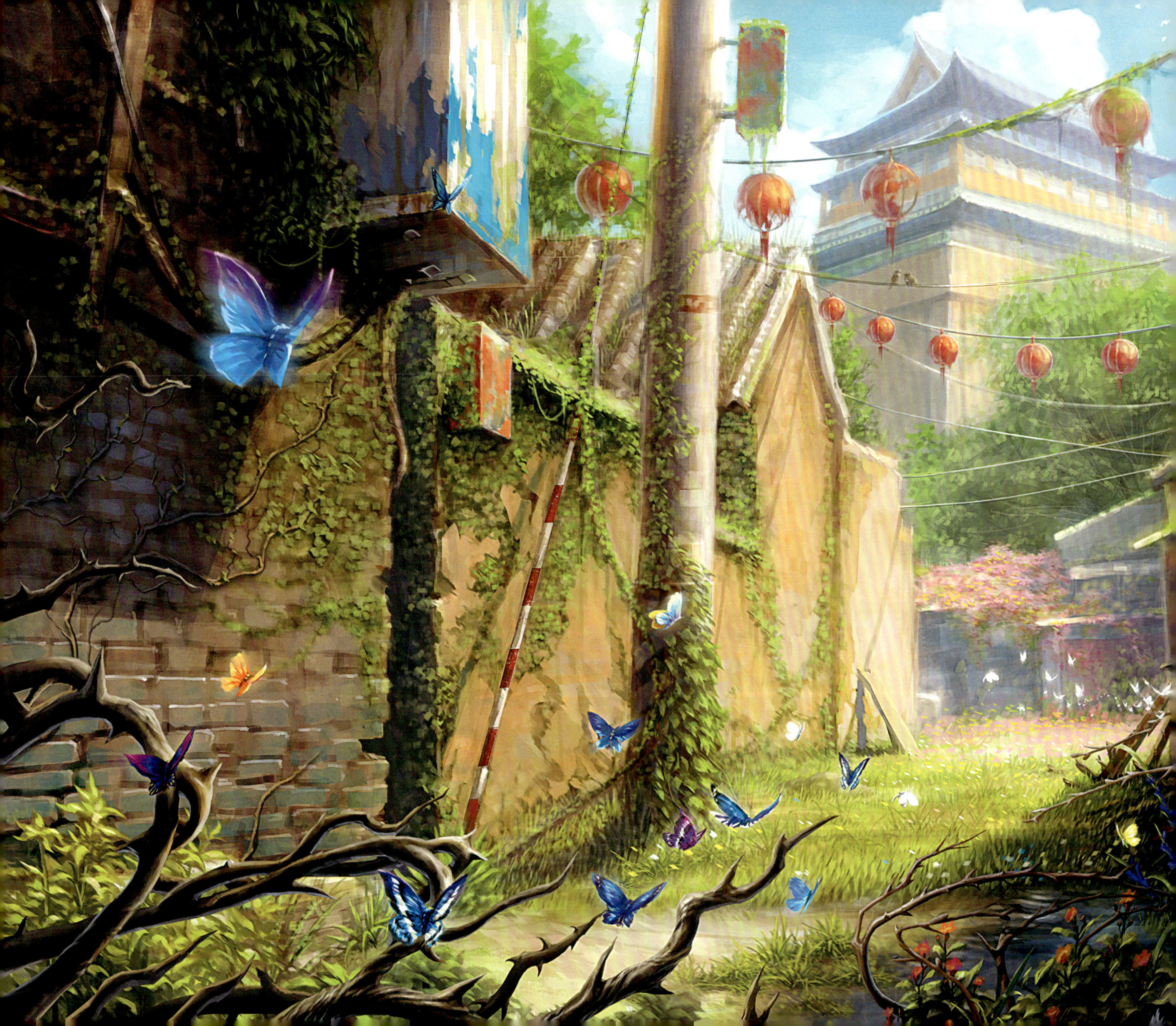

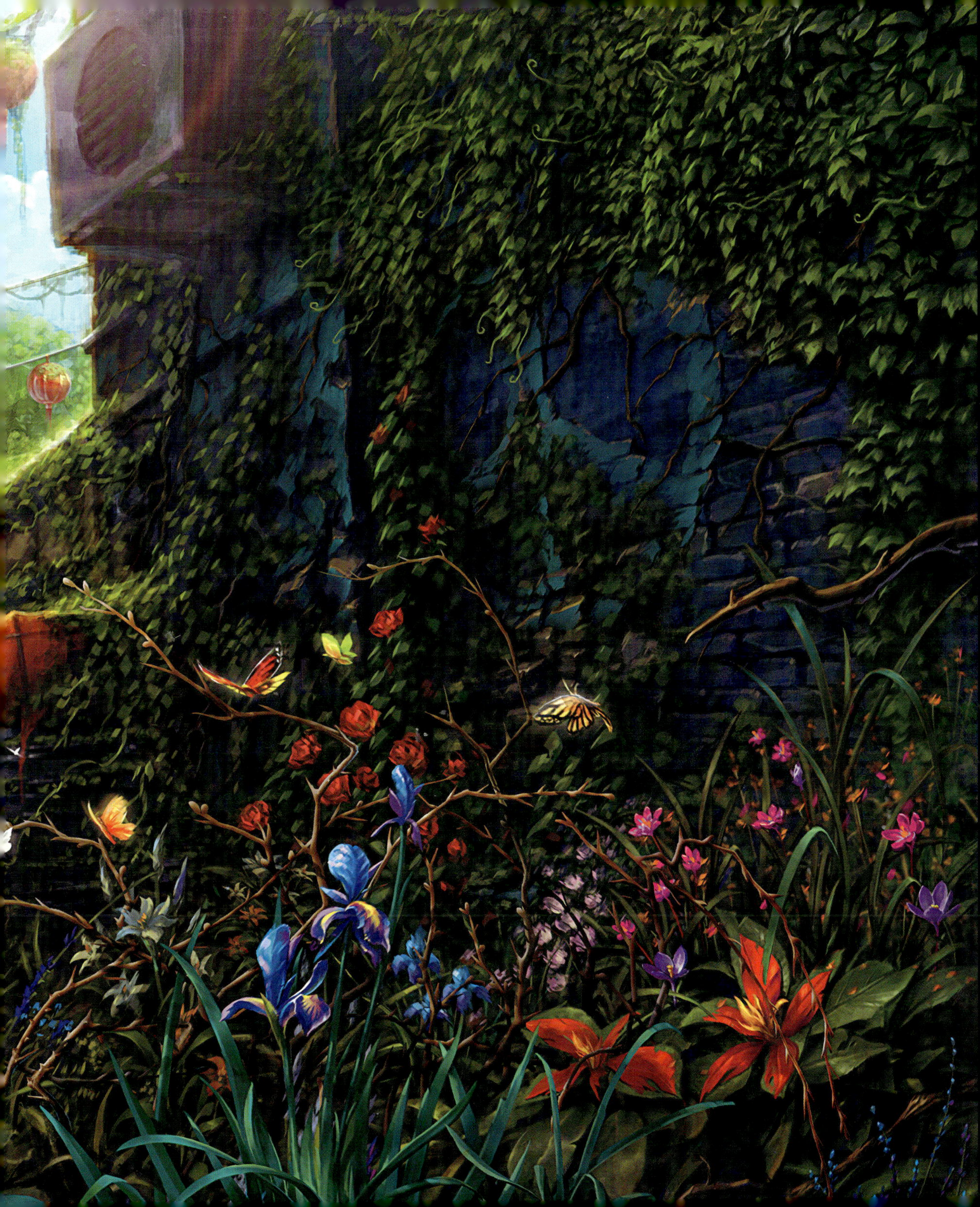

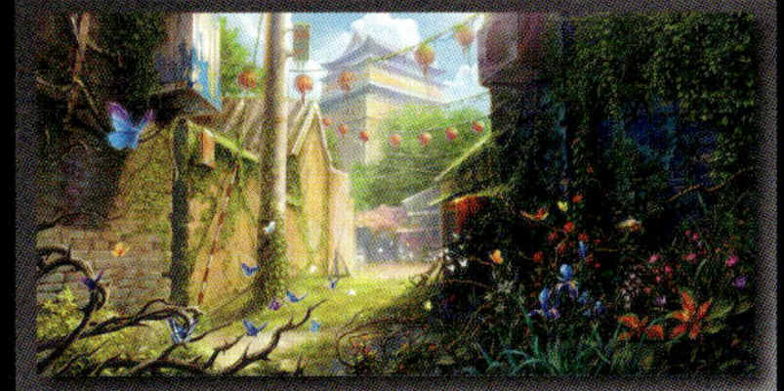

Toward the end of this creation, these butterflies are distributed across the scene according to their harmonizing effect of their colors and flight direction. Making use of the principle that objects look smaller in the distance and bigger when close-up, we can portray a flock of butterflies flying along and down the street toward its far-end. These butterflies thus embody the thematic message of the whole piece.

The street beyond appears warmer in the sunshine. Clusters of flowers climb from the ground to the rooftops. Butterflies symbolizing life and hope fly across the nearby creepers and thorns that pervade the scene, deep into the street toward the sunlit flowers. The whole scene captures an old street, untrodden since the world's end, which has finally embraced new life.

# MAIN POINTS

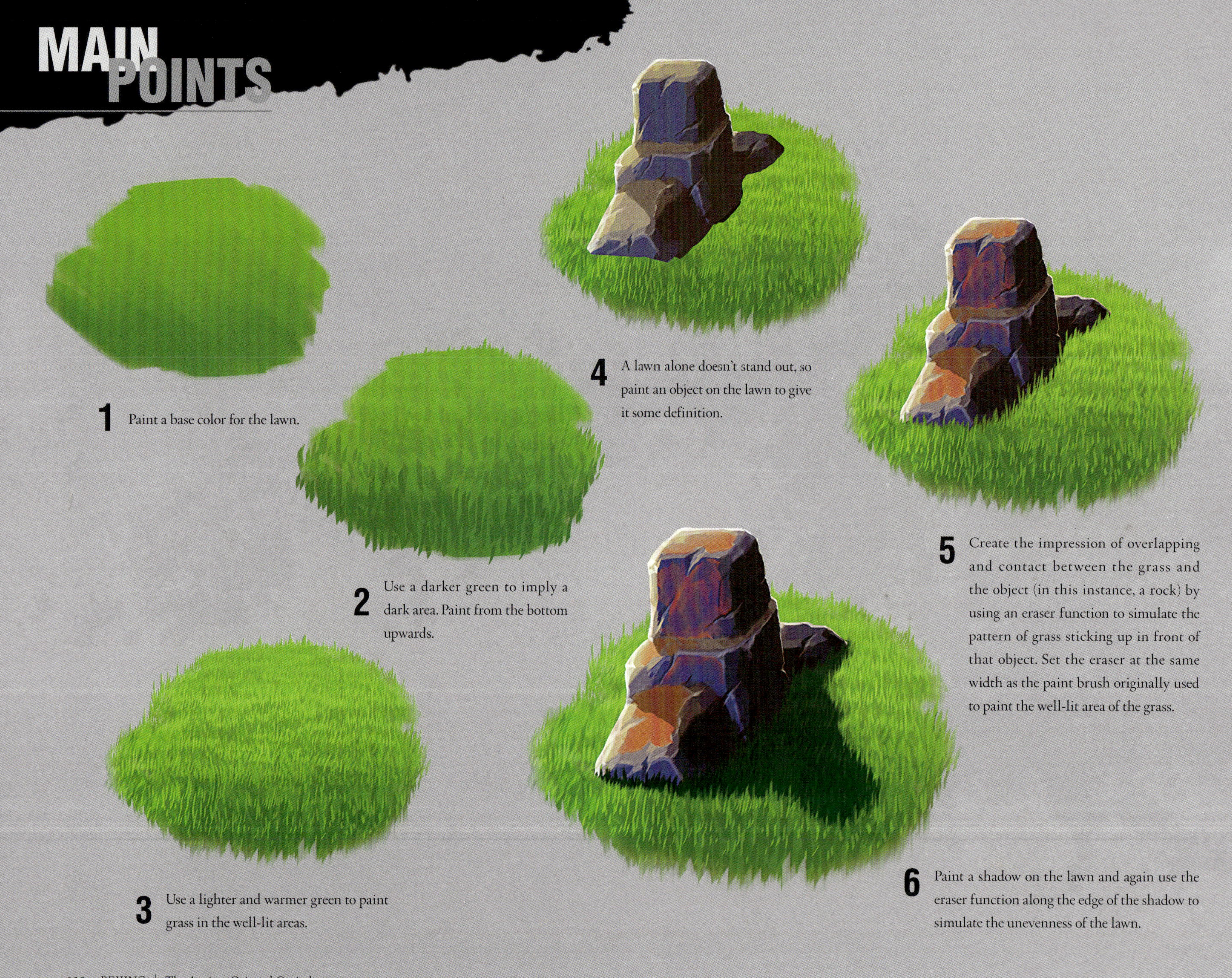

1 Paint a base color for the lawn.

2 Use a darker green to imply a dark area. Paint from the bottom upwards.

3 Use a lighter and warmer green to paint grass in the well-lit areas.

4 A lawn alone doesn't stand out, so paint an object on the lawn to give it some definition.

5 Create the impression of overlapping and contact between the grass and the object (in this instance, a rock) by using an eraser function to simulate the pattern of grass sticking up in front of that object. Set the eraser at the same width as the paint brush originally used to paint the well-lit area of the grass.

6 Paint a shadow on the lawn and again use the eraser function along the edge of the shadow to simulate the unevenness of the lawn.

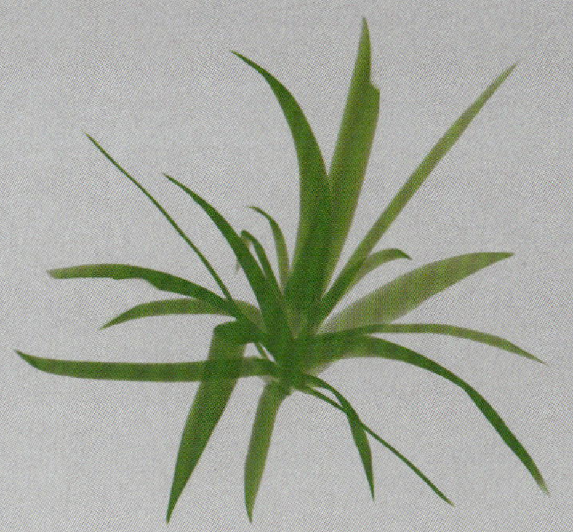

1 Paint the outline of leaves using the silhouetting method.

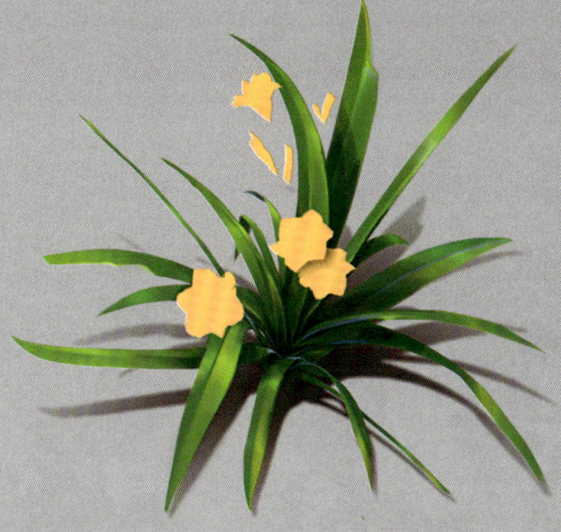

4 Use a base color while painting flowers to produce their silhouettes and fix their positions.

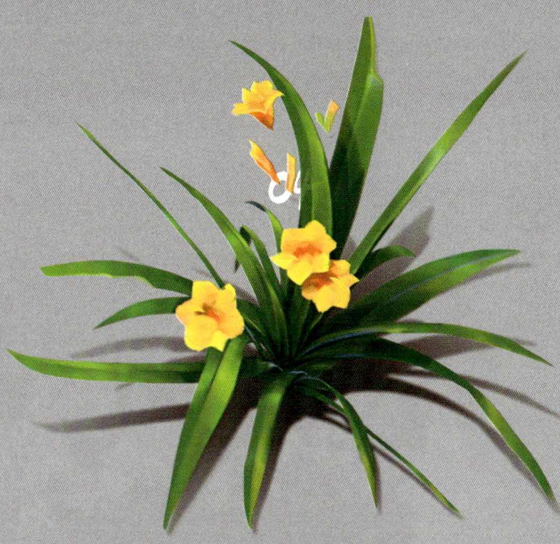

5 Add lighting that is consistent with the depth and form of the leaves.

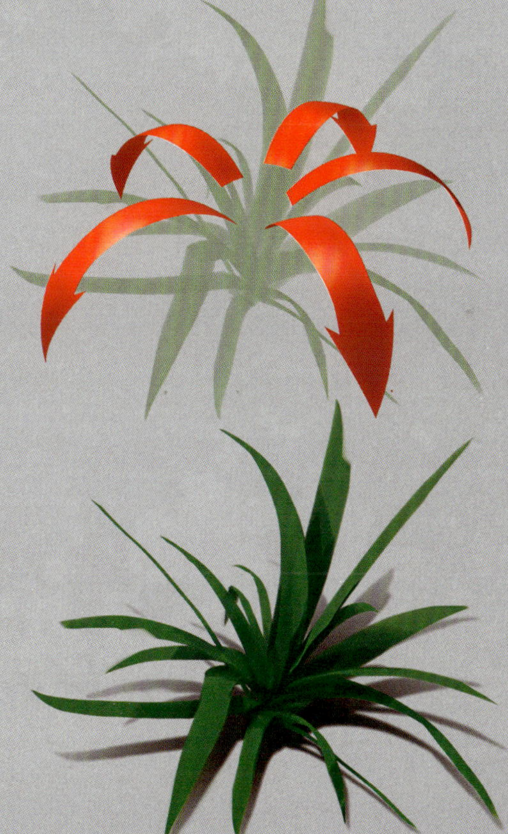

2 Since leaves grow in all directions, it's important to try to demonstrate their spatial depth and breadth.

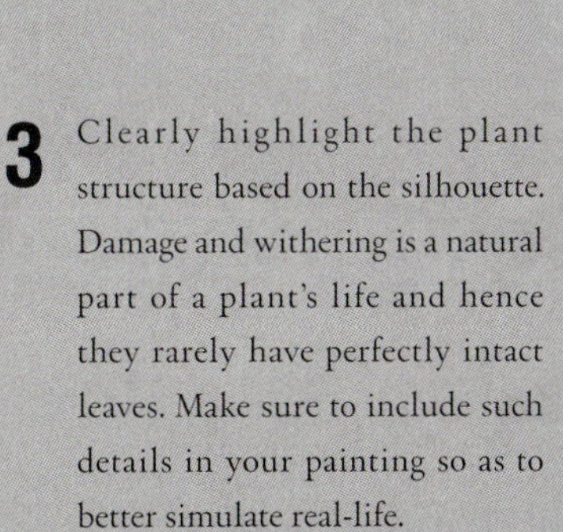

3 Clearly highlight the plant structure based on the silhouette. Damage and withering is a natural part of a plant's life and hence they rarely have perfectly intact leaves. Make sure to include such details in your painting so as to better simulate real-life.

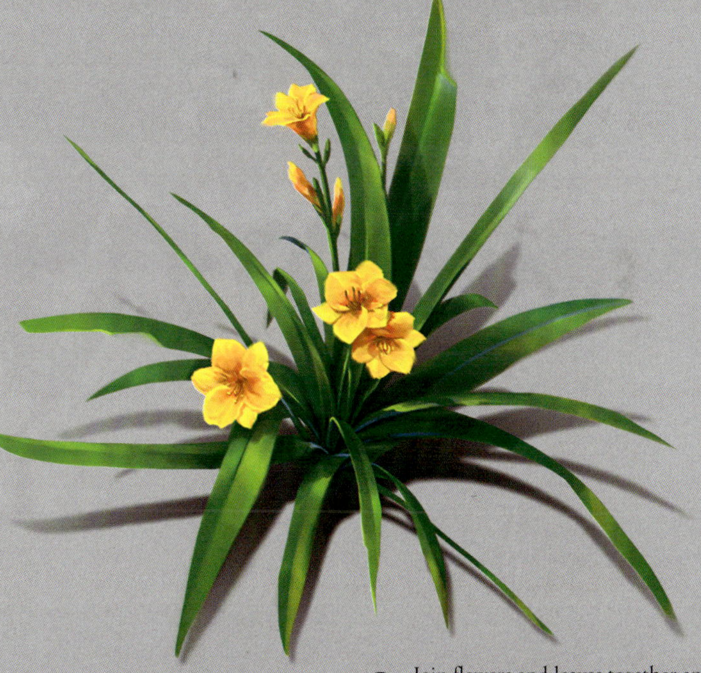

6 Join flowers and leaves together and add the final details in order to finish the work.

# The Forbidden City

Beijing, known as "Jingcheng" in ancient times, served as the capital city for several dynasties and is where legendary "emperors, generals, and ministers" resided. As the palace for the emperor—the highest ruler of China then—the Forbidden City (now known as the "Palace Museum") has become the most unique landmark of the city. This magnificent and grand historical site not only preserves time-honoured history and culture but also embodies the remarkable achievements made by the craftsmen hundreds of years ago. As a cultural heritage museum, the Palace Museum today tops the list of the world's five grand palaces. The other four are the Palace of Versailles in France, Buckingham Palace in the United Kingdom, the White House in the United States, and the Moscow Kremlin in Russia.

The splendid complex of oriental design stands as an example to the world of the architectural miracles possible even in ancient China and tells the tale of the rise and fall of several dynasties.

The piece of work *The Forbidden City* aims to convey a sense of "dust-laden" mystery hidden beneath the palace's magnificence as well as reveal fragments of the multitudinous stories which have unfolded over time within the imperial palace walls.

Creating such a work first necessitates a good grasp of the "form" of the palace before we add "spirit" into our rendering. Considering that "form" is the vehicle of "spirit", only a solid vehicle can safely hold all the contents desired. In other words, if the form of the Forbidden City was poorly represented, or if it was painted like some military fortification or structure in a weird mix of western and oriental styles, then how could we convince viewers that legendary oriental stories took place here?

So, the core question of this creation process is how to present "fantasy" to the maximum degree and concurrently recount these historical tales, whilst remaining the respect to history and culture.

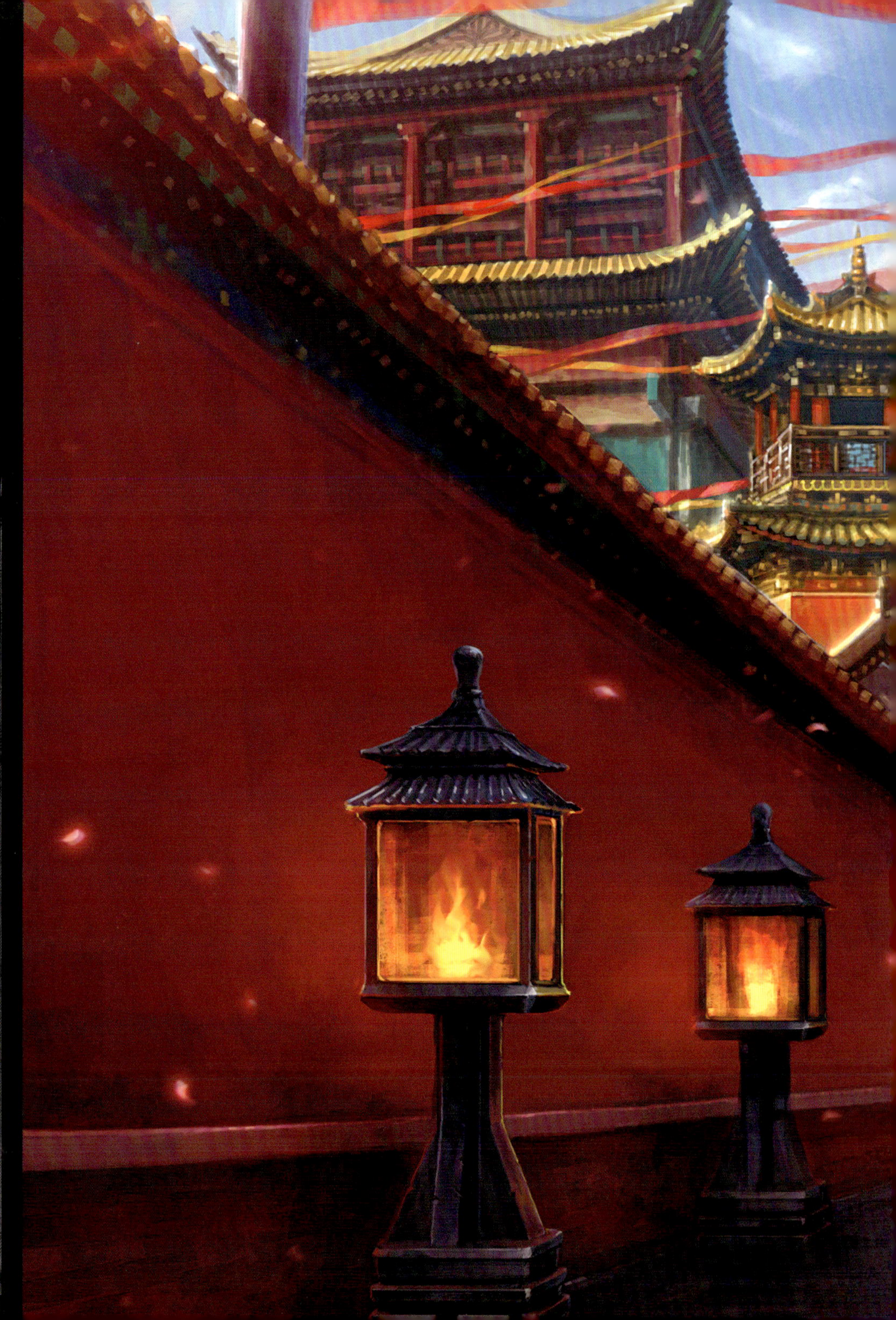

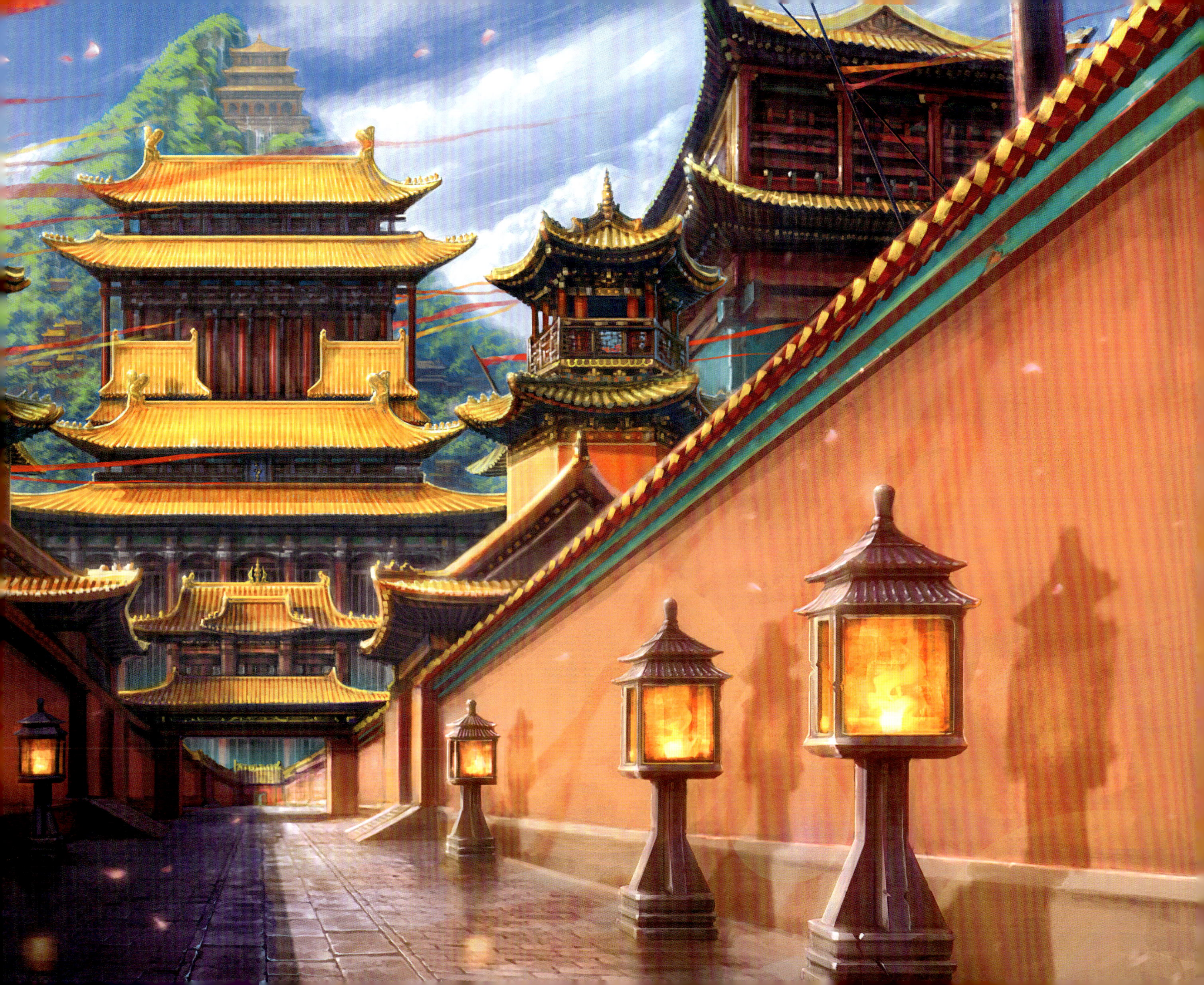

# THOUGHTS ON CREATION

*This piece takes the Palace Museum as its blueprint. In addition to the essential folklore and materials directly relevant to the structure, it's also important to collect and investigate its surrounding environment and geographical landscape as well as sort through records about related major historical events. These will become useful resources for the subsequent design, making the work appear more realistic or meaningful.*

*As a fantasy work, I do not want to simply define the theme of The Forbidden City as "majesty and solemnity" or any obvious choices. Instead, I hope to portray a stronger sense of history and legend, or even a "romantic" or "melancholy" feeling, while still capturing the "magnificence". These are the key words of this piece of work. I would like to emphasize again here: understanding the history, culture, or geography of a region can help to fill an already classic scene with more significance and depth.*

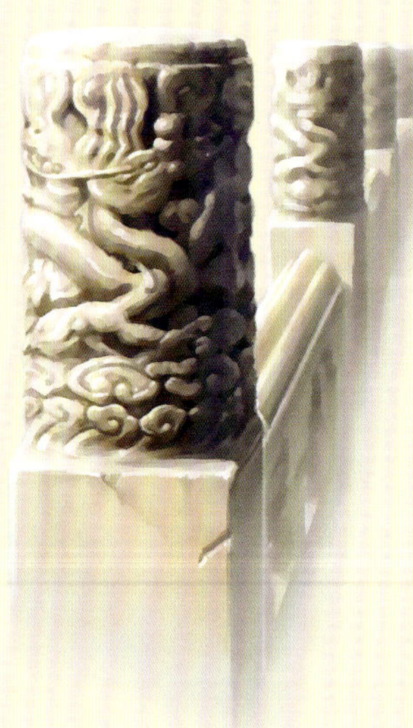

*The Palace Museum is an representation of ancient Chinese imperial palaces. The colossal and magnificent complex is a symbol of power for past rulers and emperors. Most impressive about the structure are the fine details which cover every inch. Its carved beams, painted rafters, glazes shining in various colours, flat flagstones and black bricks, and the reliefs on every marble balustrade all appear delicate and vibrant. Undoubtedly, all these characteristics give expression to the extravagance, majesty, and uniqueness of the palace.*

As a historical site open to the public and a museum for cultural transmission, the Palace Museum receives tens of thousands of visitors every day worldwide. All of them hope to experience this oriental imperial palace of grandeur. It's only when night has fallen that these travellers leave. With the palace lanterns lit to match the glow of sunset, the whole palace takes on an extraordinarily serene and profound character. It gives the illusion of having travelled back to ancient times, to that "Forbidden City" which still never fails to capture our imagination. Here in the Forbidden City, a lot of legendary stories took place, and thus everyone has his or her own deepest impression of the palace. Some may be sad or tragic, others inspiring or heroic, and even those that are infuriating or regretful... Whatever might be, one can infuse them into this fantasy as appropriate.

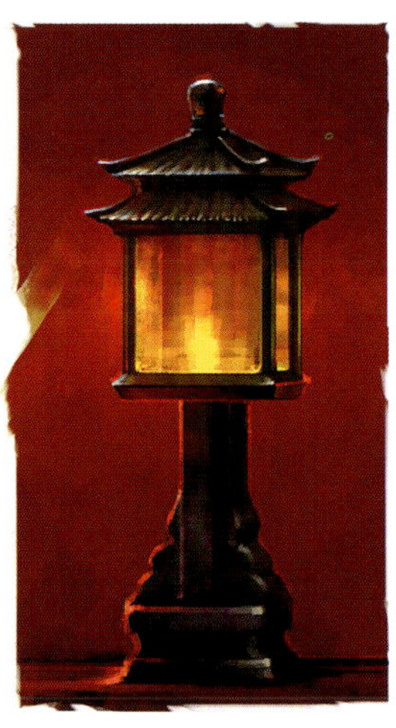

## ▼ THE PALACE MUSEUM

Covering a massive area and housing many palace buildings, the Palace Museum is one of the largest and best-preserved ancient wooden structures in the world. Only first-hand experience of it can give you a real sense of its grandeur. Whether the great turrets, palace hall, or the bronze lions standing in front of the entrance, its every element gives people a feeling of refinement and solemn magnificence.

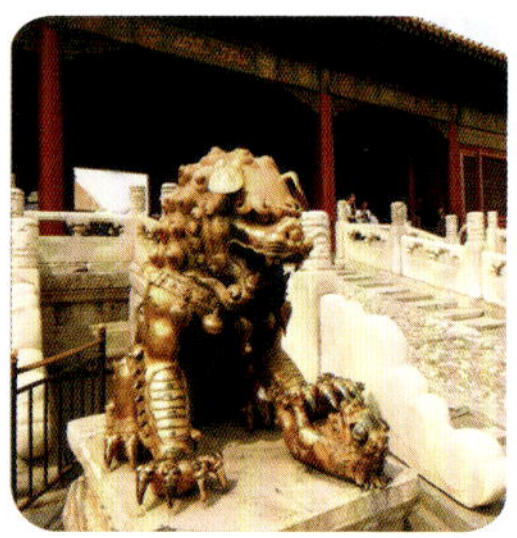

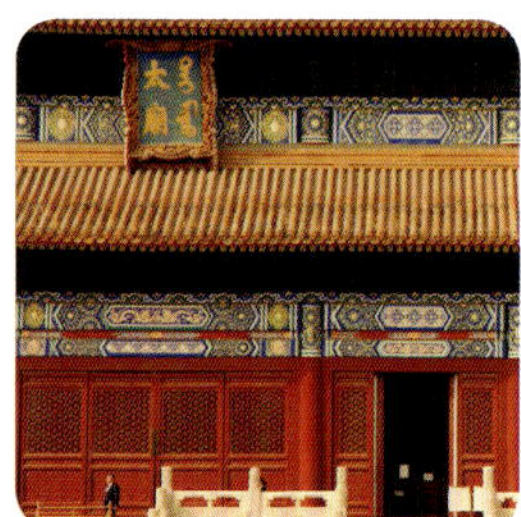

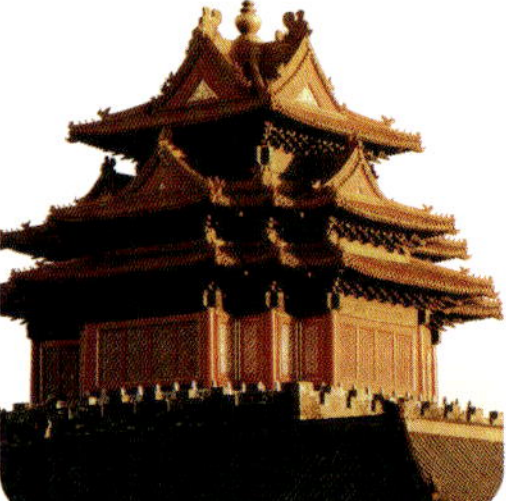

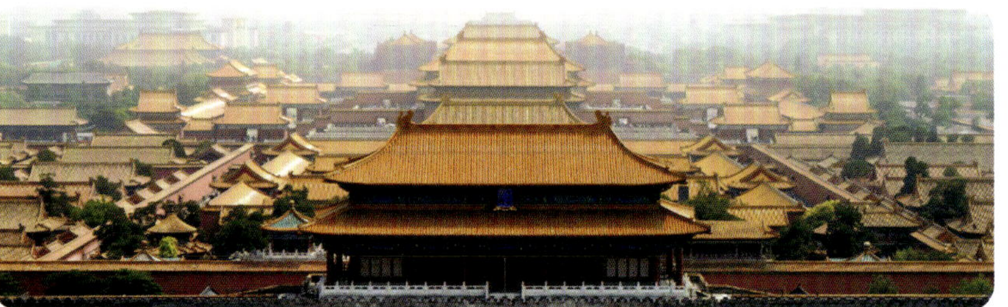

## ▼ HALLS, PASSAGEWAYS AND ATTICS

Three widely known architectural forms as major elements are chosen to be depicted, namely halls, long passageways, and attic buildings. On the one hand, these elements represent the major forms of traditional Chinese architecture; on the other hand, they are respectively characterized by largeness, deepness, and highness, and hence are highly complementary to the spatial composition of this creation.

Considering multiple objects and features we could depict, choices need to be made based on the central theme we want to express and the compositional allowances. In this way, we can achieve the "feeling" we wish to convey and avoid disorderliness or disorientation. A good work does not necessitate an all-inclusive, all-encompassing representation of the relevant contents.

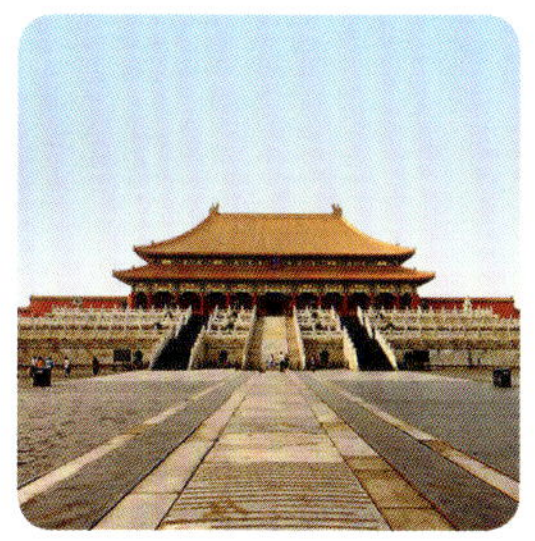

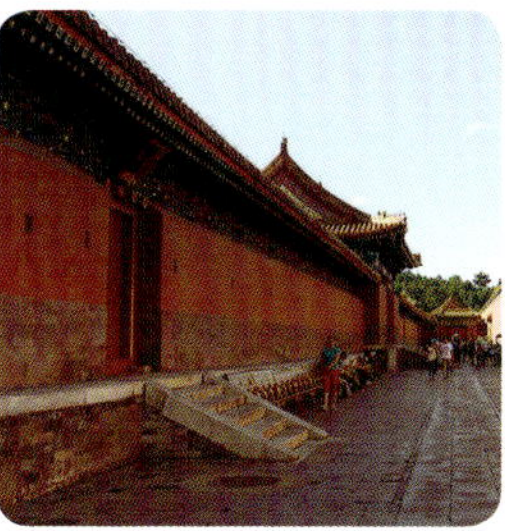

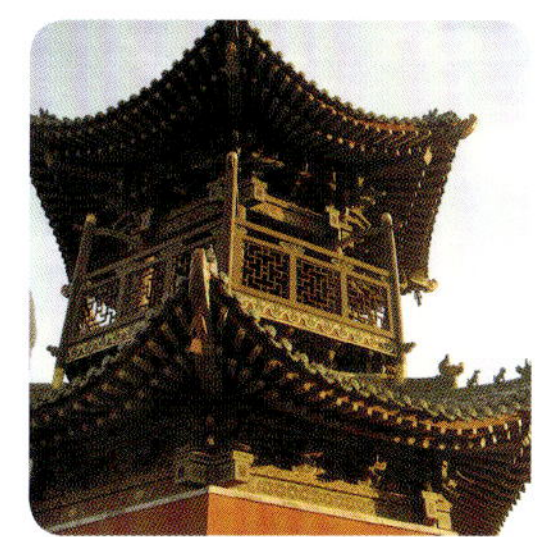

With the three selected architectural forms, I composed a preliminary sketch. Since the magnificence of the palace is reflected in the extensive area, and the wooden structures have their own limitation in height, the Palace Museum does not appear sky-scraping. In order to make the scene clearly layered, I also added an even more massive structure at the centre. To this end, I magnified the hall to a highly exaggerated degree and added structures around its bottom so as to raise it up and make it as complex and imposing as a castle. In the foreground, I placed a long passageway leading up to the hall to create a sense of depth and an atmosphere of tranquility. To the side of the frame, I inserted an attic building. This helps to avoid any large blank area and injects a sense of rhythm, of highs and lows, into the scene.

After thinking about the sketch over and over, I rejected part of the design. The biggest problem with this sketch lies in the way the hall is presented. On the one hand, the castle-style exaggeration makes up for a lack of magnificence and diversification within the limited space, but the oriental flavour is sacrificed. China's imperial palaces are usually arranged in a wellbalanced manner. This is especially true to the palaces in Beijing built upon flat plain-like land. It is often this layout working as a foil to highlight the palaces' solemnity and grandeur. In this original sketch, however, the hall is lifted up so much as to appear as high as a mountain. The truly important features of the subject are thus lost. Moreover, the main subject in the original composition is put to the right side of the scene, in a way that is often used to represent castles as it highlights their shape and size. This deviates, though, from the way that oriental palaces are normally presented. For these reasons, the preliminary sketch was scrapped.

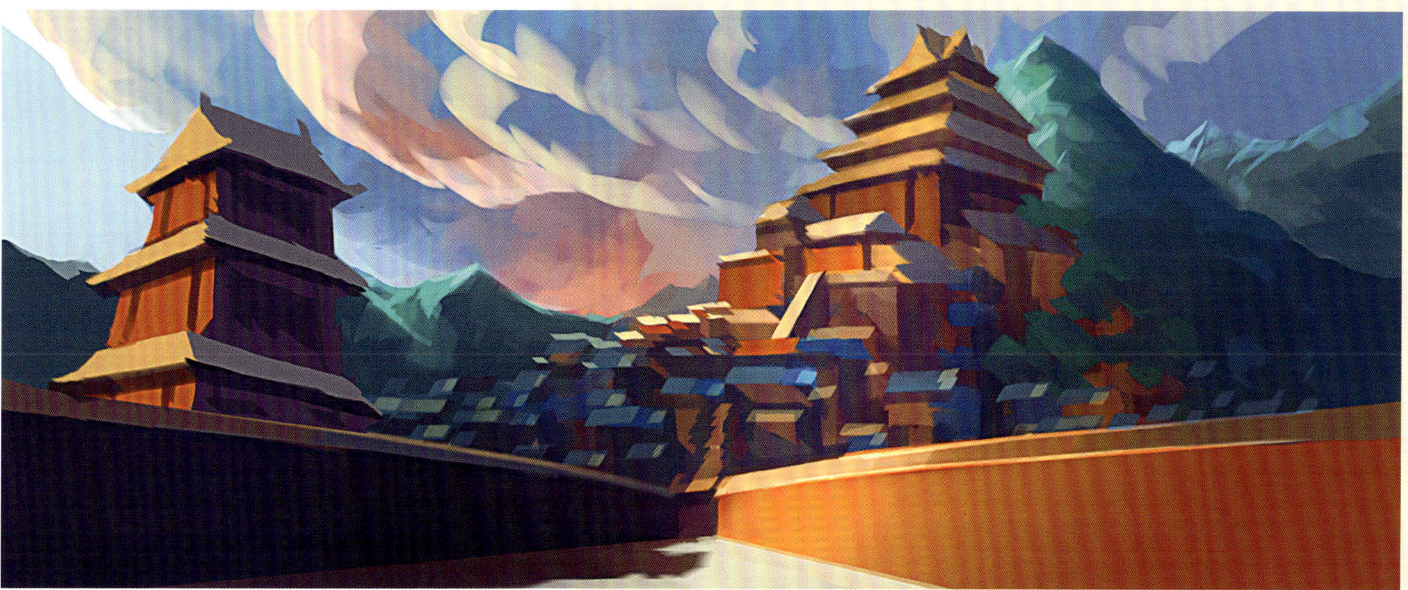

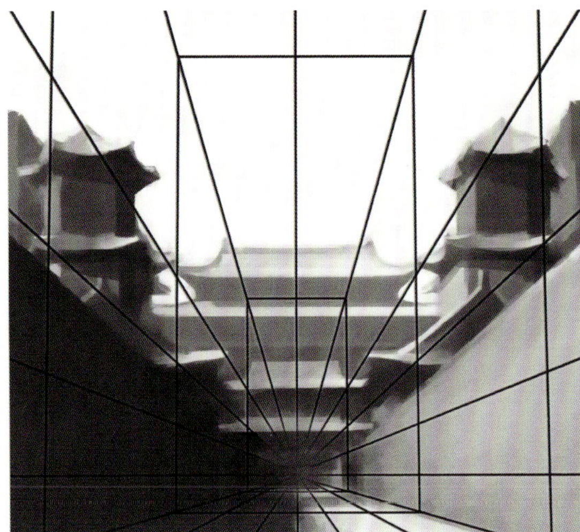

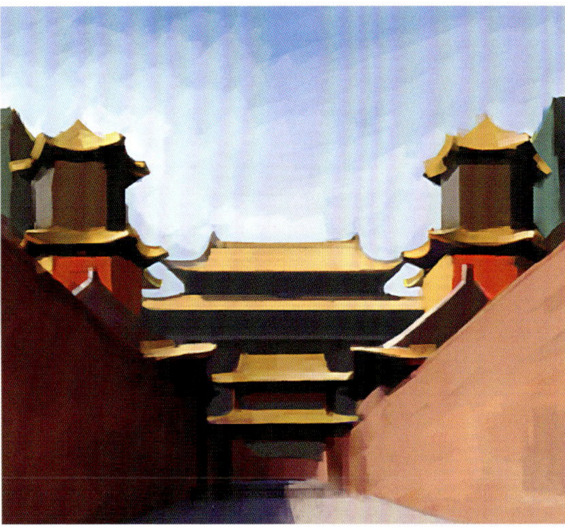

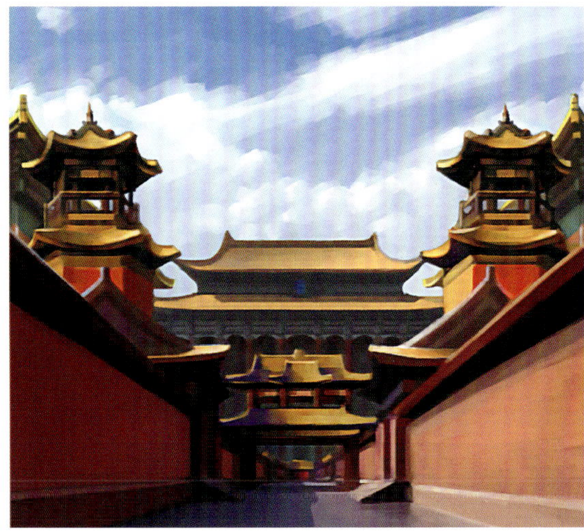

Next I turned to an "orthodox" perspective — that of looking down a street. My thinking here was quite similar to that of *Alleys and Streets of the Past*: the more common a perspective, the more likely it is to resonate with people. I adopted a slightly upward looking view, along the eye-line of any onlooker, to demonstrate the solemnity and majesty of the imperial palace.

I also inserted an imagined light source off to the side and rays of light coming in from that side to produce strong light effect and avoid too much symmetry (or mirroring effect).

Then, details were added to the scene to give the hall, long passageway and attic buildings more shape. I painted in a blue sky with white clouds, and the creation was thus oriented.

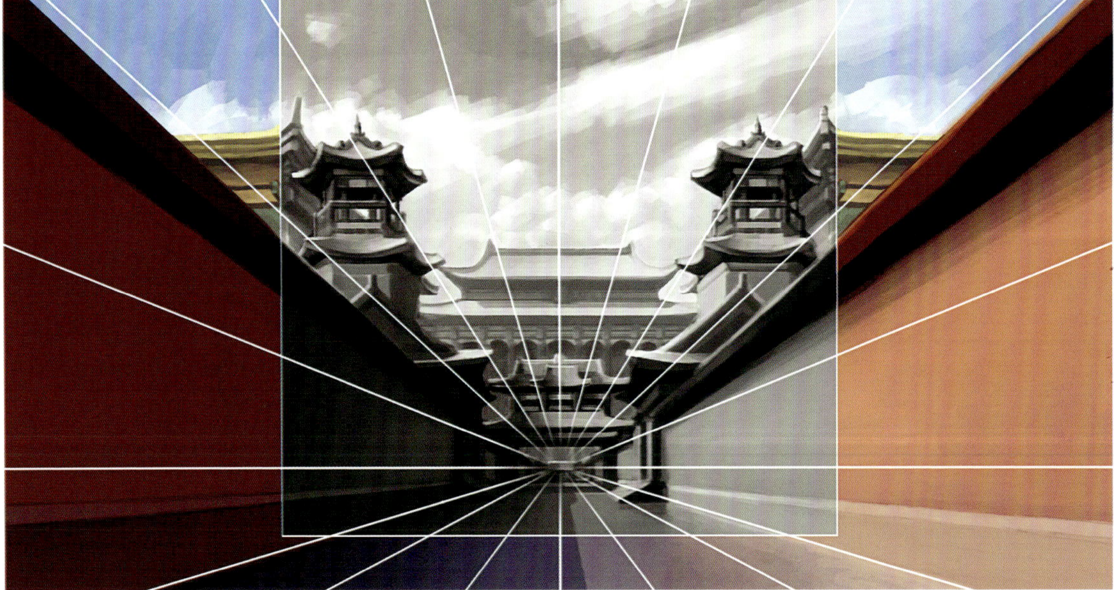

Here I noticed that in order to highlight the squareness of composition and forms within, I had changed the aspect ratio to 1:1. After the details were refined, however, I found the scene to be a little bit crowded and subsequently opted to broaden the frame to a wide-angle view. I think this accentuates the palace's nature as well.

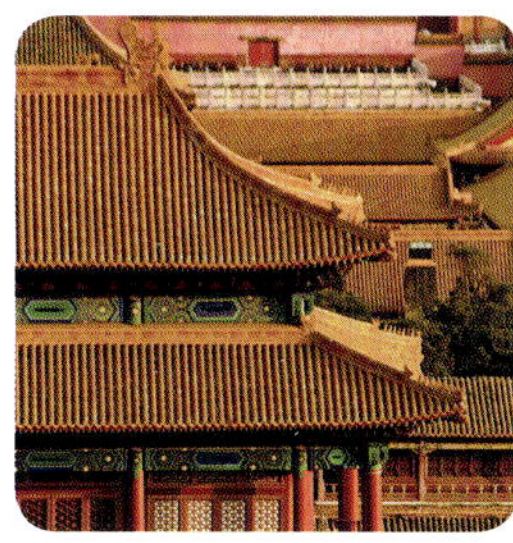

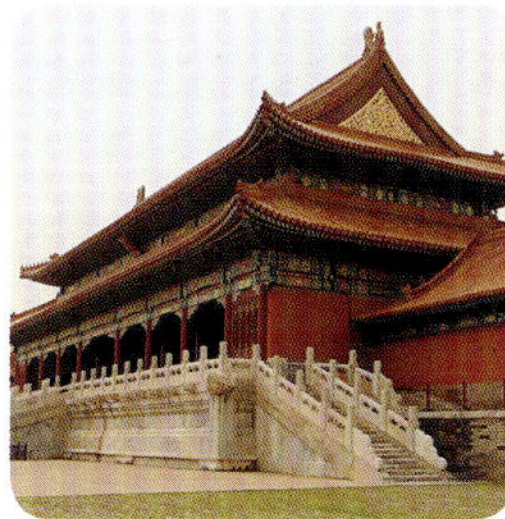

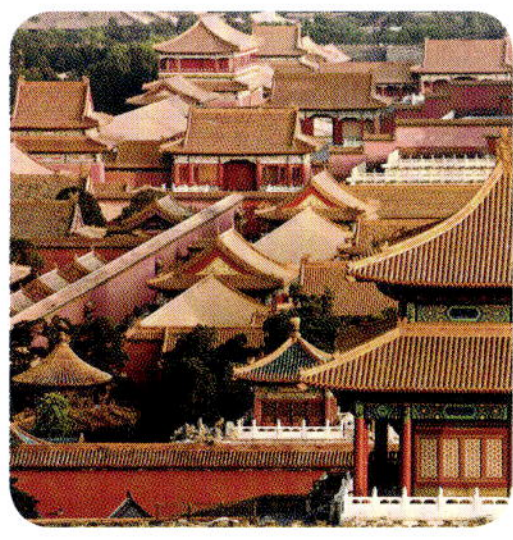

## ▲ BUILDINGS

Structures in the Palace Museum are strikingly symmetrical. Roofs of main halls are covered with yellow glazed tiles, matched with the malachite green, sapphire blue, purple and black.

On the two sides of the roof of the Hall of Supreme Harmony are two glazed *wenshou*, beasts that hold the roof ridge in their mouths, serving as structural components and ornaments of the hall.

There is a mountain in the background of the frame, and the newly added attic buildings are "enlarged" in an exaggerated way. Yet compared with the original scene of a castle as tall as a mountain, built atop a mountain , the new composition evidences more restraint on the artistic license. In addition, the point of view is that of an onlooker gazing upward, the same as that of the gate building. Enlarging objects is the most common way of injecting an element of fantasy into a piece. But what kinds of objects can be enlarged? From what kind of a perspective should they be enlarged? How much should they be enlarged? To have our works be credible and accepted by viewers, these are all questions we should ask ourselves and weigh up the different possibilities carefully.

Next, I added palace lanterns to imply a sense of silence and quietness and build more of an atmosphere. Their inclusion also seemed appropriate now that a new aspect ratio had been adopted. The final layout was thus finished. At the initial stage, it's normal for edits to be made, sections to be deleted, and then those same elements reintroduced again, perhaps in a different way. Here I have presented the creation process with the aim of showing that any modification is worthwhile, whether it is to the composition, the scale, the perspective, the contents, or the style of representation, as long as it improves the work or enriches the theme.

More objects were added to fill out and refine the broadened area of the overall layout.

Since I shifted the scene to a wide-angle view, the original attic buildings appeared small and isolated. Larger ones were thus added to make the scene more proportionately balanced. Similarly, after the aspect ratio of the scene was changed, the hall in the central distance seemed fragile. To remedy this, I added a large gate building above the hall at its back. In order to better layer the scene, I also inserted a mountain behind the gate building. For one thing, this makes the scene more diverse; for another, the mountain has its own "story" to tell, which will resonate with viewers who know about Chinese history (to be explained later).

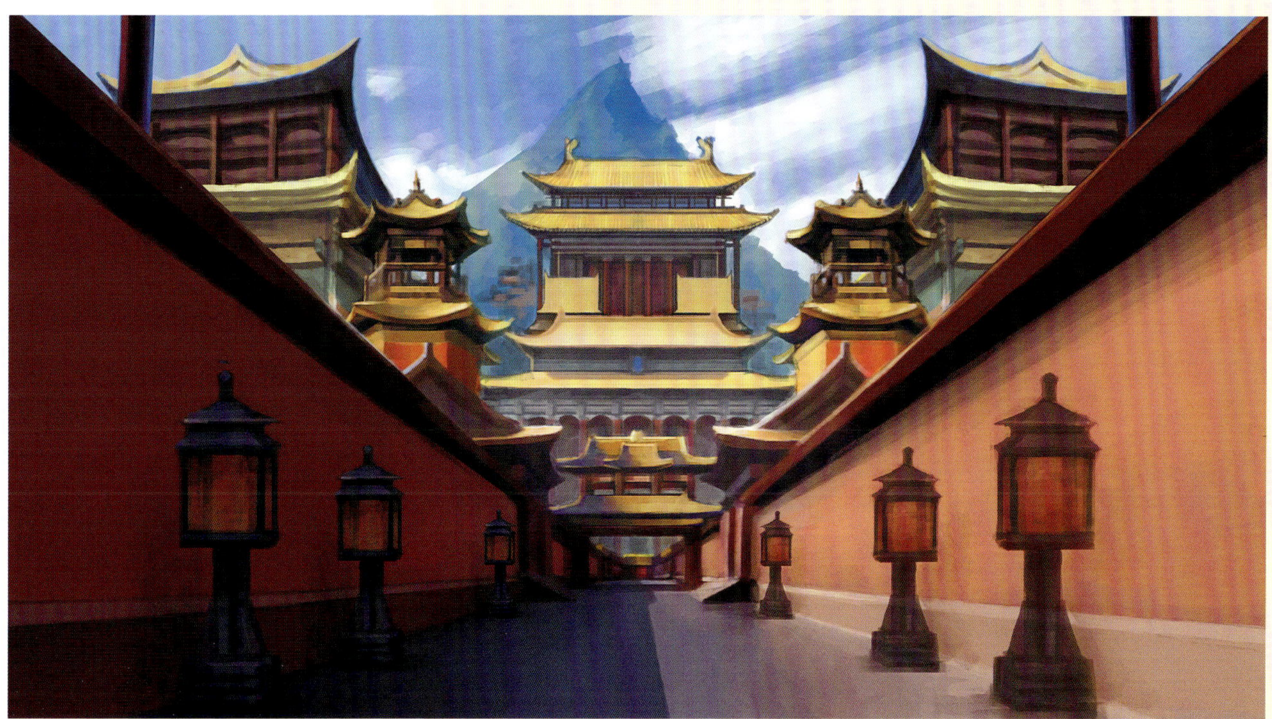

Including Wansui Hill in a piece and infusing it with the sadness of the story can tie together the whole of the piece. Meanwhile, for those viewers who know this part of history, there is an added layer of meaning for them to realise; that is, the despair of the Chongzhen Emperor at the fall of his regime and thus the knowledge that "today's grandeur may die tomorrow".

## ▶ THE MOUNTAIN

The mountain in the background refers to "Wansui Hill" (Long Live Hill) in Jingshan Park adjacent to the Palace Museum. In the Yongle era (1403-1424), Emperor Zhu Di of the Ming Dynasty decided that there should be a hill to the north of the Forbidden City where, according to the saying that "the Azure Dragon, the White Tiger, the Vermilion Bird, and the Black Tortoise are guardians of the four directions," the black tortoise guards. Therefore, earth was excavated from the Tongzi River, the Taiye Pond, and the South China Sea to form five peaks together known as the "Wansui Hill".

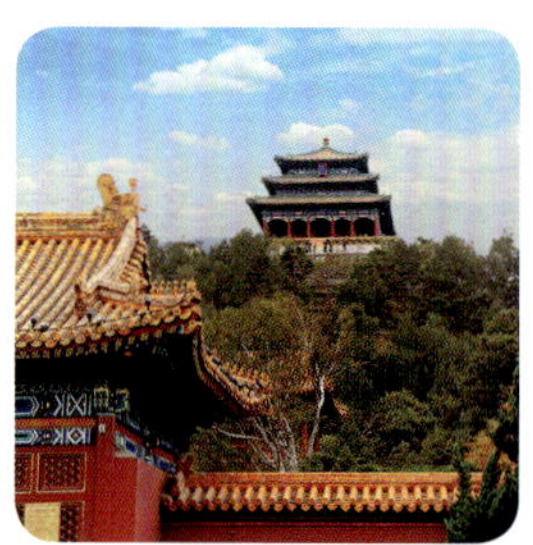

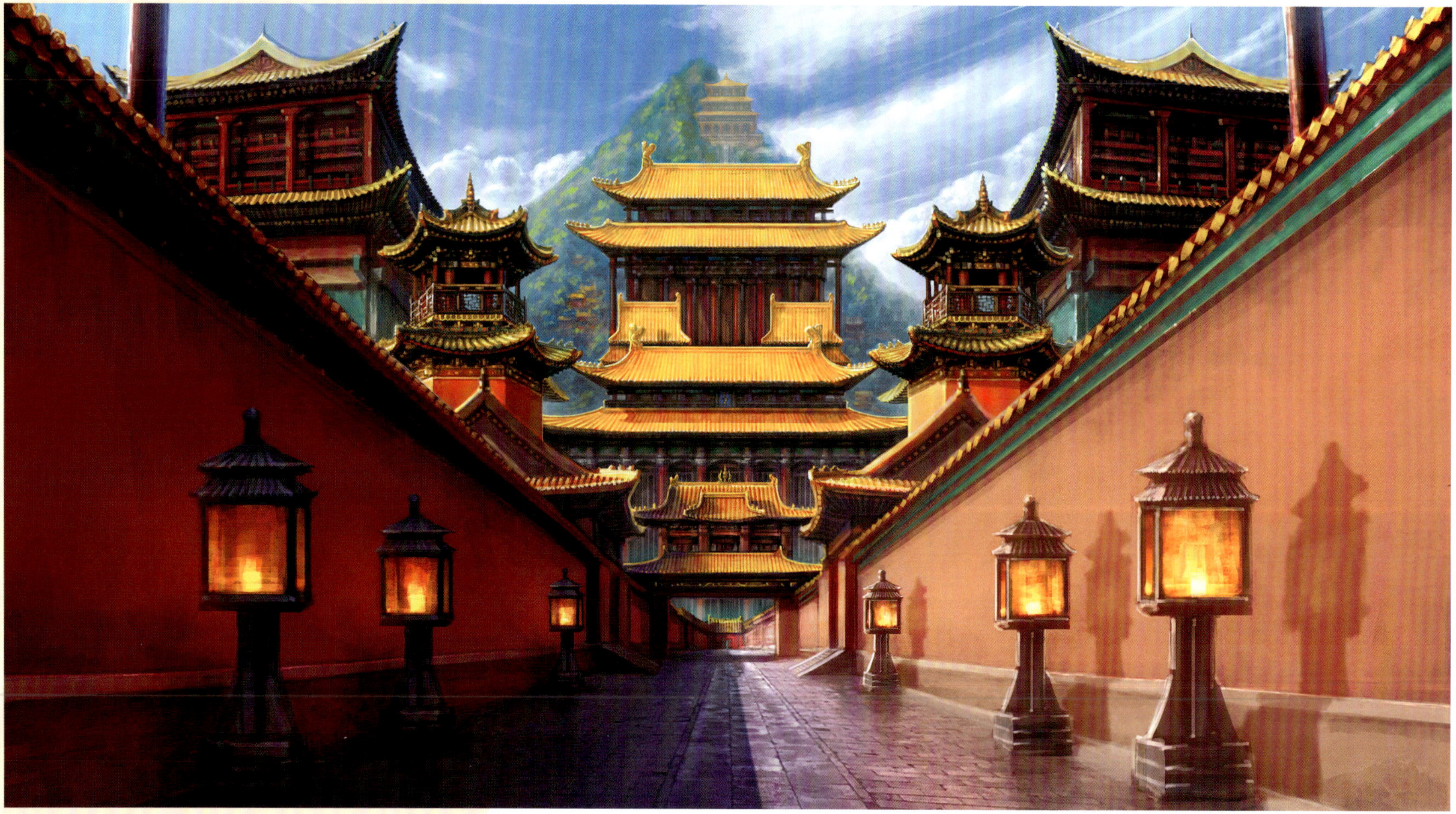

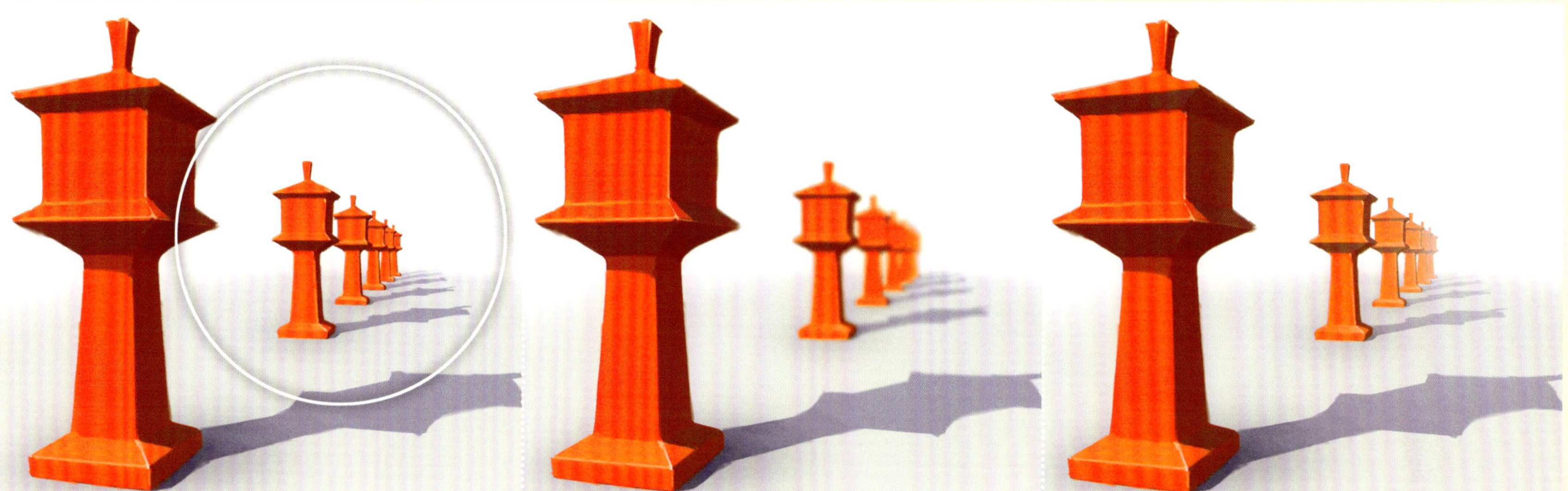

I continued to refine certain details in objects, such as the palace lanterns with the goal of fleshing out the desired atmosphere. Objects similar to each other on both sides of the frame were made consistent in shape using the mirroring method. However, some of the objects required re-painting as they have different shadows.

As the scene became richer in content, the relationship of depth between objects and refine non-focal parts should be considered. To this end, there are two methods: one is to simulate depth with the blurring method; the other is to use mist effect to make the work appear more layered. Since I hoped the scene could remain consistent in clarity and sharpness, I chose the latter.

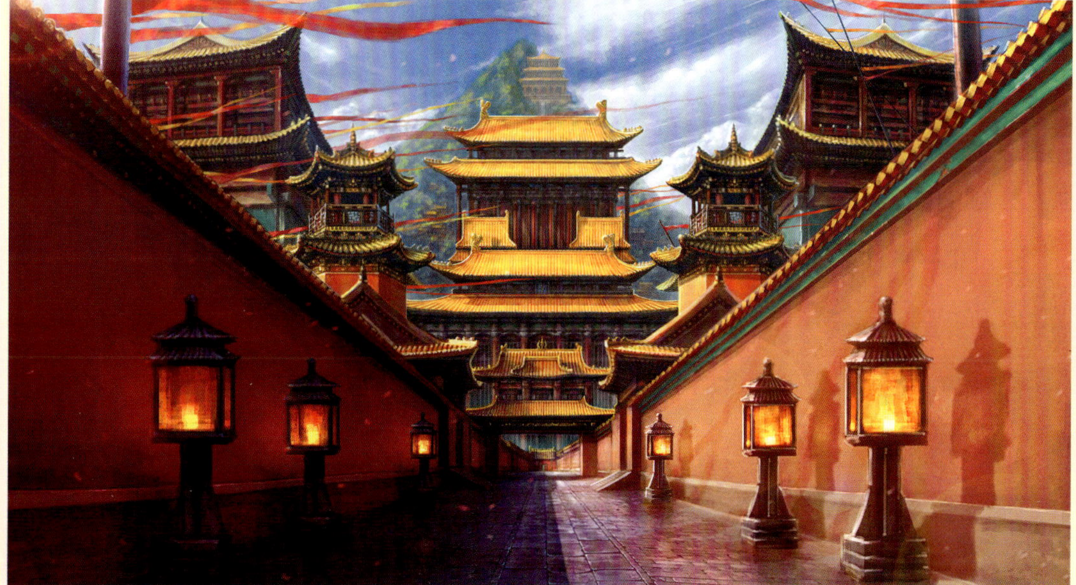

After the mist effect was produced, I continued to refine details and added elements which would strengthen the atmosphere: flying coloured flags and fluttering flower petals. These inject a sense of dynamism and movement to the static scene and convey the happiness of being caught in a cool breeze during warm spring.

(Note: objects subject to the influence of wind should be in the same direction. Any obvious logical mistake in a scene is immediately noticeable to viewers and makes it difficult for them to resonate with it.)

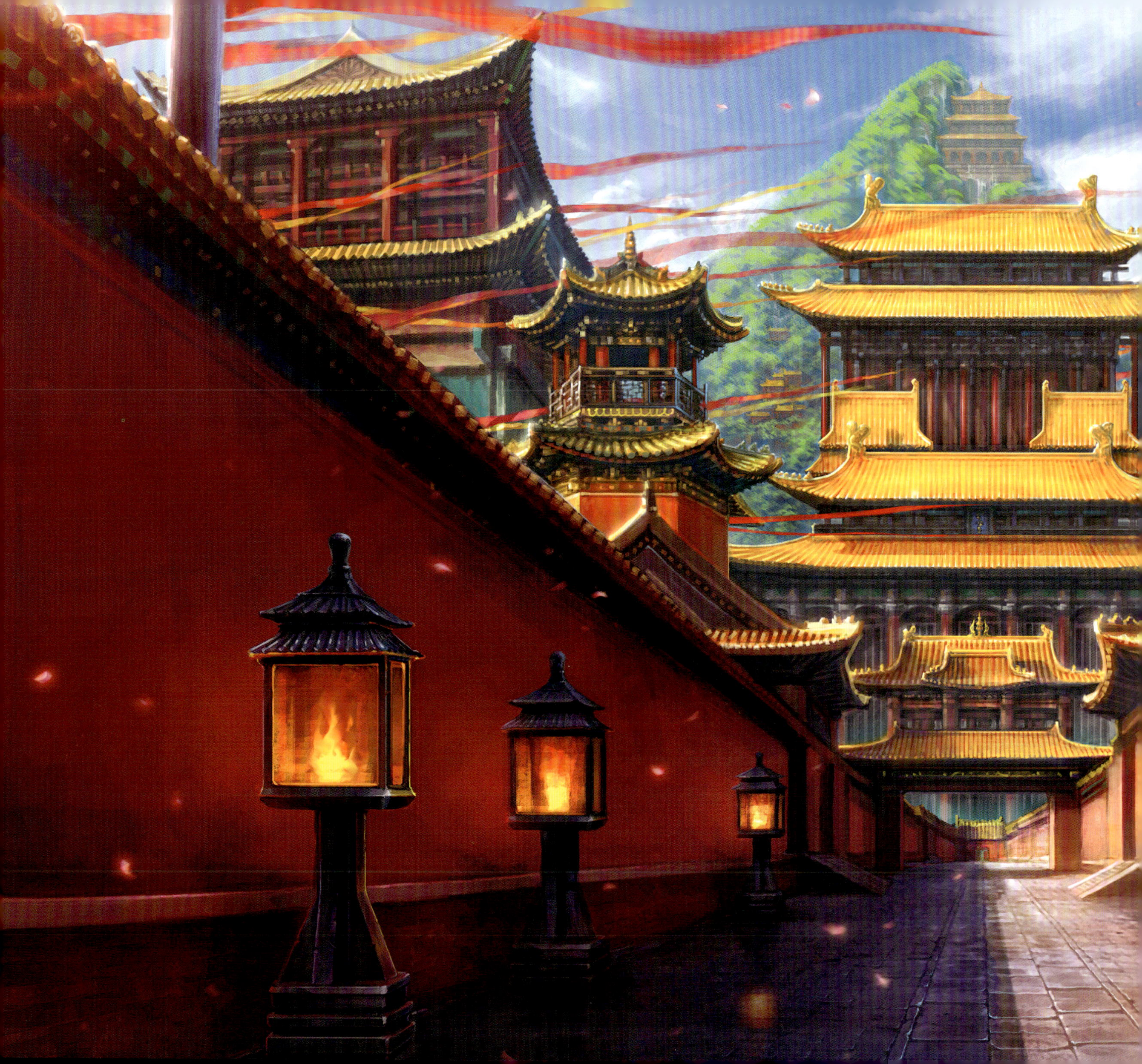

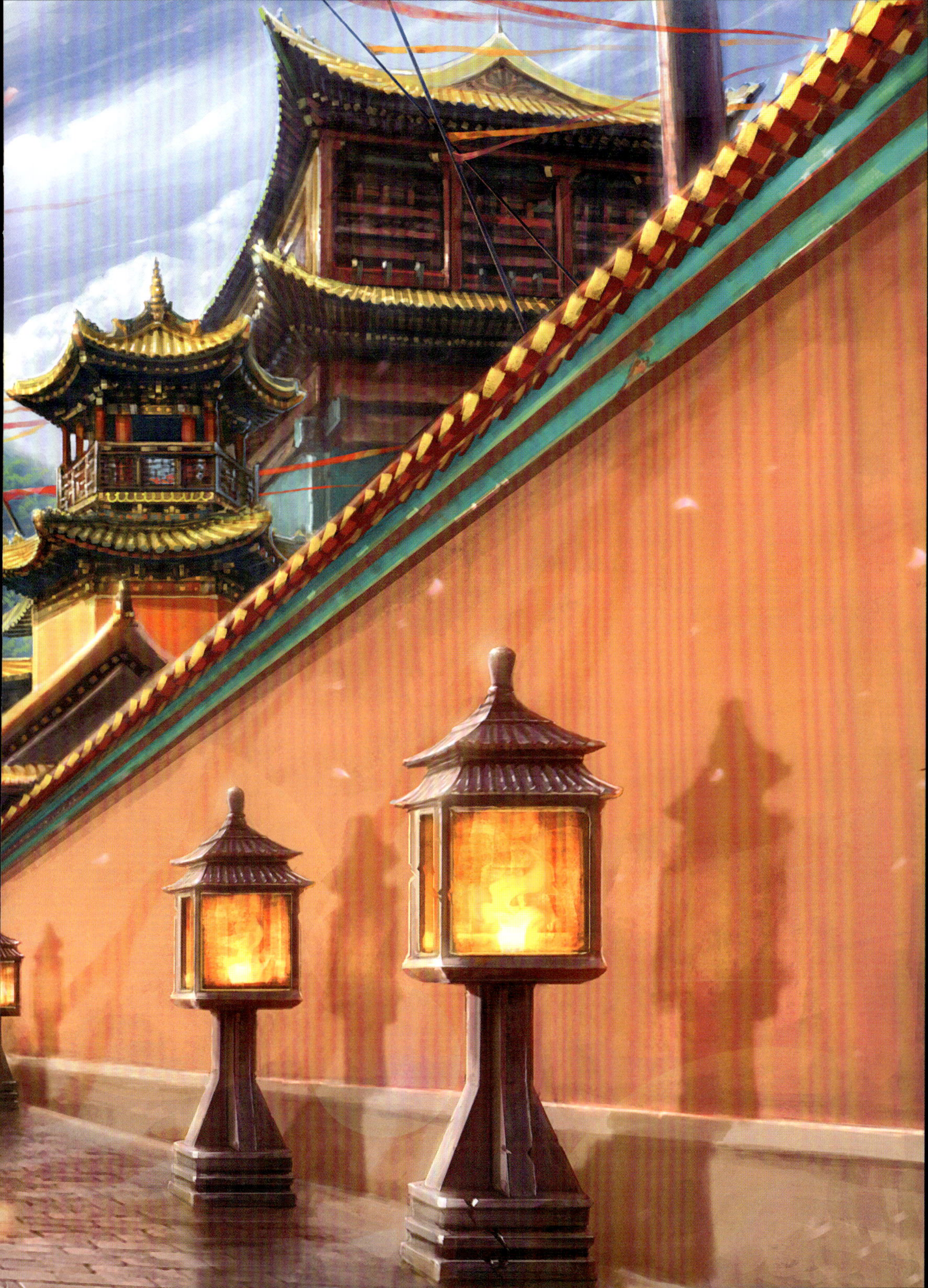

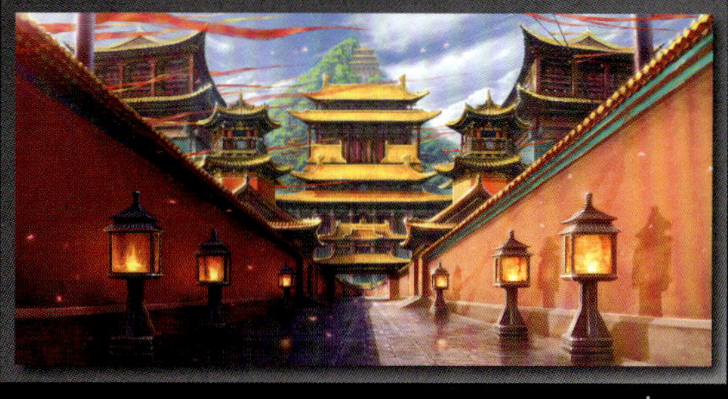

The piece was then checked for mistakes. For instance, since the rest of the palace lanterns were originally copied from a single lantern I painted for quick effects, there were serious problems with these lanterns' perspective. In painting the fluttering flower petals, I only considered their composition and direction of movement but failed to keep them at an appropriate distance from each other… After such problems were solved, I adjusted the lighting and colouring of the scene, making the warm sunshine stronger and the candlelight of the palace lanterns brighter. Finally, I created glow effects (adding dim light reflected from the highlighted areas) in the well-lit areas where reflection might occur. These effects improved the overall atmosphere, enlivened the interplay of light with objects, and injected the scene with a sense of movement. *The Forbidden City* was thus completed.

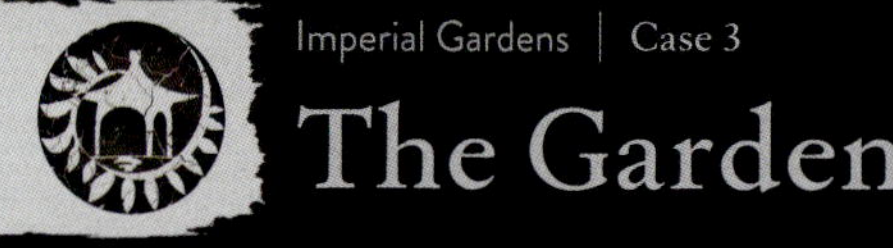



# The Garden

Beijing was called "the imperial city of the past", and the "imperial gardens", known in ancient books as "yuan", play an essential part of the fabric of Beijing. As one of the most important parts for the emperors and their families, the imperial gardens thus served as both retreats offering recreation and rest and symbols of absolute imperial authority, distinguishing themselves from other types of gardens.

Imperial gardens are characterized by their large scale, architectural magnificence, purposeful locations and a combination of the best features from other gardens. They are usually located by mountains and waters to create a landscape of poetic and pictorial splendour which is secluded from the real world. An imperial garden is usually divided into several interconnected scenic spots, each of which is distinctive. Designers used objects such as ornamental perforated windows, open doorways, bamboo forests, and rockeries to create the illusion of disconnect among adjacent areas, making them complementary to each other, while at the same time independent of each other.

*The Garden* tries to present the viewer as many characteristics as possible. Meanwhile, I hope that this work can push myself to achieve, and even improve on, the "sense of transcending ordinariness" that our ancients aspired to. This is the first example in this book depicting natural landscapes, though I will still be infusing the scene with cultural elements. Ancient Chinese gardens can be understood as refined natural landscapes, where beside the obvious addition of architecture, seemingly natural mountains and waters have been polished and shaped to appear more "poetic".

To the minds of ancient people, imperial gardens embody a perfect combination of fantasy and reality. They either take dreamlike fantasy lands as their model or attempt to create a microcosm of the great landscapes of ancient China by transplanting their shrunken forms to a garden. Adding to the special architectural forms, diverse trees, flowers and grasses, and winding paths and rivers, a garden is interwoven with the designers' emotions and dreams.

With the ancients' pursuit of the imperial gardens, we need to give expression in our creation. During conception and our search for materials, we need to touch upon this blend of fantasy and historical reality.

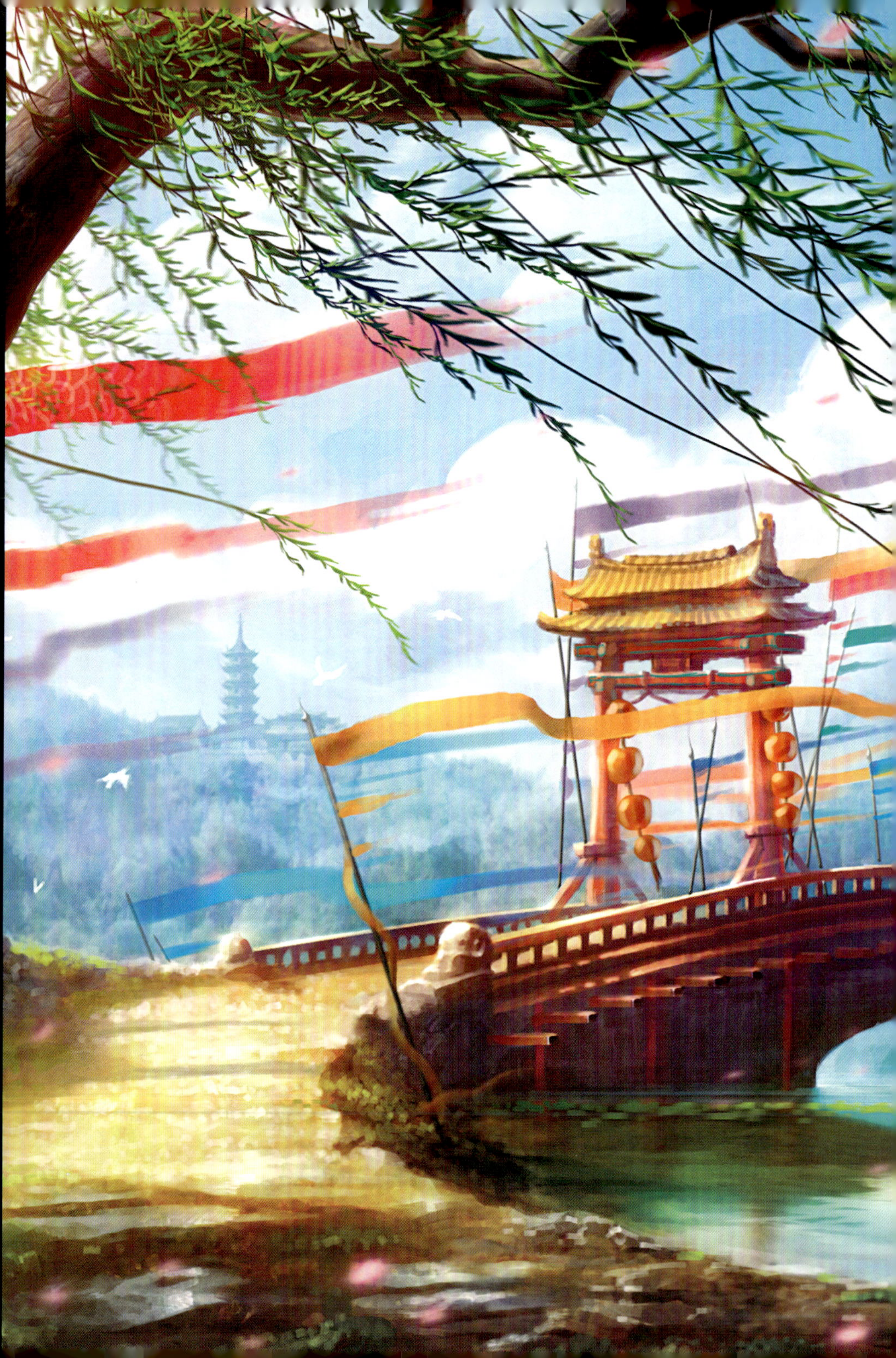

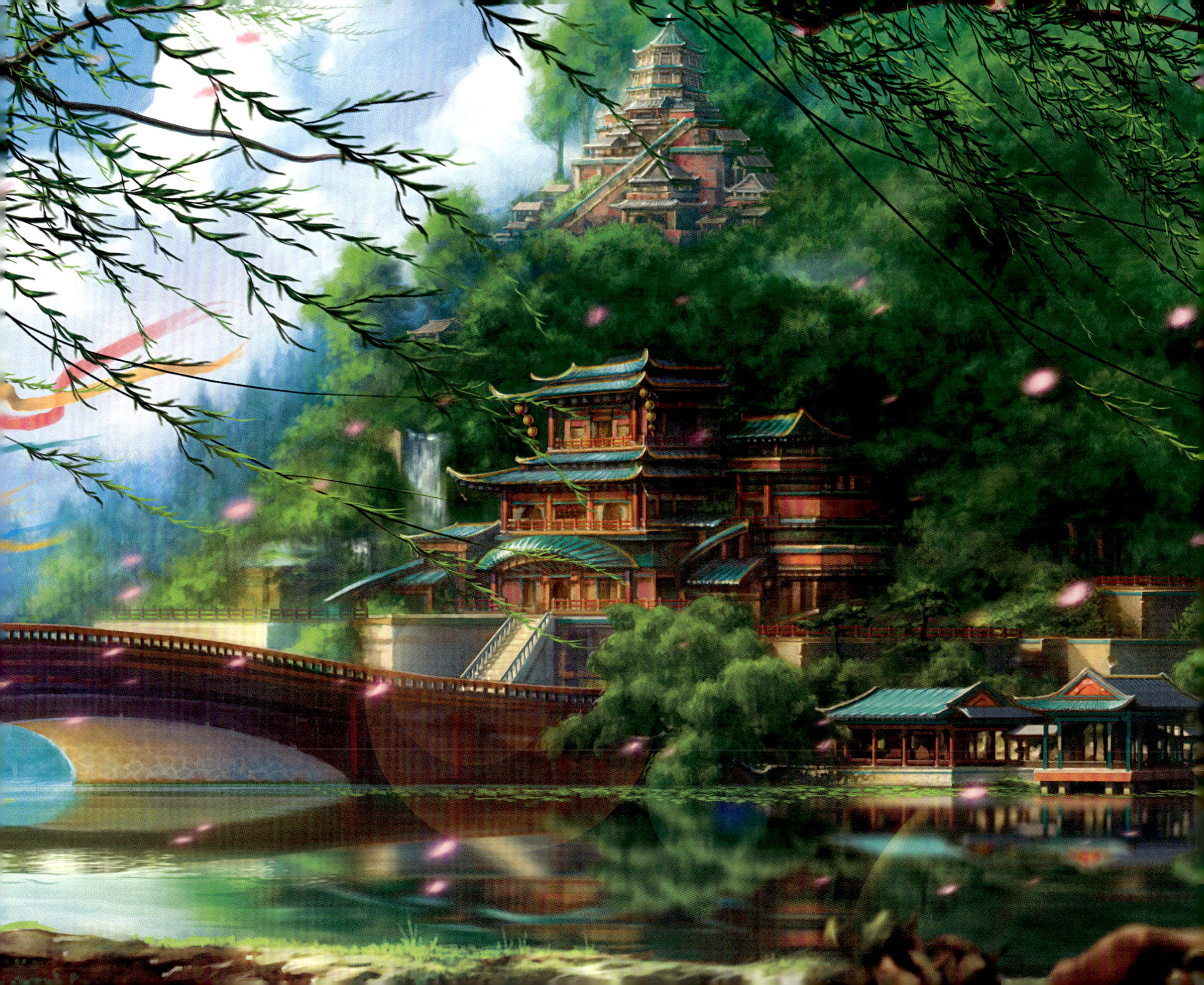

# THOUGHTS ON CREATION

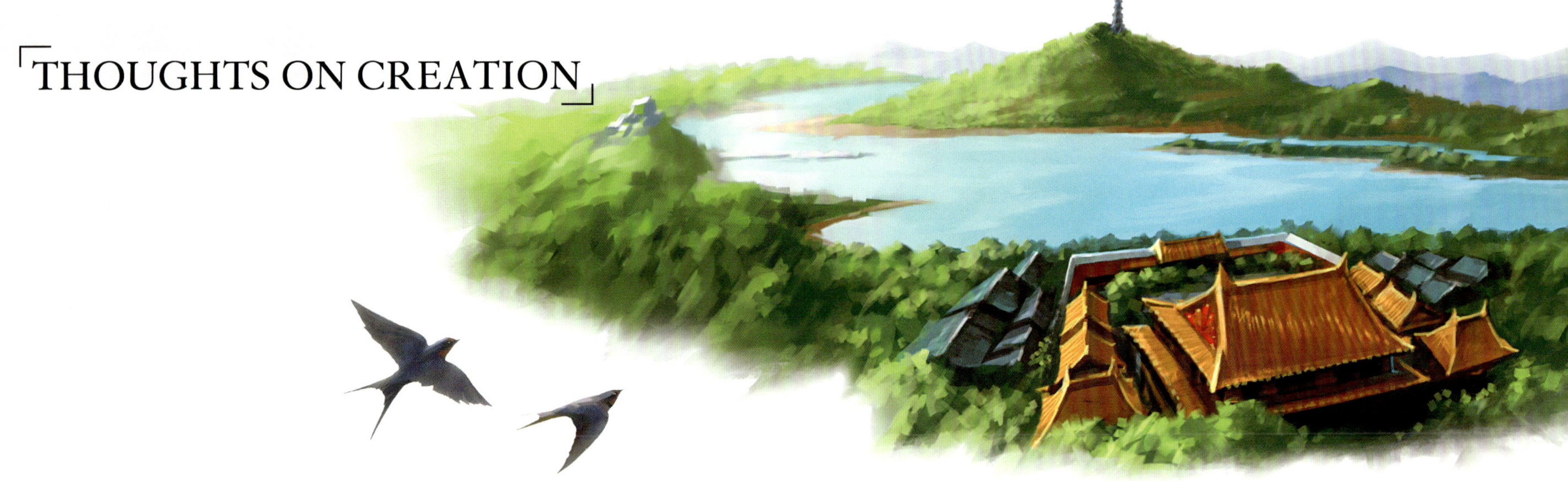

*As a highly representative composition method used for classical Chinese gardens and architecture, "borrowing scenery" is the method of incorporating the vista of an adjacent scenic spot into the composition of a new space. The spaces created with this method appear layered, profound, and colourful from wherever you view them. Moreover, the result of borrowed scenery is optimised when the site is as exceptional as those chosen for imperial gardens. Compared with ordinary gardens, imperial ones are larger in area and boast a richer variety of elements. Nevertheless, borrowed scenery allows a garden space to transcend its own limits, providing indefinite possibilities in a definite space.*

*For instance, there is a pagoda visible from most areas of the Summer Palace — it is the Jade Peak Pagoda which is built on the main peak of Jade Spring Hill. Though it is not a scenic site located within the Summer Palace, the pagoda has become an indivisible element of the garden as a whole. In the foreground of the imperial garden scene are pavilions; behind those, at eye-level, are willows by rippling lakes; and in the distance are continuous mountain peaks and a quiet pagoda. This is a typical case of "borrowing scenery" and the "spirit" with which the technique can imbue a scene.*

*Ancient Chinese freehand landscape paintings and Chinese garden design all pursue "spirit" in the same way. As the paintings pursuing resemblance to scenery or vice versa, "form" for freehand painting and landscaping is not important, whereas "spirit" is the soul of an artwork. For an imperial garden of oriental design, the lack of "spirit" is seen as an inadequacy. On this account, I adopted the "borrowing scenery" method and freehand landscape painting skills to depict a fantasy realistic work that would be considered full of "spirit".*

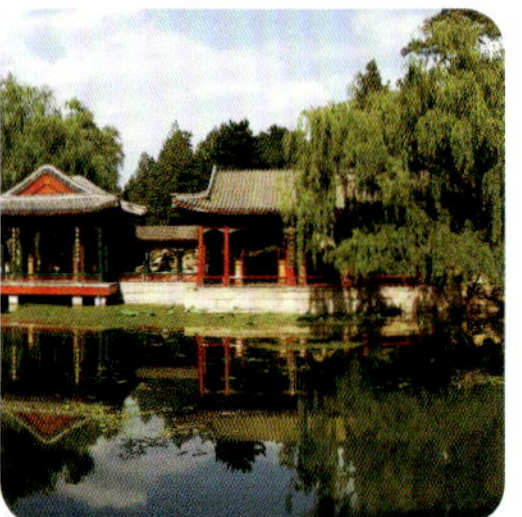

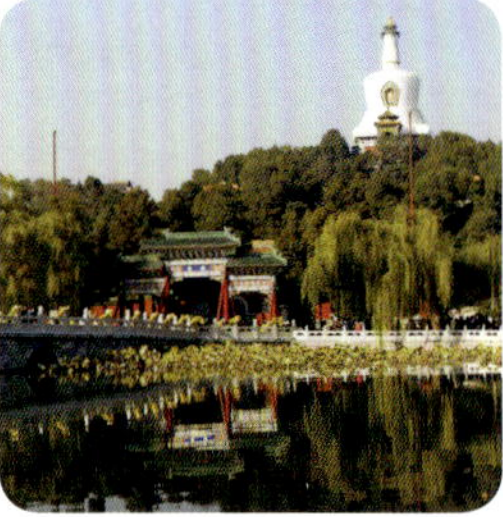

## ▲ WATER

Another essential element of classical Chinese gardens is "water". From small ponds to large lakes, a garden cannot go without water. According to our ancients, "where there is a mountain there is a garden, but where there is no water there is no scenery". Objects in a garden, when reflected in waters, appear clearer and more profound. When there is no wind, the waters will appear clear and calm. When wind blows, the waters will sparkle. When it rains, the waters will ripple. And when it snows, they will freeze. Varied forms of water container can inject a totally different spiritual essence into a garden. That is why water is so vital.

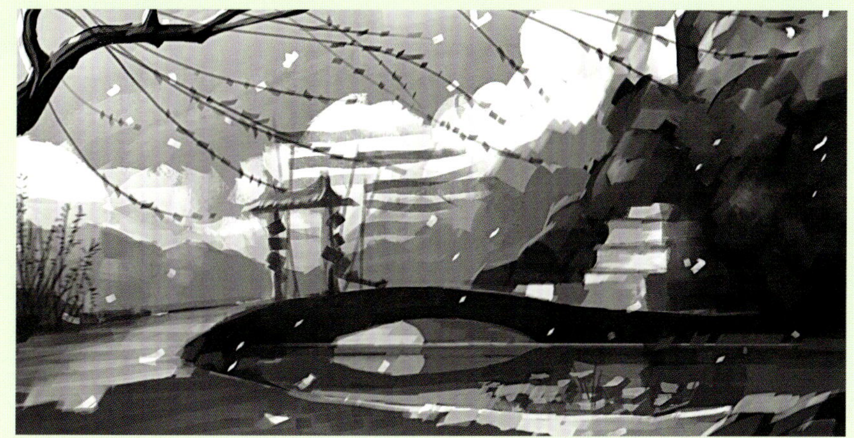

This painting takes an imperial garden as its subject matter, as such, I resorted to skills applied in traditional Chinese landscape paintings. As "freehand landscape paintings" is predominantly an artist's expression of a particular spirit or space, what first came to my mind was the inverted reflections in the lake surface and an ancient arch bridge connecting objects on the two sides of the lake. These would serve as the "form" of the imperial garden. In addition, a clear and cloudy sky and warm afternoon sunshine were chosen to inject "mood" into the garden; the mountains and pagoda in the distance present the element of "borrowed scenery"; and the fluttering willow branches and flying flags were added to the foreground as my last attempt to convey my desired "spirit": happiness in serenity.

When there are too many key words available, and images in your mind are rather vague, you will find it impossible to effectively design the piece while thinking. In such case, you need to draw some rough concept sketches to record elements you want to present. Meanwhile, you need to organise your train of thought and intent before deciding upon a final layout.

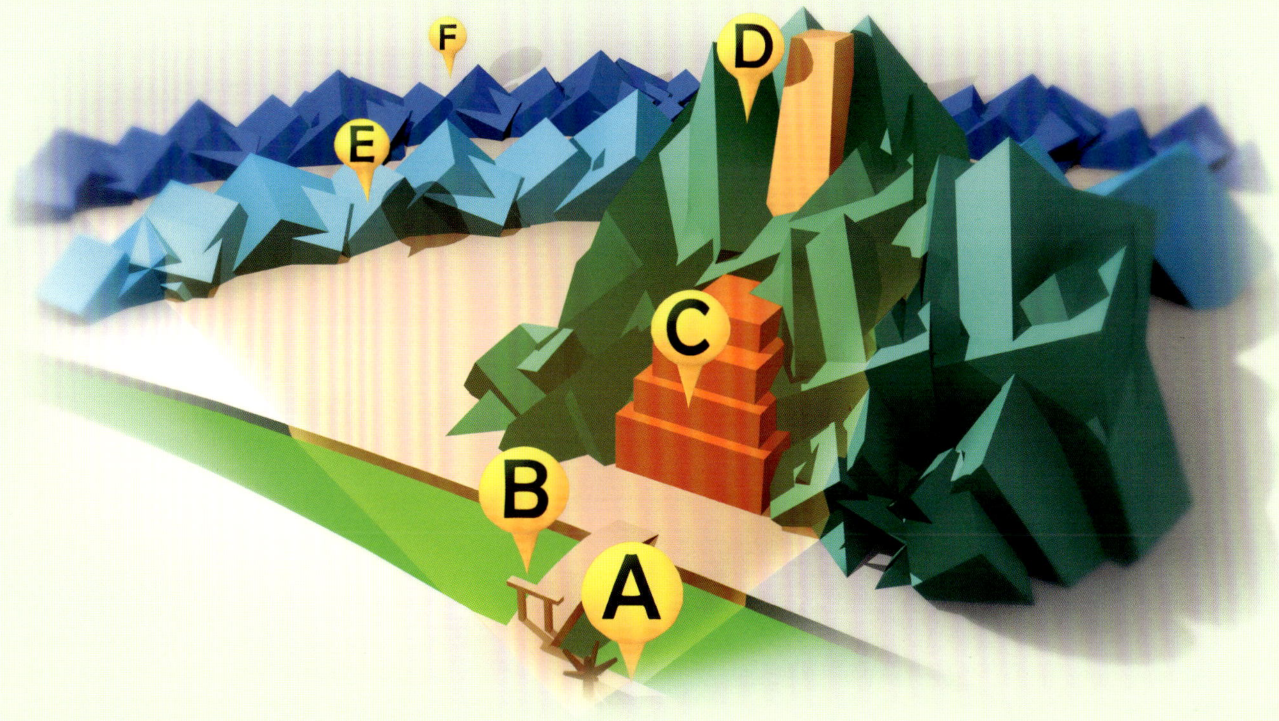


Take this preliminary draft as an example. We should not only consider how to combine different scenic elements together, but also conceive of their spatial relation to the whole environment: A is a willow tree by the lakeside, B is an arch bridge, C is a building on the far-side of the lake, D is a building on a mountain top, E is the mountain range where the pagoda stands, and F is the range far beyond that. With this in mind, we have an accurate idea of the perspective ratio of objects and the distance between them.

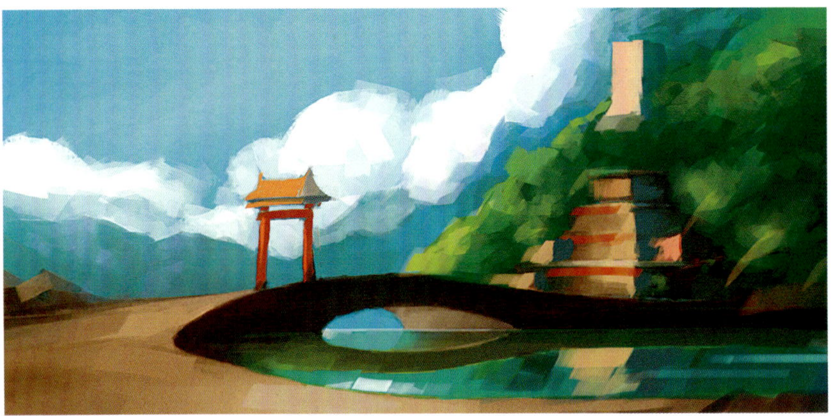

Now, painting begins! Based on the preliminary draft, the main objects in the frame were reshaped and colours were applied. A blue sky, white clouds, green mountains, and blue waters were composed.

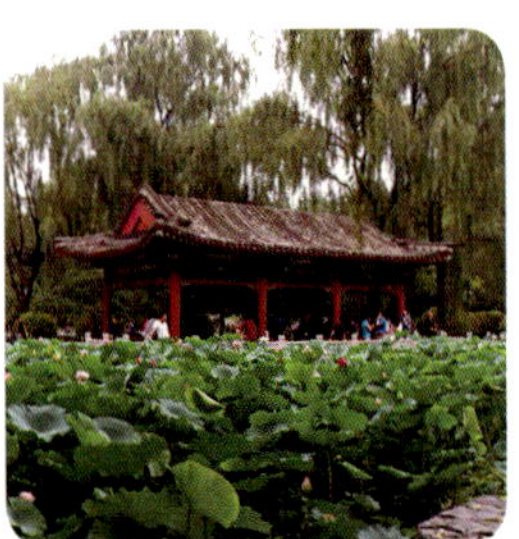

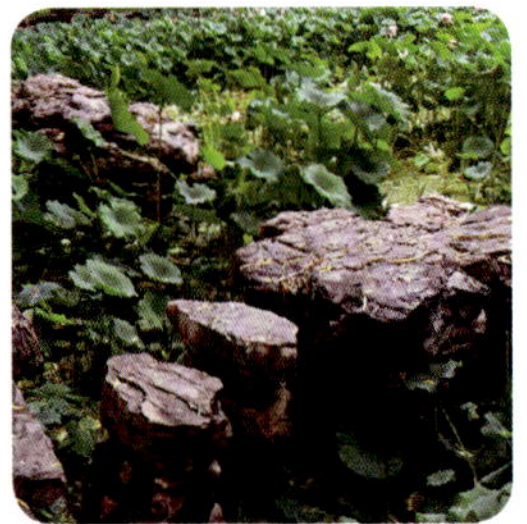

## ▲ LOTUS AND WATER LILY

In traditional Chinese gardens, areas of water are usually filled with aquatic plants to avoid inverted reflections and enrich water landscapes. In addition, ornamental fish such as the Koi carp is often kept in these ponds or lakes.

The large areas of water within imperial gardens allow for large quantities of aquatic plants to thrive. Come midsummer, these plants can grow to cover the water's surface. When lotus flowers and water lilies blossom, the view is as beautiful as that of the Jade Lake on Mount Kunlun.

To complement these landscapes, the two oft-used man-made elements are that of classic architectural structures such as pavilions, corridors, and towers and artificial rock formations around the banks of the lake. Since the function of them is as a place where people can appreciate water lilies and lotus flowers, they should be spacious and open. Rocks of different types and sizes should be used to construct the banks of the lake and match well with water lilies and lotus flowers, forming a contrast between "hard" and "soft".

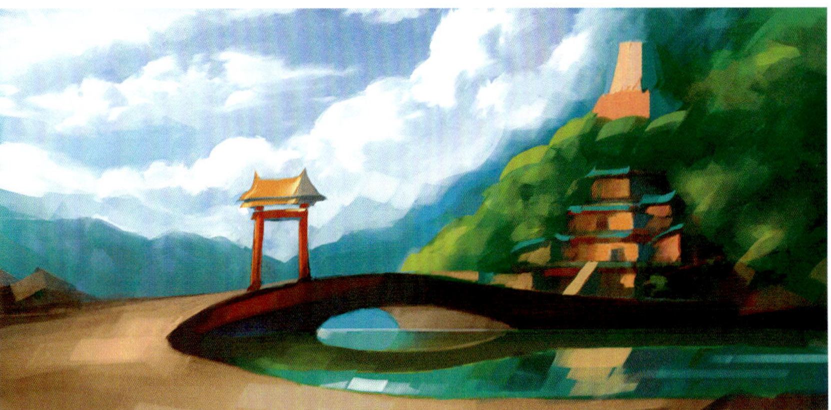

Then, I continued to refine the work. Personally, I like to paint the sky and the background elements first. On the one hand, this determines the weather, direction and intensity of light, and ambient light colour by which all the effect of the follow-up refinement will be influenced. On the other hand, if there are too many objects in the foreground, the sky and background vista will be covered up. Even in layered painting, it is difficult to fully describe nearby objects upon an undetermined background.

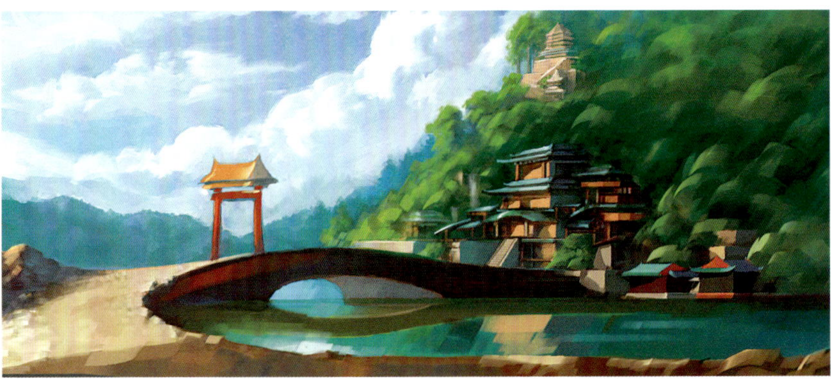

I added the pavilion, corridor, and tower on the opposite side of the lake and surrounded the lake with piled rocks. I decided to add the leaves of lotus flowers on the surface of the lake at a later stage, after the inverted reflections were completed.

Ancient beliefs dictate that a good resort should be located by "mountains and waters". In this creation, beautiful and luxuriant mountains act as a foil to the buildings and add a sense of mystery to the scene. The building on the mountain top is created with reference to the Tower of Buddhist Incense in the Summer Palace.

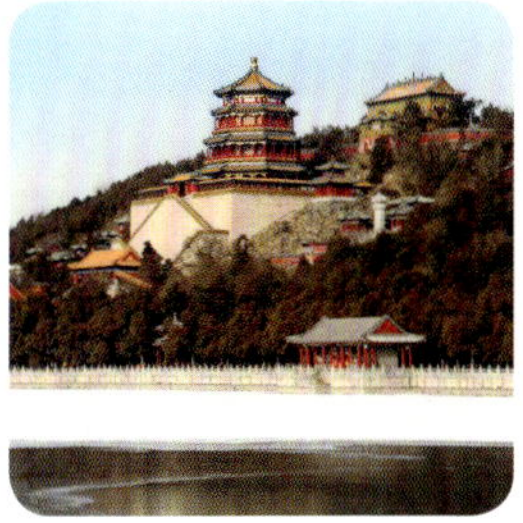

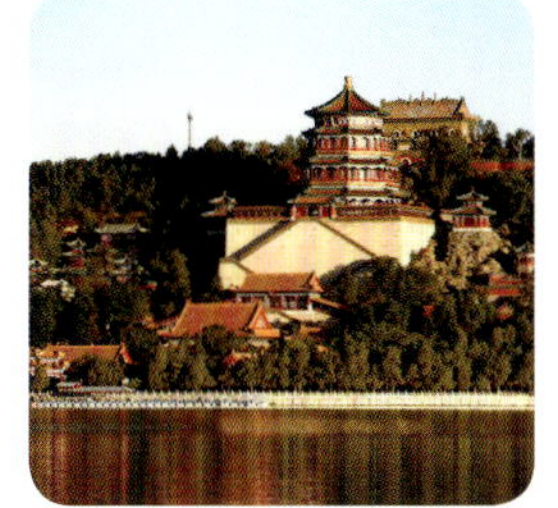

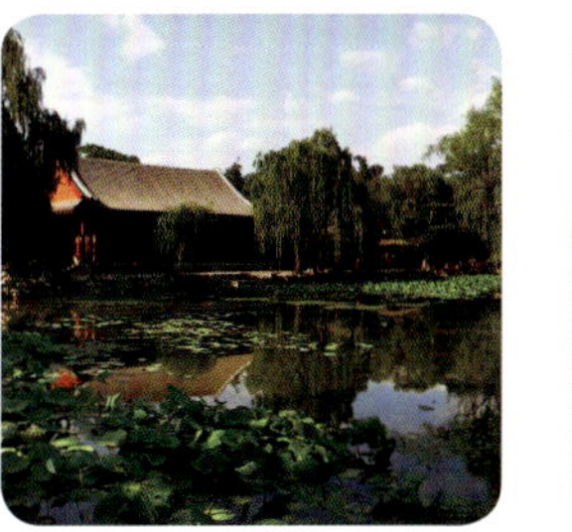

## ◄ TOWER OF BUDDHIST INCENSE

The Tower of Buddhist Incense is a typical imperial garden complex located by Kunming Lake in the Summer Palace. At the centre of the complex is a colossal pagoda-style tower flanked by many small buildings arranged in an orderly and symmetrical way. The magnificent tower evokes images of the moon surrounded by a myriad of stars. In contrast, Beihai Park is lined with willow trees providing shade and contains an antique lakeside building and a lake of luxuriant water lilies. The diverse elements create a feeling of harmony in the park.

I created this piece of work with reference to the view along the lake and the lakeside building in Beihai Park. I hoped that this would inject into it a sense of serenity and peace. I also alluded to the majestic Tower of Buddhist Incense and Longevity Hill as these increase magnificence and extravagance of the scene. The diverse objects all integrated into one piece of work both form delightful threads of interaction with each other while demonstrating their own individual significance.

Independent objects in the foreground and middle-ground were refined to near completion, thus preparing the space for other related objects to be added. The shadow within the nearest plane of ground, for example, was prepared for the later depiction of a willow tree by the lakeside.

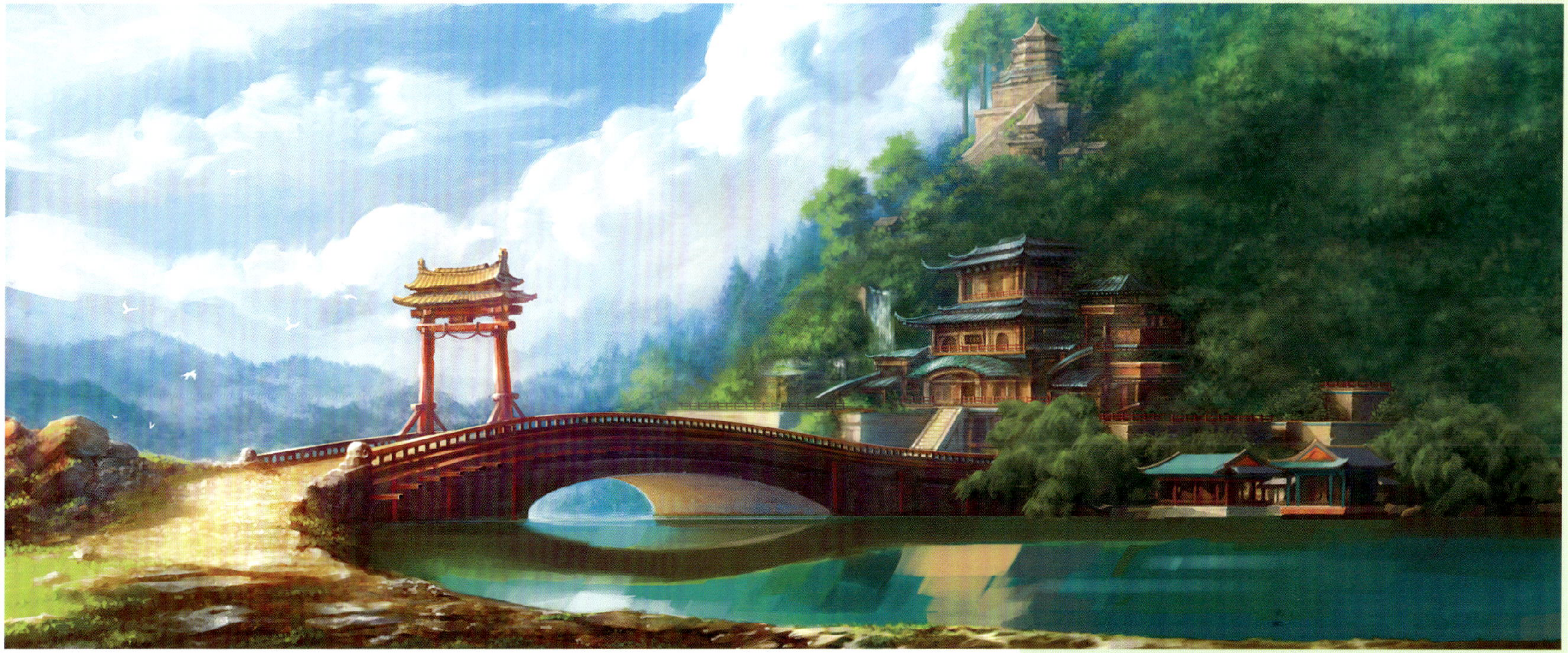

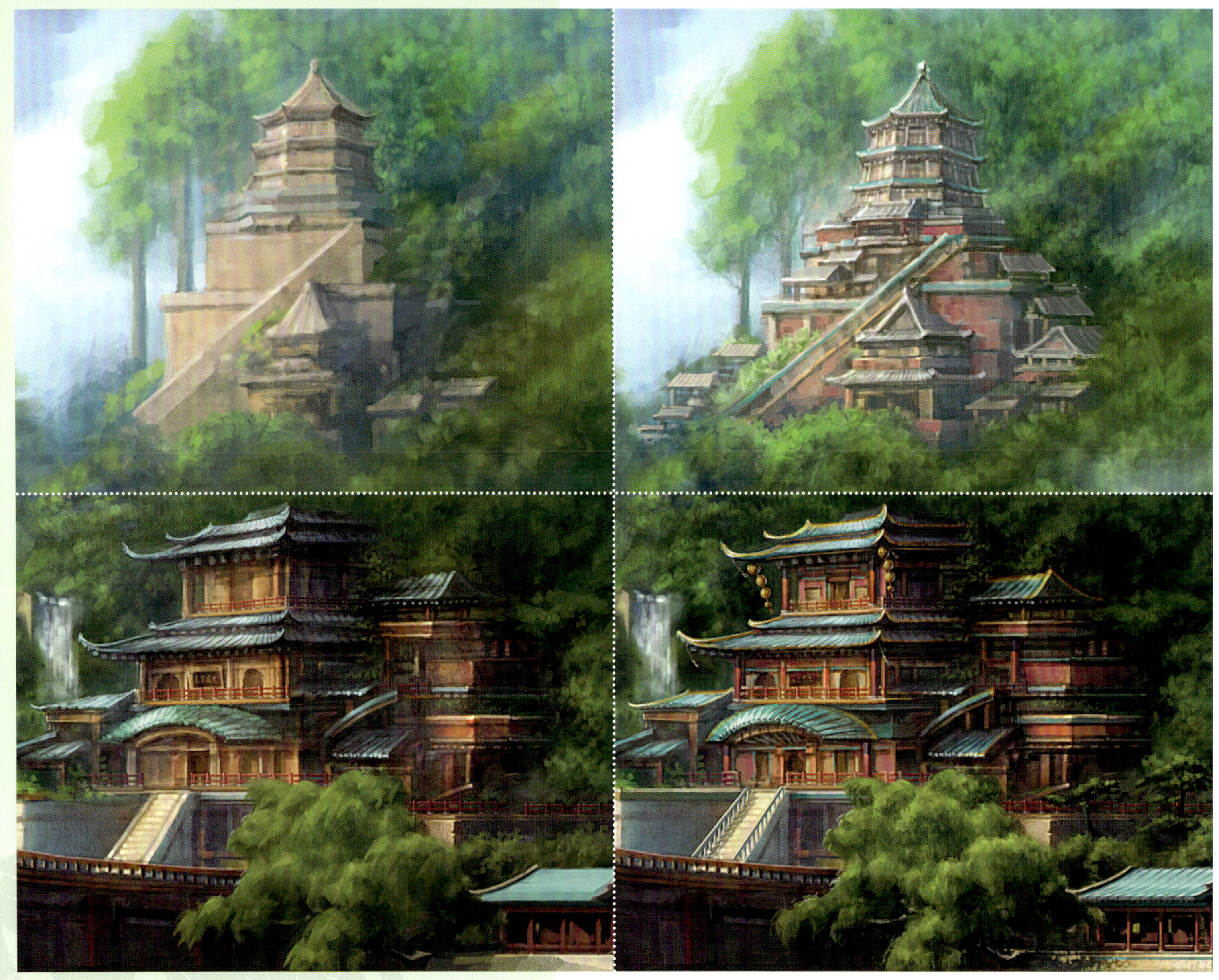

Here you can contrast the pictures on the left and right sides to see the refinement process. The buildings were given red walls and green and yellow glazed tiles. These colours represent imperial dignity. Plants on the mountains were clarified according to their distance so as to increase the sense of depth and foreground the main subjects. Beside details such as highlighting areas of the handrails, railings, and tiles, the addition of dynamic features can also instil a scene with a sense of life. Such features could include fog rising from the mountains and trees and strings of lanterns swaying in the wind.

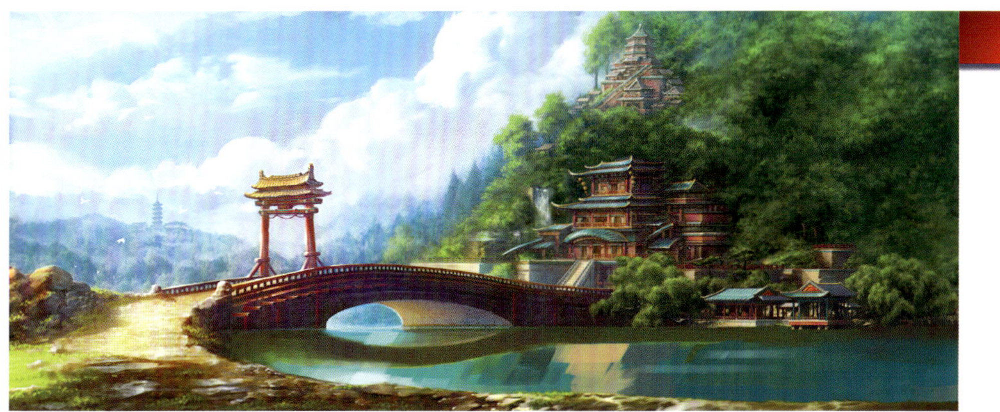

At this point, I began to depict the water surface and inverted reflections upon it. First, I extracted the water area as a "mask" for later adjustment.

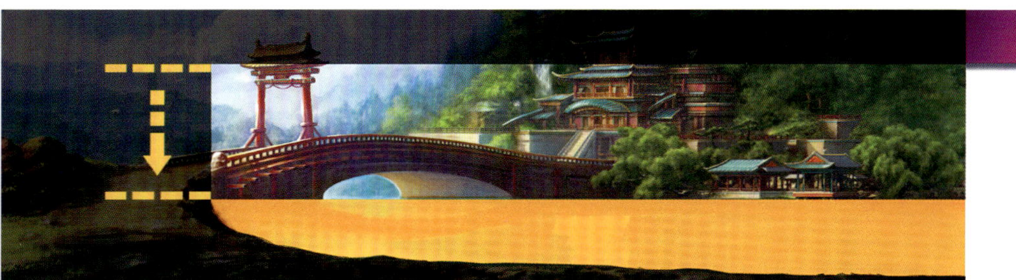

Second, I selected the section about 1.5 times the height of the water area "mask" from above the surface and extracted the scenery. This served as the material to be inverted for the reflection.

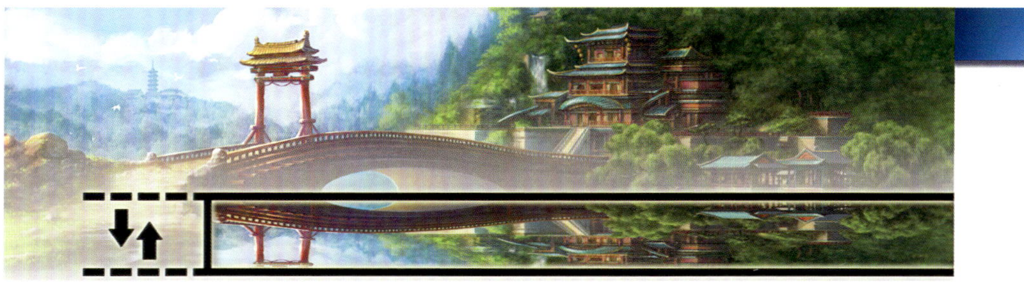

Third, I applied the mirroring method and compressed the extracted section down to a size ratio of 1:1 with the mask before pasting it onto the mask.

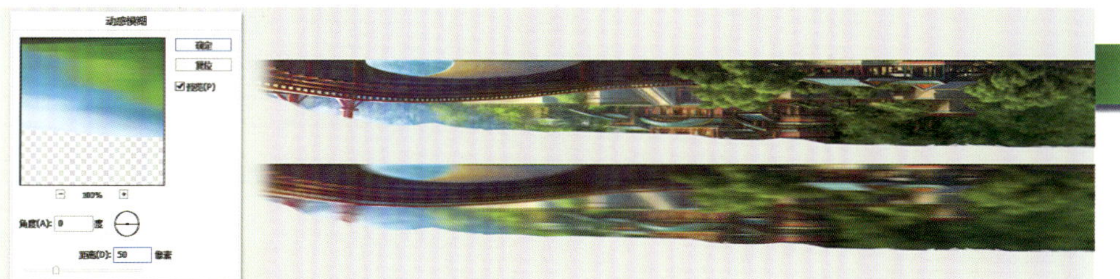


Fourth, I applied the motion-blur method to the materials to create the appearance of "inverted reflections in a calm lake" and then cut out surplus parts using the mask limits.

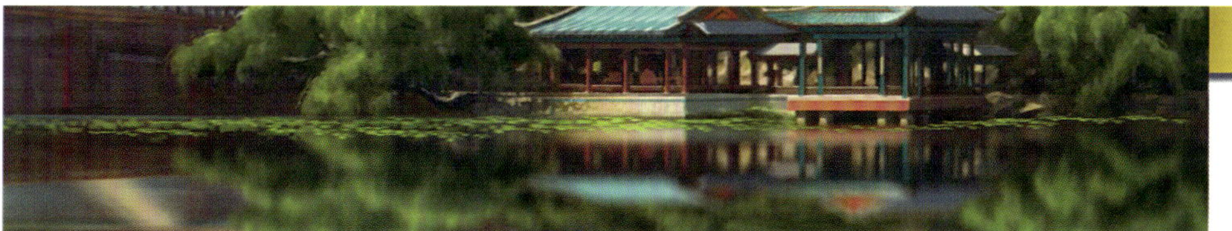

Lastly, I reconnected the extracted part with the base picture and added water lilies on the water's surface. The water and reflections were thus finished.

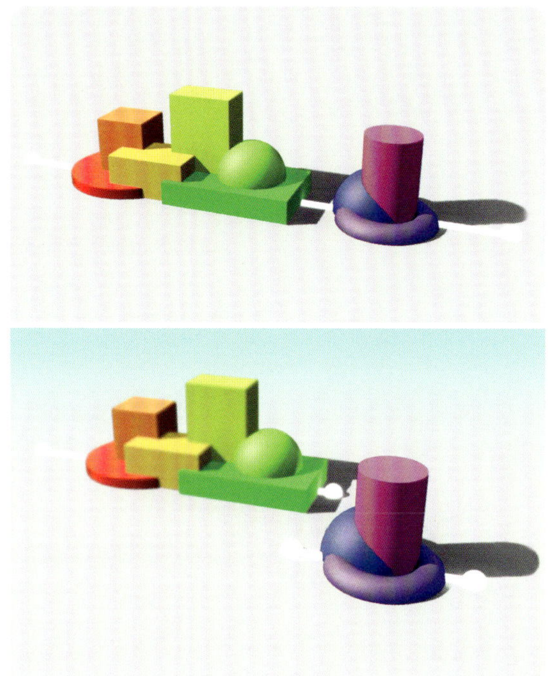
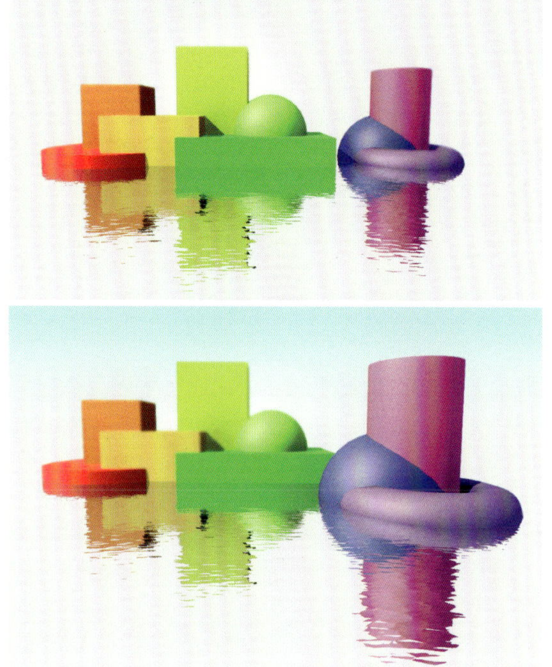
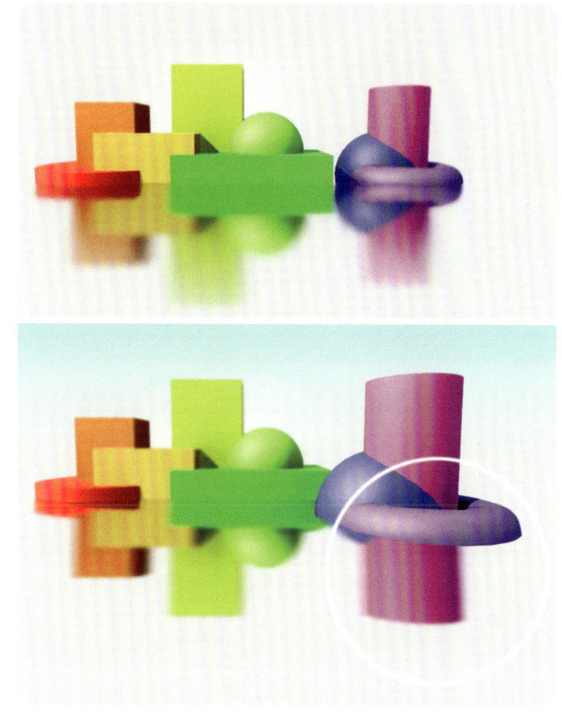

There is one more thing you need to pay attention to with creating reflections. Using the mirroring method to achieve them is only applicable in this case because all the objects to be reflected are located on the same horizontal line and are reflected in the water on the same visual horizon. When inverted reflections are not located on the same visual horizon, the mirroring method is not suitable; instead, special objects should be extracted for independent treatment. To decide whether an inverted effect is reasonable, you need to apply a simple method: observe whether each object that needs to be reflected can be entirely mirrored from its bottom. [The first column of images in the above graph shows groupings of objects put on the same and different parallel lines; the second shows the real effects obtained using a 3D simulator programme when the objects are viewed from the parallel perspective; the third one shows the simulated reflection using the 2D mirroring method. Apparently, direct mirroring will lead to the distortion of objects on different parallel lines.]

Willow branches and a pagoda on the distant mountain were added. From the preliminary composition, you can see that such objects shouldn't be reflected in the water, so they are depicted after the reflections. The whole scene is close to completion. The "shape" of the tree branch and the "position" of the pagoda were designed to balance the scene.

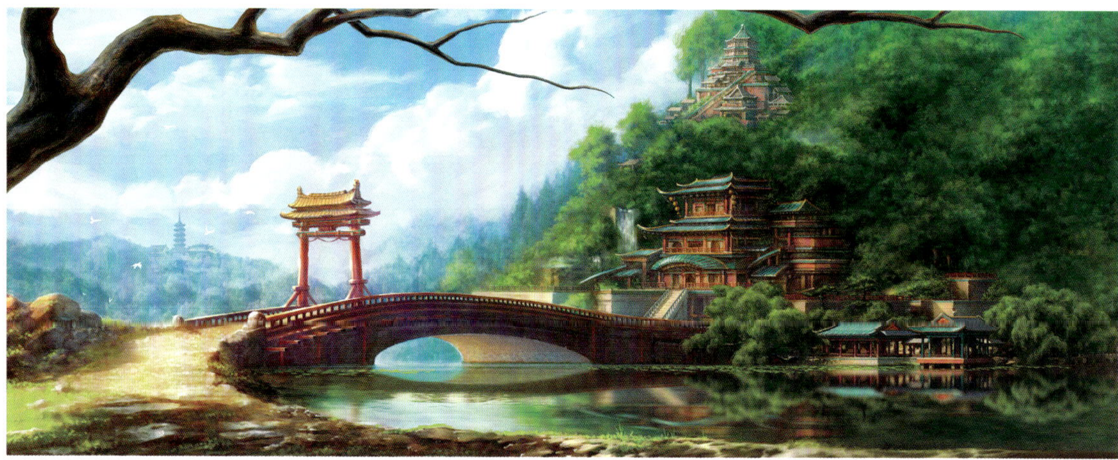

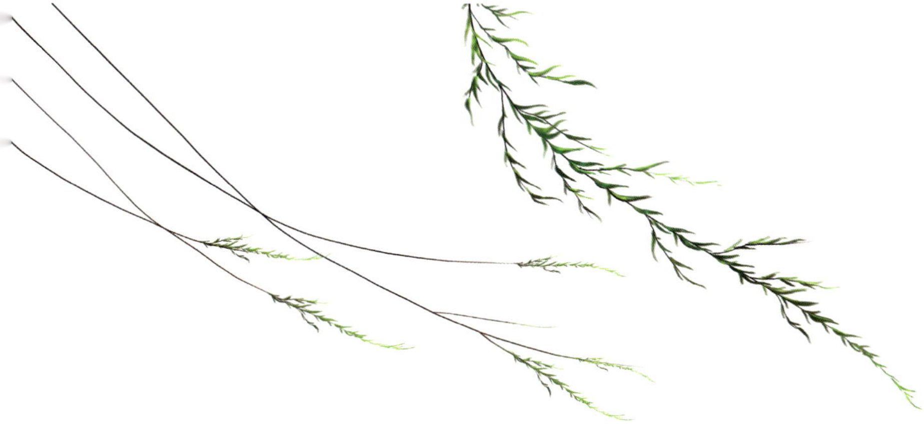

As for painting the willow branches and leaves, first, I used lines to sketch major branches, making their shapes soft, beautiful, and natural as if wavering in the breeze. I then tried to emulate the natural growth of willow leaves by depicting the tenderest and the smallest new leaves at the end of a branch with warmer colours. The points which would sprout new branches in the future as being moved along with the wind were then changed. Then I added leaves to all the branches and adjusted the lighting effects to create different layered textures. The branches and leaves farthest away from viewers were silhouetted to foreground the closer leaves. Last, I added some special branches whose leaves grew only at their tips as well as some jumbled broken leaves to reproduce the imperfectness of the real world. I feel these details enlivened the whole scene and bestowed it with a natural appearance.

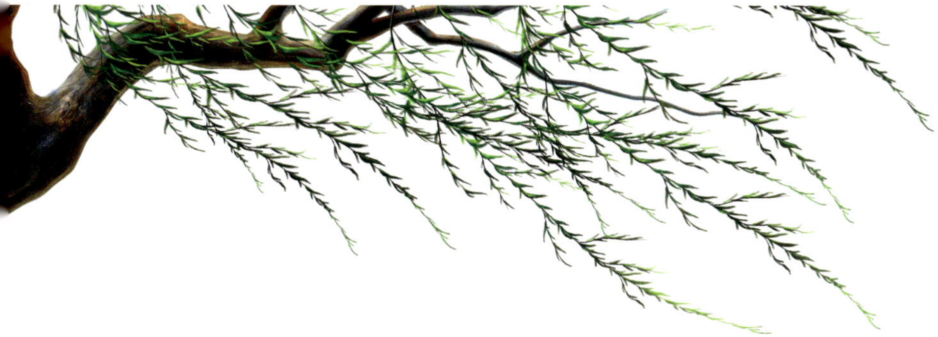

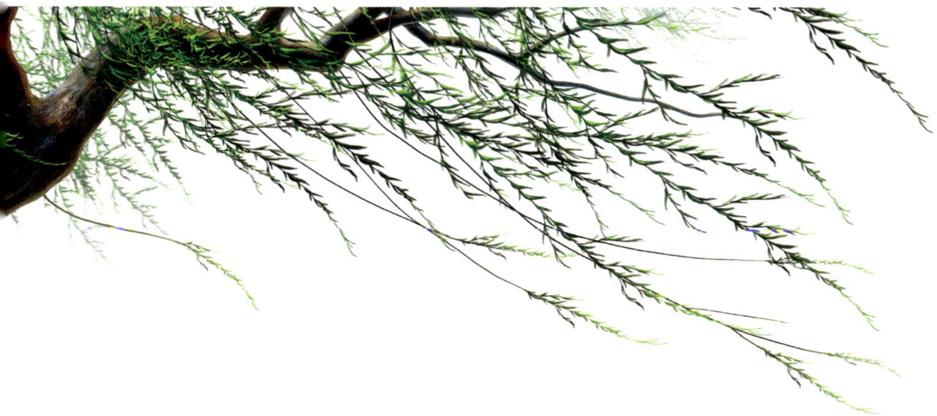

Adding the willow leaves blowing in the wind gave the scene a sense of movement. By the lakeside, a section of plants was added to echo the willow branches opposite them and balance the whole composition.

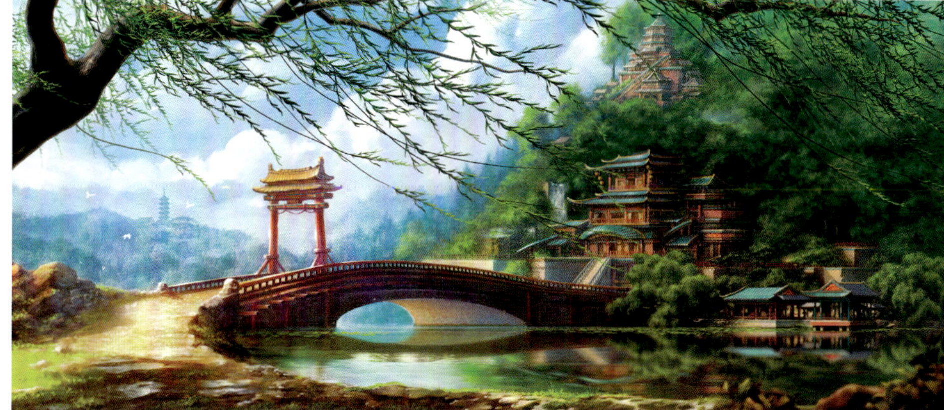

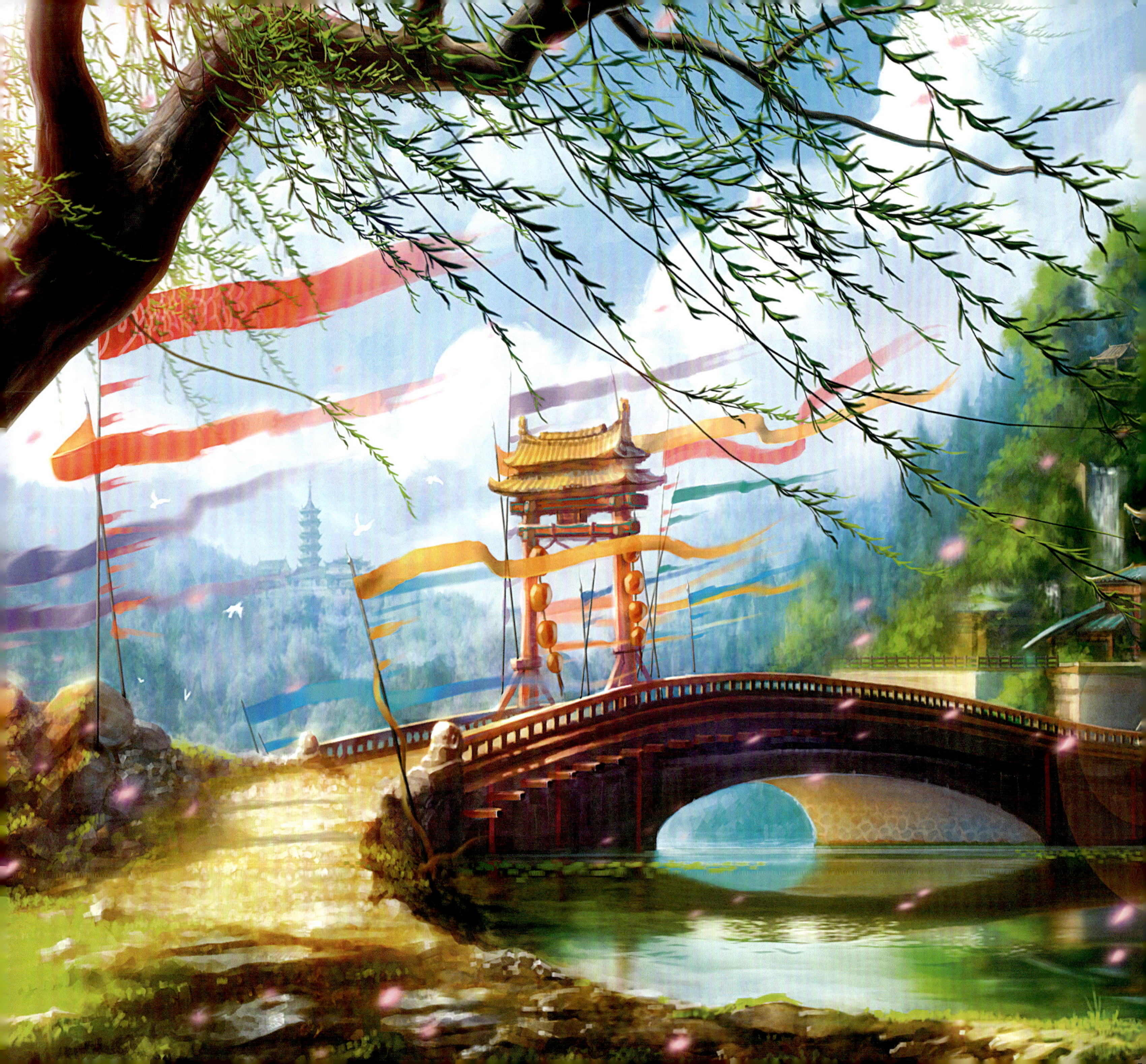

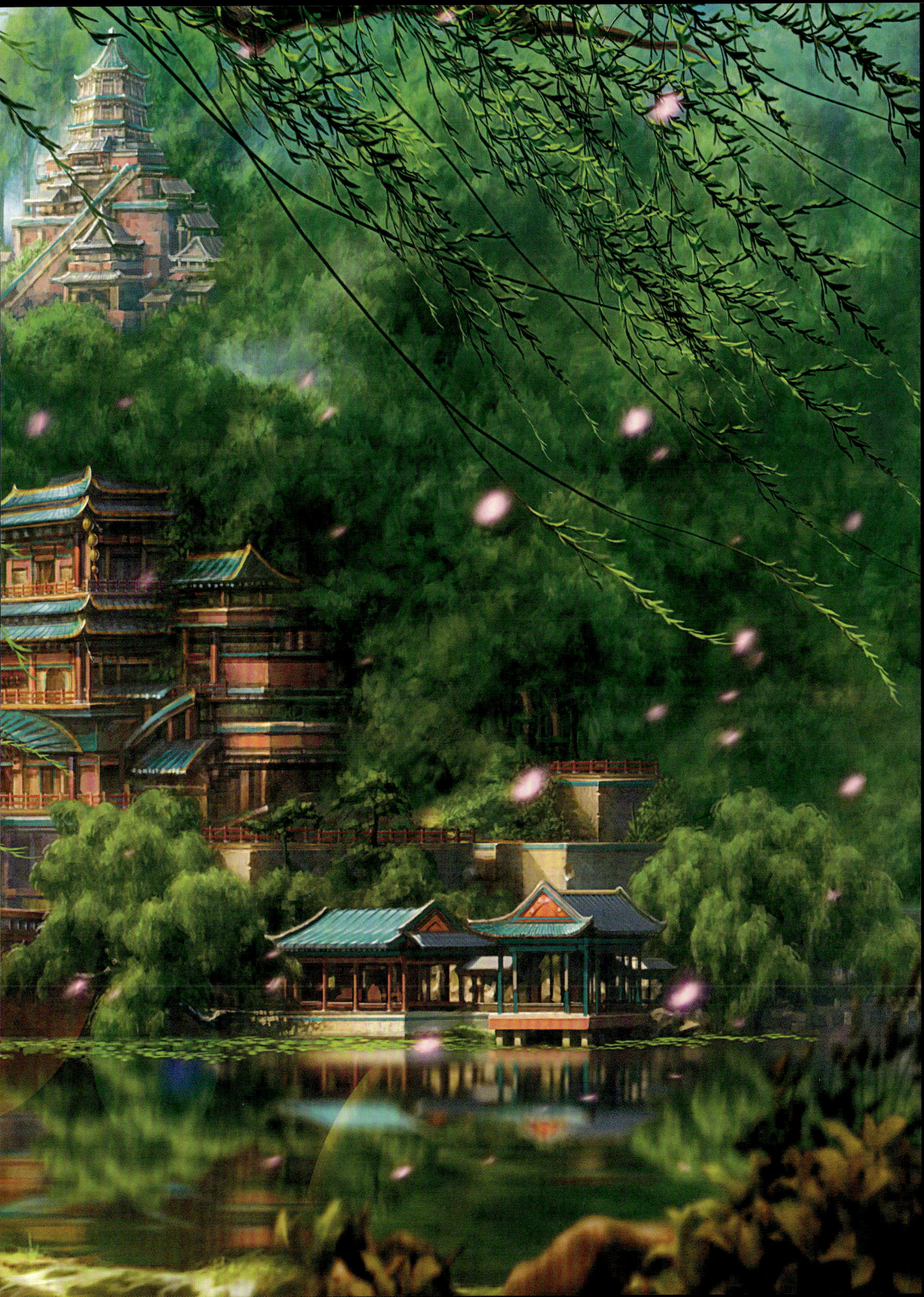

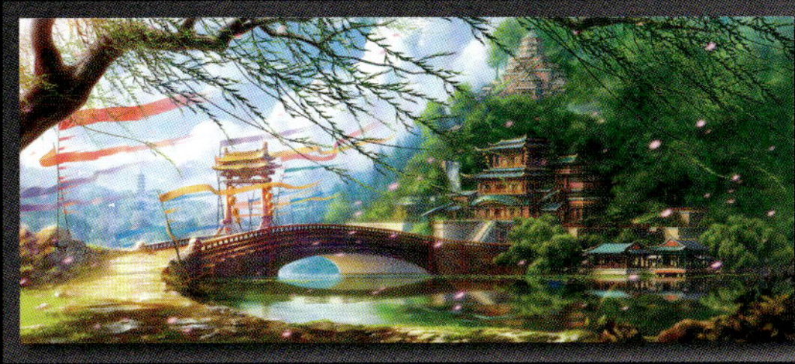

Finally, I added coloured flying flags, flower petals and rays of sunshine crossing willow branches to shed light on the lakeside. These transformed an otherwise serene and solemn imperial garden into a "secluded land of idyllic beauty" that appears both pleasant and relaxing.

# Museum

Beijing's ancient residences, imperial palaces, and gardens stand as reminders of a bygone time to the endless streams of people who come and go every day to wander their grounds. Casting only passing glances at these sites, however, people may wonder how their structures appear inside. Perhaps exploring the interior of a renovated ancient residence can satisfy this curiosity and provide a deeper understanding of architecture of antiquity. This objective is a perfect starting point for a creation too!

Chiefly wooden structures, classical Chinese architecture adopts timber pillars and beams to form their supporting frames. The older an ancient building, the higher the cost of maintaining it and the longer it takes to renovate it. Hence why many plans to renovate ancient buildings have been discarded. For safety reasons, unrenovated ancient buildings cannot be put into use or opened to the public, denying visitors to scenic sites access to the building interiors. Nevertheless, there are some ancient buildings that have been renovated and now stand as examples of what once was, where people can experience and learn about past dynasties and eras. In addition, there are museums that display antiques and stores that sell folk relics and curios.

The artwork *Museum* is a piece of work of indoor scene that shows the renovated interior of an ancient building. In this section, besides exploring ancient Chinese architecture and museums' functional characteristics, I will also show you the skills for composing and portraying an indoor scene.

Indoor scene design is entirely different from outdoor scene design. There are many limitations on spatial composition that require unique methods of representation and lead to singularly charming results. How an interior space is portrayed is determined by regional cultures, historical background, the size of the space itself, lighting, and layout. A scene can either be gorgeous or dilapidated, bright with sunshine or eerily gloomy. It's important to consider how to present your desired scene and emotion within a fixed space while adhering to the theme and subject matter.

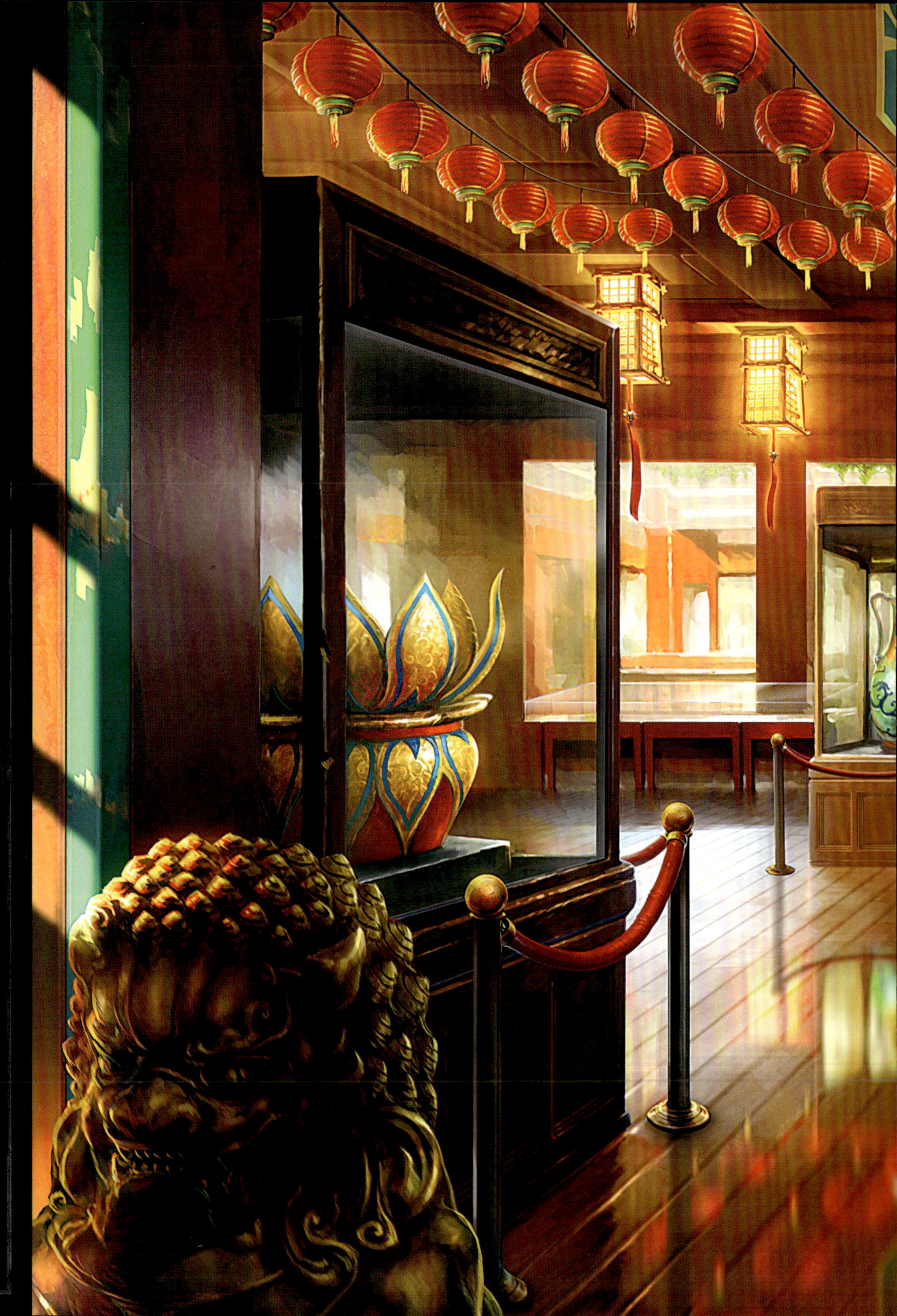

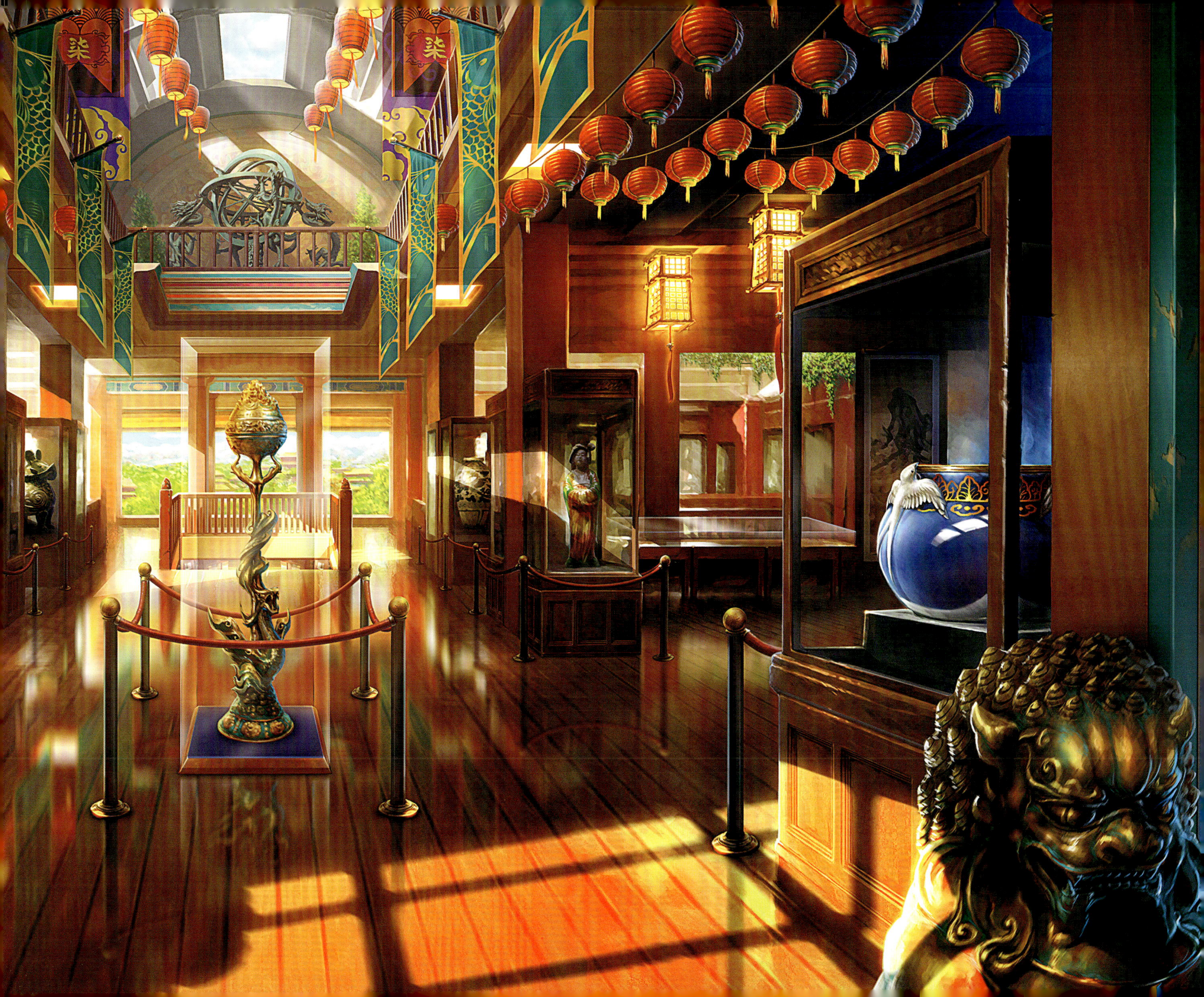

## THOUGHTS ON CREATION

*Museums in most countries are places where historical relics are exhibited and dynastic tales told. Some of them are housed within reconstructions of local ancient buildings. Ancient architecture provides exhibits with some contemporary context while its furnishings are a perfect foil for the artefacts on exhibit. In fact, the ancient buildings themselves are colossal relics begging to be explored. Antiques and artworks are suitable pieces for museums reconstructed from ancient buildings. They share a similar sense of history with the setting. In addition, the unique lighting often found in old structures is good for the appreciation and preservation of exhibits.*

*Preserved ancient buildings are the products of contemporary state-of-the-art construction processes. In ancient times when there were no modern facilities, people resorted to careful engineering design to ensure buildings were not only warm in winter and cool in summer but also capable of natural ventilation and being well-lit.*

*The question is: after their repairs, are ancient buildings straight away suitable to be used as museums? Of course, the answer is no. Despite their superior qualities, ancient buildings require modern equipments to be fitted to support these features and ensure the preservation of exhibits under any weather conditions. Considering the free flow of visitors and the need to clearly display special exhibits, the spaces' lighting also needs to be adapted and security facilities updated. Only an artistic representation of a museum which includes all these elements would be suitably realistic.*

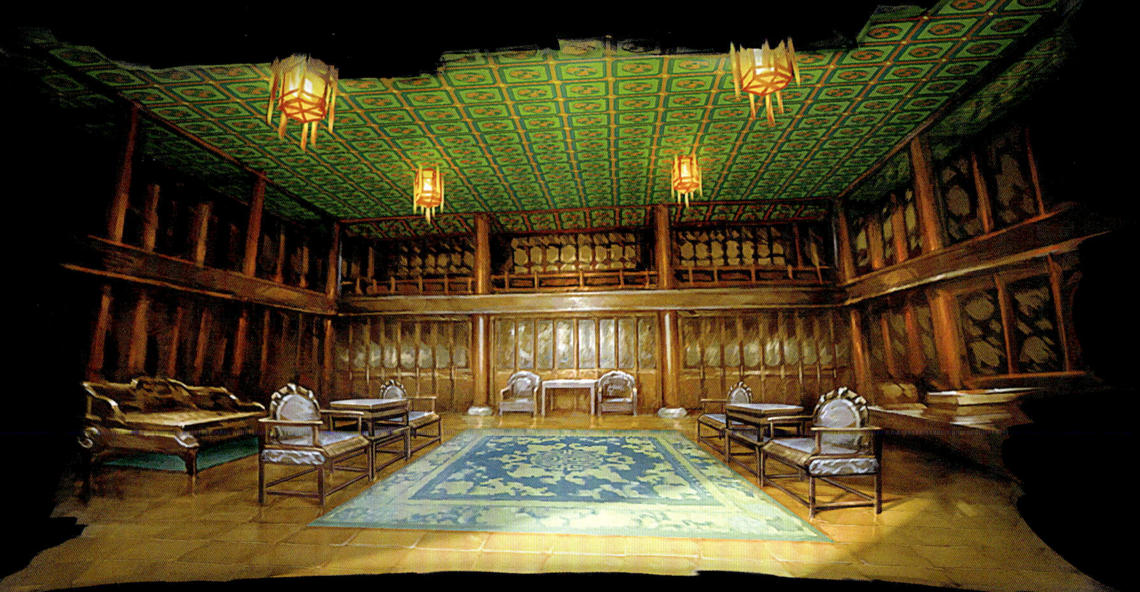

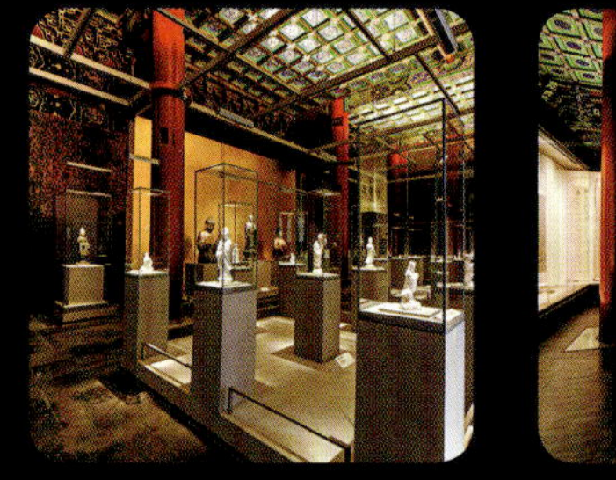

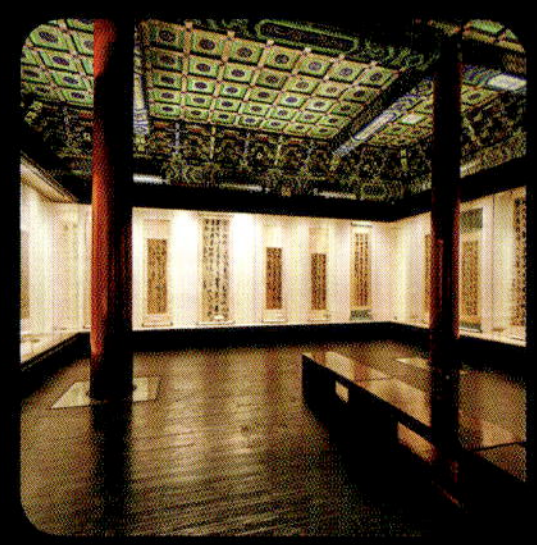

### ▲ LITERARY BRILLIANCE

The Hall of Literary Brilliance in the Palace Museum is now an exhibition hall. A combination of green glazed tiles and red pillars demonstrates the majesty and magnificence of imperial palace interiors. Exhibition counters, glass cabinets, spotlights, rails, and a dazzling array of exhibit pieces all remind visitors that the ancient-building-turned museum they are visiting is rich with history.

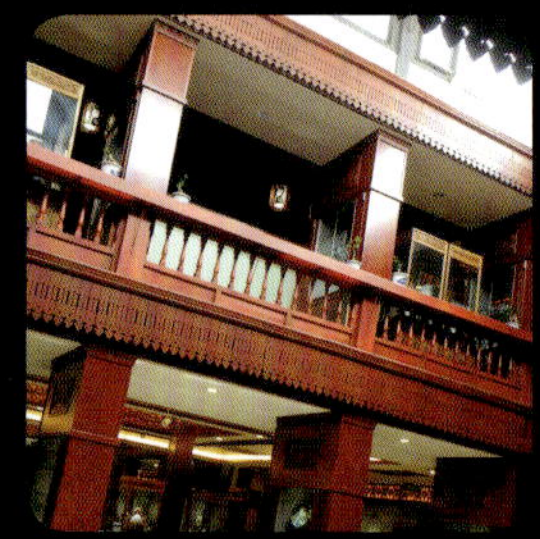

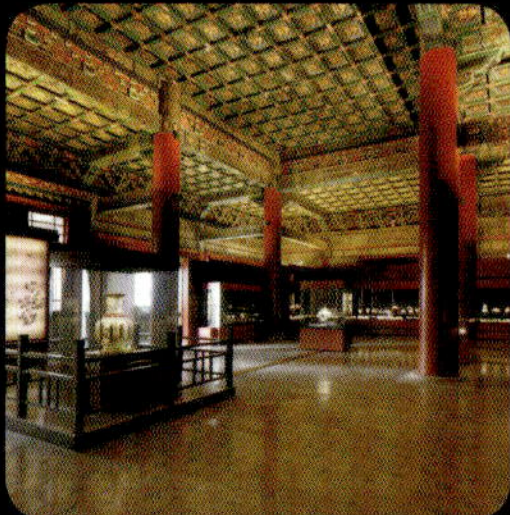

### ▲ EXHIBITION HALLS

In addition to national exhibition halls like the Hall of Literary Brilliance, there are other exhibition halls scattered across the city of Beijing, which are reconstructed from residences and courtyard houses. These refined spaces tend to be less tall and spacious than the Hall of Literary Brilliance, yet despite this, can be renovated as freely as possible, often resulting in a number of compact partitioned areas containing a diverse range of exhibits.

## ▲ CORRIDORS

Exhibition halls can be grouped into several categories according to their structures. For example, "corridors" are suitable for thematic series such as scrolls of calligraphy and paintings from one artist or era to another. Spacious "halls" can be used to house large or a large number of exhibits. "Atriums", their skylights, and surrounding floors exist for the purpose of admitting daylight. Each of these elements has their own distinctive characteristics which should be presented in this creation.

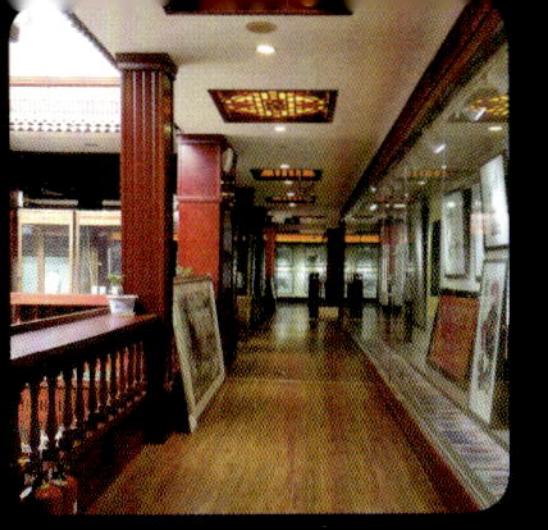

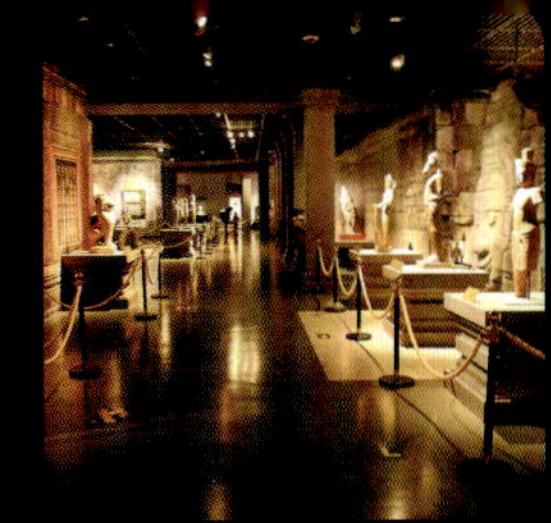

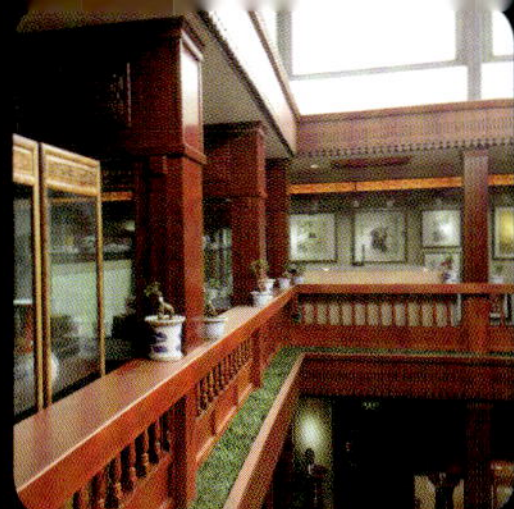

This piece's main feature is a front hall as this is often the highlight or the most eye-catching area of a museum. This space allows us to present the museum's interior structures as well as a variety of exhibits and the signature interplay of lighting in such old structures. This combination element provides sufficient diversity for the piece of work to be an aesthetically pleasing piece.

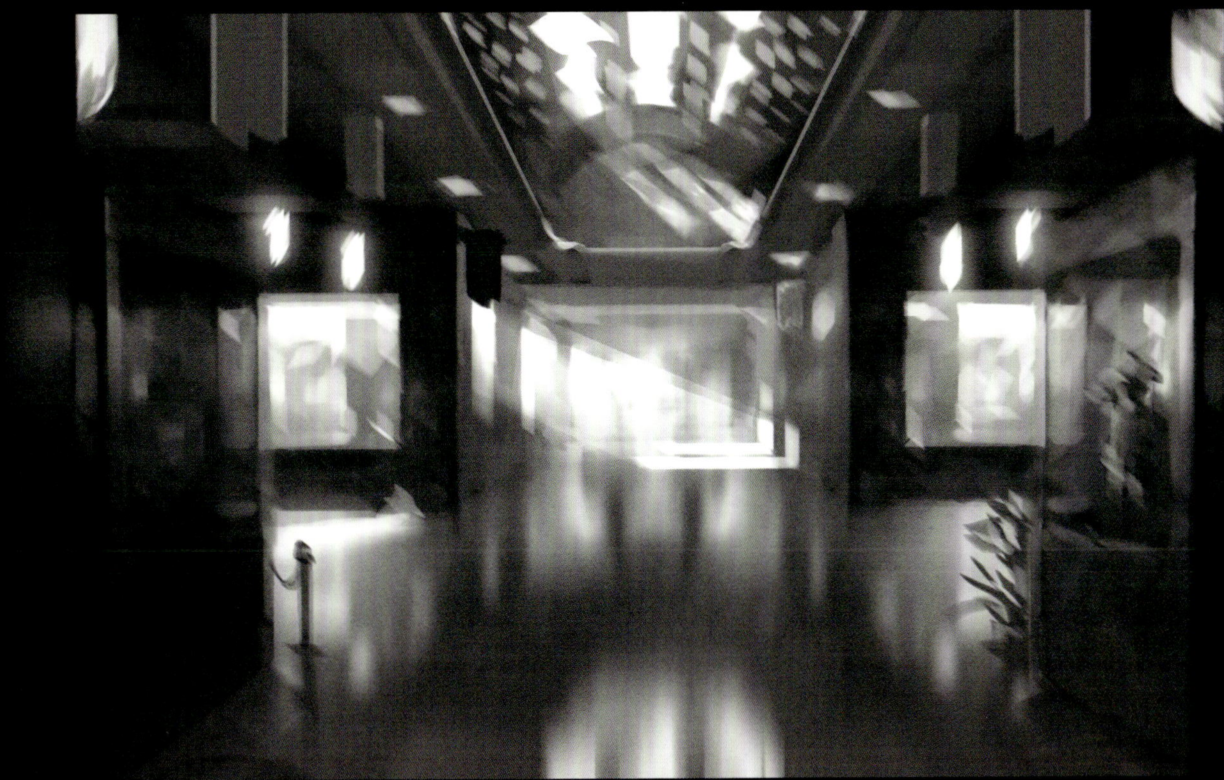

I sketched the front hall in a manner similar to how I approached *The Forbidden City*'s composition. Although the museum is not as majestic as an imperial palace, it is important to give expression to its solemnity and serenity. A parallel composition serves this purpose well. At this early stage, designing a symmetrical scene saves a lot of initial effort and allows us to jump into other details.

The sun slants through the ceiling spaces and skylight, casting light and shadow across the floors, walls, and other furnishings. This treatment could make objects on the left and right sides of the scene appear asymmetrical. In addition, the reflection of light on old-style wooden floors could enrich a simple indoor layout. Promotional banners along with the ornaments under a certain exhibition theme show traces of a commercial public space, producing a meeting of past and present.

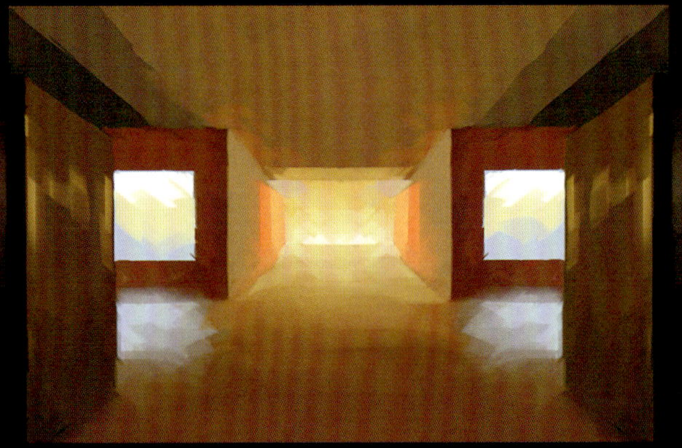

Now, let's begin to draw a colour sketch. The main hall has a square layout. In the middle of the scene, two skylights are included on the left and right to admit daylight. In this initial draft, the ceiling is drawn level to avoid influencing the current shape of the hall. For now, the hall is presented as a single-storey room (on the premise that the final layout of objects has been determined in the initial draft).

The overall tone of the scene is yellowish brown, the hue of wood. At the end of the hall, warmer colours such as yellow and orange are applied to create depth of colour and prepare for the subsequent addition of lighting. The skylights and the reflection of light on the floors in front of the skylights feature the hue of sky blue. This cool colour forms a contrast with the scene's warm colours, thus avoiding an overall atmosphere of anxiety that could be caused by too many warm colours. Moreover, the greater diversity of colours makes for a richer scene and establishes the flow of colour temperature.

Exhibition cabinets, exhibit pieces, and lamps are added. The structure of the skylights is clarified. Windows at the end of the hall and staircases leading downstairs are also further refined. Owing to outdoor scenes' diverse scenery content and the abundance of outdoor light, drawing them with the mirroring method just appears extremely unreal. The mirroring method is applicable only to the initial stages of sketching when light and shade effects haven't yet been added. When designing an indoor scene, there are only a few specific light sources. Thus, it's reasonable to adopt the mirroring method, and to do so can improve the efficiency of completing the scene's preliminary drafts.

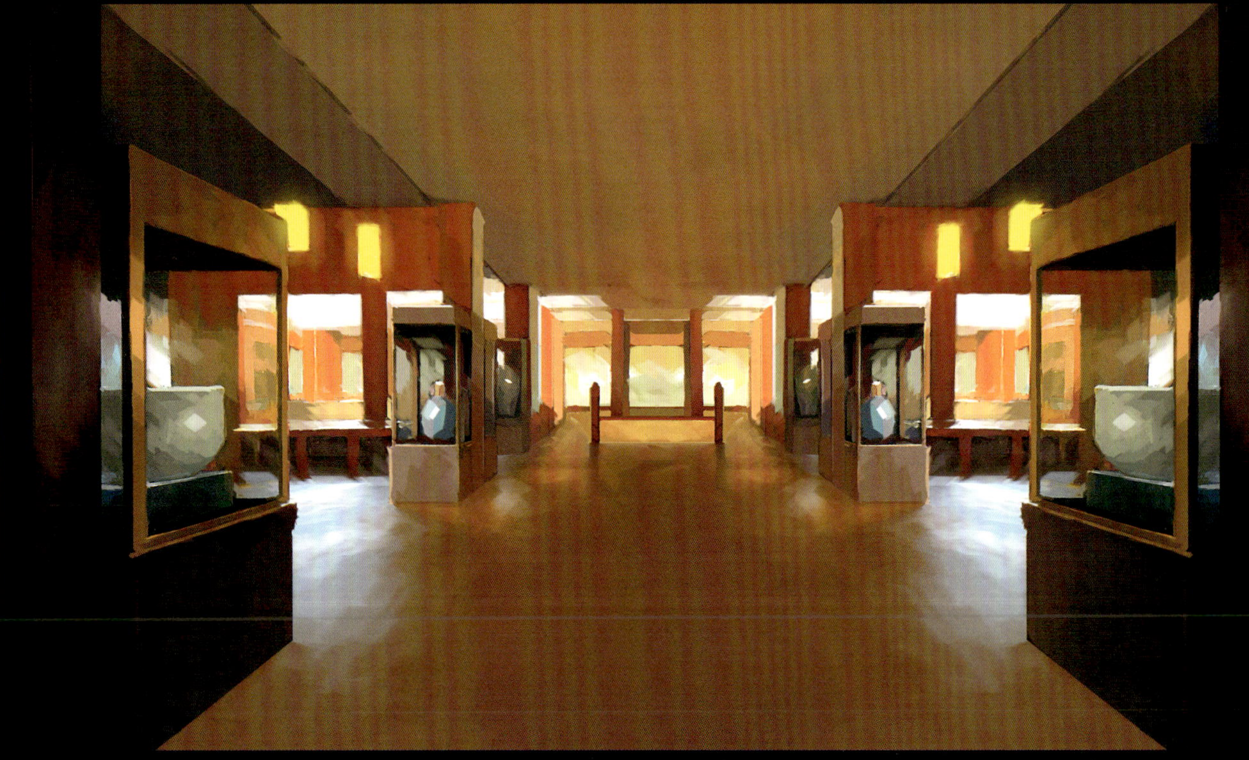

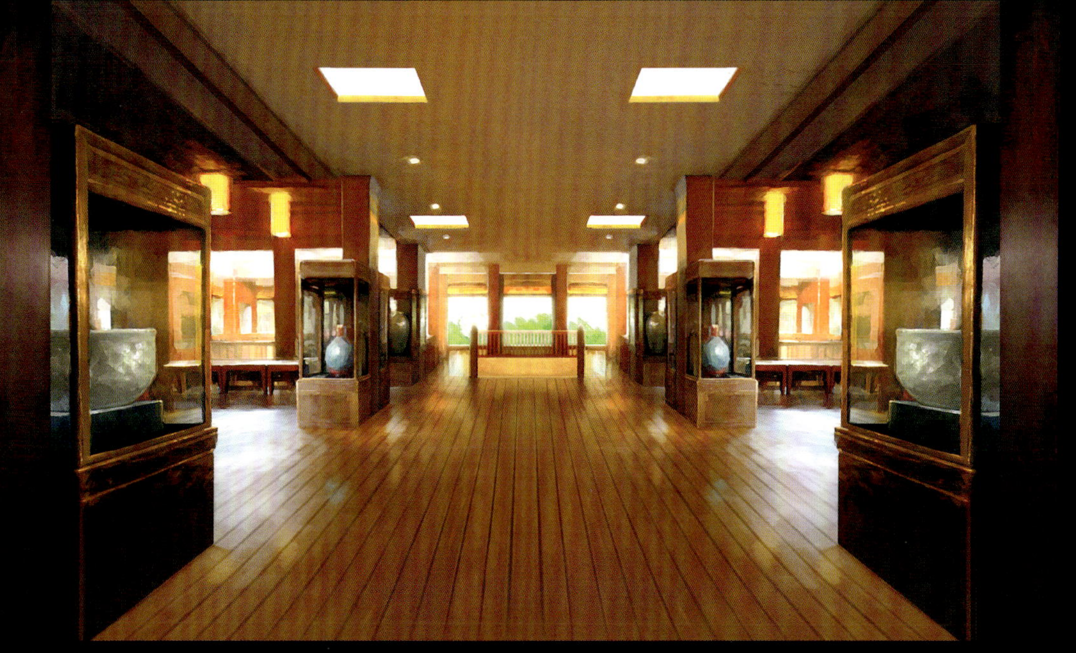

I then added the texture of the wooden floor and the simple shadow effects upon it, before refining certain details on the furnishings and architectural structures.

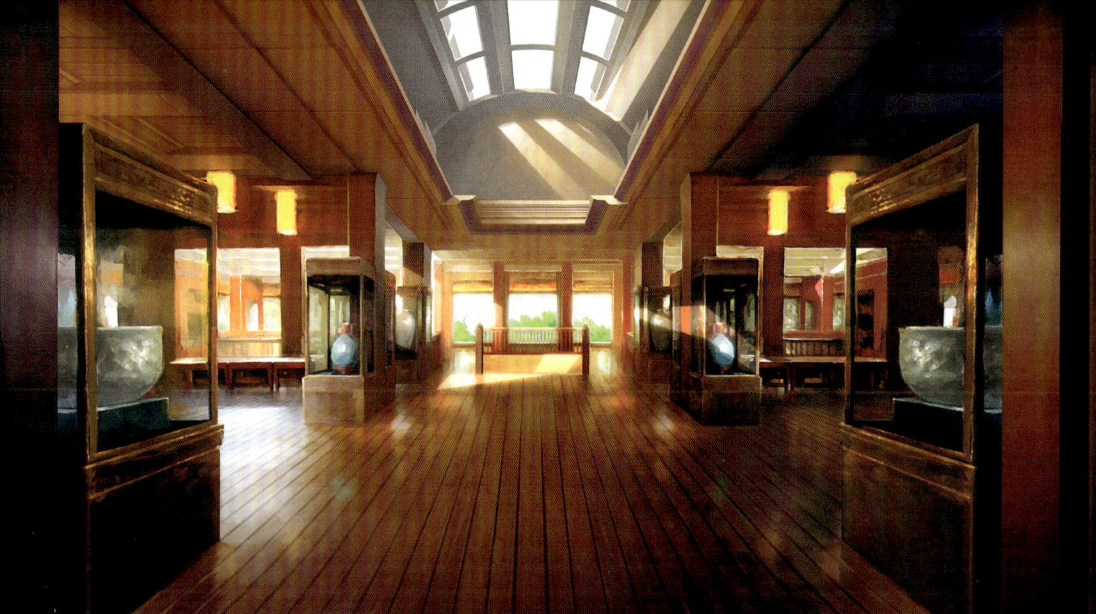

From this point forward, the mirroring method becomes unsuitable. The second-floor structure has now been factored into the overall composition, and with the addition of daylight, objects on the left and right no longer appear symmetrical.

To remove traces of the mirroring effect, I added glimmers of light cast on the floors and walls according to where the daylight enters the scene. On the right side, I added a cold-light source to diversify the overall atmosphere. As daylight comes in from the left and extends to the right, the quality of the light declines.

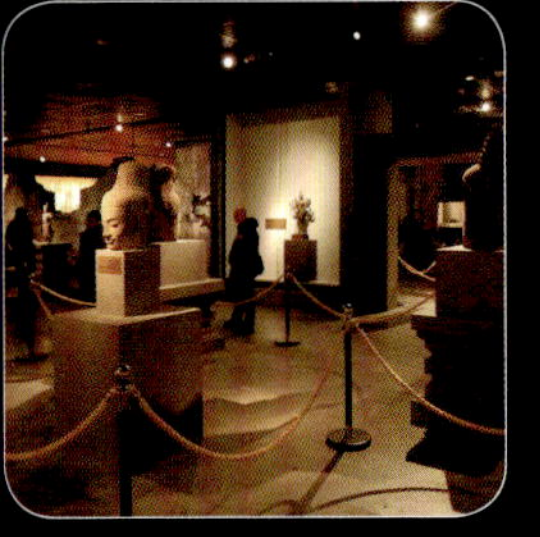

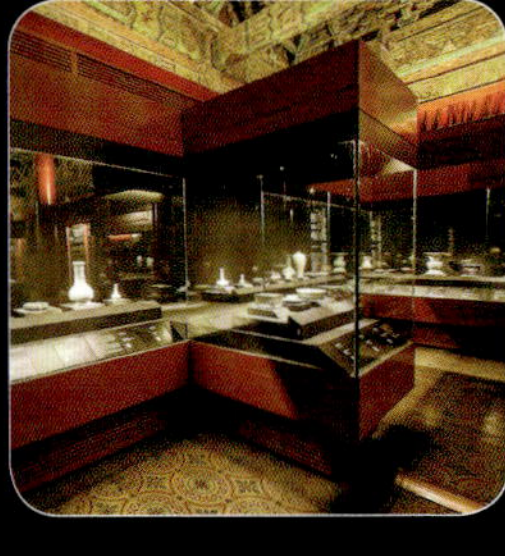

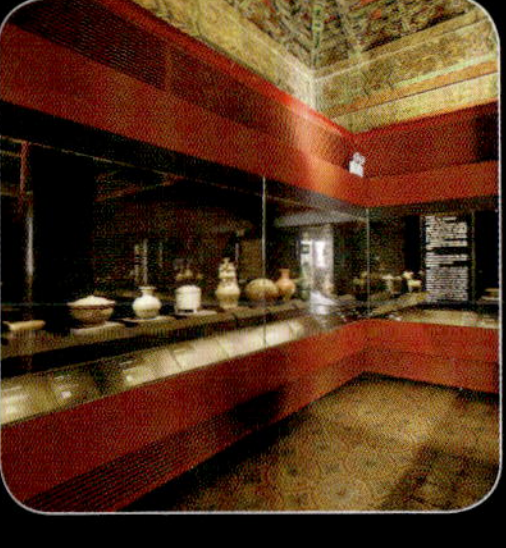

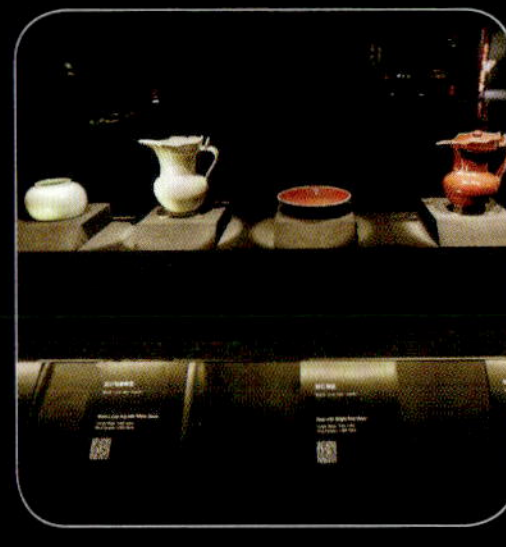

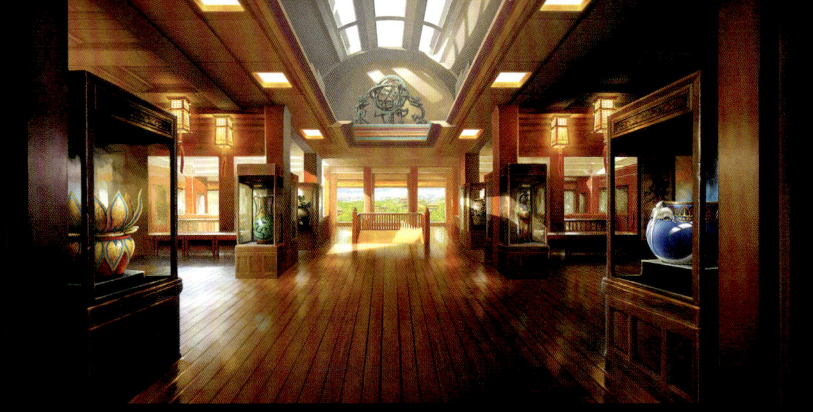

I placed an armillary sphere at the centre of the second floor, which can be seen clearly from the viewer's perspective. And then, I added the colour of patina to the sphere. This is a common technique in scene design. The purpose of which is to create an even distribution of different colours without isolating any single colour (there are those creations which require single block colours as well). The exhibits contained in the glass cabinets were then varied. Similar shaped objects were chosen and then coloured with either warm or cool tones, consequently rendering the whole scene more colourful and adjusting the rhythm of colours as well. The four exhibits on display, from left to right, are a red lotus seat, a green vase, a brown pottery figurine, and a blue porcelain jar. They each shows a combination of warm and cool colours.

## ▲ ANTIQUES AND RELICS

There are a diverse array of antiques and relics to choose from. Most exhibits housed in museums feature a certain theme. They either come from the same region, date from similar periods, or belong to the same religion. Alternatively, they could all belong to a certain category of artefact, such as ceramics and lacquerware.

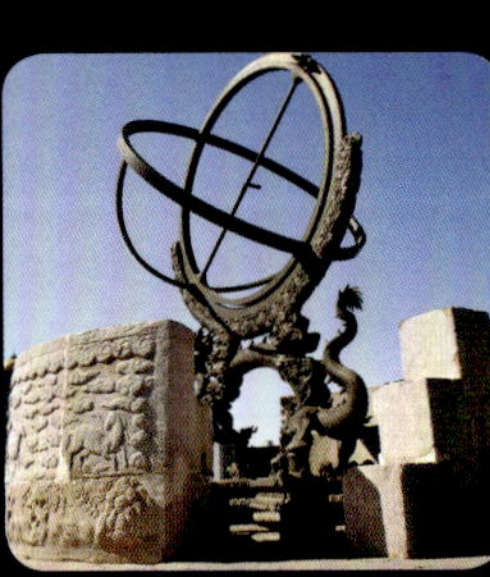

## ◀ ARMILLARY

Invented during China's Western Han Dynasty (around 100 BC), the armillary sphere is a device used to measure celestial coordinates. Its invention demonstrates the importance attached by the ancient Chinese to celestial observation and research as well as the technical sophistication of the time. Its delicate shape, huge volume, and significance make it a signature exhibit for a museum.

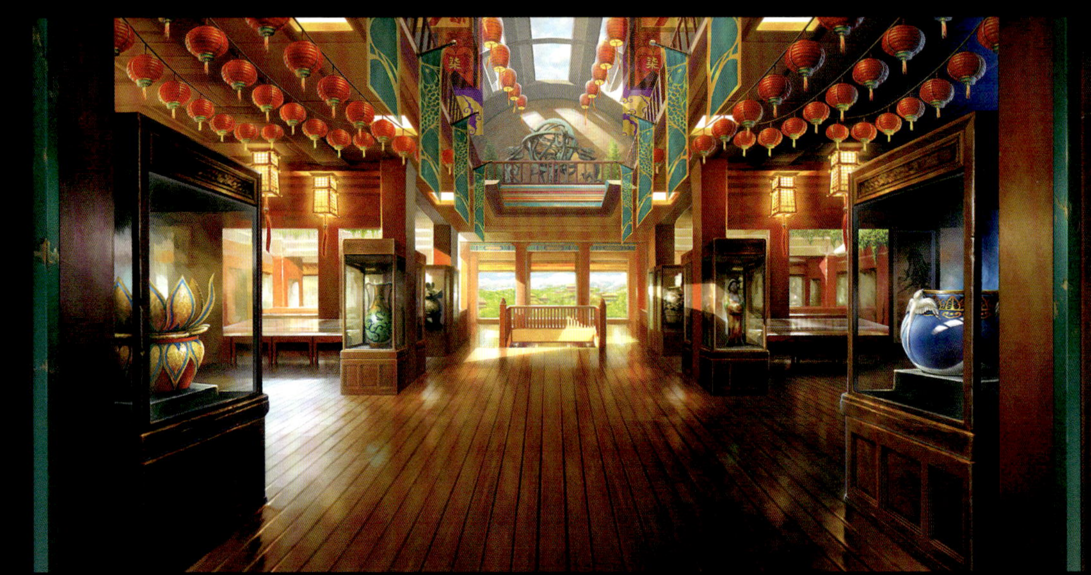

The "bluish green" colour, which represents the "vitality of life" and was common to Chinese imperial palaces in ancient times, is applied to diversify the predominant tone of yellowish brown. I subsequently added banners and other decorations to serve as canvases for new colours which match the colour palette. This also bestowed the scene with a notion of commerciality distinguishing it from pure "ancient building interiors".

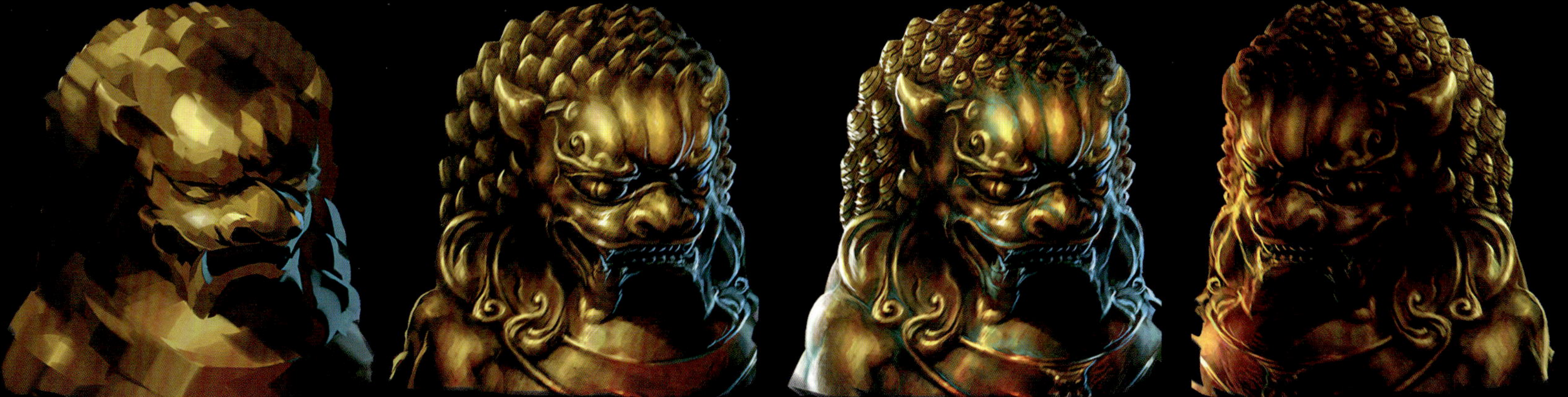

The uniquely shaped copper lions with a short muzzle point to one aspect of Chinese history and culture. In the process of drawing them, attention should be paid to changes of light and shade across the form as well as the difference in colours between the left and right sides.

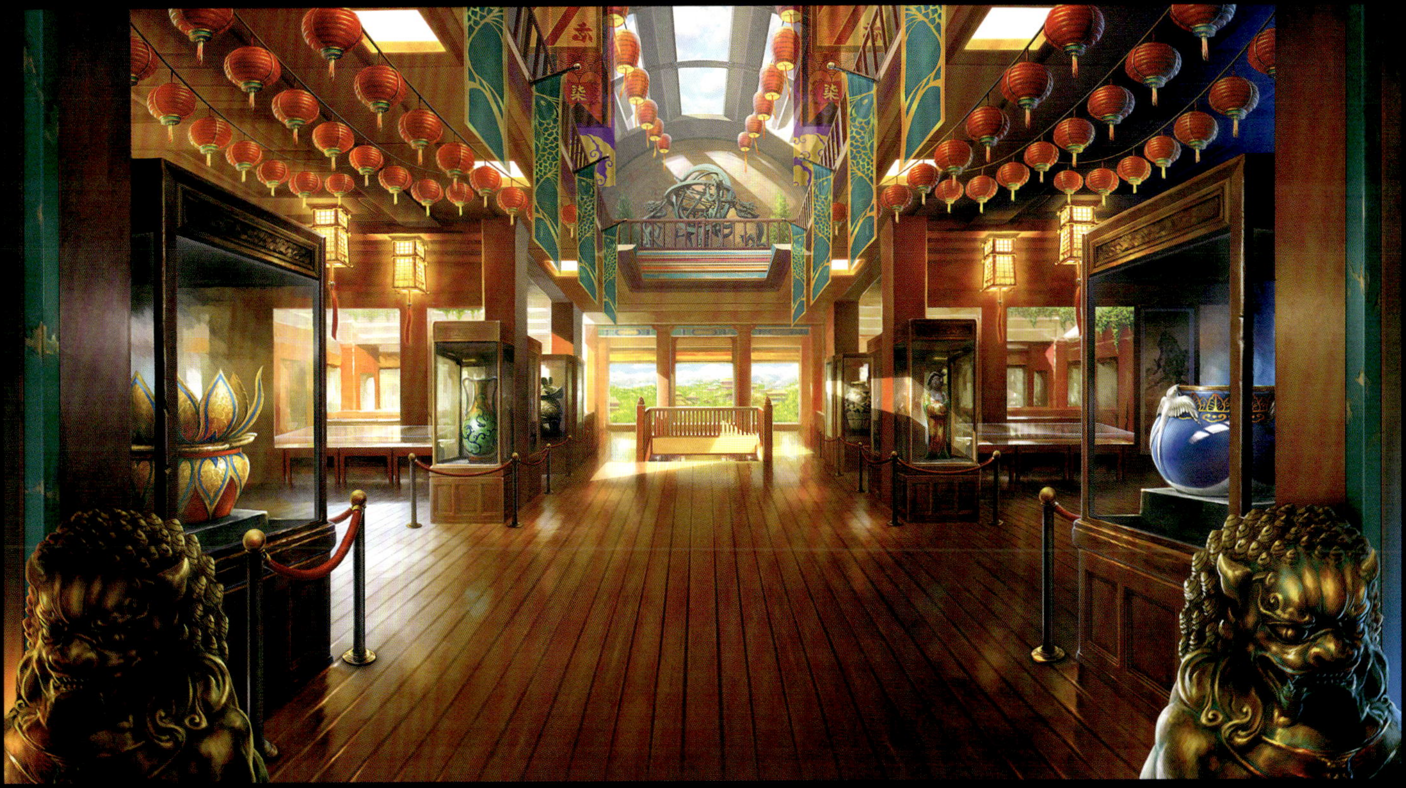

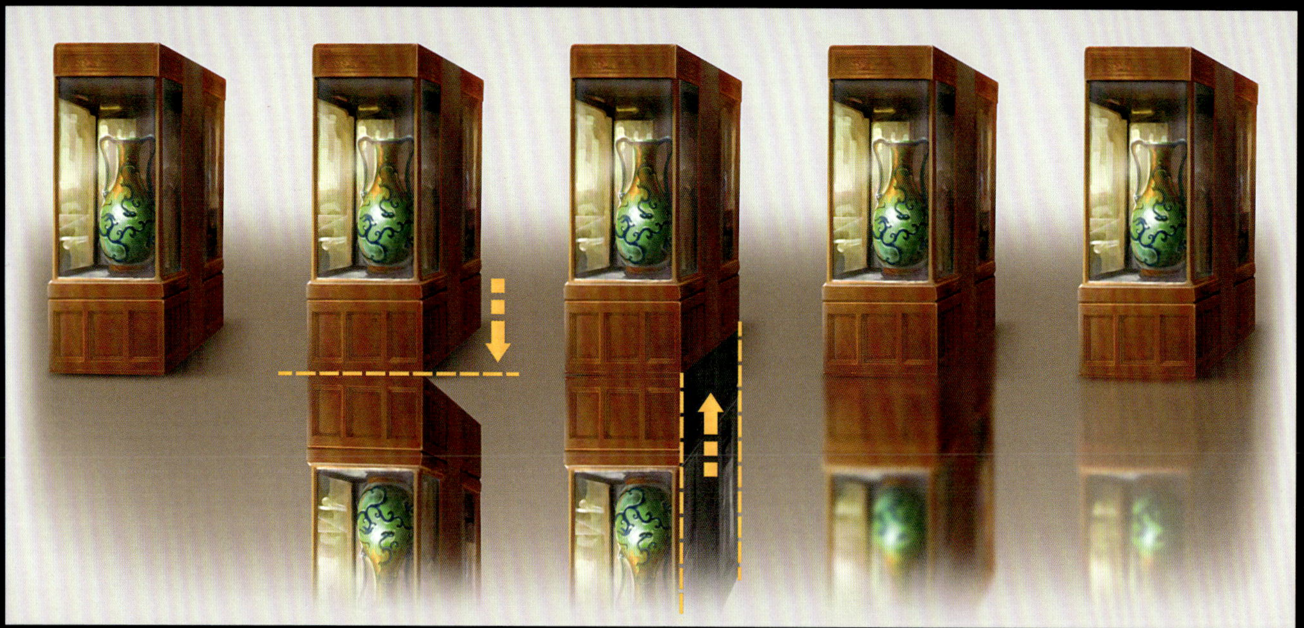

If objects are not parallel to each other or are not seen from a parallel perspective or a big wide angle, then the mirroring method will not perfectly line up the mirrored images with their originals. Thus, each object needs to be singled out for special treatment to ensure a lifelike representation of its reflection.

Like exhibition cabinet, it's necessary to pick out the reflections which haven't lined up with the original object via the mirroring method and carefully replacing them in the correct position before blurring the reflection to cover up any minor flaws. Finally, according to the texture of the floor and the degree of reflection you hope to portray, you can choose between translucence and superimposition for treating the reflections.

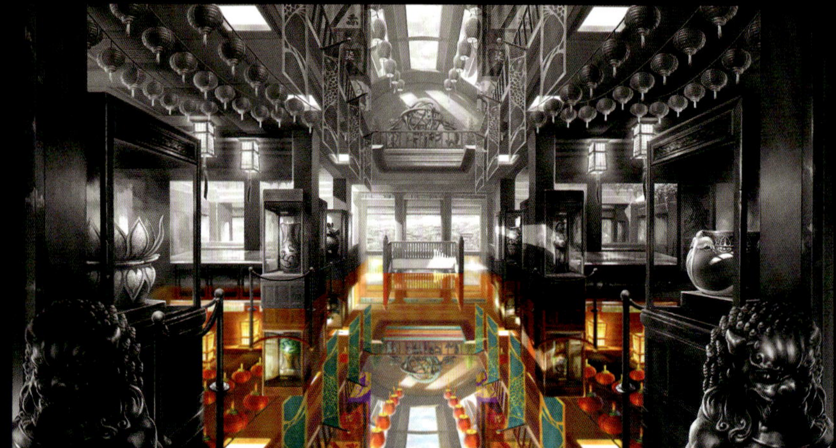

In this picture, the coloured part shows the rough effects of reflections created using the above methods.

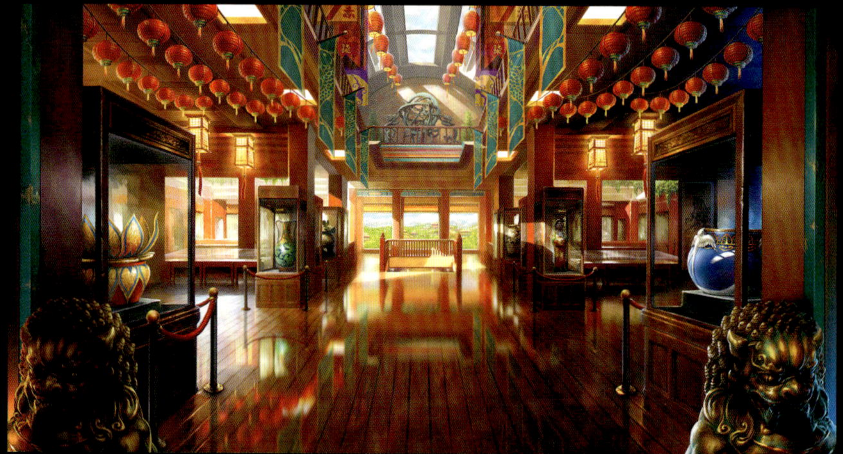

This picture shows the effects of superimposing blurred reflections onto the floor. Reflections that are not easily reflected or are likely to be weakened in the process of reflection were wiped out. The overall effect of the reflections on the wooden floor is thus completed.

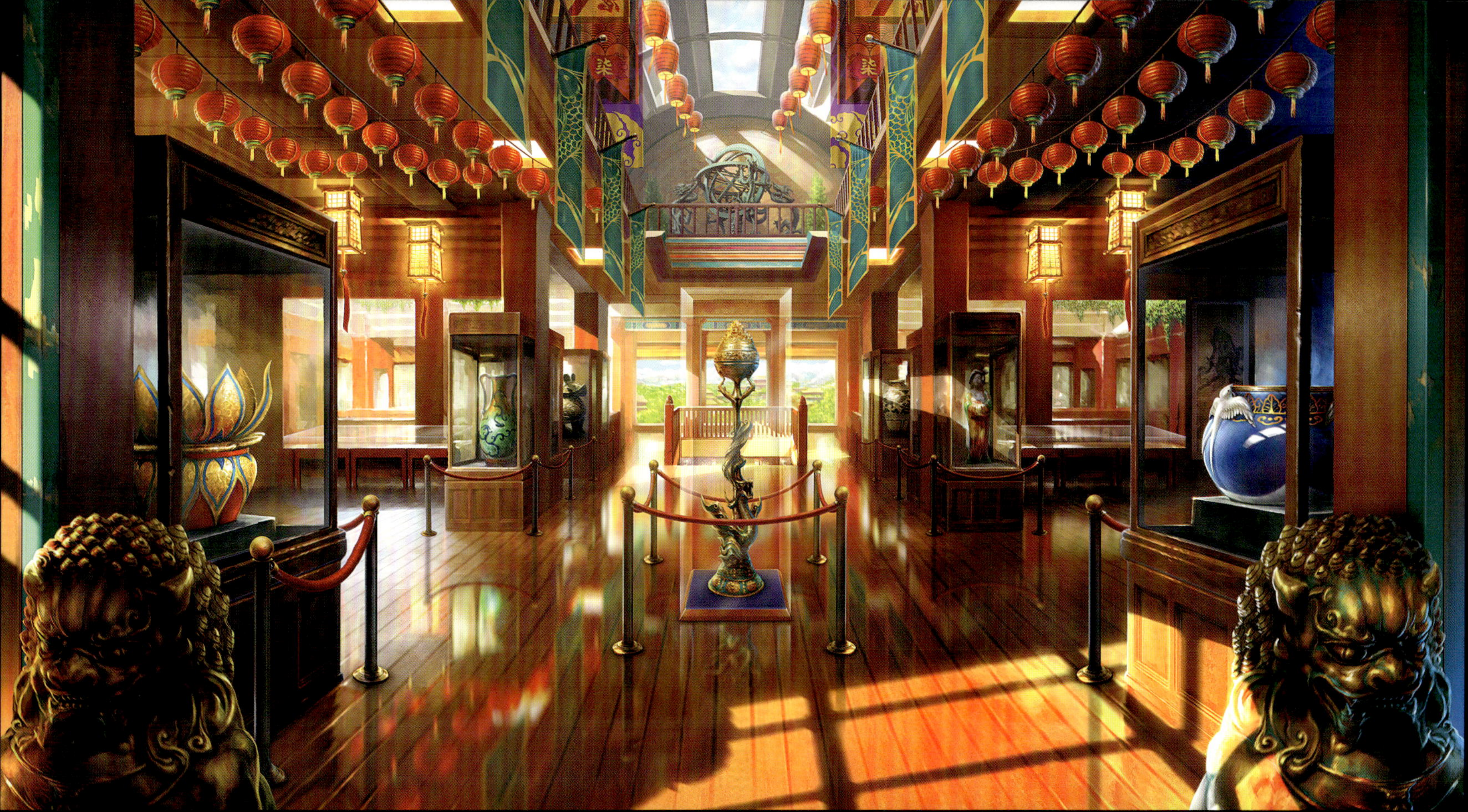

Sunshine is projected onto the floor of the foreground. A delicate, special exhibit which was designed so as not to block the view of the background was set up in the centre of the hall with its reflection on the floor. These two elements could not be added until the rest of the reflection had been added, because as foreground elements they are likely to influence the initial reflection effect.

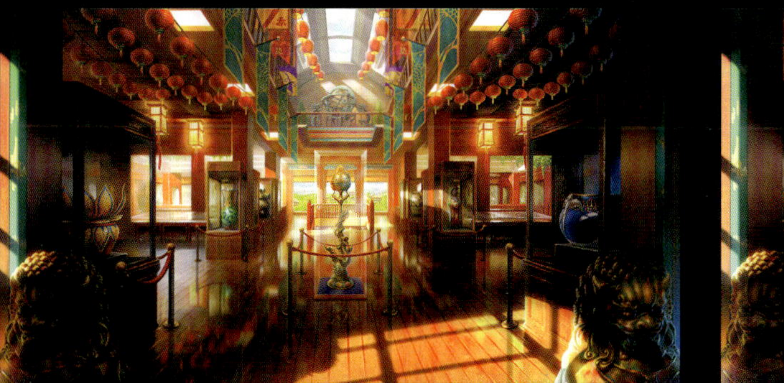

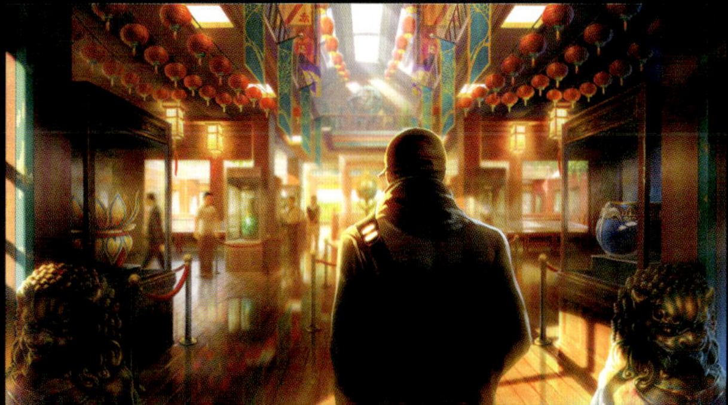

Changing the overall contrast of such an indoor scene by exaggerating its bright and dark spots and backlight effects will make the scene more real. Moreover, adding a figure looking in could also make the scene look as if it was a situational creation.

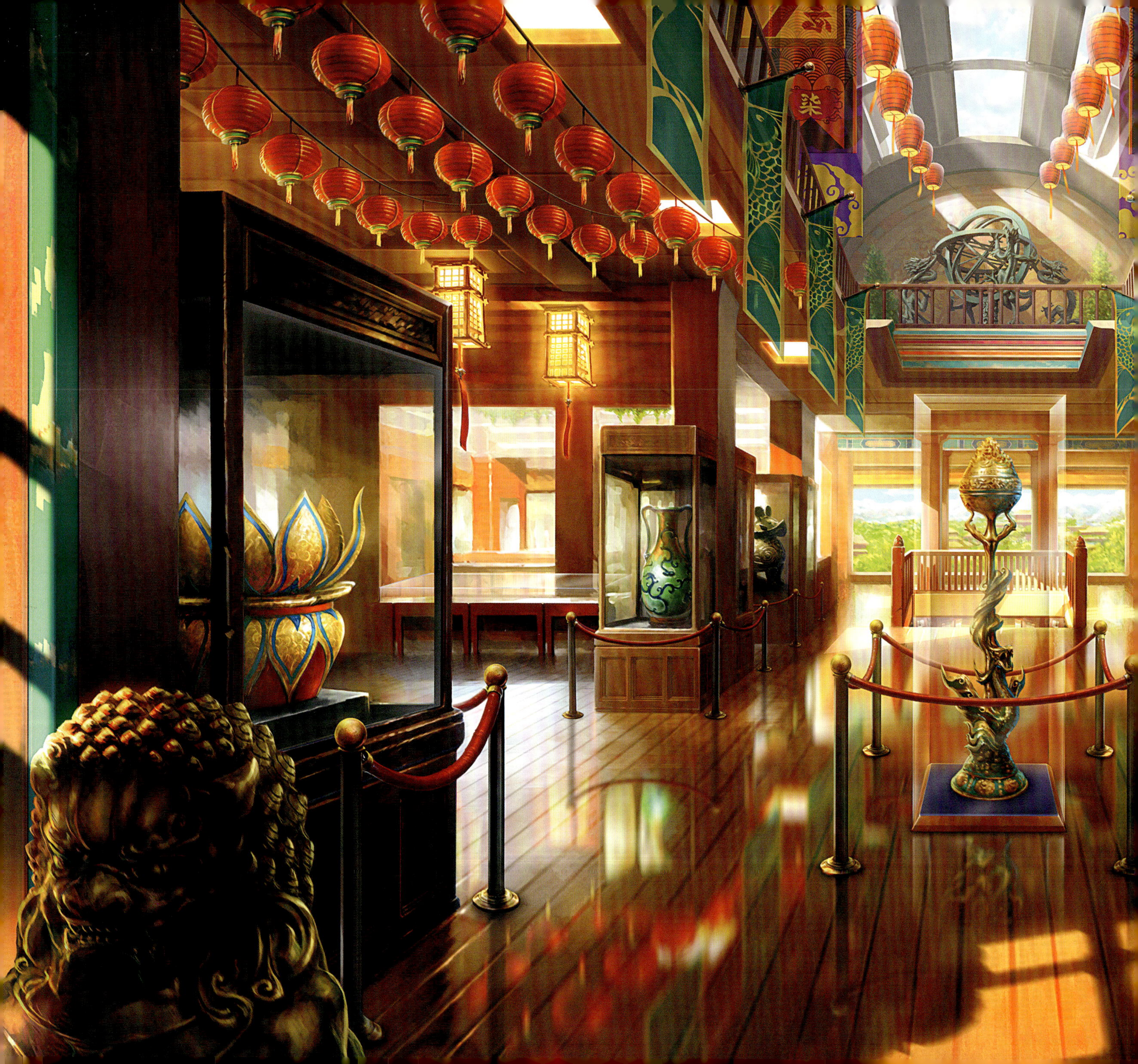

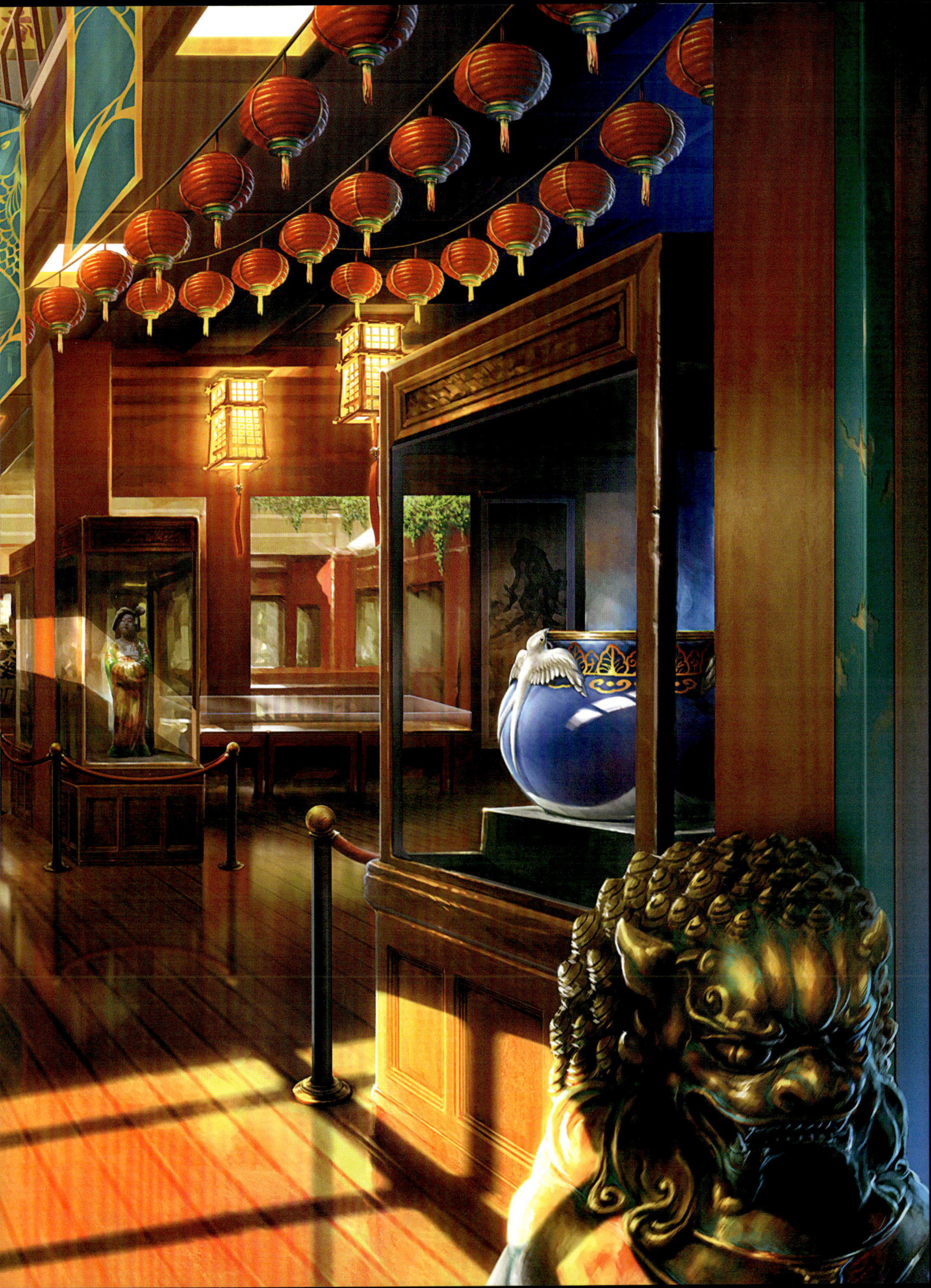

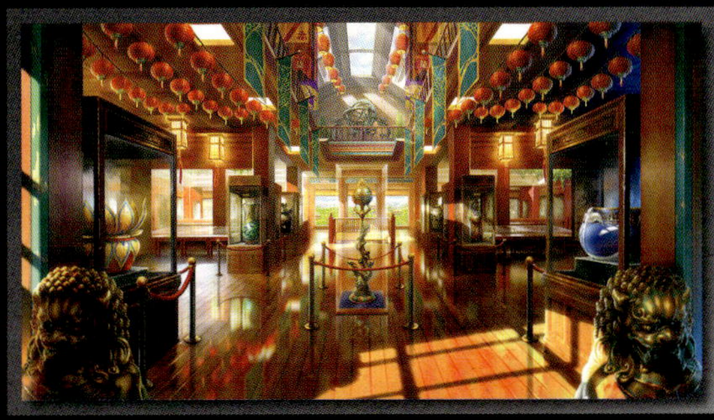

Finally, I adjusted the overall light and shadow effects. Glow effects were added to the areas exposed to light, and the volume of light coming in from the ceiling was increased. Till now, this work is completed.

# Old Temples in the Wild

Throughout history, "museums" have served as records of the social conditions and trivialities of popular life from former times. For some people, China leaves an altogether different impression. It is an impression not of resplendent palaces or gardens of green willows and red walls but of old temples situated amongst high maintains and dense forests where bells toll and birds flock. These are the retreats depicted in martial arts novels where Kung Fu masters live in seclusion and train.

Freeing themselves from the fetters of the mundane world and secluding themselves away, martial artists live a life unbounded. Now, in a society characterized by hustle and bustle, people restricted by regulations and rules of all kinds and hindered by diverse burdens are longing for such a life. In light of their wishes, I created *Old Temples in the Wild* as a symbolic retreat from the modern world.

As a representation of buildings hidden deep in forest mountains, this work of art is entirely different from the outdoor scenes of previous chapters – the narrow street, magnificent Forbidden City, and man-made gardens. New methods are applied for completing the piece, including stratified depiction and associated representation. If I used previous methods for this piece, we would first draw a large stretch of luxuriant forests and then erect a temple in a space among the trees. The result would be a "superficial" representation of the theme established by merely depicting two relevant token objects. Such a design really doesn't require much thought to achieve and lacks any systematic conception, inevitably meaning that painters of different understandings and expressive abilities would produce highly divergent ideas about how a theme should be presented.

An appropriate means of conveying the spirit and theme of a work can significantly improve the efficiency of producing it. The alternative is a slower progress or a final piece which has strayed from the initial conception. Therefore, it is necessary to carefully analyse relationships between major elements in the frame and the theme of a work at the initial stage of creation so as to identify certain "tailored elements" which can be adapted and integrated into the work.

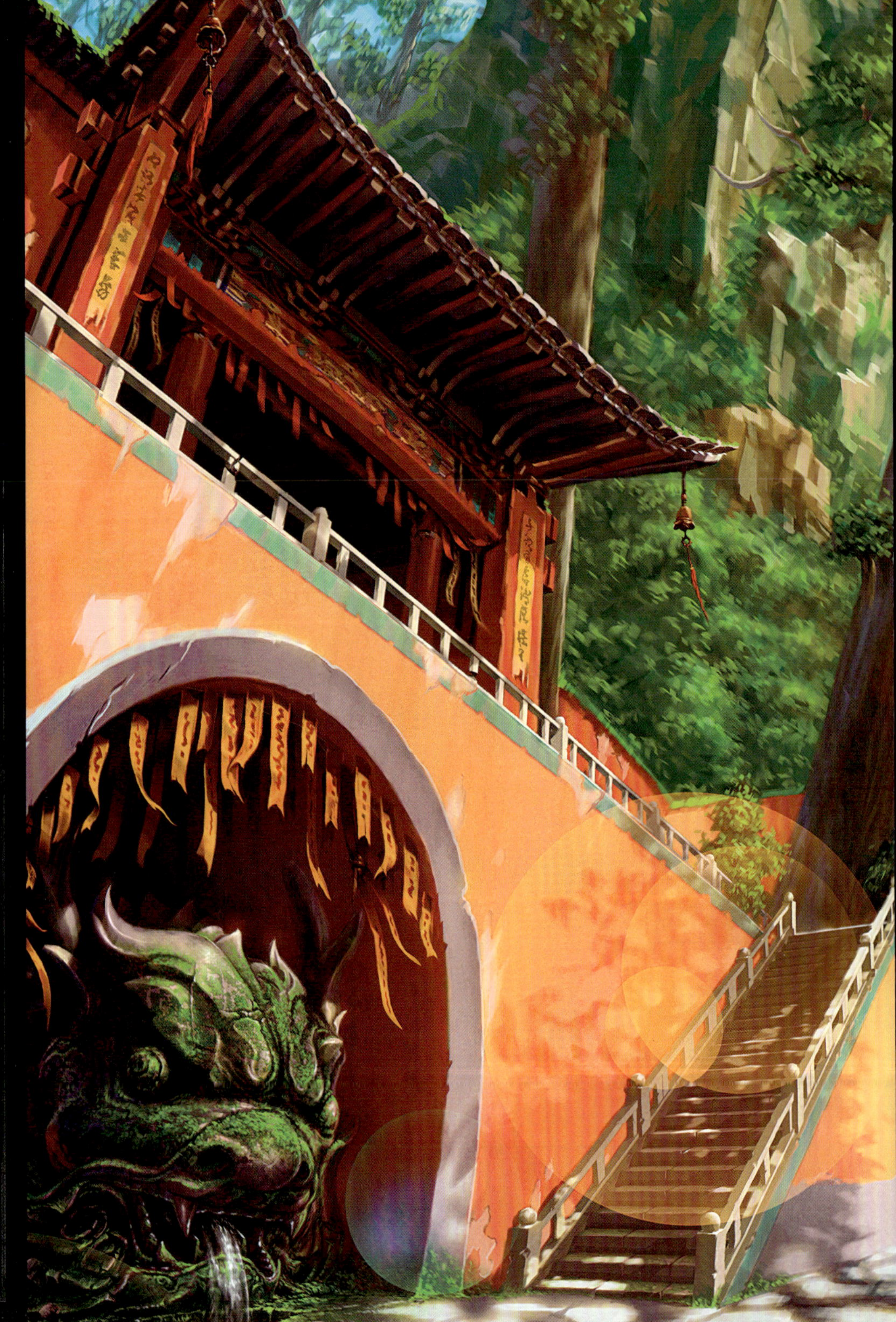

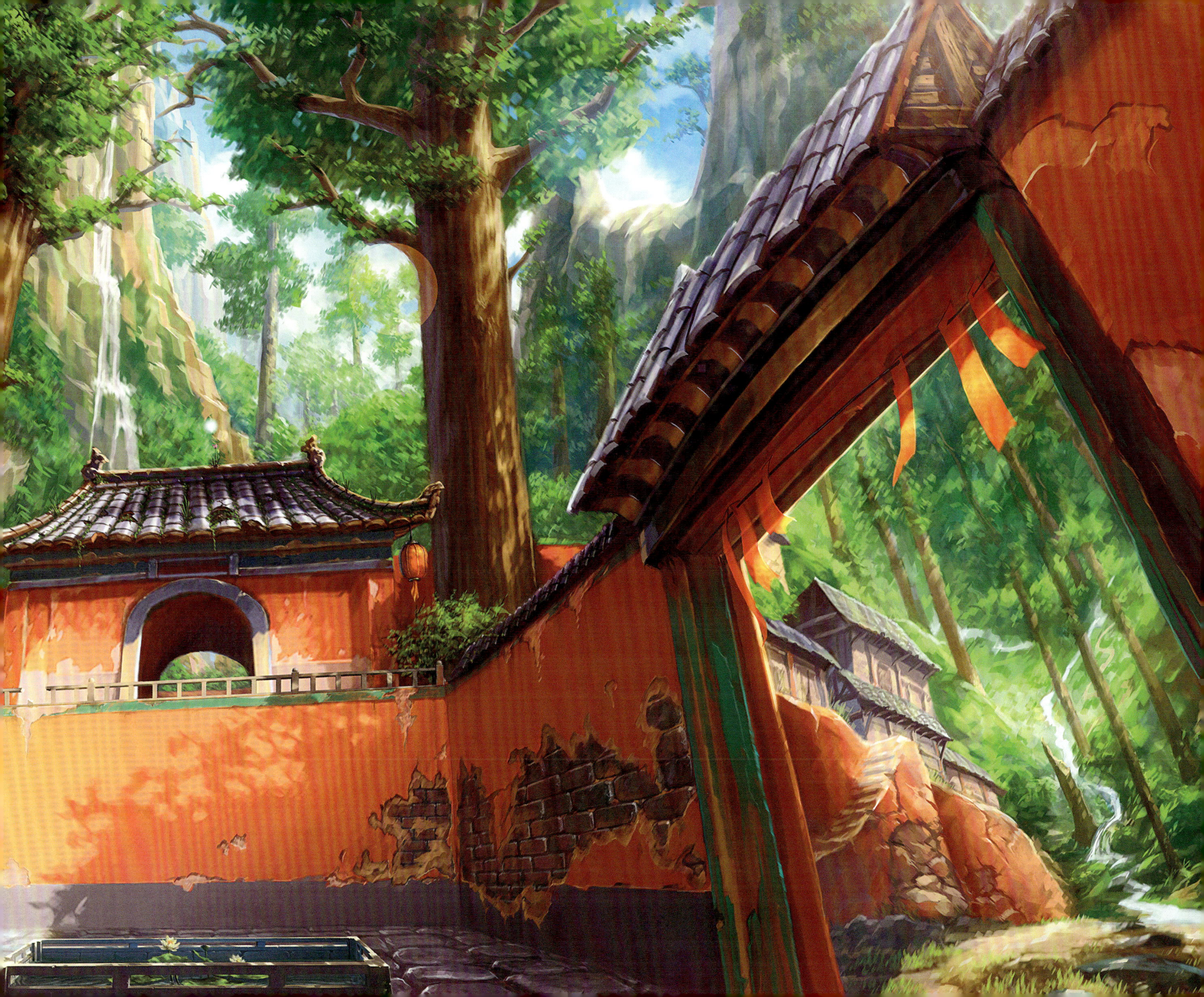

# THOUGHTS ON CREATION

*It is the representation of overall atmosphere which determines the kind of resonance a piece arouses with viewers. Therefore, without figures or an unfolding situation, one needs to make full use of light effects, dynamic effects, fog effects, colour pallets, and colour temperatures to highlight a certain atmosphere or make up for the shortage. Among them, dynamic effects are the most difficult to achieve. Adding a sense of movement into a static piece necessitates careful planning and appropriate pairings of different objects.*

*Imagine, for example, a copper bell hanging from a branch is swinging in the wind. There is a ribbon tied to the bell that is fluttering along with the motion. The desired illusion is for a viewer to hear the crisp sound of jingling on seeing this image. Such a simple scene leaves a lot of room for imagination. The static and silent scene is transformed into dynamic space filled with sound and rhythm, displaying a thread of serenity. More such elements need to be integrated into the design so as to strengthen its sense of movement.*

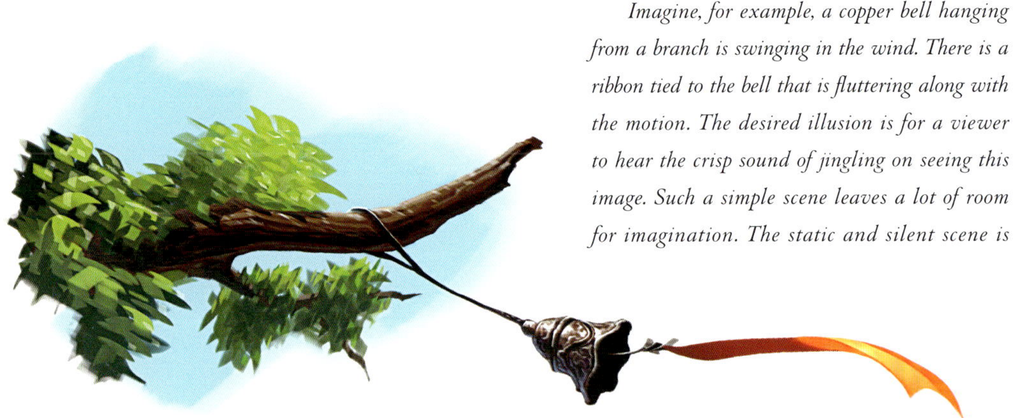

*If you consider the "atmosphere" of a work of art as its "soul" or "spirit", the enlivening factor which most resonates with viewers, then the "contents" or "objects" can be said to be its "body". The spirit is contained within the flesh. Thus, the flesh should be strong and sturdy to serve as a solid foundation for containing spirit. Even the simplest objects carry with them their own unique characteristics, which require research, analysis, and investigation to uncover. The payoff of these endeavours is a final piece that is closer to nature and more likely to be accepted.*

*Old temples usually have long and rich histories. In the shade of surrounding trees, their red walls and grey tiles really draw the eye, bringing people to think of the same dignity and solemnity associated with imperial palaces. Red and grey are commonly used colours at Buddhist temples in China. Located in mountains and forests, both often quite humid environments, moss grows over the temple stone steps while the red walls of the structures are cracked and faded by exposure to the winds and sun. Naturally, this gives a strong sense of the site's age.*

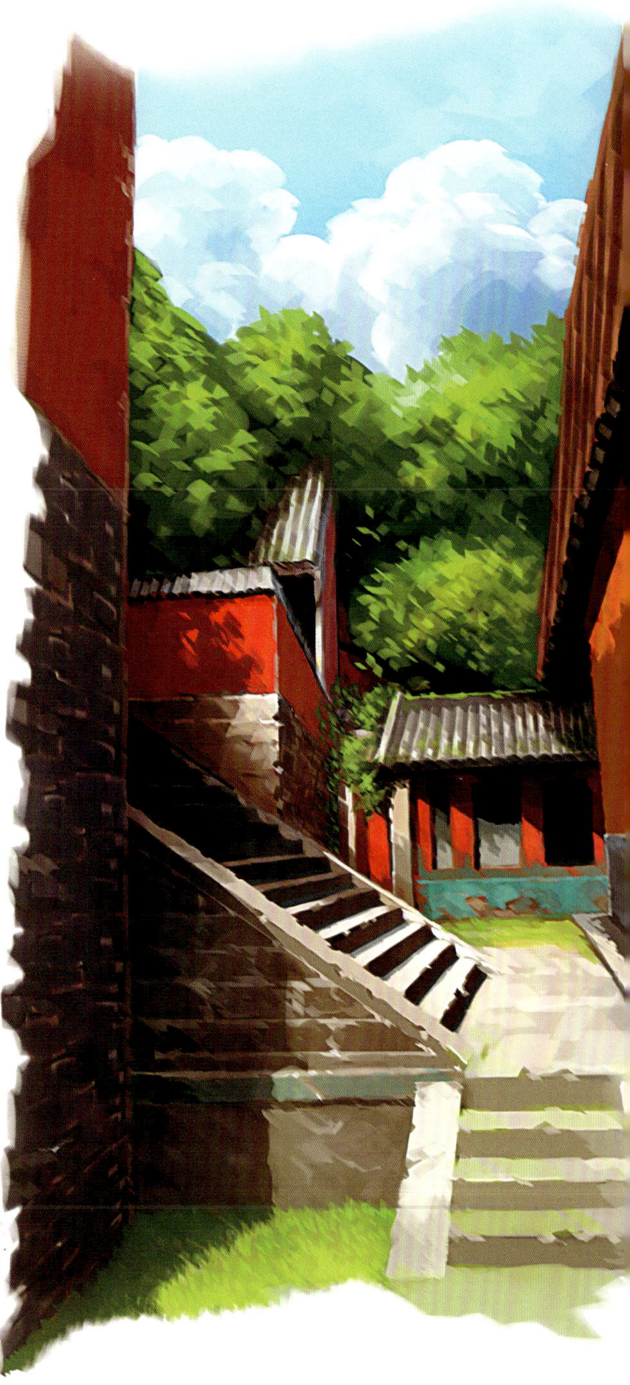

## ▼ EIGHT GREAT SITES

The *Badachu*, or "Eight Great Sites", is a famous complex of eight old temples built in the Western Hills of Beijing in ancient China. I took the *Badachu* as the primary model and the place to collect materials and inspiration for this creation, because Badachu is comprised of a complex of temples both concentrated into one area and representing a diverse range of types.

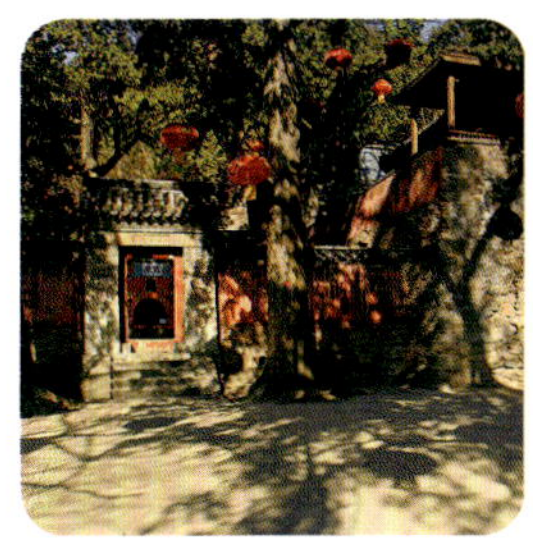

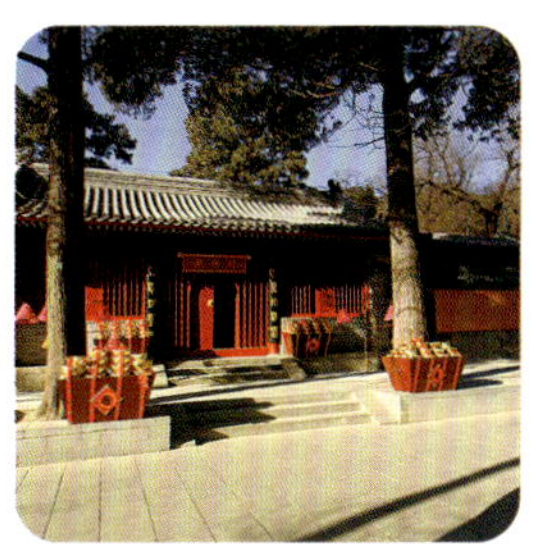

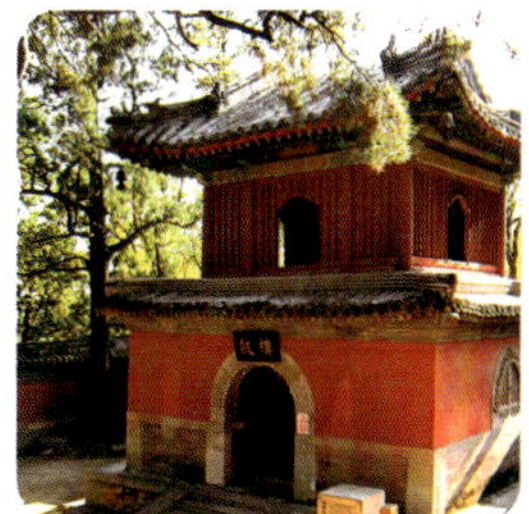

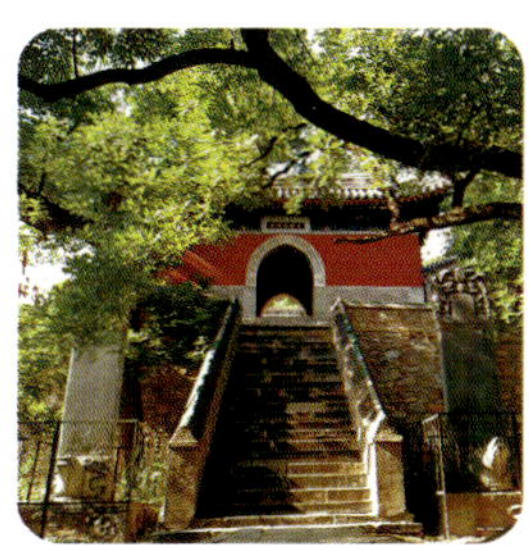

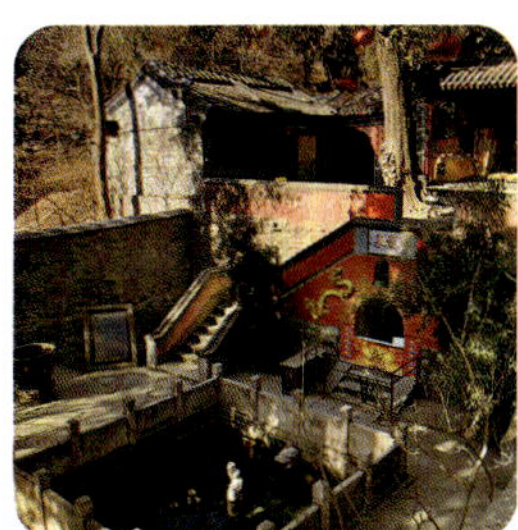

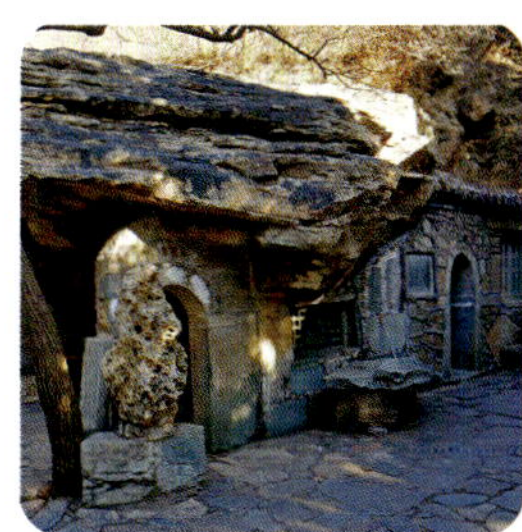

## ▼ CENTRAL BUILDING

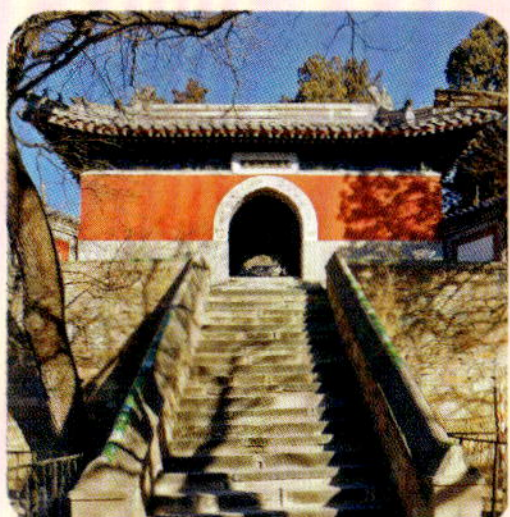

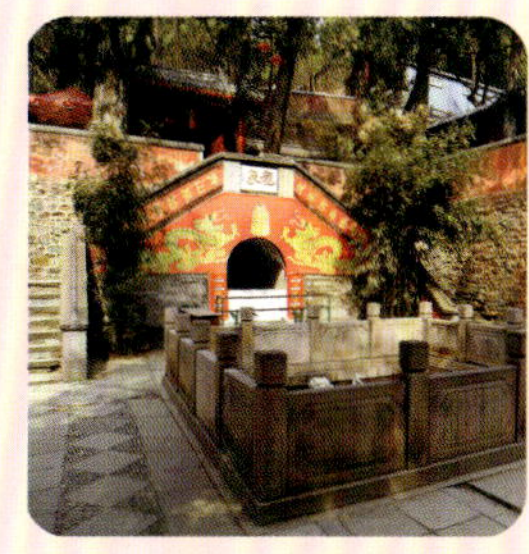

Beside the main hall serving as its central building, the average Chinese temple usually also has a mountain gate, a front hall, a main hall, a back hall, a sutra repository, and an abbot's chamber. They are all flanked by a bell and drum tower and side halls. Small temples hidden deep in the mountains don't receive as large flows of visitors as big temples and so have simplified layouts, like the Longquan Nunnery, one of the Eight Great Sites.

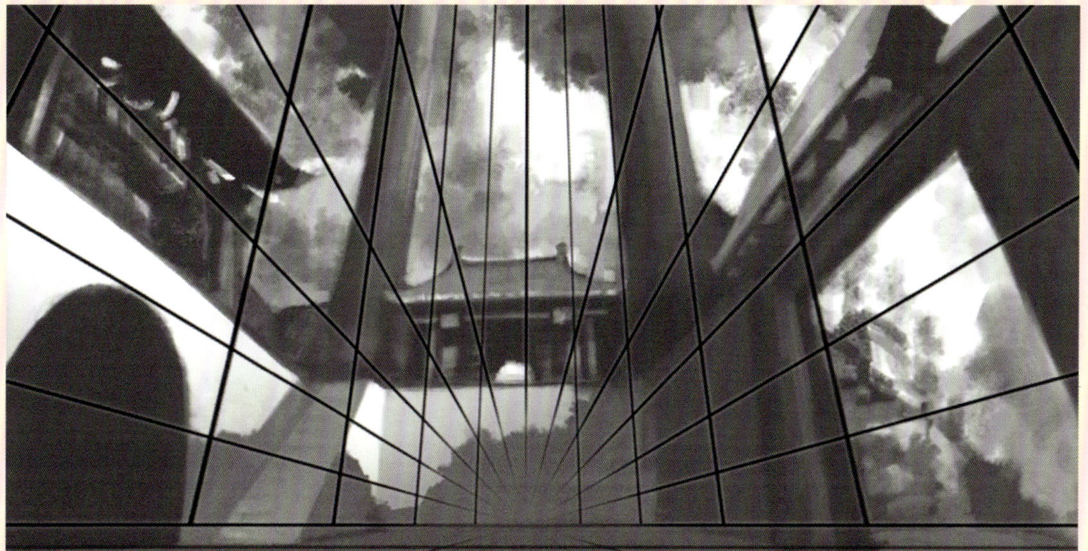

Inspired by the orderly layout of the Longquan Nunnery, an upward perspective is adopted to make objects in the painting appear tall and large, strengthening the grandness and denseness of the forest enveloping the temple. Moreover, this perspective helps with exaggerating the piece's sense of space as it requires us adjusting the arrangements of the structures, tall trees, and mountains in the distance.

Considering that building walls all around a temple tends to give an oppressive feel, I opened up the structures on the left and right of the frame, inserting there a spring where water flows and an open mountain gate, respectively. In addition, there are stone steps leading to the structure above and rays of light coming in from a side angle produce numerous, fun interplays of light, injecting a sense of liveliness into the steadiness.

The "bird's eye view" perspective can bring out the whole range of desired content within a single frame. However, this approach is inferior to the previous composition for a number of reasons: depicting a large stretch of trees, for example, requires considerable effort because of its scope and if any part of the structure is blocked by the trees, the structure loses its sense of scale and fullness. Neither does this presentation of space easily allow for layering and gradation between areas of the frame, therefore no sky and mountains in the distance and no highly detailed foreground to appreciate. All these disadvantages lower a design's effectiveness.

From my research I found that temples in Northern China are characterized by red walls and grey tiles. Therefore, I stuck to this colour scheme. In the process of applying the colours and refining the image, I separated the green mountains and trees from the buildings to instil the image with a greater sense of mystery. Such represents the process of the "new forms of creation" I mentioned at the beginning of this section, namely "stratified depiction and associated representation".

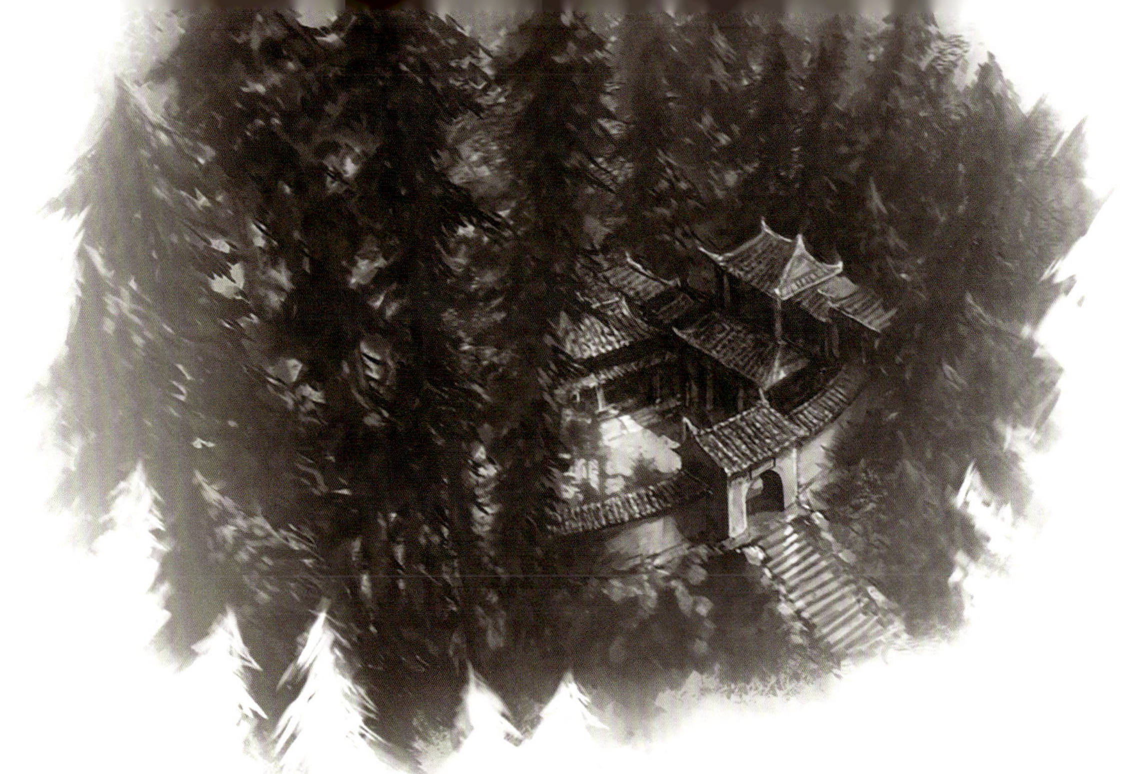

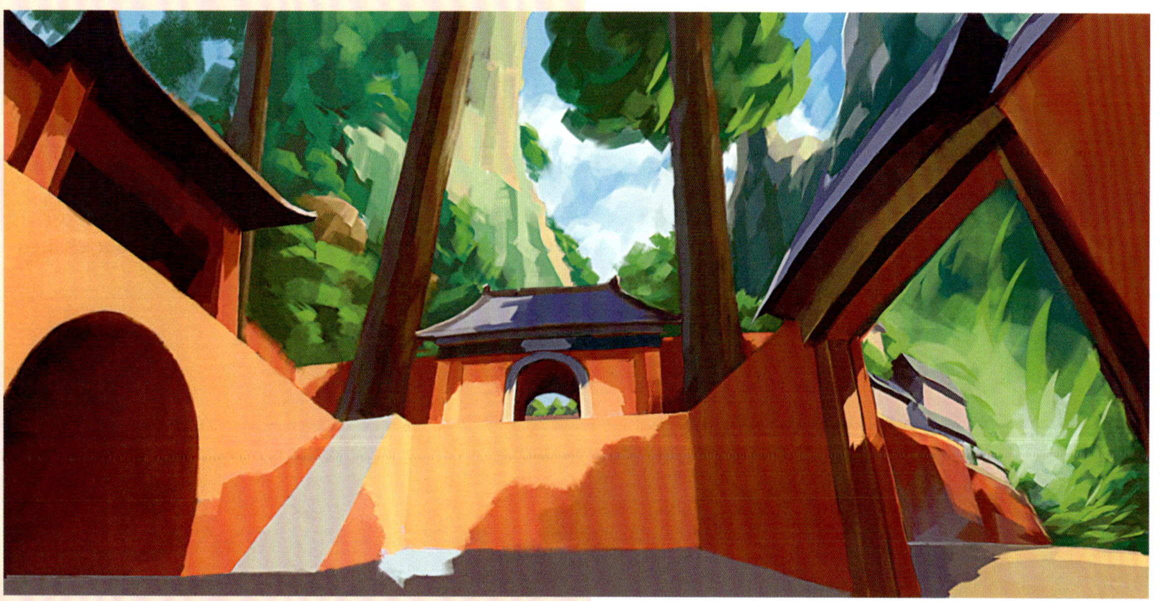

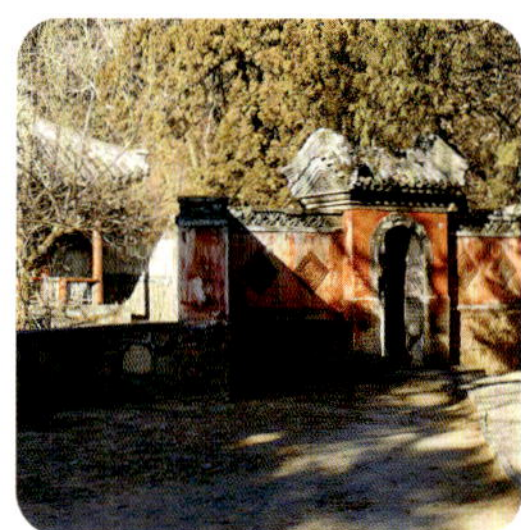

## ► A MOUNTAIN GATE

A mountain gate is a gate at the front of a temple. In early times, temples were mostly built in mountains and forests to remove them from the secular world. Hence here is the name of "mountain gate". Though many large temples have since been set up on plains or in prosperous, developed areas, the name has been kept until now.

My next step was to clear up the mountain gate. As the temple itself is small, I kept the gate simple. The focus of the piece is really the pronounced difference between the outdoor and indoor scenery. There is neither interaction nor crossover between the temple and the mountains and forests in the background. The only link is the mountain gate.

The mountain scenery at the back of the temple is depicted to match the scenery seen through the mountain gate. I also ensured I leave enough areas of clear sky visible so as to avoid overall oppressive feeling. Though the background only exists as a foil to the foreground, it is necessary to coordinate the light effects as they are of course located in the same space. The shadows of trees were added to remind viewers of their closeness.

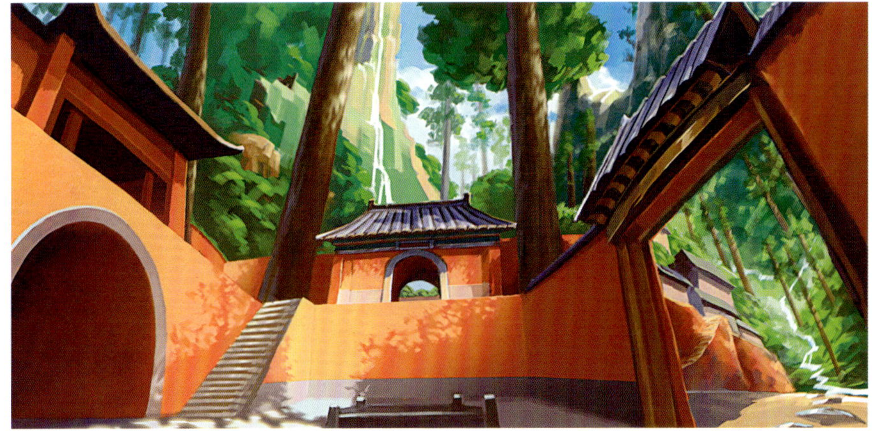

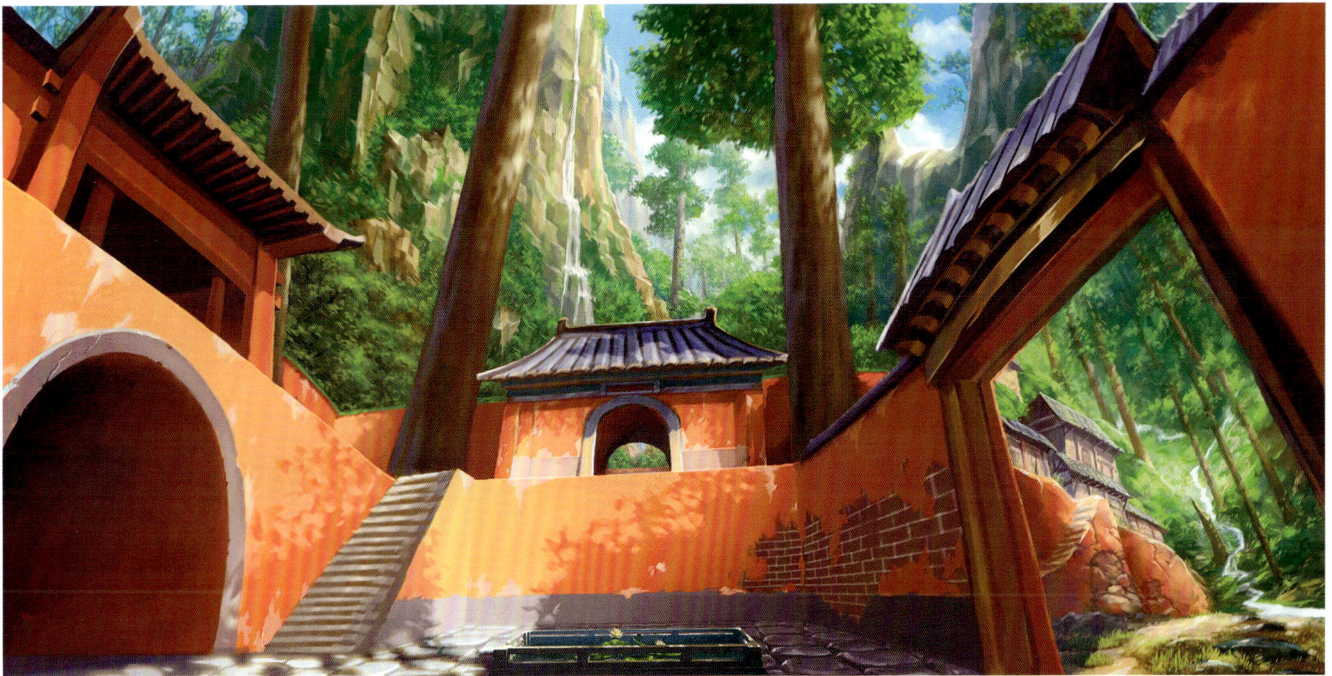

Then, more details were added. Damaged areas on the walls were defined in an even distribution to capture the effects of natural erosion. Objects that required no further revision such as the square pond, distant mountains, and tree trunks in the temple were refined to the point of completion.

The overlap of tree shadows, fluctuations of the mountain peak, and water flowing from mountain streams and cliffs highlights a sense of being in the depth of a dense forest.

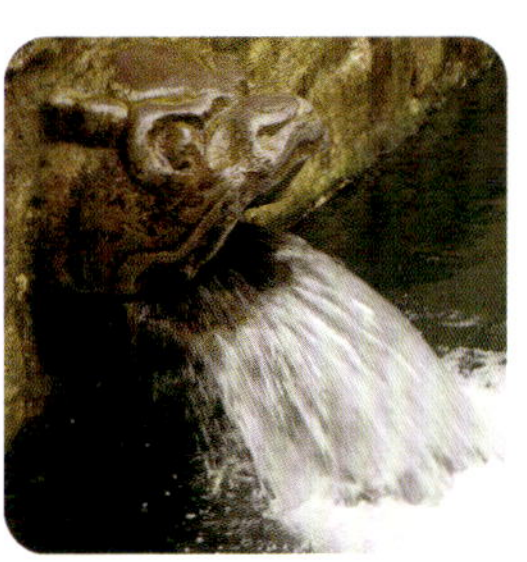

## ▲ LONGQUAN

Spring water from the "Longquan" flows out of a carved stone dragon's head with great force and liveliness.

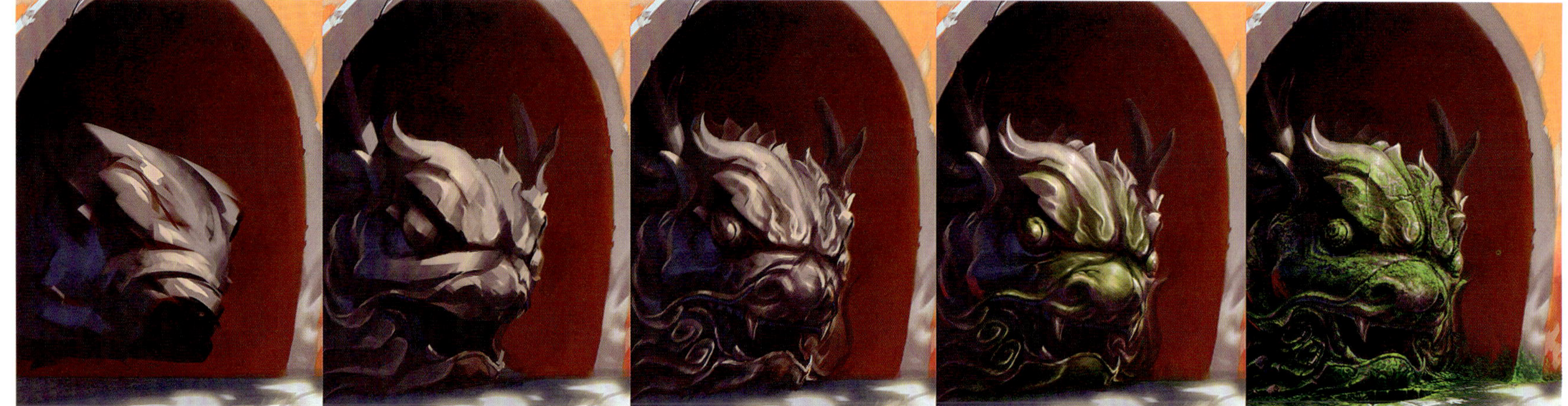

When sketching the dragon head, I made sure to mark the bright and the dark areas as well as the warm and the cool. A more aggressive expression was chosen to leave a deeper impression on viewers. I continued to add more details after the head was enlarged. In applying the colours, it was important to take into account how they might have changed after a long period in the humid environment. Finally, elements that show traces of age, such as moss, were added to create a sense of mystery.

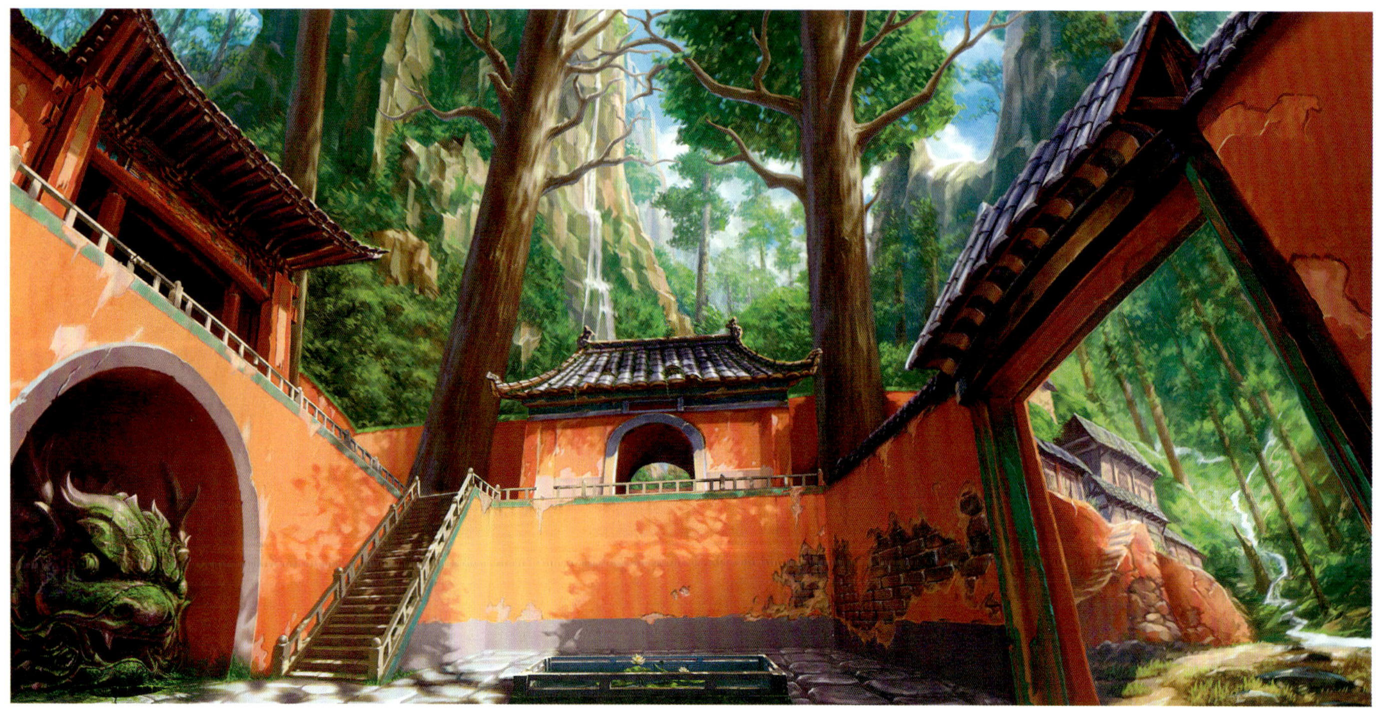

Based on the above changes, I then began to refine the remaining sections till they accorded with the stylistic and atmospheric choices so far.

## ▶ RED RIBBONS

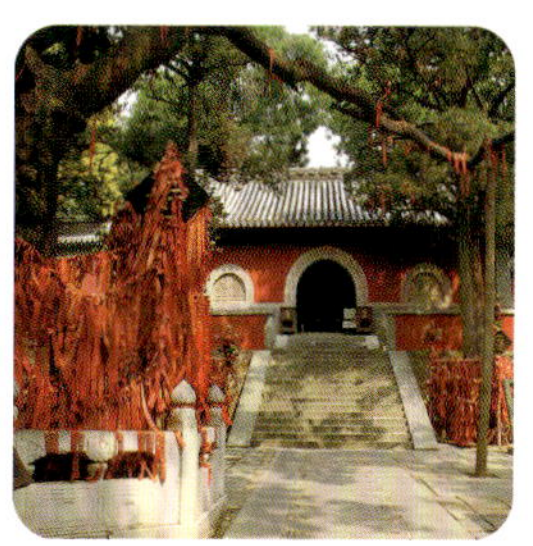

Usually, there are many red ribbons hanging in temples, carrying up on them the wishes of pilgrims and prayers for blessing. Each red ribbon represents an individual's wishes. The more incense a temple burns, the more people who visit to cast their wishes. Sometimes, the ribbons hanging on tree branches have become so numerous and thus so heavy as to bend the branches, creating a unique sight.

A copper bell swinging from the eaves, ribbons fluttering in the wind above the spring, red lanterns hanging on the side hall, and the luxuriant leaves of the old trees to the sides all reveal some traces of human activity and presence. In addition to adding some atmosphere, they also remind viewers that the old temple dates back to ancient times but in no way is dilapidated or lifeless.

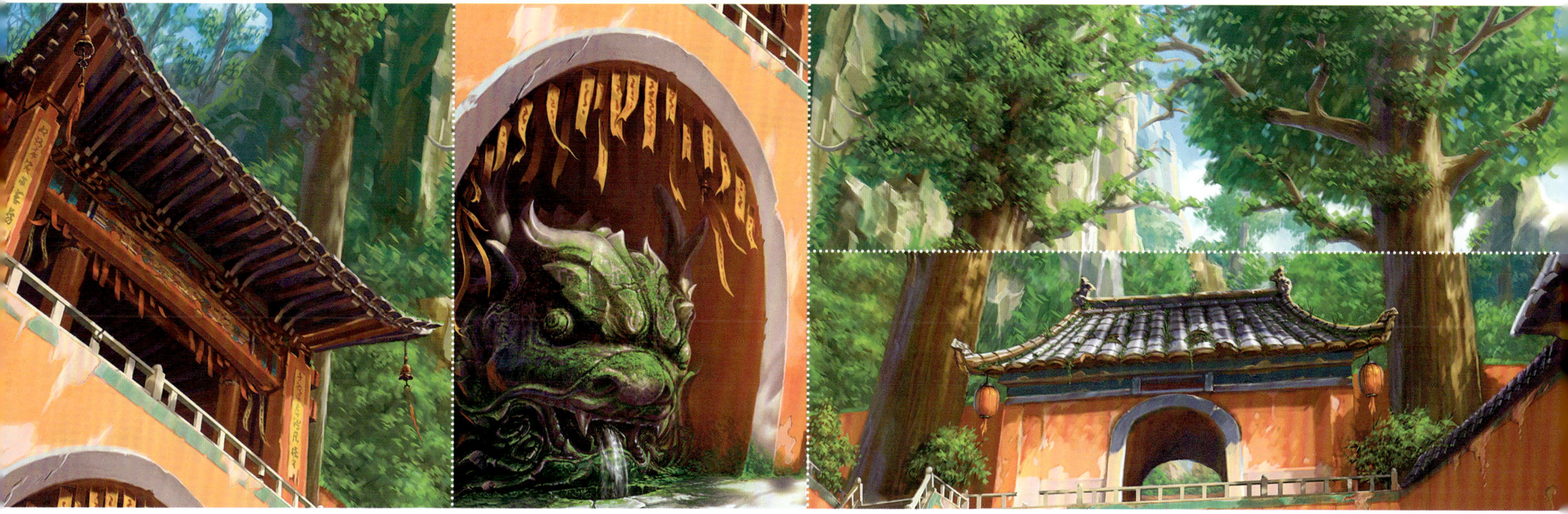

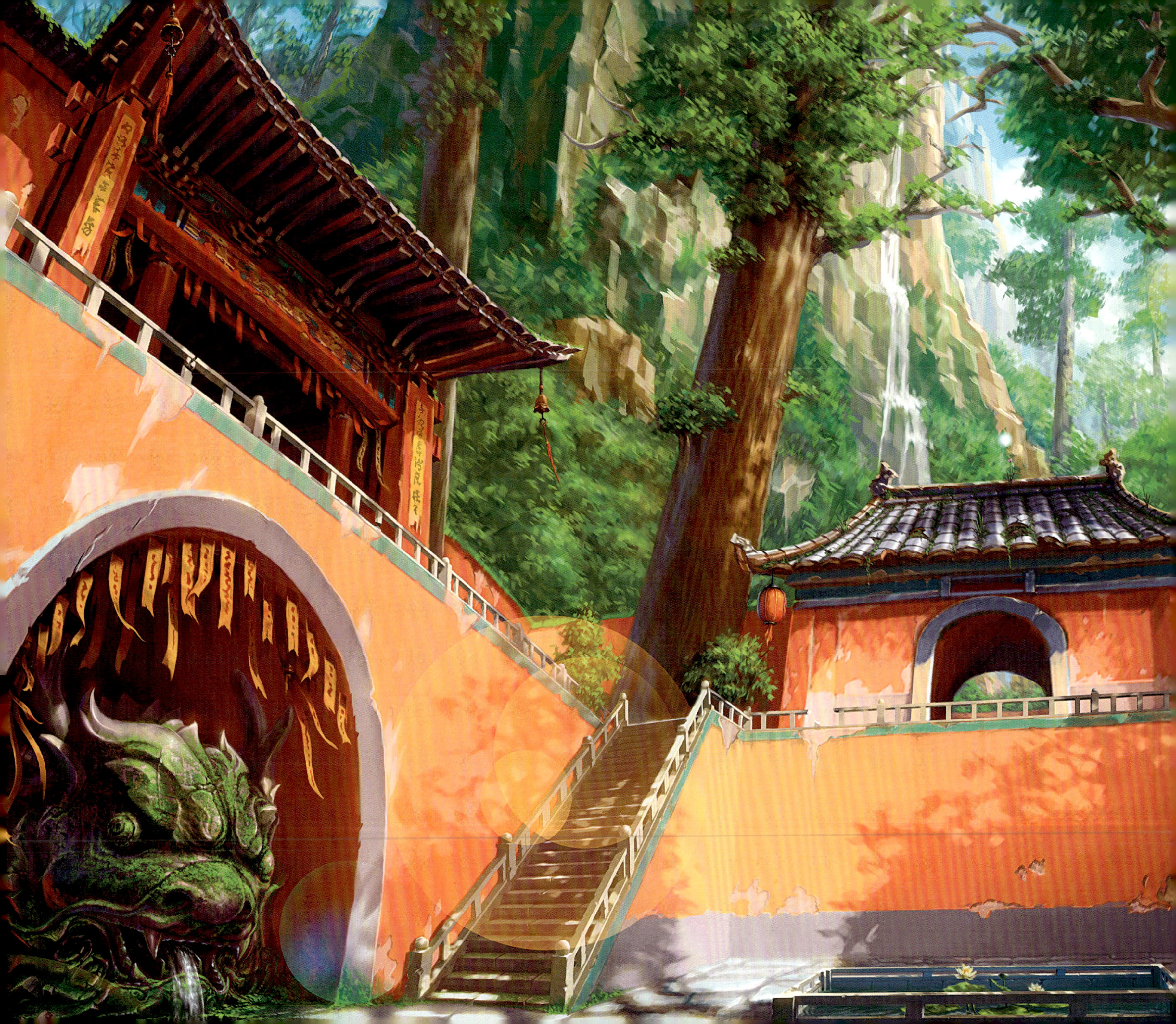

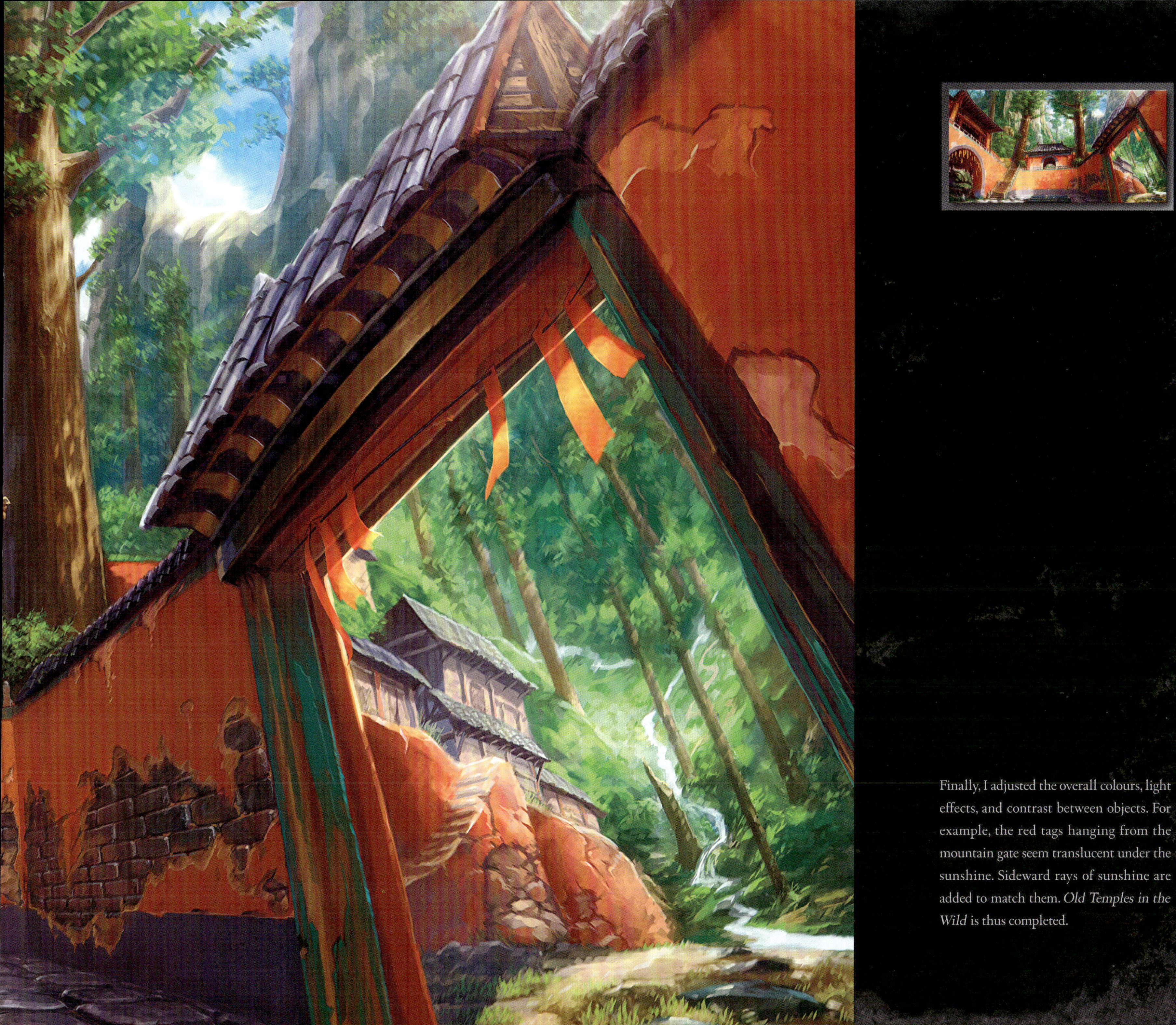

Finally, I adjusted the overall colours, light effects, and contrast between objects. For example, the red tags hanging from the mountain gate seem translucent under the sunshine. Sideward rays of sunshine are added to match them. *Old Temples in the Wild* is thus completed.

# MAIN POINTS

▼ Here is a step-by-step illustration of wall structures and how to paint damage effects to them.

**1** Bricks are often arranged in a pleasingly asymmetrical way. Lines of different depths are used here to show backlighting and the lit areas of brickwork joints, producing a sense of depth. The first illustration shows the effects of a façade with small brickwork joints, while the second captures that of bricks featuring big joints and rough surfaces usually seen on temple walls.

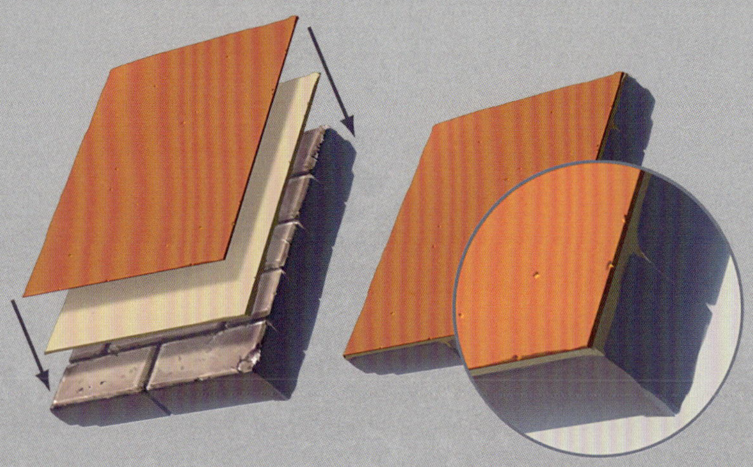

**2** Such brick walls are first covered with mortar (plaster) which is then followed by a layer of paint. The purpose of applying mortar is to fill brick work joints to make the surface of a wall level. A layer of paint is aesthetically pleasing, rainproof, and resistant to types of erosion and weathering.

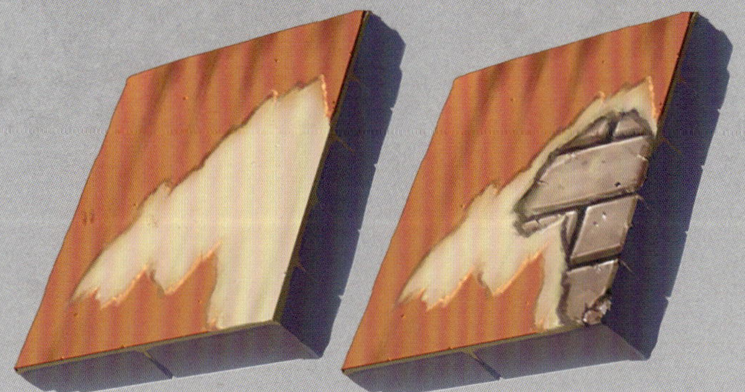

**3** Made of a mixture of cheap loess and sand, mortar applied to brick walls has such a weak adhesive property under the effects of strong external forces over a long period of time, it is likely the outer layer of paint will come off, and even subsequently, the inner layer of mortar to peel as well. Therefore, areas of non-human damage to paint and mortar should appear different.

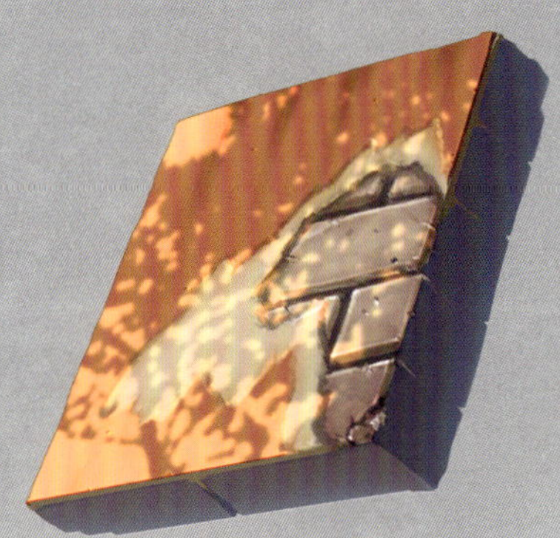

**4** Then, tree shadows are added to the wall, as shown above.

## ▼ The effects of natural cracking and two different effects of external damage.

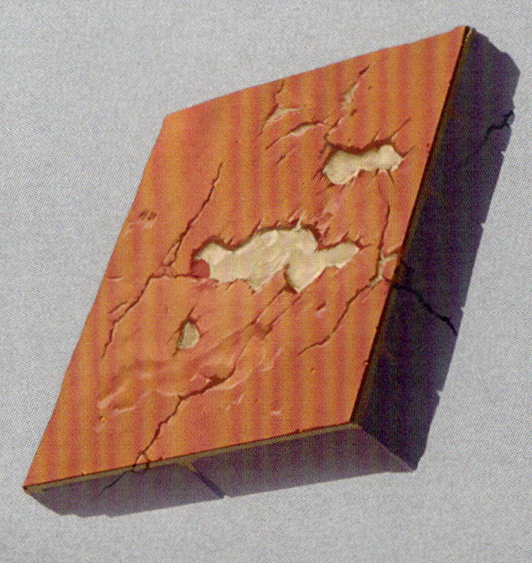

**1**

Cracking and peeling are similar. Due to the action of weathering, paint comes off and cracks, making the surface of the paint uneven.

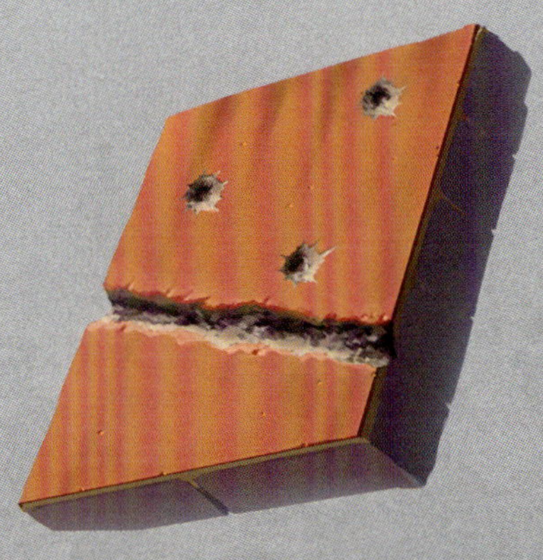

**2**

The above shows the effects of a wall impacted by sharp objects or objects moving at a high speed (e.g. bullets) and cut by blade-shaped objects (e.g. a cast knife).

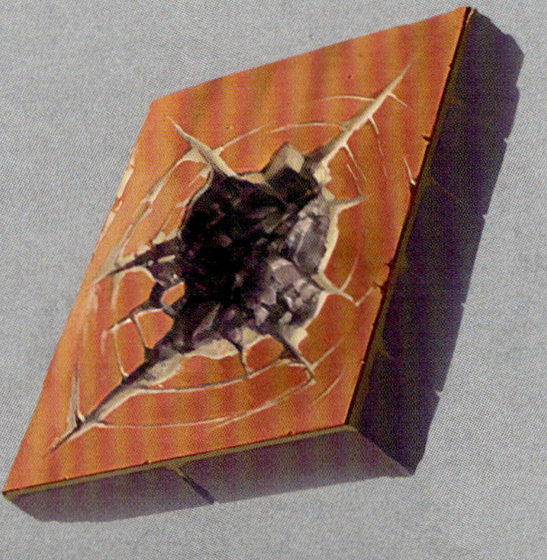

**3**

This captures the impact of an explosion. There is a deep pit in the bricks, the outer circle bulges slightly, and cracks radiate out in different directions.

## ▼ The effects of aging and damage to a painted wooden structure.

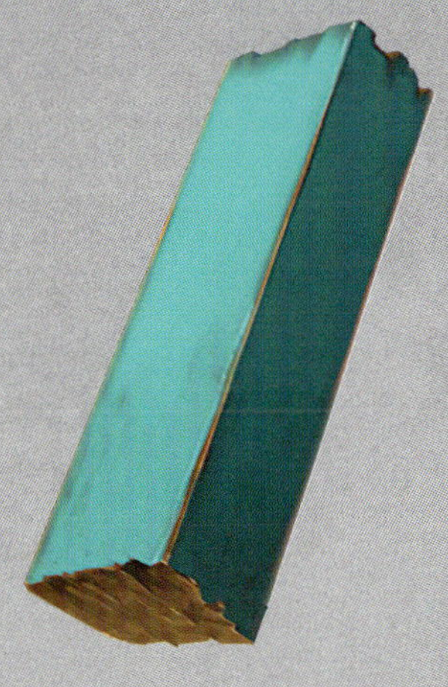

**1**

The effects of aging and damage to a painted wooden structure are different from those to walls. The first difference lies in the properties of paint. Moreover, wooden structures have a delicate texture and don't need any base coats to be applied before the paint. The surface is directly coated with a layer of paint that possesses durable adhesive properties.

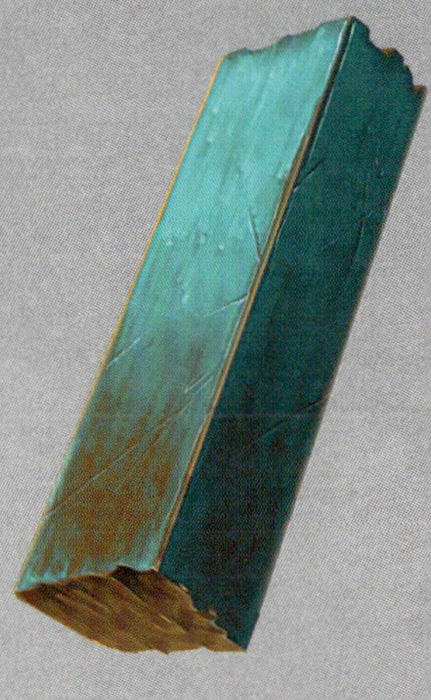

**2**

There are two paths to end up with painted timber that appears old. The first involves scraping some paint off the structure to show the wooden texture beneath, while the second results from paint cracking as the wooden surface cracks. Unlike brick or cement walls, wooden structures age and decay as the surrounding humidity changes and time passes, leading to cracks and damages.

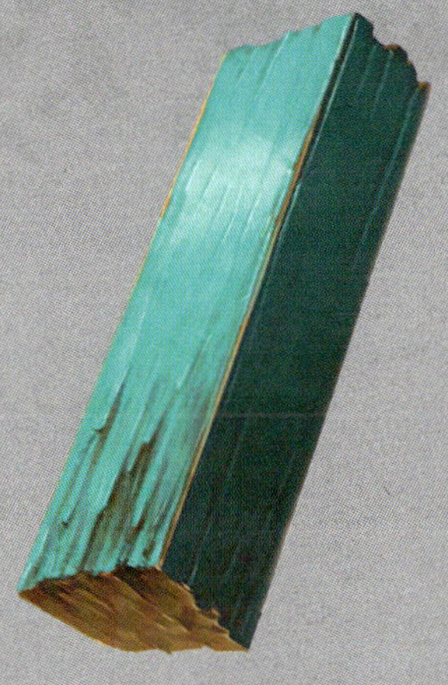

**3**

This section shows that the appearance of coloured paint can differ as much as the materials and structures on which it's applied. In order to capture the most realistic characteristics of the objects chosen for a scene, we need to understand their properties, construction, and how they change under damage.

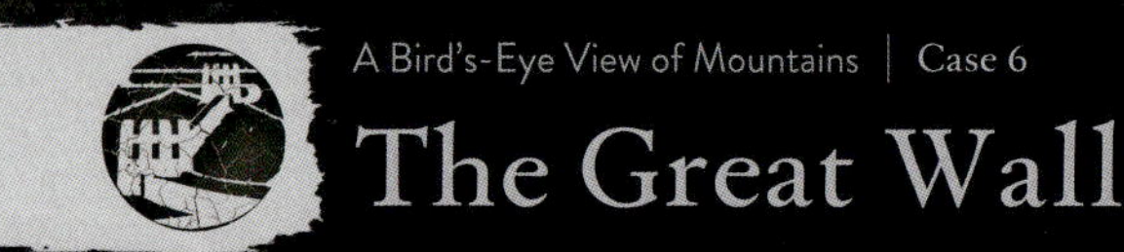



# The Great Wall

The Great Wall, known as one of the Seven Wonders of the World, stretches from the East to the West for tens of thousands of kilometres. Its history dates back to thousands of years ago. Most sections of the Wall are built upon precipitous cliffs. Its great length, long history and architectural ingenuity, together with the significant role it has played in ancient military defence and the aesthetic value it still possesses in modern times, have all earned it an exceptionally important place on the World Heritage list.

The history of the Great Wall can be traced back to the Western Zhou Dynasty (c. 1046-771 BC). It was during the Spring and Autumn and the Warring States periods (771-221 BC) that such beacon towers and walls began to be collectively referred to as the Great Wall and used for military defence by different powers struggling for hegemony.

The full breadth of the Great Wall's magnificence cannot be fathomed in your first step atop it. Due to its extensive coverage, even those sections not far from where you begin your journey will be blocked from view by mountains. Only those who are patient enough to ascend to higher lookouts will experience the surprise of looking down upon superb mountains seemingly dwarfed by the wall. In order to bring out the magnificence of the Great Wall and inject some "spirit" into our portrayal, this section attempts to capture it from a bird's eye view.

This perspective permits a broader view of a subject and is highly suitable for depicting sublime vistas. However, due to specific positioning of a bird's eye view, it's difficult to gather enough materials to accurately depict this perspective through mere document investigation and difficult to achieve other means of observing the original site without "external support" (e.g. the support of a drone). Therefore, the creation of this piece of work necessitates a deeper understanding of the site's geographical formation and shape, coupled with reference to relevant materials.

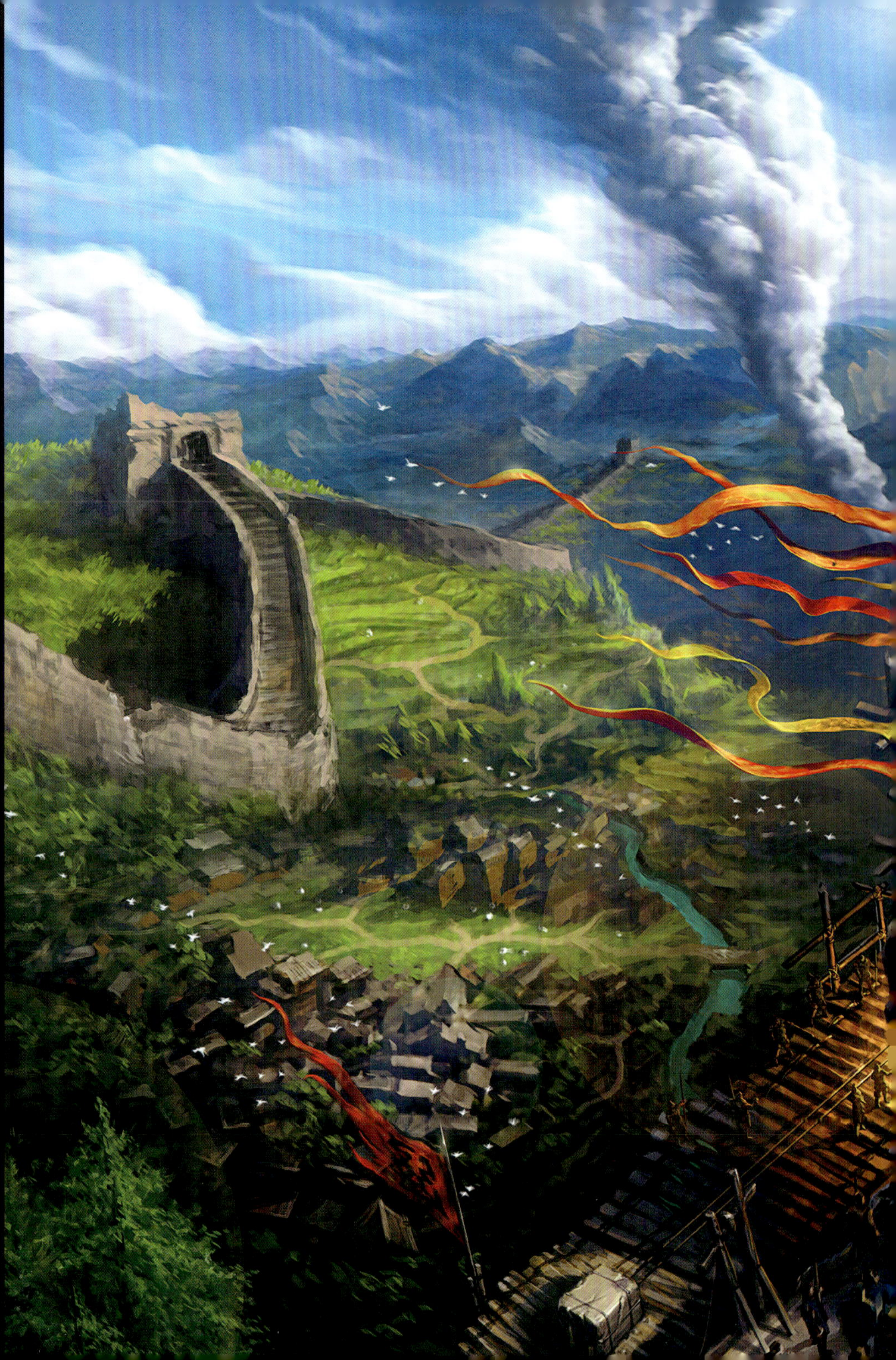

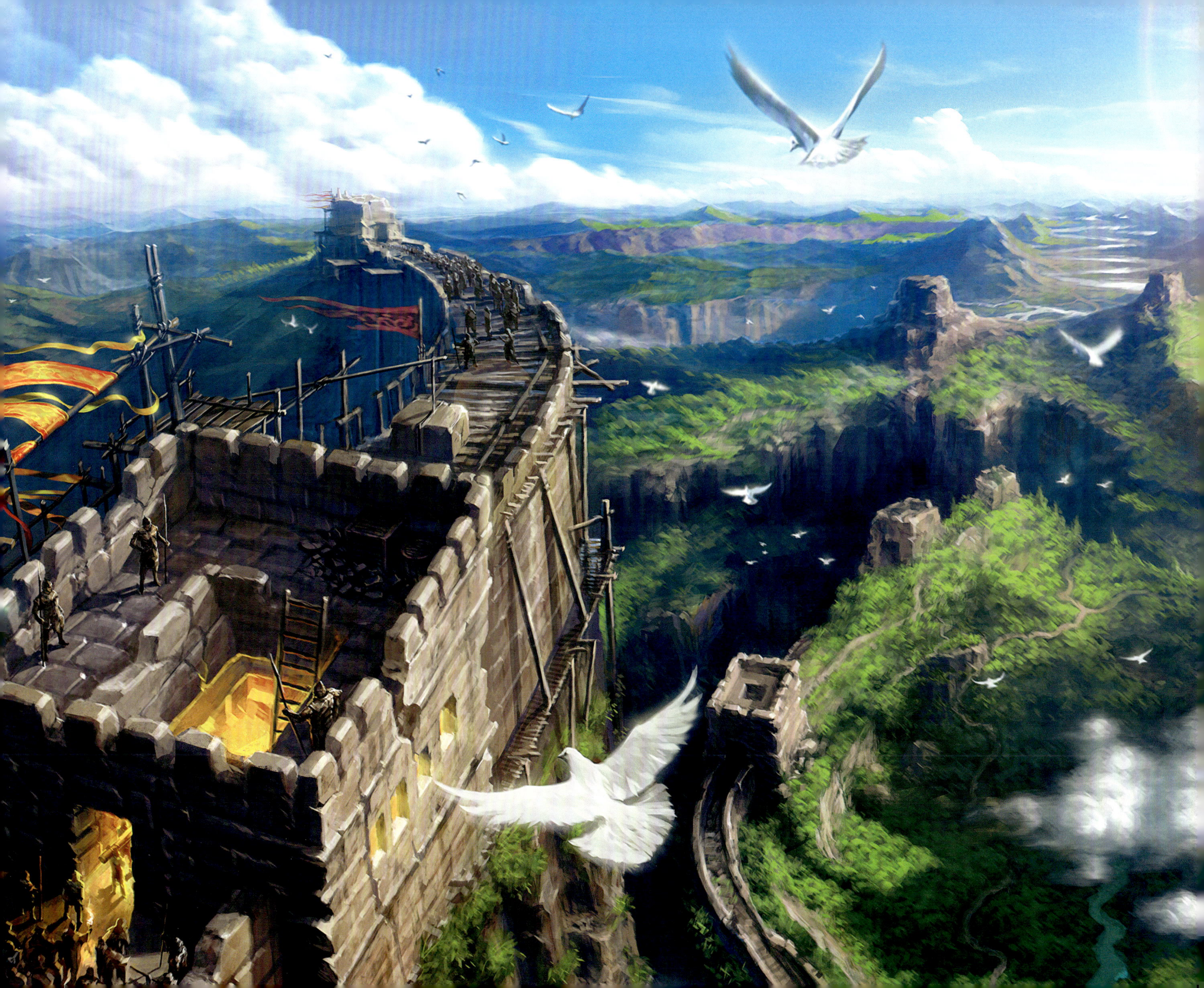

# THOUGHTS ON CREATION

*What is unique about the Great Wall is its great length stretching for tens of thousands of kilometres. This wonder was made possible thanks to people's perseverance.*

*For reasons of heightened military defence, the majority of the Great Wall is built on mountain ranges in a series of zigzags. When ascending the Great Wall, you may feel confused by the zigzags as to the direction the Great Wall stretches. Some sections of the Great Wall with "crenels" on both sides (an architectural form for defence) make it even harder to tell areas beyond the wall from those within.*

*You may also find it difficult to discern the route along which the Great Wall stretches if you take aerial photographs of a limited space. In your design, how could you ensure walls zigzag in a reasonable way? Among the great number of photographs of the Great Wall available, there are only a few relevant to our design. But that does not mean there is nothing to draw upon. Considering that the Great Wall is built on mountainridges, it is advisable to refer to images that show a bird's eye view of a mountain region. After the mountain region is composed, we can draw a wall atop it which has a reasonable zigzag.*

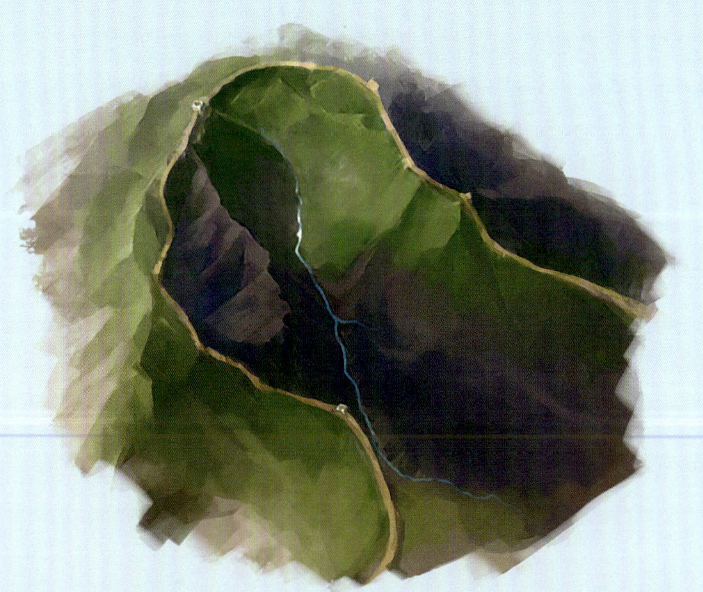

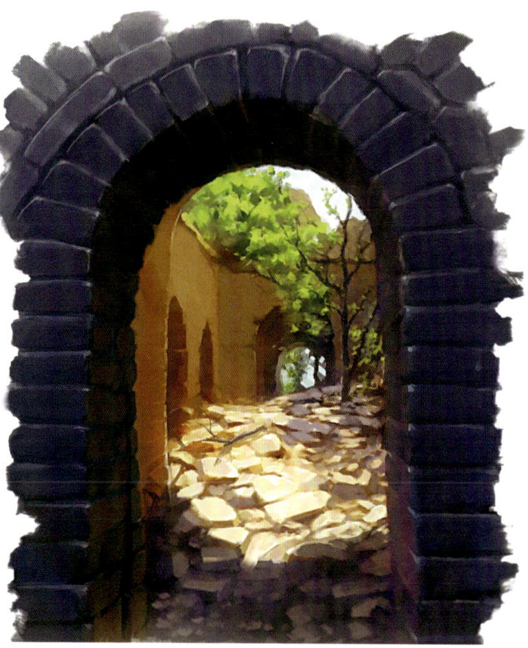

*Much of the extant remains of the Great Wall are dilapidated. In years of peace, the Great Wall, no longer used for military defence, was left exposed to natural erosion. Except for famous passes that have been repaired for the purpose of attracting tourists, most sections of the Great Wall are not as well preserved as those shown in photographs of repaired sections. The Great Wall captured in such photos appears clearer and more orderly, in stark contrast to its surrounding natural landscapes.*

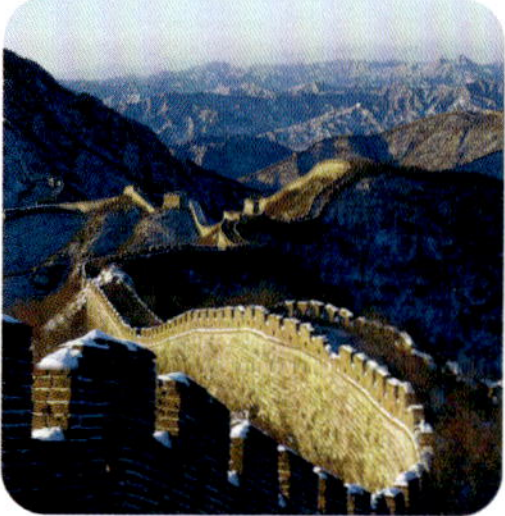

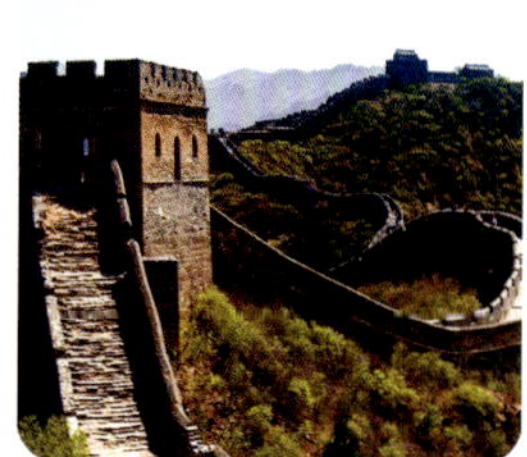

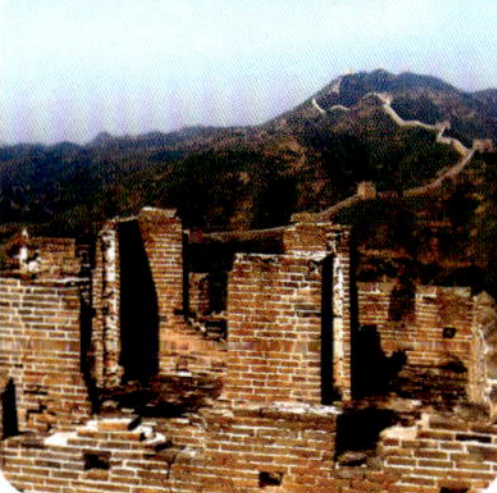

## ▲ GREAT WALL

A diverse array of landscapes surrounds the Great Wall. The combination of buildings with mountains and forests expresses some fantastic harmony between humanity's magnificence and nature's splendour. Different seasons, time, and weather conditions can bring a variety of feelings of an entirely different nature to the scene too.

One winter, I climbed up a wild section of the Great Wall. Atop the wall and looking out at the bare branches of trees, their swaying shadows, and the golden sunshine cast upon broken walls, I was hit by a feeling of inexplicable misery. When I returned after heavy snows several days later, the bleak and desolate landscape appeared as if shrouded in a purely white quilt and felt comforting.

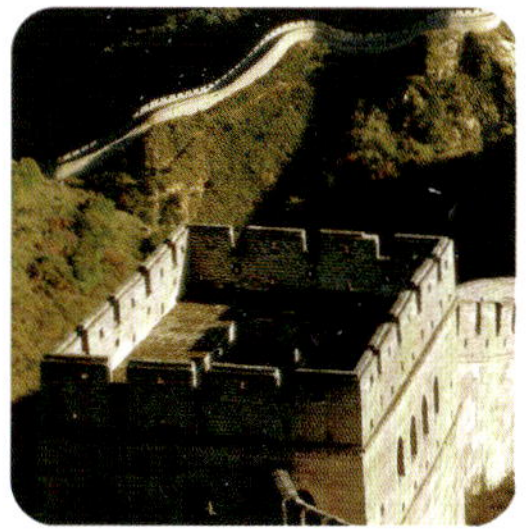

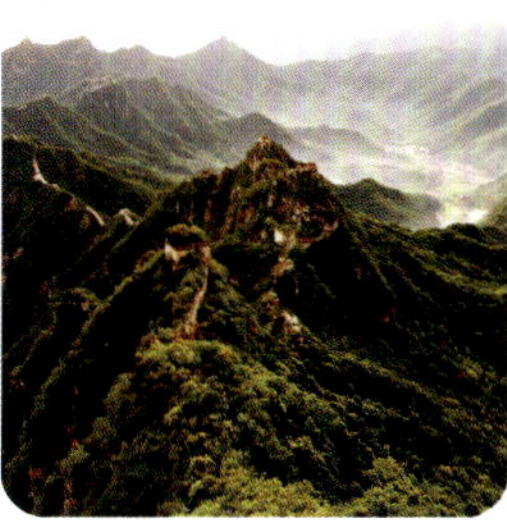

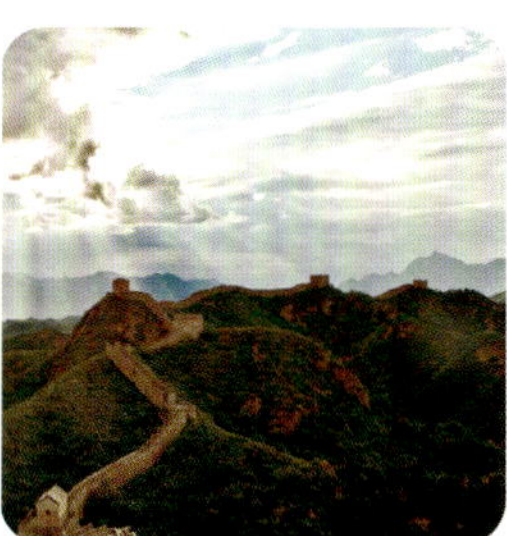

## ◀ WATCHTOWERS

Watchtowers and beacon towers are major structures along the Great Wall. We need to search for materials showing a bird's eye view of such structures as well as photographs showing internal details from different perspectives in order to be able to paint a full picture of these features.

Looking at resources on beautiful mountains and extensive landscapes are useful for finding inspiration to create the desired atmosphere. In cases where photos showing a bird's eye view of the Great Wall are not available, you may find it convenient to refer to pictures of other mountains. It should be noted that we should avoid referring to beautiful pictures of mountains located in Southern China when drawing mountains of Northern China where the Great Wall is located.

We need to figure out the regular ways buildings are constructed on mountains so that we can consider how to draw the Great Wall onto mountains of any form. Before starting this design, it was important to collect all the necessary materials at the initial stage. Adequate preparation ensures that things will work out smoothly in the later stages.

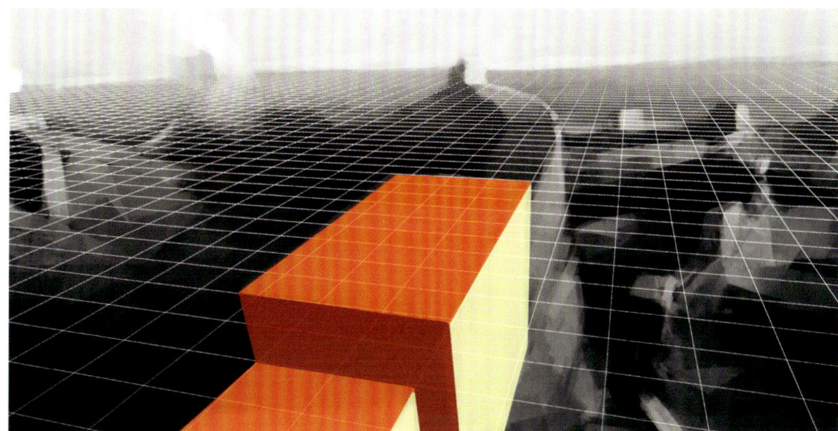

Although I adopted a bird's eye view for this picture, it was still necessary to show the horizon and the sky. A top-down perspective is suitable for scenes of great depth and height but doesn't allow for a scene's broadness without a skyline. A watchtower, the main subject of this design, is put in the centre of the scene to draw people's attention and separate areas beyond the wall from those within. In order to make the scene asymmetrical and appear more flexible, I adopted a side skewed perspective.

Why a bird's eye view suits this design most? The reason lies in the position of the main subject. In a bird's eye view or a top-down perspective of old temples built among forests, much of the temple is blocked by tall trees. In contrast, a bird's eye view composition of the Great Wall built upon mountain ridges high above trees actually increases your scope of vision and frame.

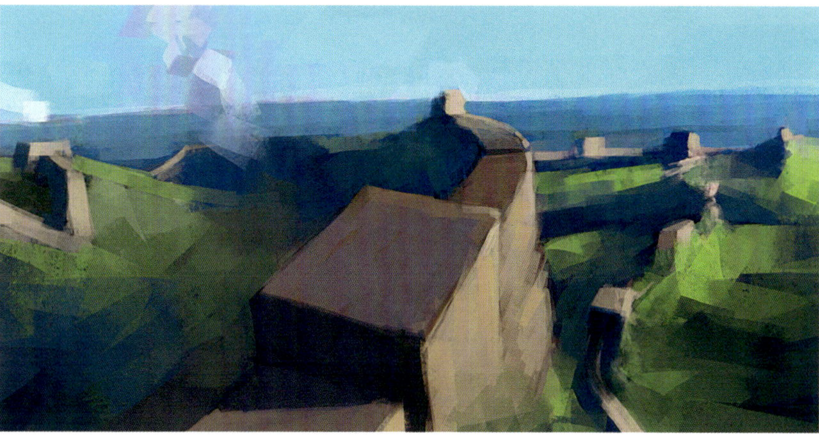

Next, I gave shape to the mountains and the sections of the Great Wall winding around them. Green is highlighted to give a sense of the verdant luxuriance commonly seen in the height of summer. This is matched with a blue sky. The design is intended to show a section of the Great Wall under construction during a period of peace, the objective being to neuter any notion of the cruelty of war and the pains taken by the wall's builders.

A drawing is an epitome of reality. A Great Wall marred by fire and blood in times of wars will create stronger effect than that in times of peace. Destroying things is always far easier than creating them. Remember, though, it is the painter who has the right to decide the theme of a painting and I myself prefer a scene of peace.

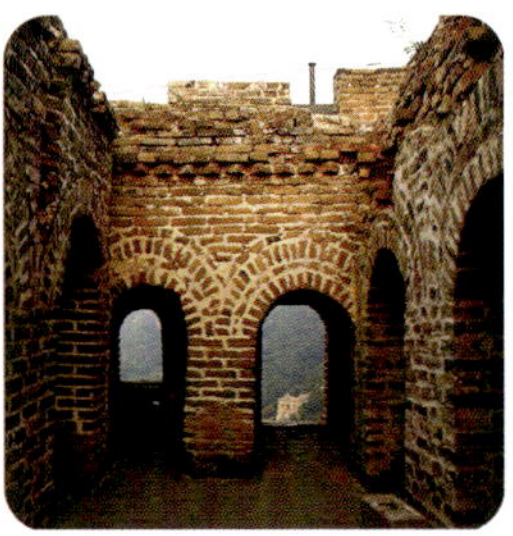

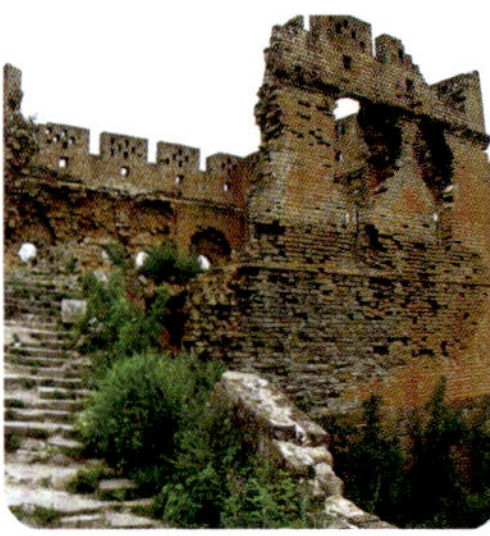

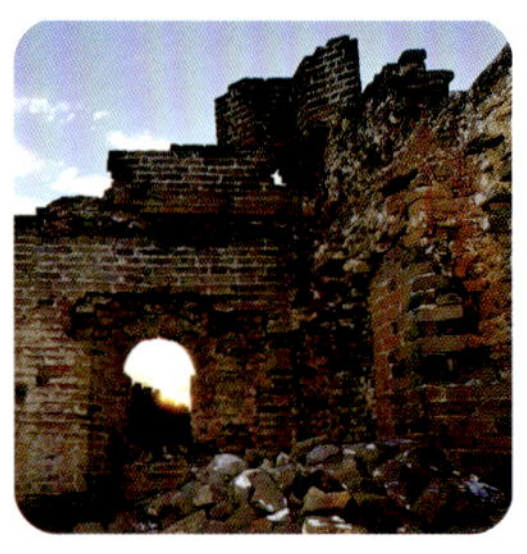

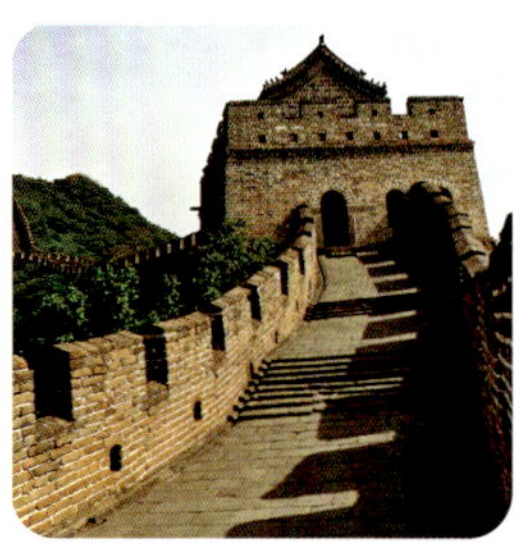

## ◀ A WATCHTOWER

A watchtower is a tower on a wall used for defence against enemies, where soldiers watch out for encroachers and give commands. It also serves as a place where armies defending a city can rest and store their equipments. With these functions in mind, I attempted to reconstruct the appearance of the tower before it was ruined. Refering to materials showing watchtowers from different perspectives was also helpful.

As I refined the various architectural structures, the Great Wall began to take shape. Scaffolds are set up around the watchtower under construction. This treatment highlights the theme of the design and enriches the foreground with more elements.

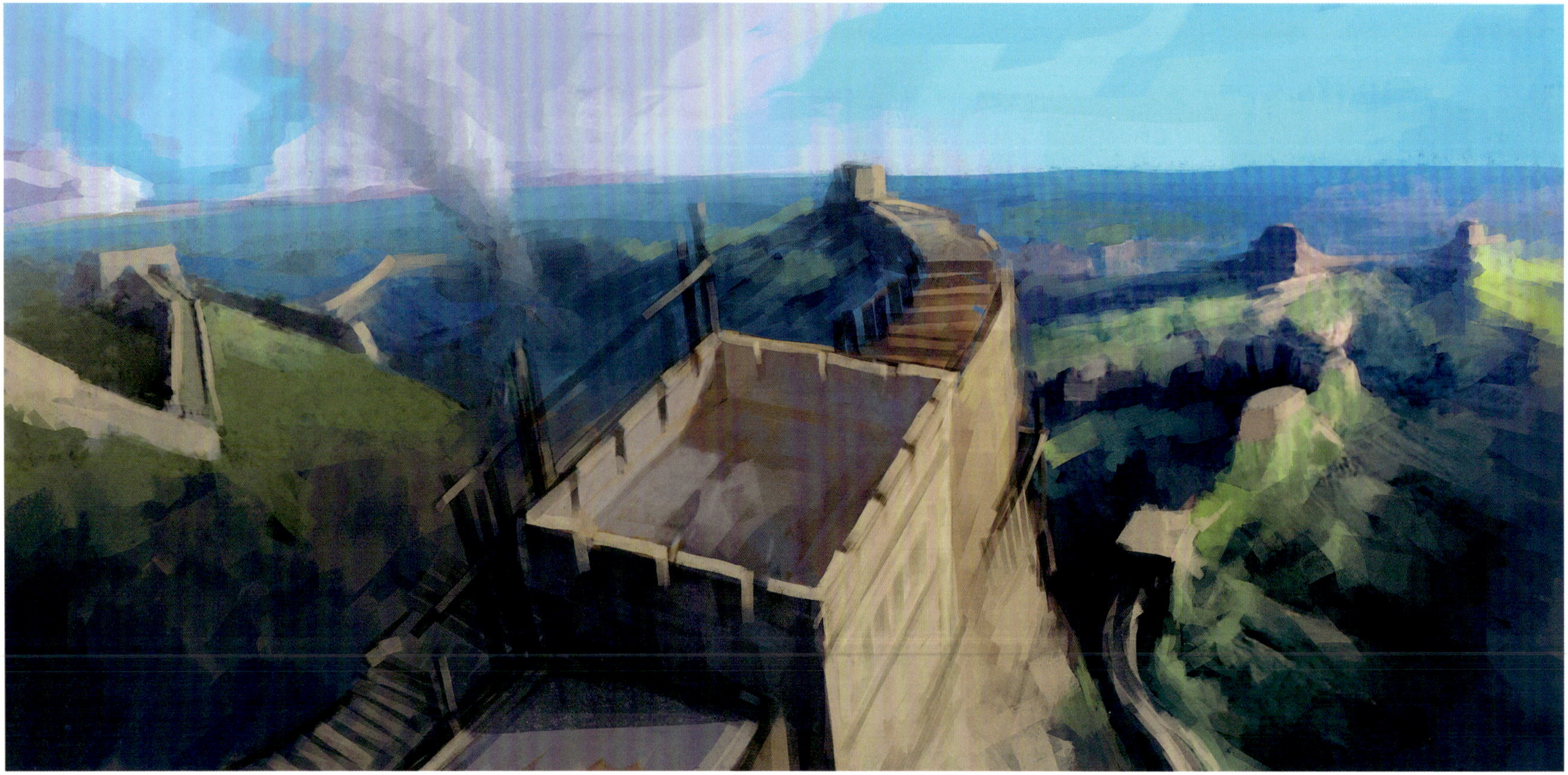

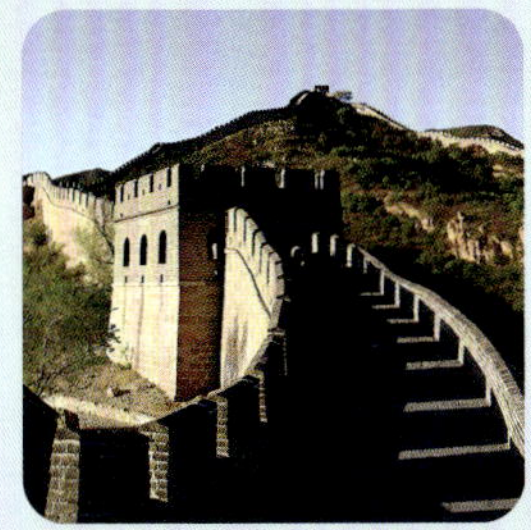

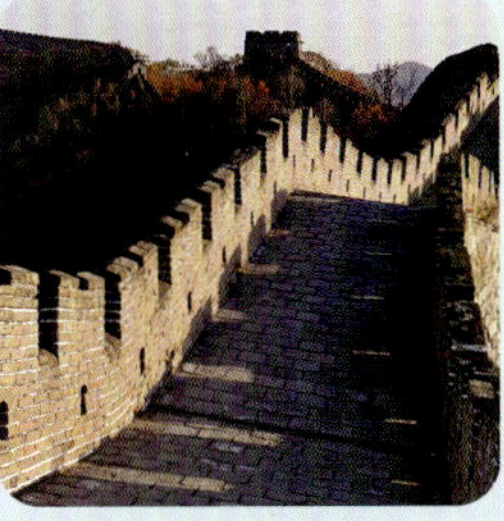

## ▲ A STRUCTURAL FEATURE

The undulating Great Wall is crenelated on both sides — a structural feature that helps soldiers watch out for enemies and remain in cover while shooting out at them. Most sections of the Great Wall are crenelated on a single side facing areas beyond the wall in need of defence. There are some special passes built with crenels on both the sides.

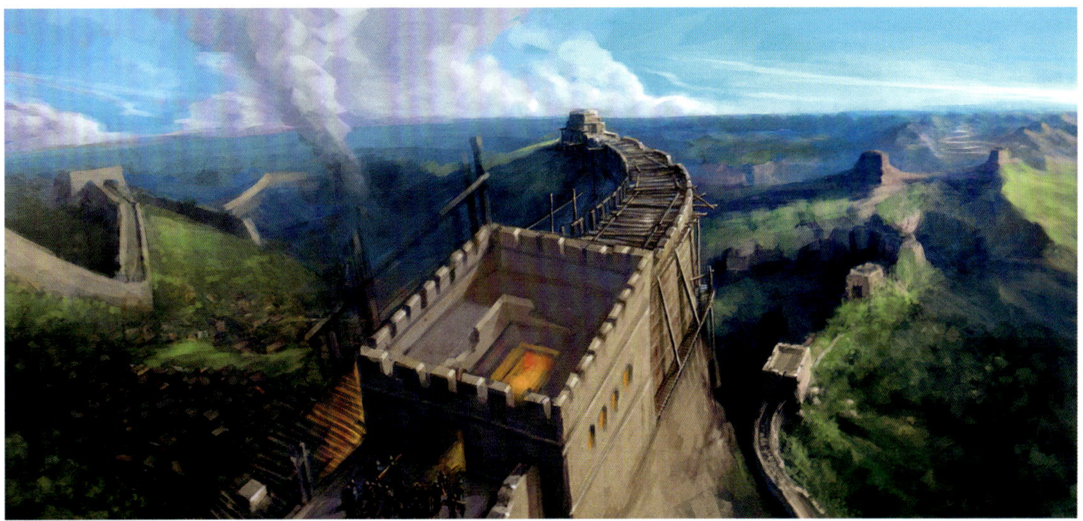

I then refined the details of the crenels and clarified the watchtower in the distance. On the left side, a village was added to highlight the height of the watchtower on the right. Moreover, the village on the left indicates the function of the Great Wall as a means of protecting and shows which side is under protection and which is without.

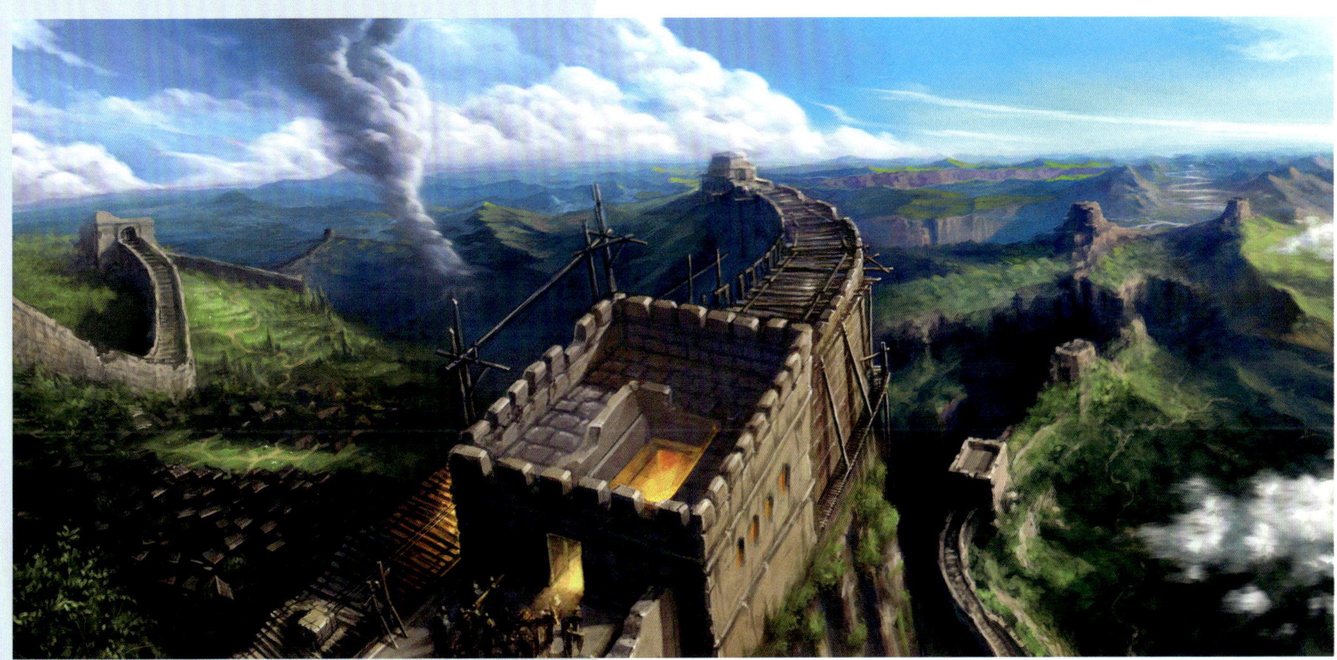

Clouds and smoke are added to give the scene a sense of depth and gradation. Then, watchtowers in the mid-ground and foreground were drawn in at specific intervals chosen so as the distance between them increases the frame's sense of length and depth.

The texture of the walls was refined and the watchtower structures were improved. Lighting coming from the watchtower interior indicates that builders are busy with their construction work.

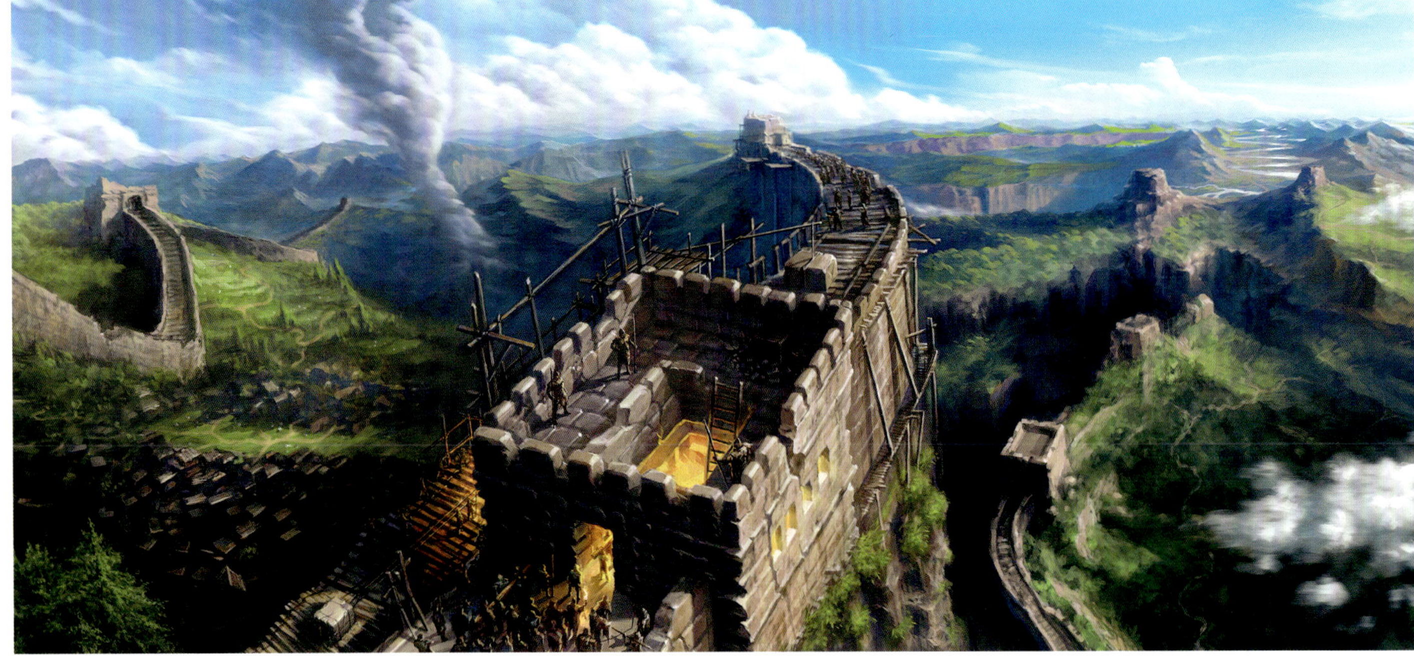

The process of depicting a believable village at the foot of the Great Wall involved improving the stereoscopic effects of the houses, adding a path between houses, a river stretching through the village to ensure the population has water access, and incorporating other elements which indicate human life, such as terraces and short trees.

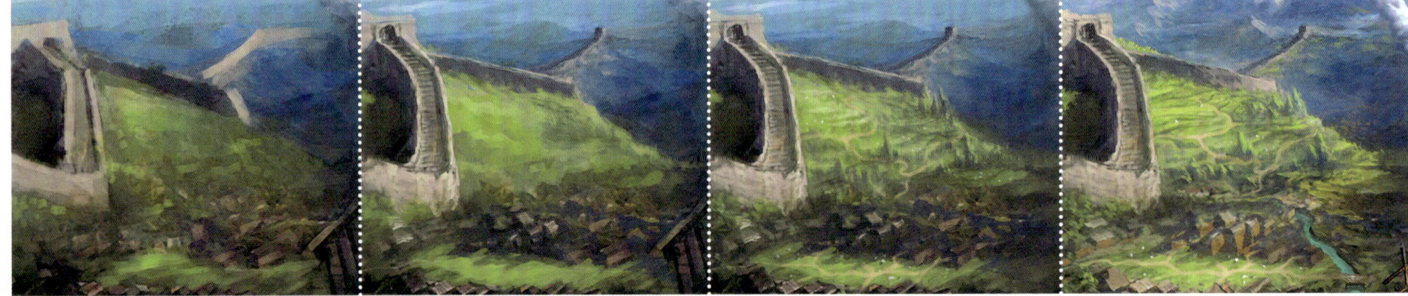

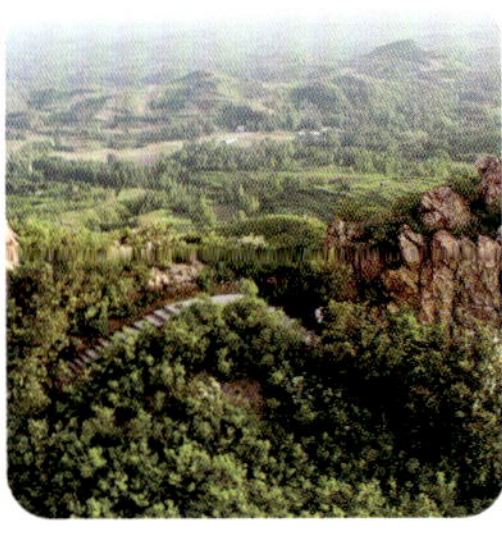

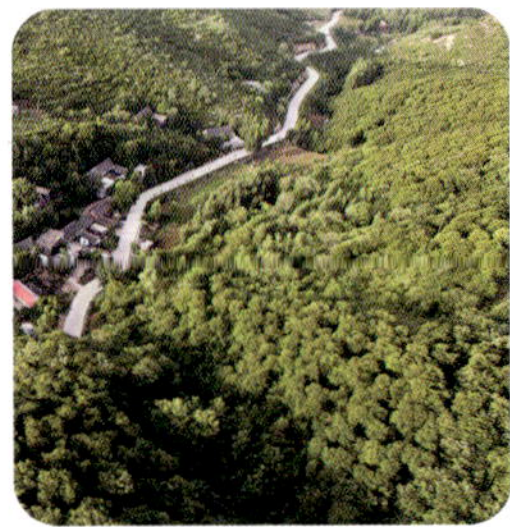

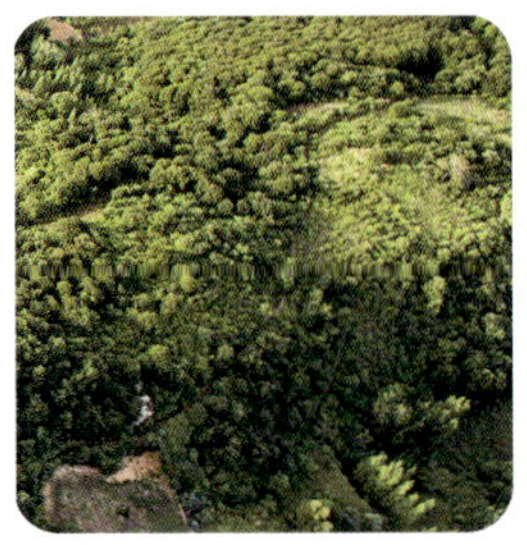

## ◄ TREES

This is a bird's eye view of trees as captured by aerial photos of mountains and forests. The trees look as small as "granules" because the photos were taken at a great height.

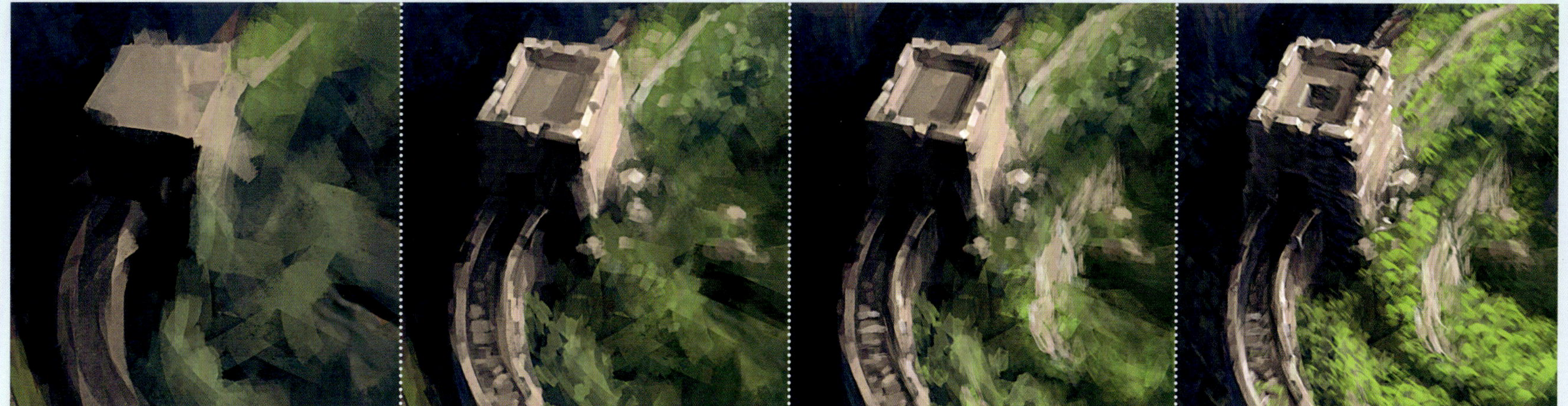

The area beyond the Great Wall is made more bleak and desolate. There is nothing in the area but plants and stones, forming a stark contrast to the village. Plants covering the area are painted to look like green granules irregularly spreading across the undulating mountains.

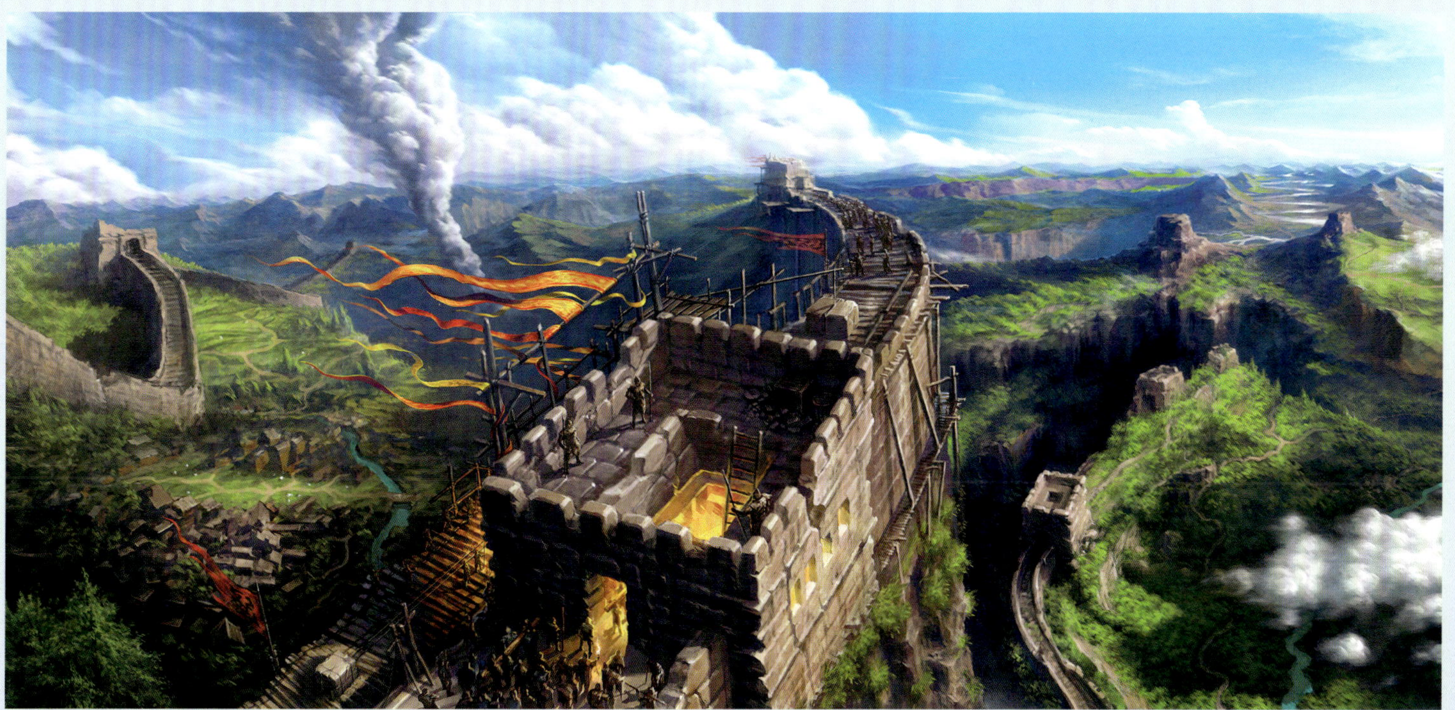

Final refinements were then completed. I added flags flying in the same direction as the clouds and smoke plumes are moving. Elements showing traces of movement fill the scene with vigour.

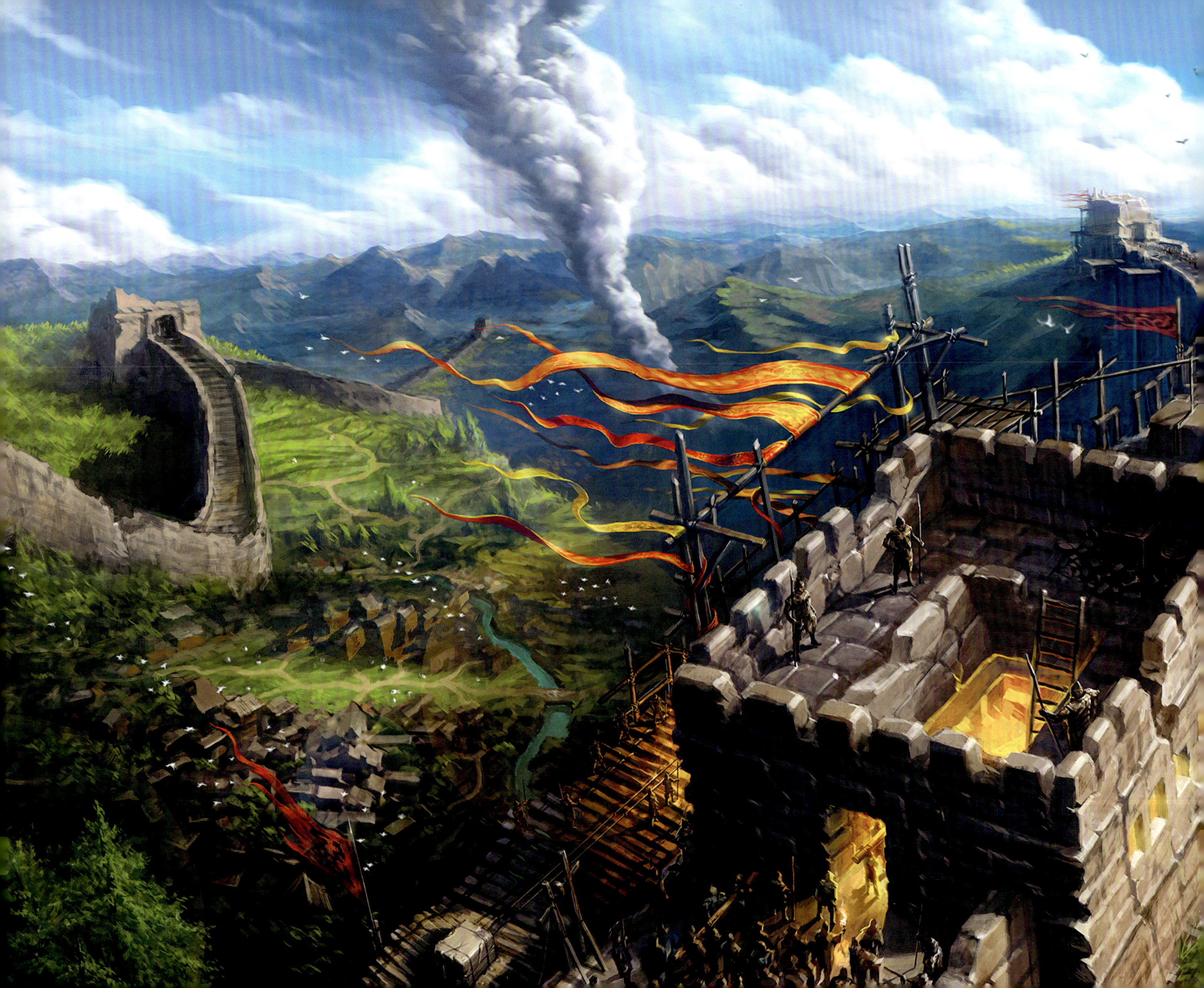

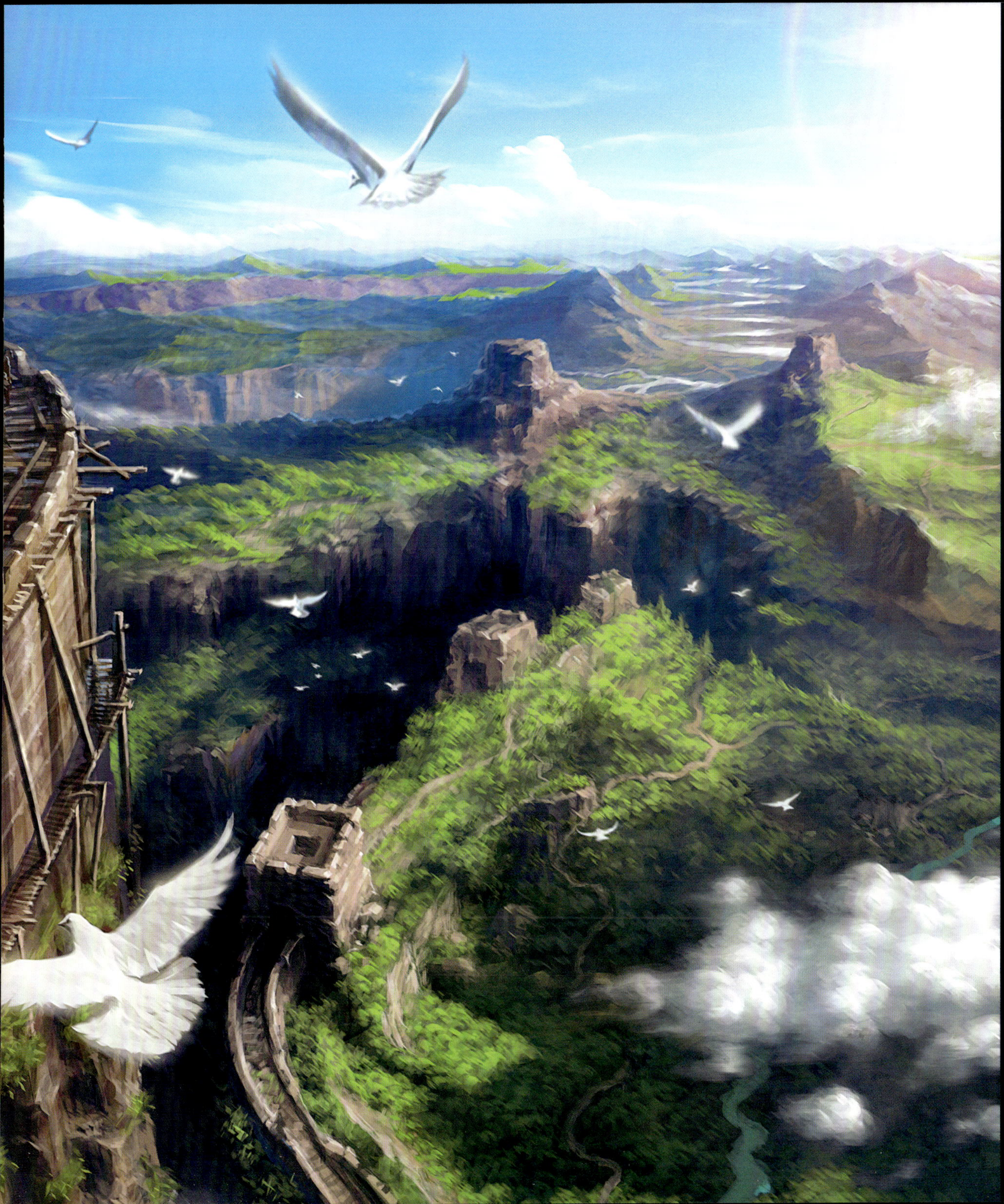

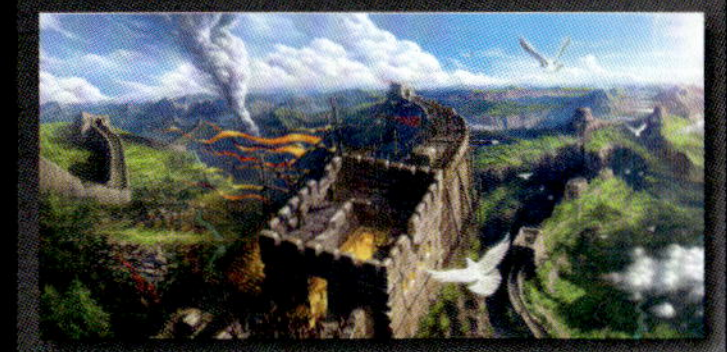

Lastly, a flock of doves are painted flying across the sky from where the halo of the sun radiates out. These final touches further strengthen the sense of layering and vitality and symbolise hope for peace. It is the very existence of the Great Wall — a structure used for military defence — that has brought people everlasting peace.

Dubai lies in the middle of a flat stretch of desert on the southeast coast of the Persian Gulf in the central Arabian Peninsula. Since its early development is heavily reliant on oil revenue, it has grown into a centre of tourism, real estate, trade and finance in the Middle East, as well as a major transport hub, famously known as "the Pearl of the Gulf" and "the City of Trade". I see Dubai as the "City of Miracles". Now not entirely depend on oil for economic growth, it has become a super metropolis of unparalleled grandeur. The city's pioneering efforts and persistent ability to make valuable progress continue to produce miracle after miracle.

Dubai is home to an array of the world's most stunning attractions, including the world's tallest man-made structure, the "Burj Khalifa", with a roof height of 828 metres, the world's first 7-star hotel, the "Burj Al Arab" (also known as the "Dubai Sailshaped Hotel"), the world's largest artificial island, the "Palm Jumeirah", and one of the world's most beautiful gardens, the "Dubai Miracle Garden". These are miracles created by the Dubai people in the spirit of innovation and with the determination "to be No.1".

For fantasy artists, there is much to be derived from a trip to Dubai. Creating fantasy art is a process of giving expression to miracles. "Miracles" are "unprecedented" and "nearly impossible to realise". For a concept to come into being out of nothing, it must first be visually imagined and shaped before, perhaps, eventually taking form and being recognised as a "miracle". Similarly, phenomena that defy easy expression are sometimes called "fantasies". Therefore, the design of "fantasies" and the birth of "miracles" go hand in hand. As a city that has made numerous "fantasies" into "miracles", Dubai is as enlightening to us artists as a textbook.

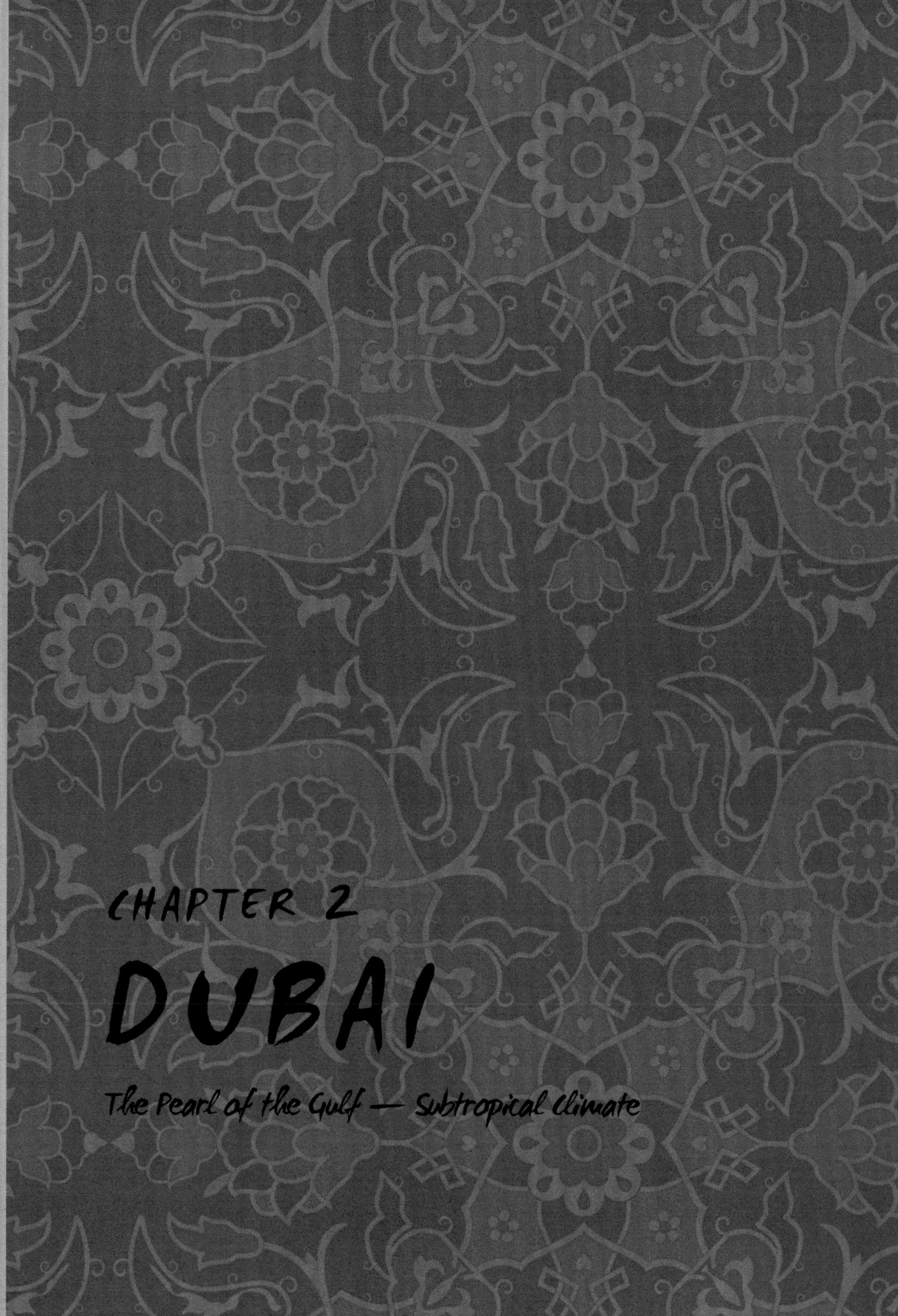

CHAPTER 2

# DUBAI

The Pearl of the Gulf — Subtropical Climate

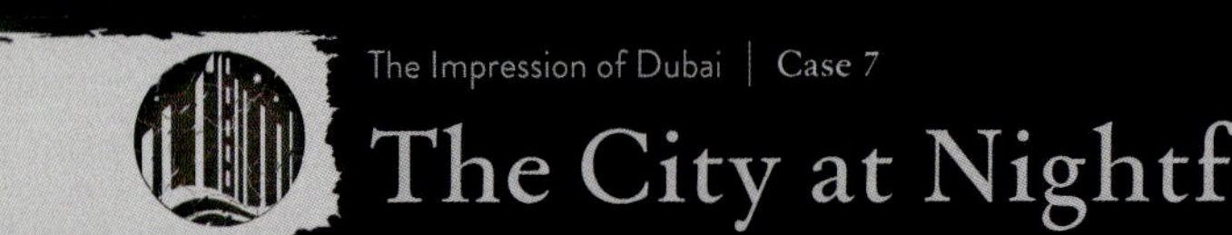



# The City at Nightfall

As with earlier designs, this first design about Dubai also begins with street vistas, the best indicators of the appearance of a city. For *The Alleys and Streets of the Past*, memories of my early life in *hutongs* (the lanes in the old towns of Beijing) were drawn upon to represent the greatest impressions of familiarity that Beijing had left on me. Standing on the streets of Dubai, I observed and pondered the environment without such long-rooted conceptions as those I held about my hometowm Beijing. My understanding of the city came directly from what I saw and what I heard. It was based on my very first feelings about Dubai as a by-stander that this "fantasy" was weaved.

The Sheikh Zayed Road is a highway stretching across Dubai, similar to Beijing's Chang'an Avenue. Together with the light railway nearby, it not only serves to relieve urban traffic congestion but also increases the efficiency and speed of road traffic. It is lined with an array of landmarks such as financial and trade centres, famous hotels, the Burj Khalifa, and the Dubai Mall, a line of sight-seeing across the city of Dubai. Driving on the road, you can see a dense complex of skyscrapers from your window and tens of thousands of lights packed far denser than the stars in the sky shining out from the many high-rises. Around this complex of buildings located along Sheikh Zayed Road, however, the feeling is entirely different from other cities. Covering 12 lanes with two-way traffic, the road's great width weakens the sense of being blocked in by large structures, thus distinguishing Dubai from its counterparts.

Representing the apex of a region's advancement, a city's architecture demonstrates its unique features shaped by the local culture, political orientation, religious belief, geographical position, climate and traffic planning. These features are unique marks of a city. *The City at Nightfall* uses this road of remarkable distinction, the Sheikh Zayed Road, to express the first impression that the Dubai metropolis left in my heart.

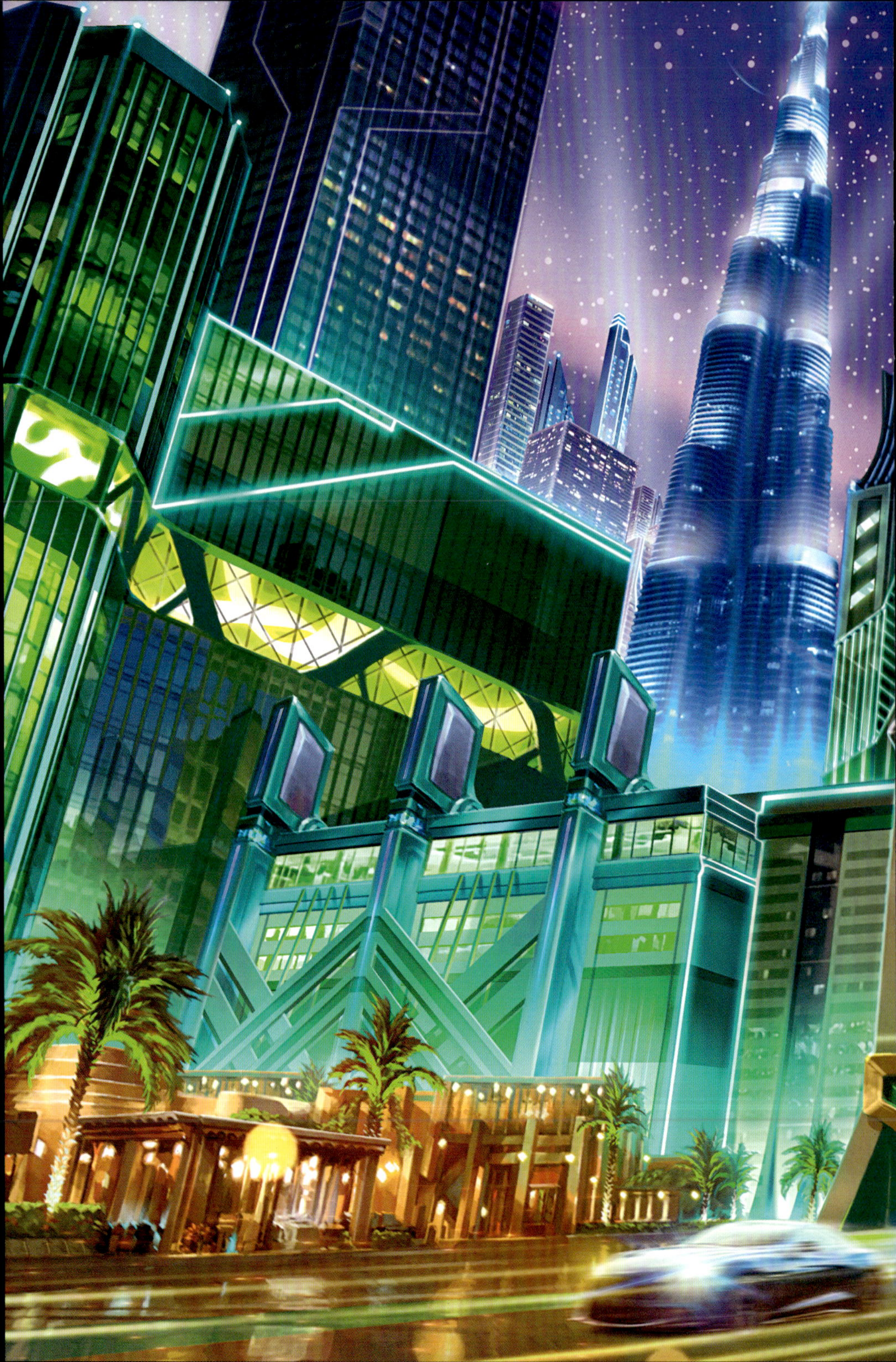

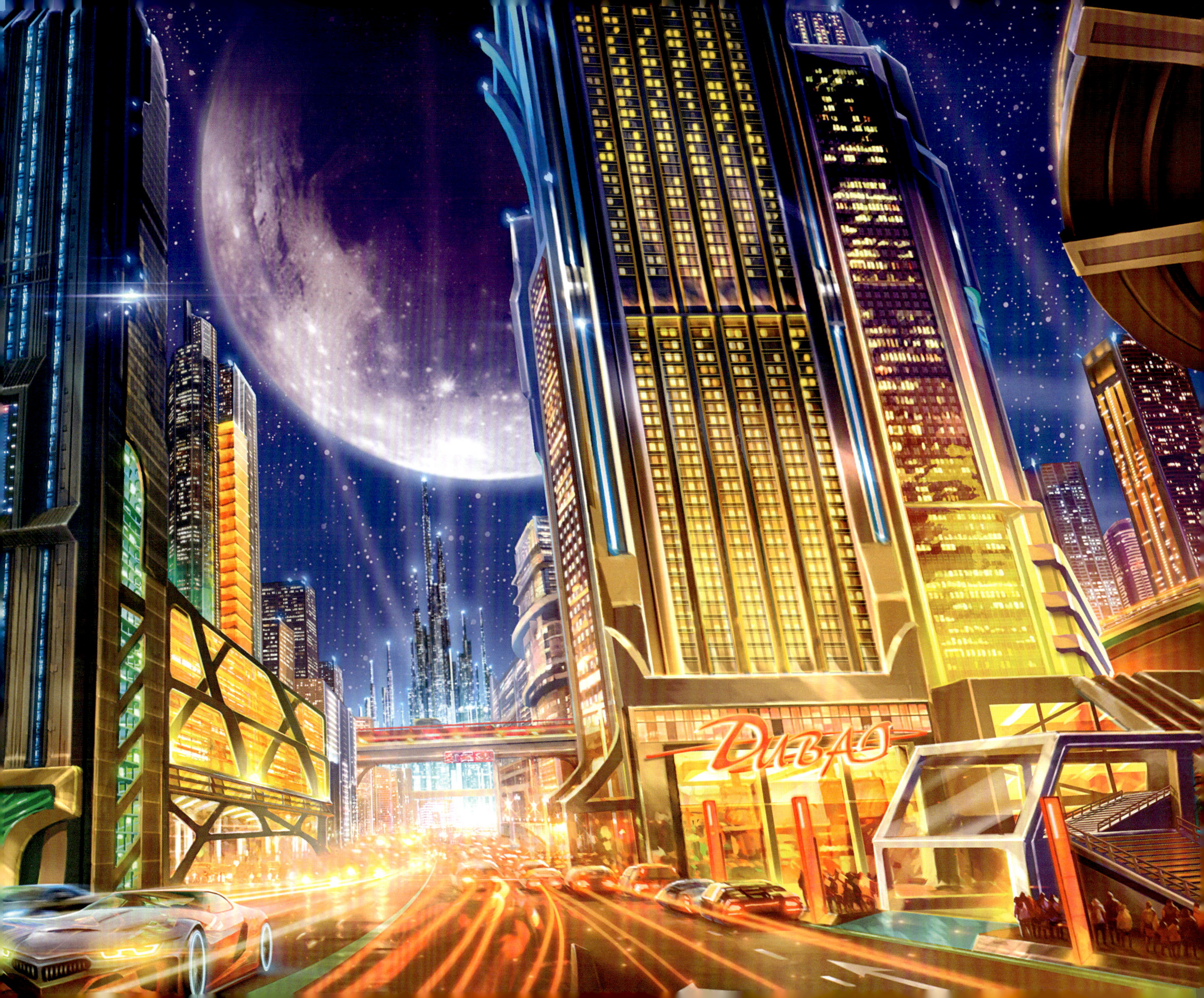
DUBAO

# THOUGHTS ON CREATION

*It was nightfall when I arrived in Dubai. As the plane was flying across clouds, and the orange rays of the setting sun came into the cabin, I looked down upon the city bright against the night's darkness. At the time, I was not much in the mood to appreciate the beautiful scene below. Jetlag and fatigue had me in their grip. However, as I walked out of the cabin door, I was suddenly sobered by a wave of heat. A long-time inhabitant of a northern city in China, I was not accustomed to an outdoor temperature above 40 degrees Celsius. Thankfully, I immediately realised how scientific the planning of the city is. Adequate facilities are available to relieve discomfort brought about by heat and the inconveniences it can cause to people's daily life and travel.*

*I took the opportunity to appreciate the urban view of Dubai as I left the airport taking a bus along the road. Palm trees and road signs of various lighting effects looked like musical notes giving rhythm to this subtropical coastal city. Modern and extraordinarily distinctive high-rises of various types form a pleasant contrast to traditionally-shaped mosques, big and small. Along the road there are closed bus shelters in which air-conditioners and other facilities provide passers-by with shelter from hot weather. The elements combine to shape the landscape of Dubai, a metropolis that integrates natural, modern, religious and cultural elements.*

*Although Dubai's economy is not dominated by oil, the motor vehicle culture has developed rapidly in this young city thanks to the abundance of oil and convenience of car trade at harbours. The temperature at night feels more comfortable than that during the day and so when evening falls, residents go out in their cars, filling the city with roars of motors and horns. Flashing car lights and reflective car bodies add greater lustre to the night view of the city.*

*These were my first impressions of Dubai as a traveller. Through the strength of my imagination, I magnify each of the impressions to create this work of fantasy art, The City at Nightfall.*

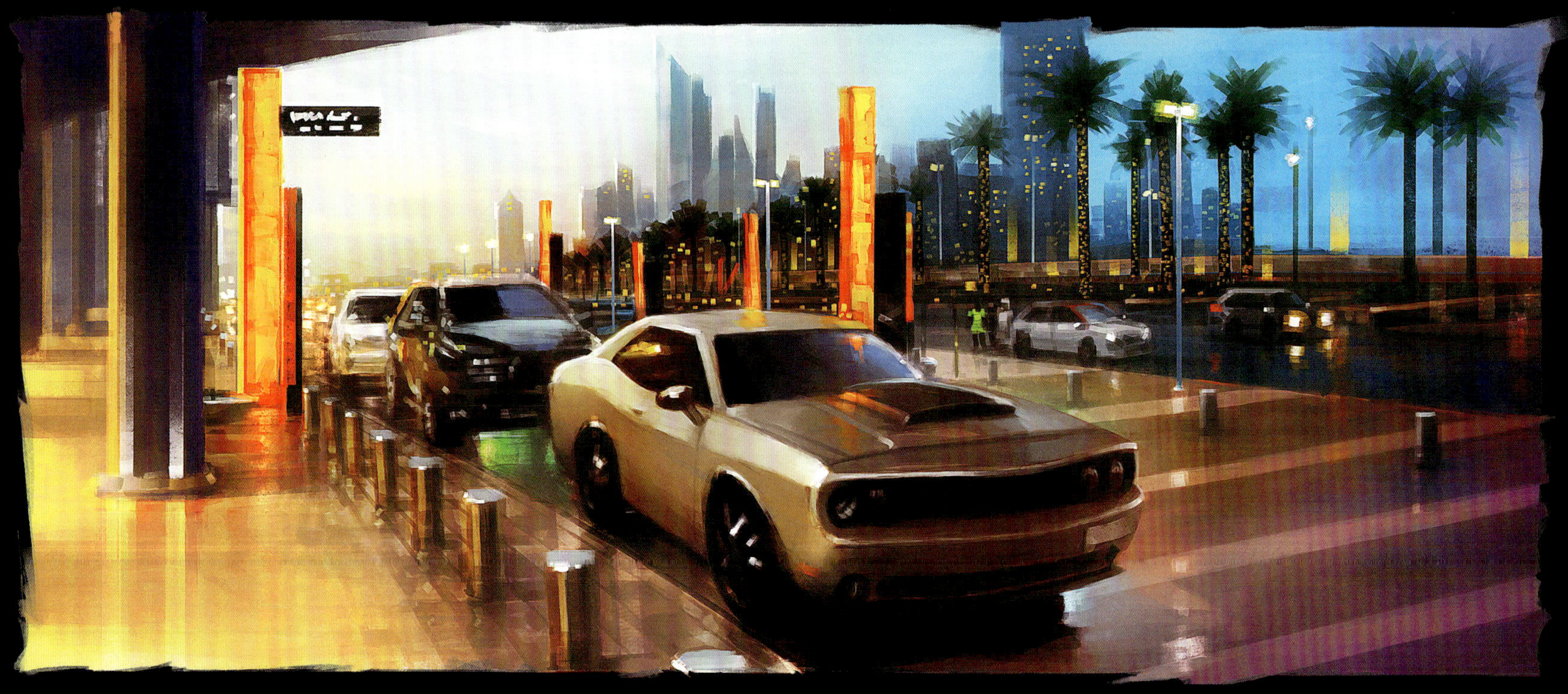

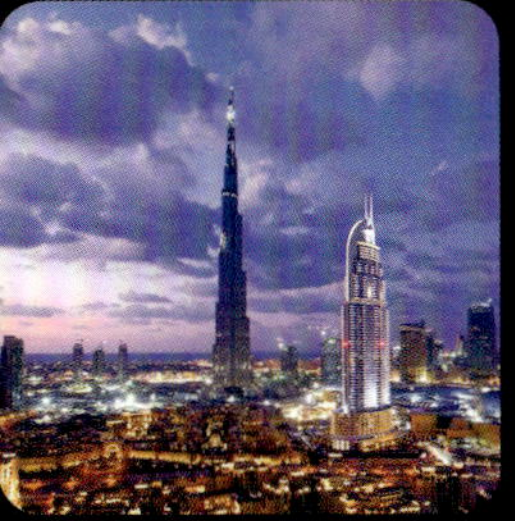

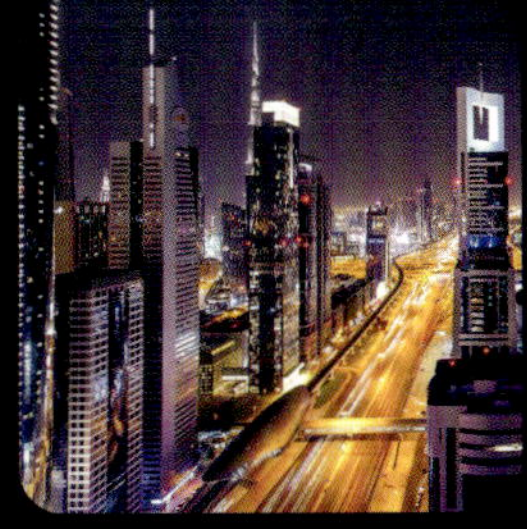

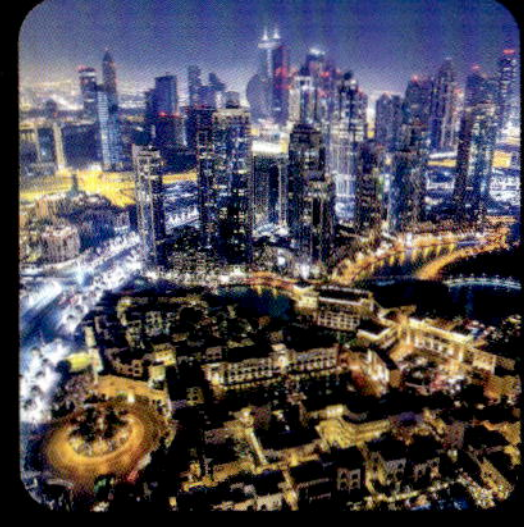

## ▲ NEWNESS

The young city has another prominent feature — its "newness". There are no dilapidated or old buildings within Dubai's downtown, the area captured in this design that the Sheikh Zayed Road intersects. As the symbols of Dubai, the Burj Khalifa and other skyscrapers lining the Sheikh Zayed Road, serve as the major players in city scene. They come nightfall while the traditional style low-rises harmonise with the palm trees to evoke the region's classical culture. These are "main elements" of *The City at Nightfall*.

The above elements are best depicted from the familiar perspective of an onlooker on the street. Originally, the centre of the road seemed to be the best viewpoint, but for safety reason, the perspective was modified with reference to night views of other metropolis.

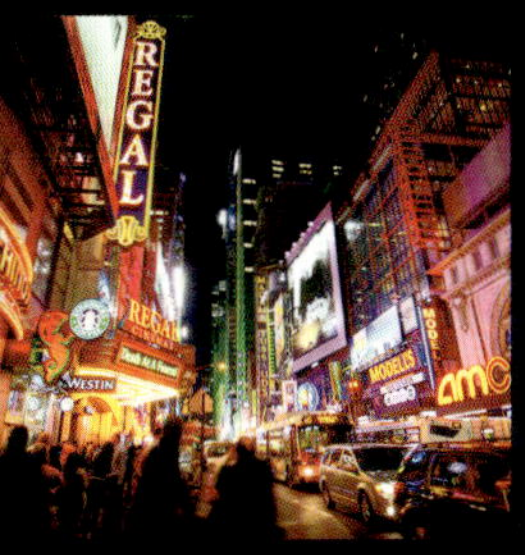


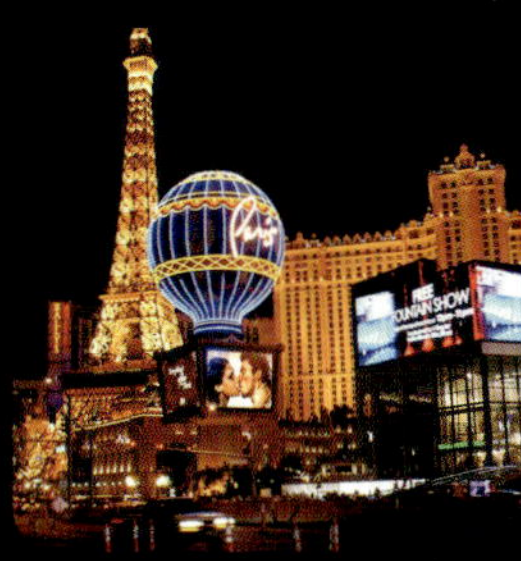

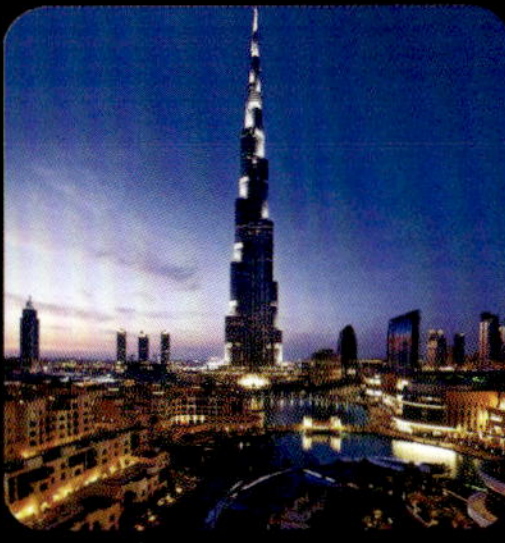

## ▲ SLEEPLESS CITY

When referring to similar night views, it's important to consider whether their features align with the final image that we want to depict.

Take other modern city streets as examples; including the Times Square and the Las Vegas strip. They aren't helpful templates for our design. In Dubai's new downtown, you will find few neon shop signs, even on the busiest streets. Due to differences in cultural habits or urban planning, these elements are missing in the "sleepless city". So, it's vital that we check not only the obvious, surface details of any reference materials for applicability but their background, hidden areas too.

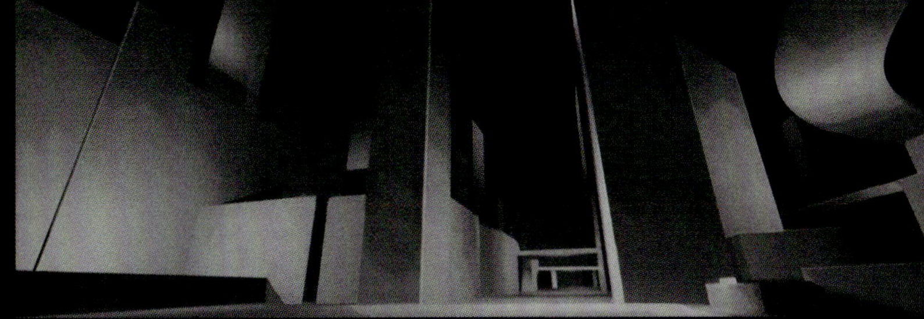

Compared with our previous street designs, this current design adopts a wider angle shot and an adjusted upward view so as to involve a greater number of objects and the taller buildings.

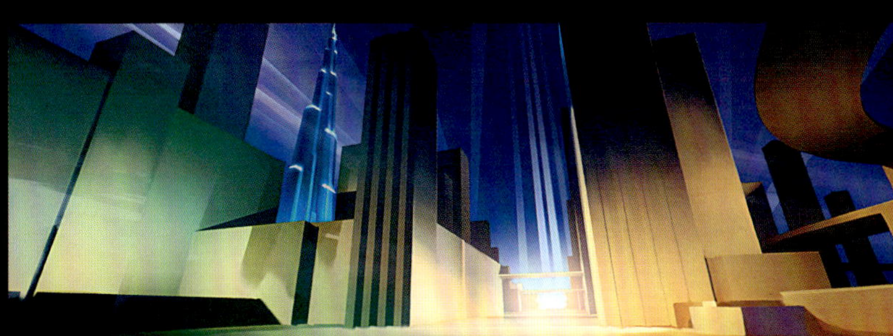

The background features a cold blueish violet as it pairs well with the warm lights shining upon the buildings and road in the foreground and mid-ground. At the intersection of the two areas, the transition between the warm and cold colours is kept subtle so as to appear more natural and improve the overall sense of spatial depth.

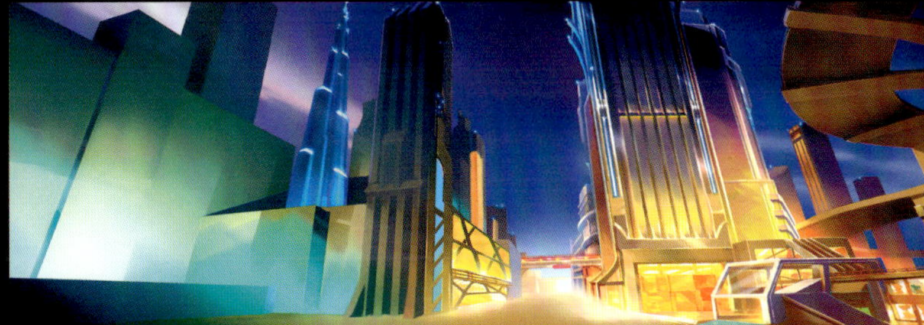

Once the lighting effects are defined, we need to adjust the saturation of the entire scene. This mirrors the fresher and brighter appearance of typical "young" cities. The sky is also coloured in to prepare for the shaping of the background at later stages. Buildings in the foreground are designed first to serve as standards against which other buildings should be shaped.

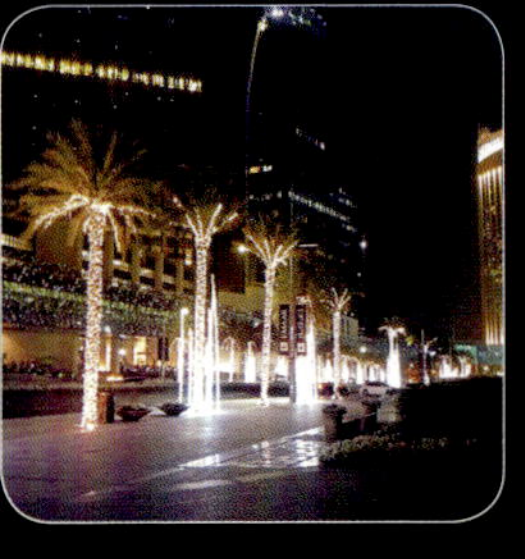

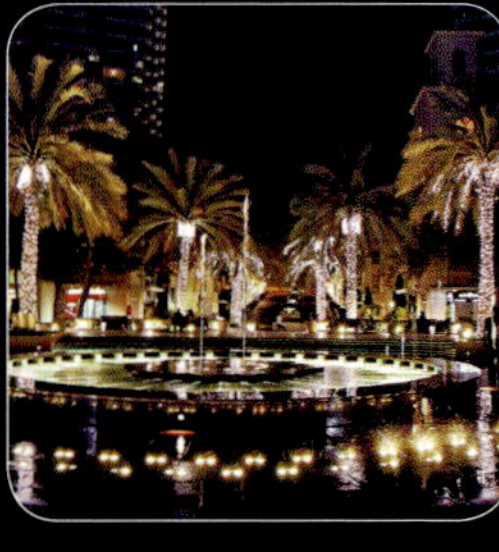

## ▲ PALM TREES

As a subtropical city that faces the sea and lies in the desert, palm trees are Dubai's choice of greenery. Near the business centre, there are palm trees decorated with light bulbs at night. They give off an extraordinary glare against the darkness. This may be the reason why Dubai's new downtown seems sparkling even in the absence of neon lights.

Then, certain elements are refined, including buildings in the foreground. Due to differences in the shape of buildings and the likelihood of their deformation caused by the wider angle, we need to take extra care while drawing to maintain relative congruence. One effective method is to treat the buildings like boxes of different shapes and sizes and draw a diagonal line coming from each of them as reference for the perspective. Another technique is to repeatedly use the Mirror Canvas function to observe whether there are any problems with the perspective that need to be corrected. Here we should also add palm trees and some cars to help define the proportional relationship among different objects. By doing this, we can make adjustments before further refinement.

A huge moon is added in the sky to enhance the "fantasy" flavour. All special fantasy elements should match the rest of the subject material, the design composition, and the world view a scene hopes to represent, while at the same time being compatible with the environment and overall tone. A colossal spacecraft, for example, would not be a good fit for the city that features no scientific elements at all. Similarly, a bizarre flying creature would disrupt a generally realistic style. Such out-of-place elements divert viewers' attention away from the chief theme of an urban night view; whereas a moon against the night sky is quite reasonable and perhaps expected. With a simple colour and shape, the moon hangs in the background and doesn't intrude into the foreground.

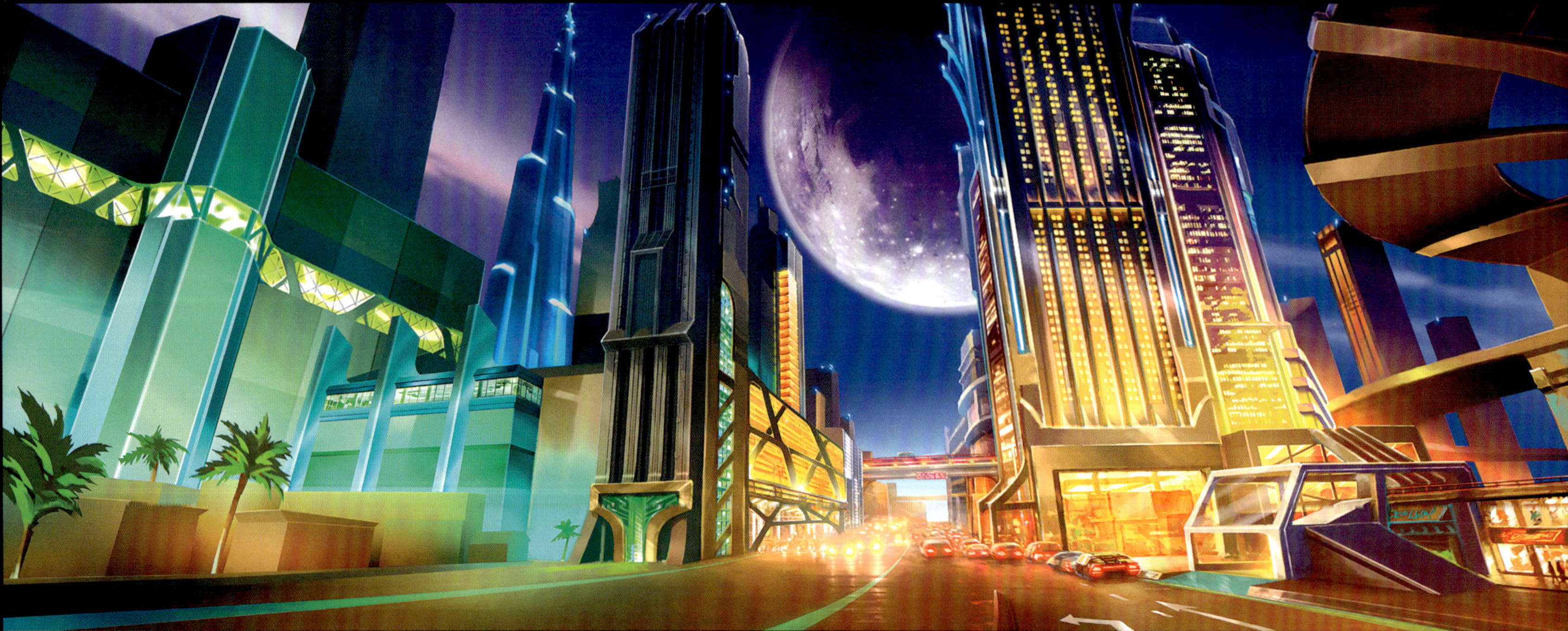

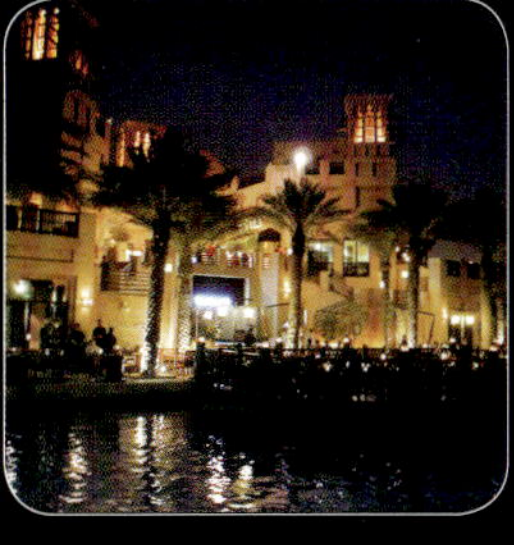

## ▲ LOW-RISES

Palm trees and traditional style low-rises contrast starkly with the modern high-rises, thus giving a sense of the city's multi-layered character and a peak at the regional culture.

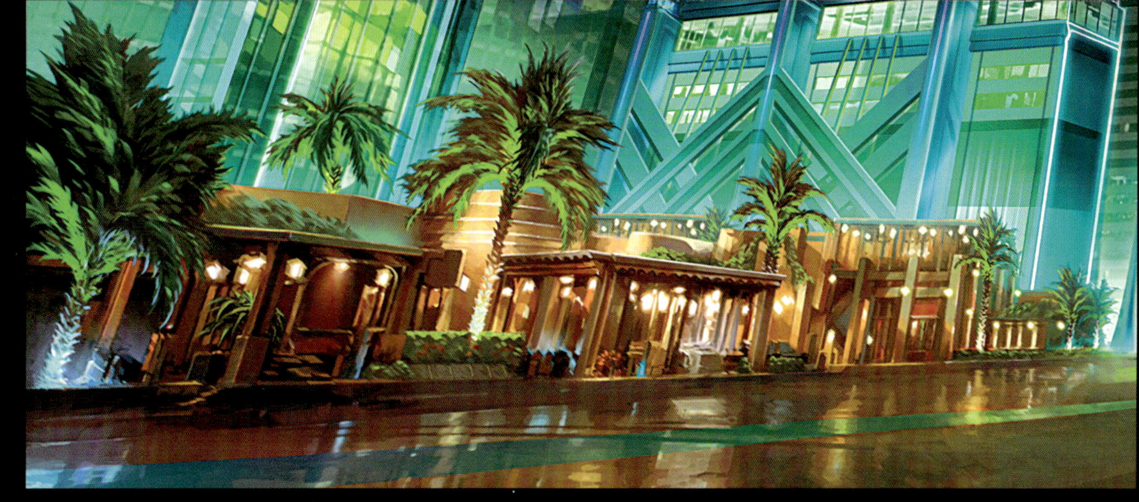

That is the moment captured by the current design. And to further draw viewers in, "realistic" details that show traces of daily life are added. The result is to move the scene away from the "fantasy" and create greater potential for viewer resonance.

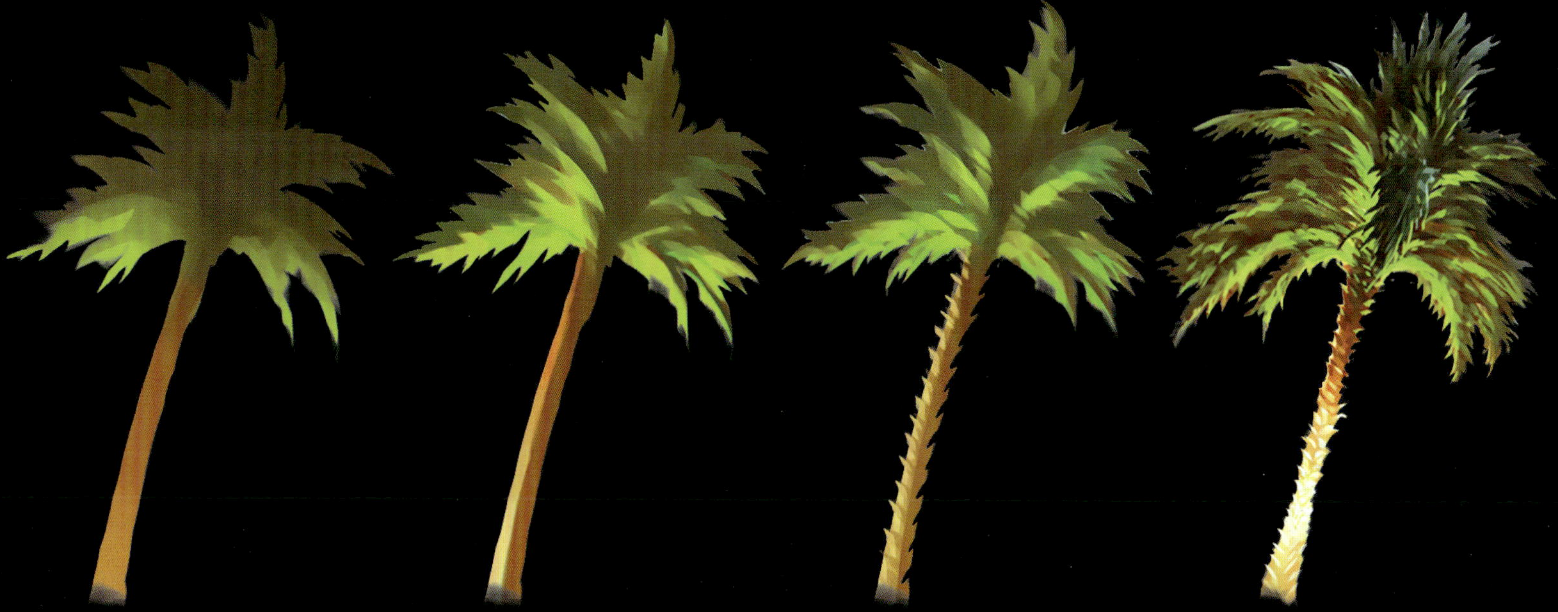

At night, all objects take on distinctive lighting effects. As such, the lighting of the palm trees is also a point for consideration. The silhouetting method is applied to outline the general shape of the palm trees. Then, leaves are outlined with brighter or darker colours according to the desired lighting effects. Details are added to the tree trunks to bring out a sense of depth and, finally, extra physical-details enhanced by the lighting are added according to where each palm tree will be located. Sometimes, over-exposure is used to showcase particularly strong visual effects.

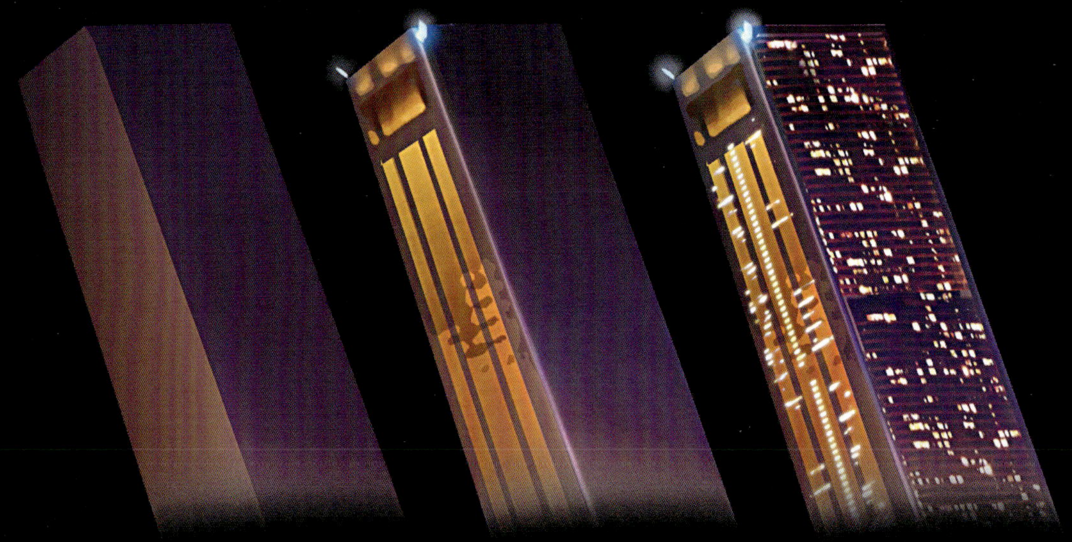

At night, great arrays of lights turn on in the buildings. As it would be time-consuming and skew the perspective if we bothered to depict each and every of them, material superimposition is adopted to complete.

Lumps of colour are painted in to bring out the colour of buildings, the spatial perspective, and the lighting before spotlighting is applied to the main buildings or structural changes are made. Finally, we superimpose separately prepared materials onto areas where lights need to be presented.

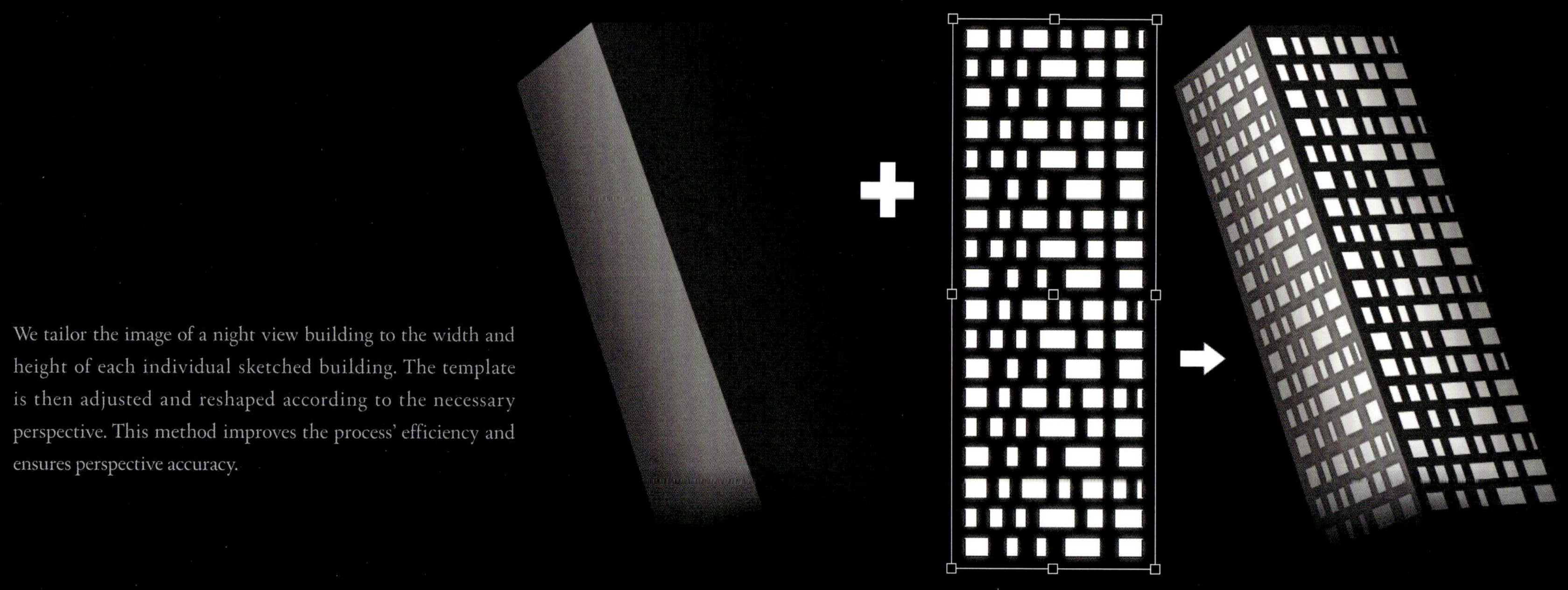

We tailor the image of a night view building to the width and height of each individual sketched building. The template is then adjusted and reshaped according to the necessary perspective. This method improves the process' efficiency and ensures perspective accuracy.

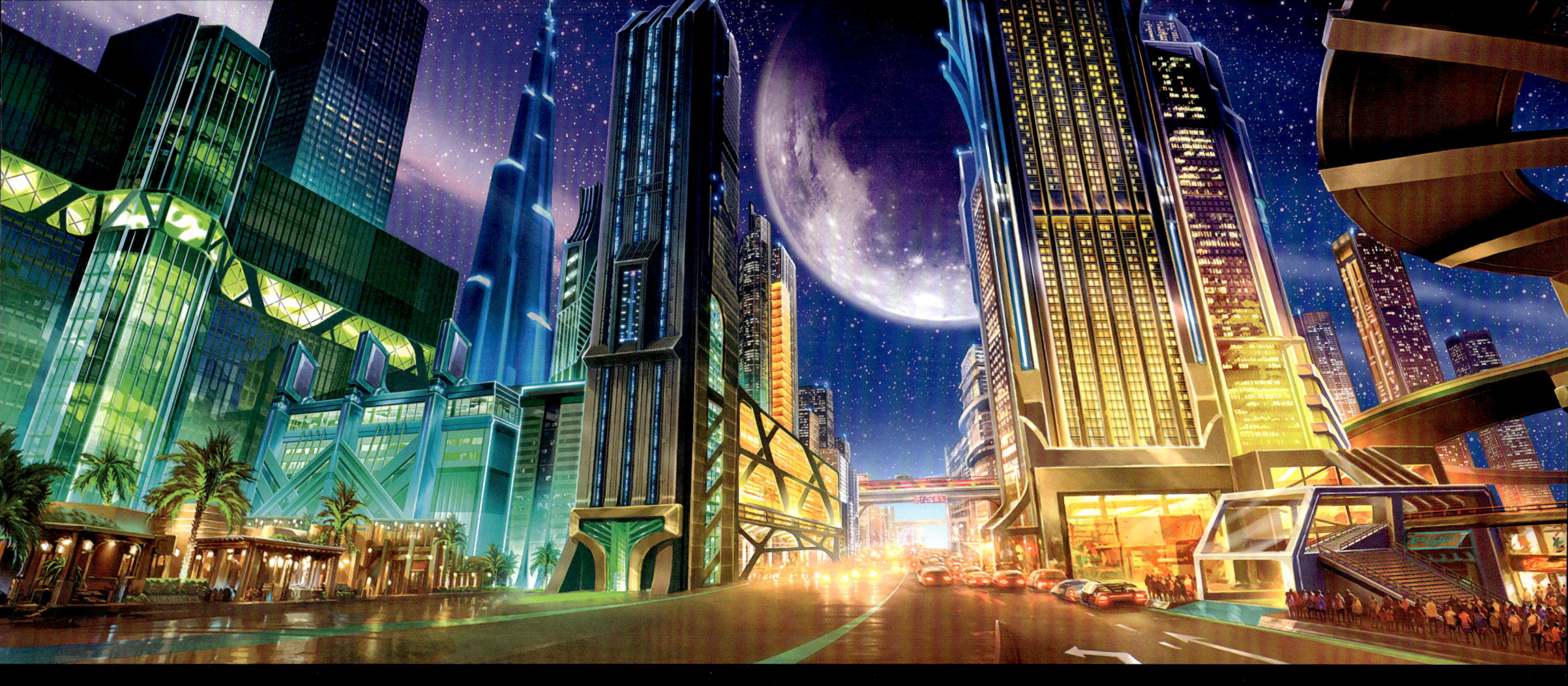

Those are all the methods used for completing the foundations of *The City at Nightfall*. But a few more features should still be needed.

This design features a diverse array of content. It is a busy scene. As such, one or two objects of a certain kind will not suffice to bring out the desired effect. Often, the necessary repetition to achieve an effect can lead creators to become bored, maybe even influencing them to find the painting process mechanical and uninteresting. My only suggestion is perseverance. There is always an end to every task no matter how many elements are involved. Plus, more often than not, it's worth the time and effort. By finishing one area at a time, the work will gradually progress toward completion, and the creators will be rewarded with a sense of accomplishment each time they see

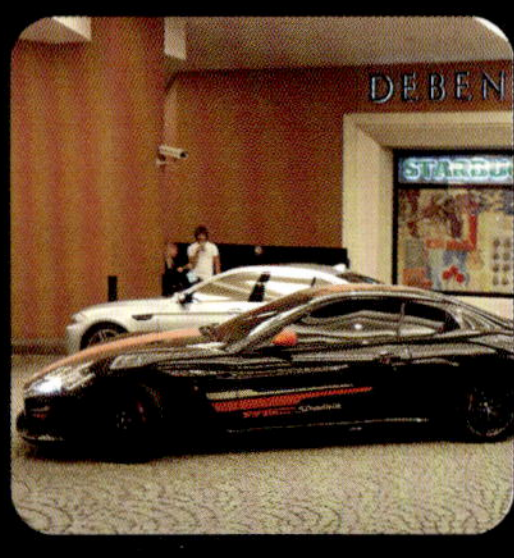

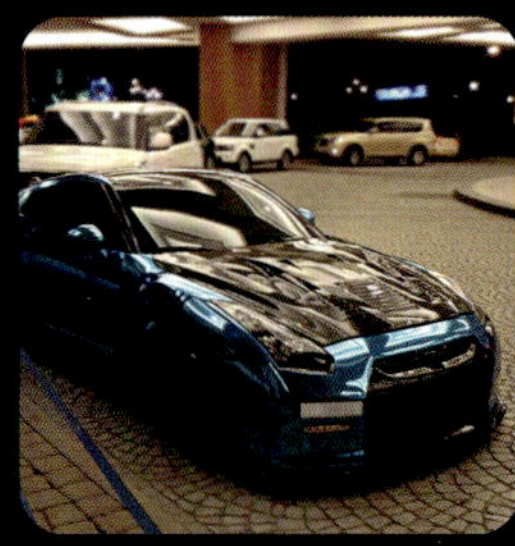

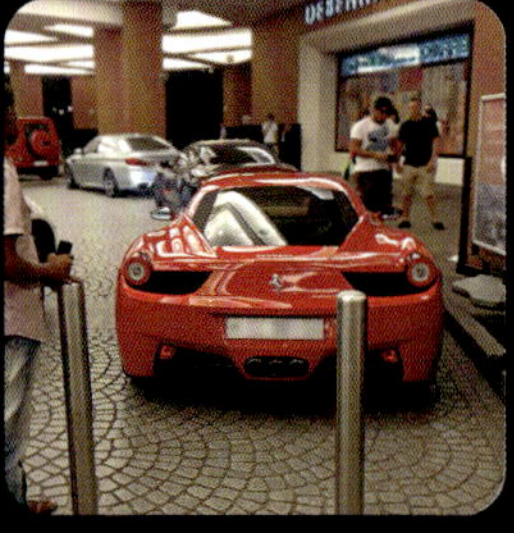

## ▲ LUXURY CARS

To most of the world, Dubai is chiefly regarded as a city where limited edition high-performance racing and luxury cars are ubiquitous, for generally wealthy residents in Dubai have high expectations for their living standards. However, it's an exaggeration to suggest that such cars are "ubiquitous". As a matter of fact, due to the high temperatures, residents in Dubai usually go out at night, as such, only then can you find luxury cars, bright in colour and sharp in shape, parked at the doors of large shopping malls and other entertainment and catering establishments.

In order to highlight this side of Dubai life, two to three super cars are necessary additions. To depict their shape accurately we need to use reference materials. The blue-glow of the rims and streamlined bodies hugging the ground provide a strong sense of the refined technology involved in their production. Moreover, this keeps in line with the theme of the entire scene. To give a more fantastical appearance, the cars could be made to levitate in the air or fly with fire coming out their back. However, such fantastic elements do not fit with the current composition. In fantasy art, different objects should simultaneously be exaggerated and rendered believable.

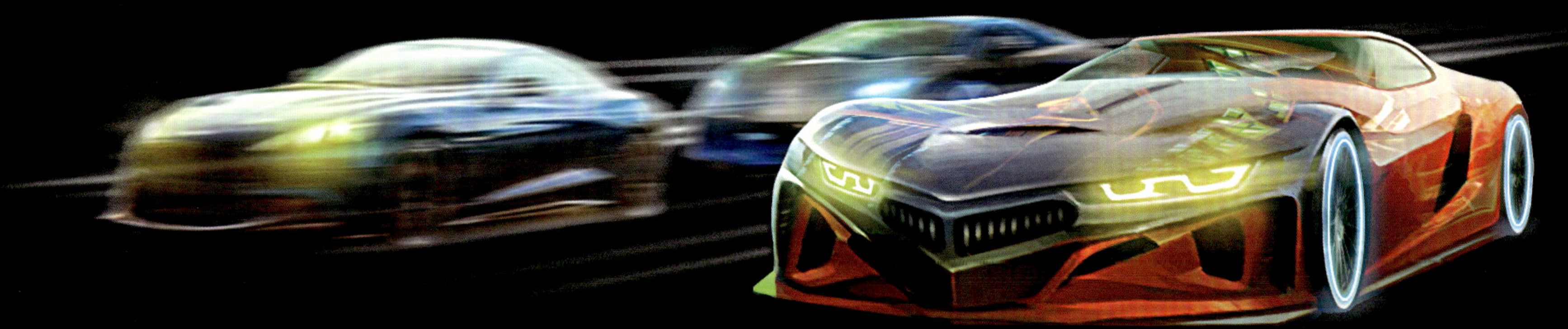

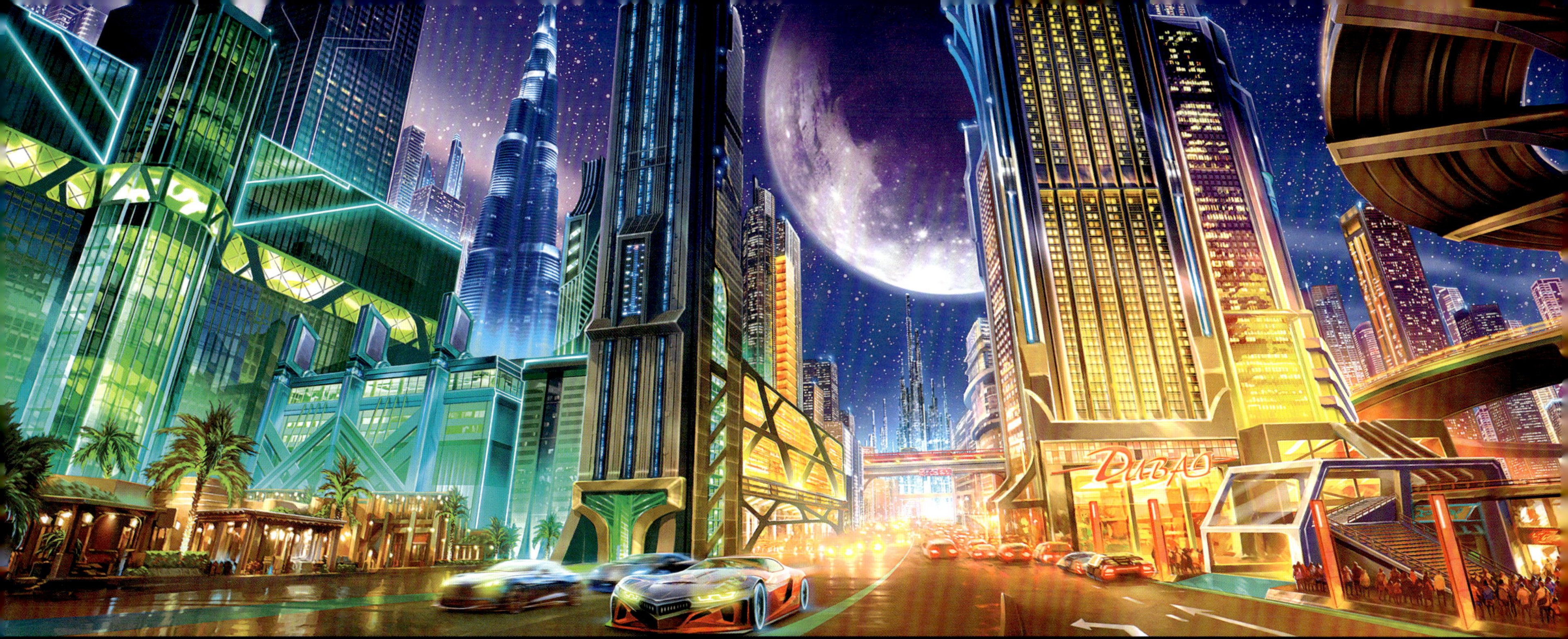

The motion-blur effects created for the cars give a sense of their speed while surfaces of the bodies reflect the inverted and deformed images of nearby buildings.

Next, the landmark structure, the Burj Khalifa, is refined and more high-rises are added to improve the sense of gradation and reinforce the design's theme. As Dubai becomes more developed in years to come, the Burj Khalifa will no longer be the tallest building. Fittingly, the skyscrapers at the end of the road stand as the representation of the new era.

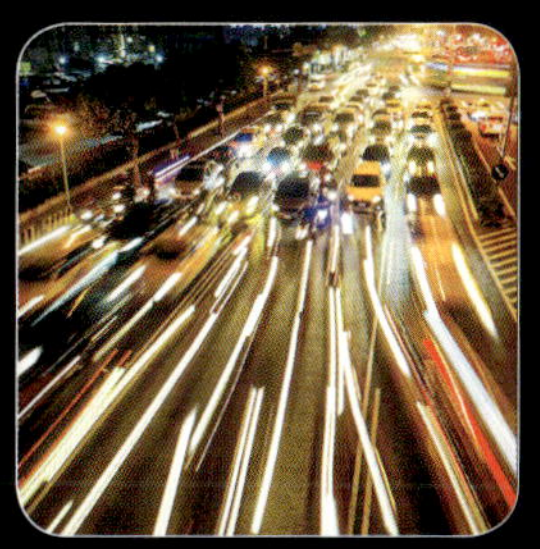

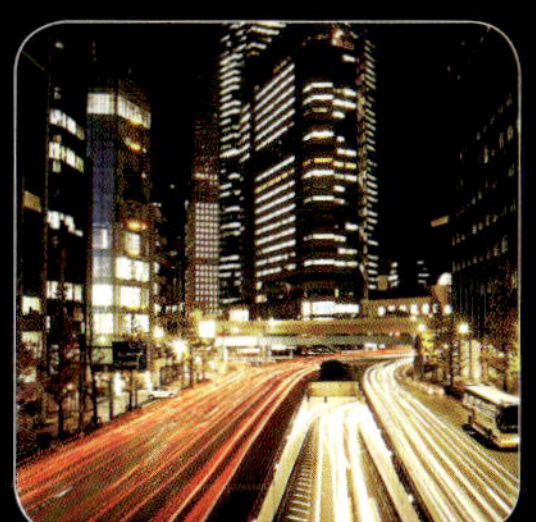

## ▲ GLISTENING

When you think of an urban night view, you might imagine cars shuttling past on the road with long glistening trails behind them. The above picture captures that movement using slow-shutter and long-exposure photography. In our painting, different colour taillights and headlights create a diverse glow on the dual track of the road. Then, the "colour fade" method is adopted to create a similar effect

## ▲ GLOWING LIGHT

Glowing light depicted in a variety of colours and shapes serves to enrich the scene. These special effects are readily available. Using the "colour filtration" method, we are able to replace the black background with a cacophony of glowing effects.

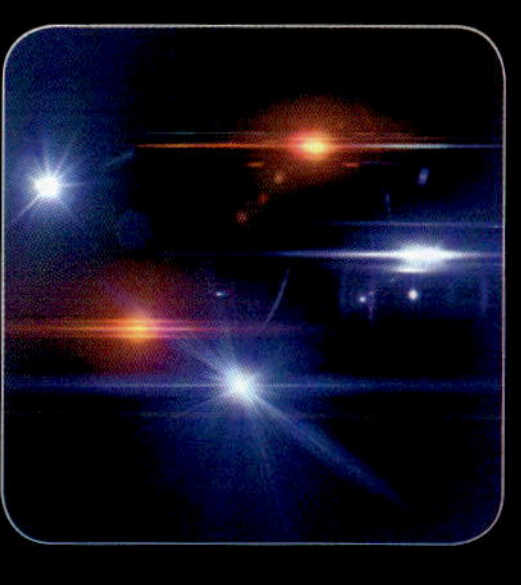

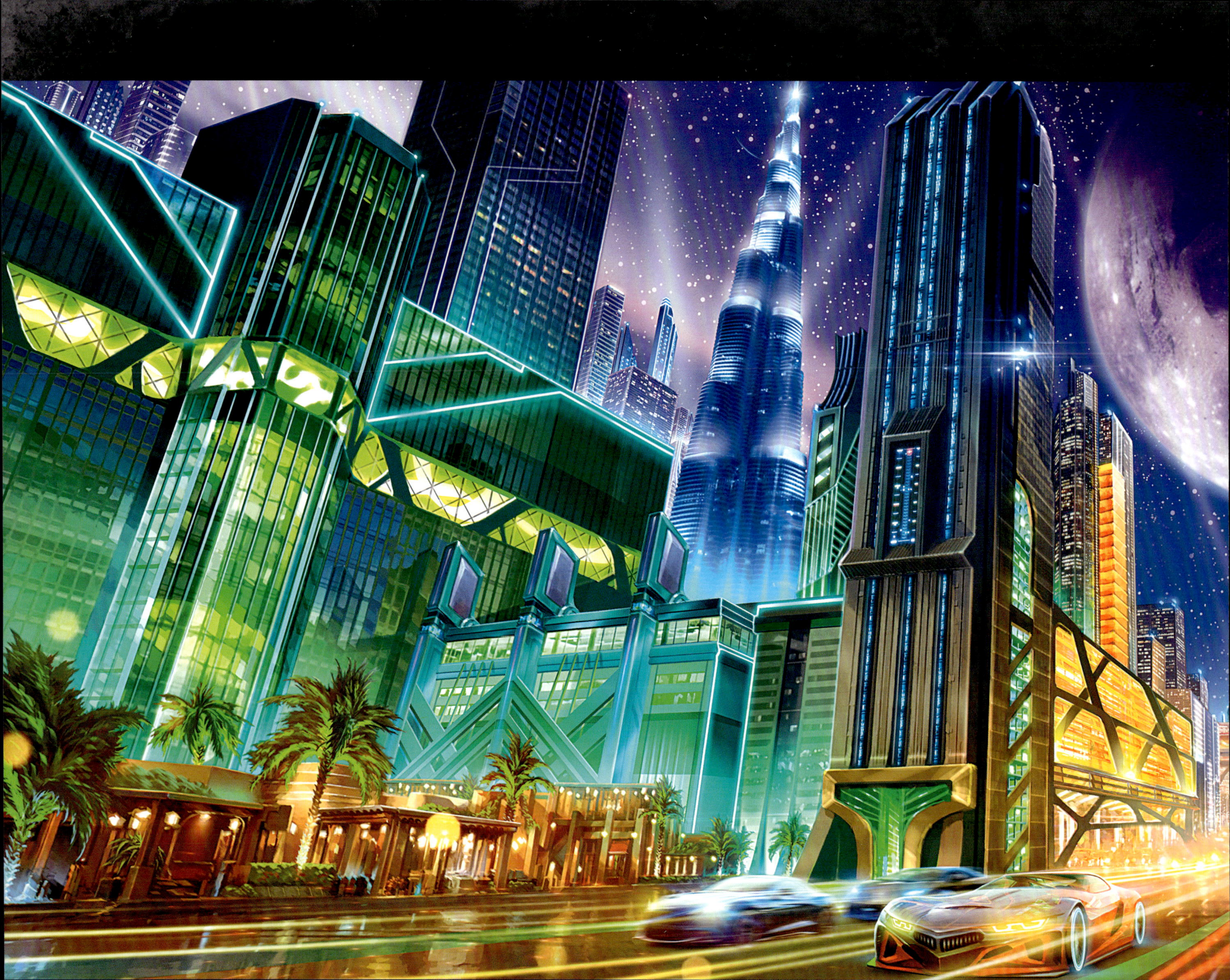

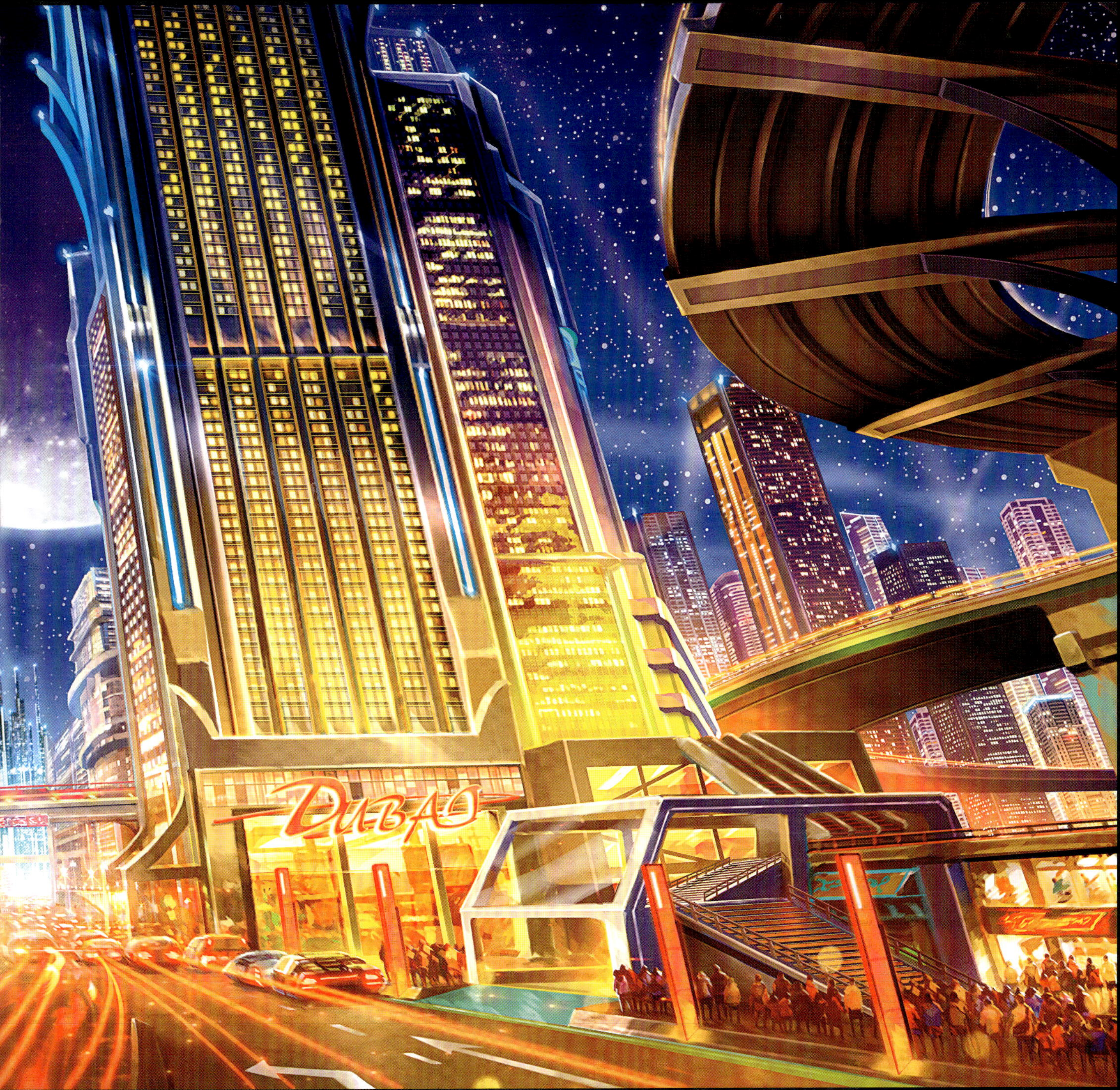

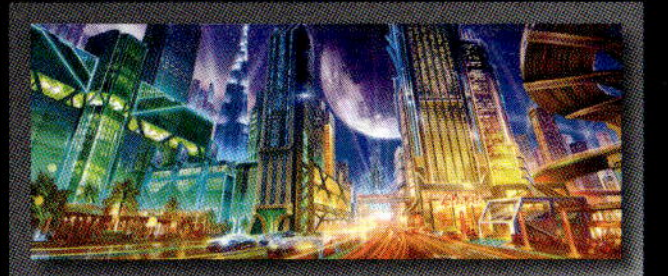

The atmosphere surrounding the scene is refined based on the above visual effects. My first impression of Dubai is thus depicted in *The City at Nightfall*.

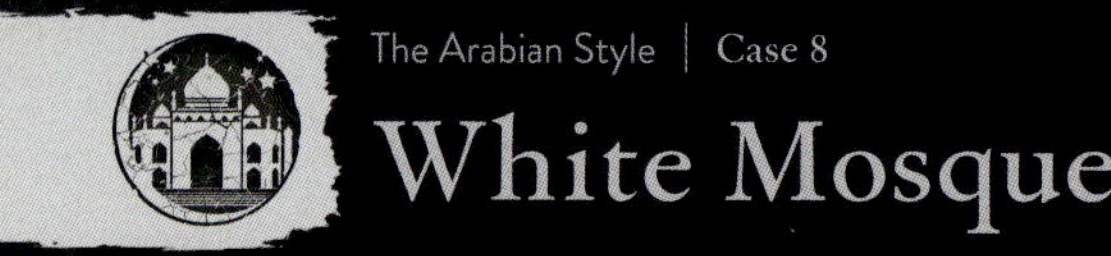

The Arabian Style | Case 8

# White Mosque

Mosques are indispensable in the Middle East. Compared with those in ancient cities such as Istanbul and Isfahan, the ubiquitous mosques in Dubai, whether big or small, wear few traces of age yet stand with a greater air of purity and holiness.

The Jumeirah Mosque is the largest and most beautiful mosque in Dubai, an exemplar of the glory of unique architecture. Located in Abu Dhabi over hundred kilometres from the Jumeirah Mosque, the Sheikh Zayed Grand Mosque ("Zayed Mosque" for short) is another must-visit attraction for travellers touring around Dubai. Though not located within Dubai, it is inextricably connected with the city thanks to its renown as a scenic spot and importance in religion and architecture.

Modelled after the Zayed Mosque, *White Mosque* integrates some traditional Arabic architectural structures with characteristics of Dubaian residential layout into the design and, as such, exhibits features of regional religion and cultural environment. The composition adopts a super wide-angle perspective and gives objects subtle gradations, making the building complex far more spectacular. Moreover, the addition of fantasy elements injects some diversity and rhythm into the scene that would otherwise appear overly regular.

In my view, the Zayed Mosque is a colossal work of art. The meticulous construction techniques and refined craftsmanship evident from the mosque's overall appearance, internal structures, and even the ornaments in each of its corner, hint at the constant strive of artisans and designers for perfection. Once there, you may find your eyes busily chasing its every detail and the exceptionally picturesque views available from whatever angle. Parquet marble floors, decorated and colourful carpets, traditional patterns across the walls, and the plethora of diverse, splendid ornaments all serve as reminders of the mosque's unparalleled charm.

But how can so many elements be captured within one single painting? This merits further consideration as we continue through the design.

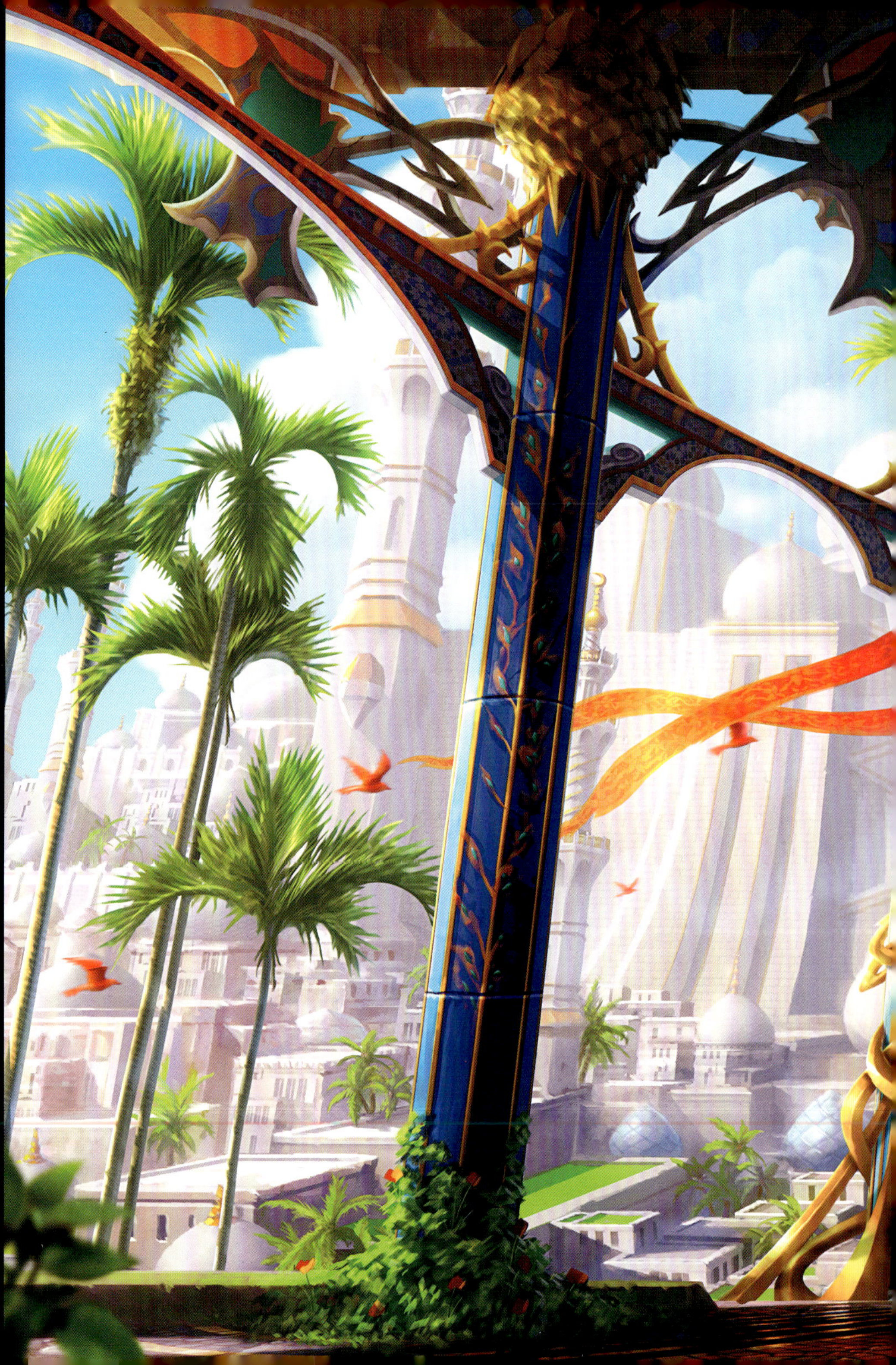

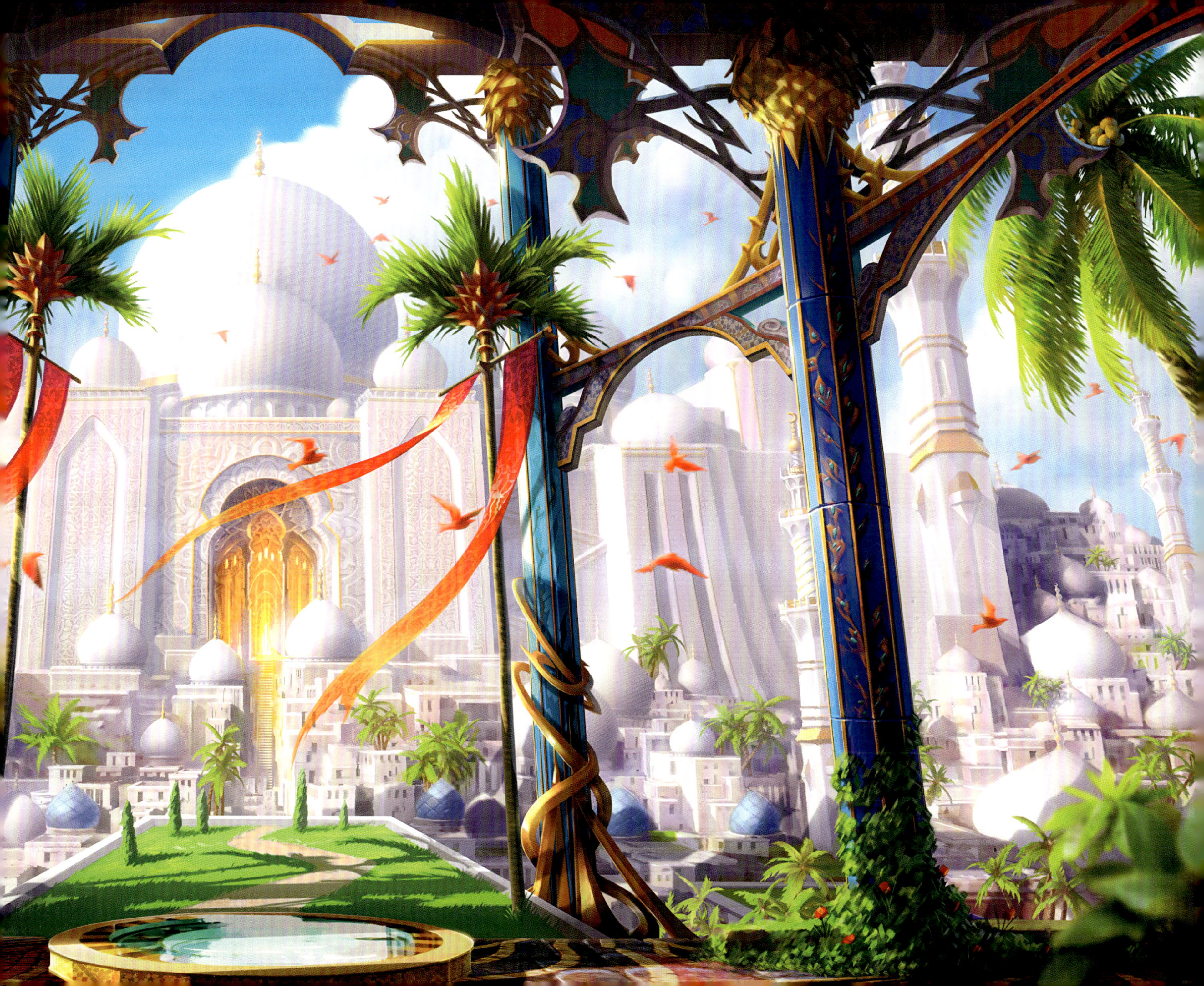

# THOUGHTS ON CREATION

*The Zayed Mosque is famous for its grandeur. Its external walls are constructed out of white marble inlaid with decorative shells and gems. Tons of gold form golden ornaments adorning the space. Its interior is decorated with crystal chandeliers, and the main prayer hall is furnished with a colourful and beautiful Persian carpet made predominantly of wool. In this extremely luxurious mosque, sounds of praying and chanting can be heard all around, giving a sense of sacredness, purity, and solemnity unknown in the common world.*

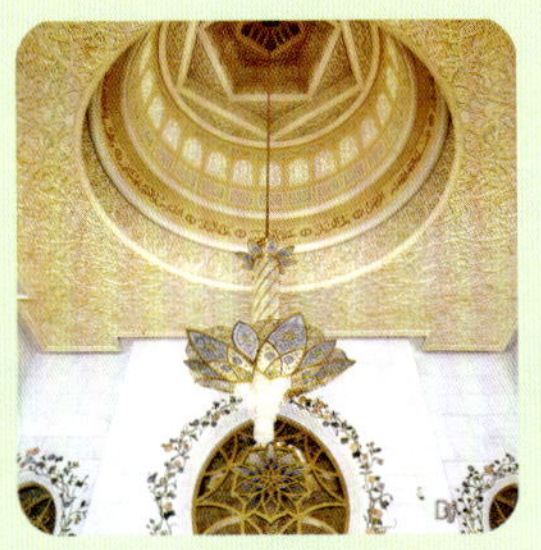

## ▲ MOSQUE

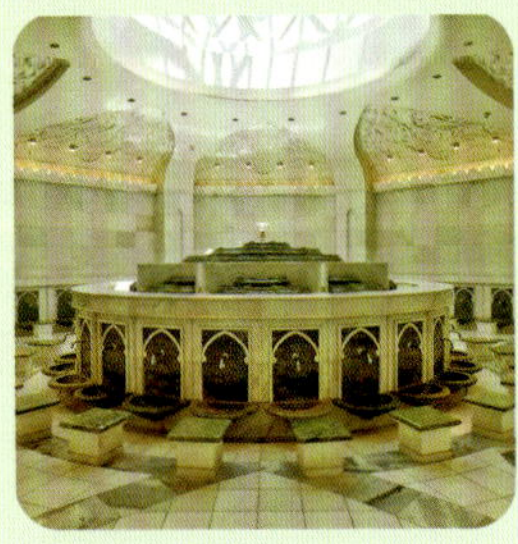

Inside the mosque, apart from a worldly famous, large wool carpet and gems of various types on the walls, there is also the world's largest crystal chandelier, the shape of which is astonishingly striking. Colourful patterns on floors and ornaments on walls alike are made of natural materials such as celestine, agates, amethyst, pearls and abalone shells. Even the bathroom, rendered in the Muslim architectural style, is spectacular.

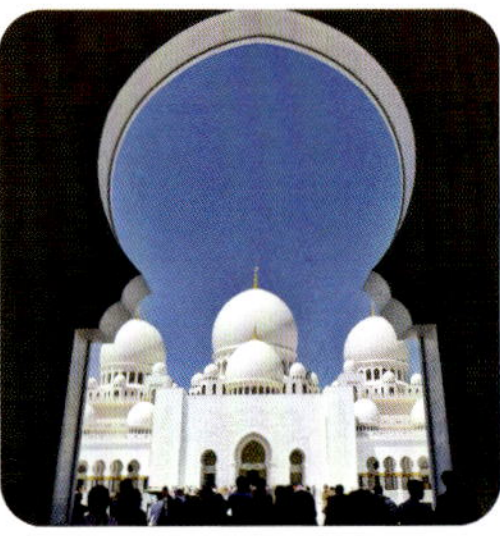

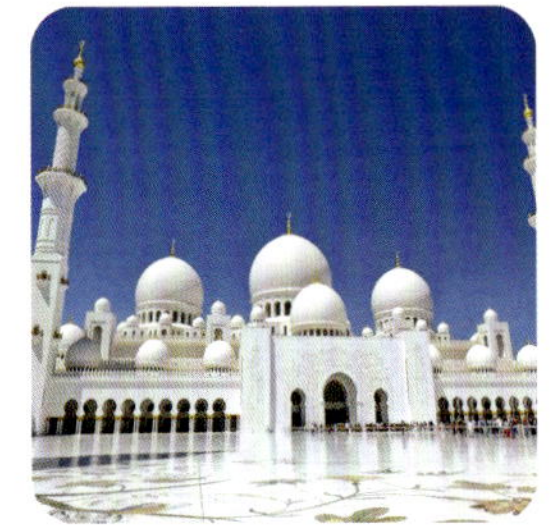

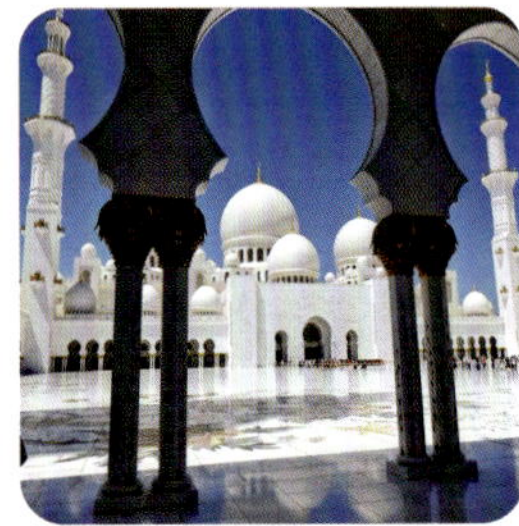

## ▲ ZAYED MOSQUE

The Zayed Mosque combines Arabic architectural tradition with design styles specific to Persia, the Mughal Empire and the Moors. Its white marble dome, walls and columns give expression to its magnificence, purity and solemnity. The colossal dome is decorated with golden patterns of crescent moons to match the golden floral designs lining the corridor of the columns, shining brightly in the sunshine. The very first impression the Zayed Mosque left on me was its resemblance to the holy palace depicted in *Arabian Nights*.

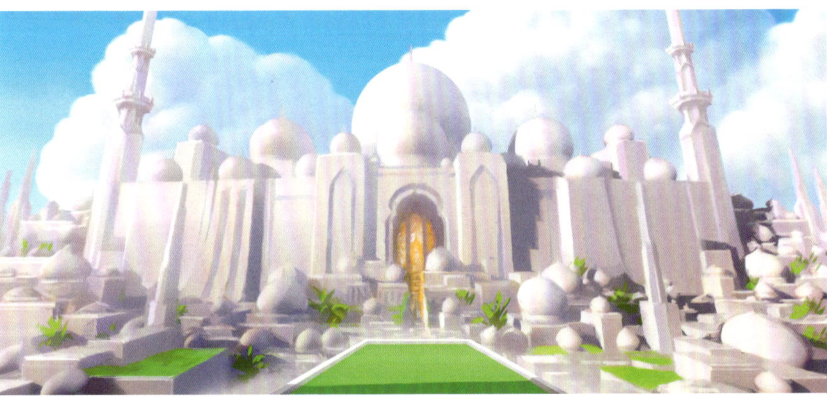

For the convenience of modification at the initial stage of sketching, let's leave the door frame in the foreground for now as it is likely to block objects in the middle and in the distance. The main complex is simply shaped based on the draft with its exact position determined in relation to other objects and the effects of light and shade.

The main structure of the mosque is designed with reference to the features of the Zayed Mosque, such as its domes, columns and towering minarets. In this work of fantasy art, these features are enlarged, as such, the bottom of the structure should be reinforced to bear the extra weight. Walls capable of bearing greater weight are used to support the entire structure, making the image more believable and acceptable.

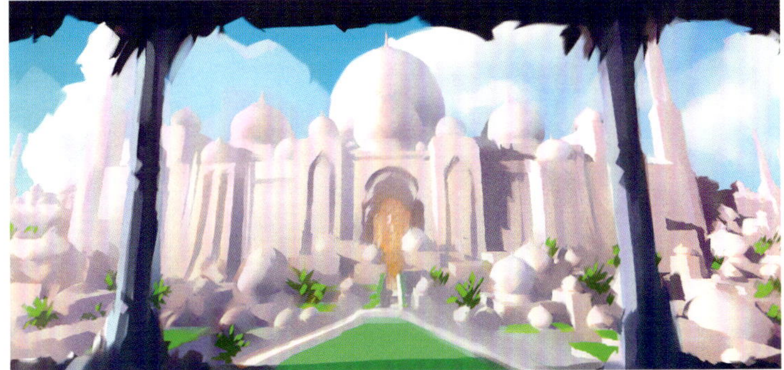

In order to highlight the solemnity and magnificence of the main structure, a slight side-on view is adopted. A "super wide-angle" perspective is also applied to extend the length of the scene so that residential complexes can be added to enrich the scene and foreground the splendour of the mosque.

To bring a sense of depth, the distant background, middle and foreground are divided. In the foreground, there is a door frame, from which it seems like the viewer looking out. The foreground is also joined to the middle ground by a meadow, for its length extends the space between the two. The height and layout of the door frame, the meadow, residences, and the main structure of the mosque are adjusted to provide different stereoscopic perspectives.

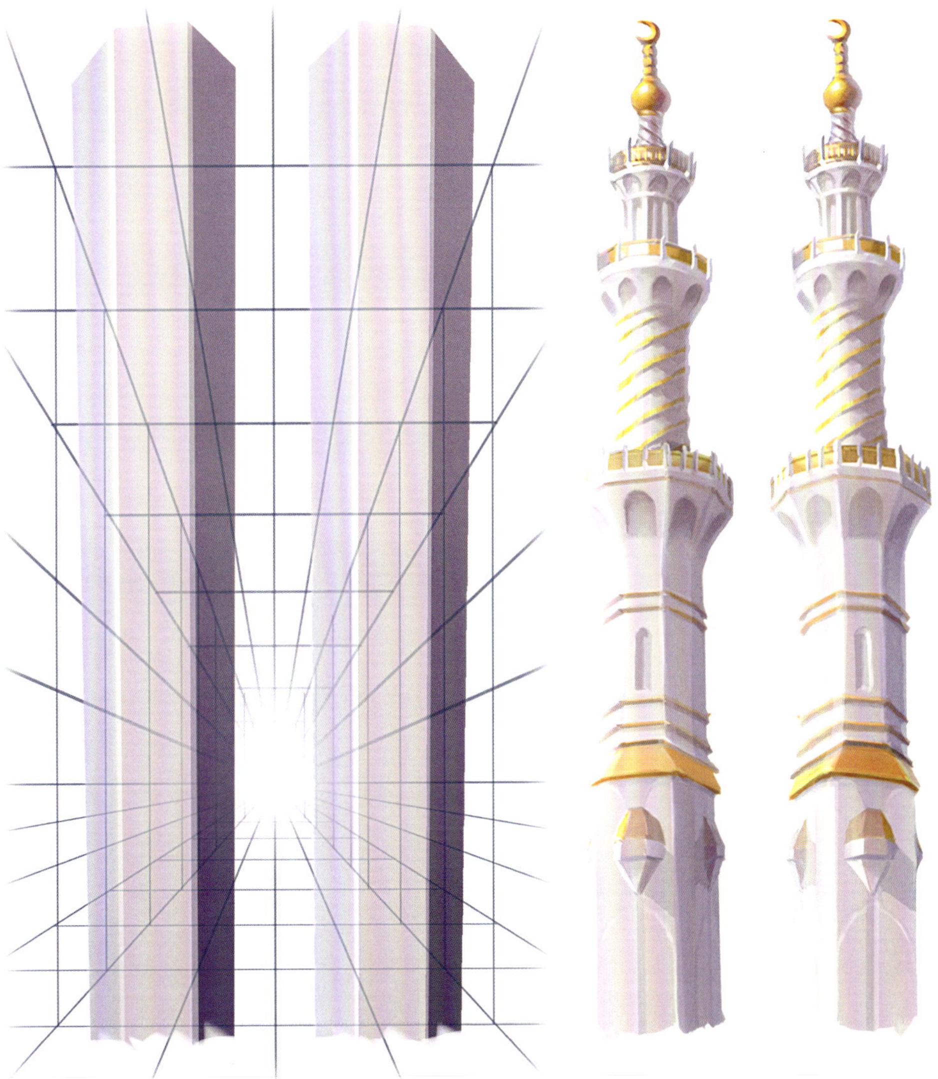

Before we go further with this design, let's take some common or symmetrical objects out of the scene for individual refinement. These objects can be used repeatedly as "resources" to improve the efficiency of creation.

For example, the minarets are common mosque structures, often set up to summon followers to pray. In this design, they appear quite frequently. Two minarets are given different side lighting effects since they vary in location and the way their shade cast.

The two minarets are drawn from a slight side view, and made of white stone like the main hall of the Zayed Mosque and furnished with golden ornaments. This combination of the exquisite with the plain has broad benefits for the overall image.

In copying one minaret from the other, it is necessary to make changes to their shapes according to their apparent distance from the viewer and where they stand in the complex. The areas where the "minarets" join other structures are painted in until the joints look reasonable.

Around the massive mosque, there are residential buildings designed in the Arabic architectural tradition, with domes and minarets of the kinds often seen in small mosques to match the main structure. The residences are scattered asymmetrically and irregularly but are balanced in density and uniform in colour.

Due to differences in height between the building complex and audience's viewpoint, urban streets seem mostly to be blocked by buildings. In order to show that these streets exist, some areas are left in view, especially the main street leading to the front door of the mosque.

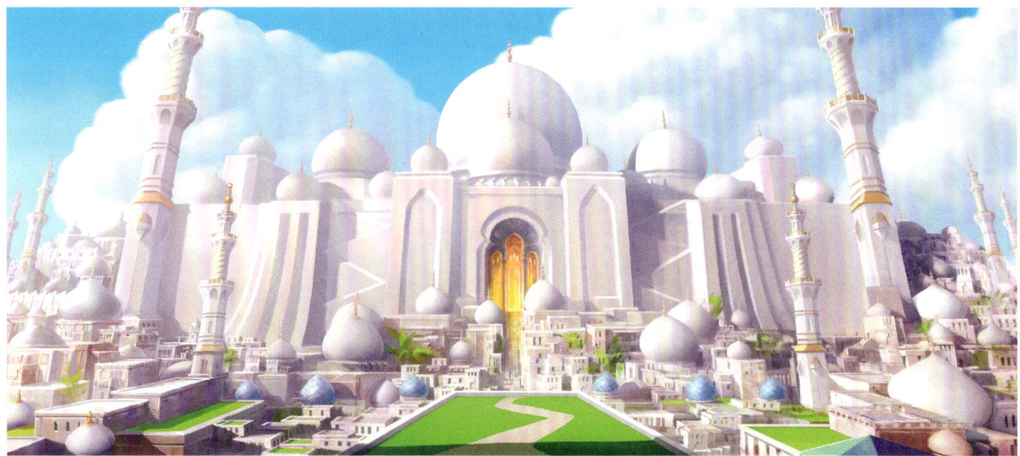

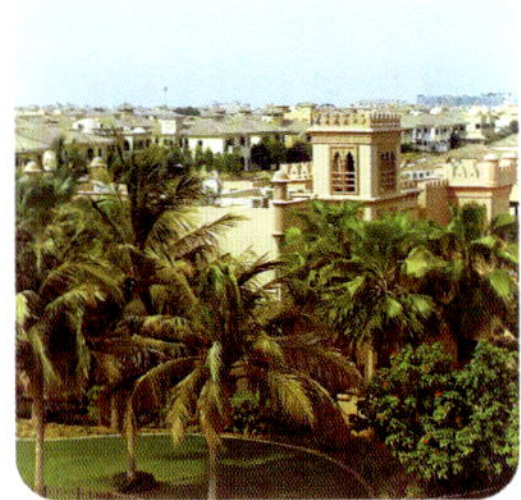

## ◀ CITIES

Dubai and Abu Dhabi are cities built on deserts, where fresh water is in short supply. However, as the saying goes, "You can tell how rich or not a family is, not from the splendour or size of their house but from how many trees and flowers are planted in their courtyard". So in addition to water resources, plants are also symbols of a luxury lifestyle. That is why palm trees that need the irrigation of a large amount of fresh water are indispensable for a luxury courtyard.

Details are refined. Simple shapes are "carved" into complex structures, which are complemented with appropriate architectural details, plants, and elements and items showing traces of life. Some leaves are added to the top of buildings to represent trees of the same height as low buildings.

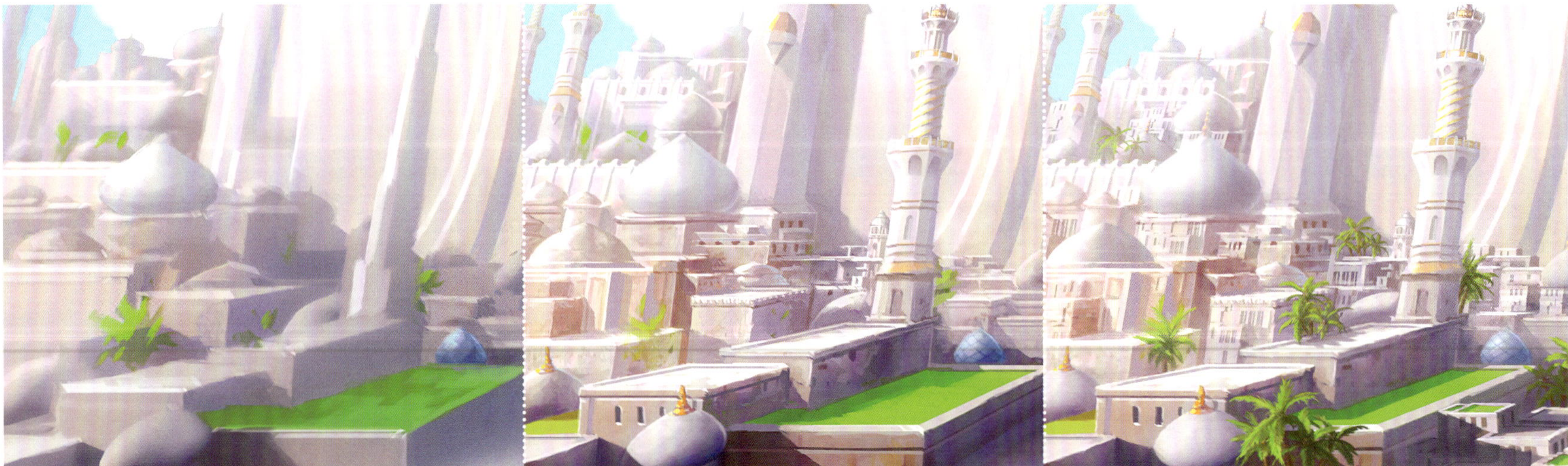

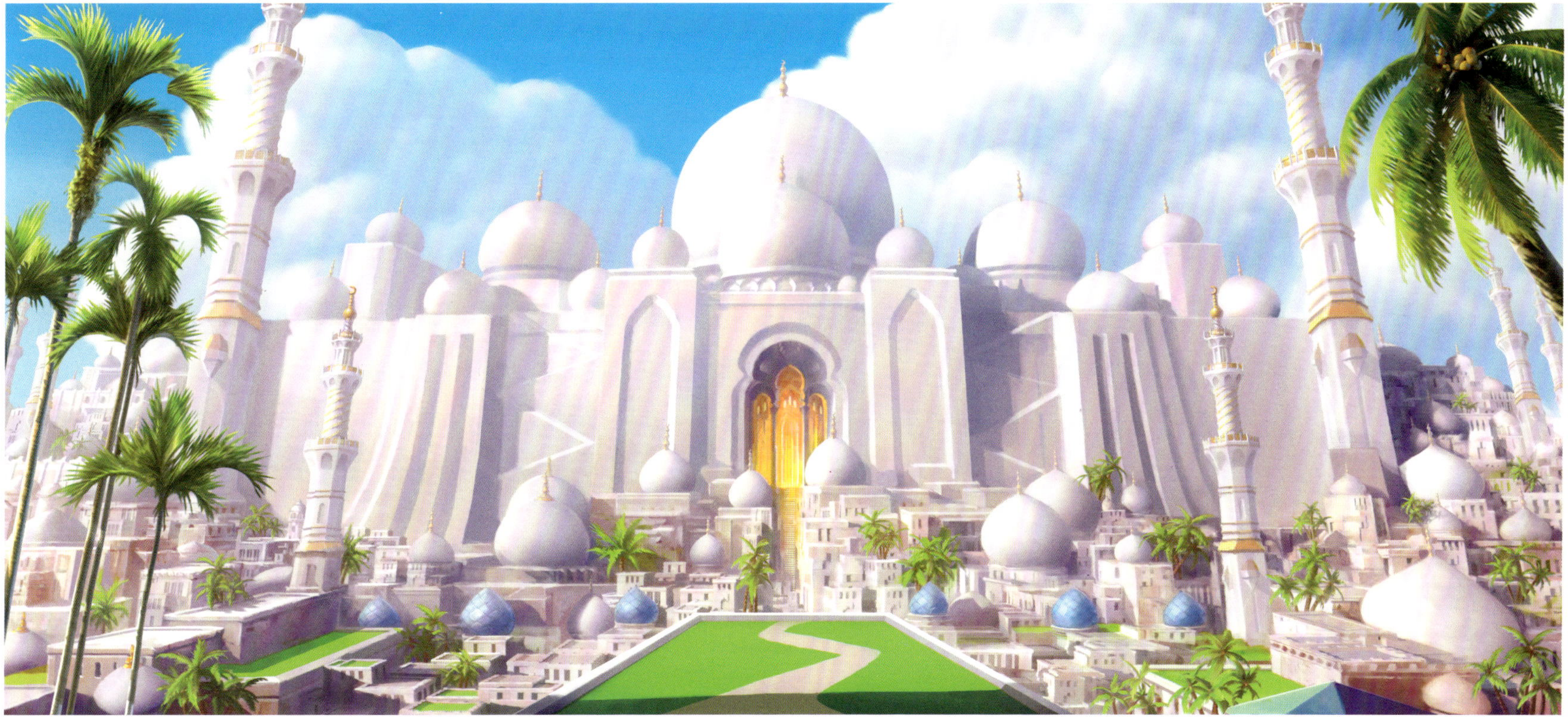

Trees dot the scene evenly, the layout of which appears well-spaced and orderly like that of the complex. Green trees serve the functions of diversifying the scene's hue, varying the density of buildings, adding features to the courtyard, and enlivening the entire scene. They are also the best references for adjusting perspective ratios. The ratio of the magnified mosque in relation to other buildings tends to confuse viewers. In contrast, the ratio of trees is relatively consistent and close to reality. The addition of such trees discourages any confusion about the relation between building sizes and makes the main structure seem all the more magnificent.

For greater diversity, palm trees of different species are painted in the foreground. A group of areca palms that feature small leaves and thin, straight stems and coconut trees with big and wide leaves and sturdy stems are put into the scene standing high. In areas blocked by leaves, objects that are highly expressive and require detailed depiction are removed.

## ▼ THE CORRIDOR OF COLUMNS

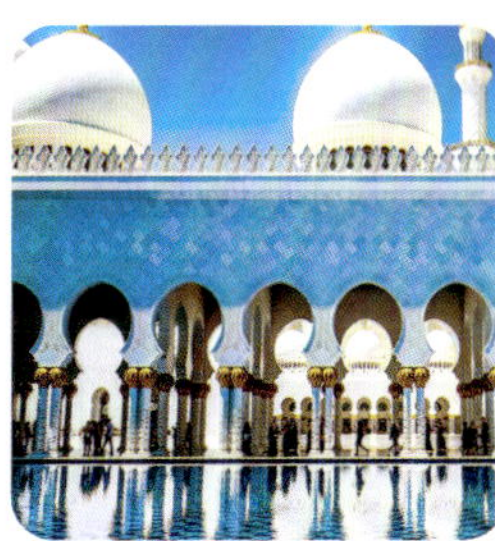

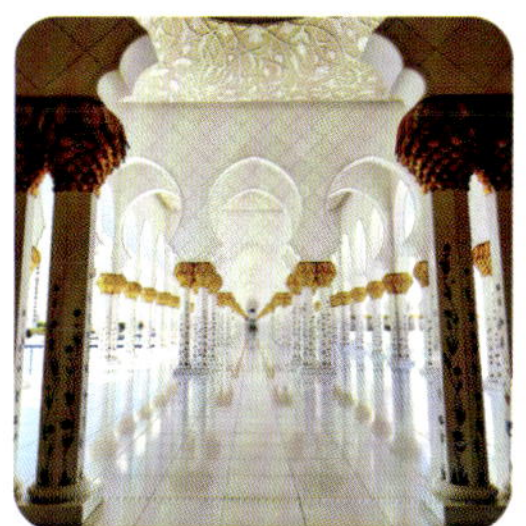

The corridor of columns is one of the features of the Zayed Mosque. The white marble columns shine brightly in the sunshine. The spotless corridor seems endless, giving a sense of unparalleled sanctity. The beams in a style specific to Abu Dhabi are decorated with golden capitals and floral patterns, producing a combination of plainness and luxurious elegance.

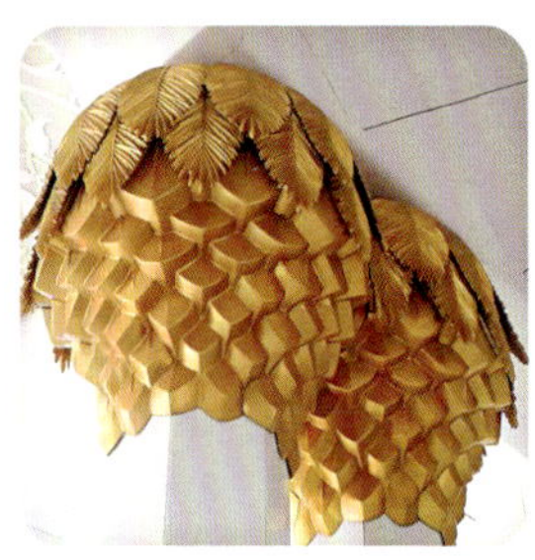

## ◀ COLUMN CAPS

The gold column caps look like the stem of date palms and as such possess strong regional characteristics. These individualised designs, when applied to a creation, will give full expression to its essence.

The outline of the door frame is drawn in the silhouetting method which is fast and convenient to modify. What should be made clear here is that silhouettes of objects and locations of objects that block views in the middle and the foreground. As with drawing the trees, highly expressive background objects are avoided.

Then, with the completion of a stereoscopic door frame drawing in silhouette, the columns supporting the door frame are painted in the cold colours of lake blue and ultramarine as perfect matches to the golden ornaments and the grey side of the white complex.

Columns not depicted for the main structure are added here to make up for the loss of one of the important features of the Zayed Mosque. Some other delicate objects inside the original mosque are also applied here to the foreground door frame such as a line-up of ornaments, coloured bricks, and the central sink in its bathroom. By applying what is inside to the exterior, this design attempts to holistically present the essence of the original.

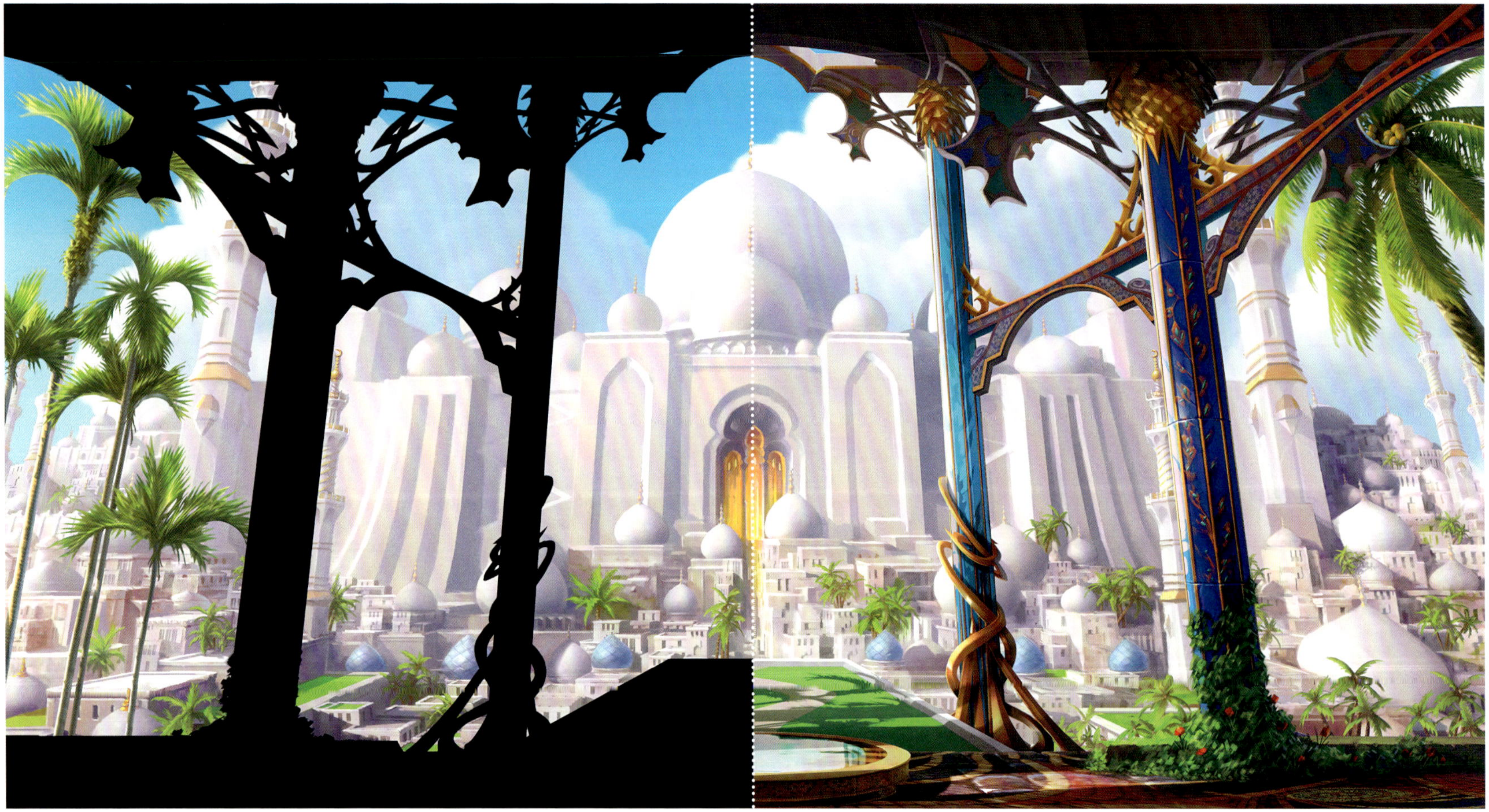

Plants are added around the door frame to enliven the scene. With two of the columns forward of the others and plants now on the ground, a single door frame becomes a more complicated corridor. The decorations shaped like palm trees near the columns under the door frame match trees in the distance. Different from natural trees in shape, the artificial trees are tied with red flags, the movement of which adds a sense of dynamism to the scene.

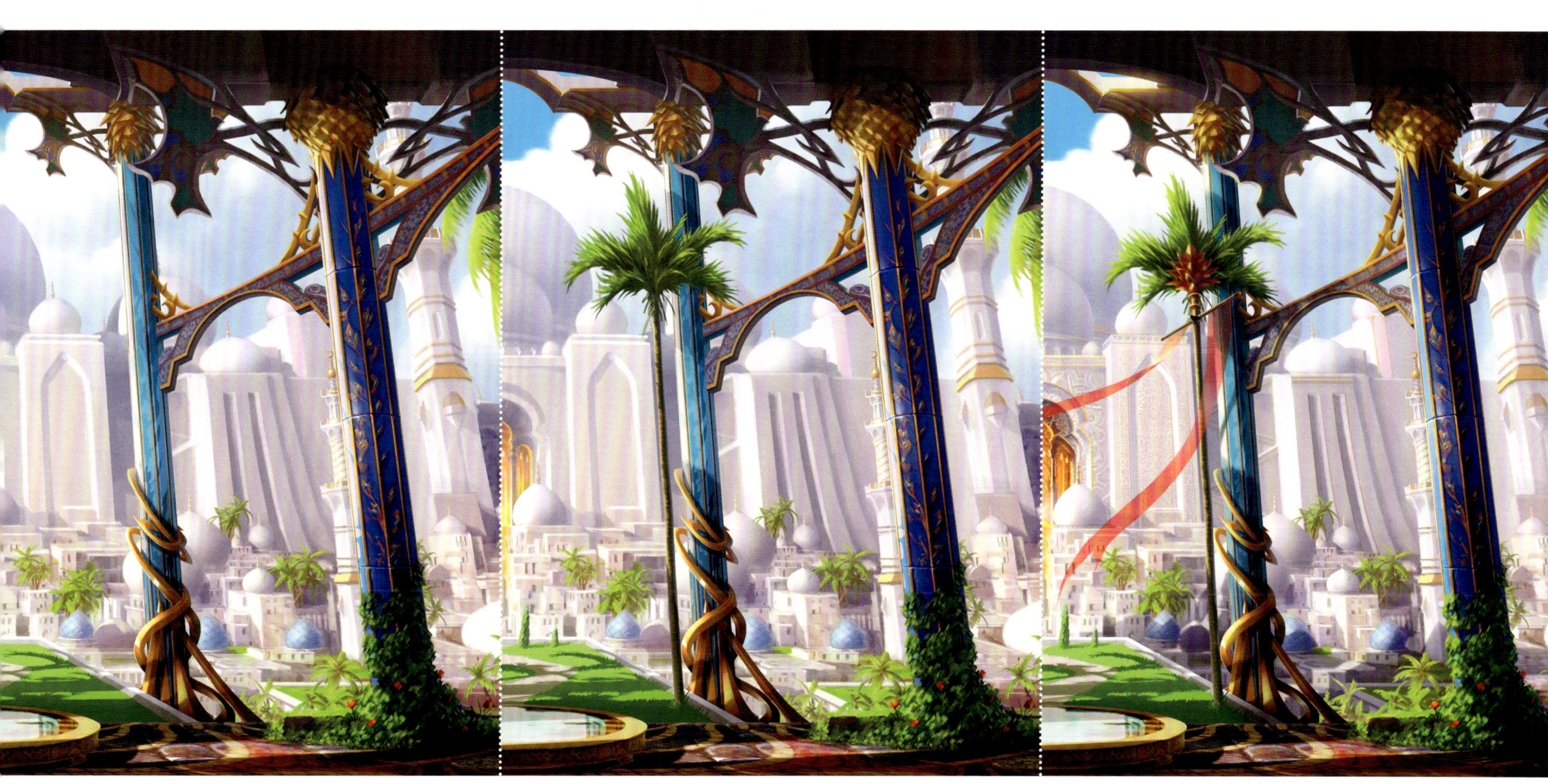

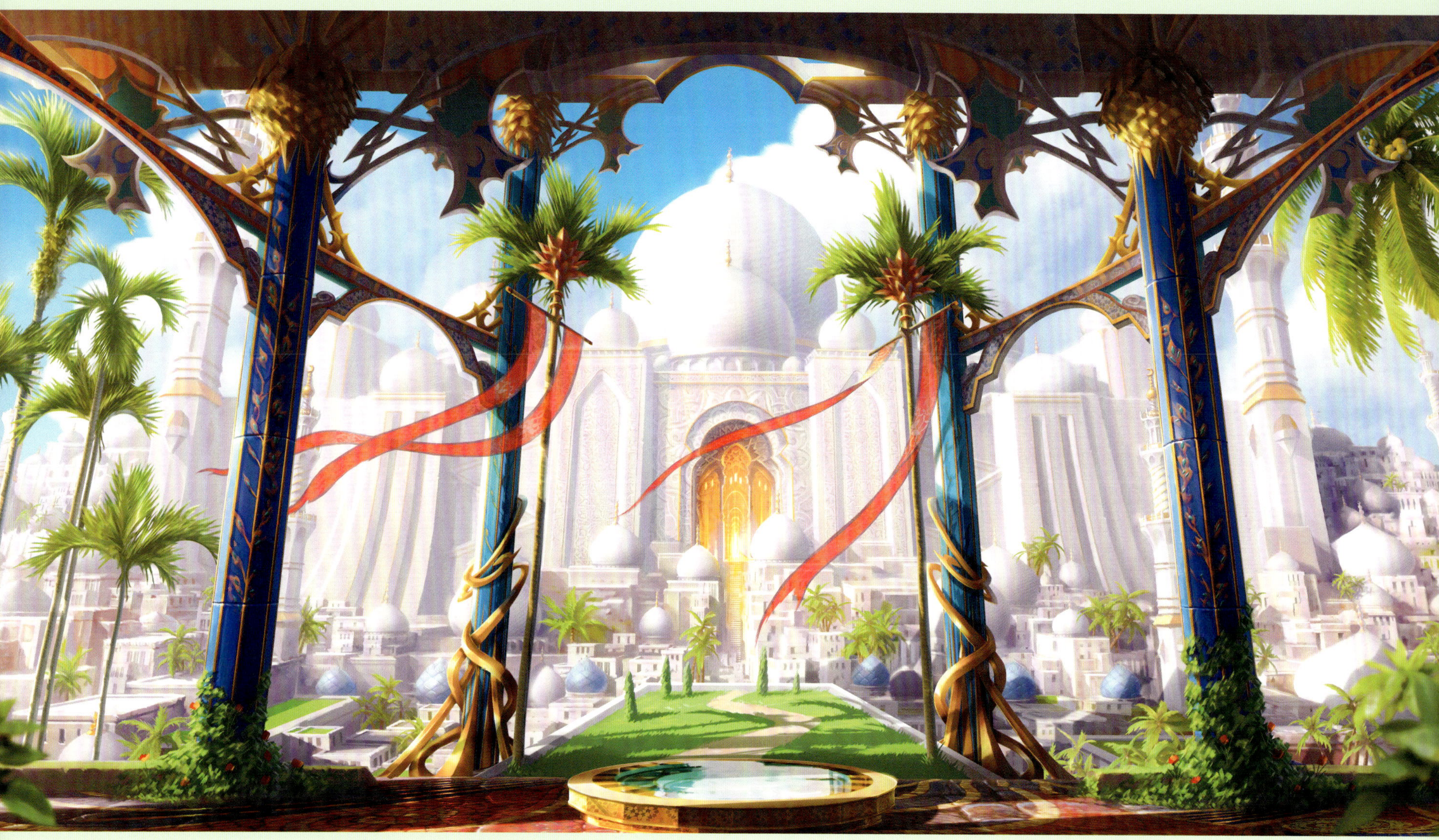

With elements in the distance, the middle and the foreground in place, we need to see whether the entire scene is balanced or not and finish all the details, such as raised floral patterns on the main structure's walls, the colossal dome, and plants in the foreground that simulate the "unfocused effects" common with this depth of field. When all these elements are ready, this piece of work is approaching completion.

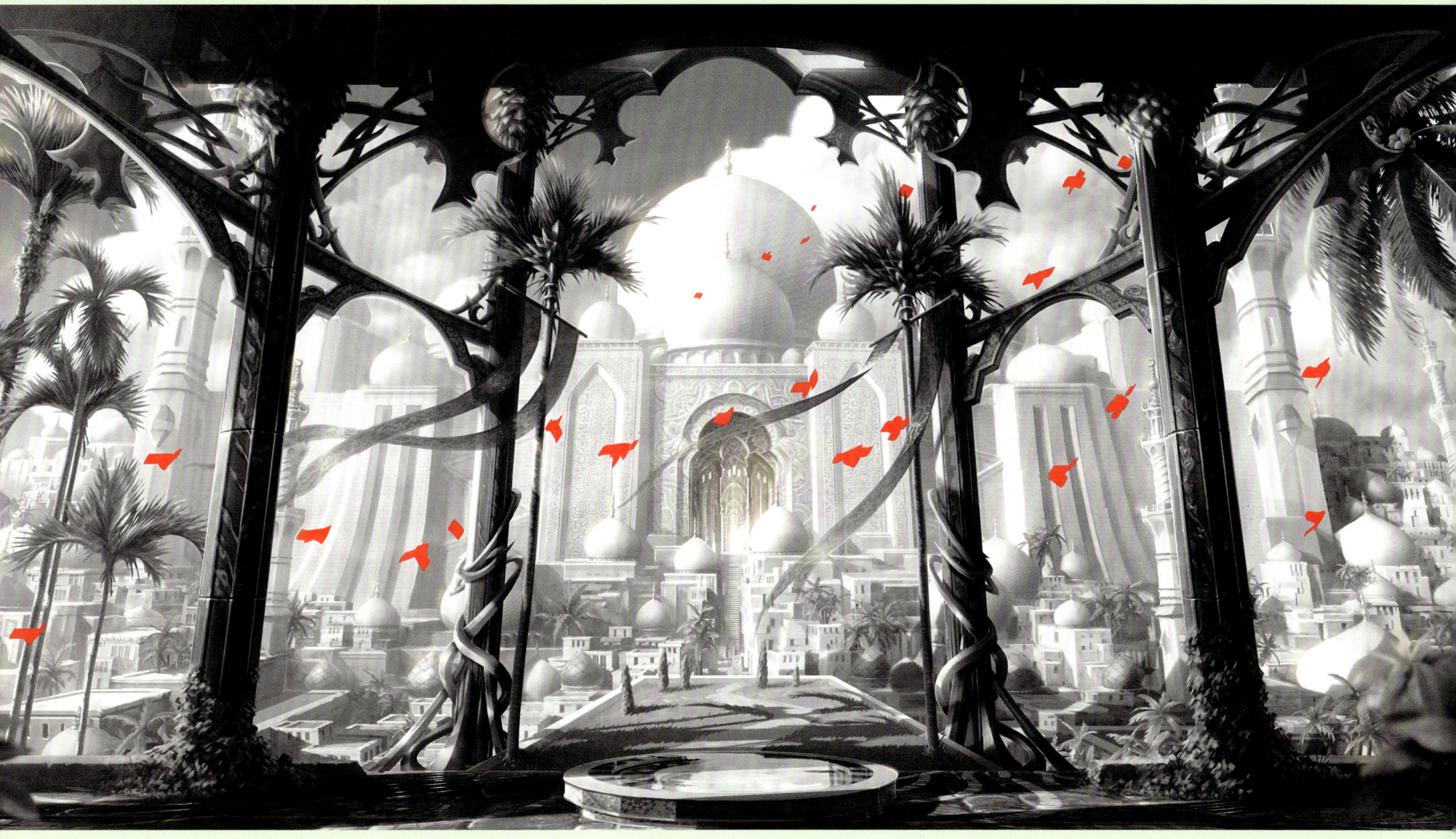

A flock of mysterious red birds is painted to provide lustre. The birds' shapes are also created using the silhouetting method to set the directions of their flight and movements. These birds are made to fly against the wind, contrary to the direction the flags are fluttering.

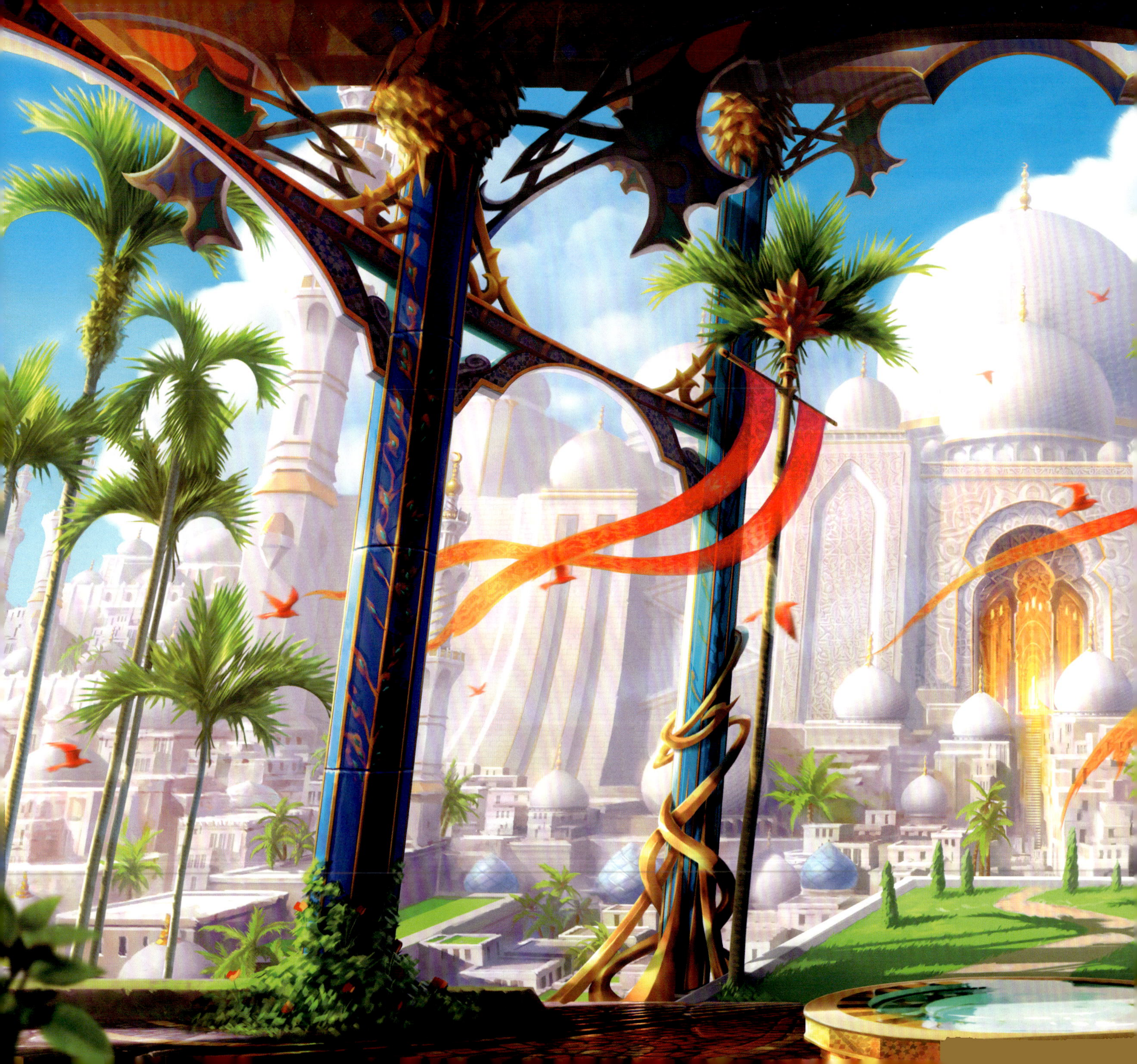

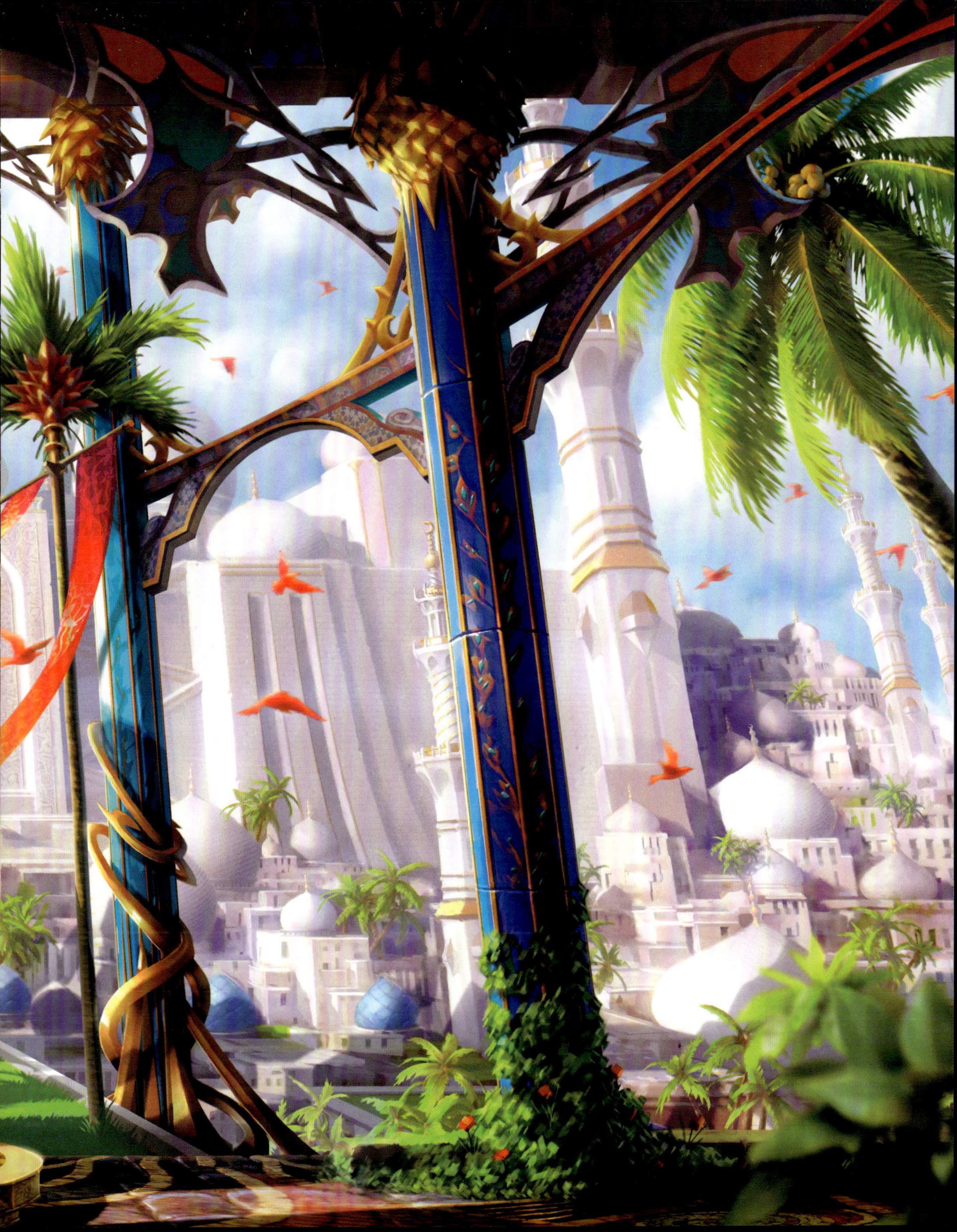

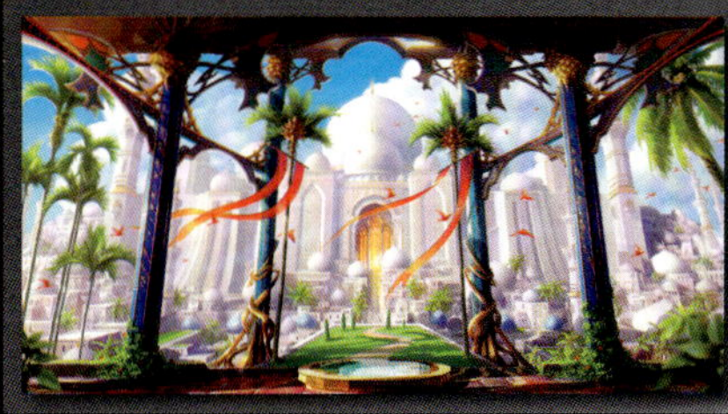

Then, adjustments are made to colours and brightness of some areas. The "glow effect" is brought out in some light-receiving areas. The work of art *White Mosque* is thus finished.

# MAIN POINTS

Global Illumination (GI) refers to the comprehensive effects of direct and indirect illumination created through numerous reflections and refractions of light from the main light source onto objects and bearing surfaces. Generally, its effects will be more obvious when it is applied to lighter or brighter coloured objects in the sunshine. The effects of GI are simulated in drawing *White Mosque*.

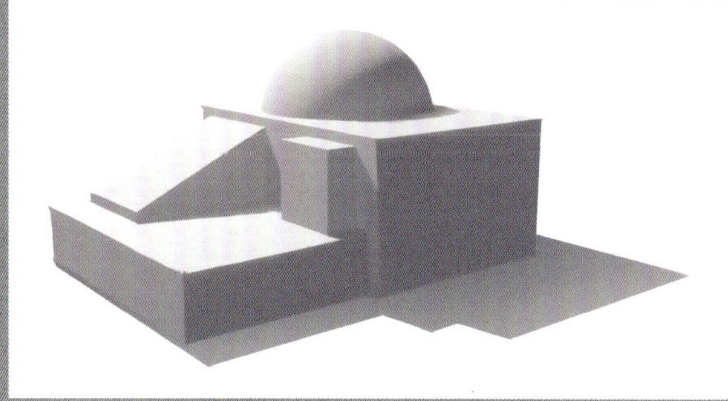

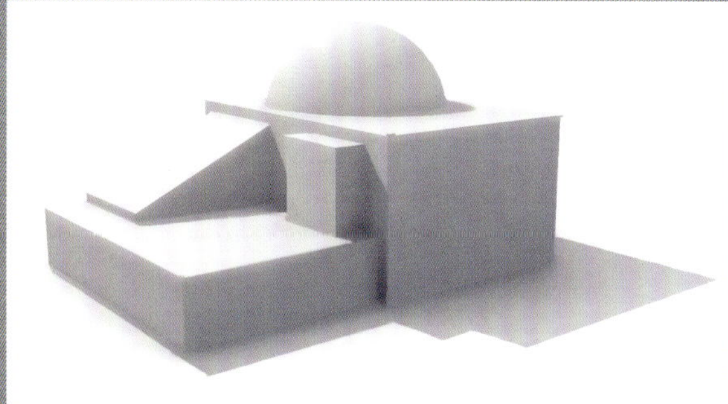

Comparing the left picture with the right, the one on the left shows normal lighting effects while the one on the right shows the effects of GI. Their difference is obvious. In the right picture, the illumination effects of the dark side increase and the declining effects of light and shade become more evident after light is reflected and refracted several times. GI from calculations in 3D software is accurate and real. When presented in painting, it requires a thorough understanding of its rationale and effects.

## 1

First, let's paint two boxes of a single bright colour. The light comes from the left to the right, which is presented in the simple method of flat painting.

## 2

Shadows of the two boxes are presented also in the method of flat painting. This is how the normal lighting effects are created.

## 3

Now, let's add more effects to the lighting. Between the red box and the green box, there is an angle in the area receiving no light. The declining effects of lighting are simulated in this area according to the depth of the angle to reinforce the tone of darkness. Similarly, the shadows at the top and bottom of the green box, due to their proximity to the light-receiving area, become less dark with more light reflected and refracted from the bright side. The tone of brightness, therefore, is adjusted according to the proximity to the bright side.

## 4

Due to radiosity, the intrinsic colours of the objects will directly influence the change of the lighting's colour after several reflections and refractions, thus bringing out the effects of GI. Light at the bottom of the boxes is influenced by their colours to make surrounding surfaces red and green, while areas close to light-receiving surfaces will become brighter in light density and colour. This is how the effects of GI are produced. This example is expected to help with understanding of how such effects are represented and applied.

## ▼ The effects of GI are also used for clouds on sunny days that feature a strong sense of volume and a white colour.

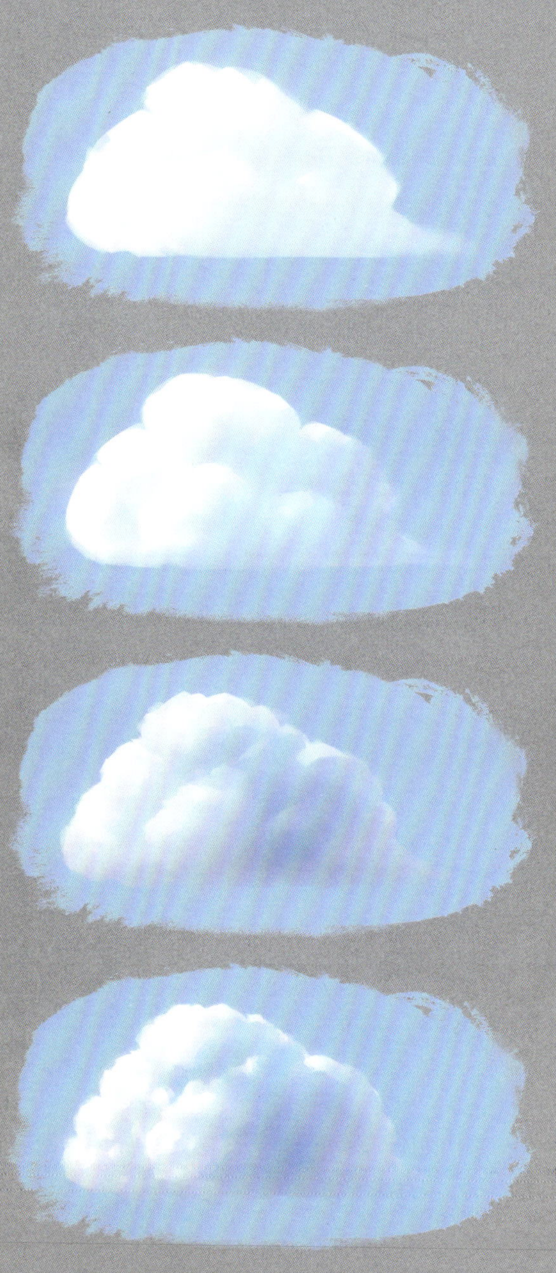

1

We start by sketching the outline of a cloud that has no clear-cut edges, as well as its intrinsic colour. Then, we add some lighting effects to the cloud.

A dark side is created for the cloud to enhance its sense of volume. However, the dark side of the cloud, as a moving object without physical bearing surfaces, should not be too dark. This is due to radiosity.

The effects of lighting are deepened, and the structure of the cloud is refined.

4

More details are added to improve the sense of realness.

5

On the dark side, a reflective hue of purple is added to give the cloud gradations and make it appear cleaner.

Clouds that seem as if they're being blown away by the wind added.

7

With the glow effect added, the thick clouds are depicted in the background of a blue sky on a sunny day. The clouds' sense of volume is strong while their impression of physicality is weak. Nevertheless, the current effects of GI will suffice since the clouds are mostly added to the scene's background.

# Souk

A bazaar is a place for trading. Since its opening hours and stand locations are fixed and the displays are orderly, each trader is able to adapt according to their personal conceptions and practices of what makes the best shopping experience. And thus, a unique space takes shape.

Most bazaars spring up along streets, whether makeshift stalls in the open air that flank a thoroughfare or a larger bazaar with criss-crossing passages like a spider's web or grid. Fixed street structures, open-air bazaars, and indoor markets with central planning and management all take the same basic structure as their template.

So far, we have drawn the "*hutongs* of Beijing" and the "business road of Dubai's new downtown", two types of "street" that are very different in essence. *Hutongs* are residential spaces that are primarily flanked by courtyard residences rather than for commercial use. They feature simple designs and shapes and a relatively tranquil environment. In contrast, the wide business road of Dubai's new downtown is lined with an array of high-rises and receives an endless stream of cars. These two types of "street" differ vastly from bazaars both in layout and in size. So how can this third type of street be presented in a painting? Despite these spaces' distinguishing features, we can still identify some similarities in them which might help us portray our bazaar. The sense of history and regional culture so prominent in *hutongs* can guide us in depicting the historical and social features of a bazaar and serve as reference for deciding upon the size of shops and the most appropriate perspective effects to use. As for the business streets of modern cities, their business and bustling atmosphere born out of the shopping culture they nourish provide a great template for representing several elements in a compact space.

Mostly located in the Old Town, bazaars in Dubai, or "souks" as our piece will be called, preserve the features of ancient Arabic architecture and layout. Even the Souk Madinat Jumeirah in Dubai's new downtown is built in an antique style. At a glance, it's clear that souks in Dubai are not purely places of trade but carriers of culture. In order to give expression to this role, we need to include aspects of the Old Town and features of traditional architecture alike.

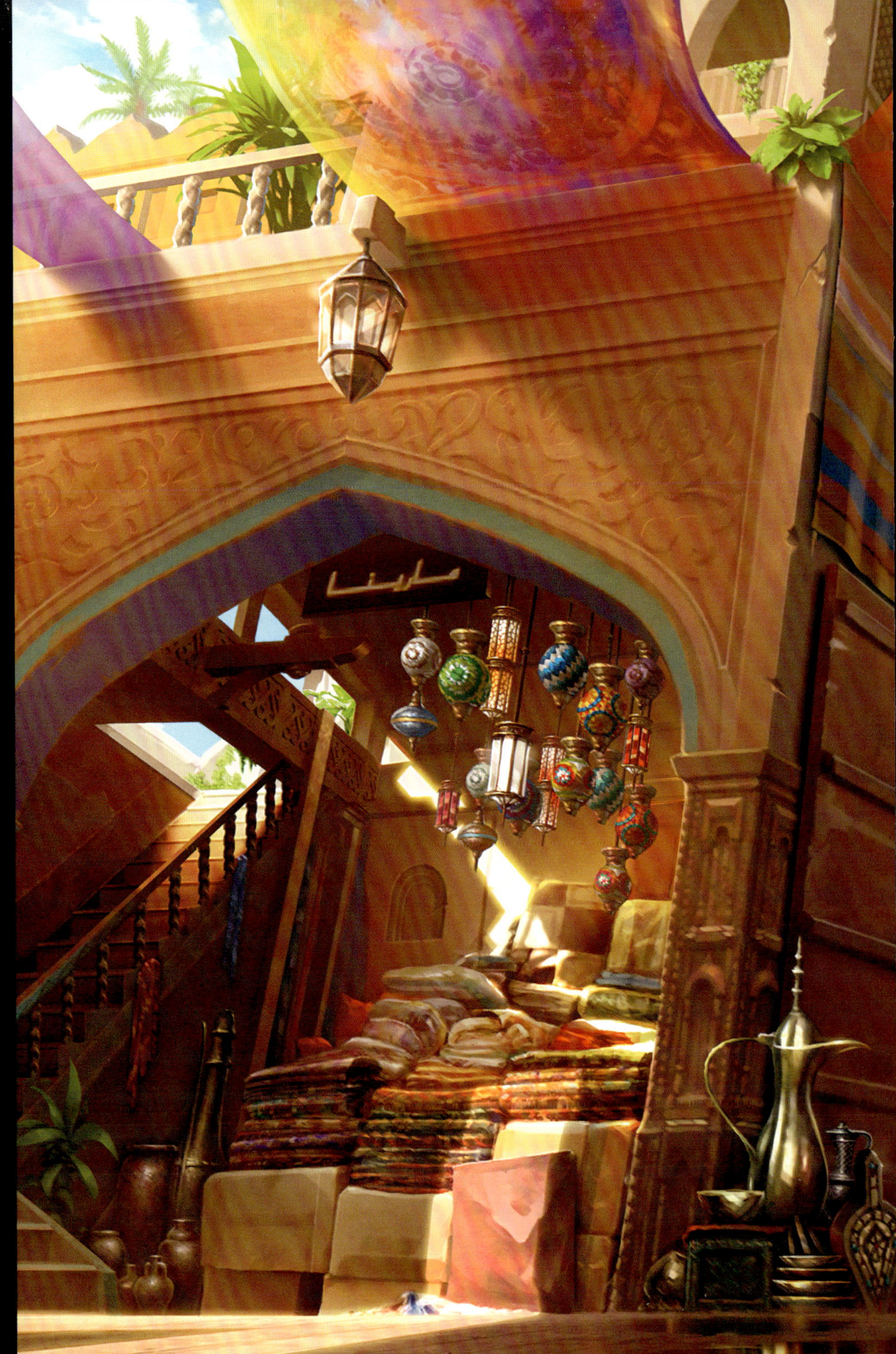

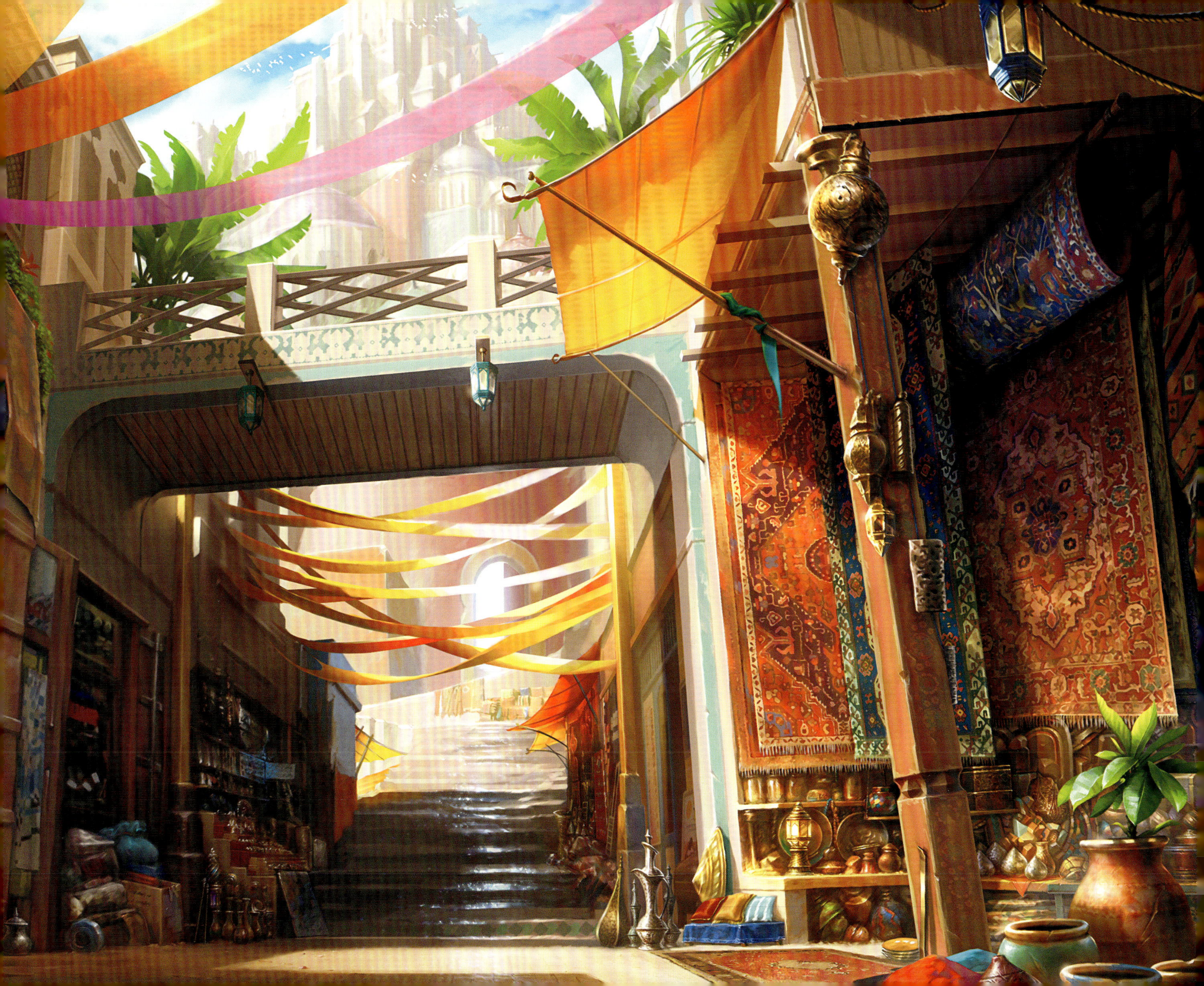

# THOUGHTS ON CREATION

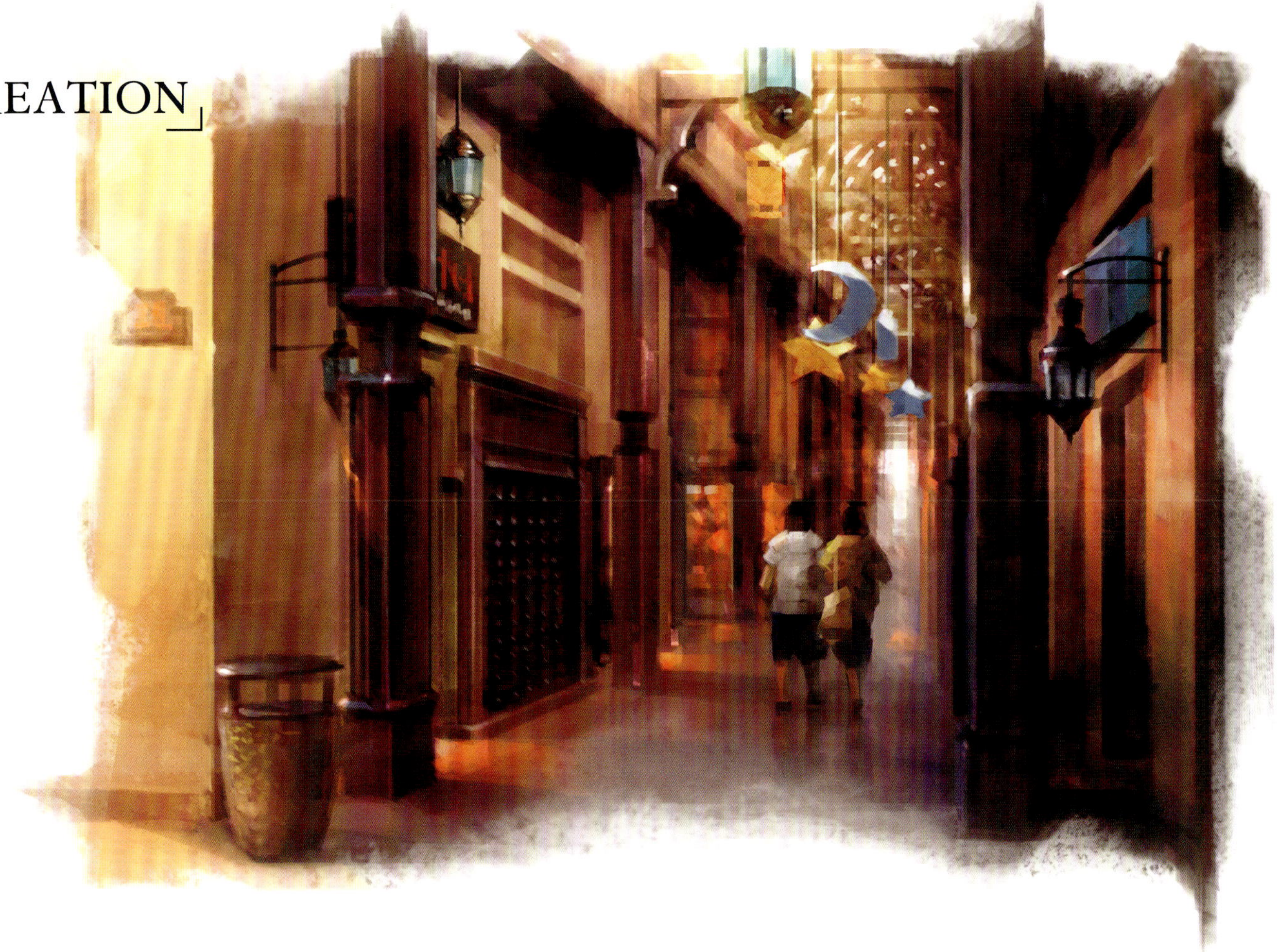

*In drawing Souk, we need to consider the surroundings, including street corners, lanes and other geographical characteristics, have a clear knowledge of customs as reflected in different types of houses, and understand the functions of certain architectural features. Then, upon a foundation of accurately captured local characteristics, we can begin to construct our fantasy scene.*

The Souk Madinat Jumeirah is a modern structure that preserves the characteristics of traditional Arab open-air souks in its vintage shapes and indoor decorations. Commodities on sale are mostly traditional handicrafts and various artefacts with Middle Eastern characteristics. The market was built to reproduce the architectural forms and shopping culture of ancient Arab souks.

Roaming the souk, you may feel you have stepped into the past. There are no shouts of hawking street vendors. From above the serene and empty souk, rays of sunshine come through an awning to cast light on the hanging moon and star-shaped ornaments. Visitors here feel frozen in the flux of time drifting along a plane all of their own.

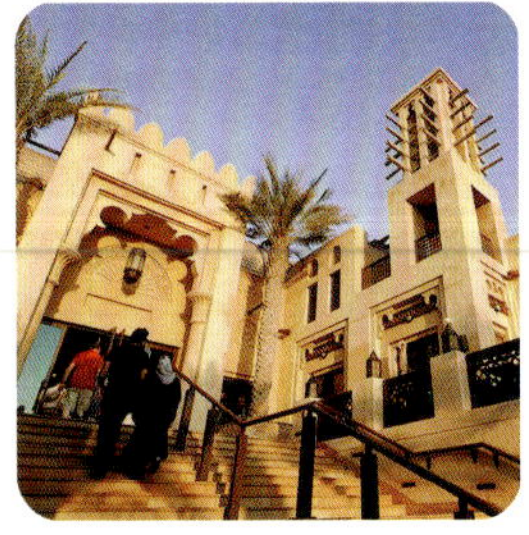

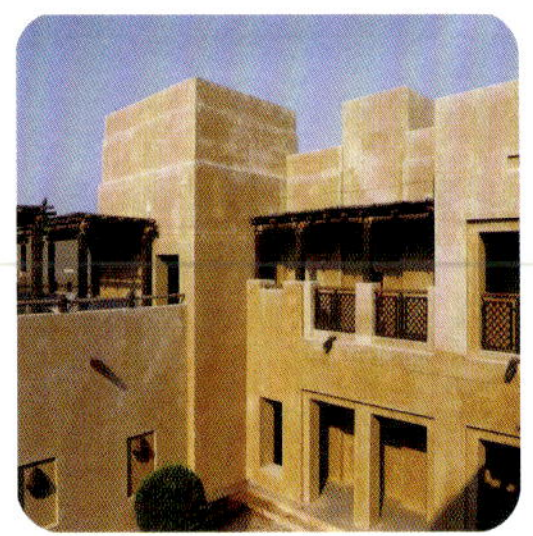

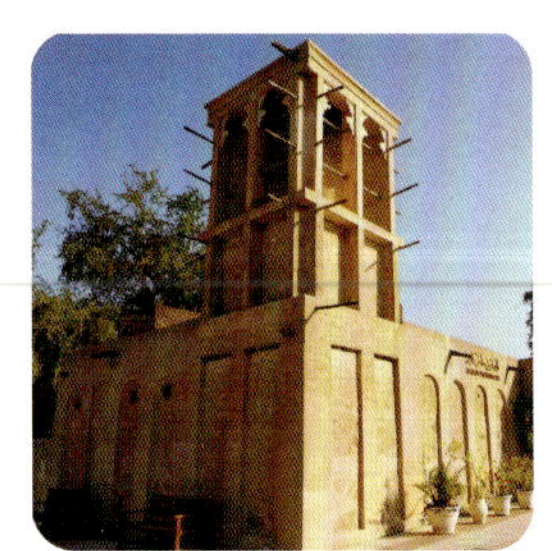

## ◀ WIND TOWER

In the Al Fahidi Historical Neighbourhood, or Bastakiya Old Town, there is a traditional architectural element called the "wind tower". It is a tower-shaped structure invented by the ancient Arabs that has openings along its sides to dispel heat in the desert, serving a similar purpose as airconditioners to pull away hot air and bring cool air to an indoor environment. Nowadays, such architectural elements remain characteristic of historical Arabic residences, visible everywhere in the modern Madinat Jumeirah.

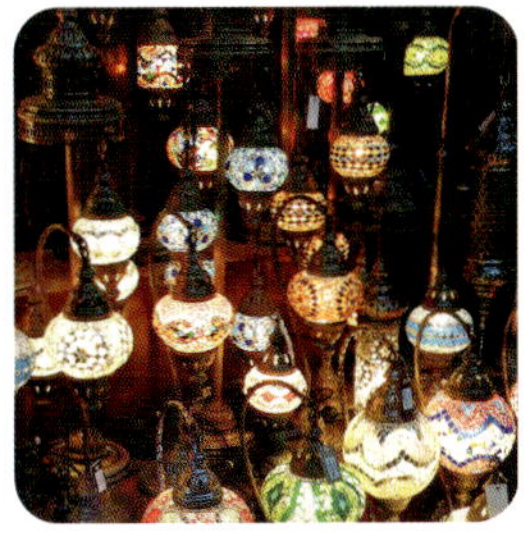

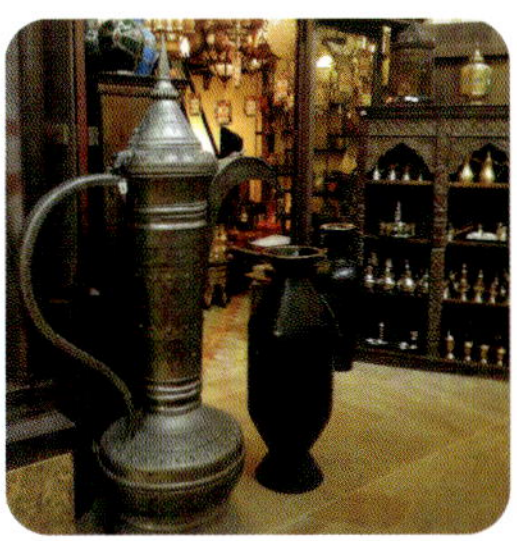

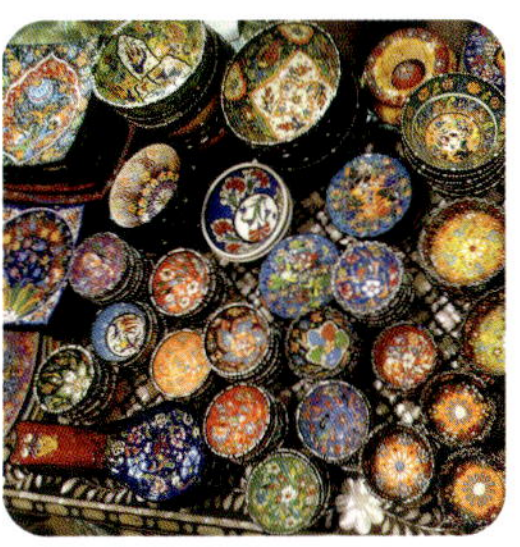

## ▲ LAMPS MADE OF COLOURED GLASS

Made of coloured glass, the lamps sold at this market bear a strong Middle Eastern flavour, and the coloured bowls and dishes boast the whole gamut of bright colours and rich patterns. Long-tubular jars and vessels, shishas, and bottled sand art popular in modern times are just a few of the unique handicrafts on sale in the Souk Madinat Jumeirah.

Souks in Dubai are more refined than the Grand Bazaar in Istanbul. No matter the traditional Gold Souk and the Spice Souk in Old Town Dubai, or the Souk Madinat Jumeirah which blends the modern with the vintage, they all cover small areas and line shorter streets with no complicated byroads between the stands. However, commodities on sale are diverse. With these features in mind, we can go on designing the layout for *Souk*.

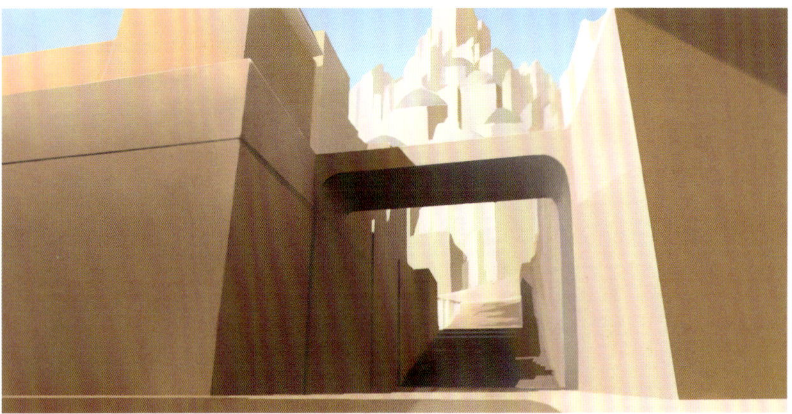

A rudimentary form is drafted. This time, the viewer perspective is to set up close to the ground at an upward angle which gives the street another axis of depth besides straight back. Like traditional souks in Dubai, the main street is given about five to six shops while multistory castle-like structures give a sense of gradation and a touch of fantasy. The two shops in the foreground dominate the scene and can be filled with a dazzling array of commodities.

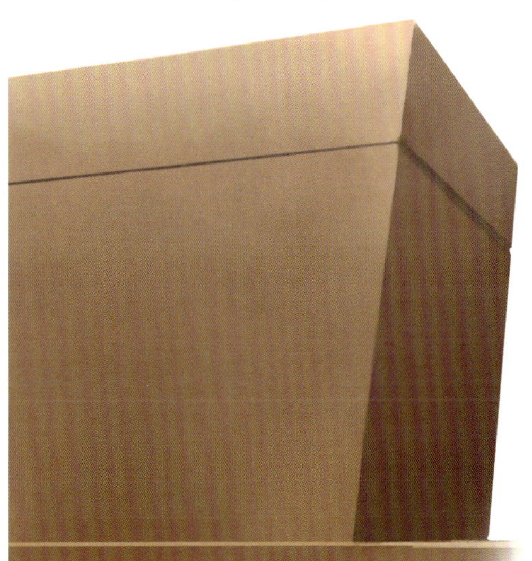

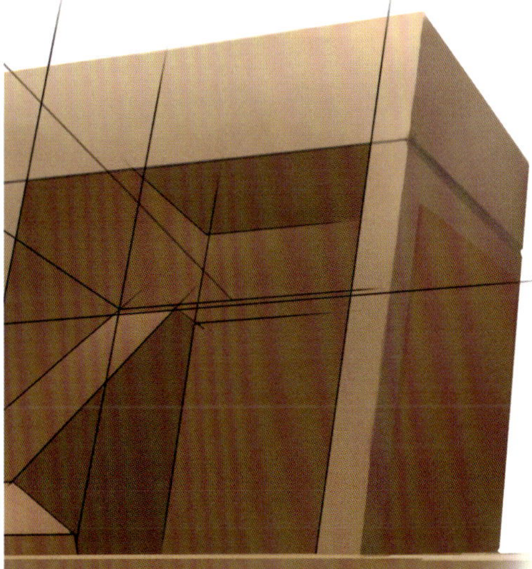

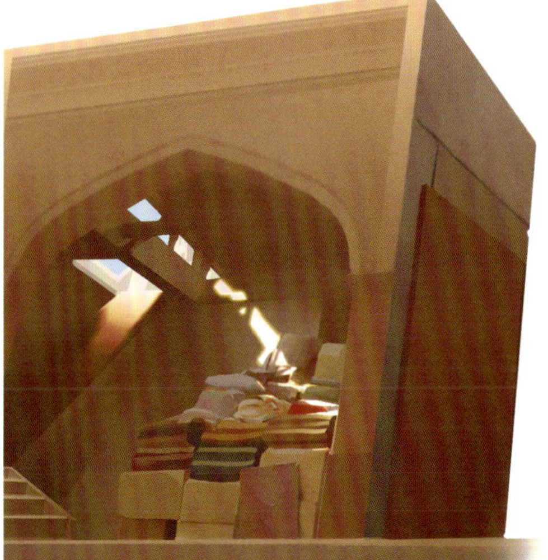

The sketches of these box-like structures are refined by using guiding lines to help with perspective. With the shop interiors and doorways completed, the souk has already begun to take shape.

The shop on the right is a semi-open shed that primarily sells carpets and crafted vessels. The one on the left is an arched structure in the Arab style selling silk and coloured glass lamps. These typical local commodities with exquisite shapes, bright colours and rich textures perfectly present the distinguishing details and theme of this design.

The shop to the right is in a light-receiving area. Given its layout, most of its commodities glitter in the sunshine. The arched structure on the left is backlit. Looking upward, we can see a blue sky peeking through the opening of the staircase leading to the top of the structure. Rays of sunshine come in through the opening, contrasting starkly with the predominant darkness of the space and adding a sense of rhythm to the entire scene.

A wind tower is drawn in an obvious but not prominent position, enriching the piece's regional flavour. Street buildings are mostly painted a faint yellowish brown. The single colour foregrounds the dazzling array of commodities in various bright colours.

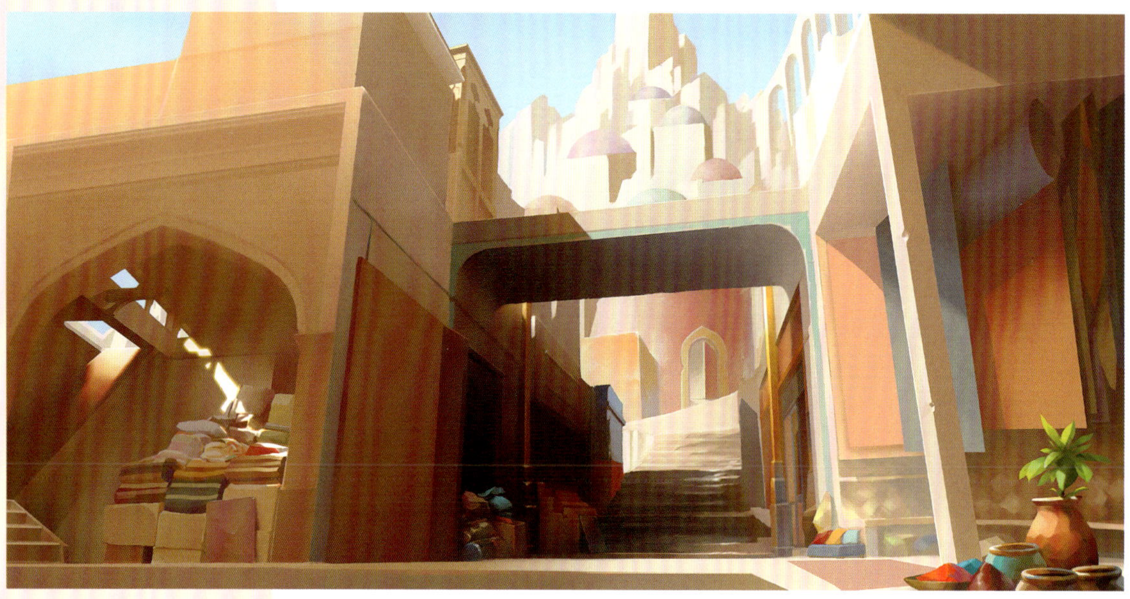

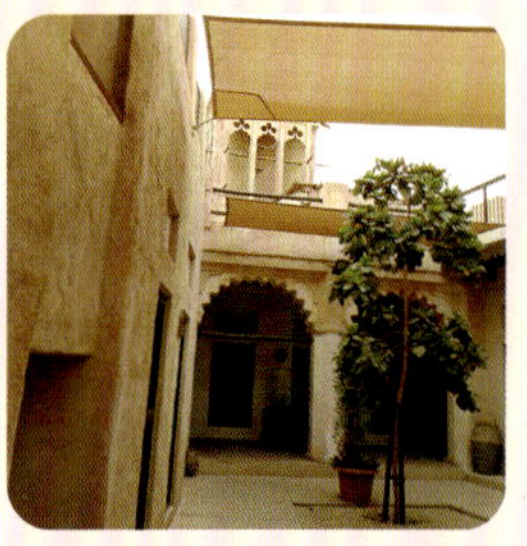

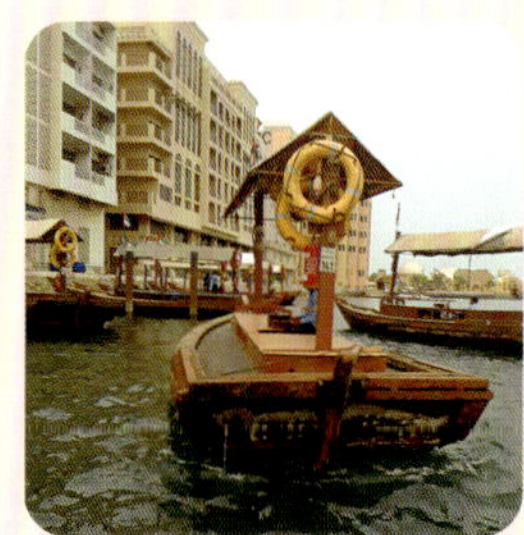

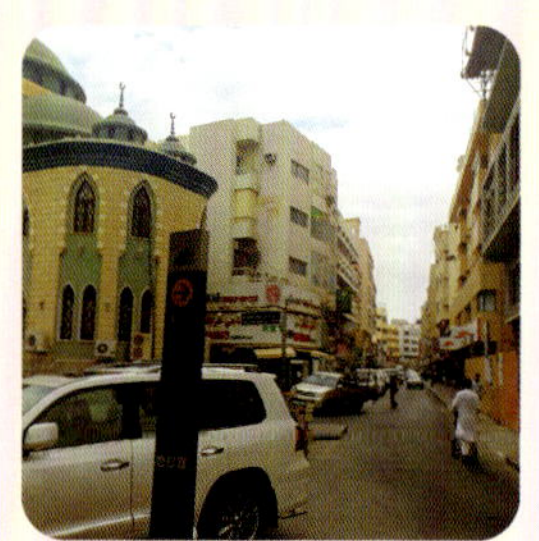

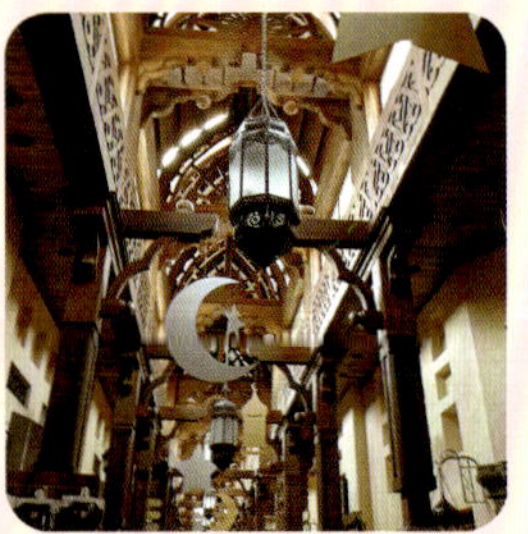

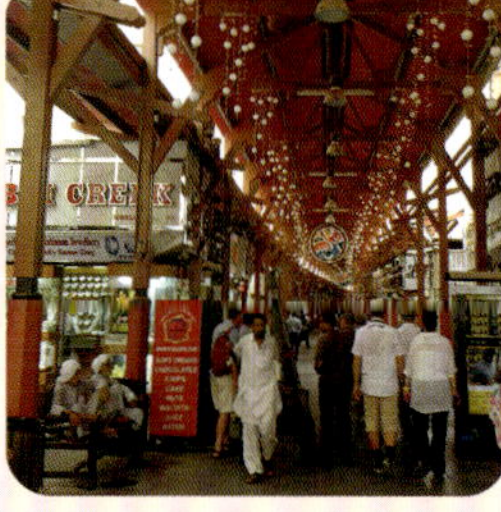

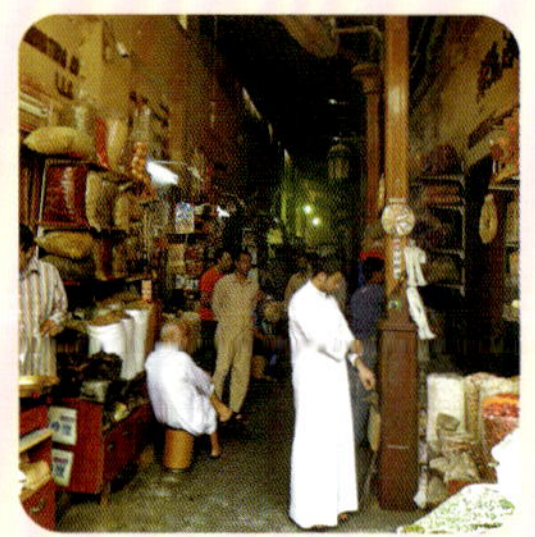

## ◀ THE MOTHER RIVER

The Dubai Creek, the mother river of Dubai, divides the city into two main sections. The west side of the creek is home to the modern new downtown with its many high-rises, while the east is the Old Town built in the traditional Arabic style. Having developed from a fishing village into what it is today, Dubai has not forgotten its "roots". Here, all historical sites are preserved and history recorded. Traditional architecture and bazaars still in use today are living proof of the vicissitudes unfolded in this city.

## ◀ SHOPPING

Crossing the Dubai Creek, you first arrive at the Spice Souk and the Gold Souk. The shopping experience here is not as enjoyable as that in the Souk Madinat Jumeirah, a new type of souk managed in a modern way. Open air souks have no other means of cooling the space except for a few electric fans when the temperature reaches 40 degrees or above. These markets are crowded with people of all races, commodities are piled up everywhere, and the entire scene bustles with prosperity.

## ▶ COMMODITIES

Compared with the new downtown markets, the commodities here, mainly the products of folk artisanship, have a more unique character. Handicrafts, gold jewellery and spices are the major commodities sold in this old souk. It's a truly dazzling array of goods.

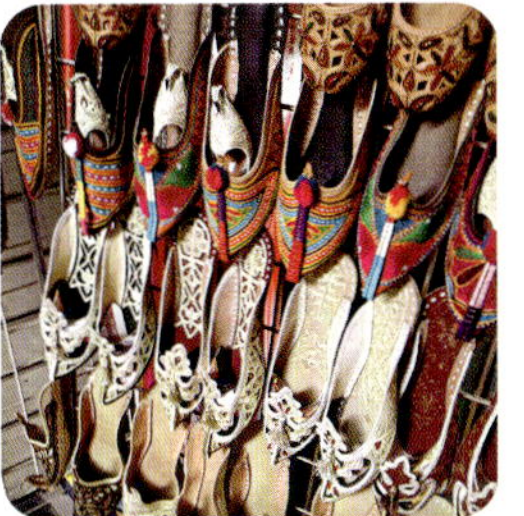

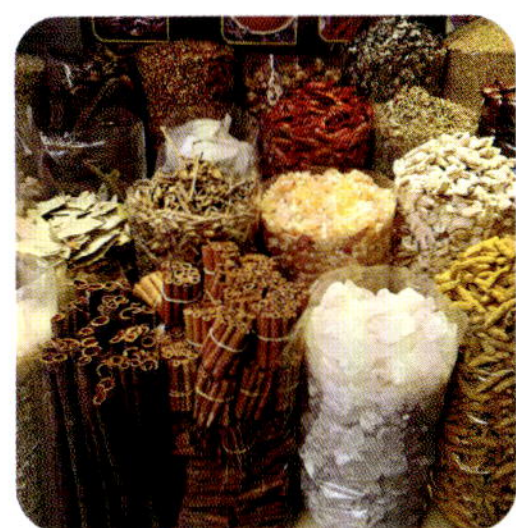

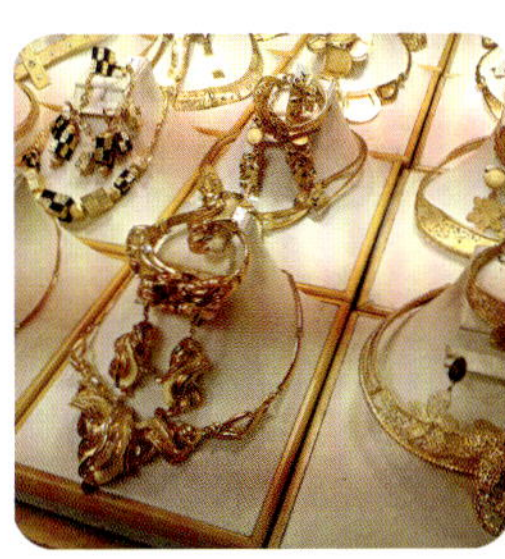

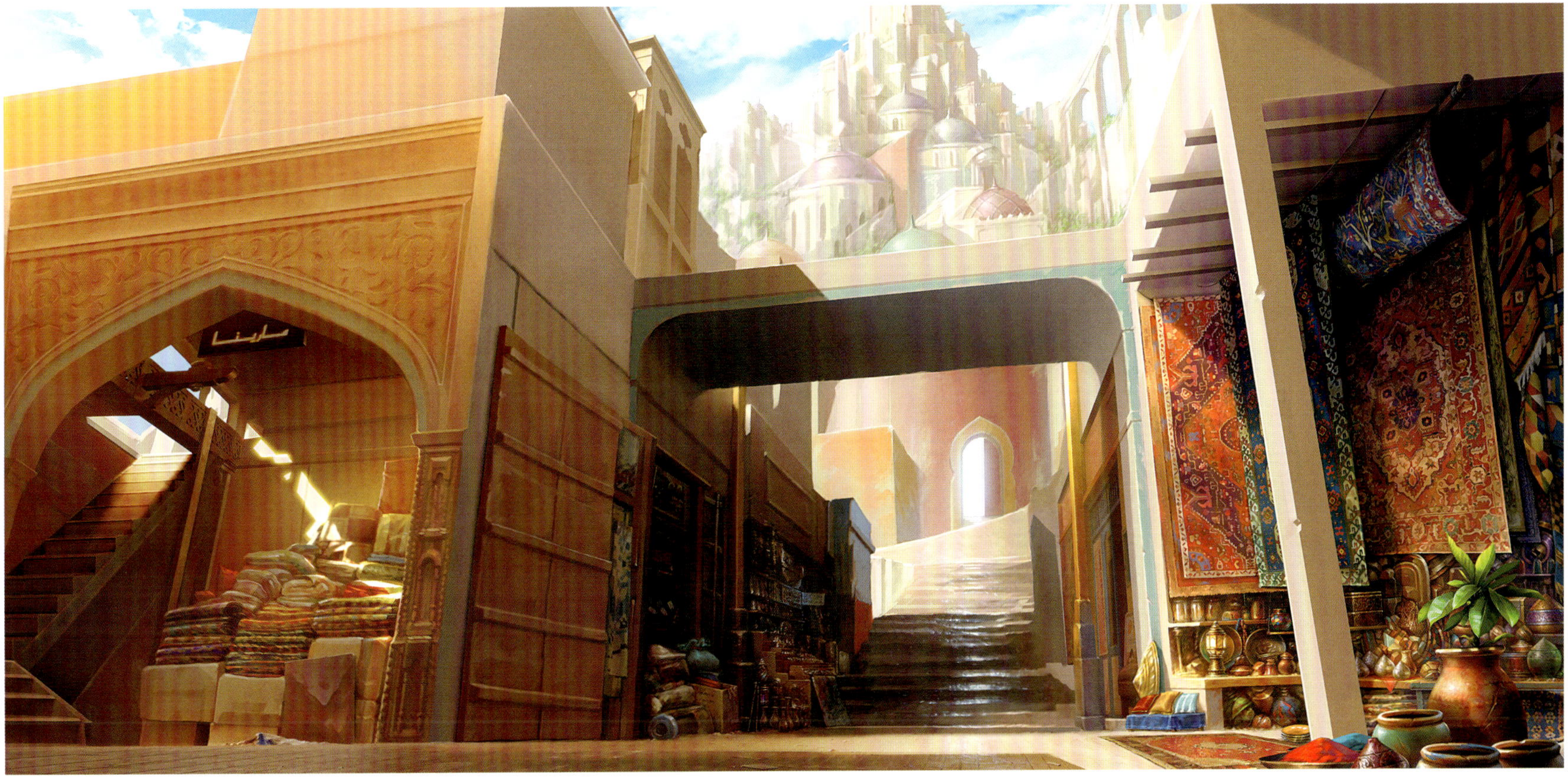

Based on knowledge and materials above, we now begin depicting the goods on display and architectural details. Commodities tend to be collected in certain places with particular types grouped together in a slightly disorderly way. While a diverse combination of colours is desirable, large areas of contrasting colours are likely to damage the entire tone of the scene and so should be avoided.

Still in the process of refinement, we continue to highlight the contrast of light and shade and the textures it brings. Light shines out through the door at the end of the street, creating a sense of mystery. To integrate this effect with the stone stair running down the centre, spots of light are added to the steps to give the impression of a wet floor texture. The sky and the building complex furthest in the background are shaped first so as not to need further refinement at a later stage. The complex is built up and connected to the foreground by the stone stair.

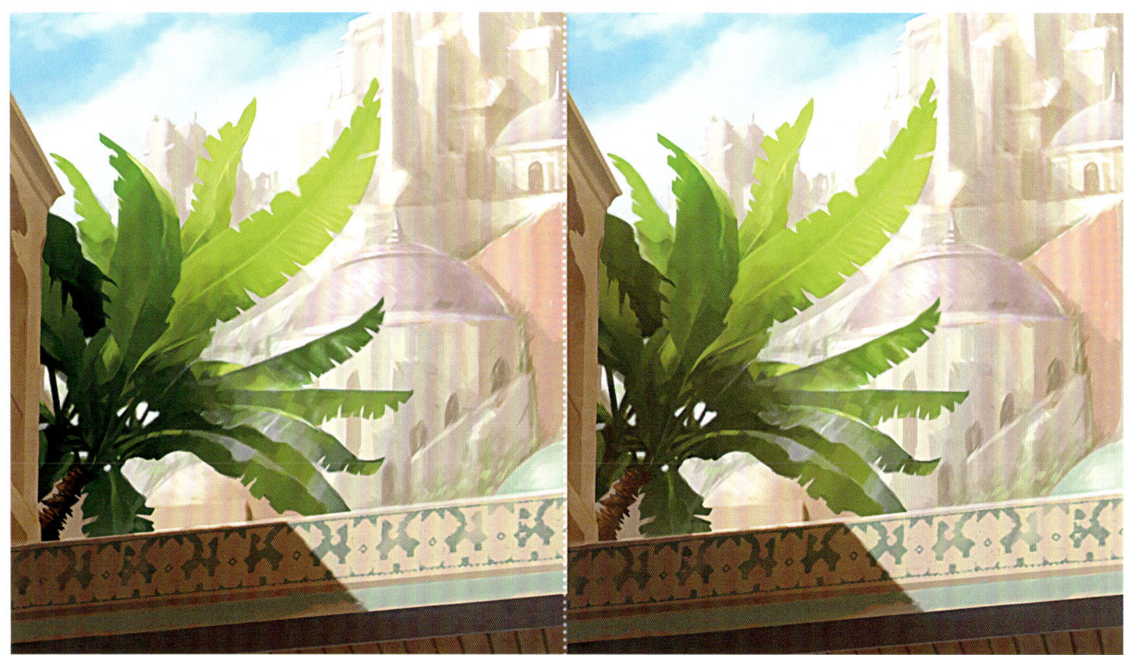

Palm trees and Musa basjoo plants are important elements for injecting vitality and more local flavour into the scene. "Frontlighting, backlighting and light-transmitting (sub-surface scattering, or '3S' for short)" effects are applied according to their positions. According to the distance of plants from the foreground, fog and colour temperature effects are adjusted to integrate them perfectly into the scene.

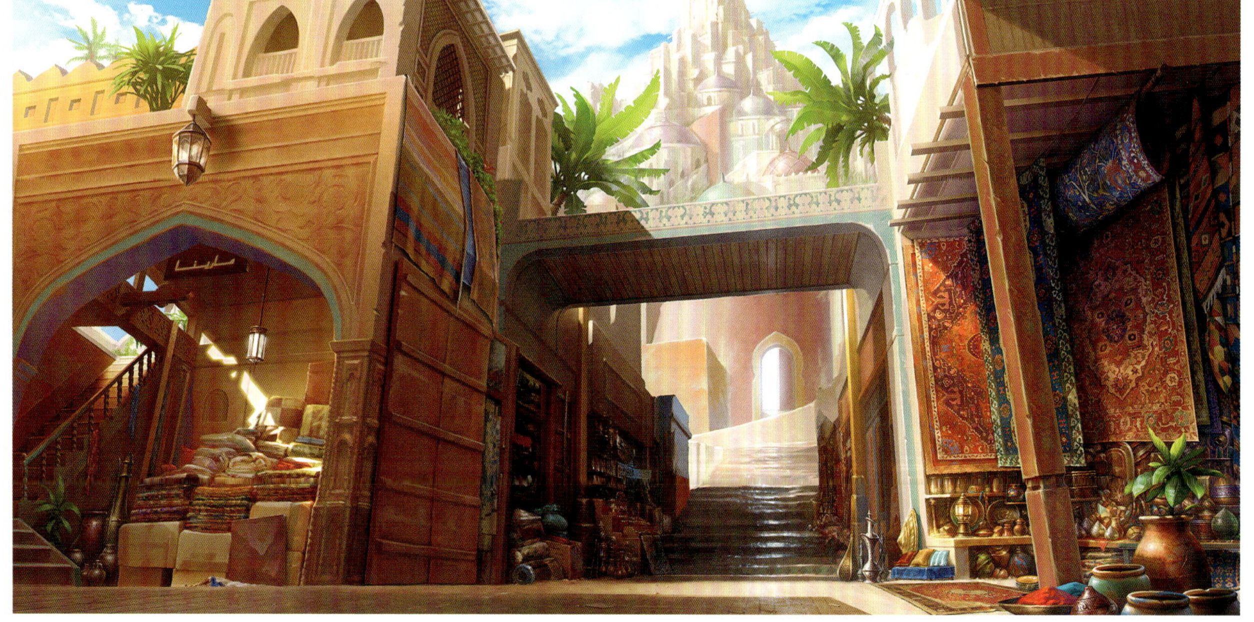

In addition to plants, we also need to refine the second-floor building structures and interior structure of the shops in the foreground, that includes the "wooden pillars, beams, and the staircase handrail". More commodities are drawn in the currently blank areas so as to diversify the scene. Floral patterns and other such details are painted on the walls and damaged areas are added to the corners of buildings.

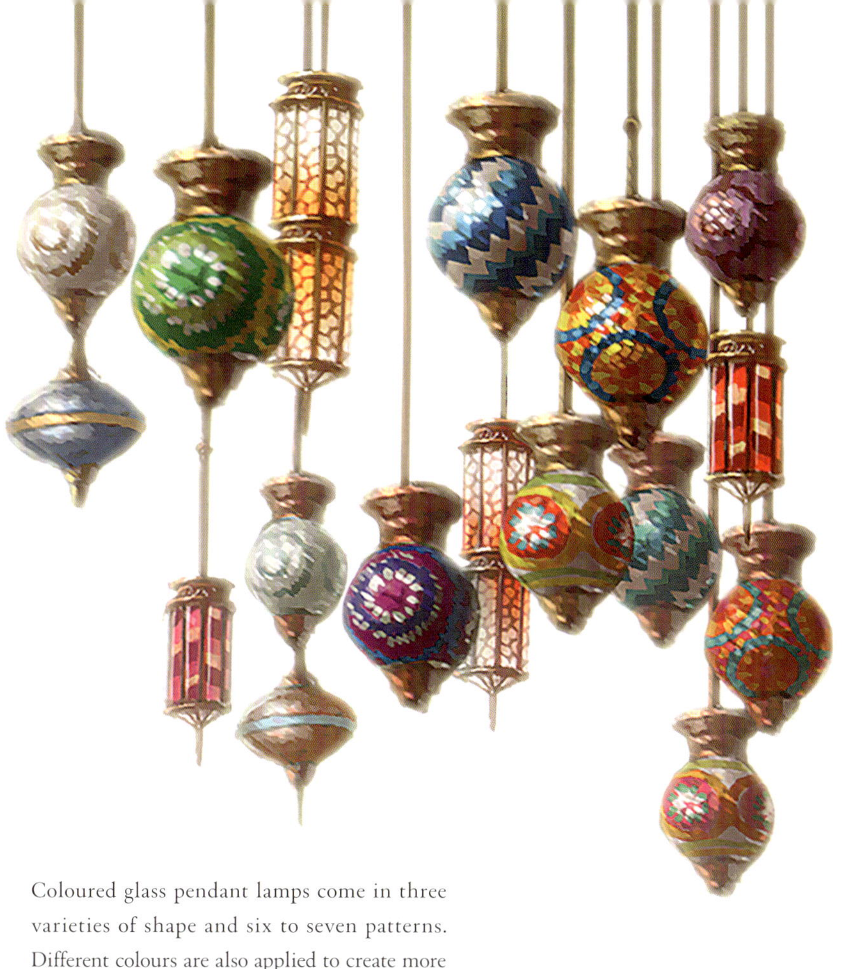

Coloured glass pendant lamps come in three varieties of shape and six to seven patterns. Different colours are also applied to create more combinations of brightly-coloured lamps.

These lamps are painted hanging from the arched shop's ceiling in a way that conforms to the viewer's angle of perspective. Similar to the treatment of plants, fog effects and ambient colours help to integrate them into the scene. In the backlit area, the coloured lamps appear all the more dazzling. It is important to shape objects in light of their expressiveness under different lighting effects and their environments.

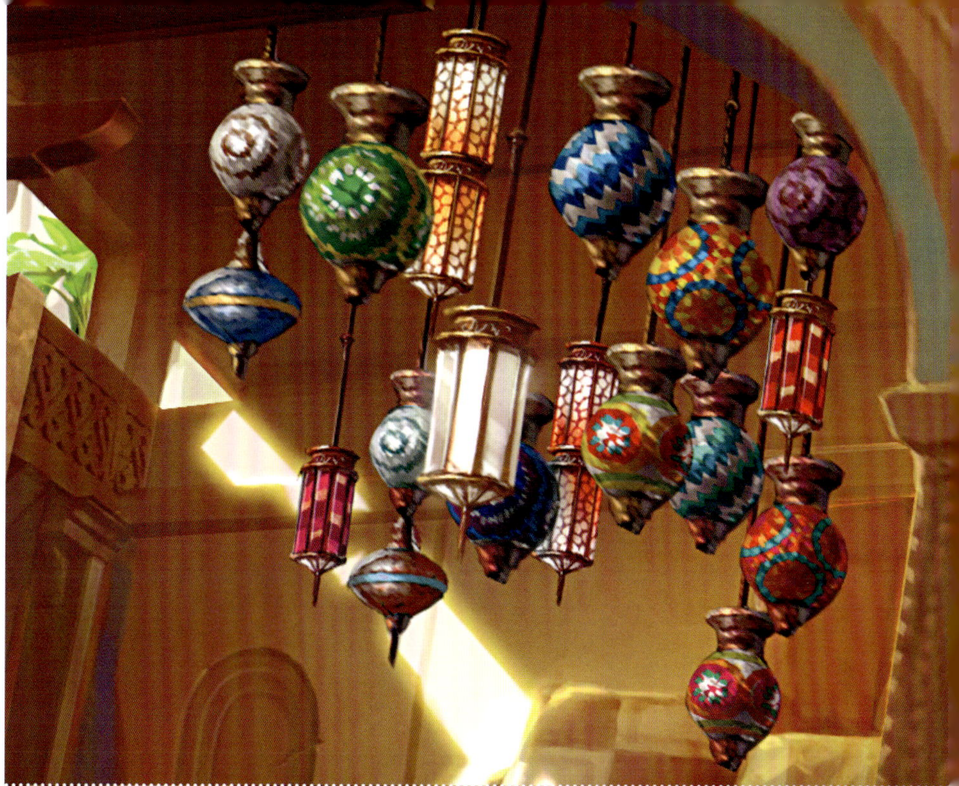

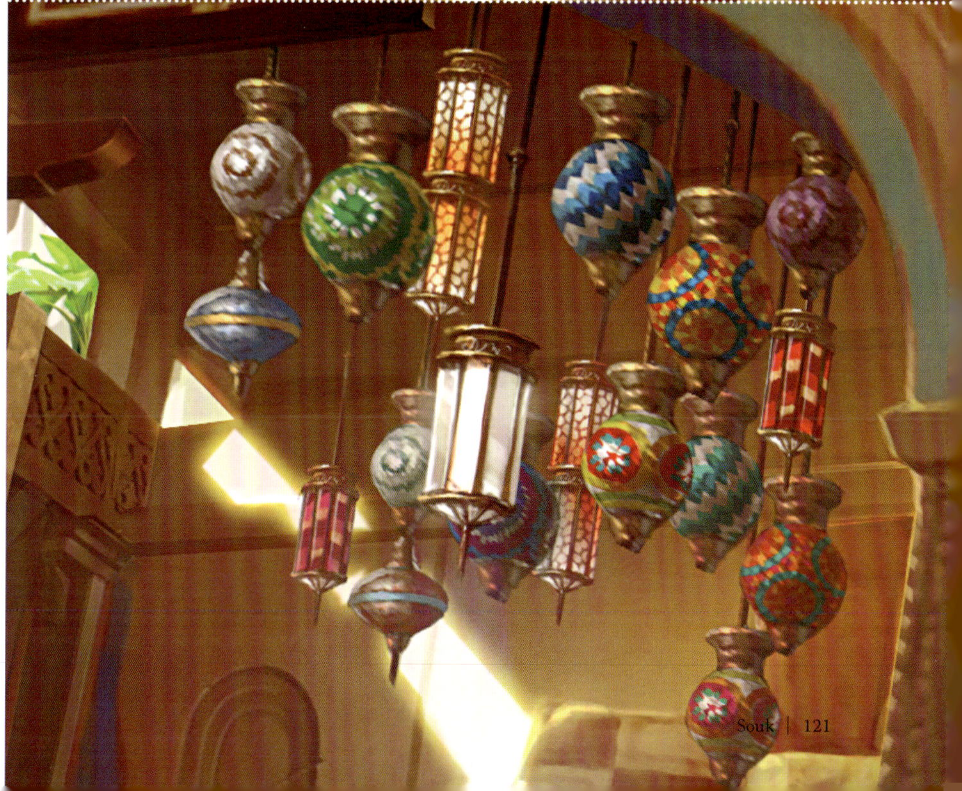

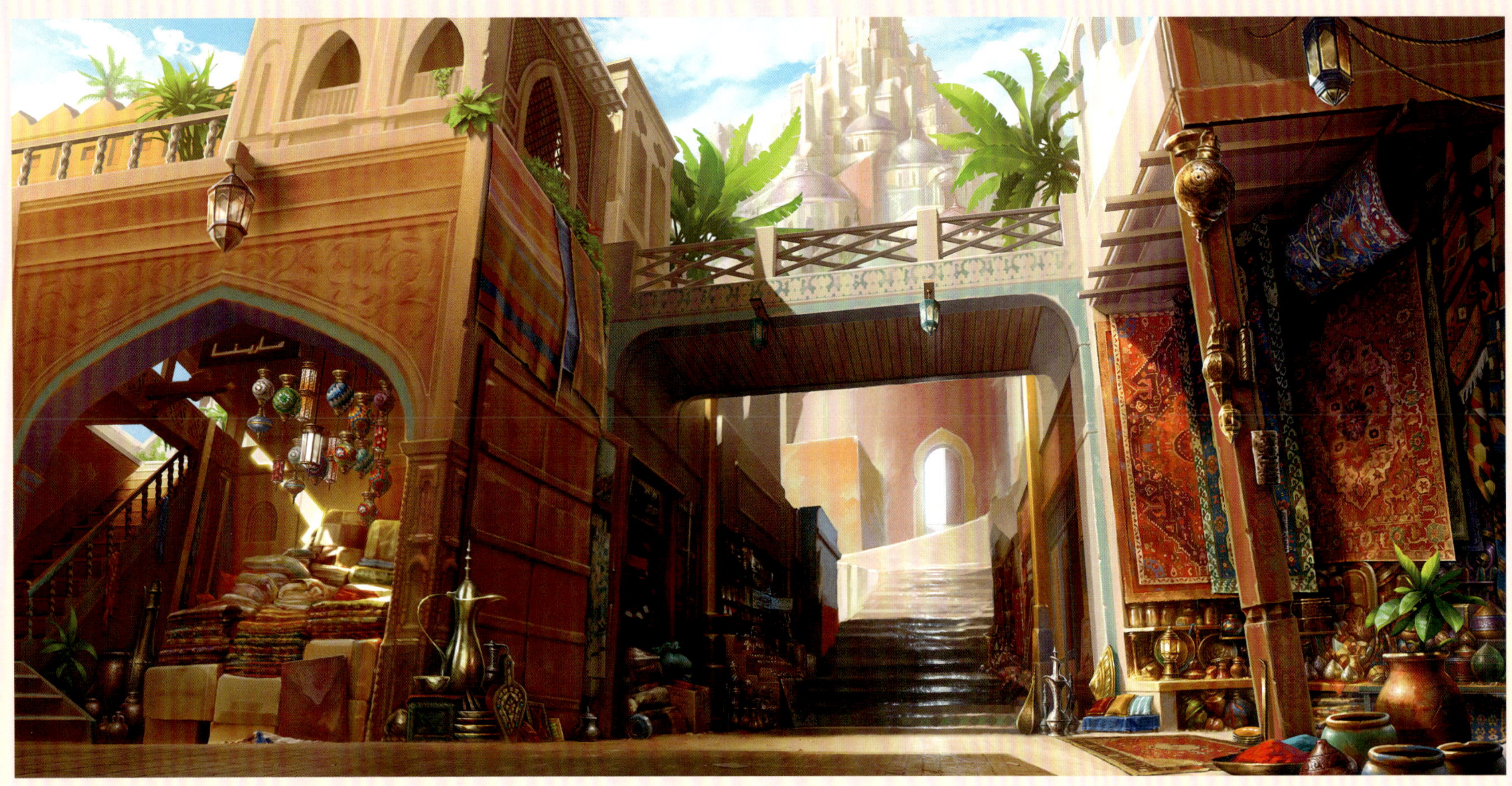

As more details are added and refined, other objects begin to appear dull by comparison. Further elements should be included in areas around these objects so as to enrich the atmosphere. This could mean drawing in a shisha pipe and antiques by the old door or metal handicrafts hanging on the wooden pillar in the shop. Also, wooden rails on the overpass and street lamps are added. At this point, the chief elements of *Souk* are completed.

Essential details are now added, such as awnings, canvases and canopies. Canvases and canopies serve the function to protect people from the sun. In terms of the design, we can also use them to balance the layout of objects and scene's colours. Apart from shops that need shade, they are also applied to any empty areas which only contain a single colour.

Canvases and canopies that are primarily made of linens are liable to transmit light and the shapes of rear objects based on their thickness. Therefore, they should not be added until all the main objects are completed, and then the material's transparency can be properly adjusted.

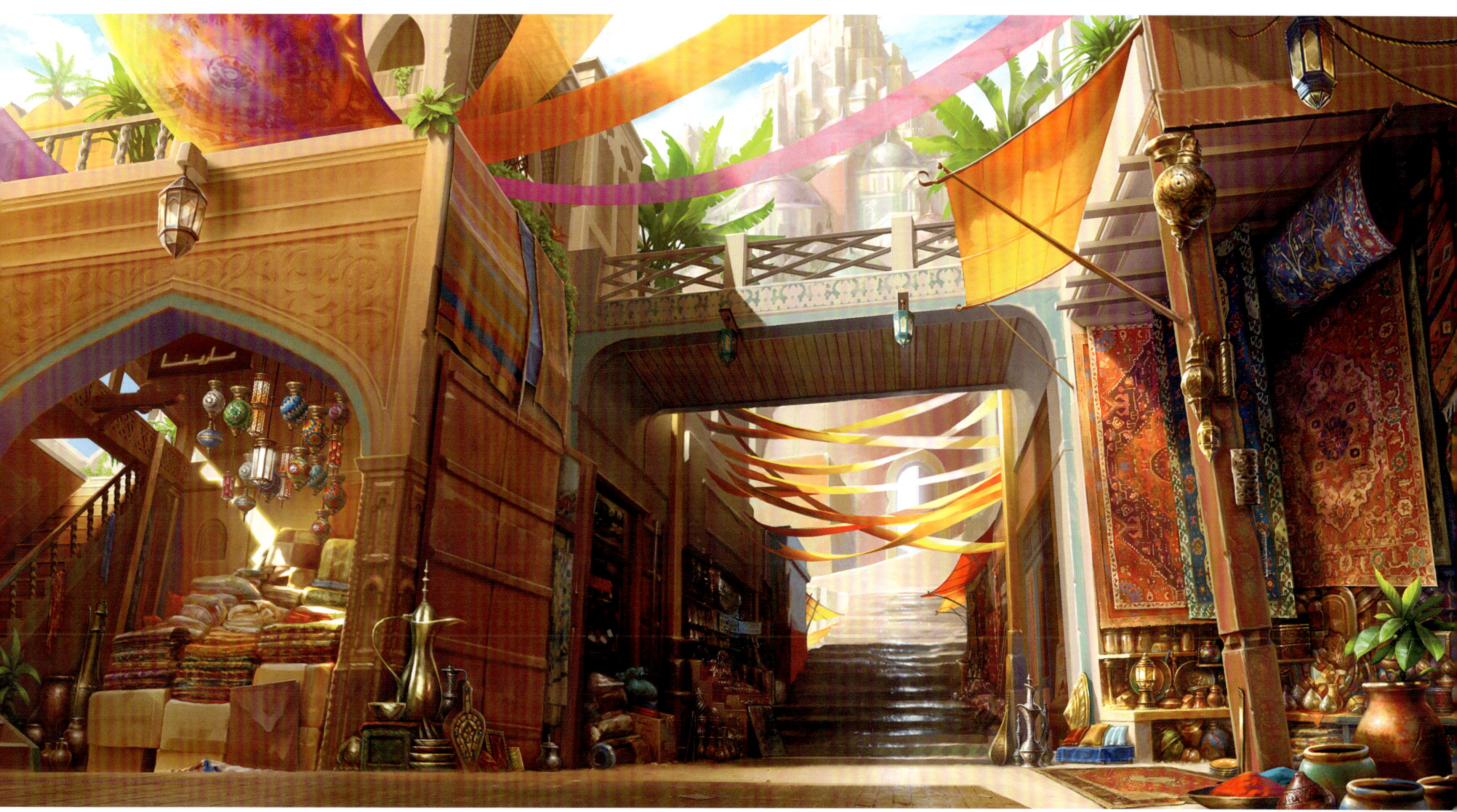

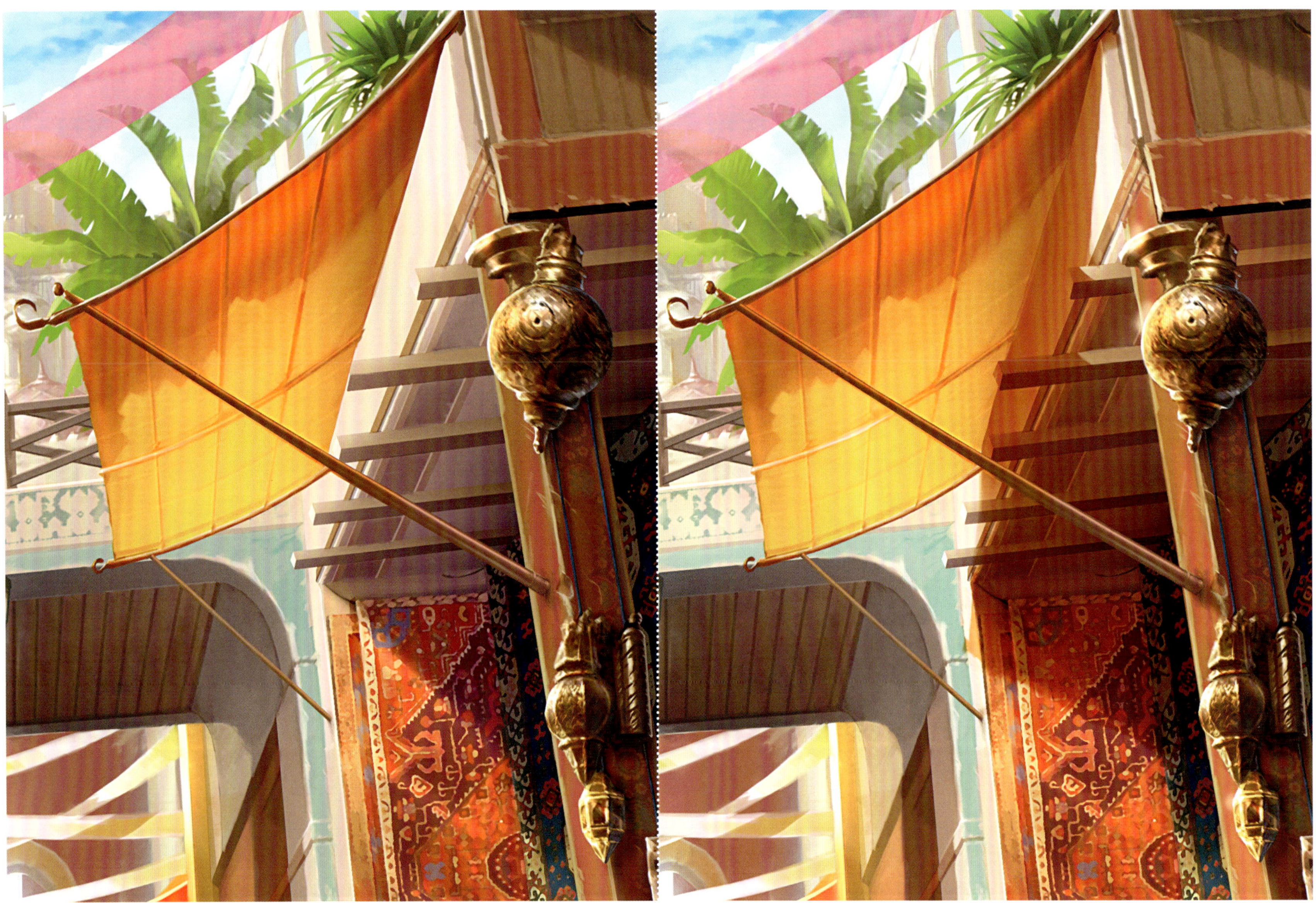

Shadows are created in the areas shaded by the awnings and canopies, and the shadows that were added earlier should be adjusted accordingly. Taking into account the transparency of awnings and canopies and the principle of "radiosity across global lighting", the new shadows should be affected by the awnings' orange colour reflecting onto them, producing a different shade of colour.

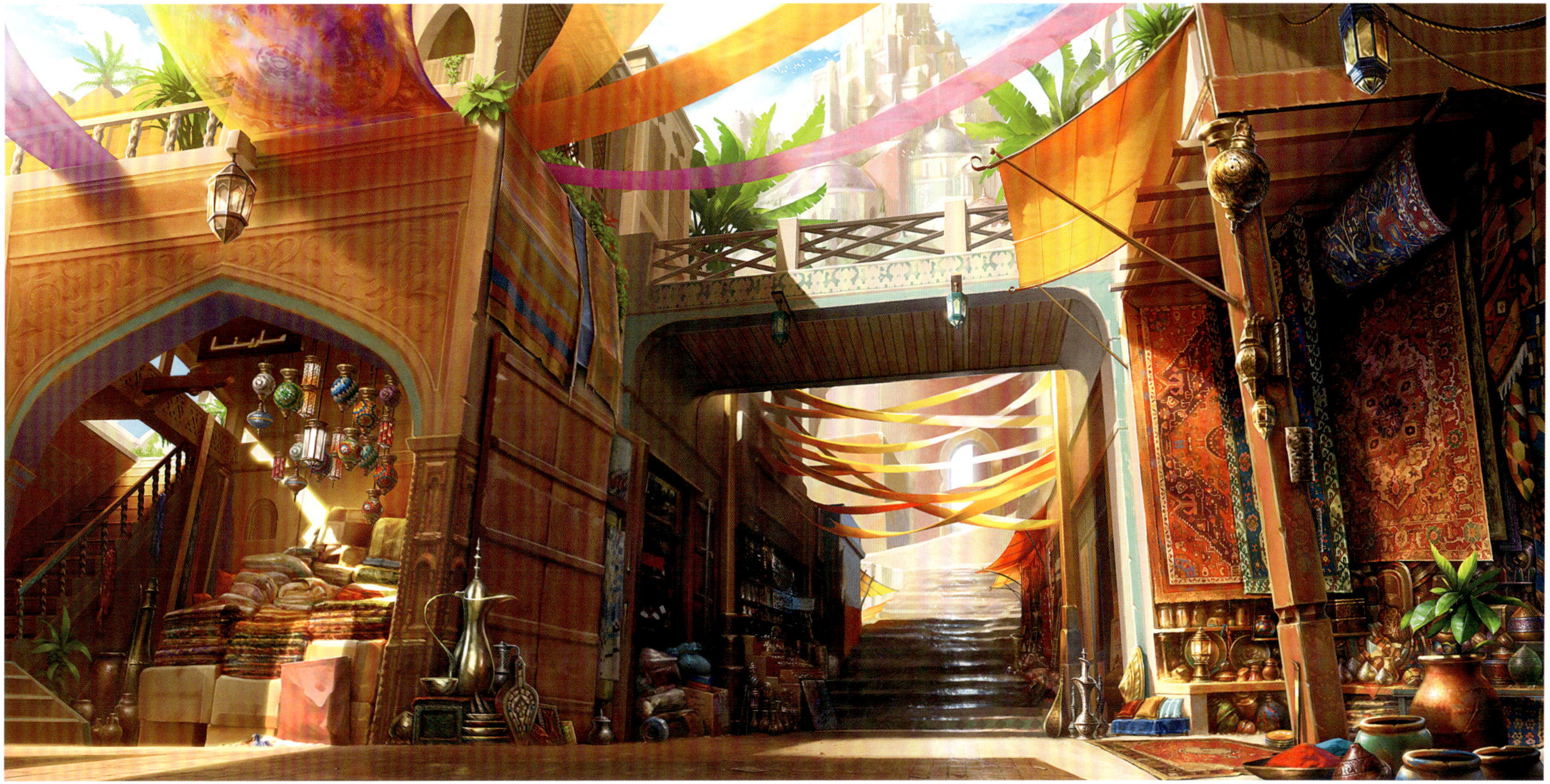

Shadows from the awnings, canvases and canopies are also refined according to the same principle, and a streak of light is added leaking into the left shop to simulate light cast by an external source to the frame.

This should solve the problem of weak brightness in this area and balance the brightness and darkness of the entire scene.

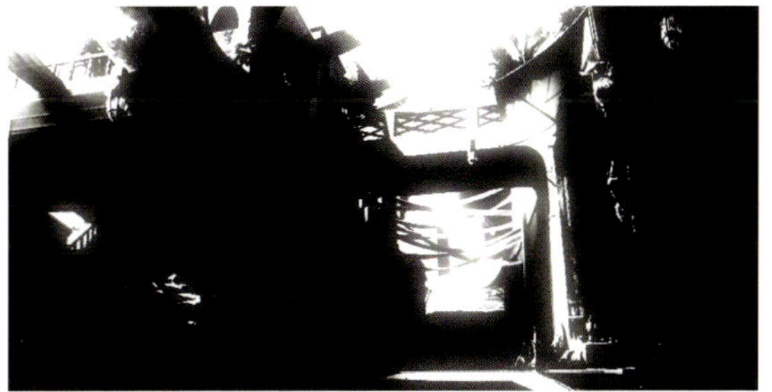

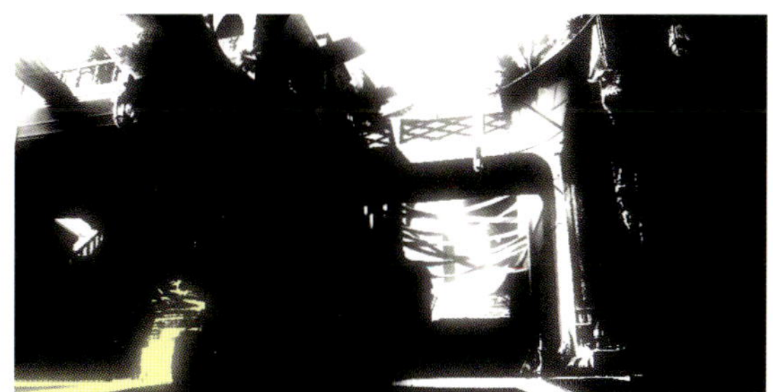

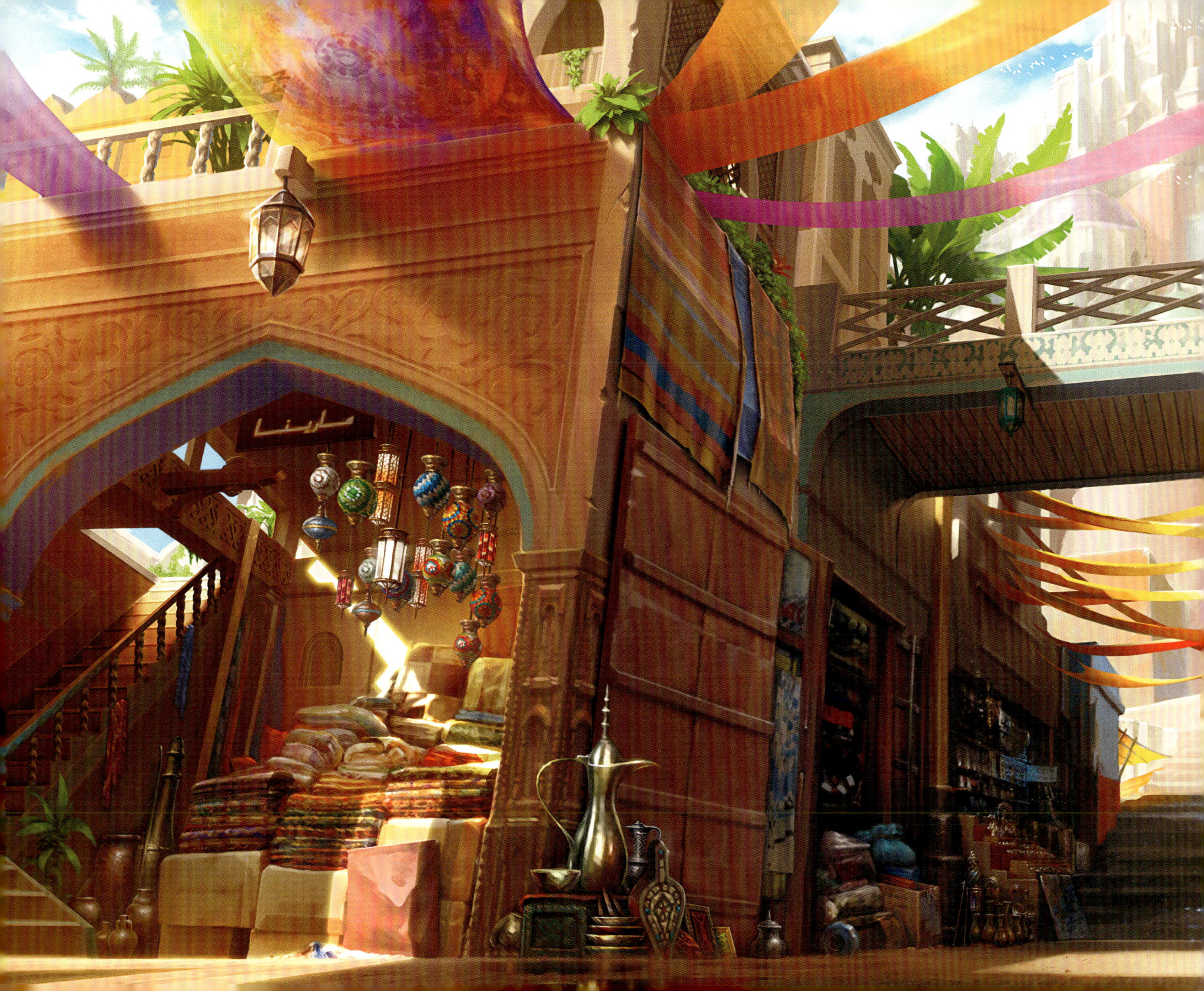

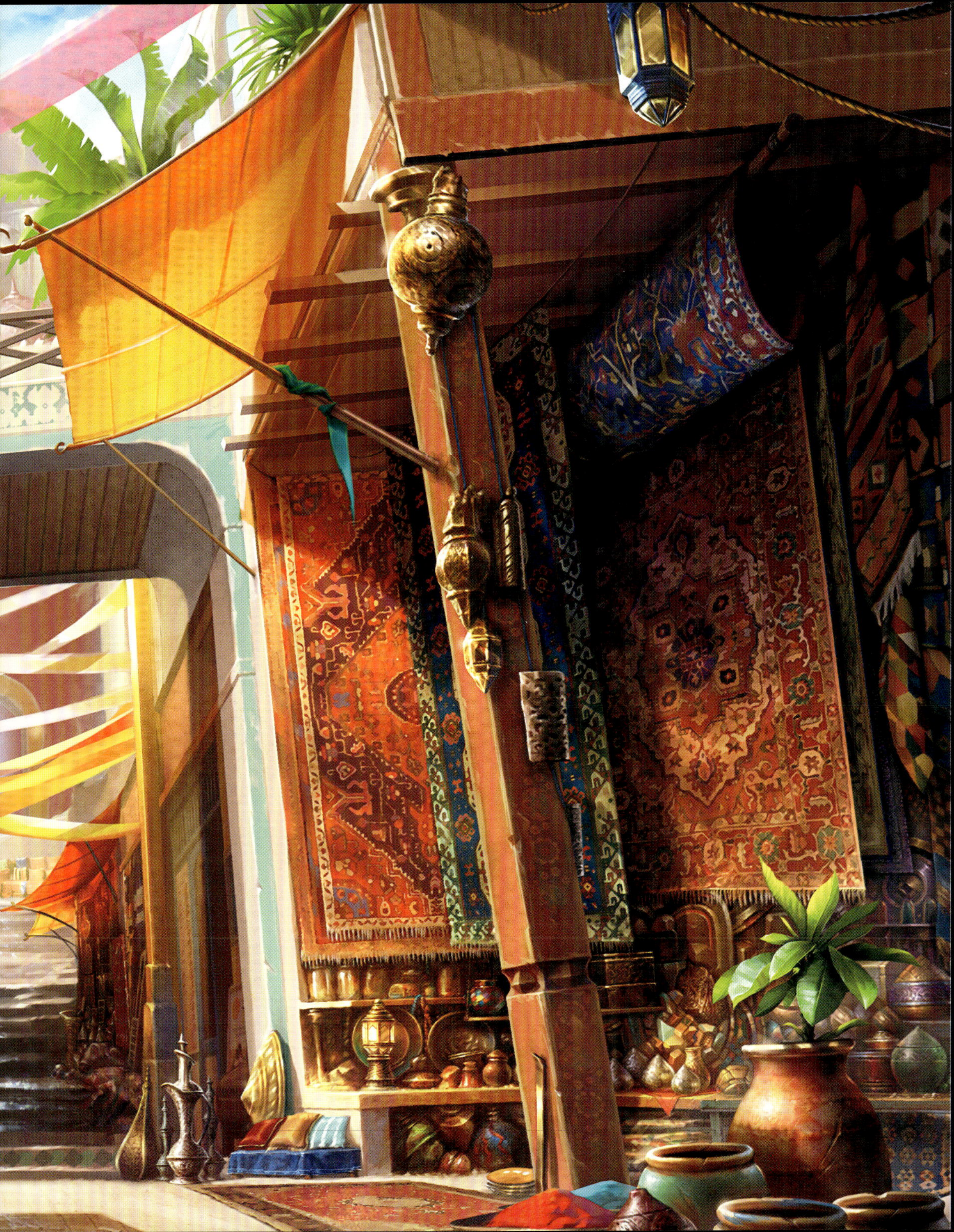

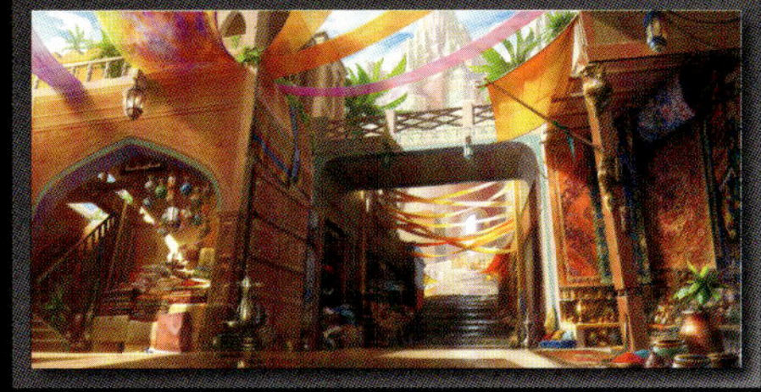

Also added are the inverted images of objects reflected in the puddles of water dotting the foreground, carpets hanging on the wall at the end of the street, dirt covering the goods and ceramic pots and a piece of cloth tied to the supporting pole of the awning. With these elements added, the overall scene adjusted and details refined, and thus *Souk* is completed.

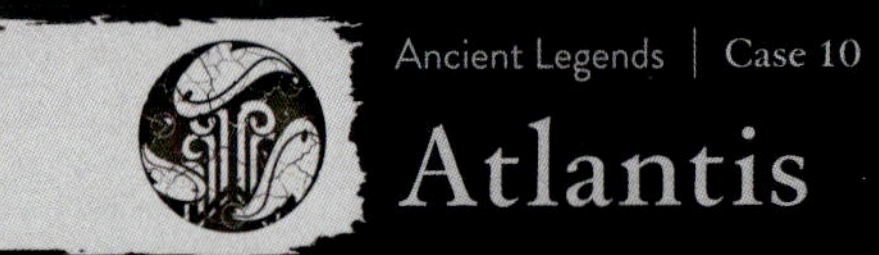



# Atlantis

Weighing up which of many hotels in Dubai to stay in, I finally settled in "Atlantis The Palm" because its theme, that of the Atlantis legend, fascinates me and as an artistic creator, I was impressed by its atmosphere. My interest in Atlantis — the ancient city of a legendary civilisation — perhaps mirrored that of the hotel's designers and builders. As I stepped inside, the mixed feelings that set in was overwhelming. The experience truly struck a chord with me. The hotel takes the shape of a fortress like those we often see on the cover of *Arabian Nights*. The shape of the hotel, its interior furnishings and the wall paintings each appears to have their own stories to tell. The colossal aquarium inside the hotel houses tens of thousands of fish, thereby bringing the fabled sea bottom up to the surface. Standing before the huge stretch of glass that contains its waters, it's easy to feel insignificant as before your eyes the end of an ancient civilisation unfolds.

Every Dubaian hotel boasts its own unique charm. Some are extremely luxurious; others picturesque; elsewhere there is cutting-edge technology; and more still can only be described as offering strange and novel experiences. My choice of "Atlantis The Palm" does not suggest that it is a superior hotel, only that its legendary architectural structure, attractive form and exquisite furnishings piqued my interest. All these features give perfect expression to the designers' in-depth understanding of the Atlantis legend and represent their bold attempt at innovation. Even those with no idea of the theme tend to be impressed by its exoticism and air of artistry. Such is the charm of fantasy art as well in that it combines fantastic elements with real structures to produce miraculous landscapes and buildings.

As a building can prompt people's curiosity for the legend of Atlantis, a work of fantasy art can immerse observers in an imagined world. For this to be achieved, designers must lay down the appropriate framework, demonstrate delicate and consistent expressiveness, develop an in-depth understanding of the main object and objects of reference, and respect each stage of the innovative process. Based on those, *Atlantis* the artwork is born.

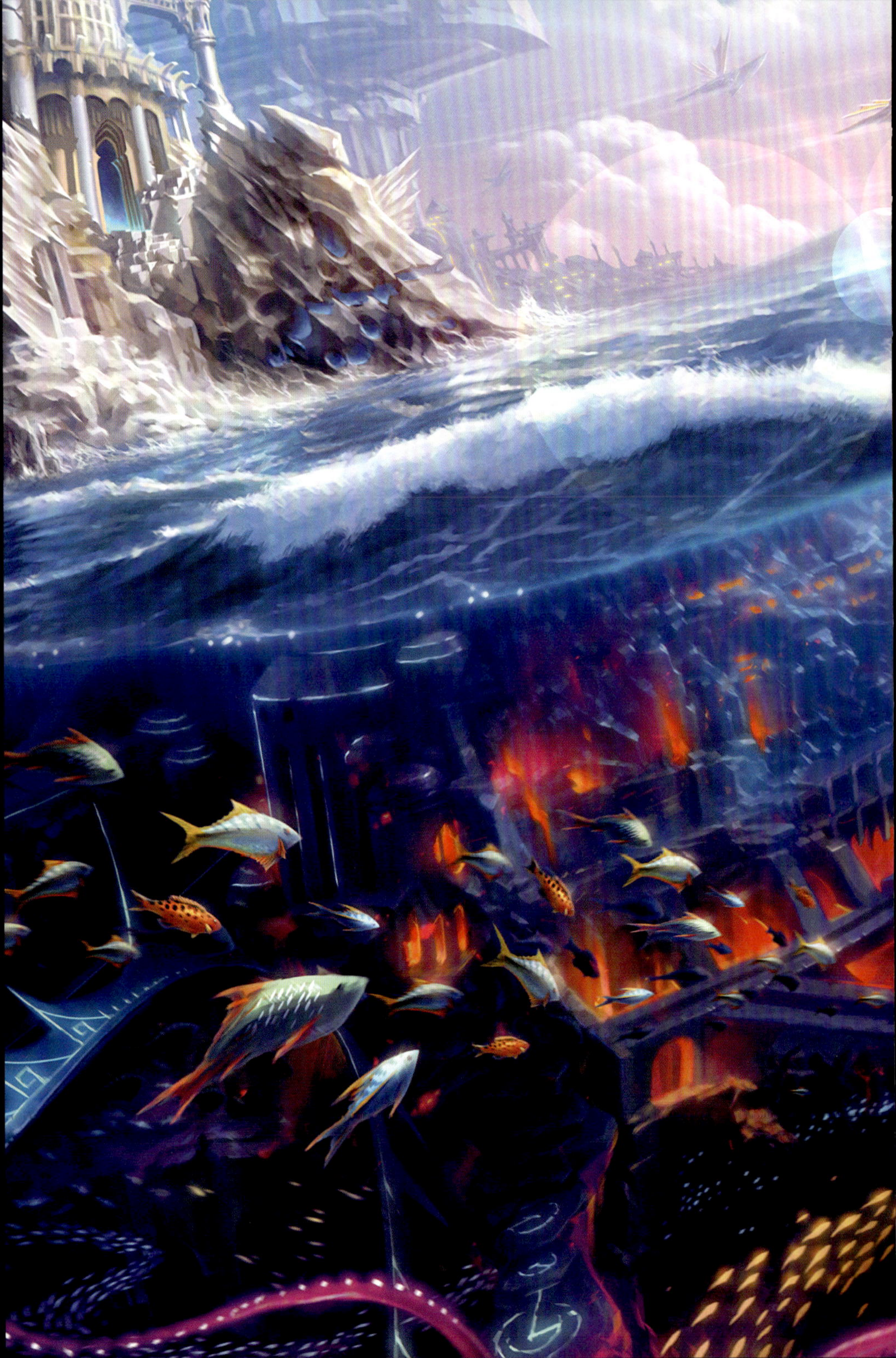

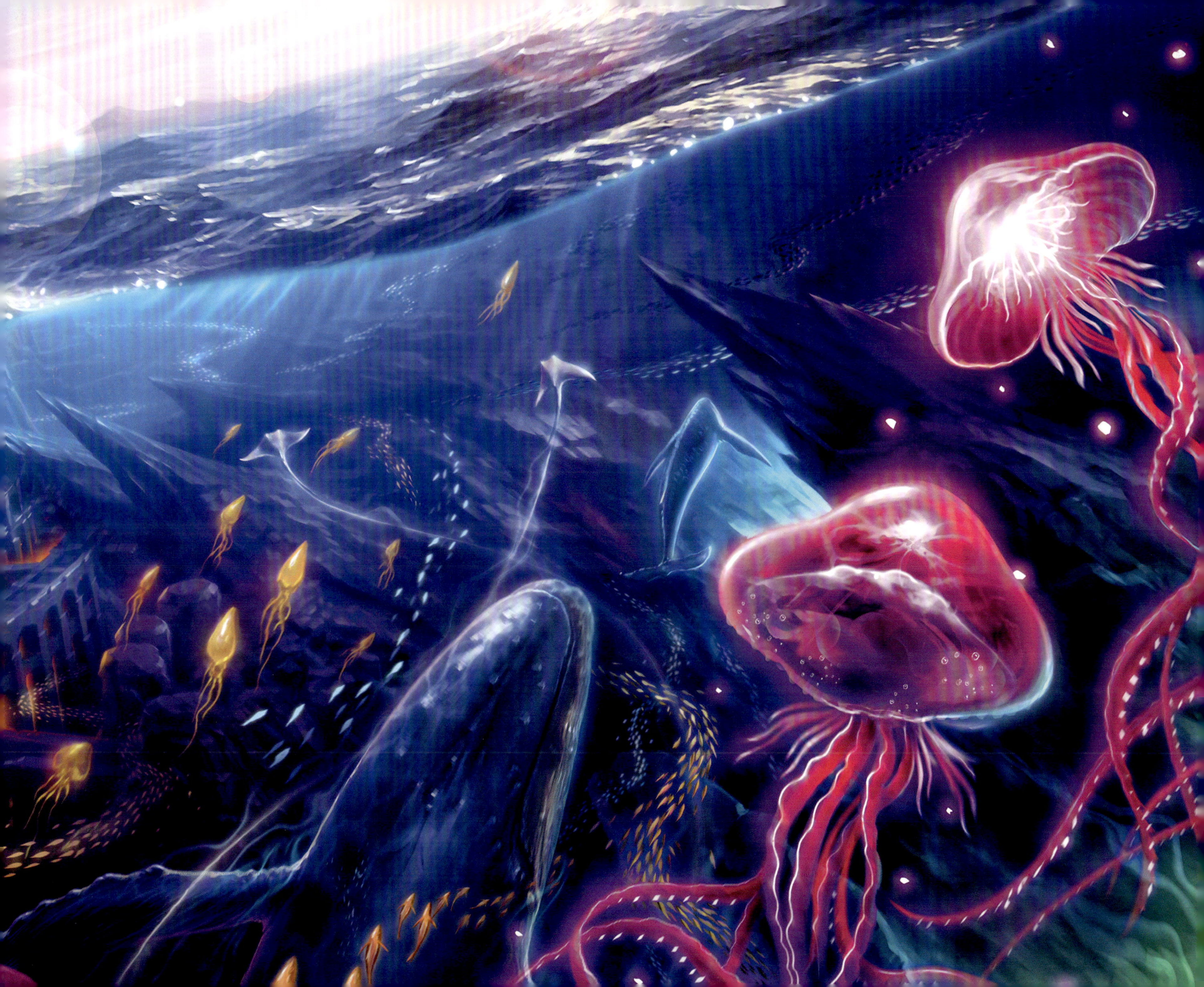

# THOUGHTS ON CREATION

*Most fantasy scenes draw on existing environments to which novel objects and elements are added, altered or re-grouped to render the final image more fantastic. Meanwhile, a close link is maintained between these additions from the creator's imagination and their physical counterparts. In this design, however, no models or template environments are available for visual treatment, and we have no choice but to peruse the hotel of "Atlantis, The Palm" for reference materials so as to better understand how our theme might take shape. A wholly new perspective and way of thinking must be adopted to reimagine Atlantis in our mind.*

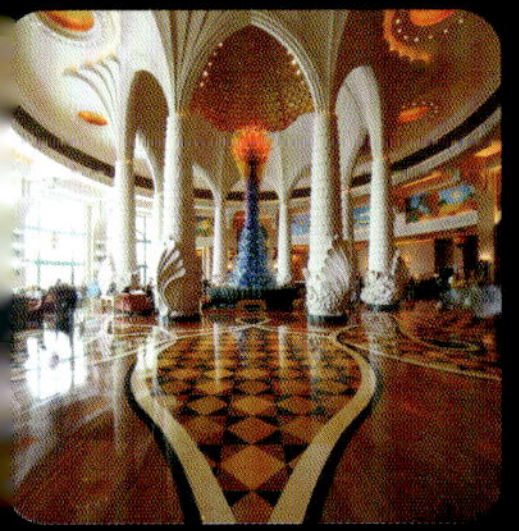

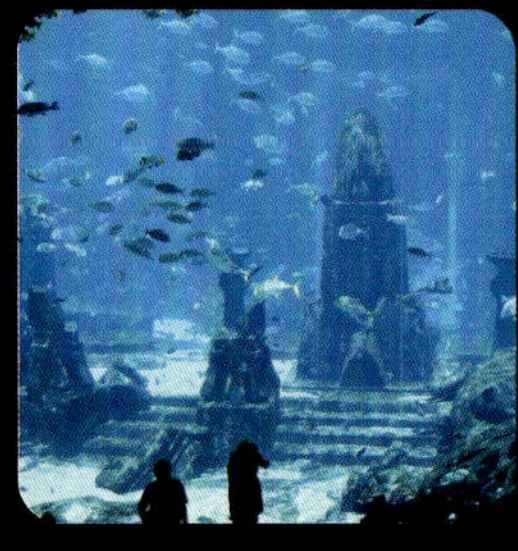

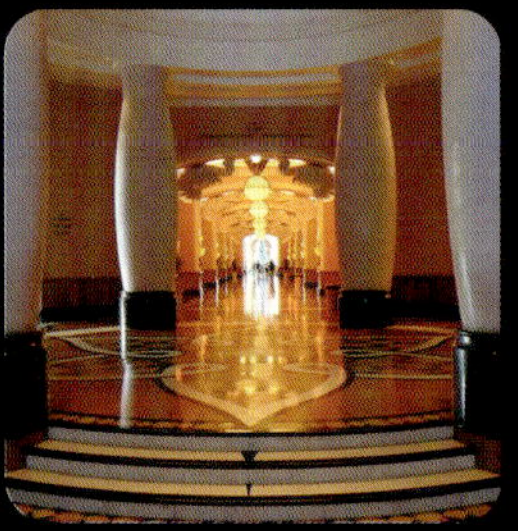

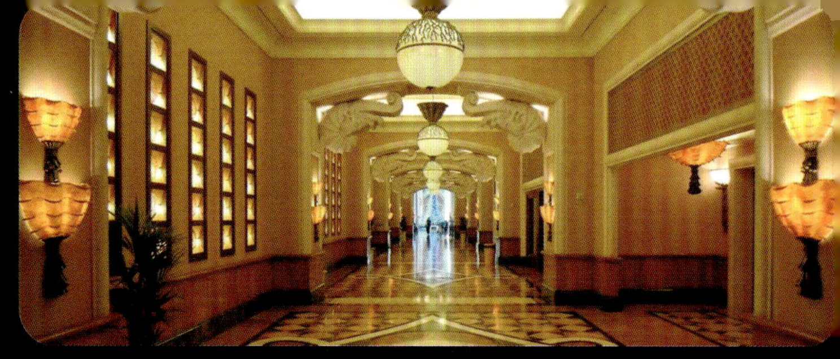

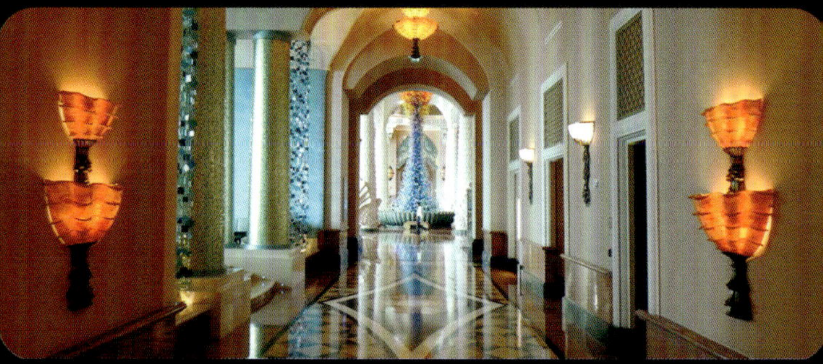

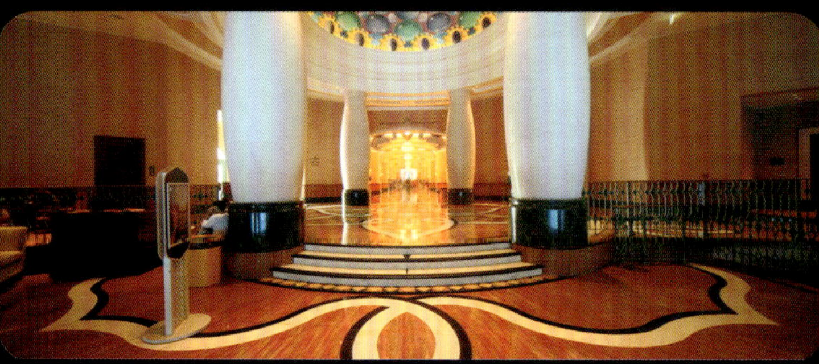

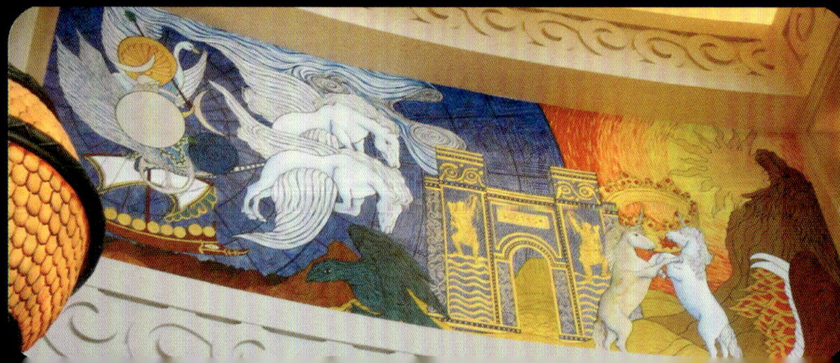

## ▲ UNDERWATER PALACE

As I walked into the Atlantis hotel, I found myself submerged in an underwater palace. Shells, conches, scales, pearls, sea animals and plants adorn every inch. In the middle of the lobby, there is a massive glass sculpture created by Dale Chihuly, a renowned American glass artist, which looks like some mysterious, colossal creature staring out at the visitors streaming in and out.

The huge aquarium inside the hotel is home to over 60,000 different species of sea fish. The interior is designed according to the theme of the lost relics of Atlantis, a magnificence and mysterious sight to behold.

The lighting inside the hotel, together with the glistening mosaic stone flooring, appears extraordinarily translucent and splendid and bestows a strong air of artistry to the space.

Corridors heading indifferent directions each seem to lead to their own distinct underwater world with unique characteristics. Delicate wall paintings tell stories about the vicissitudes of the legendary civilisation of Atlantis.

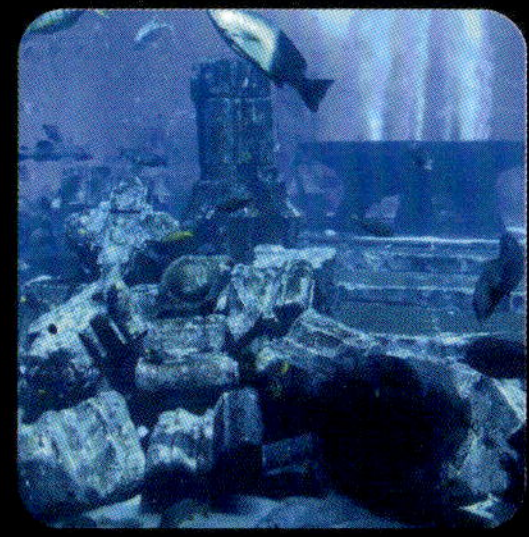

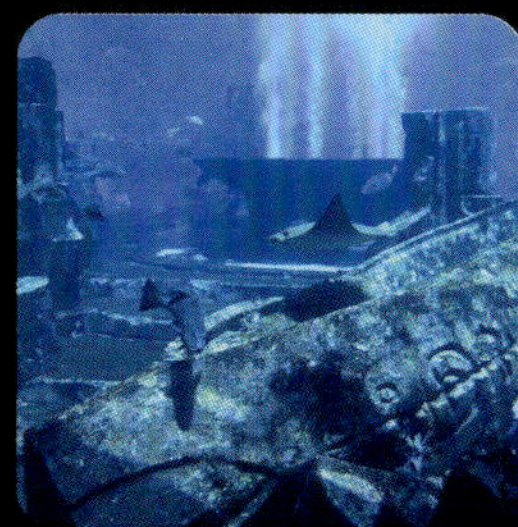

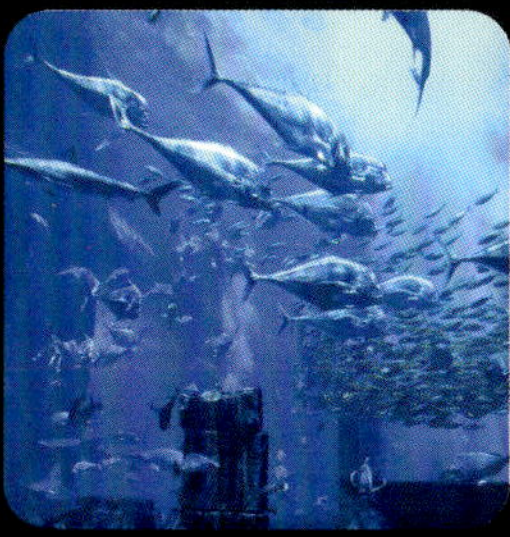

## ▲ RELICS

Relics attributed to the fictional Atlantis are scattered throughout the aquarium. These are the only suitable reference materials for our design. Greek stone pillars, altars and other irregular structures, inter-crossed with the variety of fish darting by, seem to accentuate of the impression of a sunken world. Given its space limit, it was of course impossible for the hotel to put a whole city of relics on display, so only a fragment of the "lost civilisation" can be seen.

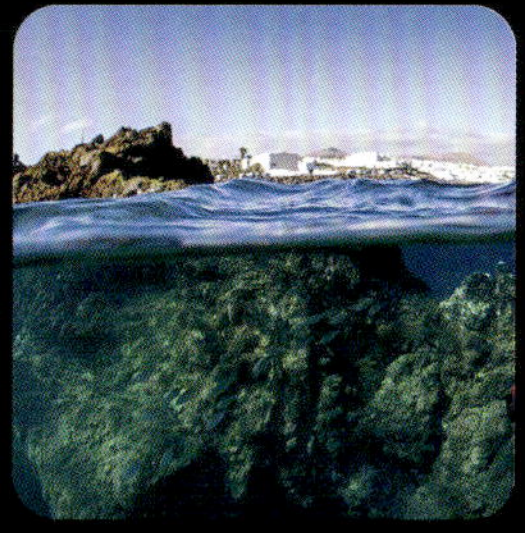

## ▲ UNDERWATER OBJECTS

This is a photograph taken from the "half submerged" perspective. It has a similar feeling to the desired result of our depiction. From this photo, we can see that the underwater part seems dark even in daytime; objects underwater relatively consistently take on the seawater's colour due to the water's transparency and lower lighting; objects near the sea surface tend to be defocused; reefs connect to the seabed; and a level division is not as interesting as a slanting one.

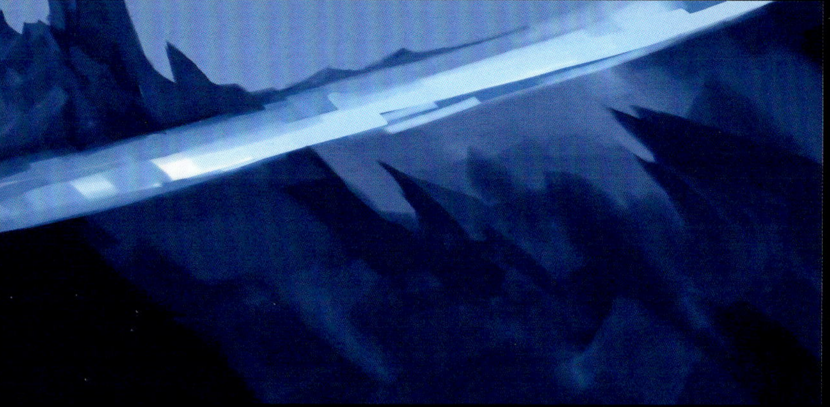

Legend goes that the ancient city of Atlantis was engulfed by the sea, making me think of a colossal relic submerged underwater, as shown in the central aquarium of the Atlantis hotel with its fantasy feeling. The one-dimensional representation here, however, is nothing new. So in this current, I am adopting a different perspective —being "half submerged". This should emphasize the ideas of myth and glory attached to this fantasy civilisation. To achieve this, perspective with photography calls for complex techniques and specialised equipment like a split dome port lens.

I chose the "half submerged" perspective to avoid the claustrophobic sensation inherent in a predominantly underwater scene. Objects are added above the water for "a sense of open air" and space to breathe, making the scene more diverse.

A special perspective alone is not enough to change the core of a creation. Different perspectives serve different works of art. Personally, I have a strong interest in ancient civilisations of legend such as Atlantis and Lemuria. What I want to express in this design is such civilisations' existence, hence the addition of the sea's surface can serve as a foil and enhance underwater world's mystery as well.

To apply the "half submerged" perspective, we need first of all to decide on where to apply the divide between what is above water and what is beneath. The focus of this design is the underwater world which occupies about 70% of the frame. The slanted dividing line frames a "key area" with an irregular shape to allow for the depiction of objects of different sizes and distances. This unique composition can improve the work's visual expressiveness.

Everybody knows that the seabed is not flat; instead, there are underwater mountains and gorges and craggy terra in which extend between the islands that protrude from the surface. These structures should be clarified when an underwater perspective is adopted. At the initial stage of sketching, we can apply the silhouetting method to decide the layout of objects before adding details to other elements and pulling the scene together into a reasonable arrangement.

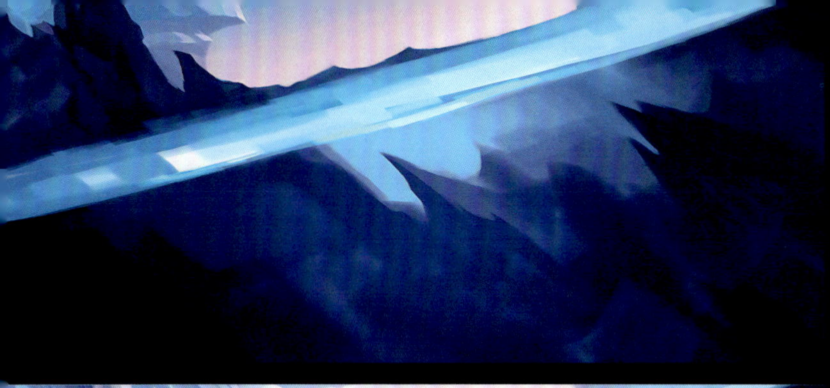

Now, let's improve the visual effect of the sketch. The centre of the scene is highlighted to signal it as the focal point running from the sky down the middle to the sea's surface and then the bottom. The sky is painted pink and purple, the colour of dusk, for two reasons: to express grief over the fallen civilisation and to ensure that the sky does not divert people's attention from the main objects underwater.

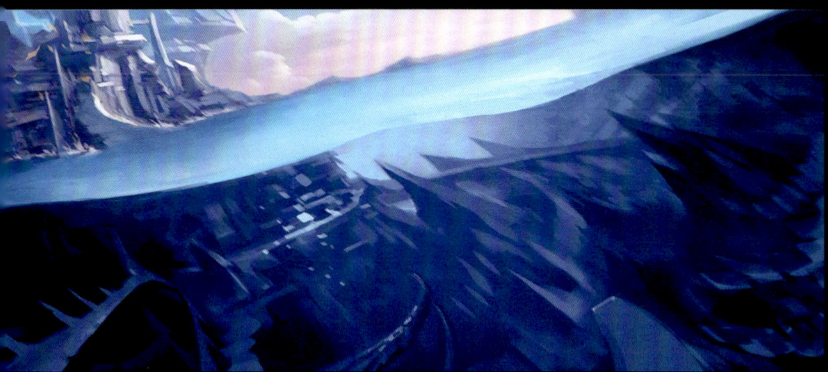

The sea's surface is depicted with a horizontal line. Above this line is a worm's-eye view; beneath it a bird's-eye view. Seas differ from most lakes and rivers in that their surface is disrupted by waves and only at its shallowest points is it relatively flat. The dividing line, therefore, should be curved to give expression to the shape of waves. Now, based on this sketch, let's paint a building atop the island in corner and relics sunk to the bottom of the sea. The building and the relics should be shaped according to their surrounding topography, especially given that the seabed is the main place that the relics have settled. Towering seamounts, undulating sea knolls and deep-sea trenches should be depicted one by one.

he island, while still part of the sea bed, rises from the sea like huge whirling cone. The building on top and the relics, as vell as the seamounts, trenches and other objects on the seabed are shaped around this cone, thus connecting the whole scene ogether in a vortex-like arrangement.

I chose the above design because Atlantisis, described by Platoas, is surrounded by a series of concentric circles, closing n from the outer ring layer by layer toward the centre. To successfully create any piece of work based on a well-known egend, it is important to understand the various descriptions and historical materials available. This will provide you with a nore accurate grasp of the people's pre-existing conceptions of he theme.

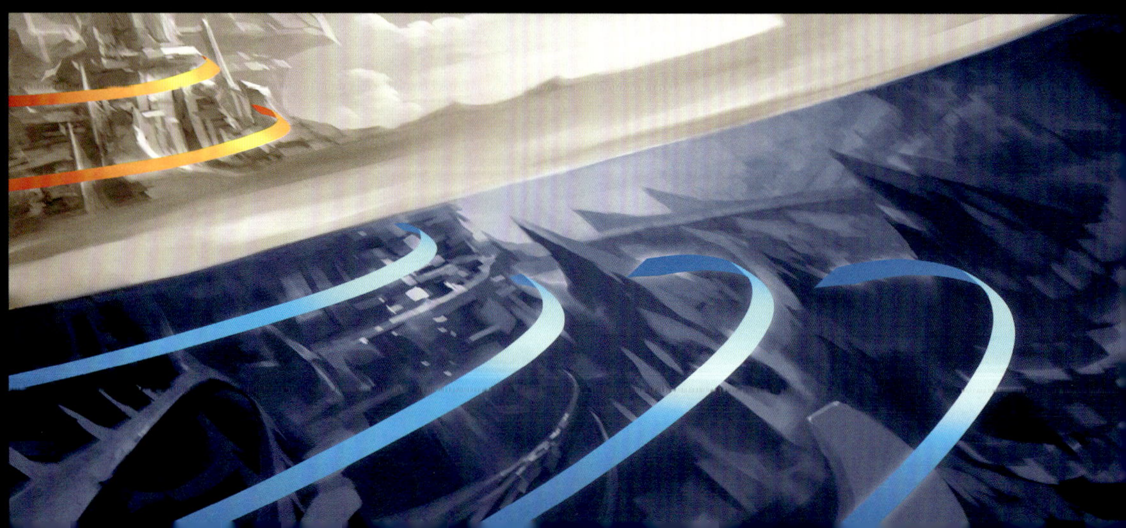

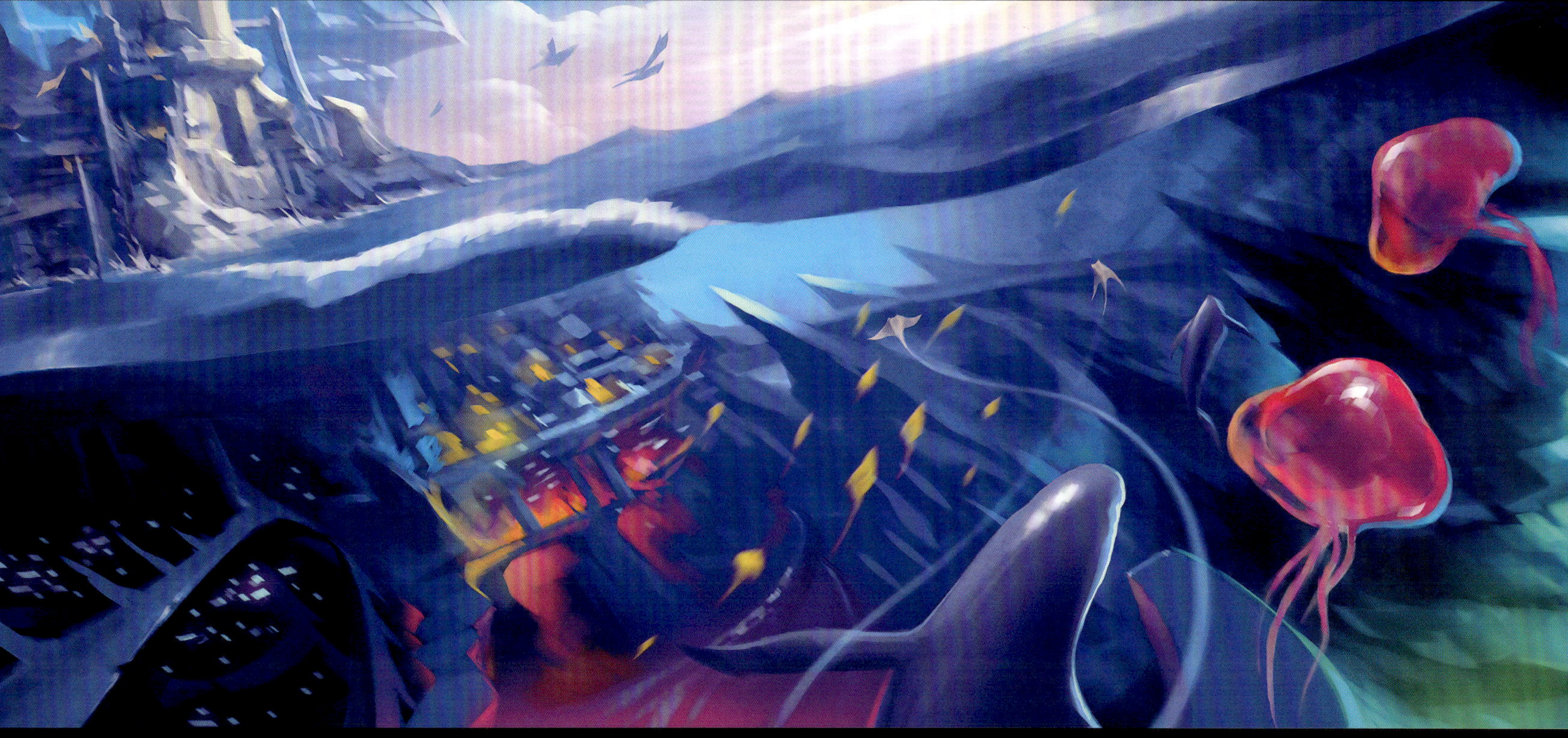

With the basic landscape ready, let's begin to depict the "fantasy" elements. To present a civilisation that has been submerged underwater but remains alive, there are a few critical details to include: the extant architectures atop the sea, the aircraft flying in the sky as a symbol of the ancient civilization's technology, and the glimmer of its treasures season the seabed. These elements hint at the survival of the civilisation of Atlantis. A diverse array of sea creatures also adds vitality to the entire scene. This work of art now begins to take on its fantasy form.

Thanks to the perspective that we have adopted, we can clearly distinguish the features of different species even hundreds of metres below the sea surface. Nearer the sea surface, we should make sure to only depict creatures that typically live in this "epipelagic zone". It would be a mistake to add creatures that only live in the "bathypelagic zone" in this part. An understanding of the types of animals and plants in different oceanic regions and depths is vital to the initial stage of this creation.

The purplish red jelly fish is placed the closest to the camera. Its colour serves to balance the tone of the predominantly blue submarine world. Its special texture allows for more effects to be added later. Different groups of fish, manta rays, and colossal whales are also included, their layout determined according to the principle that objects appear larger close up and smaller in the distance. The majority of the foreground whale's body is depicted without occupying too much of the composition or blocking other objects.

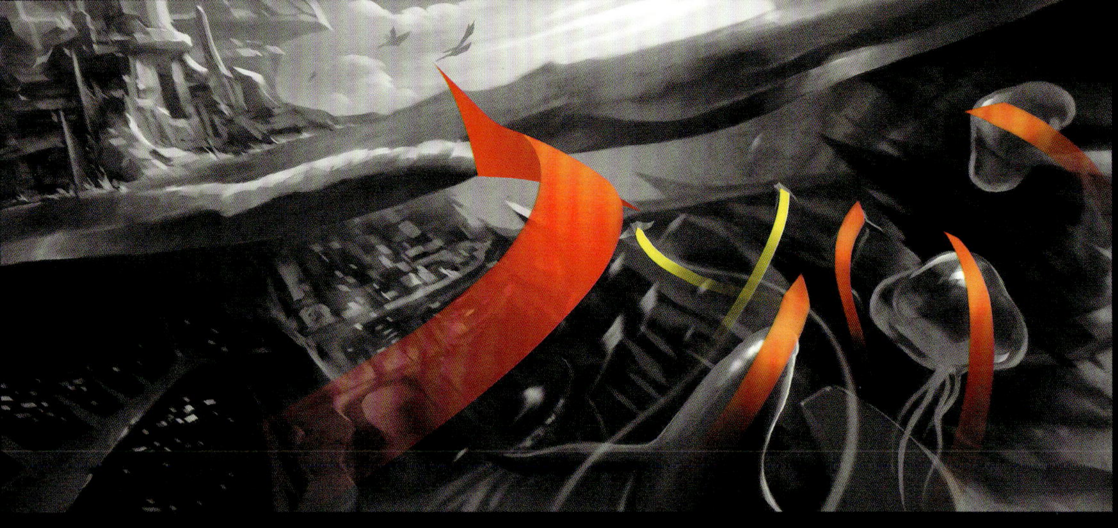

The movement of these marine creatures also follows the trajectory of a vortex. They mainly swim around the cone-shaped island, and a few are shown to be "weaving" and "interweaving" across that course.

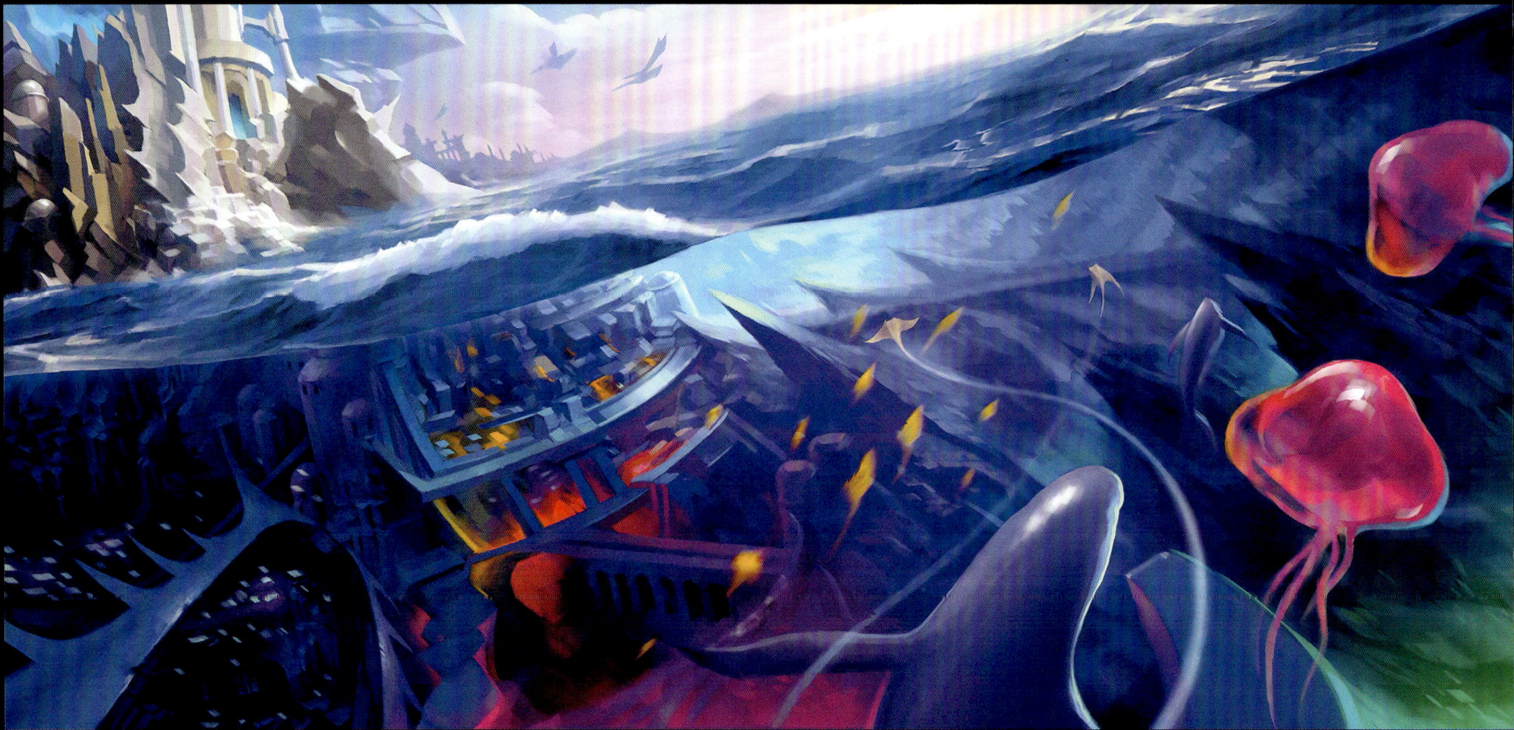

Now let's add details to other elements. The building on the island is constructed in style redolent of Ancient Greek architecture. Integrated into the mountainside and rock faces, its imposing pillars area is suitable foil for the island's dome structure. The cliffs are shaped like fins to symbolise Atlantis' worship for the sea. On the ocean's surface, the movement of waves and the sparkle of light upon it need to be brought out while beneath the water, the complex of structures should be laid out in "concentric circles".

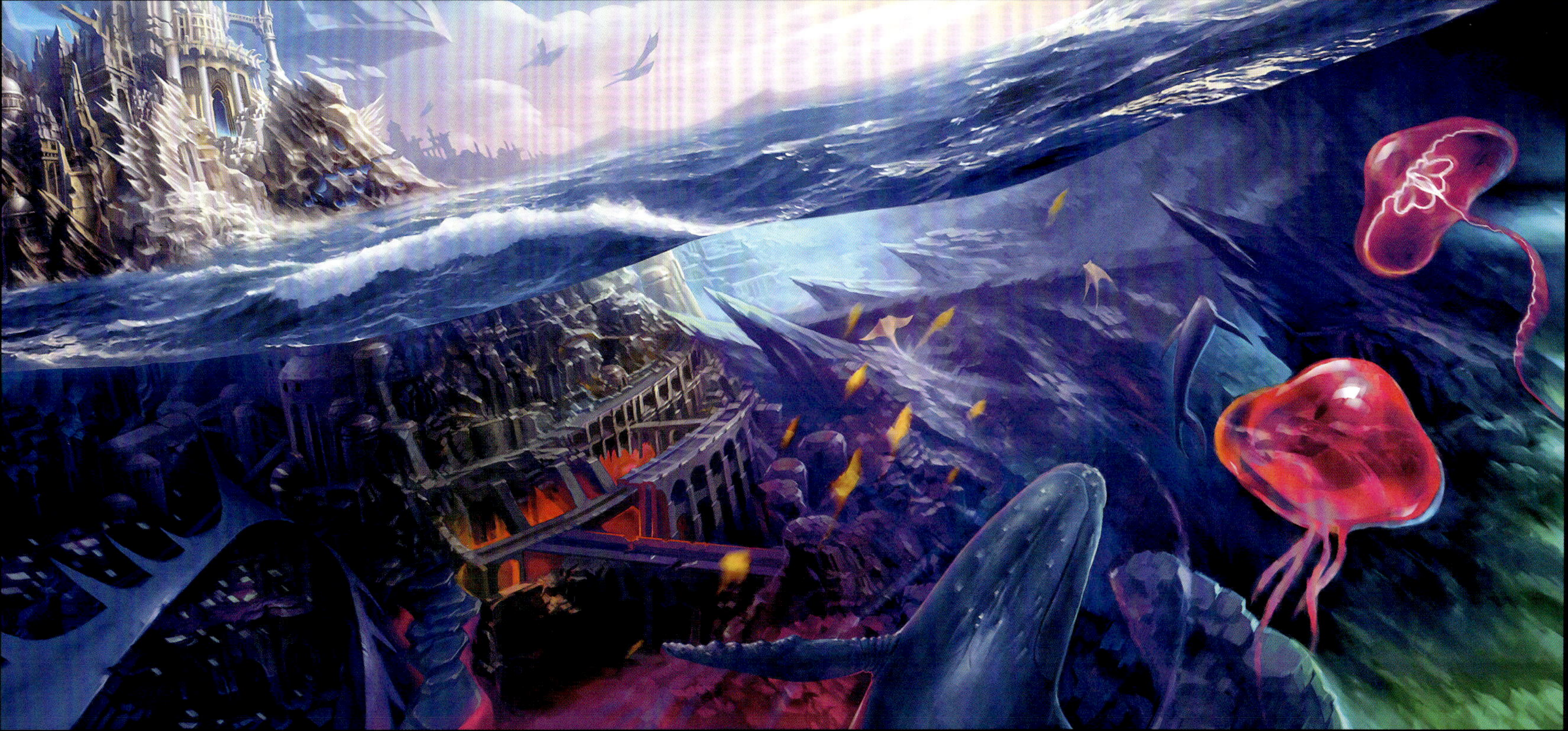

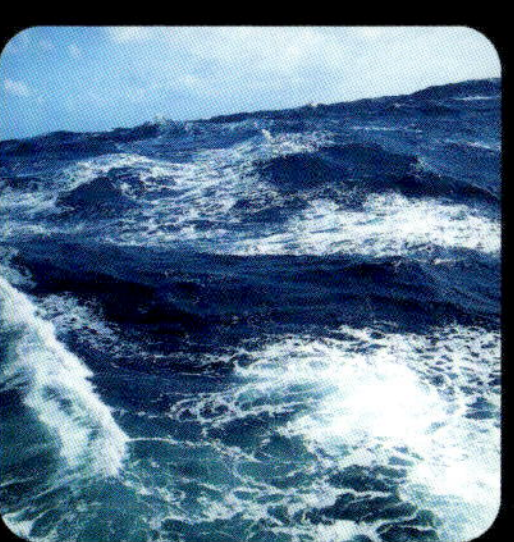

## WAVES

Waves result from the movement of sea waters, usually stirred up by winds. Their height varies according to the strength and direction of the wind, as well as the surrounding landscapes.

There are many ways of creating the impression of a wave by simply using a different visual effect: waves that rise up and slope down like dunes, white-crested waves, and white cottonlike ripples and foam that spread out at the trough of the wave. The sky's colour, sunshine's intensity, and sunlight's direction are among the factors requiring consideration when it comes to rendering the reflection visible in the waves' waters.

Once these decisions about the waves have been made, the wave details and resulting changes elsewhere upon the surface are refined. Another consideration is the inverted images of the island and other objects as reflected in the waters. Chopped up as it is by waves, the sea surface is only able to highlight the contrast between light and dark. Other details are lost because of the unsmooth plane. Although the sun is not included in this composition, its presence can be implied with sparkles on the sea surface, essentially inverted images of the sun.

The ocean's surface now completed, more details can be added to the island building and under water relics. One element that requires extra attention is the differences between the perspectives and object-to-object ratio whether on land or submerged. The seabed also needs to be shaped. At this stage most of the marine creatures are left out so as to not block other objects. Only the jellyfish and whales that occupy a relatively large part of the scene are roughly depicted.

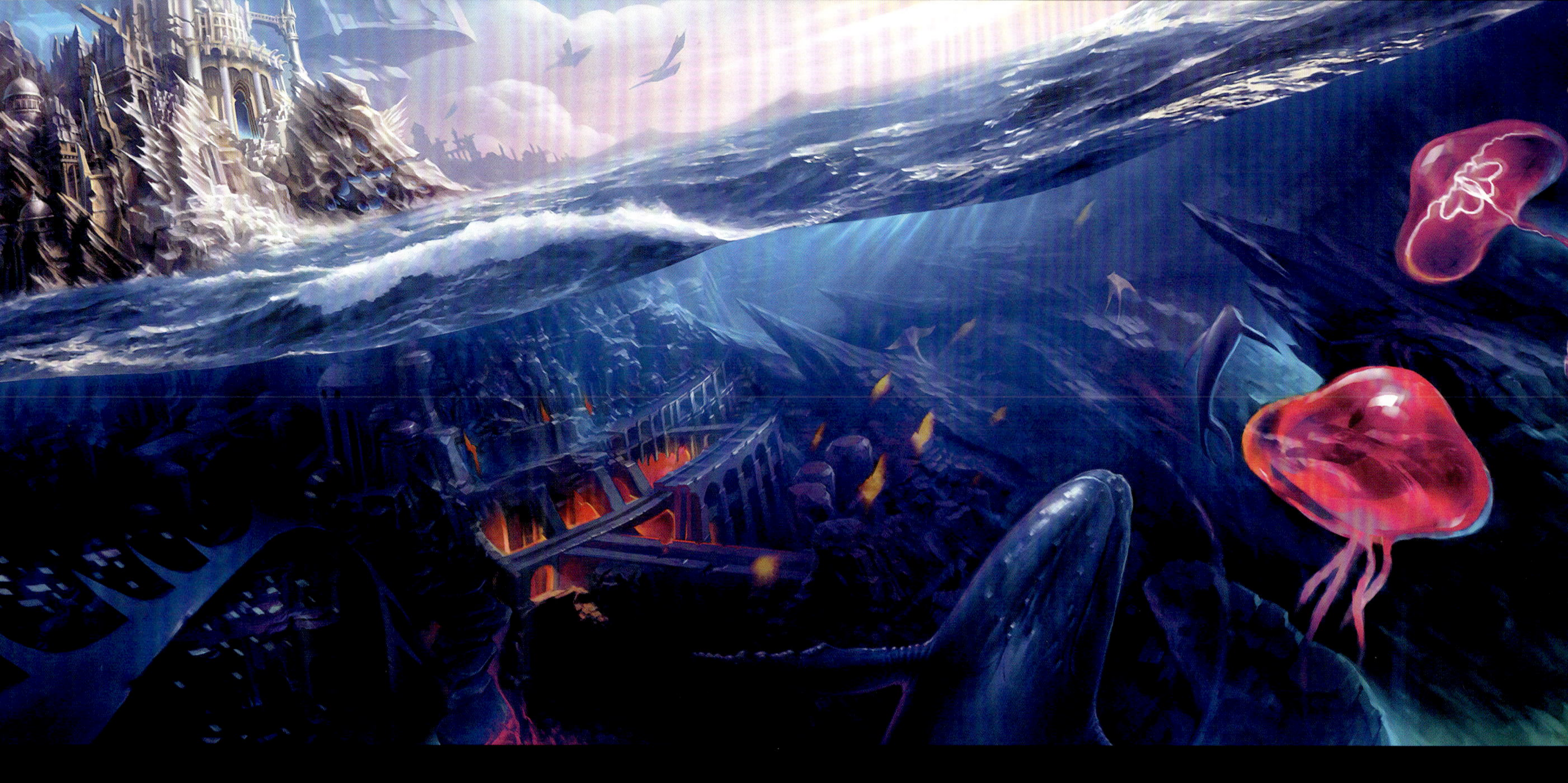

Then, the effects of being underwater are applied. Using the "distortion" function in the filter, we slightly "squeeze" submarine objects to mimic the visual distortion likely caused by their being underwater.

The profile effect applied to a sun-ocean world is different from when applied to a fish tank containing miniature landscapes and

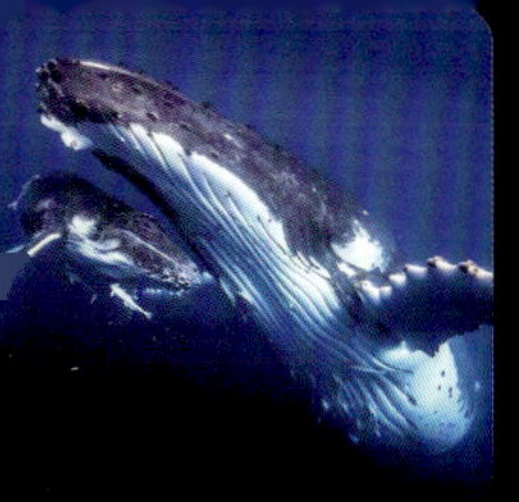
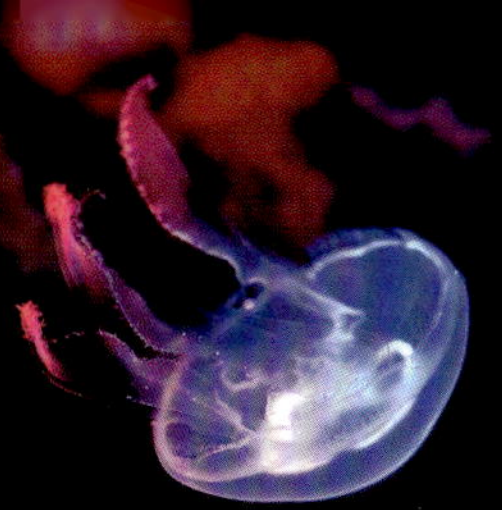
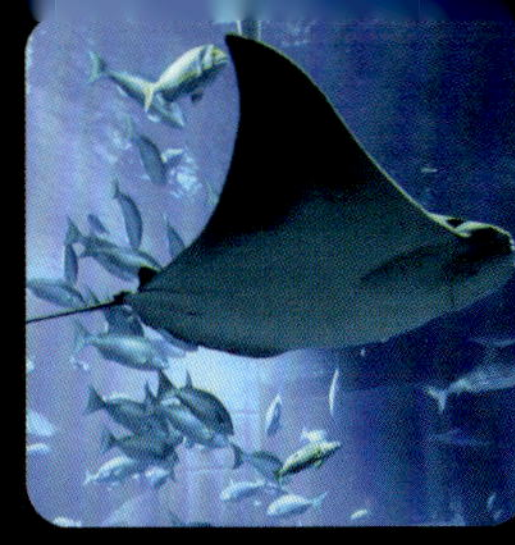

## ▲ MARINE CREATURES

Marine creatures are very diverse. Whales that are huge but move slowly sharply juxtapose manta ays that swim swiftly as if take flight. The soft movements of a jellyfish's trailing tentacles and uminal scene make them the neon lights of the submarine world. All these outstanding and nique creatures are important to our current design.

We need to learn about each of these marine animal's individual features and mak sure to give expression to every one of them. Equally important then is to conside where these animals fit in the scene according to their qualities. These feature can enhance each other or elevate the entire scene. Jellyfish tentacles stretch to th bottom right of the scene, their colour contrasting with a group of squids and th orange emanating from the relic below. Combining these colours serves the purpos of adjusting the rhythm of the submarine scene. The textures along the whale' back are brought out as well as the "defocused effects" there. Traces of waves tha are left by the manta rays' movement are added in a way that mimics that trajector of "wings" to improve the overall sense of dynamism.

As more and more underwater details are included, objects above the se shouldn't be forgotten, such as waves beating against the cliffs, the island's reflectio in the ocean water, distant mountains, the seashore, and an ancient aircraft.

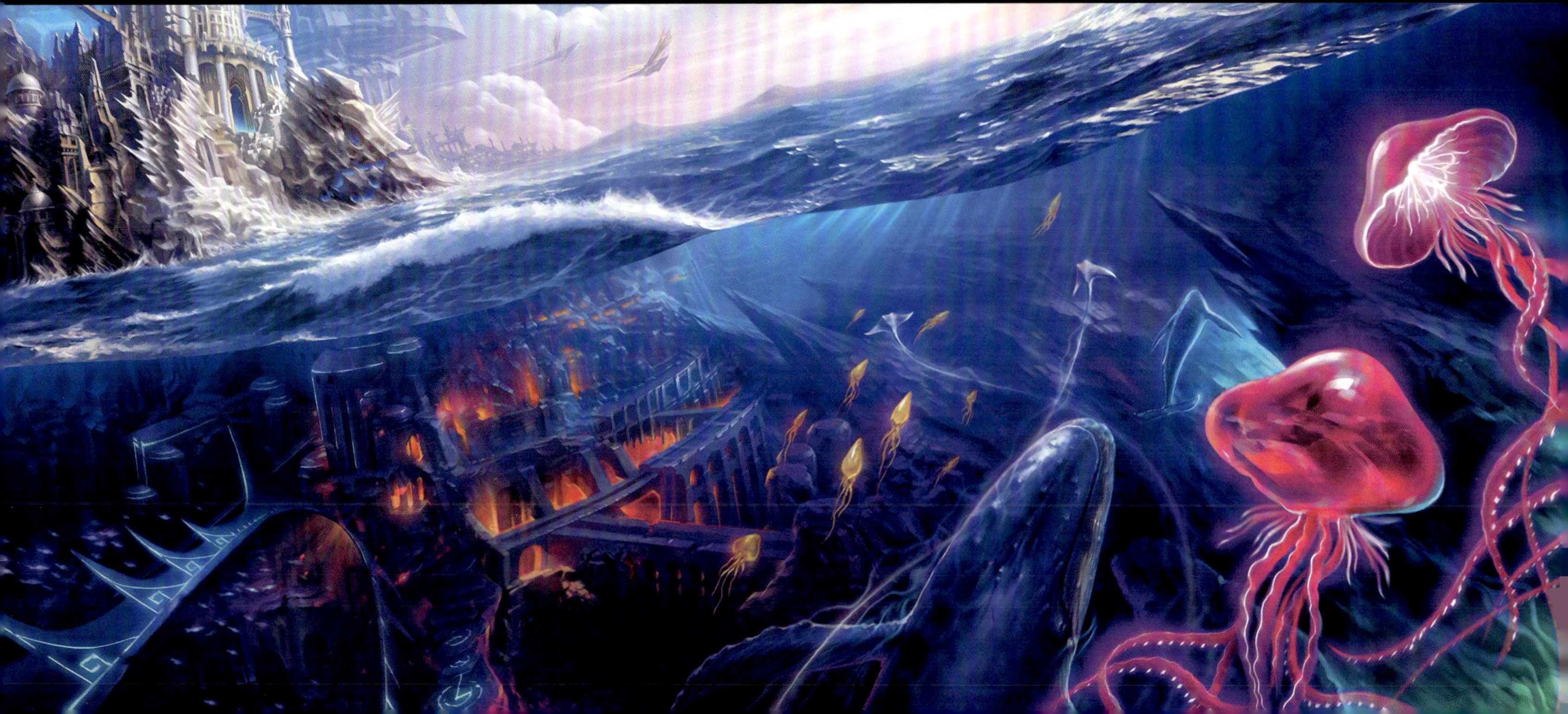

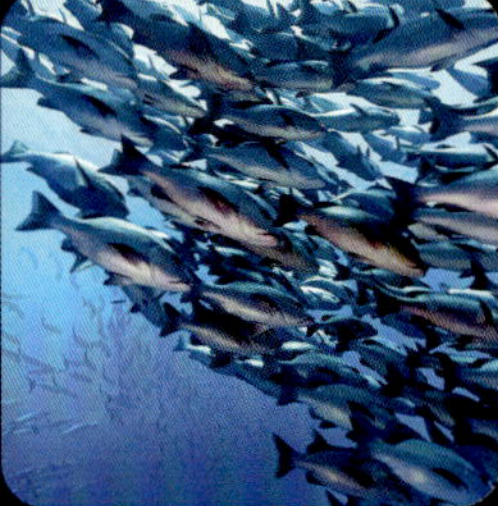

## ◄ FISH STORM

One instinctual behaviour of fish is to "storm", or swarm in a "school". This refers to impressive scenes of hundreds of fish swimming to gather in a highly synchronised and polarised manner. It is a defence strategy against predators effective for avoiding the extinction of species.

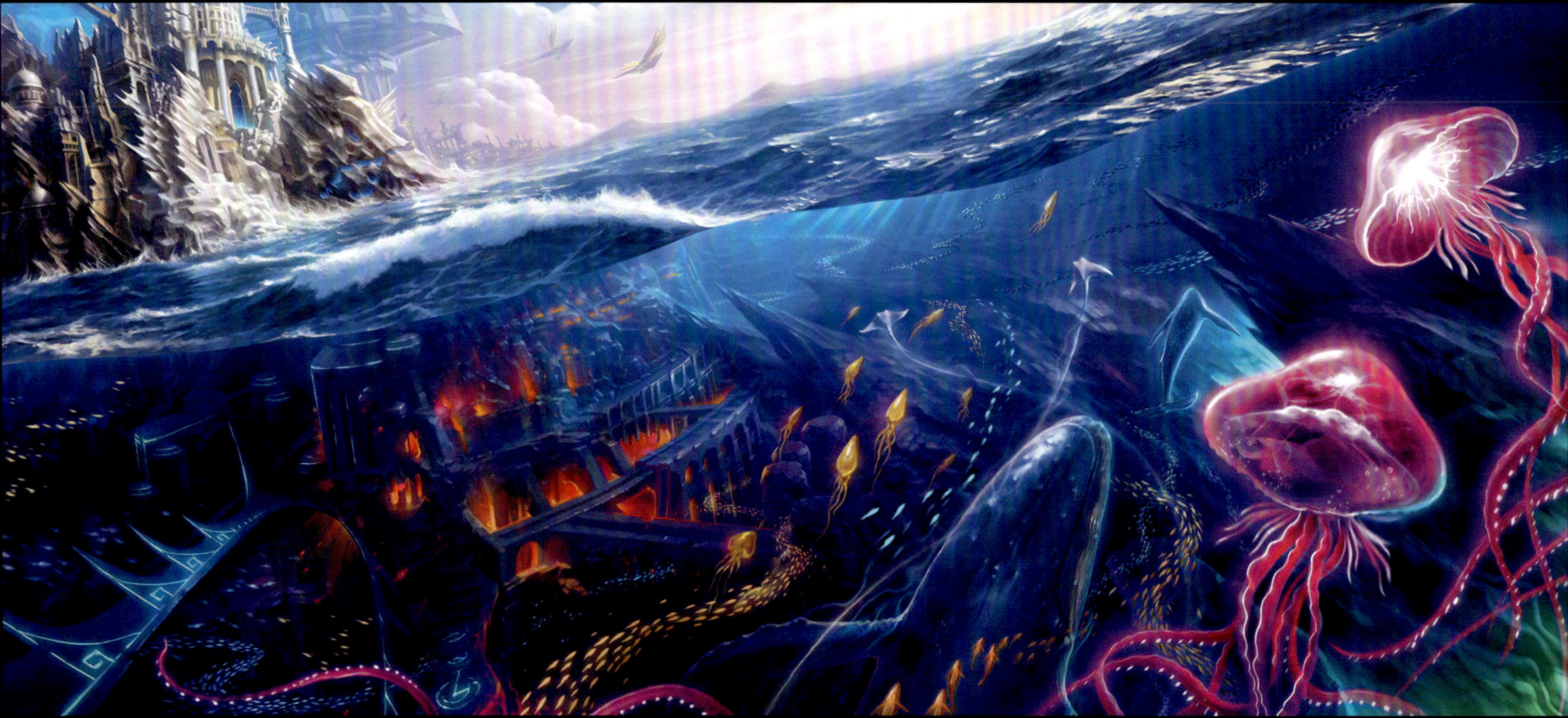

A fish "storm" can take a variety of shapes. Usually, that of a long line as the sheer numbers of fish swimming in unison gives an impression of the whole shape stretching out. I chose to include this in the design while also ensuring that the movement of each group of fish follows the trajectory of a vortex so as to highlight the concentric circle pattern of the picture's arrangement. Other empty areas are then filled with more elements, and the movement of marine creatures and various blocks of colours are refined.

Now, special effects and details are added to the jellyfish to ensure that the creature in the foreground is the most outstanding. Other objects are given declining expressiveness according to their distance from the jellyfish so as to ensure a rational sense of spatial gradation.

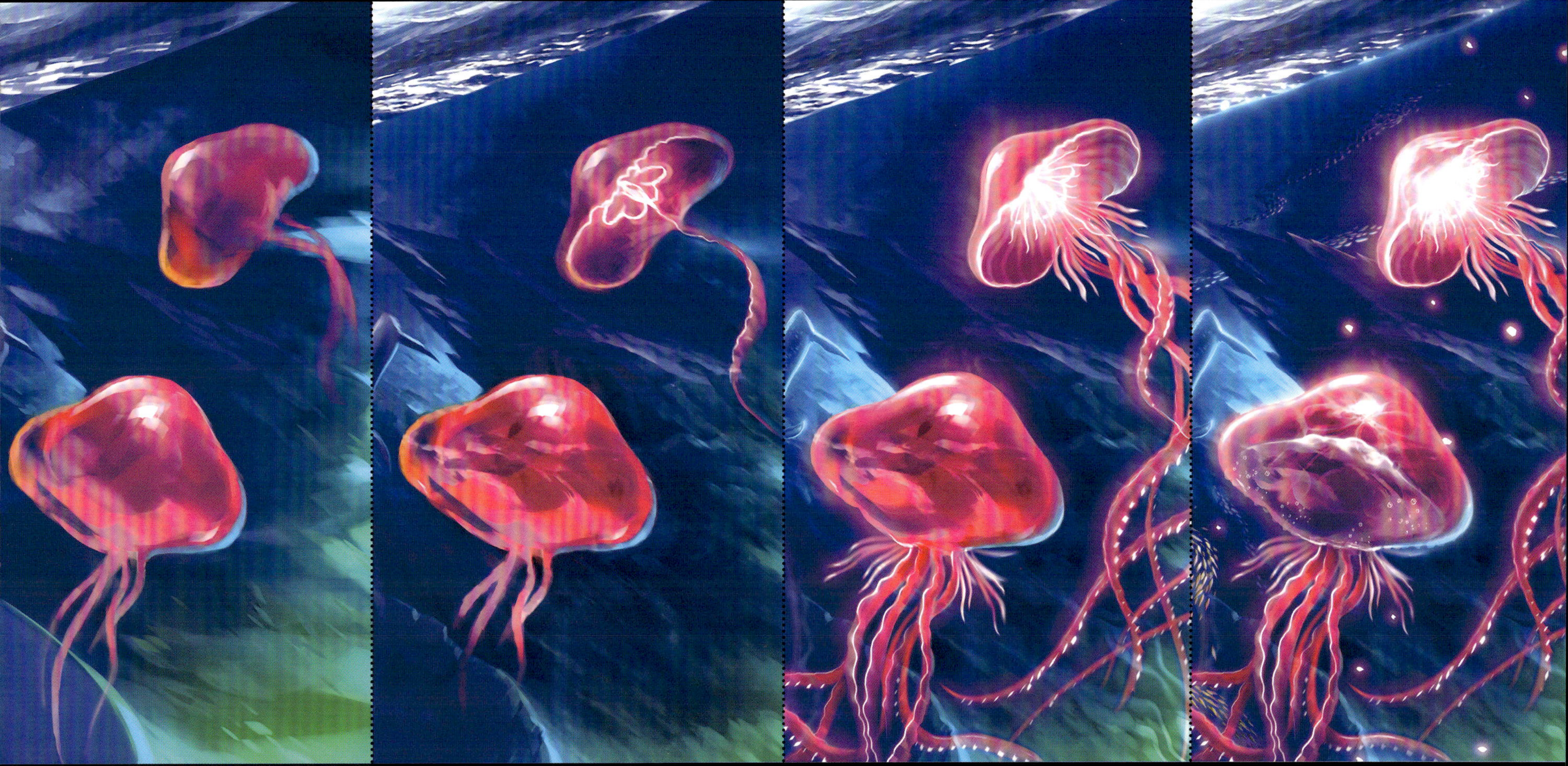

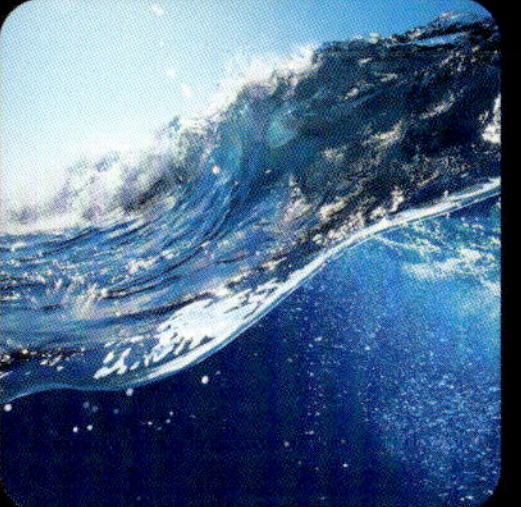

## ◄ SEGMENTED OCEAN SURFACE

This is a photo of a "segmented ocean surface " taken from the half underwater perspective. From it, we can see a great many details that differ between the parts above and below the water, such as the flare of light, the highlighted area, the uneven surface curved by the movement of water, and small and big bubbles.

With the translucent umbrella-shaped bells and trailing tentacles, jellyfish float, half their body illuminated, across the scene. To depict them, we apply the "rim light" technique and "refraction" effects to provide a strong contrast between the body's dark and light elements, hopefully accentuating the translucent quality. The movement of their tentacles decides the overall shape of the jellyfish. The luminescent quality of the jellyfish can be used to highlight the atmosphere around them and direct observers' visual focus.

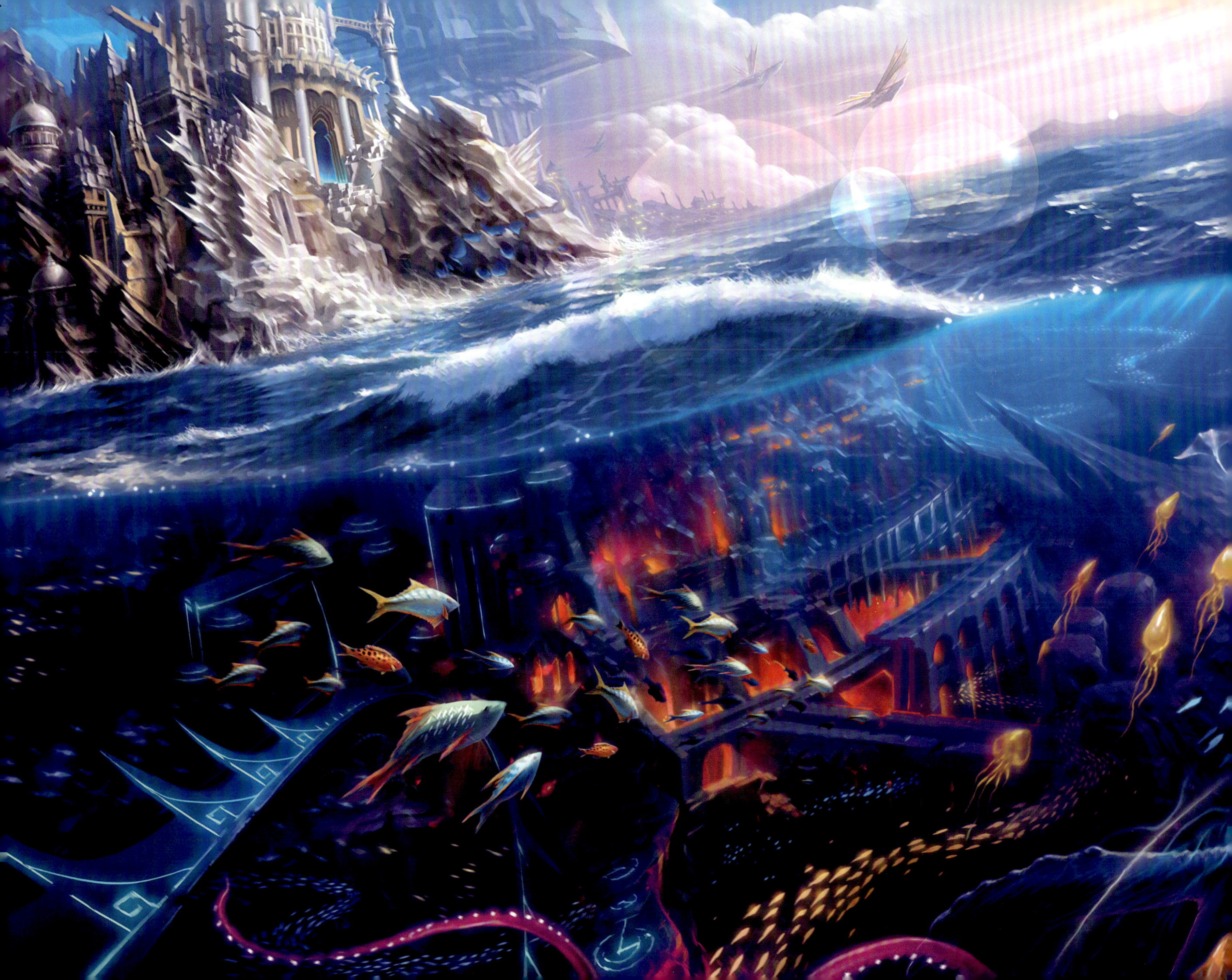

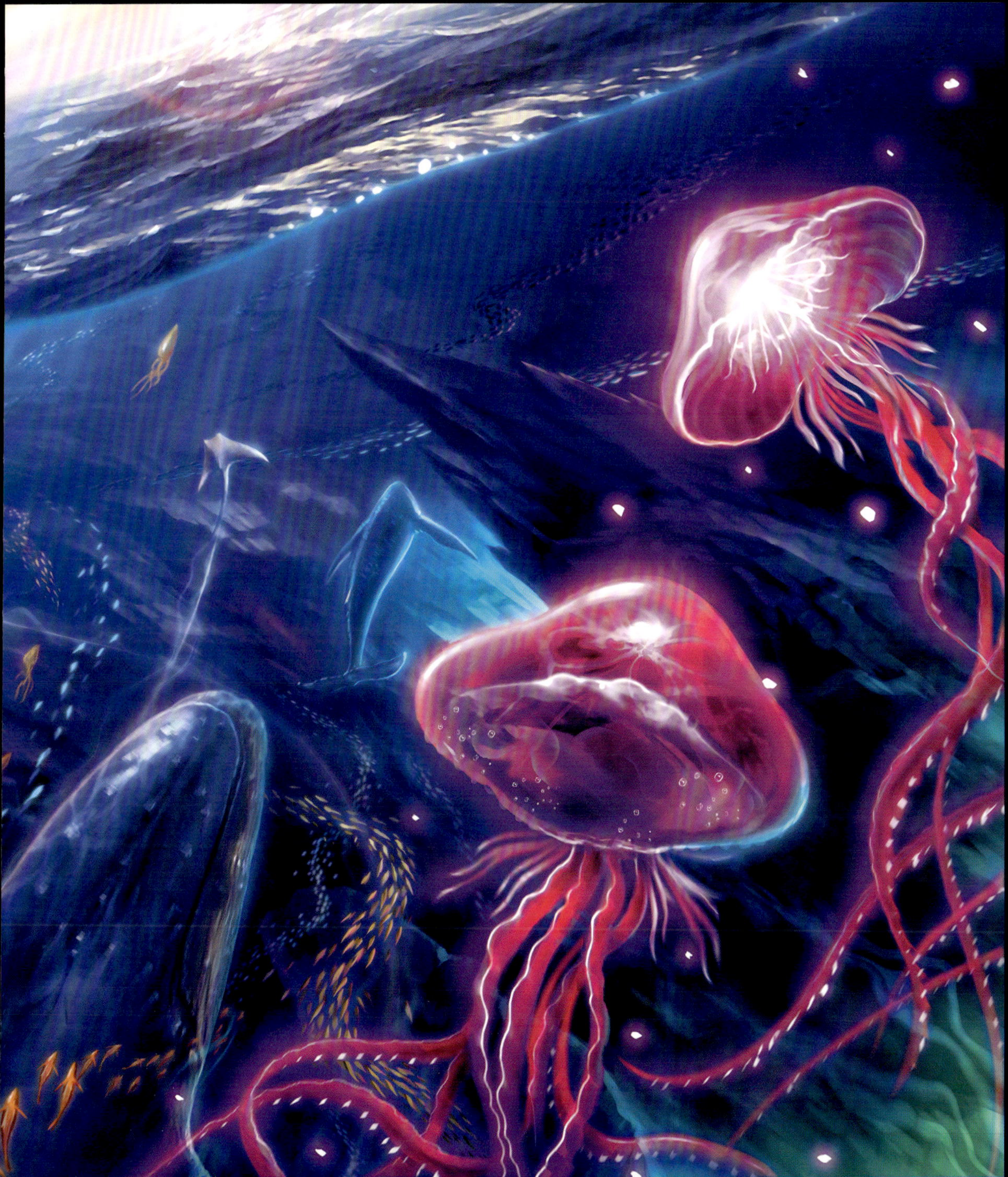

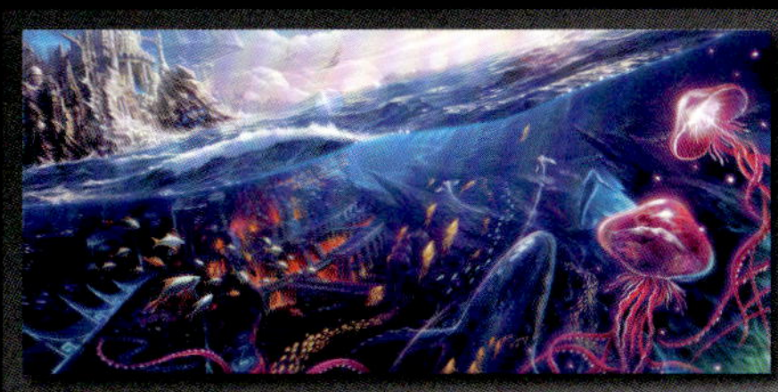

The edge of the sea is adjusted according to the lessons learnt from the above photo as well as other materials available. Sunlight flare above the surface and other highlighted areas are added in. On the left foreground of the scene, a group of fish has been included to remedy the imbalance created by the jellyfish on the right. Light and shade underwater are adjusted, as well as submarine objects at different depths. *Atlantis* is completed.

# MAIN POINTS

The "half underwater perspective" should be applied differently to different works of art. Take one of my previous works *Loch Ness Monster* as an example. How could underwater effects be dealt with now that the focal point is above water?

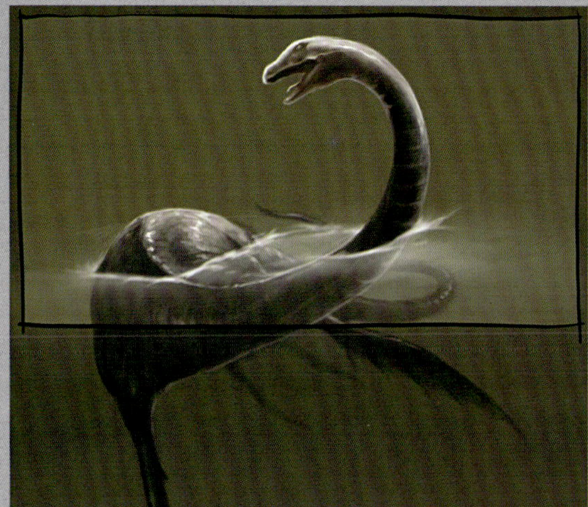

First, we need to draw the main object, deciding which parts of it are above the water and which are below.

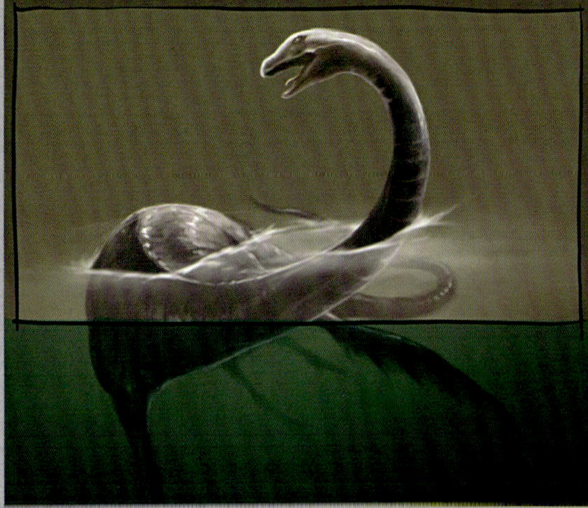

The colour, transparency and visual range of lakes differ from those of seas. As the focal point of the scene sits above the water, objects underwater should be rendered with less, and gradually declining details.

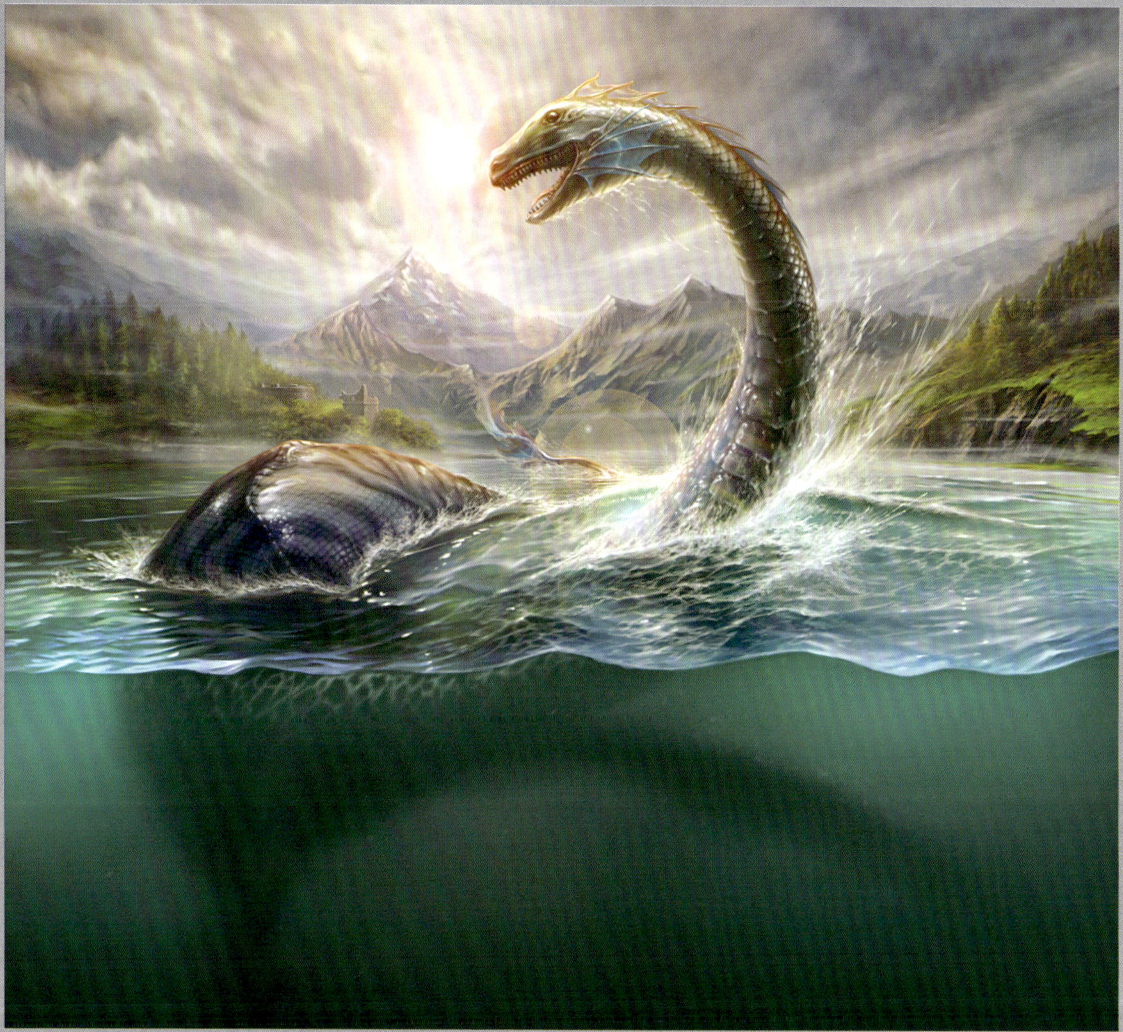

Underwater objects can be blurred not only to give a sense of turbidity to the lake water but also to form a stark contrast to the precision of the main object above water. The parts of the main object that are nearest to the water's surface should be defocused given the influence and obstruction of waves. This will improve the sense of realness. The body part underwater should be slightly enlarged and dislocated to bring out the effects of distortion caused by refraction.

## ▼ Now let's revisit the process for depicting waves.

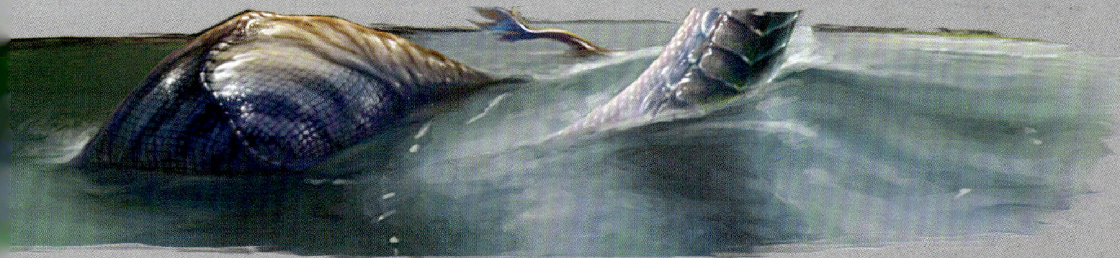

1 The water's surface in the foreground is the closest of all the elements to viewers. To stand out, it should appear as refined as the central object, the Loch Ness Monster. Greenishblue is used as the dominant tone of the water surface to form a stark contrast to the warm colour of yellow produced by backlighting and make the scene more diverse in colour.

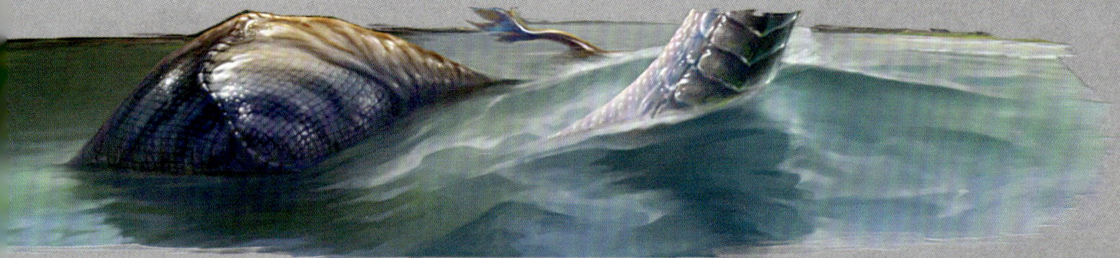

2 The backlit water surface demonstrates an abundance of effects. The reflected image in the water of the Loch Ness Monster's body pair well with the fragmented waves, producing complex colour changes. The colour should not appear "dirty", so even in the dark area, we need to apply a relatively clean, or pure, colour wash.

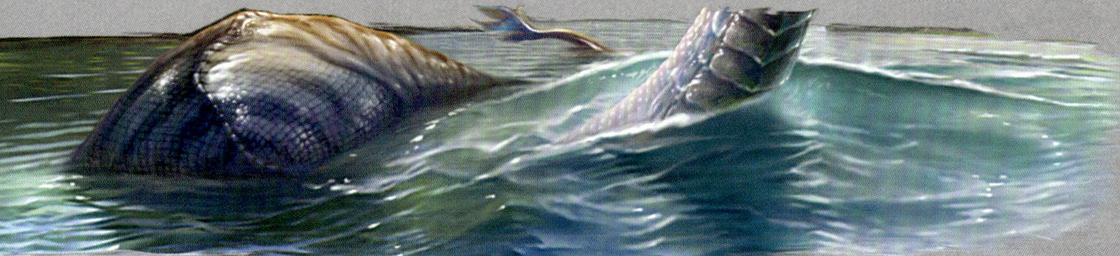

3 The crest of the wave is highlighted. Distortion to the inverted images on waves is reinforced. Thus the water is completed.

4 The Loch Ness Monster's movements should also produce white waves and sprays of water which can be painted in using white alone, given that the water is transparent.

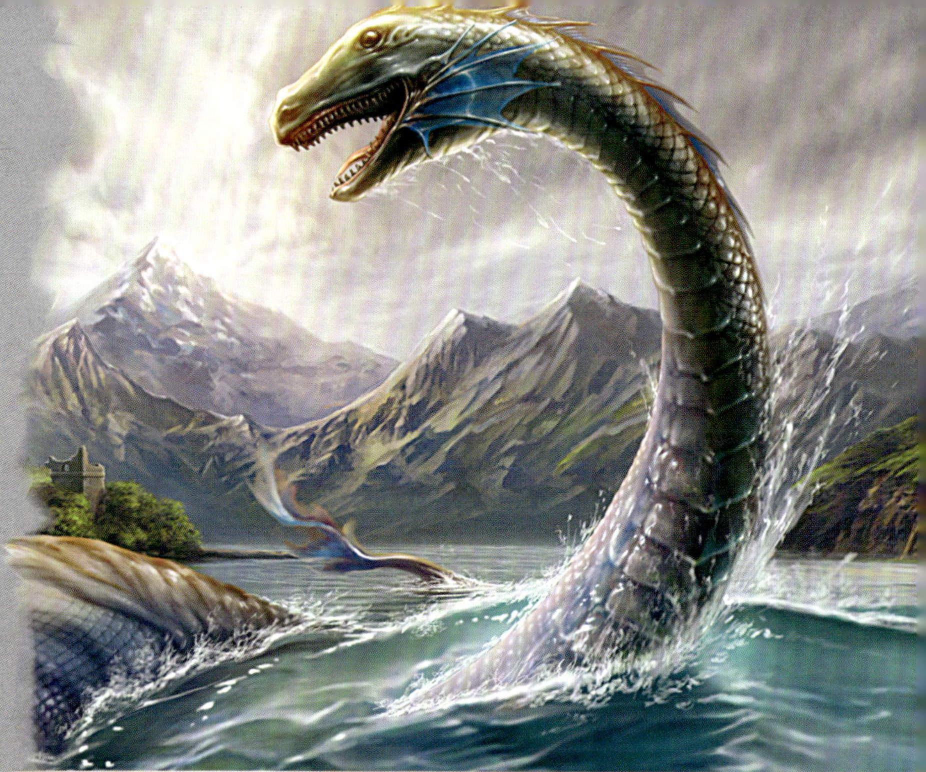

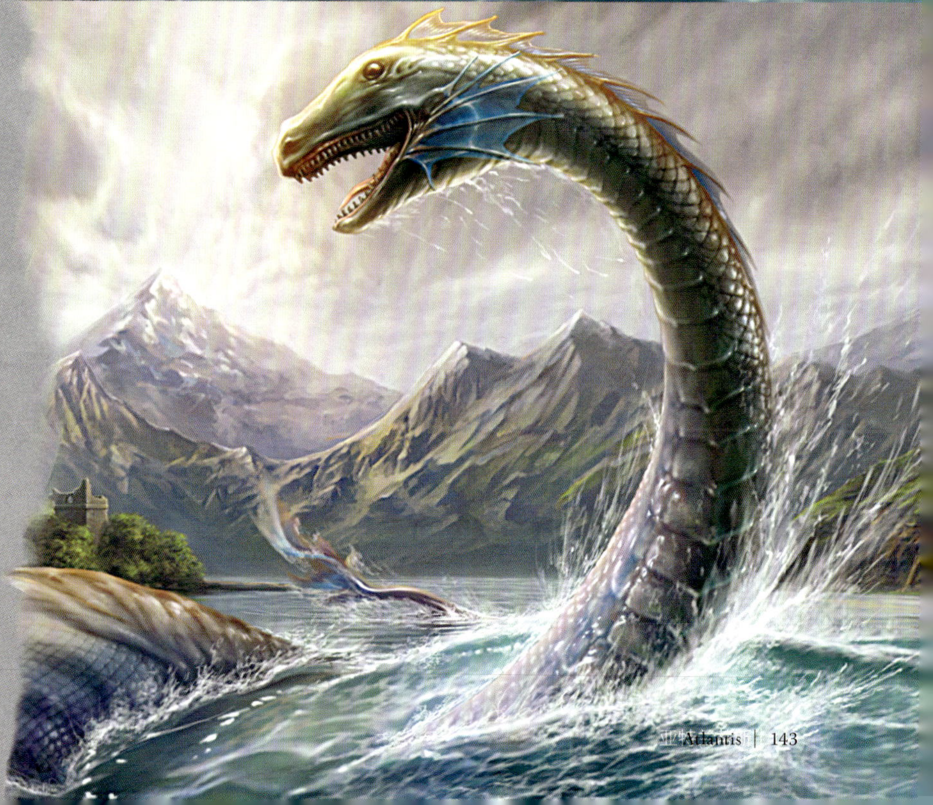

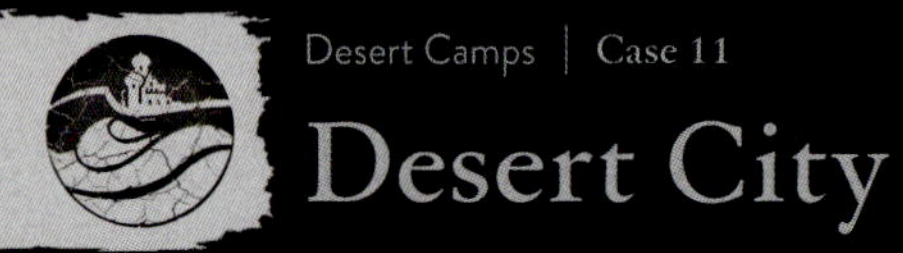



# Desert City

Given Dubai's proximity to both the gulf and desert, it is important that we stop by at the desert before departure. After a car ride through the rows and rows of buildings to the outskirts of the city, my eyes finally fell upon a boundless stretch of desert. Unlike the clean blue gulf, the desert landscape features extensive waves of golden dunes. To reach the destination, the desert camp, we must traverse the endless rise and fall of the sand dunes. A locally modified SUV is necessary for completing our desert adventure.

Riding across dunes is known as "desert safari". Driving in the depth of a desert is like sailing a small boat in the sea. As the traces of urbanity were disappearing behind us, a sense of desolate melancholy set in. The closer we were to the dunes, the more the once distant waves grew as lofty as hills. Soon, our team of cars had vanished into the endless stretch of dunes. Moving forward along the curved routes, it was thrilling to feel the car climb upward and charge downward, the unique charm of the desert was ever fascinating. Unlike that of the vast sea's "mystery" and the endless grassland's "vitality", this charm was a kind of "desolation" that of unending, deep stupor, even the roar of our fast-moving SUV failed to awake the desert sea from its deadly silence. Of course, everything changes. A sand storm, such a display of massive strength from this tranquil land, would leave us shuddering. Stood atop a hot sand bank as we took a rest along the way, we looked out to see the sky and sands merge in the distance. I let my thoughts float with them, finding myself in a world of my own.

We arrived at the desert camp at dusk. Against the setting sun, the beautiful scene of the flickering campfire against the golden expanse reminded me of something: a city hidden in a desert, its existence unknown. Outside of boundless yellow sands, there were rocks of every shape and form; once a land of pleasure, it now exists only as a legend. Like the "Iram of the Pillars" mentioned in the Qur'an, the *Desert City* takes form in my mind. Sometimes, inspiration comes from our observations and feelings, and fantasy works of art can manifest in your mind sparked by the combination of a particular environment with a specific past experience. As these diverse elements are pieced together, a scene will materialize before your eyes.

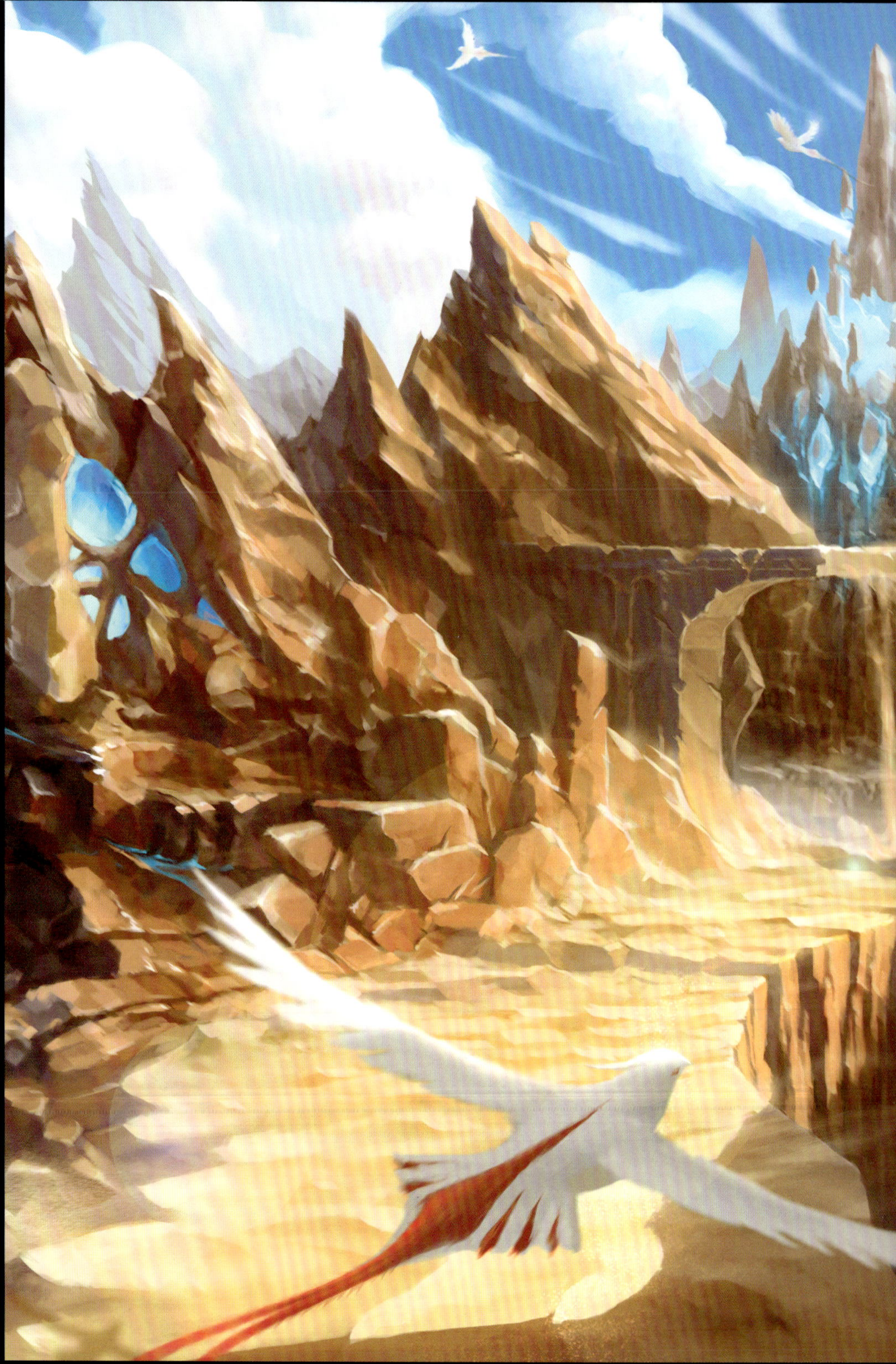

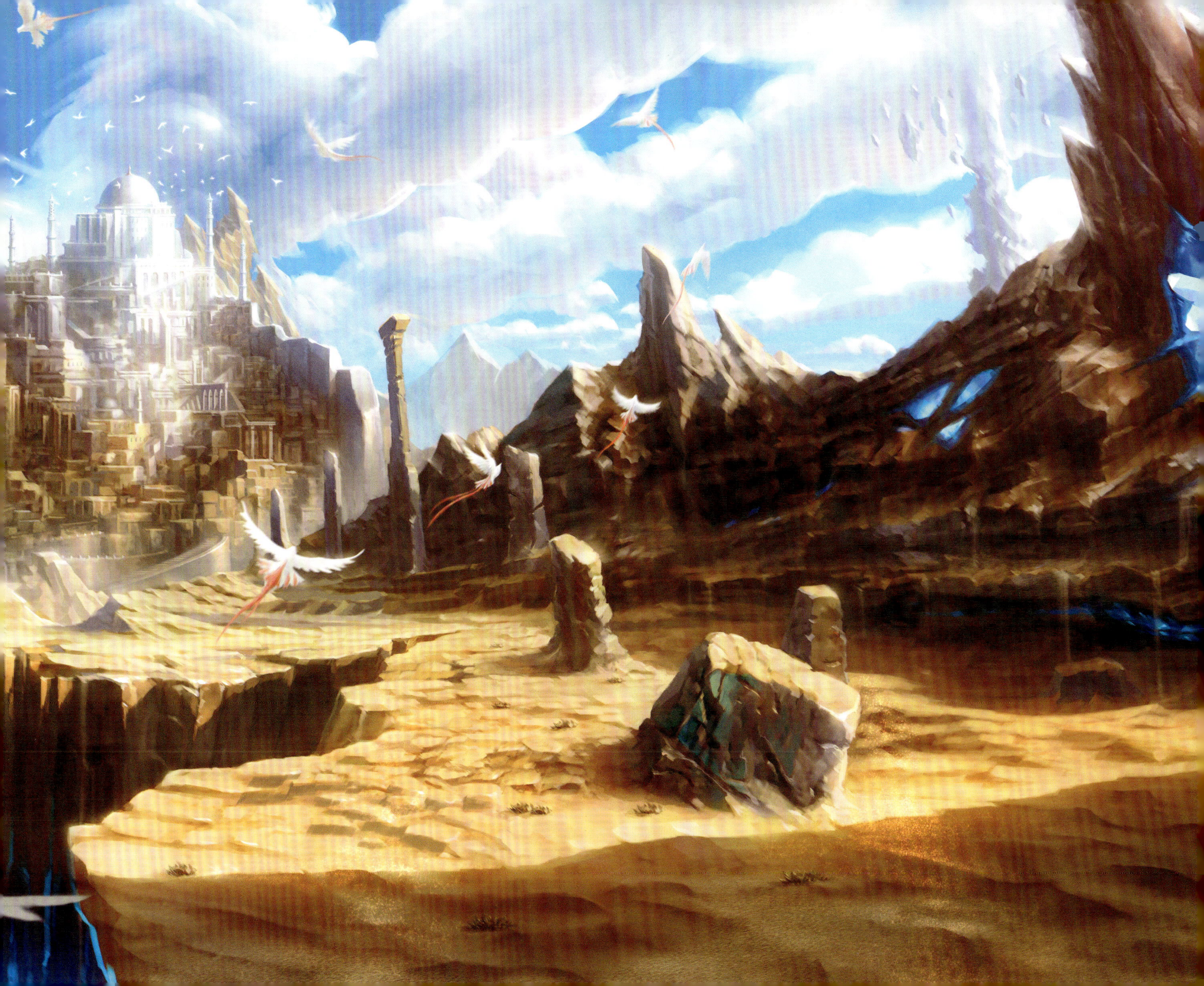

# THOUGHTS ON CREATION

*This was my first experience in the desert. It left a deep impression on me. The scenery and experience inspired this current design. Many people may have visited beaches, trampled on sands, or looked at pictures and videos of such places. They can picture the desert landscape with these resources. A firsthand experience, however, reveals that the desert is unlike a beach. They are both sandy but this does not make them similar. The feeling a picture gives you is entirely different from the one the real desert gives. That is why exploring by yourself is so important.*

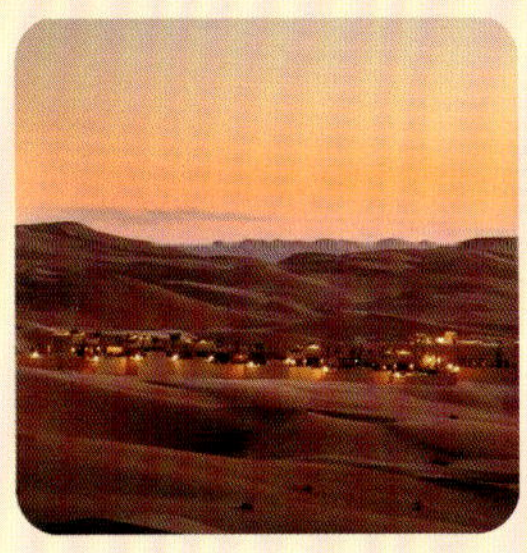

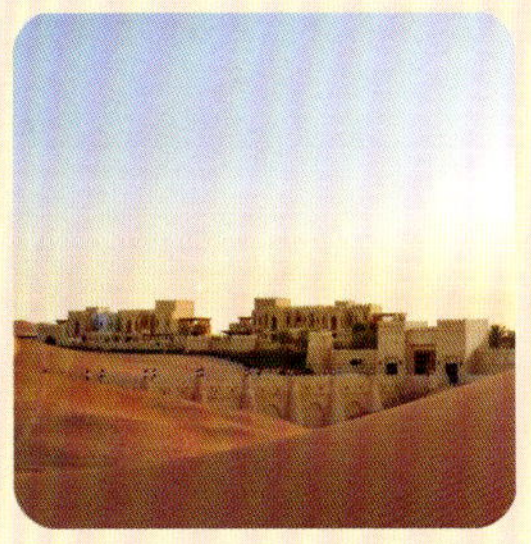

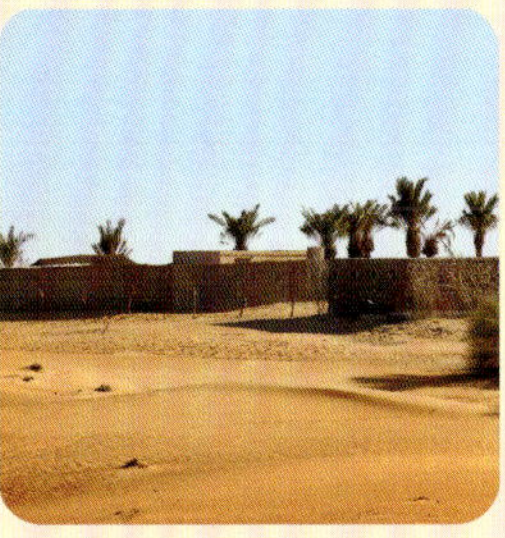

## ▲ DESERT CAMPS

Desert camps serve as places to rest for travellers to this difficult terrain. They are usually pitched in flat areas and surrounded by low walls. Besides the essential campfires, barbecues, and tents, some camps also have performances and activities like Tanoura dances, belly dancing, and henna tattoos.

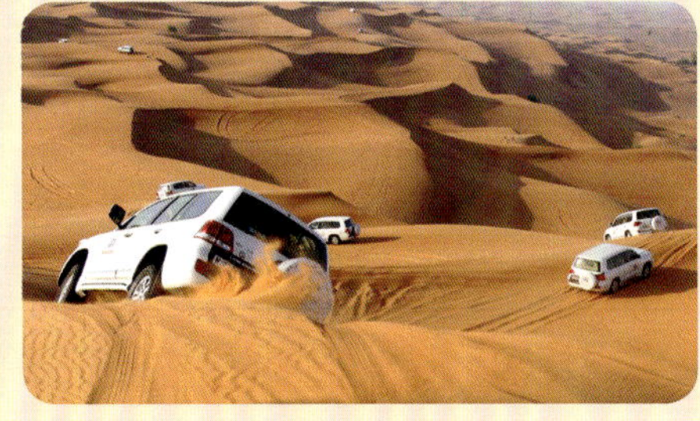

## ▶ DESERT SAFARI

"Desert safari" refers to the activity of climbing up the ridge of a dune before sliding back down from the top. The fast fall feels weightless. When you charge upward, dread of the unknown surges is within you because you can see nothing from that angle but the sky. Passengers may feel the same thrill as riding a roller coaster. I consider the "desert safari" not so much a test of courage as an attempt to be part of the desert, but an opportunity to challenge yourself and experience the fun of the desert.

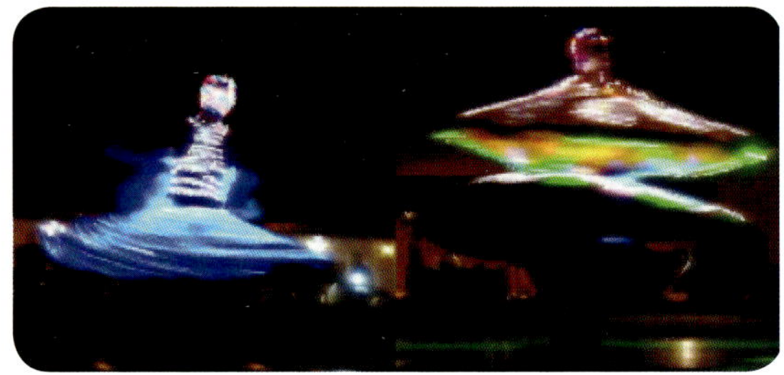

## ▲ THE TANOURA DANCE

The Tanoura dance was developed from a religious rite that involves spinning to reach a trance-like state of "inner, emotional, and spiritual" alignment. The Tanoura dance has a Turkish counterpart, but the two differ in the way that dancers spin. For me, the timing and the speed of performance and the diverse techniques of the Tanoura dance make it better than the Turkish one that I also saw in Turkey. The light installations that decorate the costumes shine with different colours when the dancer spins, making the performances aesthetically pleasing. Despite fewer performing elements and effects, the Turkish spinning dance is also worth experiencing because it feels more sacred with its dim lighting, simple and clean environment, plain music, and simple dancing form.

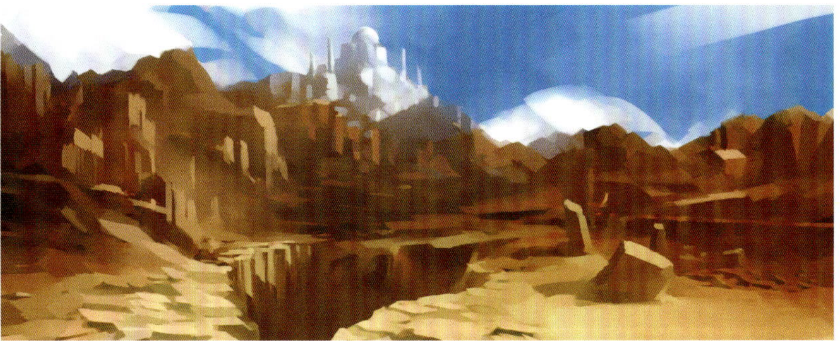

To begin with this piece, let's draw a sketch of the desert. Long stretches of desert and endless dunes might appear beautiful in their desolate way but aren't ideal for the construction of buildings. Such a composition does not lend itself to the design intention. Considering that Dubai is located in a desert of sand dunes and bare rocks, it is more appropriate to situate *Desert City* in a semi-desert and semi-rock environment. The holy, pure colour of white is applied here as the key tone of the city, paired with a bright blue sky and white clouds.

The foreground is populated with dunes, rocks, and valleys to bring out a sense of abundance and depth while scattered stones and dilapidated structures form a stark contrast to the city in the distance.

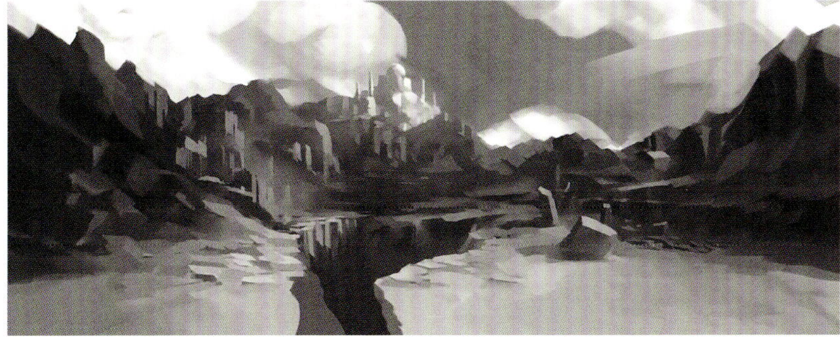

Reviewing the first sketch reveals that using a wide-angle fails to reproduce the magnificence of a desert landscape. To correct this, surrounding objects are extended to broaden the composition and improve the framing.

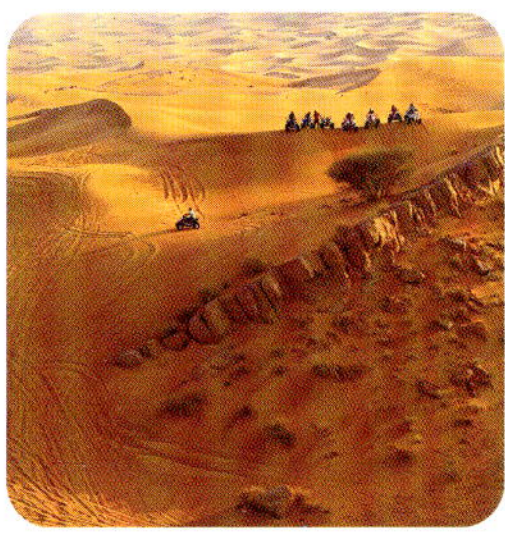

## ◄ ROCK HILLS

Rock hills in the desert exist in different forms, usually of irregularly sized rocks. Some are buried in the desert, others are half-buried, and more still standing erect like stone walls... Their colour is close to that of the desert though not identical. Side by side, the rock hills and sand dunes represent the perfect combination of the hard with the soft.

Let's refine the sketch. Sands and rocks of different textures are distinguished by their shapes and colours, and their borders are handled properly with reference to relevant materials. The location of the sun is pinpointed so to establish consistent light and shade effects throughout the whole scene. The size and layout of the city are determined. For regional consistency, this design adopts aspects of the *White Mosque's* composition. The main structure in the distance features a dome, surrounded by buildings and streets. The gradient tool is applied to make the colour of buildings near the rocky area close to that of the rocks themselves so that the white city does not appear sudden and out of place.

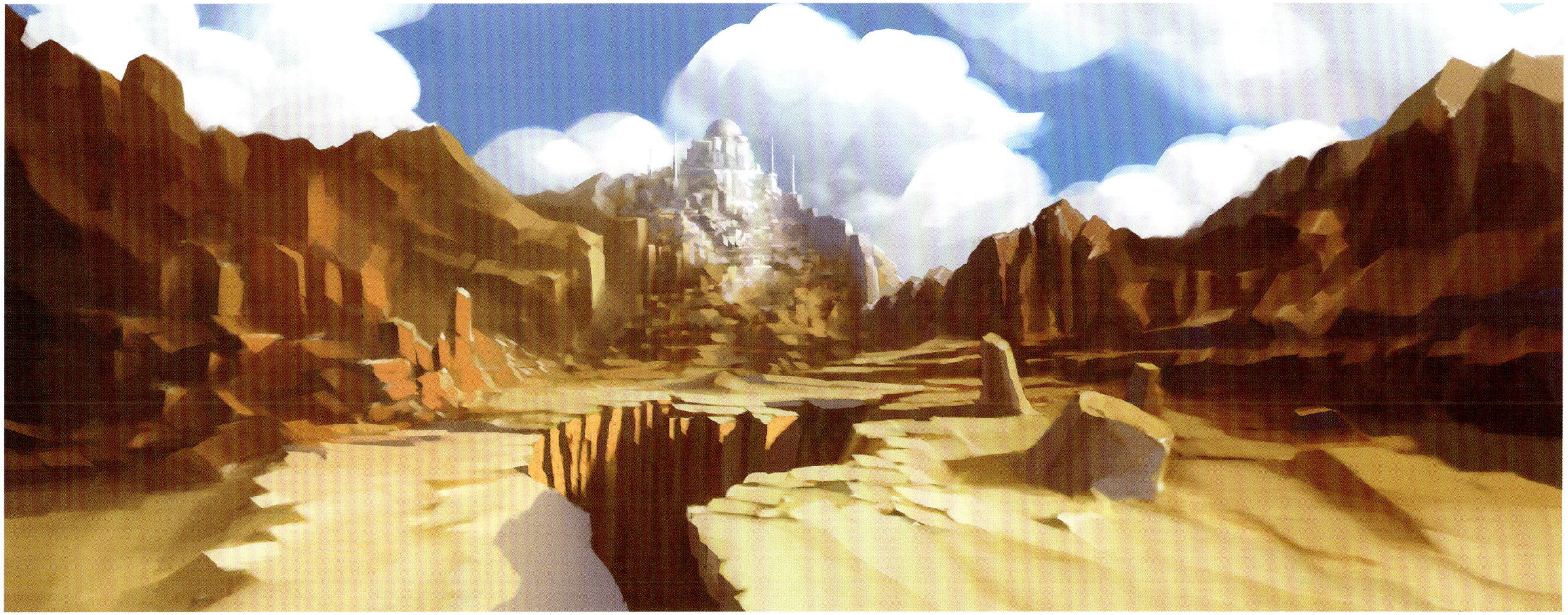

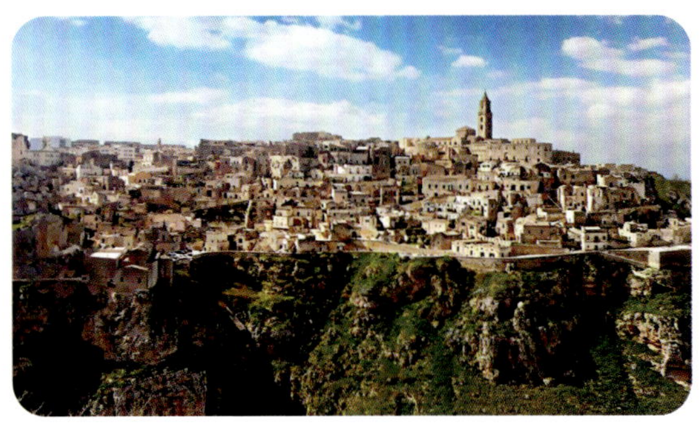

## ◀ MATERA

Many architectural complexes in the world resemble the old town of Matera, a multi-dimensional complex of structures. Most of the reproductions depict natural landscapes situated near mountains. This town was also used as a reference for this current design.

Let's continue with our refinement. Clouds in the sky are rendered in a diverse array of shapes. They hover over the city and in sections, spiral around its structures, their movement changing under the influence of winds. This treatment centres the "city" as our focus, around which other objects will be depicted.

Then, the city is refined with reference to relevant materials. Rational structural layout and the consistency of light and shade are key considerations during this process.

Rock hills are drawn near the city. Their different heights and shapes serve as a tool for regulating the "rhythm" of the scene. Some "sharp peaks" are added to show the dangerous nature of the environment. A patch of shade is added to the area of dunes closest to the viewer where sunlight is blocked by rock peaks. This treatment makes up for the relatively monotone foreground that features only a large area of yellow sand. Purple is added to the shaded area to match the warm yellow colour and, in turn, making the dark area clearer and more colourful.

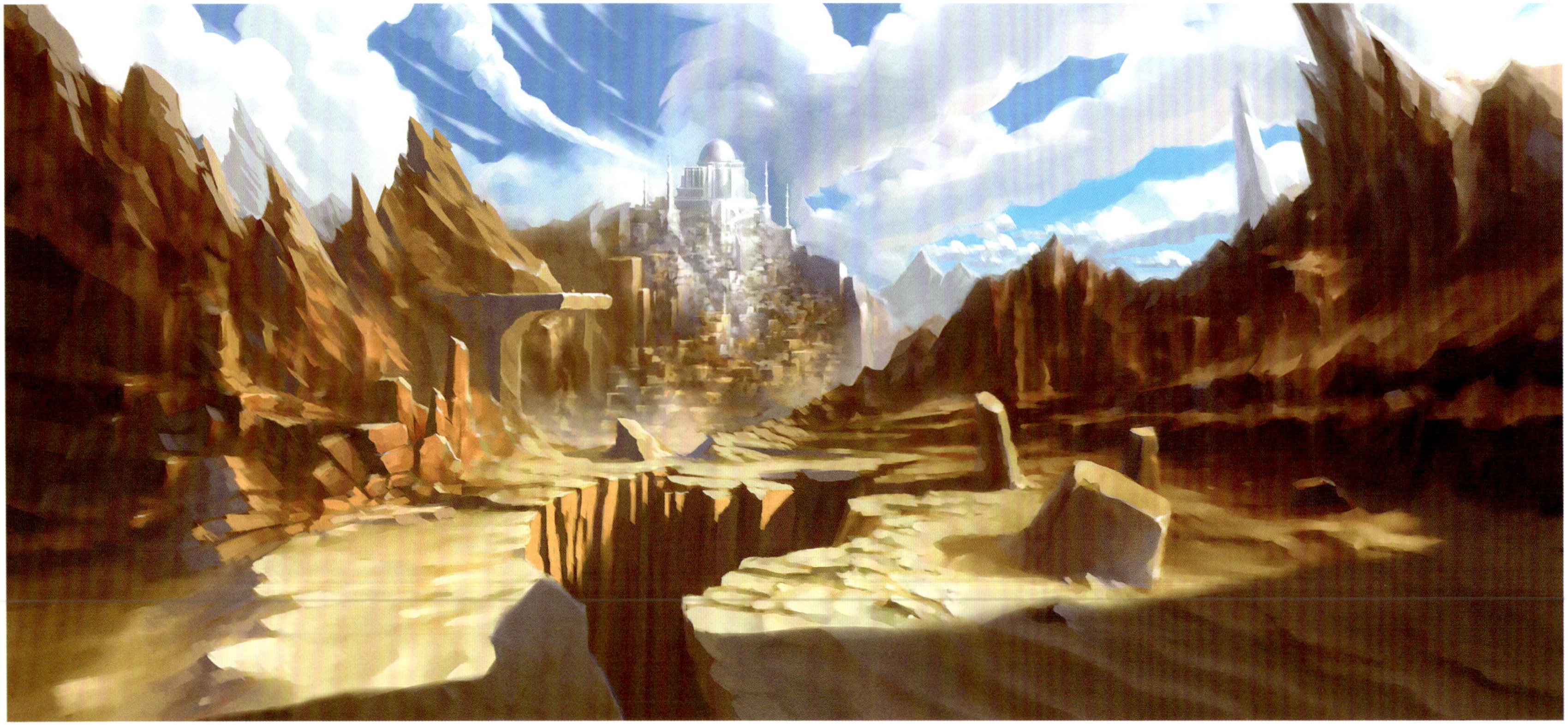

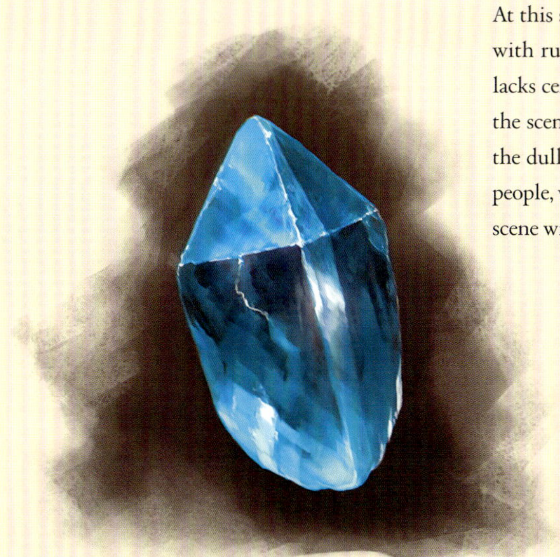

At this stage, the city heaped like a mountain in the distance, and its surrounding rock hills piled with rugged and weird stones already appear "surreal". As a fantasy work of art, however, it still lacks certain content. A cold ice blue is added here as a complement to the warm colour of yellow, the scene's dominant tone. The translucent texture of the shining crystal forms a stark contrast to the dull sands and rocks. Considering that crystals and gems are a favourite treasure of the Dubai people, we will use crystals in the following design as a central fantasy element, thus refreshing the scene with an entirely new twist.

Crystals of ice blue are fitted into the crevices of bare rocks. The light they give off is reflected by the nearby rock walls, providing a more diverse range of colour and harmonising the palette. These new elements mean that other objects must be adjusted and refined accordingly. The rolling clouds in the sky are taken to a point of near completion. The crevices near the city are given that same blue glowing as the foreground. More pillars, stone towers, and rock peaks are inserted to balance the composition's proportions.

Suitable fantasy elements can be used to fill a design with an entirely new air. In this design, for example, the rocks protruding around this city situated in an initially desolate desert now glitter with some mysterious and apparently rare mineral resource that shines in the sunlight and even seems to huge stones float in the air…

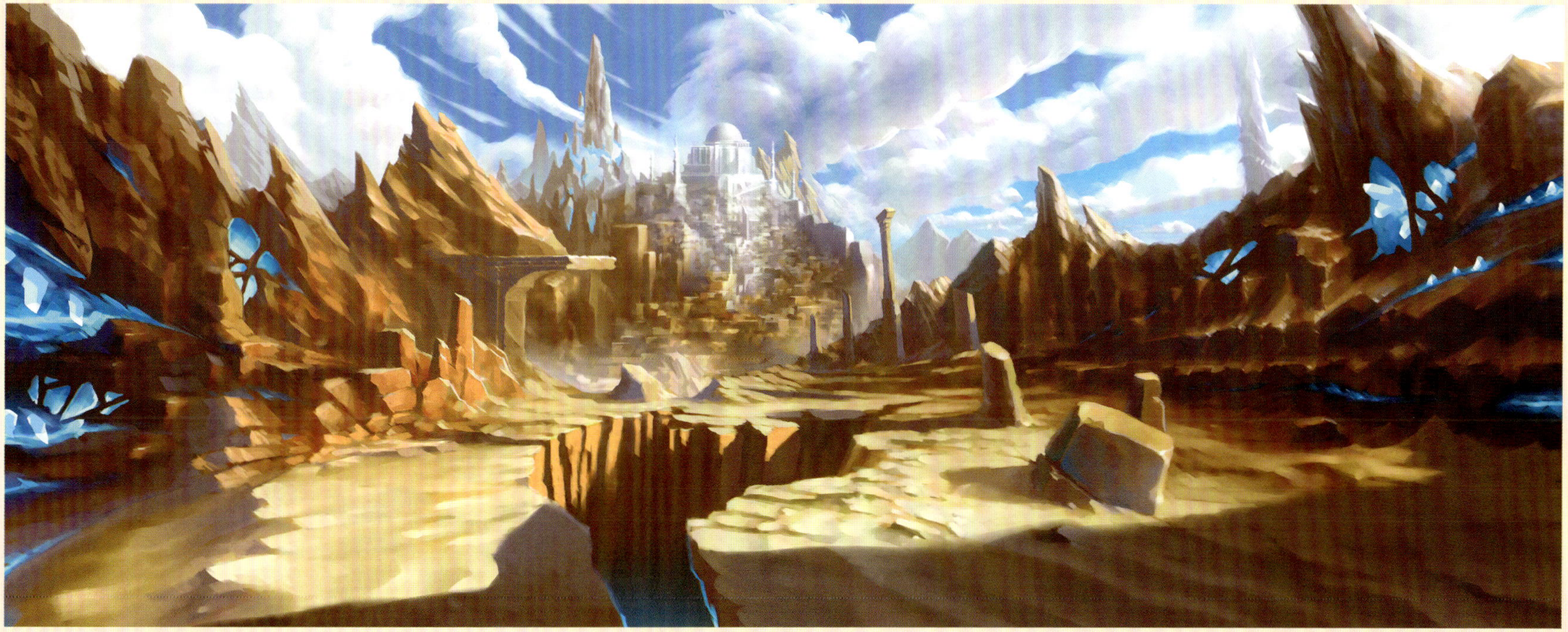

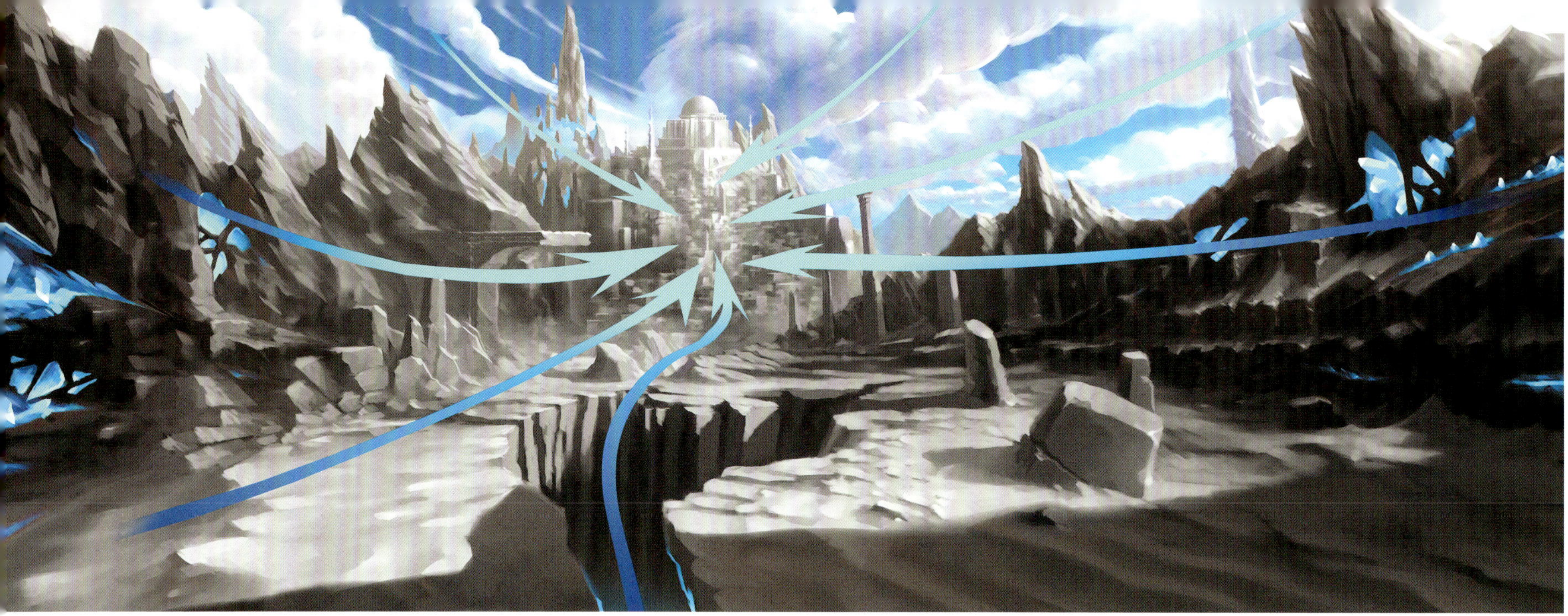

As mentioned above, all the elements of the scene are focused around the city. This is also true of the newly added fantasy elements as "kyanite ore", whose convergence extends from far to near as you see.

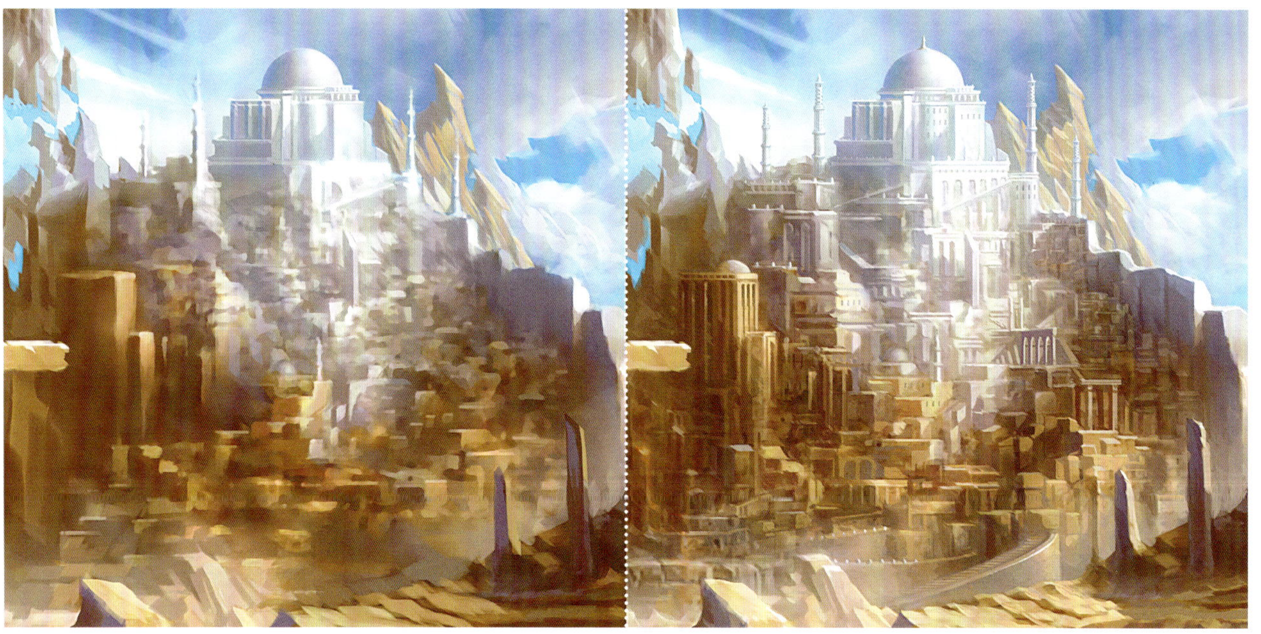

Cities that extend towards a central point require the full capture of their magnificence and structural rigour. It is important that we clearly distinguish the individual location and function of the various types of building on display, as to merely pile them up one on top of the other would result in a featureless mess of boxes. The relationship between different buildings requires special attention at a later stage and can often be ignored when starting out. It should be obvious from the city's layout that to wander through it leads from the bottom upward. As far as the scale allows, we can add roads and streets to this effect. Each building should be handled according to its shapes and functions so as to create distinctive features while maintaining consistency throughout.

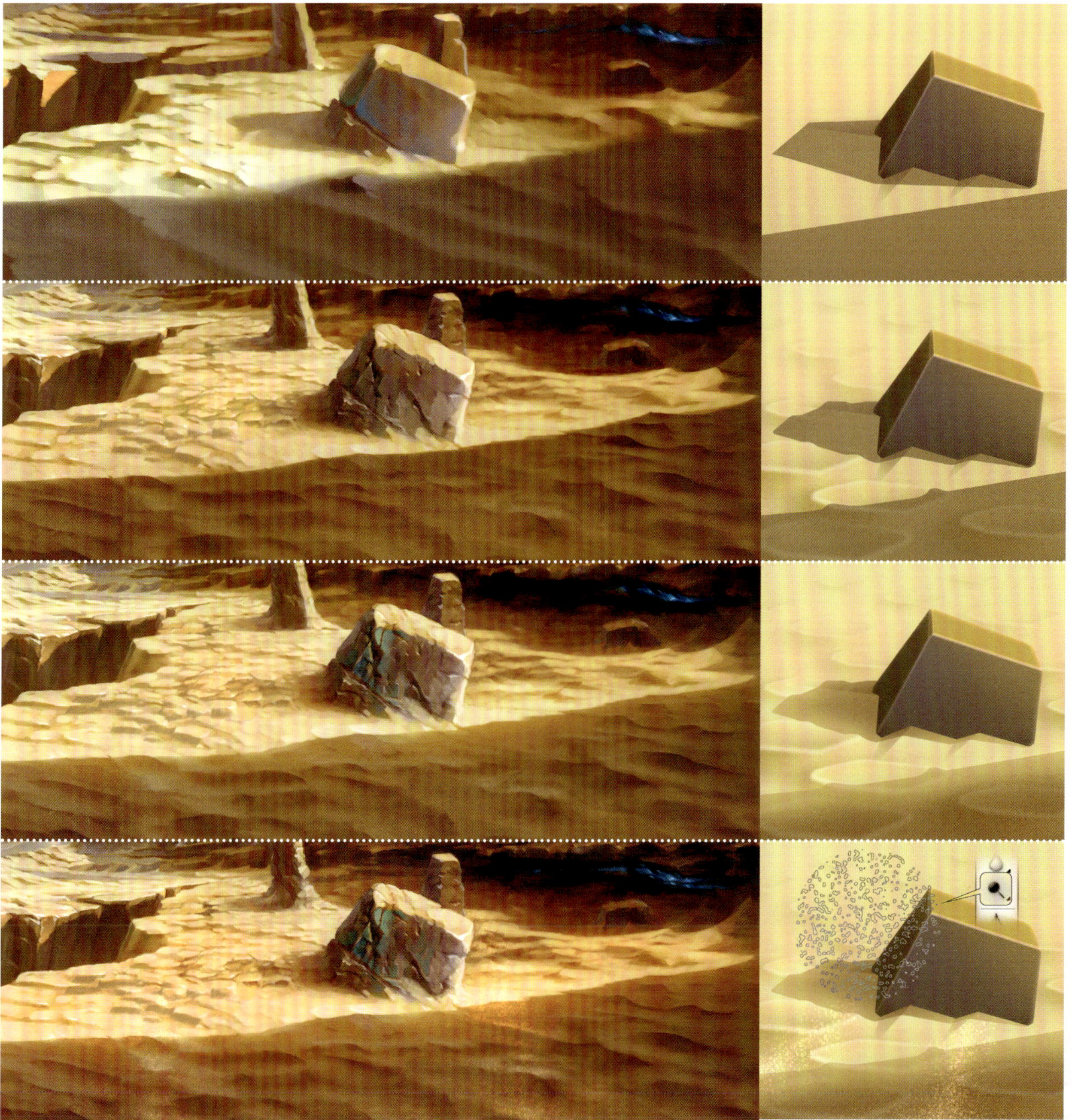

Stones and sand are then depicted in detail. We first need to create a basic shape and apply light and shade effects. The desert scene should appear rugged and the sand need to be uneven because of the objects buried under it.

The texture of the dune surface is also adjusted. More elements are added to make the surface irregular such as "sandpits" and "rubbles", and the influence of shifts in climate on the surface of the earth are shown. The cracking texture added to stones gives expression to the passage of time and ever-changing nature of life here.

The borders of the shaded and light-receiving areas are highlighted to bring out the influence of global lighting effects on the dark areas. Stones are given "damaged" effects and painted in light green so that the scene becomes more colourful, and the debris hints at something artificial that may have once been here.

Granular and strip-like highlight effects simulate the light reflection upon the sand. The texture of the sand land is thus improved. We can use the "Scatter" effect under the "Dodge Tool" option on Photoshop to brighten the scene.

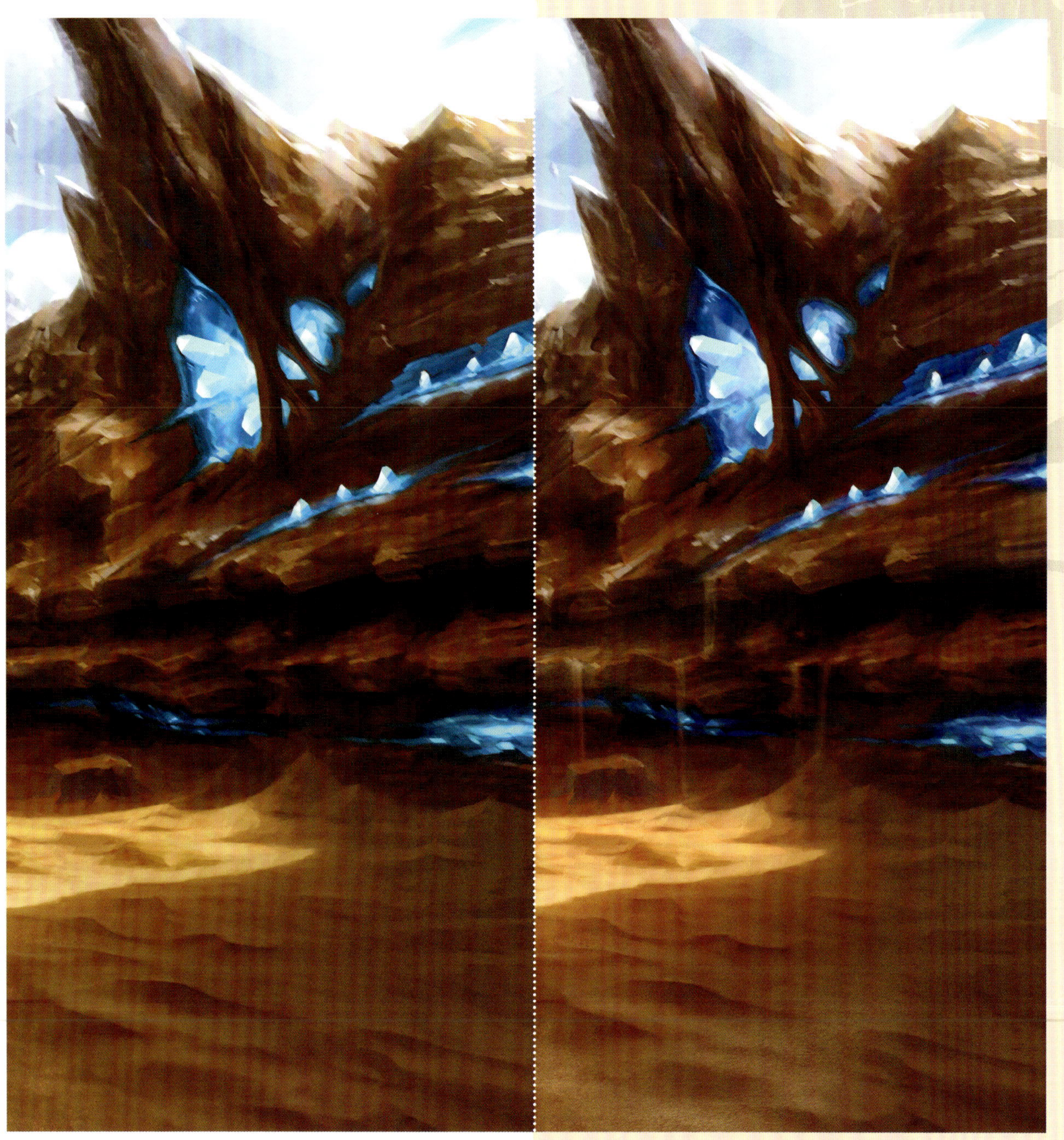

I realised that the glow of the blue crystal was close to the colour of the sky, so I adjusted it to "ultramarine" and changed the sky to "sky blue", thus avoiding the blending of similarly coloured sections and a single colour dominating the scene.

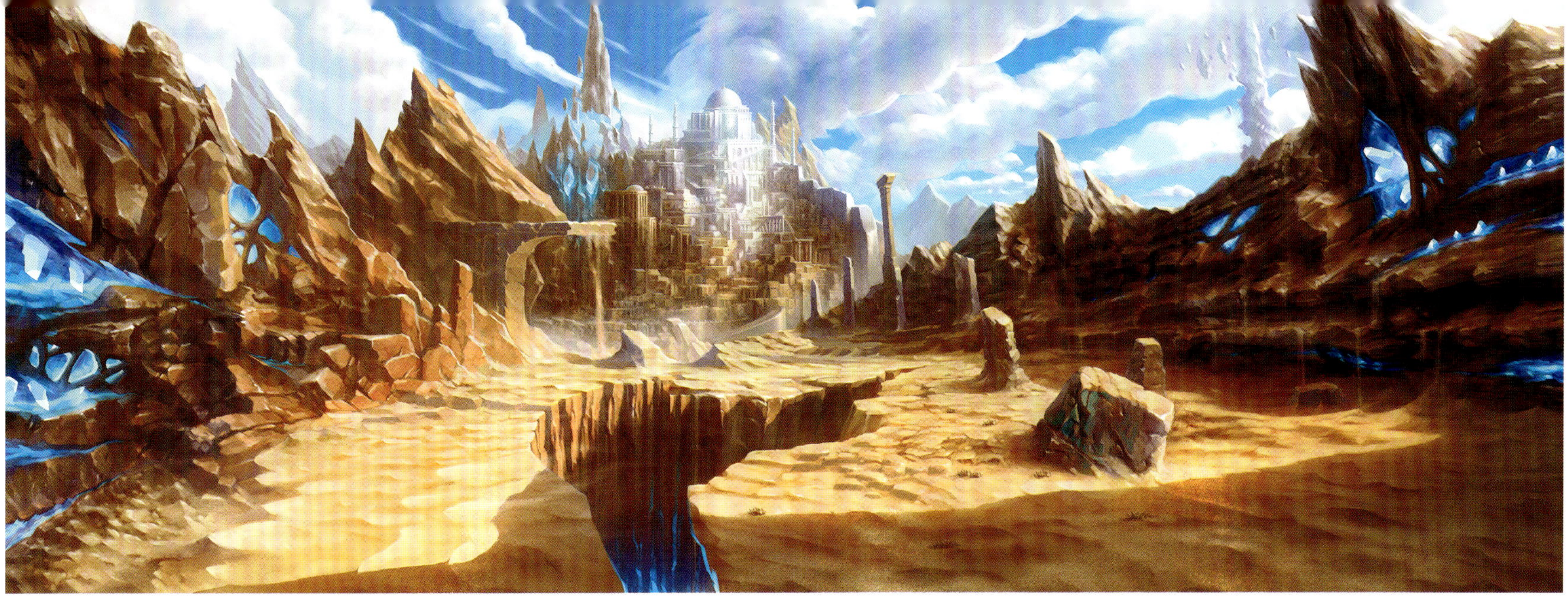

The colours of other objects are adjusted along with that of the crystals. On the right, the colour of the sand is deepened to appear closer to an "orange red" as its appearance is being influenced by backlit objects. The scene thus becomes diverse while consistent in colour. After adding flying dust, sand falling from rocks and plants withering, the scene of *work Desert City* is mostly completed.

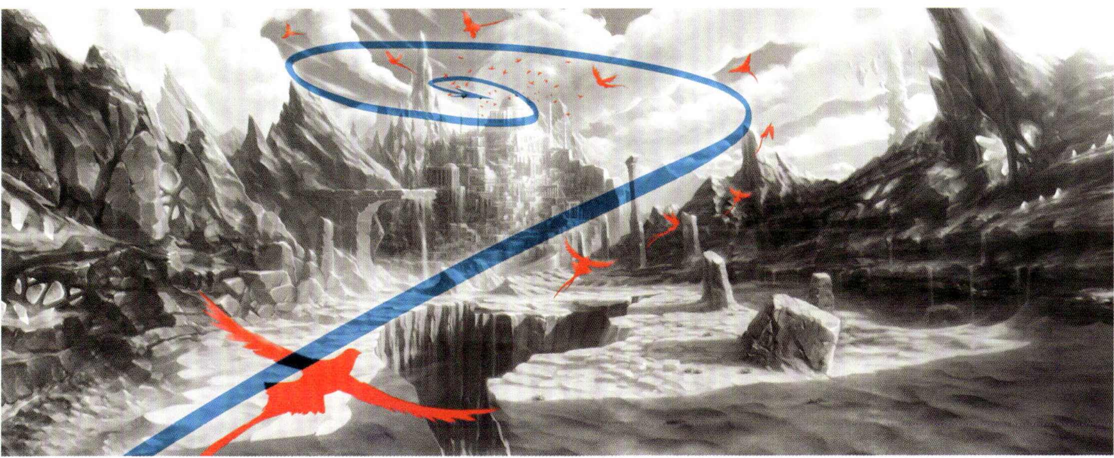

The scene may now contain the fantasy elements necessary for a fantastical scene. But it appears a little dull, for dynamic elements that inject vitality into the static space have not been added.

At the beginning, I envisioned using the distinctive activity of "desert safari" to improve the current design. But the vintage buildings and the fantastic crystals make it difficult for mechanical elements to be integrated. Finally, I chose the "all-purpose" dynamic element of "flying birds" as the final character.

Following the idea that "objects are composed around the city", a flock of birds is added hovering above the metropolis along the trajectory of the blue arrow. The flying birds are "allpurpose" dynamic elements because they are free from spatial limits. Added in a random manner, they are more flexible than racing cars or fast-running animals. Each bird is added according to a certain "rhythm" and the trajectory of their movement fills the blank areas, which works to further diversify the scene. The silhouetting method is applied here for fast revision.

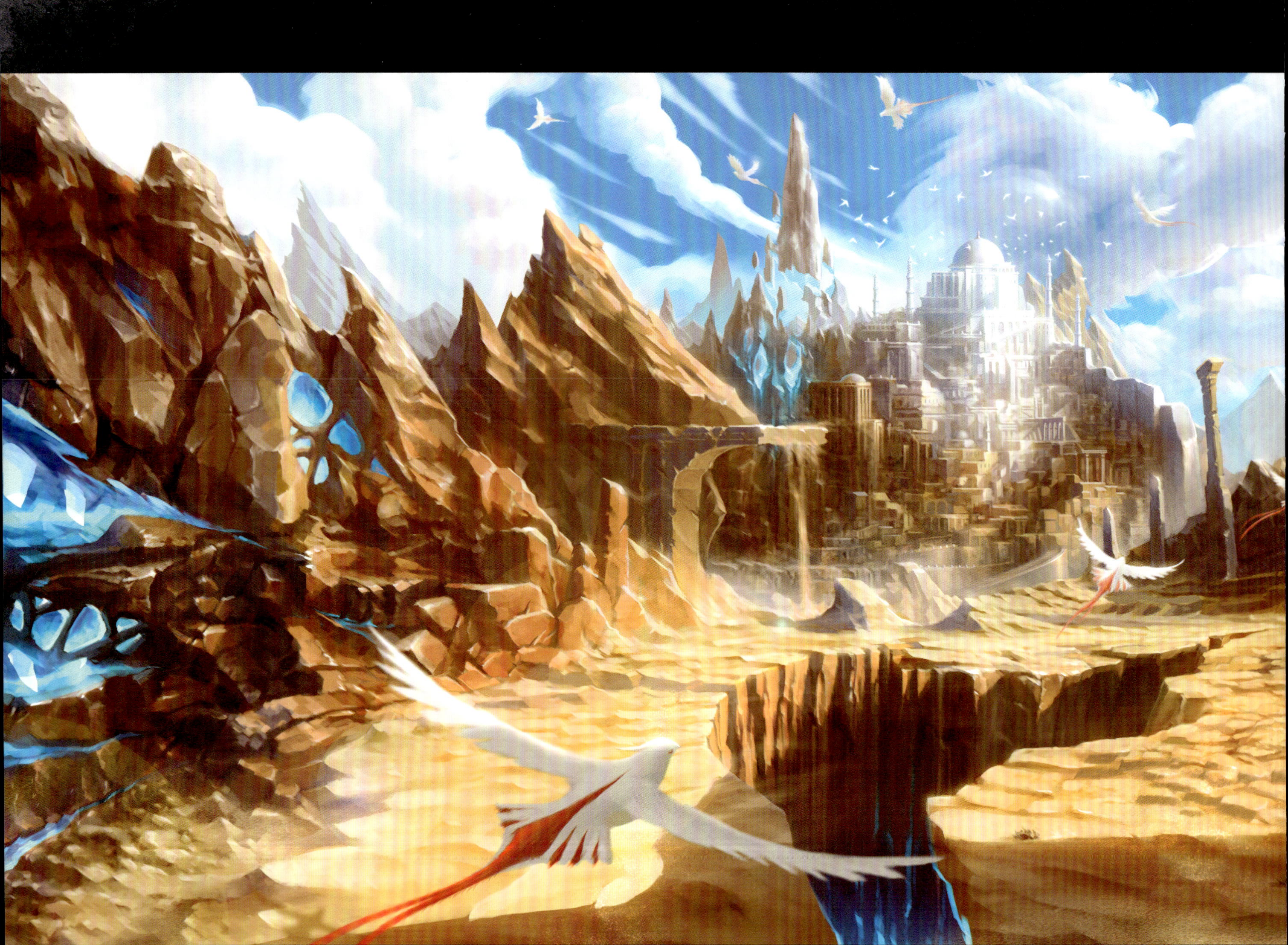

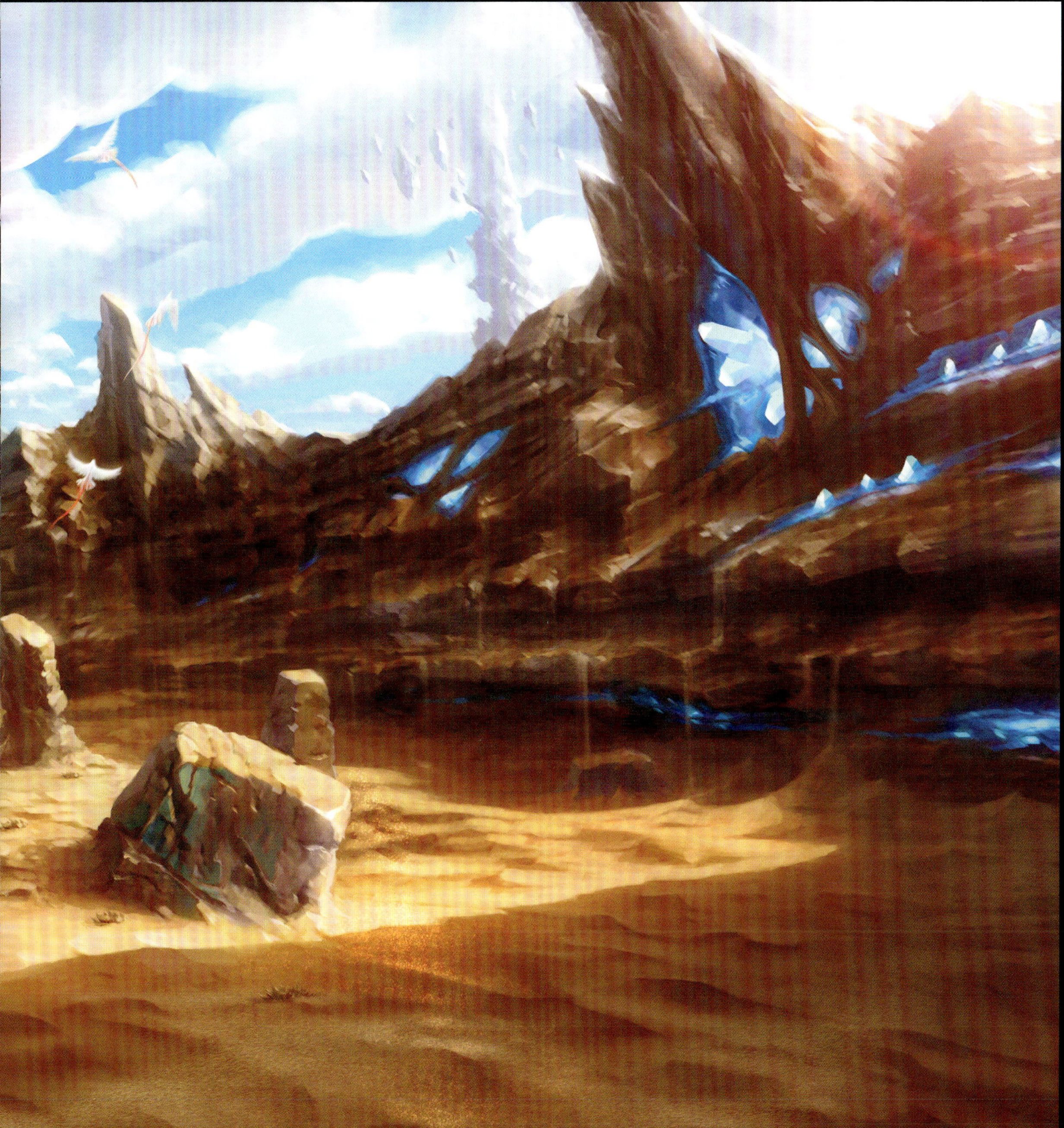

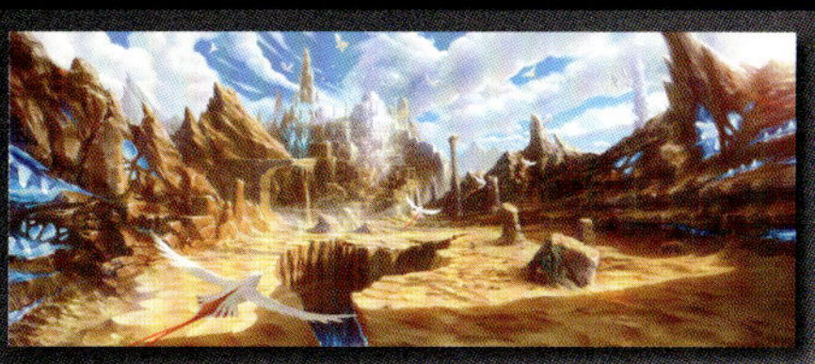

Using the silhouetting method, the flying birds are painted with a white body and a long red tail. This matches the colours of the scene and gives the birds an air of the fantasy. The foreground bird is influenced by the shadows of other objects (whatever new objects are added, we should consider the knockon effect to the overall lighting and insist on drawing objects according to the colour and light effects of the surrounding environment).

With the flying birds in place, glow and flare effects are applied to the environment. Our *Desert City* thus comes to life. With diverse kinds of fantasy world possible, an individual design should follow one consistent direction to ensure it does not deviate from the theme, like a long standing city in the desert.

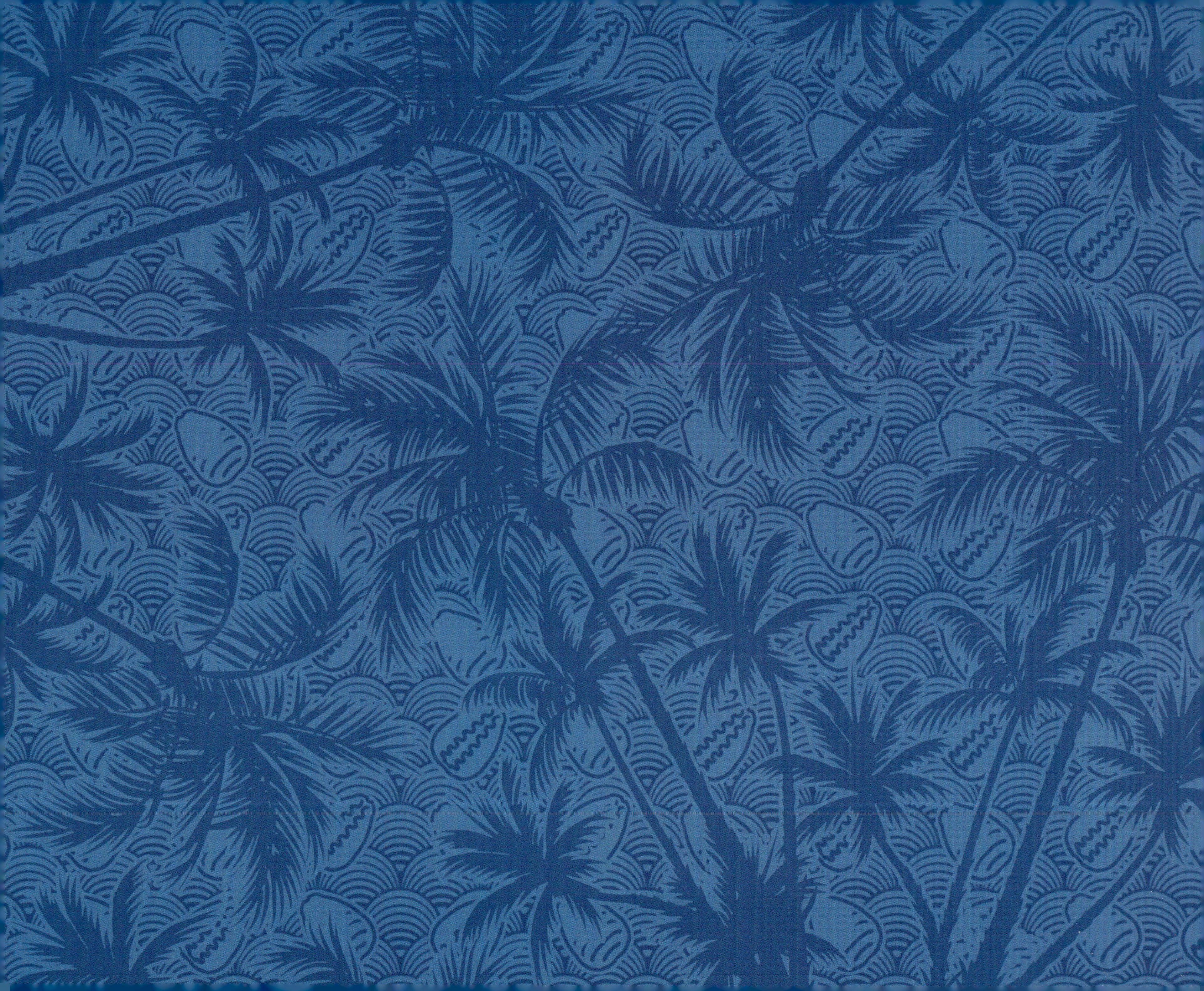

Maldives is an island country of the Indian Ocean, comprised of about 1,200 coral islands. Famous for being an earthly paradise surrounded by blue and clean seawater, it is home to hundreds of species of coral reef fish. Thanks to little human interference, ecosystems here are well protected and boast a purity of nature untainted by industrialisation. The pristine beauty of the archipelago tends to give people the feeling of being in the Garden of Eden.

White beaches surround the coasts of the islands. Refuge from the heating sun is beneath the jungles of luxuriant palm trees. The blue sky and sea are serene and fresh. Lizards of bright colours and herons fluttering their huge wings populate the rainforest plants. The scenery at sunset and sunrise rouses the same awe as a star-filled night sky. Numerous species of plankton transform the moonlit beach into a sea of stars, a true fairyland. Here in Maldives, you can dive to play amongst the coral reef fish or shoals of dolphins. This island is a paradise on the sea.

When it comes to designing fantasy artwork, the untamed landscape of Maldives resembles a flawless photographic negative on which designers are free to let imagination colour. Its unique natural scenery is an unbounded source of inspiration for artists to create stunning fantasy scenes.

The previous chapters present the "history" of Beijing and the "miracle" of Dubai, respectively. This chapter aims to capture the "pure nature" of the Maldives archipelago. These labels serve as helpful guides for pinpointing individual features of each region and thus instilling them into a fantasy design.

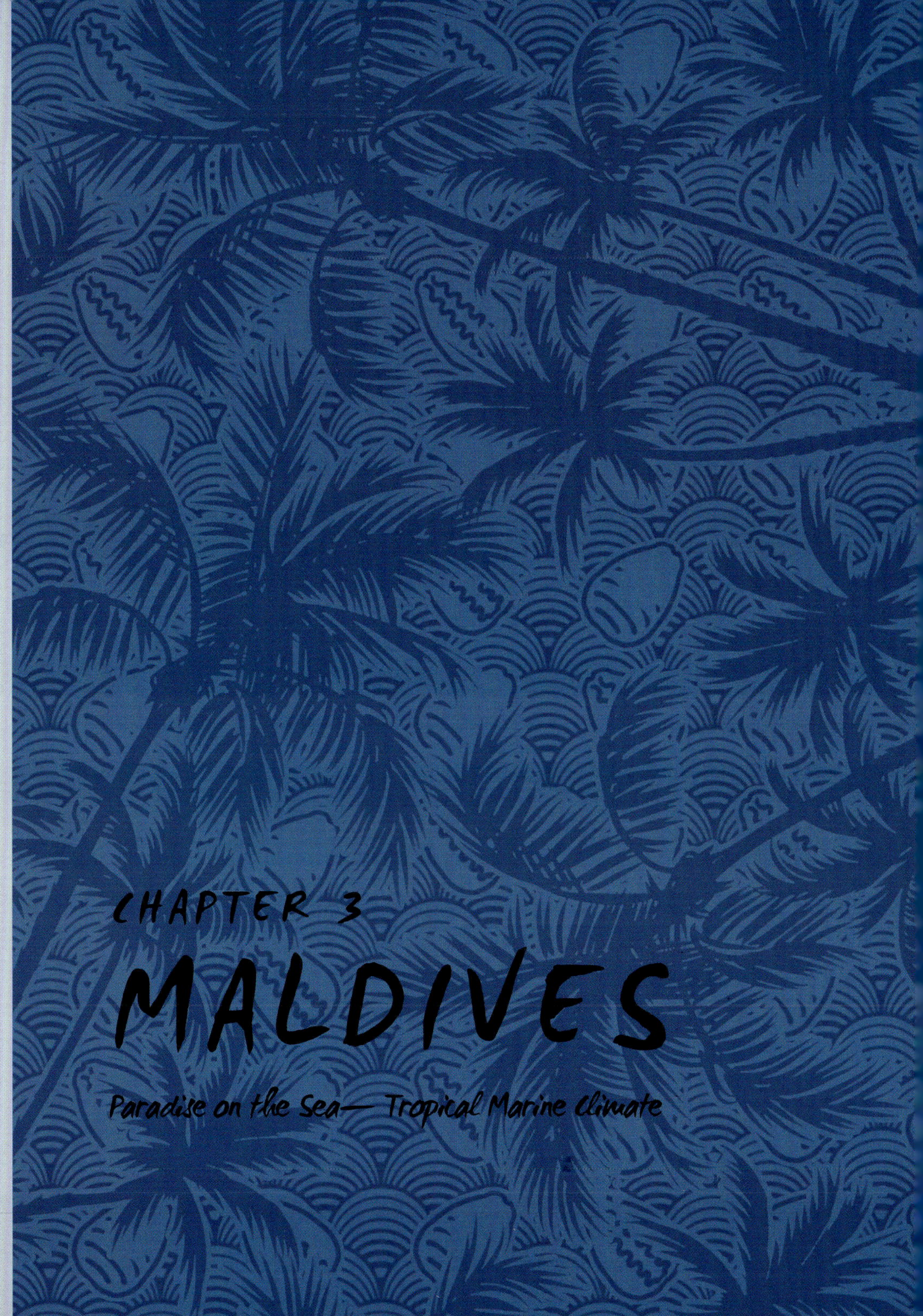

CHAPTER 3

# MALDIVES

Paradise on the Sea— Tropical Marine Climate

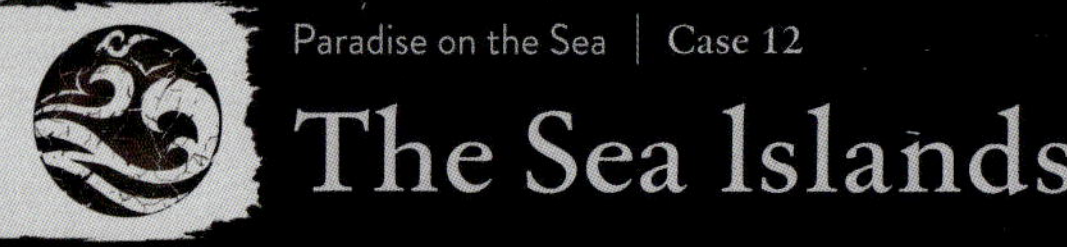



# The Sea Islands

This is the last stop of this book – the beautiful Maldives islands. From Beijing to Dubai, we were able to produce a diverse series of fantasy scenes with local characteristics. In this chapter, the geographically independent cities are replaced by a group of islands. Maldives is the smallest country in Asia, and Malé as its capital is only one of the whole island's collection. Despite its importance as the administrative, economic and cultural centre, Malé does not represent the entire archipelago. By choosing to depict a group of islands, it is possible to distance our design from the social nature: "man-made", "industrialised", "historical" and "legendary". The source of inspiration of this design is the original "nature".

A sea island is a small landmass surrounded by seawater. Usually small in area and simple geographically, it is a secluded environment with a single ecosystem immune from the damage of over-development. Efforts should be made to reduce as much as possible all man-made elements with preference given to those that create a natural and fantastic air.

Paintings first emerged to serve as records of people's life and environment, gradually developed to touch upon topics as diverse as sacrifices, societal constructions and religions. Given that its subject matter sits the closest to a state of "pure nature", *The Sea Islands* should express an understanding of the world very different from that of fantasy artworks with urban spaces.

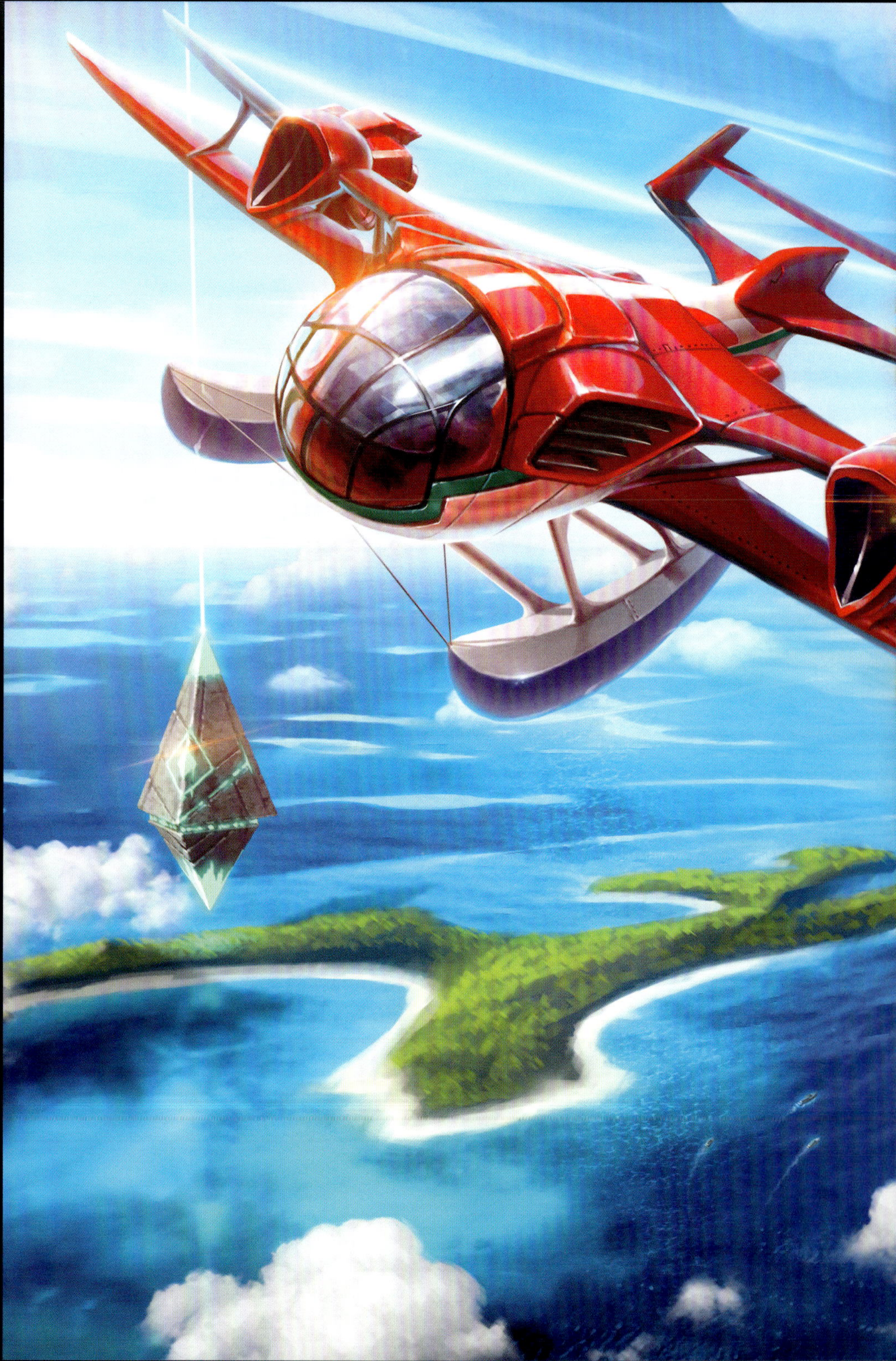

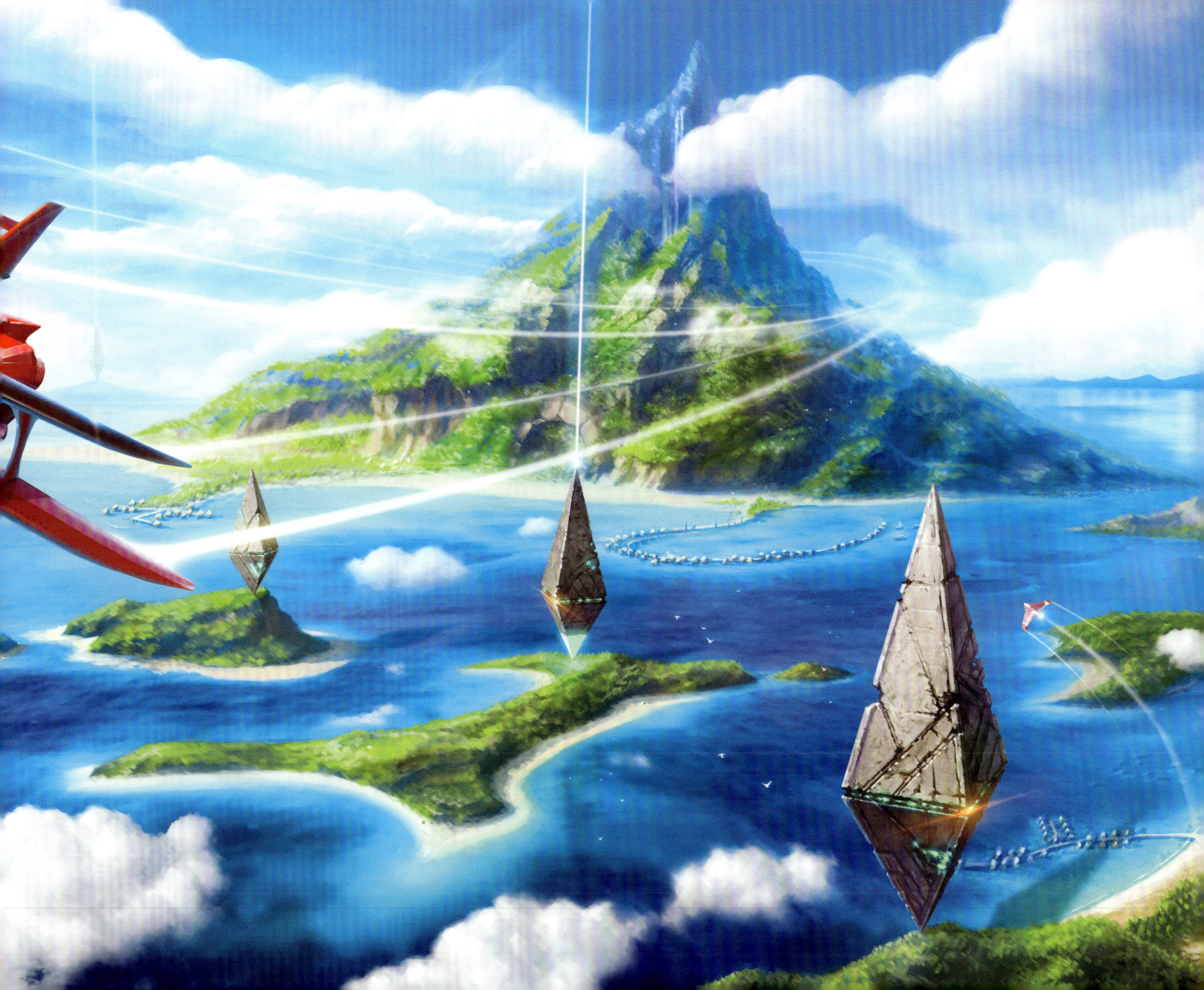

# THOUGHTS ON CREATION

*A five hours flight took me from Dubai to Malé. Maybe because of the refreshing blue sky and sea or the sea breeze that sweeps away heat waves, Malé's climate feels comfortable despite being in the tropical zone. As I headed for a seaplane anchorage, the beauty of the waterscape became immediately apparent. For the first time, I experienced a "clean blue". Upon arrival, my anticipation for the journey ahead was fit to burst when I saw seaplanes bobbing in the water.*

*After a short wait, I took a plane to the hotel. Each hotel has its unique features. Some have large swathes of beach, others can be driven around, and more still boast great fishing spots. The farther an island is away from Malé, the better protected its ecosystems are and the more pleasant its scenery is. Flight by seaplane is different from that in passenger planes. Its height is just right for overlooking the landscape. This design was inspired by my seaplane flight.*

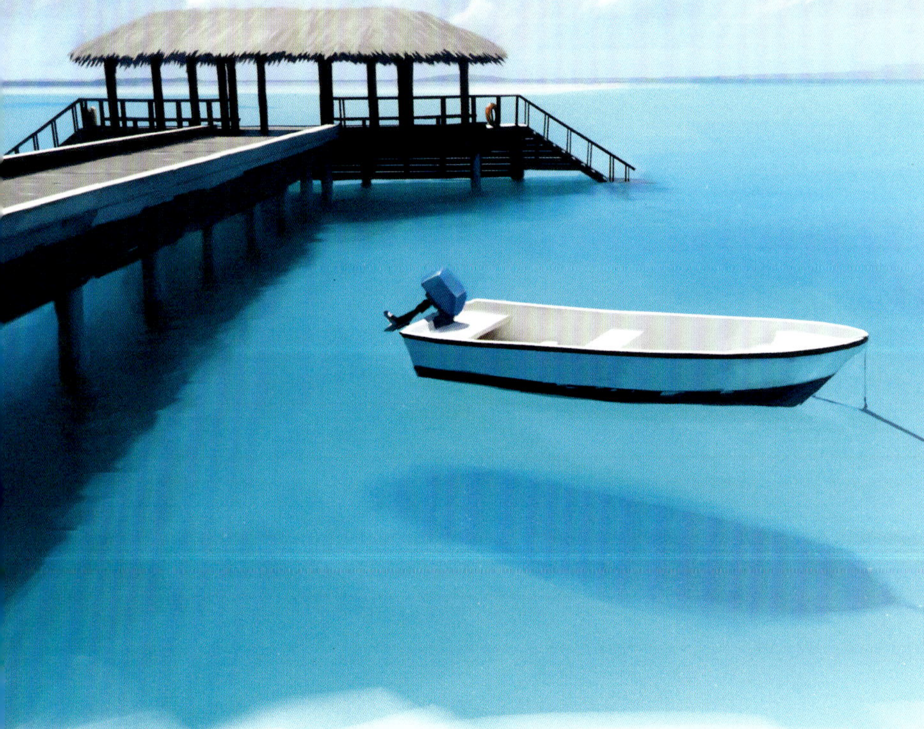

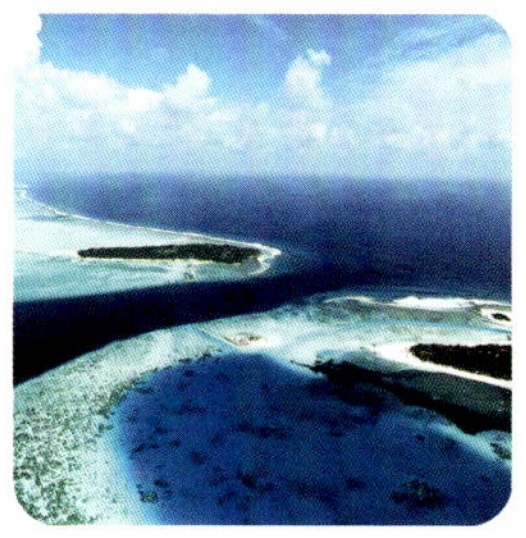

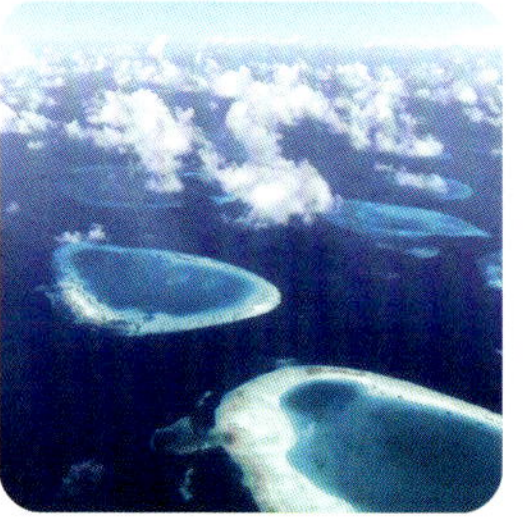

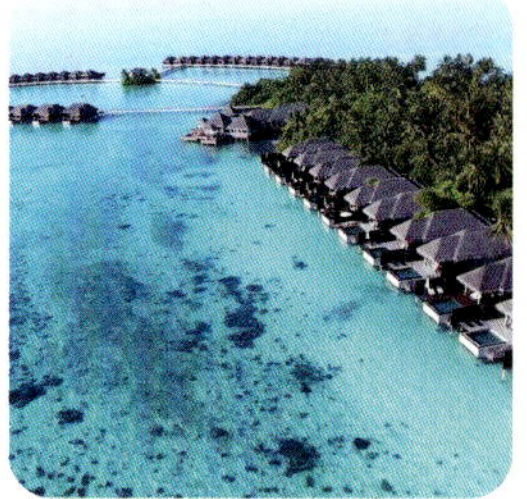

## ▲ CORAL ISLANDS

Maldives consists mostly of coral islands. The flat islands are dotted with plants and surrounded by white sands. From an aerial view, the islands appear small and densely forested. Some of the hotels on the islands provide simply furnished accommodations, creating a harmonious atmosphere.

The blue sky, white clouds, azure seas, turquoise shoals and green trees combine to make Maldives beam with colour like a canvas of toppled paint cans.

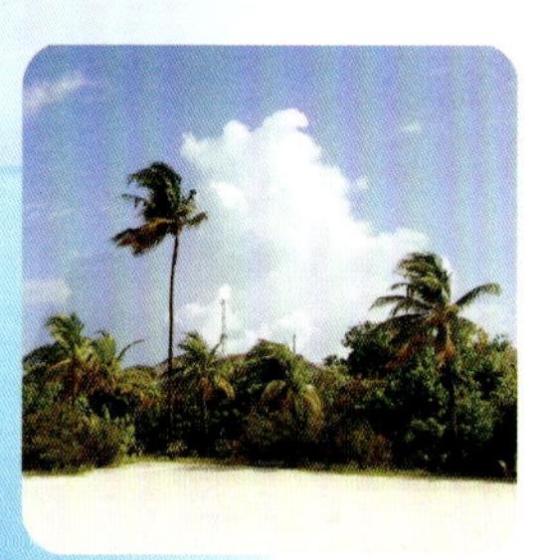

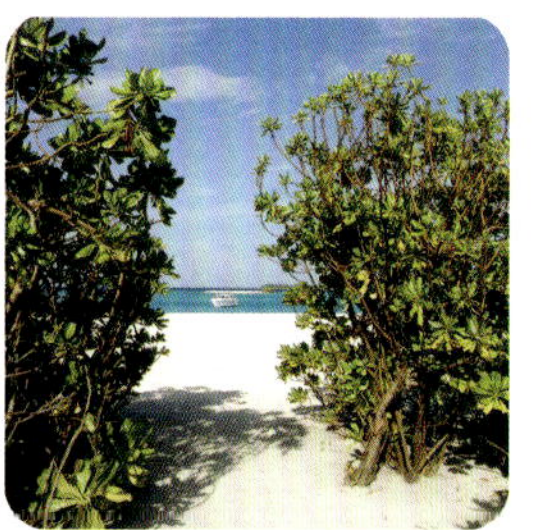

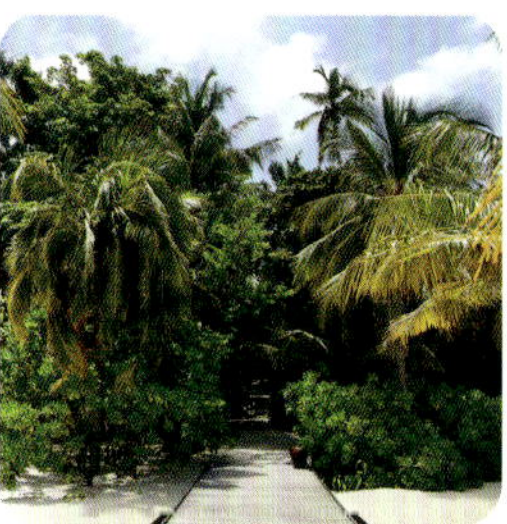

## ▲ PALM TREES

The island flora is mostly palm trees, as well as shrubs and scrubs, growing luxuriantly. Penetrating into the dense foliage, there's no need to hide from sunshine. Glancing through the green at the bright blue sky, the sea and white beaches gives an entirely different feeling.

When the sun is right over head at midday, no light can be seen reflected off the sea and the water's surface along the coasts is calm. Small boats parked at the harbour look as if floating in the air with their shadows clearly in the water. Such a fantastic sight is common in Maldives.

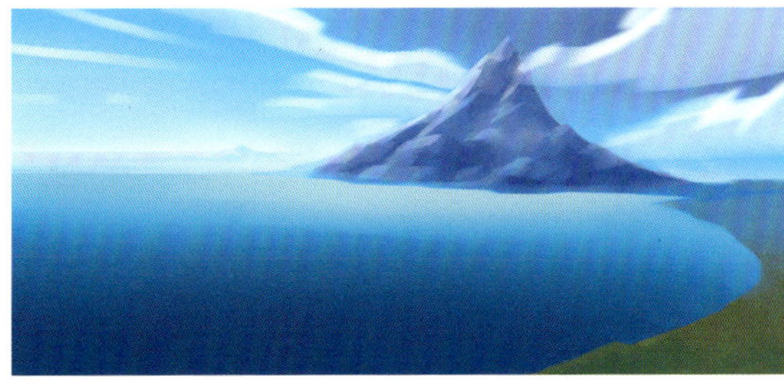

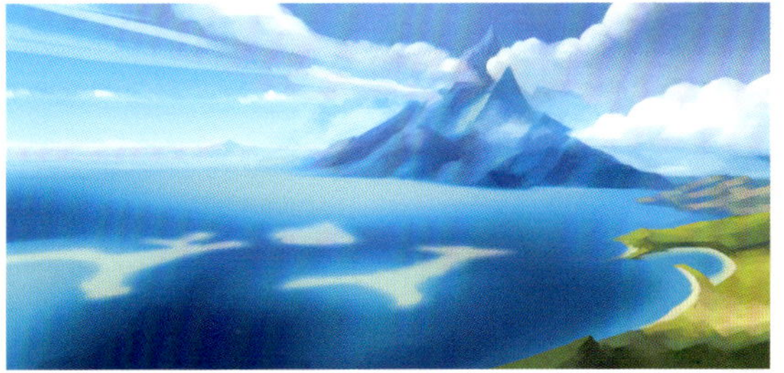

First, let's paint an island as the background of our canvas, with a colossal mountain in the centre as the core object. In reality, there are no lofty mountains on the Maldives archipelago. But to create a focal point and begin the layering process, it was helpful to add one in. Around it, I will add blue skies, white clouds, and a gulf.

This design adopts a bird's-eye view instead of the "vertical view" seen in *The Great Wall*. This time the perspective is closer to a level plane with only a slight decline. Now, objects won't simply be piled up. At this point, I chose to leave the left side and the sea's surface blank to be filled in later.

According to these notes, let's continue depicting the background environment and identify the locations and shapes of several small islands on the sea. For the convenience of repeated revisions, the silhouetting method can be used to fill in the beaches' colour and finally produce a shape which would naturally occur.

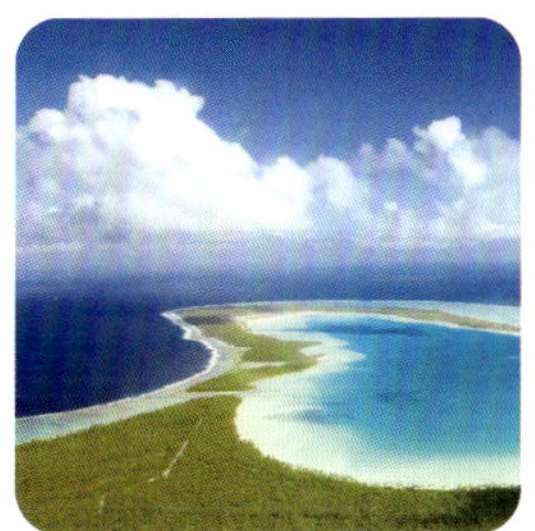

## ▲ ISLANDS

Reference materials provide the following conclusions: the Maldives islands are not limited to an oval shape but ribbon. Shoals surrounding the islands appear "light blue" beneath the sunshine, and shallow seawaters closer to beaches tend to be a lighter colour. Not all beaches connect to shoals. Some descend directly to the bathyal zone and thus look "ultramarine" and "dark blue" from above. Plants on the islands are densely packed with some stretching right up to the water's edge.

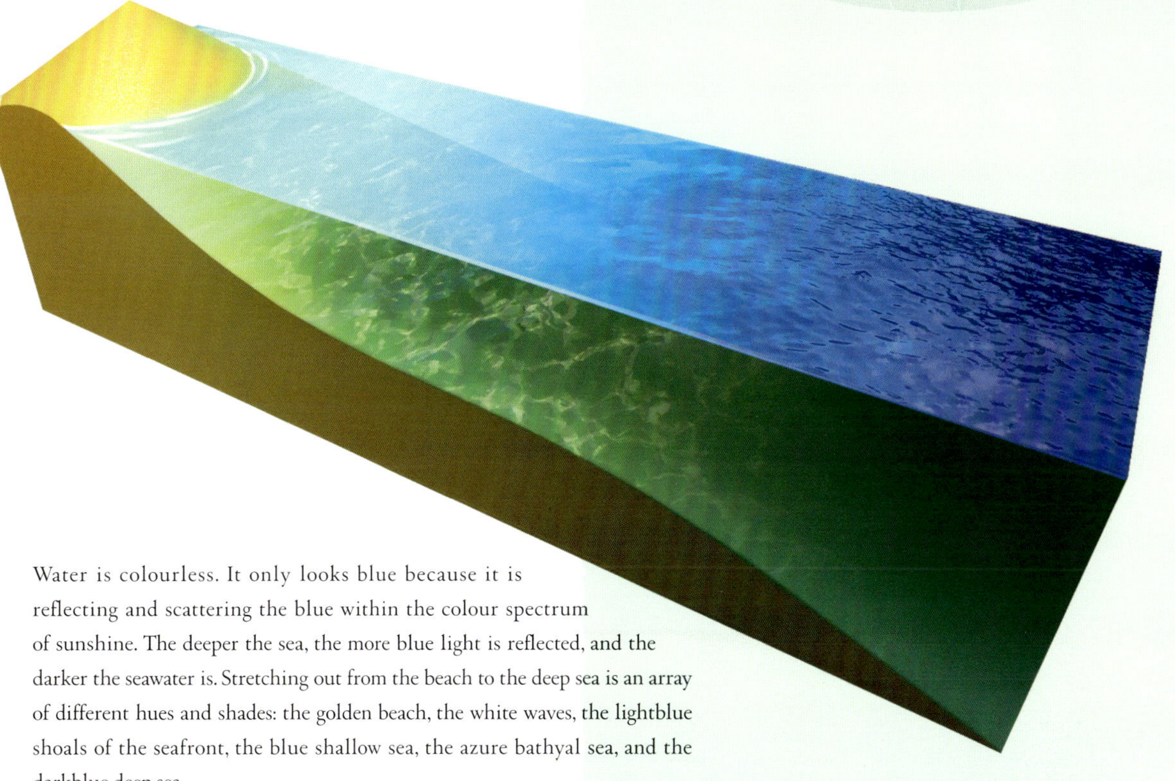

Water is colourless. It only looks blue because it is reflecting and scattering the blue within the colour spectrum of sunshine. The deeper the sea, the more blue light is reflected, and the darker the seawater is. Stretching out from the beach to the deep sea is an array of different hues and shades: the golden beach, the white waves, the lightblue shoals of the seafront, the blue shallow sea, the azure bathyal sea, and the darkblue deep sea.

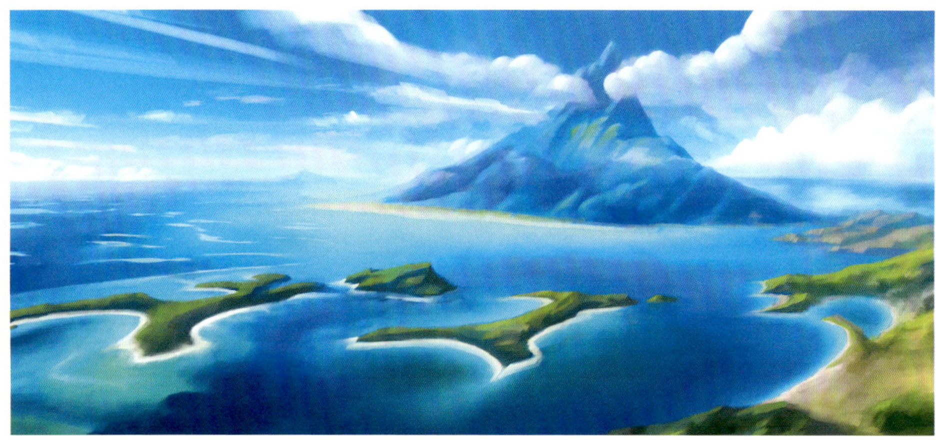

The remaining sections of the island are then shaped using the silhouetting method too. The luxuriant stretches of plants are depicted in patches to create a sense of volume. The shoals (as shown above) are identified by the change of colours to the water. A mottled shoal effect is added in the blank sea areas (the areas in the middle left of the scene). Around the island with the mountain, beaches are added to link together the mainland and the large area of shoals surrounding it.

The islands and surrounding sea areas are refined to smoothly connect up the beaches, shoals, and deep-sea areas. Regardless of the size of the islands, "plants, rocks, and sand areas" should be distinguished according to their colours and textures. As each object is refined, the light and shade effects upon it are adjusted accordingly.

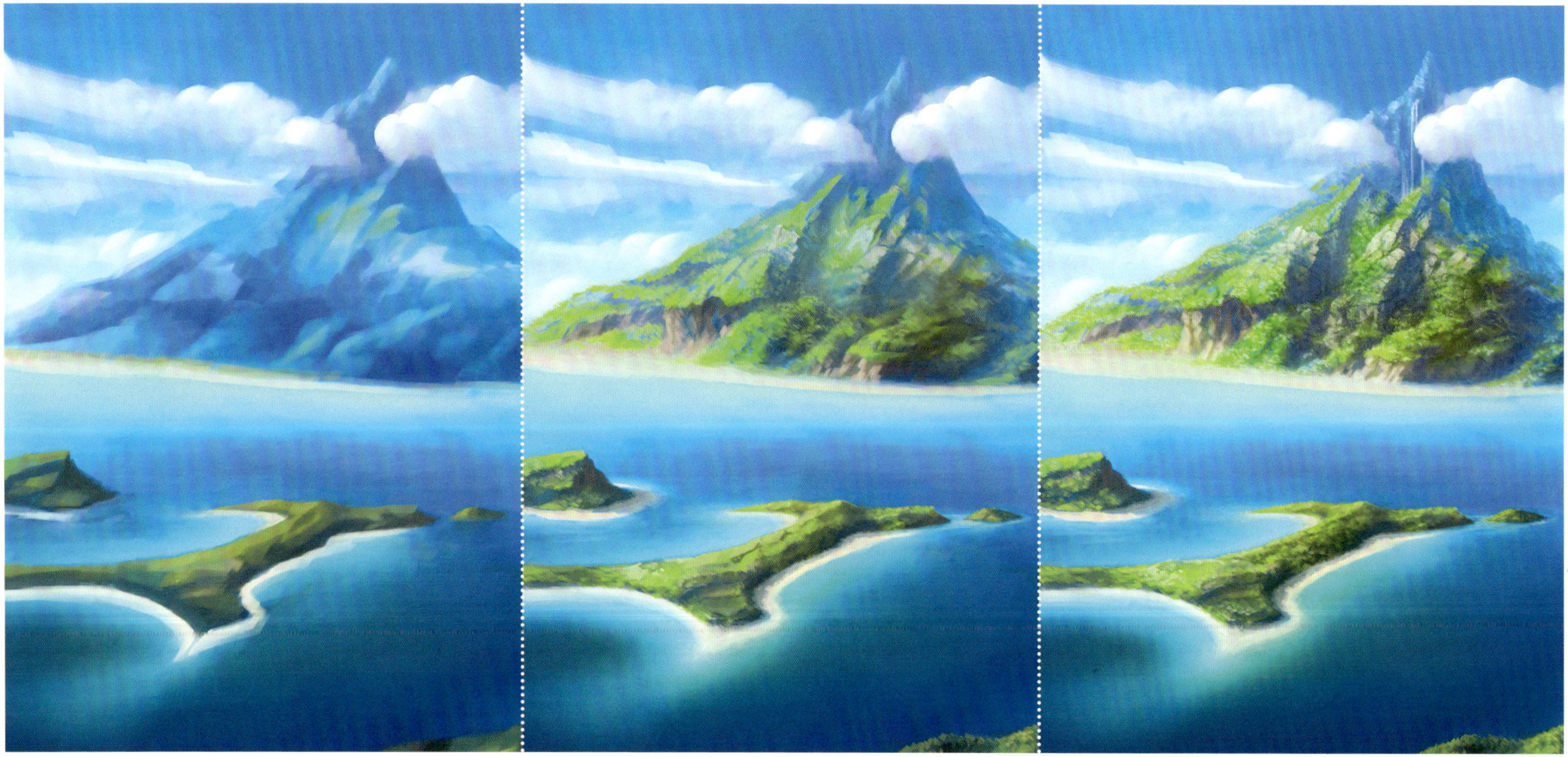

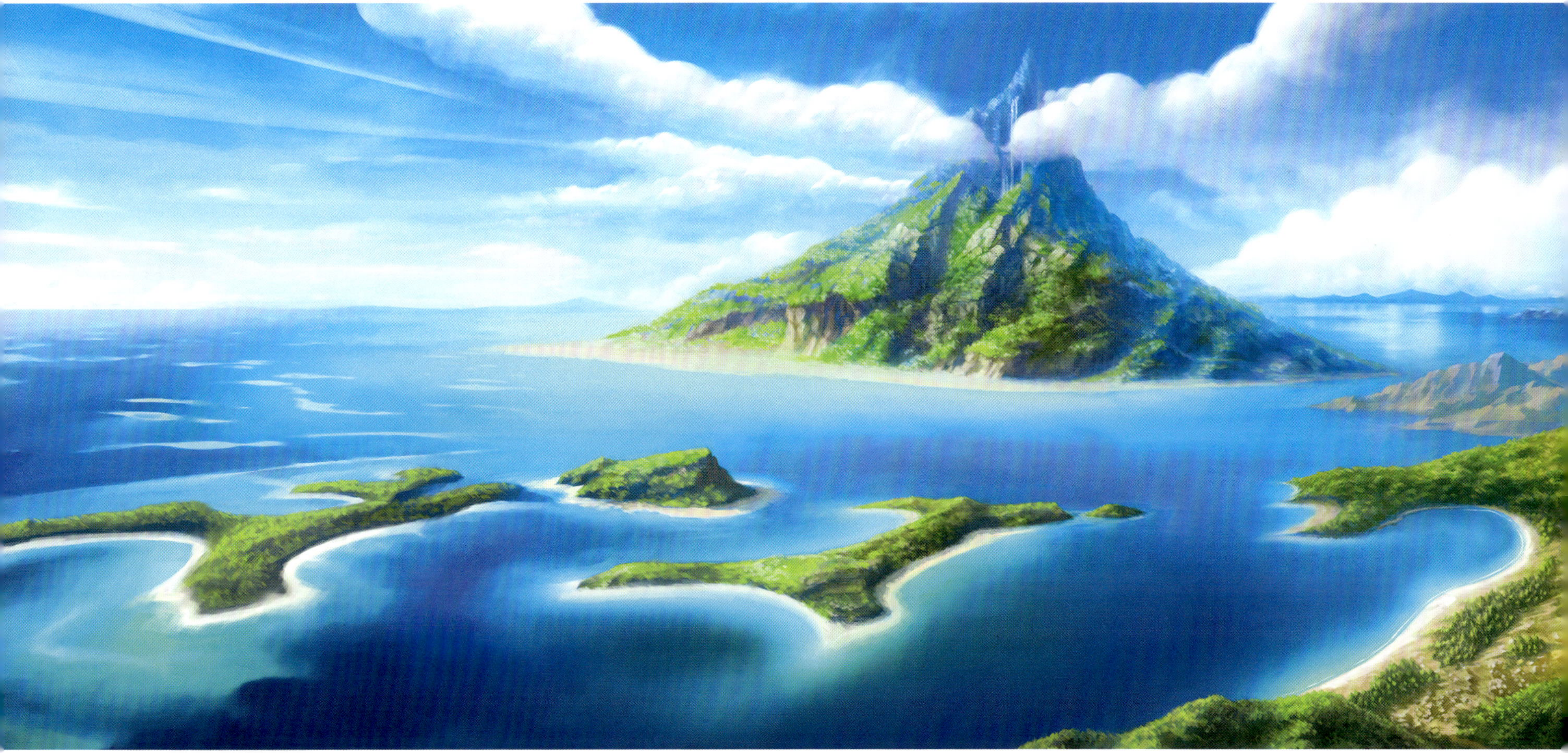

Now to refine some of the other objects already presented in the scene. Clouds, reflections, and the contours of landforms on the horizon are all treated as well as the land area surrounding the gulf.

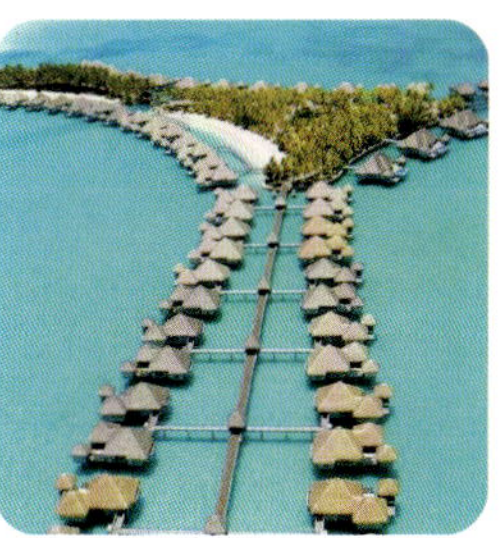

## ◄ WATER HOUSE

The "water house" is the best accommodation available on a tropical island due to the uniqueness of its structure and location. Imagine a cosy house standing in water, beautiful scenery right outside its windows; you may fall asleep to the soft sounds of waves, watch the sun as it rises from the sea, leap from the balcony and plunge yourself into the sea's embrace to dance with fish beneath a marvellous sky. Thus, this form of architecture is an essential element of the Maldives experience.

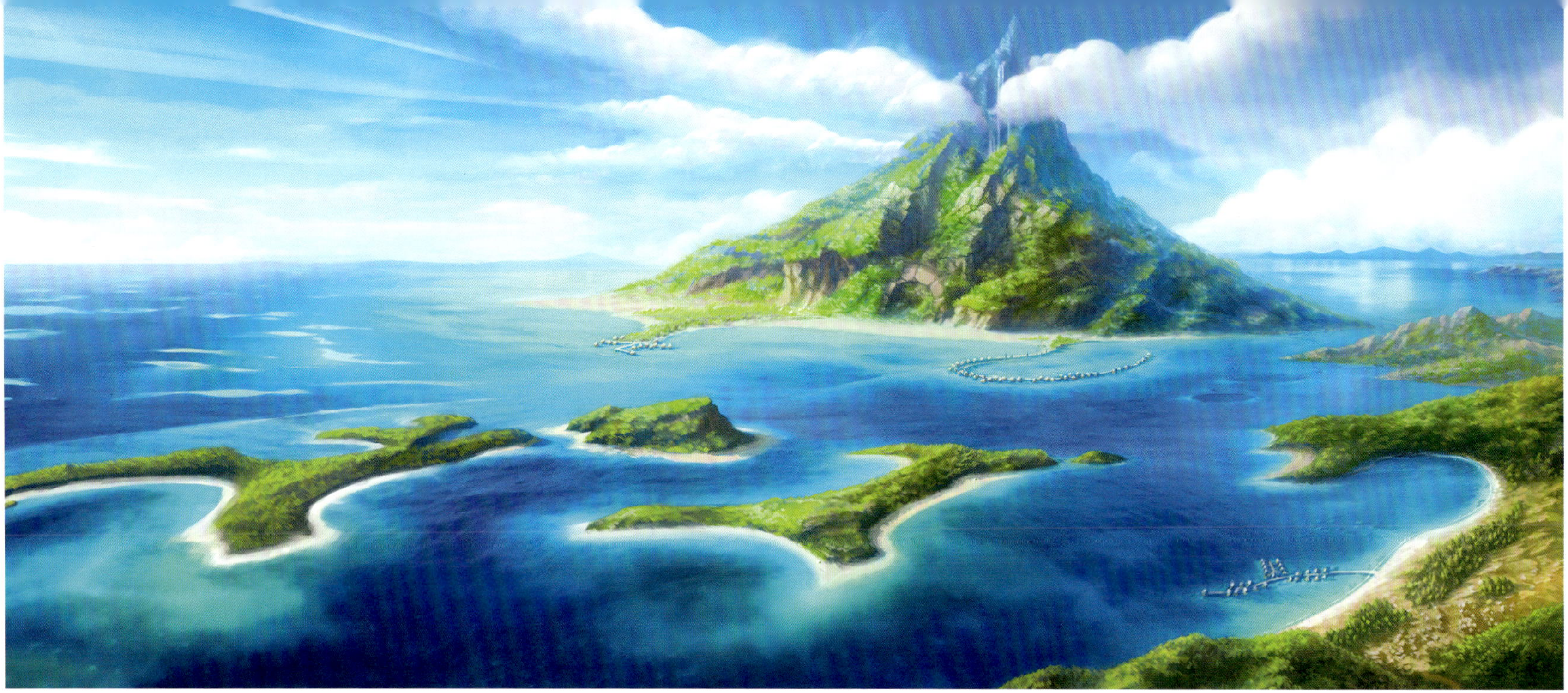

With its strong local characteristics, the "water house" is integrated into this design for the purpose of enhancing its realness and establishing some proportional relationships between different objects (as the structures are located near the ground, they serve as effective points of proportional reference). Additionally, the depth of the shoals is adjusted. Underwater elements such as reefs are added as well. And the undulations of the sea waves are brought out. Now, we have a realistic scene on which to build.

On the mountainous island, a huge faintly visible relic is drawn. Next, designing the fantastical side of the work begins.

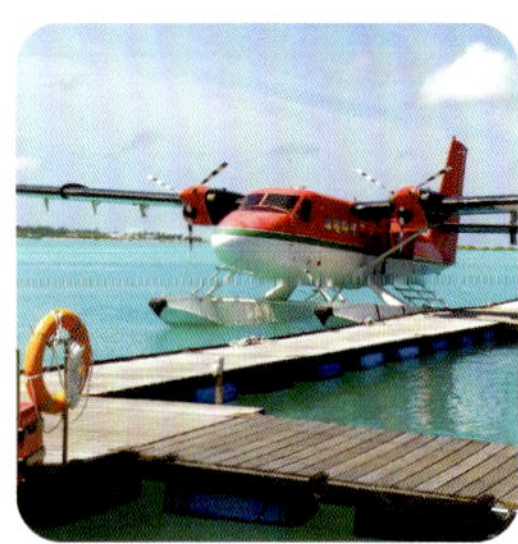

## ◄ SEAPLANE

Since there are large spaces between the different islands of Maldives, the seaplane is often turned to as the most convenient means of transport besides boats. Not only does it shorten the travel time, but beautify its passage between the sea and the sky.

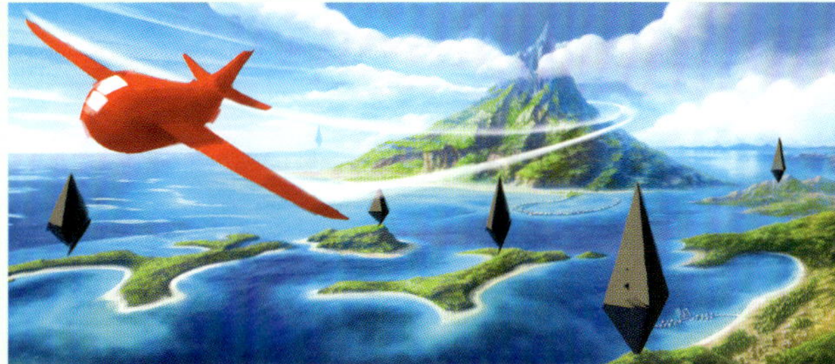

There are many different colours of seaplanes in Maldives. Between the blue of the sea and the sky, red produces the most eye-catching sight. The huge stone structures shaped like a diamond floating above each island are inspired by a saying popular among the local people, "The Maldives are a necklace fallen from heaven", referring to how the string of islands collectively appears. I used a more concrete object to manifest this idea.

This fantasy design features a seaplane flying through clouds and past the different size structures floating above the islands. This is why the left side of the scene and the sea surface were originally left empty.

As with the rest of the world in design we're creating, the shape of a seaplane should have something illogical. In this design, a vintage style and a sci-fi perspective are applied to produce a simultaneous and contrasting blend of uniqueness and familiarity.

1. Let's draft a seaplane. First, reference lines are drawn for perspective.
2. Light and shade are added to enhance the sense of depth. The colour of the cockpit is distinguished from that of the body.
3. The corners and contours of the seaplane are refined. A grid framework (as with a World War II bomber) is inserted for the cockpit, as well as inlets and other parts.
4. Two wings are added in the vintage style. The sense of texture is enhanced.
5. High-tech engines are installed in the centre of each wing flanking the seaplane. Floating undercarriages, the most iconic part in seaplanes, are designed.
6. In order to match the two wings, the empennage at the rear is altered, and more structural elements are added.
7. Reflections along the body and interior details are inserted. Our fantasy seaplane is thus completed.

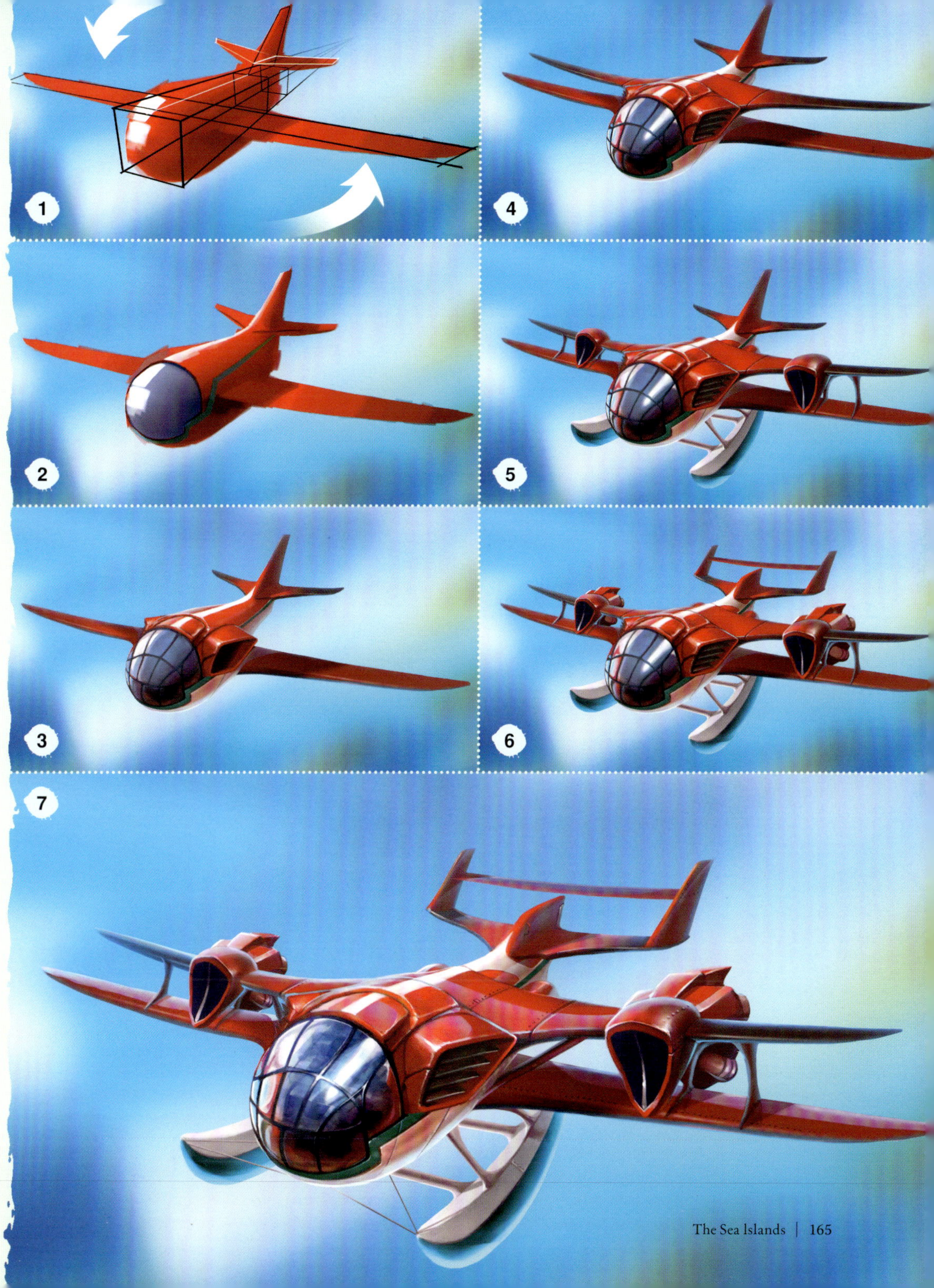

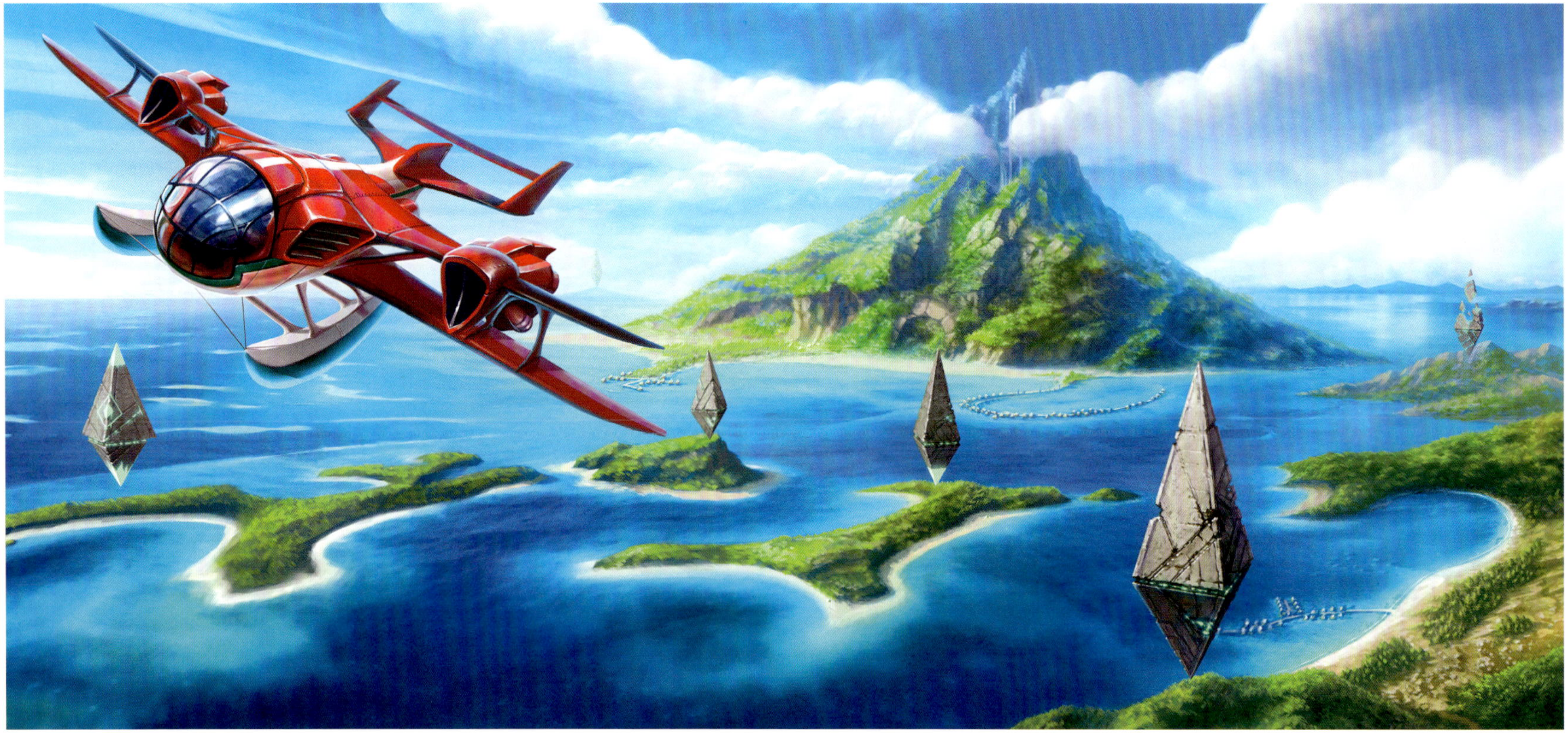

With a finished seaplane and floating structures in place, the scene feels fuller and lived in. I added a bluish-green glow in different areas to improve the feeling of fantasy and distinguish the structures from other objects in the frame.

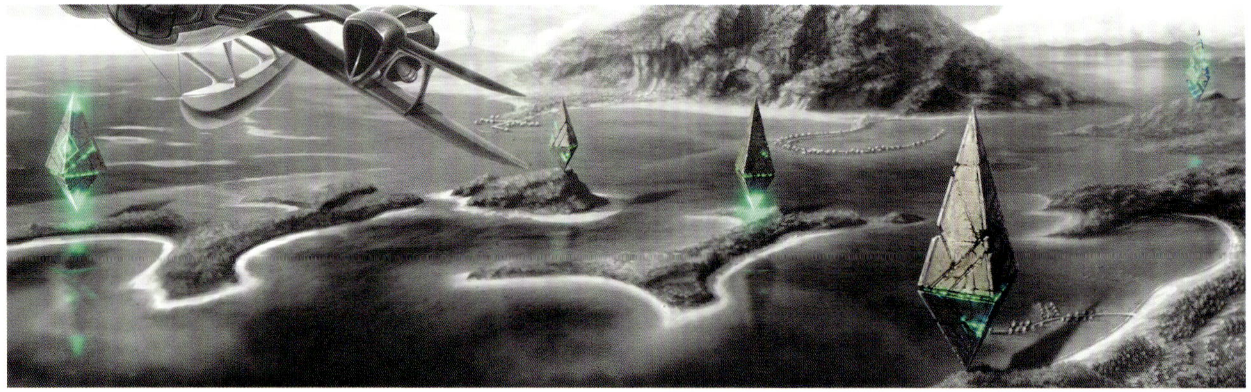

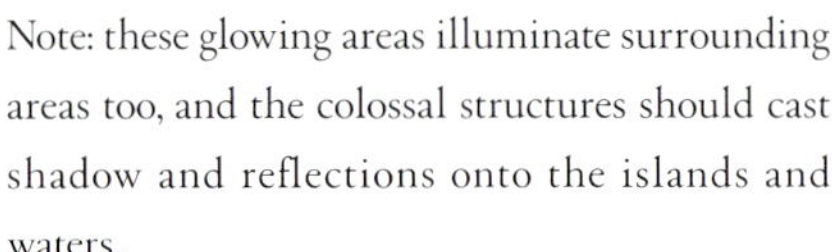

Note: these glowing areas illuminate surrounding areas too, and the colossal structures should cast shadow and reflections onto the islands and waters.

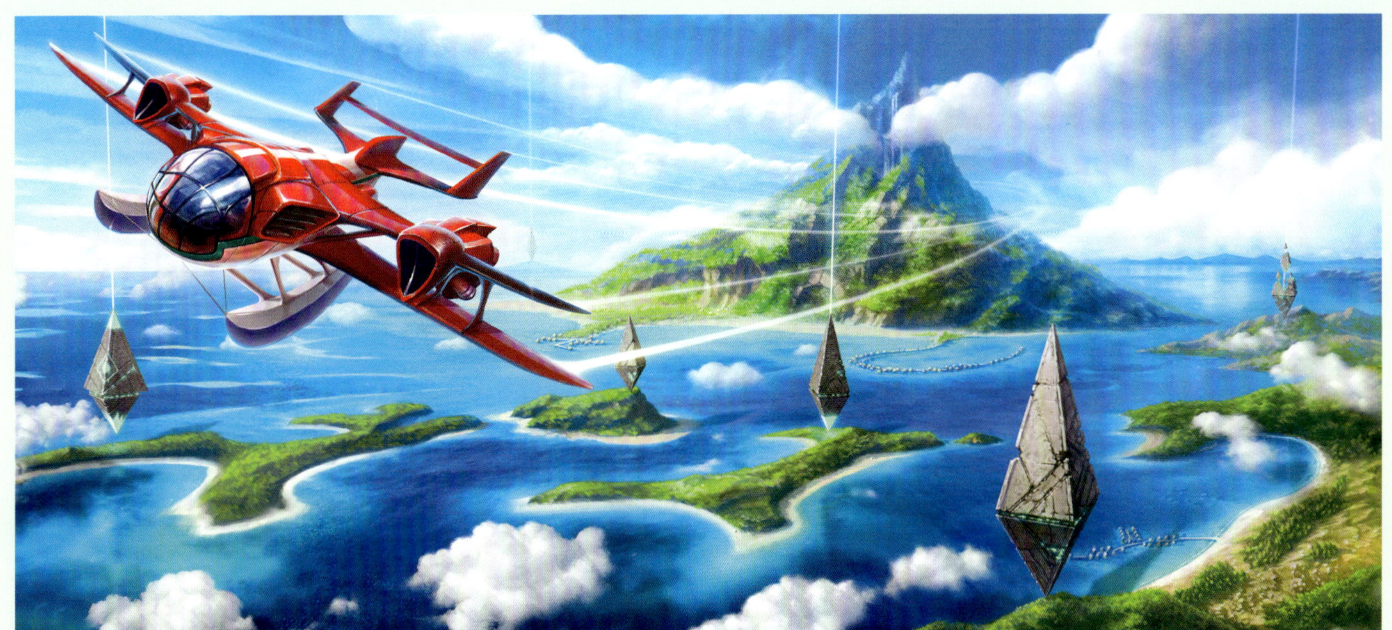

"Low-level clouds" are added to provide further layering, making the floating structures appear all the more magnificent. Trails in the sky left by the seaplane's wingtips portray movement. Some of the floating structures send rays of light into the sky as if they were bridges to outer space.

At this stage, the floating structures have been refined, their glowing effects brought out, and their reflections added in; low-level clouds and their shadows have been drawn too.

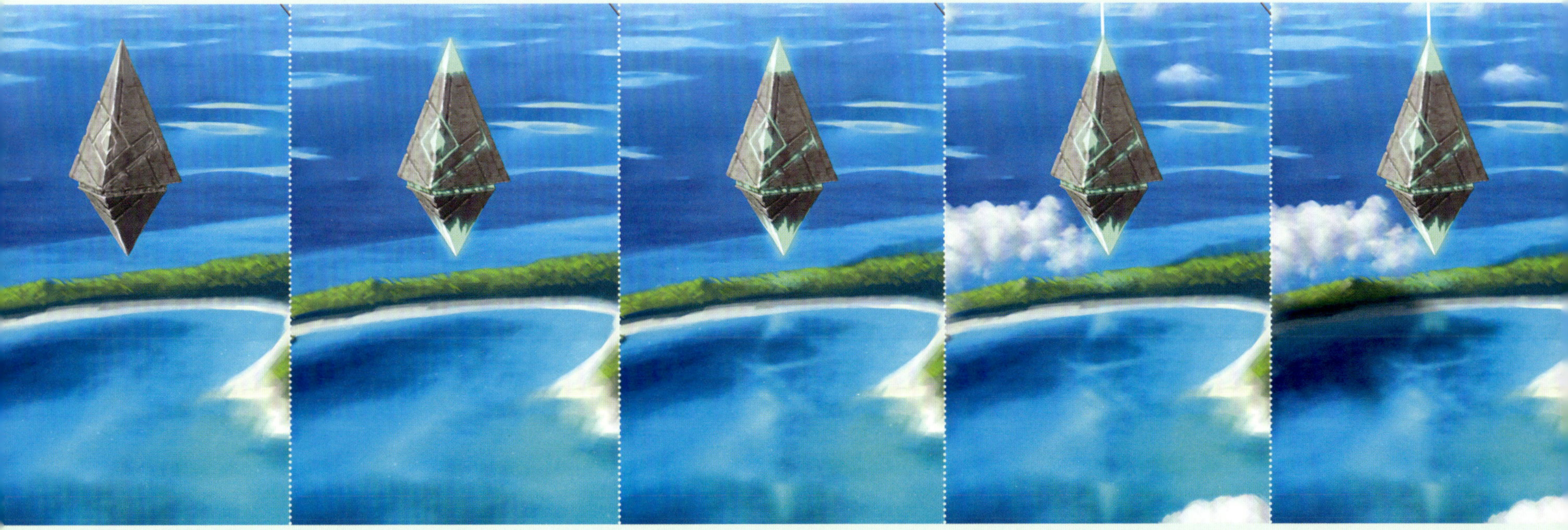

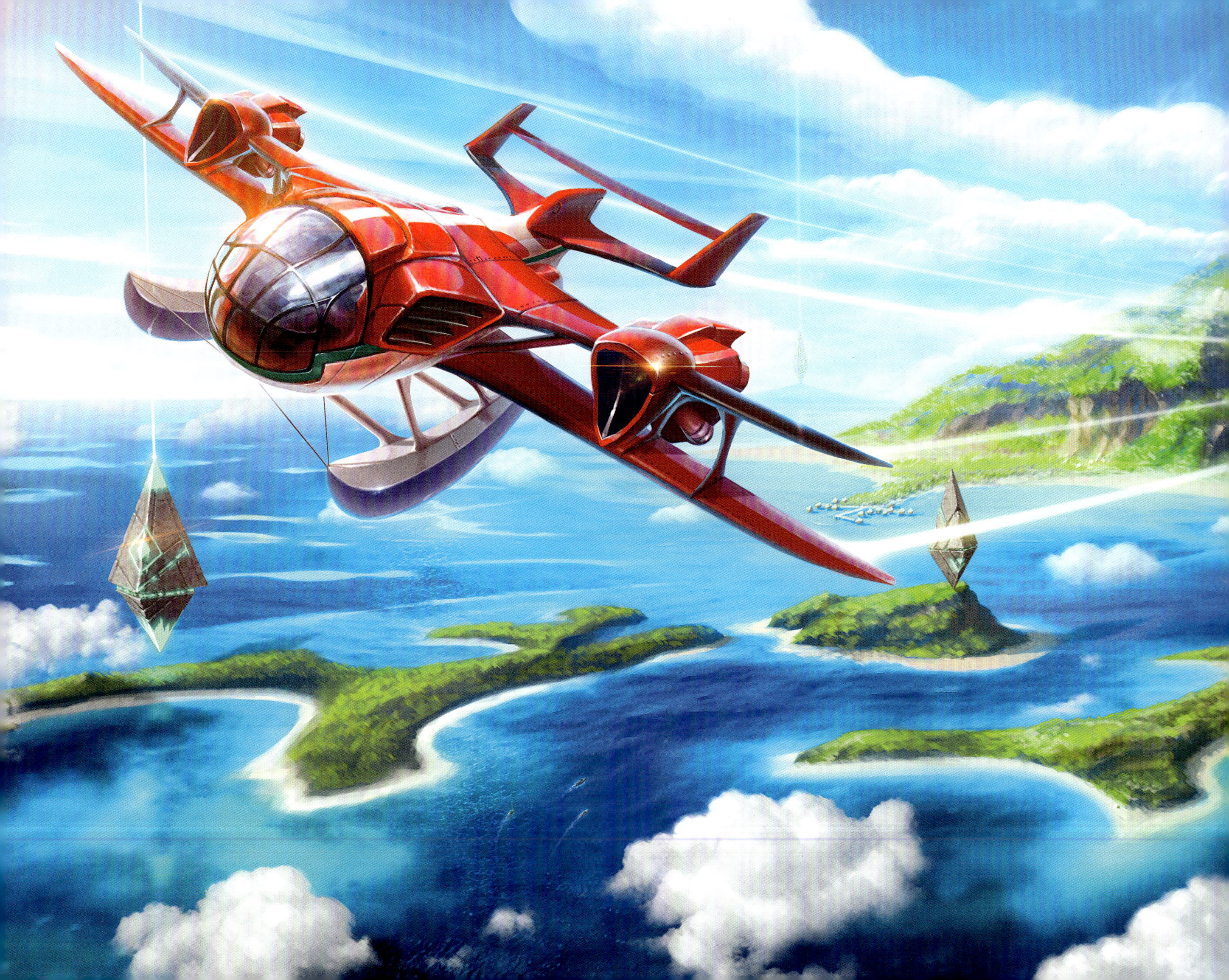

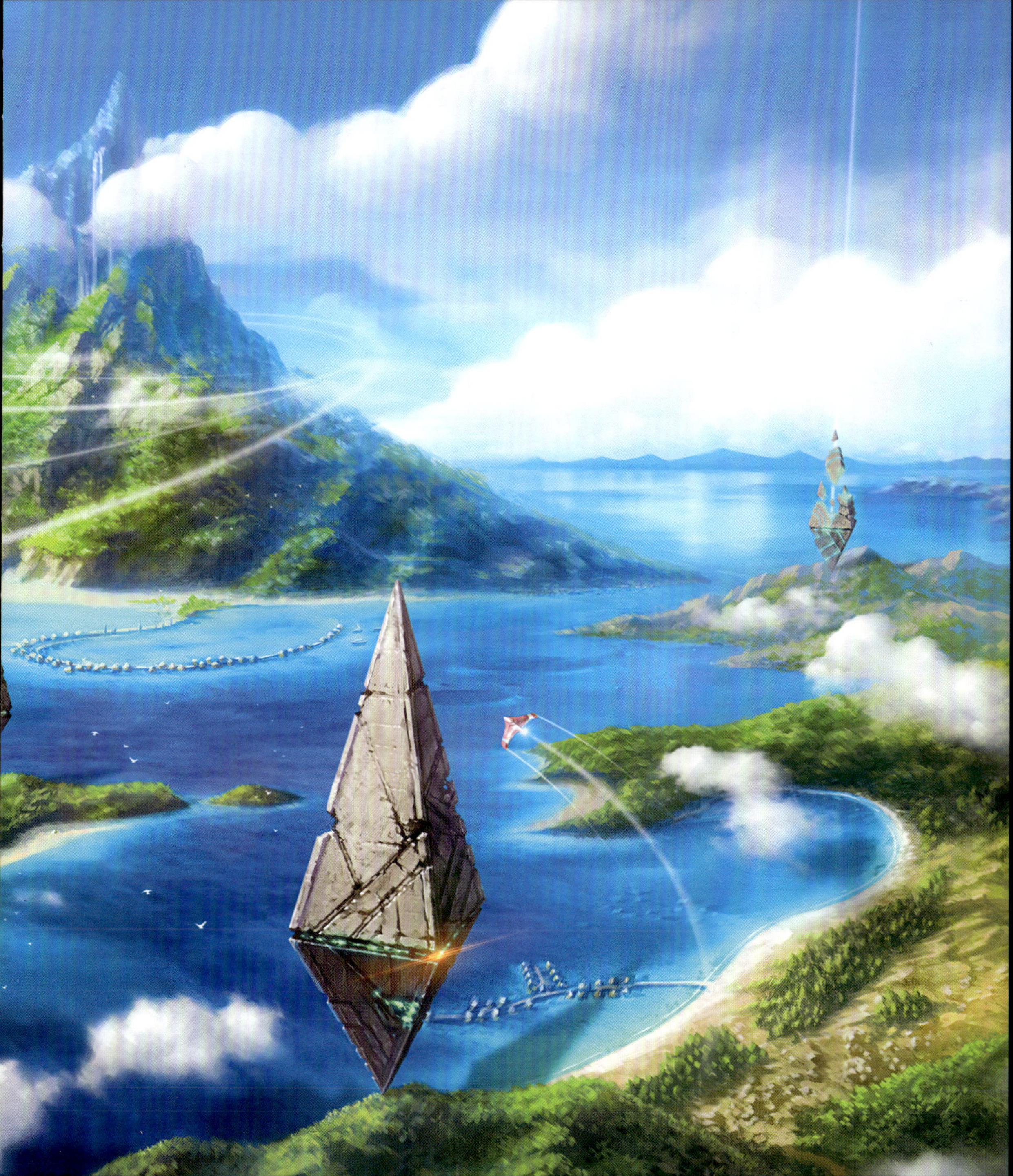

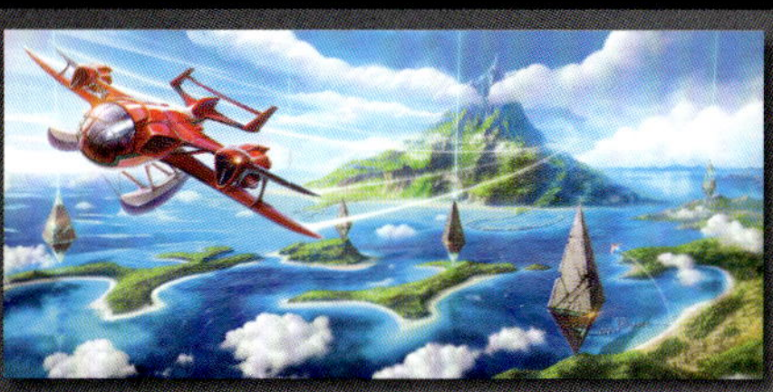

Light and colour at the left side of frame are altered to take into account the sunlight. Flare and glow are painted onto the plane. Boats, an extra seaplane and flocks of birds are included in the distance to enrich the scene. *The Sea Islands* thus comes to life with a heavy dose of the fantasy – a snippet of my first impressions on arrival to Maldives.

# MAIN POINTS

## 1

This sphere is a demonstration of one aspect of the design process. As with the seaplane body, a lacquer varnish texture is first simulated.

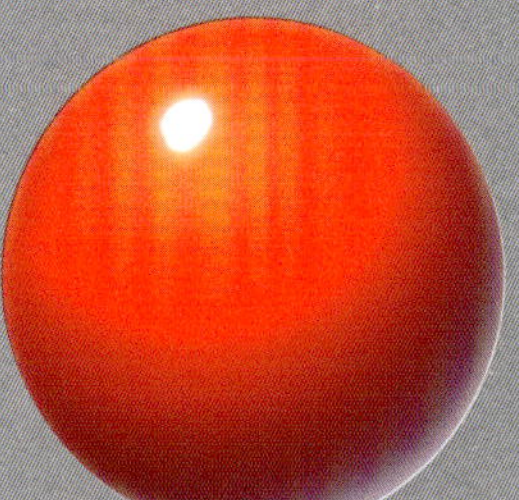

## 2

The smoother an object, the larger the area of brightness will appear beneath light. On the dark side of the object, a slither of light is painted onto make the object stand out.

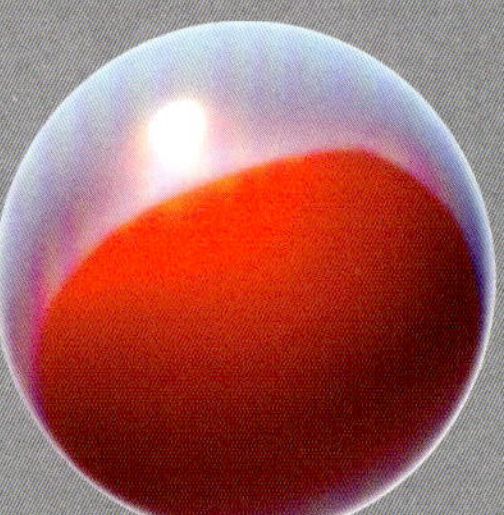

## 3

As if light is shining down on it from the sky, a glossy reflection is added on the sphere's top side. Influenced by the blue sky, the red colour becomes purple. Around the red ball, rim light is added to enhance the sense of texture.

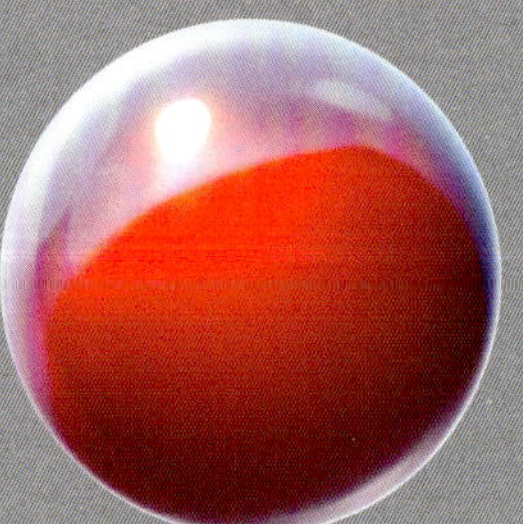

## 4

A light spot is added to the glossy reflected area to simulate the realistic scenario in which multiple objects surround the sphere. To further strengthen the realness, the intensity of rim light is adjusted according to the light source's relative position – vertically over the object. In certain areas, the light is reduced, in others it is intensified. Now we have a believable lacquered red ball.

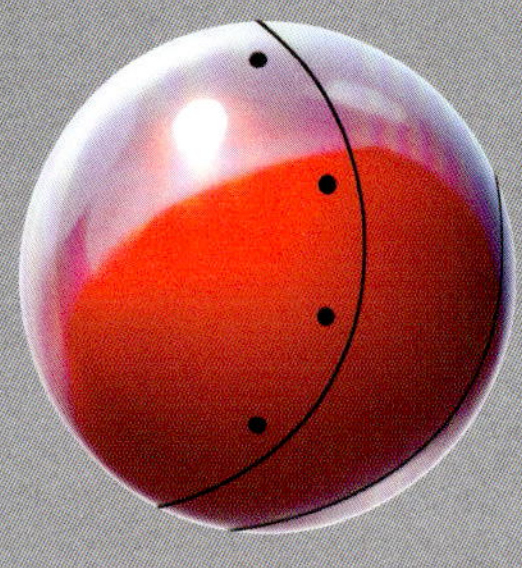

## 5

Black lines and dots suggest the screws, distinct components, and assemblage which comprise the sphere are added.

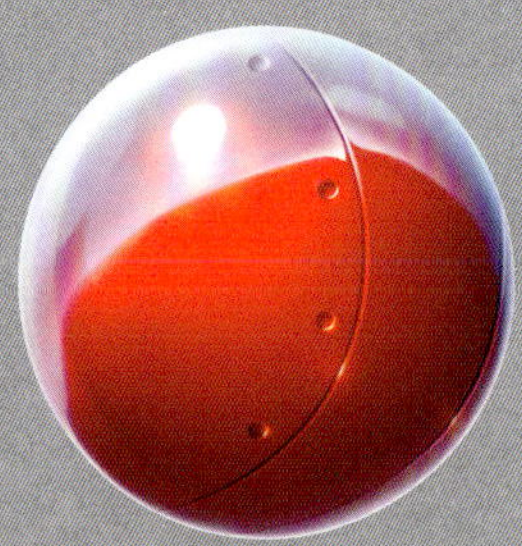

## 6

Where the lines and dots have been drafted, grooves are produced on the surface of the shell. It should be noted that creating grooves destroys the smoothness of the surface, distorting the reflections in the affected areas.

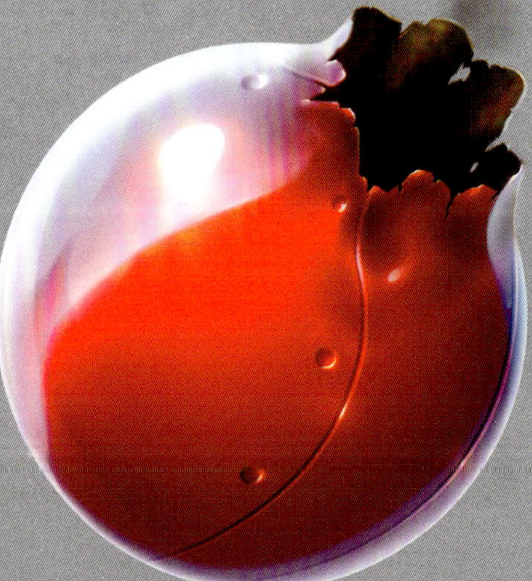

## 7

Reflections become more distorted as the object does. That is just what happens when a glossy surface is distorted.

## 1

By contrast, "matt limestone", an entirely different material, acts completely different.

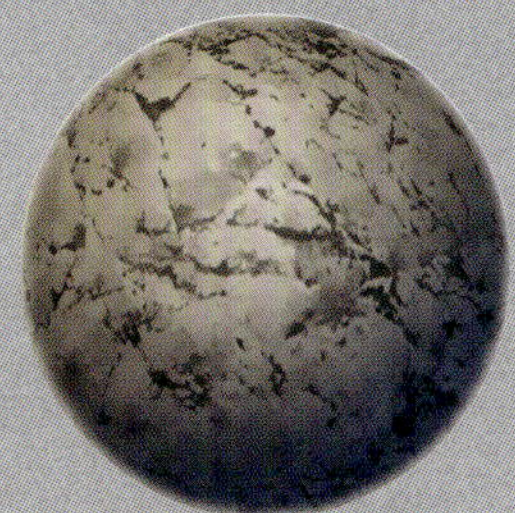

## 2

The texture of rough stone is superimposed onto a grey ball. Before further treatment, let's choose the "Distort" function under the "Filter" option to "Spherize" the texture, giving the object an obvious roundness.

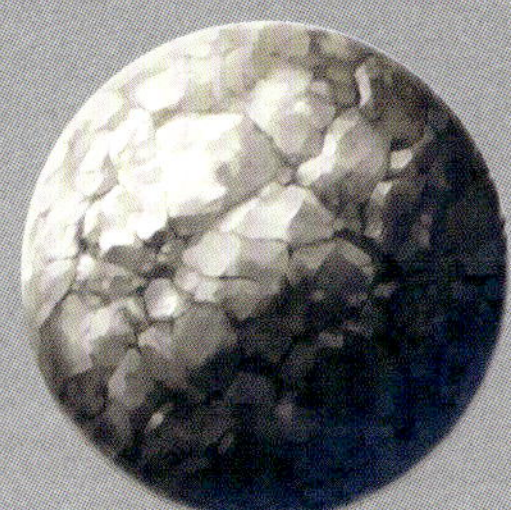

## 3

Upon that base, let's create the effect of an uneven surface. In the dark area, a cold colour can be applied to give the image some light.

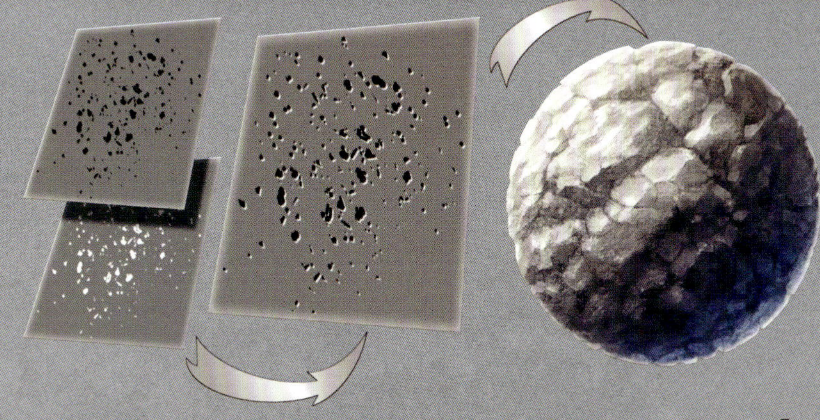

## 4

Finally, a section of the stone ball is cut away to produce a flat surface, leaving some cracks on the exterior. Scratches and dots are then added. Glowing effects coming from the object's inner core are painted through the use of sharply contrasting colours and brightness levels.

Bringing out a material's texture is an important part of the process for convincingly depicting it, whether light or heavy, smooth or rough. Only expressing its shape is never enough. The play of light and shade, the intensity of reflection and refraction, the highlighted areas, and the texture's lustre are all central elements. Visual effects such as transparency and luminosity should also be remembered.

## 5

The contours of the stone ball are refined according to its raised and depressed areas. Brushes of different sizes are applied to create black and white dots at the top and bottom. "Holes" of different sizes are randomly marked on the stone ball to suggest granules on a rough surface. That is the way to create a rough limestone effect.

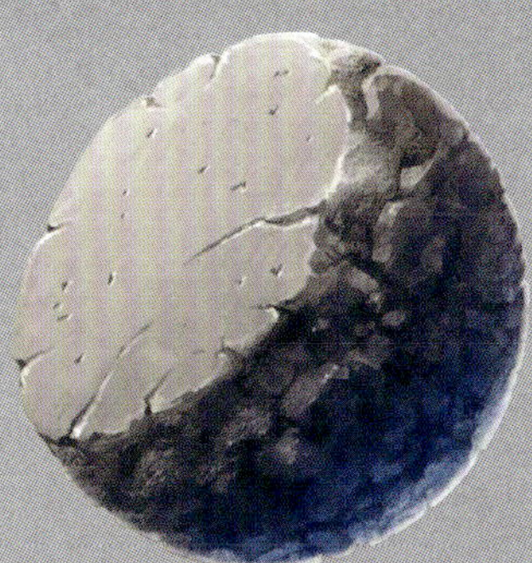

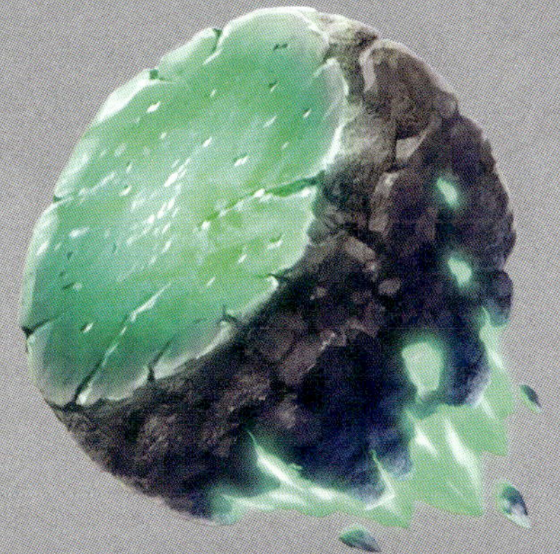

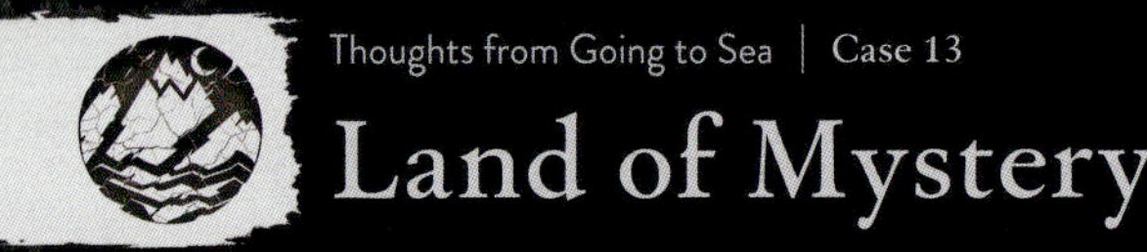



# Land of Mystery

Time spent in a hotel on an island is all about the comfort that it provides. You are free to indulge yourself in the beauties of nature, watching the sun rise, listening to the sound of sea waves, swimming or taking a walk during the day, or observing the starry sky with the sea breeze blowing around you. Here in Maldives, apart from seeing a vast oceanic world, experiencing "a lucky dolphin tour" is more exciting. Finding dolphins is all about luck, dependant on environmental factors, ocean currents and weather conditions. Yachts used are usually small with decks near to the sea surface for adventurers to better appreciate the dolphins. Experienced captains know the areas with the greatest chance of seeing dolphins and make certain sounds to attract groups over. Once one or two dolphins have been drawn close, it's not long before more follow.

The voyage took a long time to reach the deep sea area and not a trace of land was visible. The captain began to lead us passengers to clap our hands and whistle. Soon after, several dorsal fins flashed across the sea surface nearby. The water was a clear lens through which to observe a handful of dolphins chasing behind the yacht, playful as children in a park. Then, a more spectacular scene emerged as the dolphins multiplied into their hundreds, all in hot pursuit of the boat. Some leapt out of water, spinning in the air as if showing off their dancing skills. Seeing this happen out in nature is an entirely different experience from in aquariums. The "freedom" those dolphins were evidently enjoying washed over me in a sense of relief.

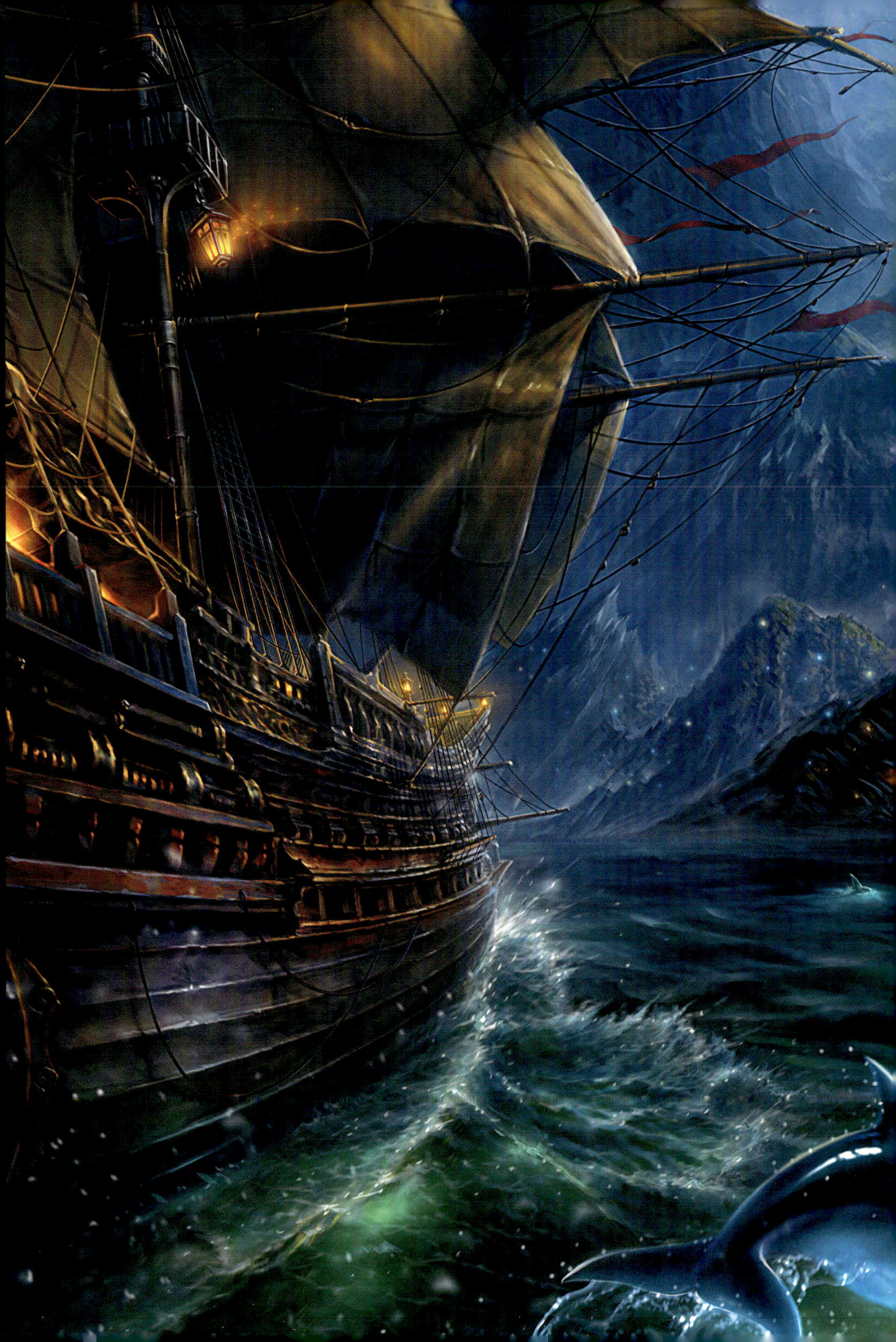

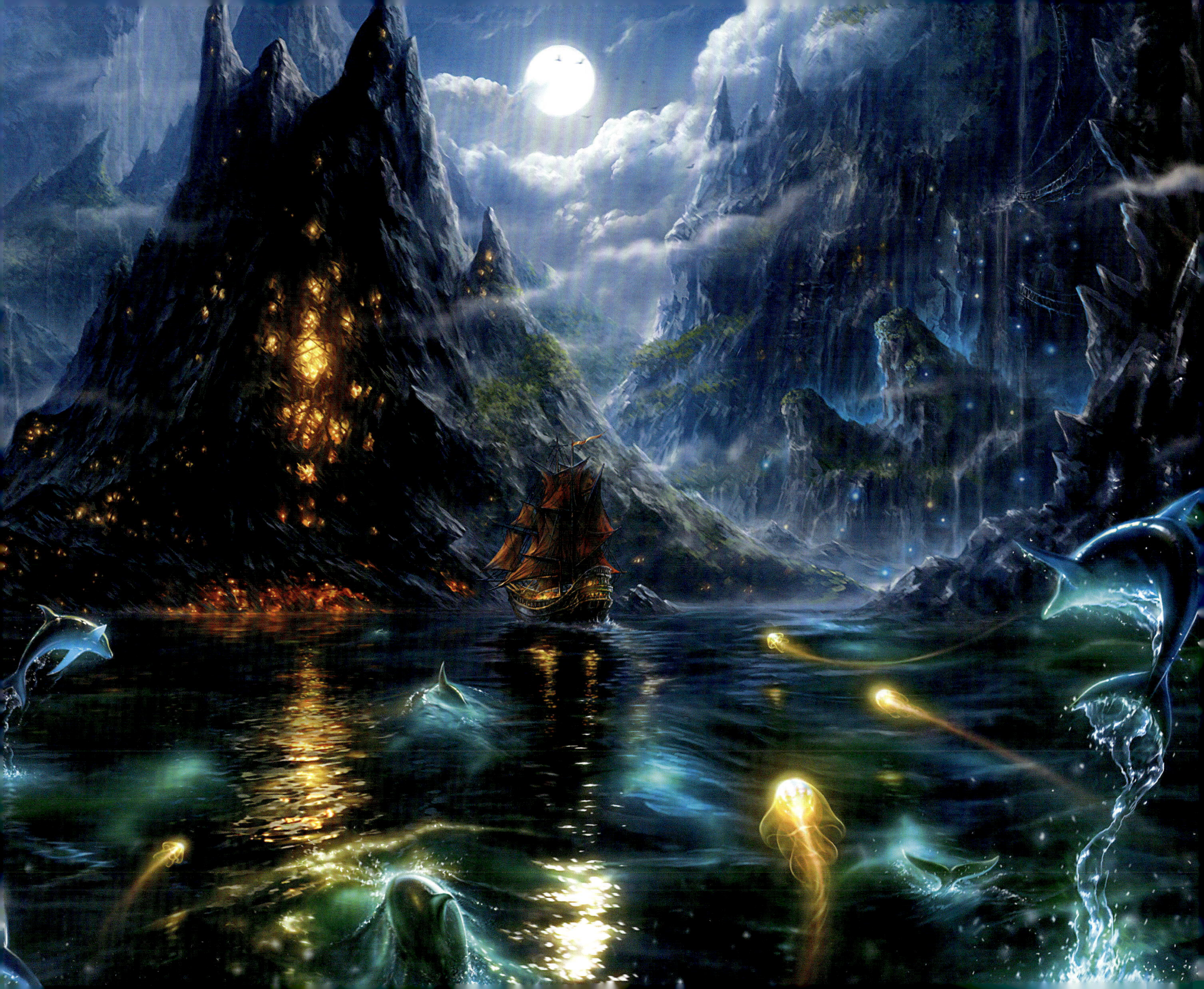

# THOUGHTS ON CREATION

*Time flied as did the dolphins. As the sun approached the horizon, the dorsal fins and rippling sea surface flashed with a golden shine. Deeply moved by the beauty, I began to consider capturing such a scene and experience in a painting. This was the inspiration for Land of Mystery.*

*When inspiration defies easy expression, it is practical to set aside the most impressive elements in your mind to be treated when you have accumulated the ideal material to match them.*

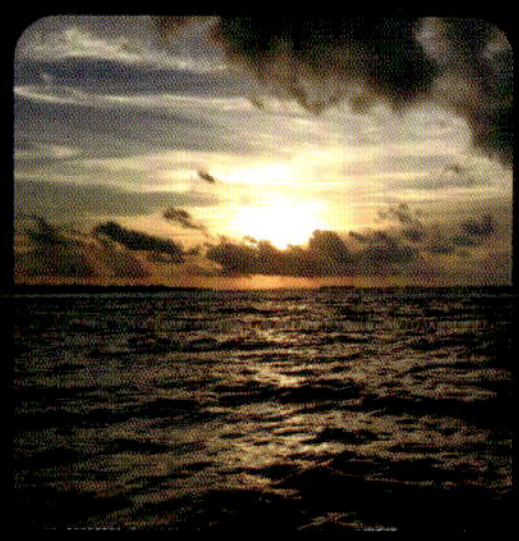

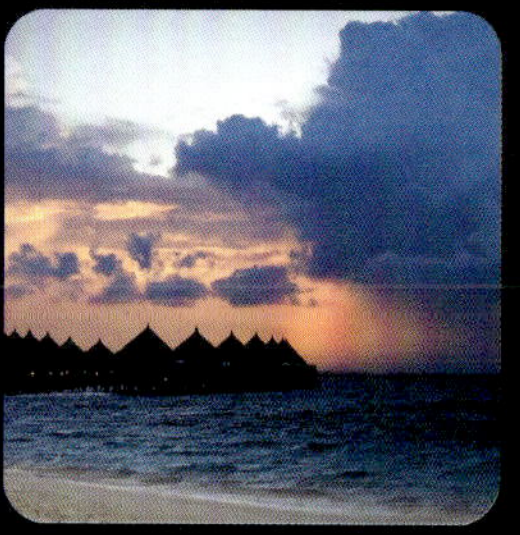

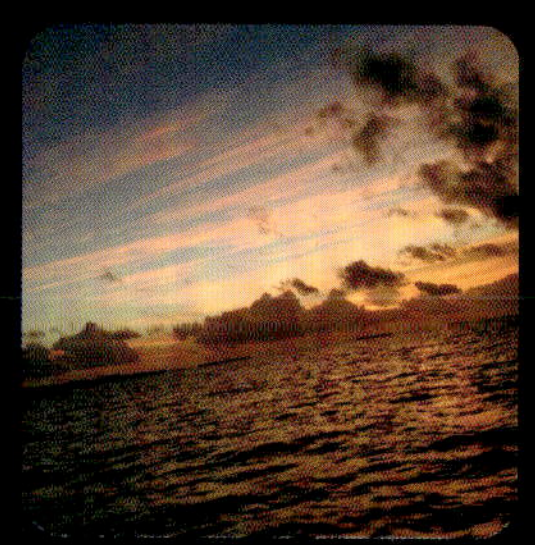

## ◀ SETTING SUN

Against a setting sun, the sea is multi-directional in the backlight. The high degree of contrast created by the light's reflection serves as a focal point, similar to what happens on moonlit nights. However, cameras struggle to fully capture natural scenes at night, so source material is sparse, and I used images of dusk in their place.

No matter how clear the water is, if deep and low-lit, it tends to appear dark blue.

Reflections directly influence the intrinsic colour of the sea water. For example, sunglow in the sky typically colour the water's surface below with a jacinth hue.

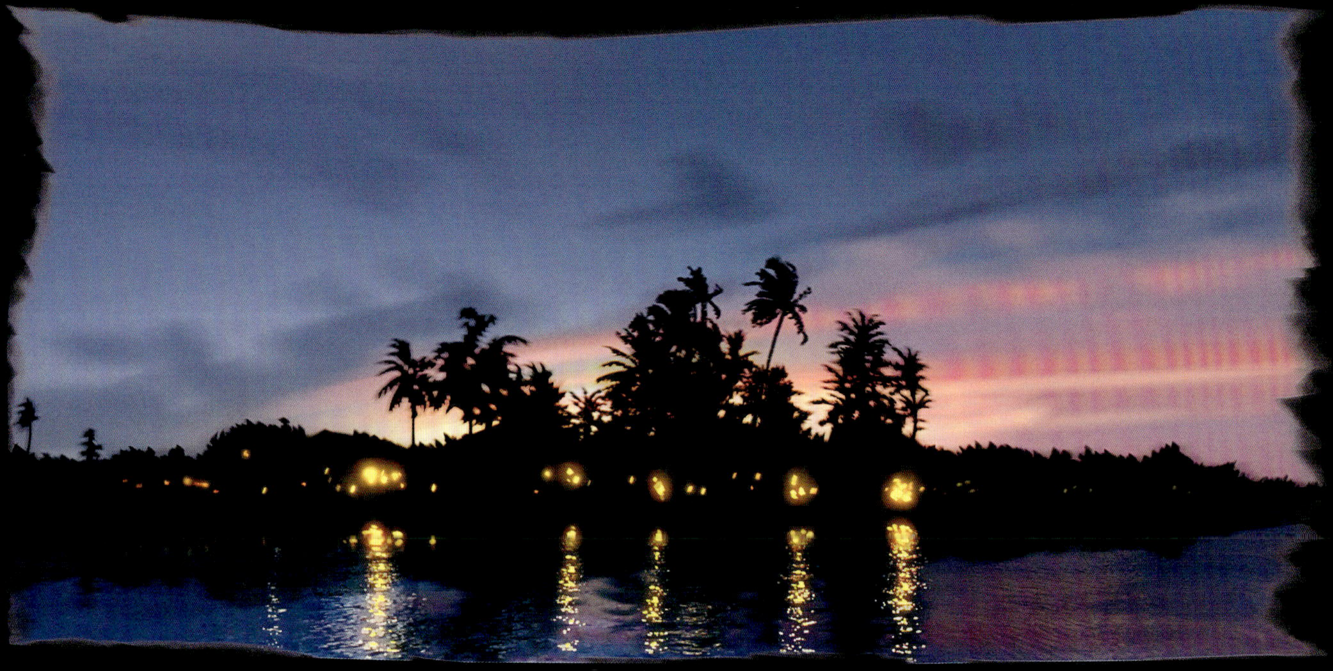

By nightfall, our yacht was already making its return. The distant afterglow of the remaining sun framed the silhouette of the flattish coral islands around us. Those which were home to luxuriant rainforests grew to look like rising hills. Lights dotting the island coast injected vitality into the dark silhouette, reminding me of the effect provided by smoke curling from chimneys. Perhaps the extended time at sea had left me confusion or fatigue, either made the desire to be ashore ballooned within me. Not merely a resort, the island seemed a haven of peace.

Once settled, the appearance of the dolphins suddenly returned to my mind. If the dolphin is an embodiment of "freedom", then the setting sun is a symbol of "return". Despite their differences, the two remain closely connected by some ineffable force. Hence the name, the "Land of Mystery", is to prompt viewers to interpret themselves what that force might be.

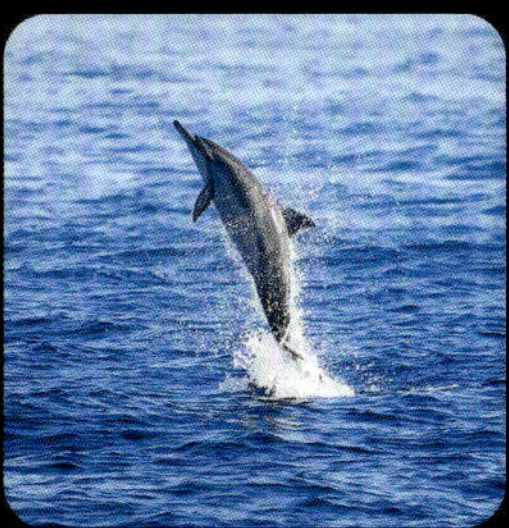
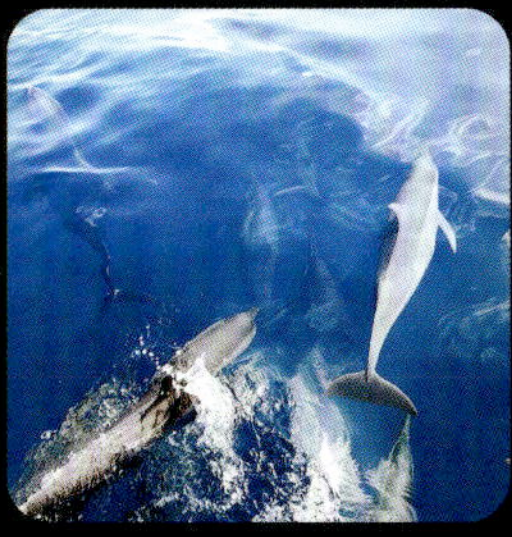
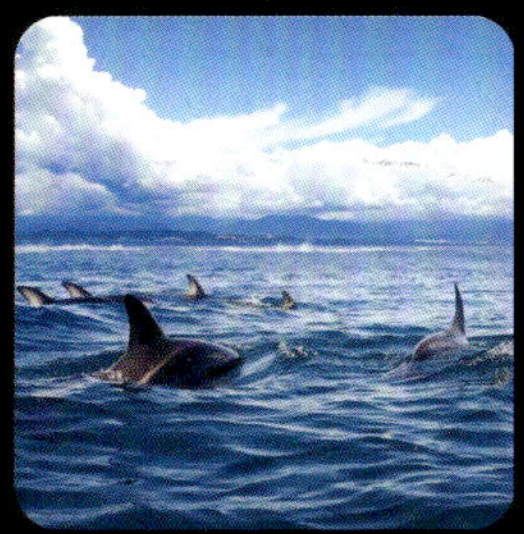

## ◀ DOLPHINS LEAPING OUT OF THE WATER

There are many scientific explanations for why dolphins leap out of the water, but the "performances" they give alongside boats – like the one I had the privilege to enjoy – are mostly considered a form of play. This "spinning ballet" of the Spinner Dolphin – leaping out of the water, spinning in the air and descending back beneath the waves – is unique in Maldives.

Dolphins breathe with lungs so they need to leap out of the water to take breaths. Standing on the deck of a boat and finding the boat surrounded by arrays of dorsal fins, we couldn't help but feel a sense of magnificence and magic.

First, I drew a concept sketch to capture the night view of a bay area. The viewpoint is focused on the sea surface (from near the observation point at the stem of the boat, the same perspective that I experienced on my own excursion out to sea). The centre is a bustling island with myriad lights that separate it from its darkened surroundings. A large boat, creatures flying above the water, and dolphins move in the same direction toward the island, as if some unknown force is attracting them.

My understanding of the term "mysterious" – that which is visible but difficult to ascertain – fills this design. The island is characterised by an air of "mystery", of something that flouts reason, thus the remaining elements to be depicted as aligned with this core theme.

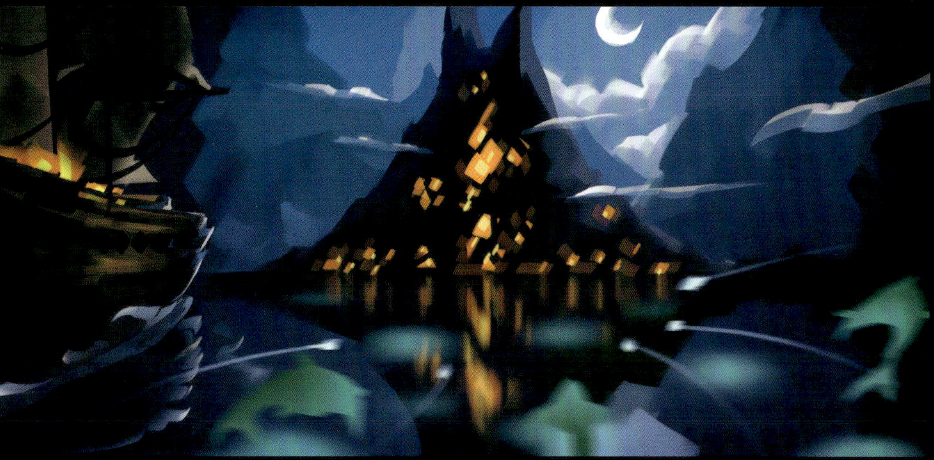

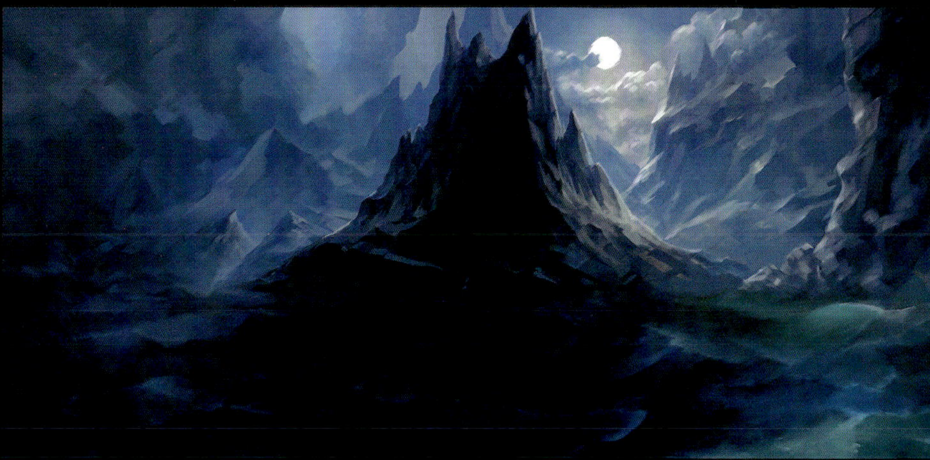

Based on the concept sketch, "a full moon, layers of clouds, and distant mountains are all drawn to complete the background of the scene. The brightness of the moon could bring out the silhouette of the back lighted central island. The structure of the mountain standing on the island is depicted taking into account its size all the way around.

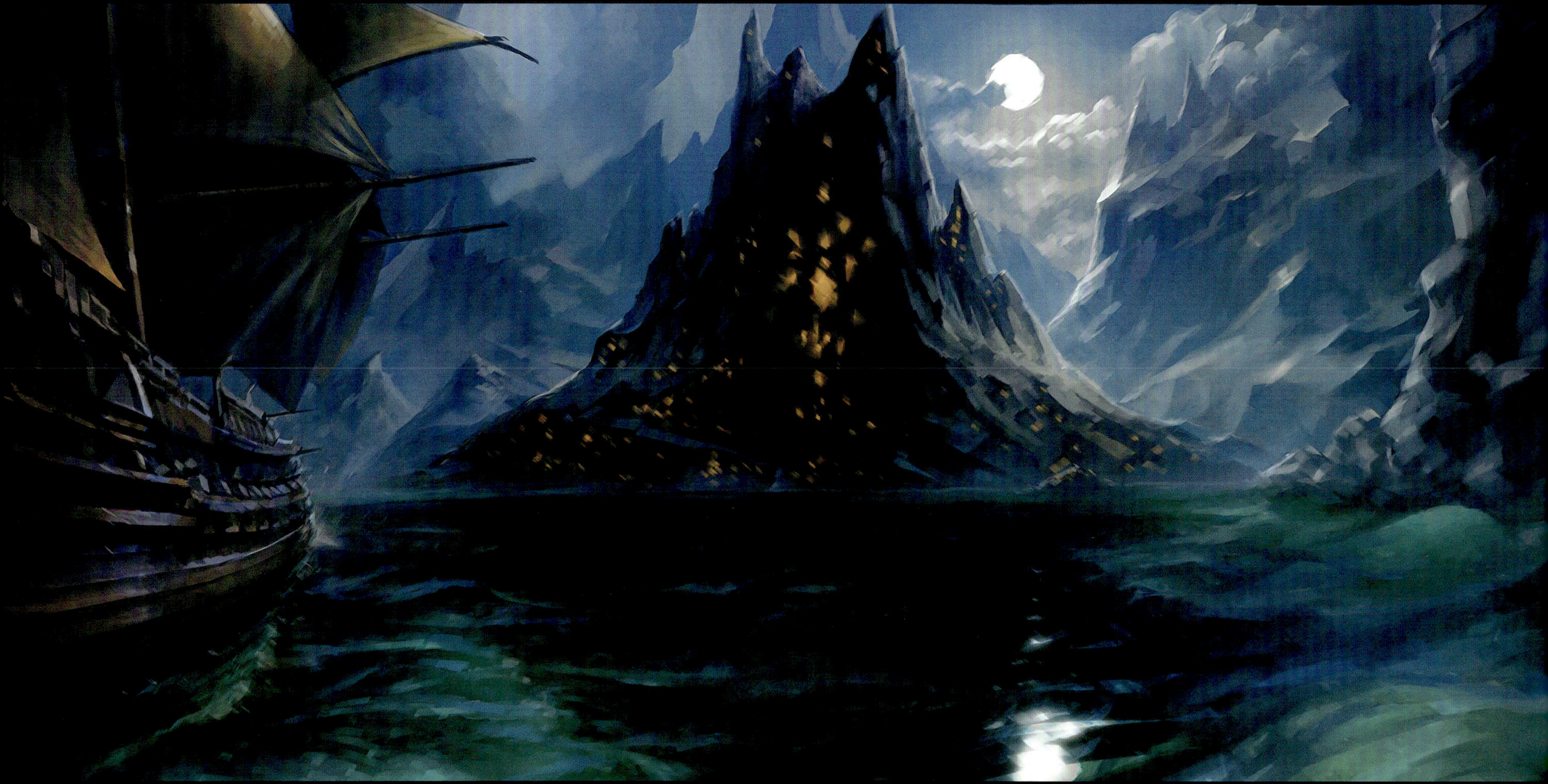

Reflections produced by the moonlight and of the island are added to bring out the sea surface details. With these new elements in place, the foreground boat's position and shape can be determined to maintain a reasonable special perspective. In addition, different sized dots of yellow lights are placed along the cliff of the mountain within its structural lines.

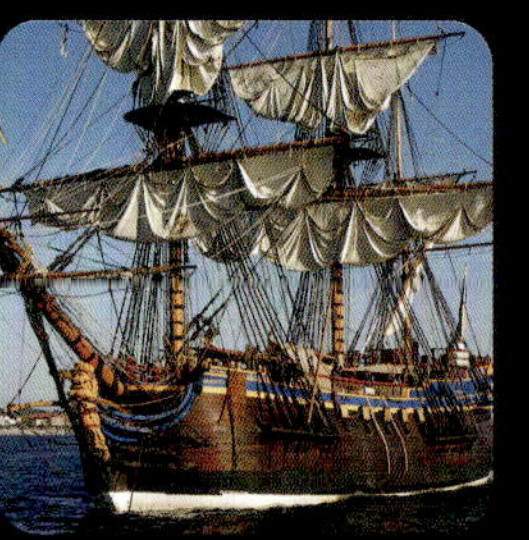

## ◀ LARGE SAILING BOATS

Large sailing boats carry a strong sense of history, making them ideal for fantasy scenes. The complicated structure and abundant texture of such a boat could provide the scene with a significantly greater scope of detail. The ripples and waves and the shape of its sail in the wind create a sense of movement.

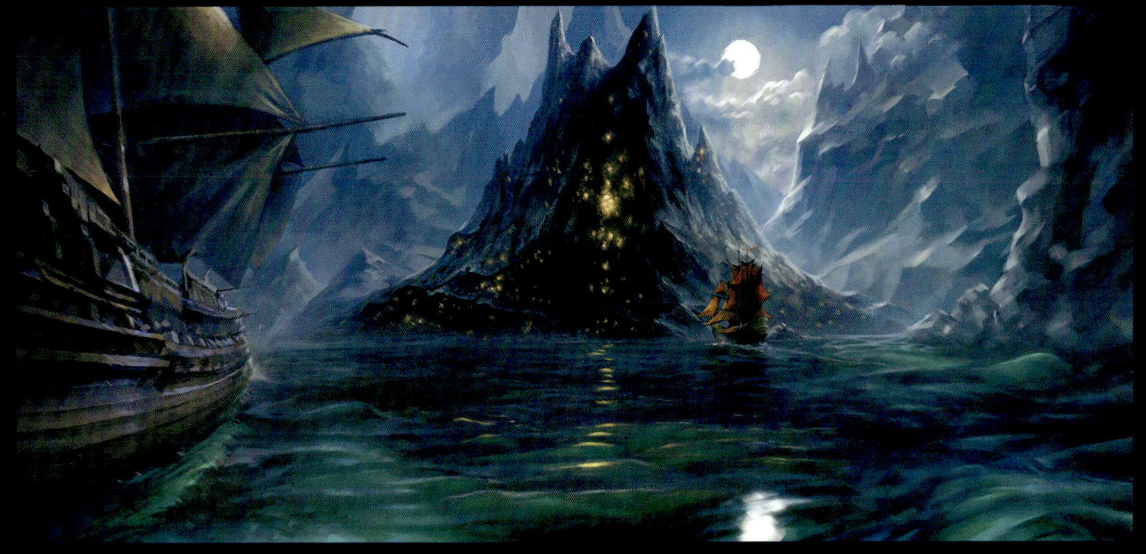

The cliffs of the central island and the layout of the lights are adjusted to make the densely dotted lights seem as if shining from within the mountain, lifting a sense of mystery.

A sailing boat is added atop the rising and falling waves to fill out the middle of the scene (as if a purposeful warships marching to the island) as well as balance the layout of elements (a single boat on the left would appear lonely and pull too much focus).

This newly added sailing boat does not need too detailed depiction, but its overall shape and bearing should not be so different from the foreground ship and therefore still requires attention. Its body and sail should be depicted clearly. According to its position, smog effects help to blend it into its surroundings. Masts, cables, lights and other elements are also added to complete the boat.

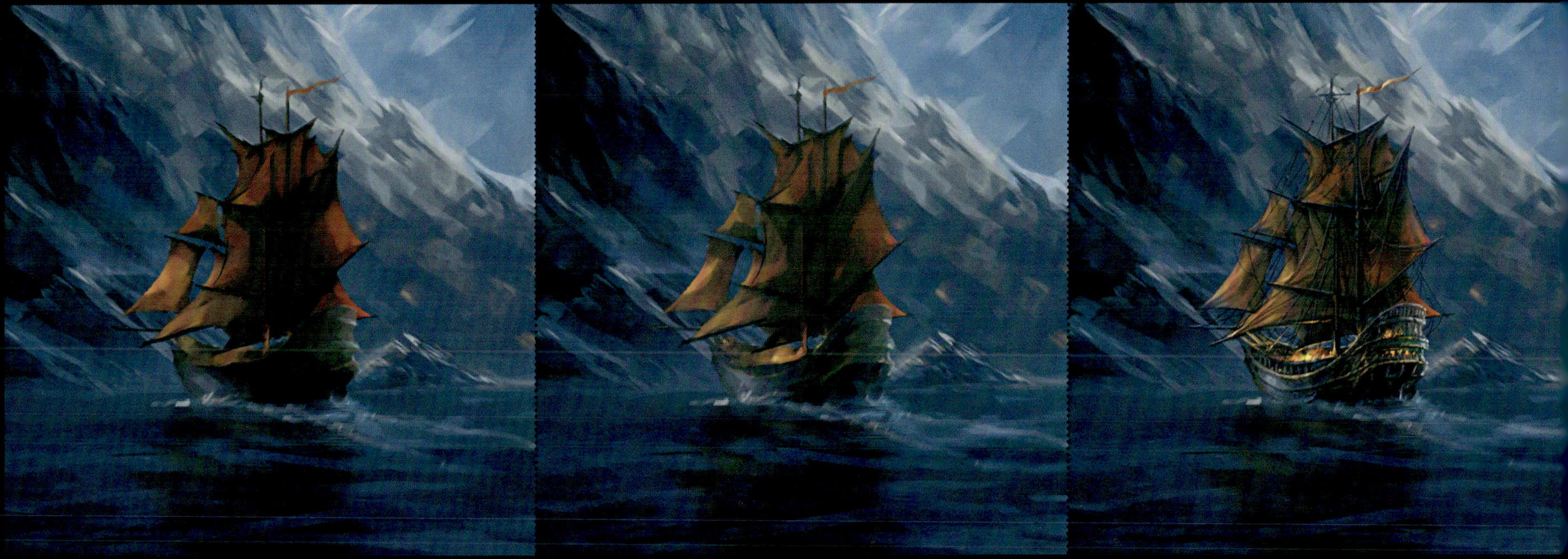

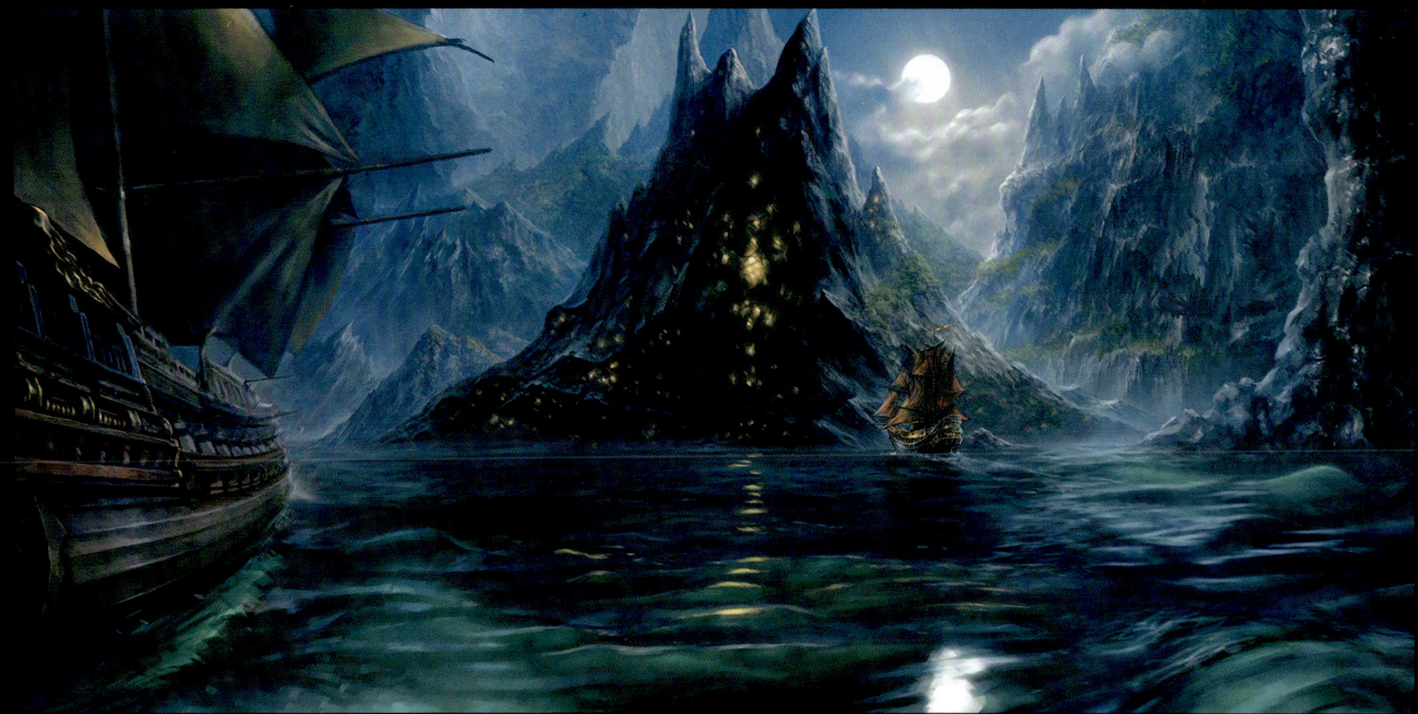

The moon, cloud layers, distant mountains and the boat in the foreground are refined to make the overall precision of the scene consistent.

Here is a comparative example of the effect that a luminous object might have on the water when placed at different positions: there is an instance of ambient lighting, near-lighting, the luminous object floating on the water, and the luminous object submerged beneath it.

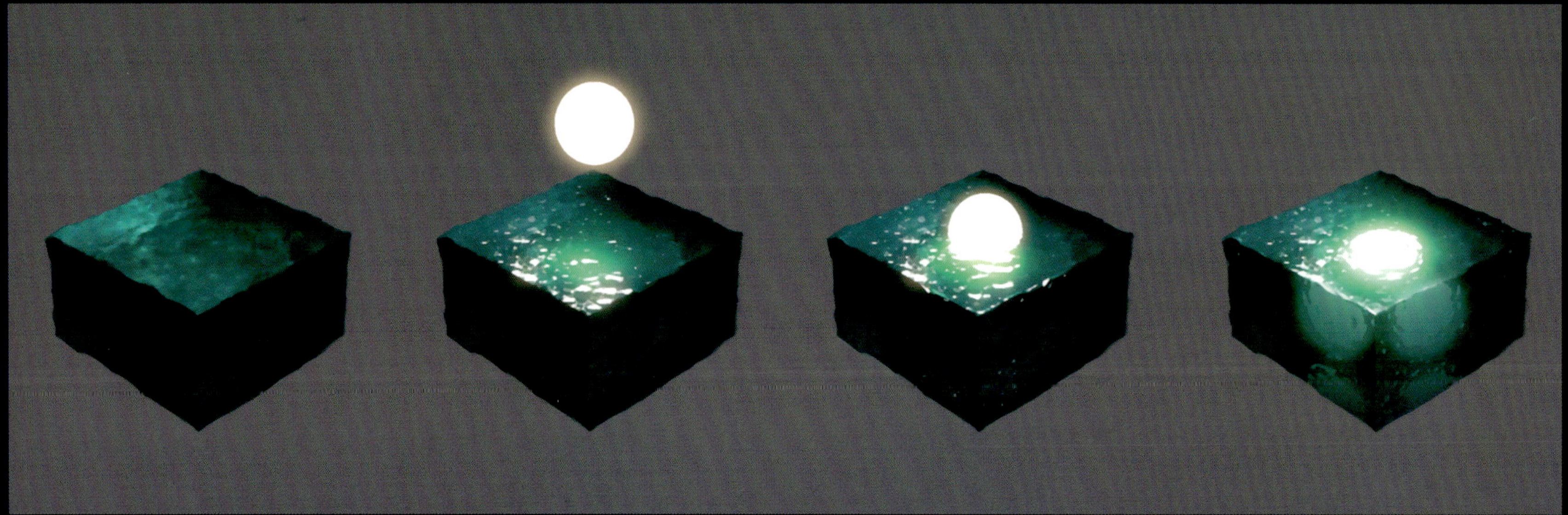

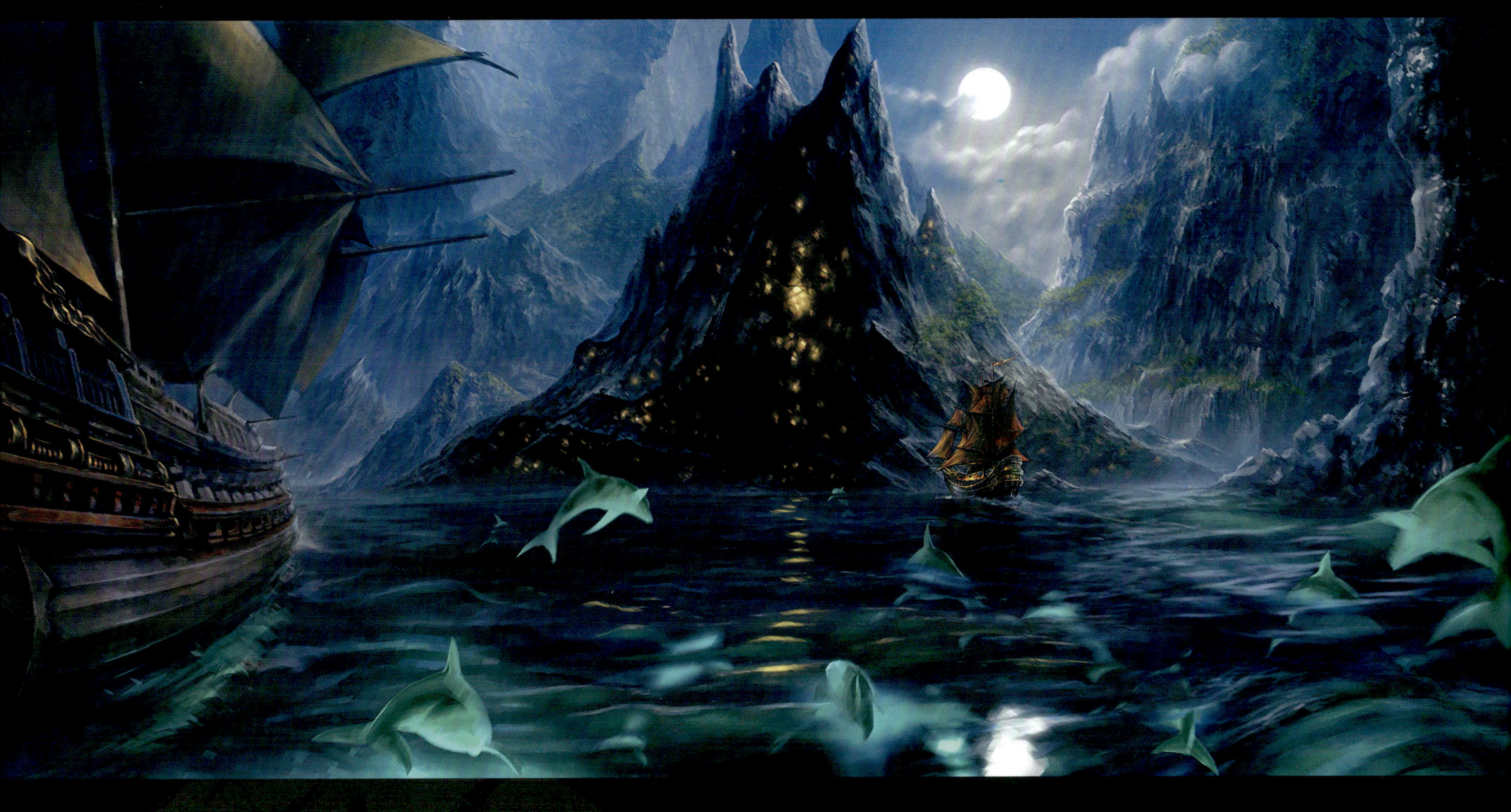

The above effects are accordingly applied to the fluorescent dolphins in the scene. First, the movement and position of the dolphins should be decided, as well as their distance from the sea surface. Considering that the effects of the sea surface are not final, layered treatment should be applied for the convenience of subsequent adjustments.

## ◀ WARSHIP

Here is the profile of a warship including its masts and cables. I searched for images of a warship with its sail down for us to better understand the vessel's structure.

With all the main objects in place, let's now refine the scene.

With reference to relevant materials, details are added to the warship in the foreground. Apart from improving its structure and texture, it is also important to strengthen the lighting effects. Lights can bring out the texture of light-receiving objects and regulate the tone of the warship so as to highlight the intended atmosphere.

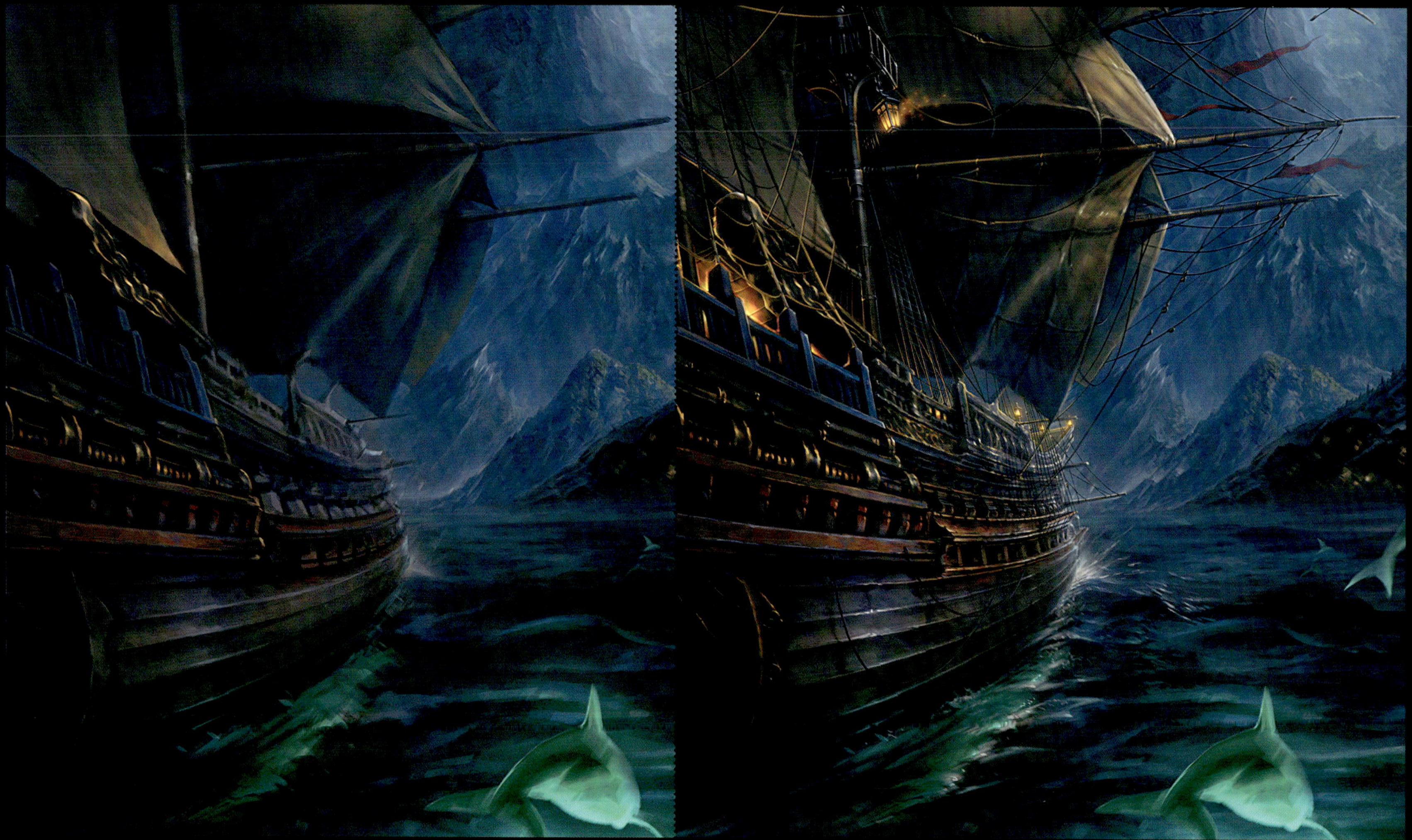

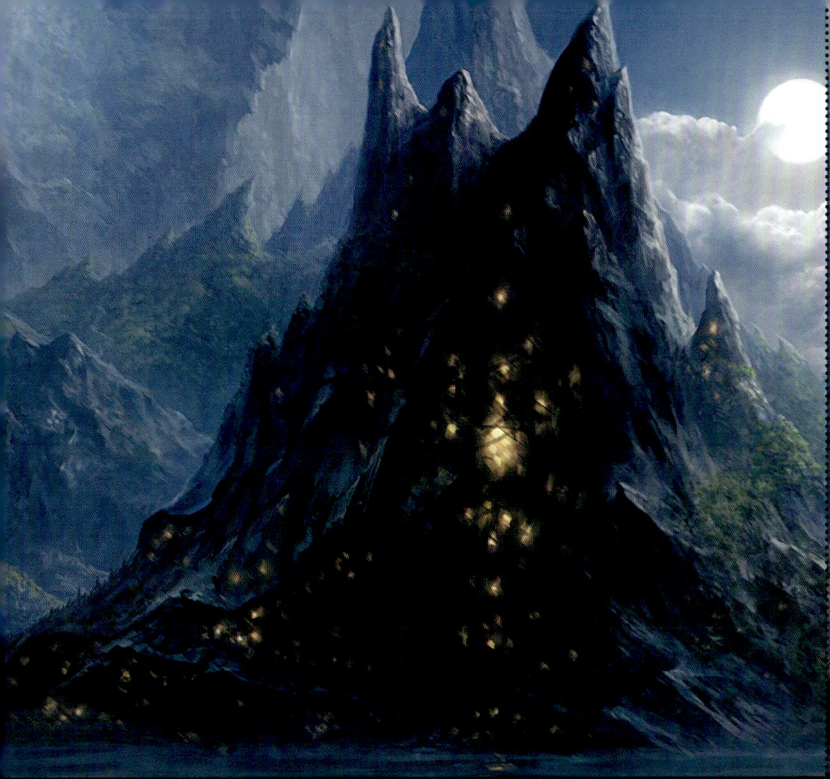

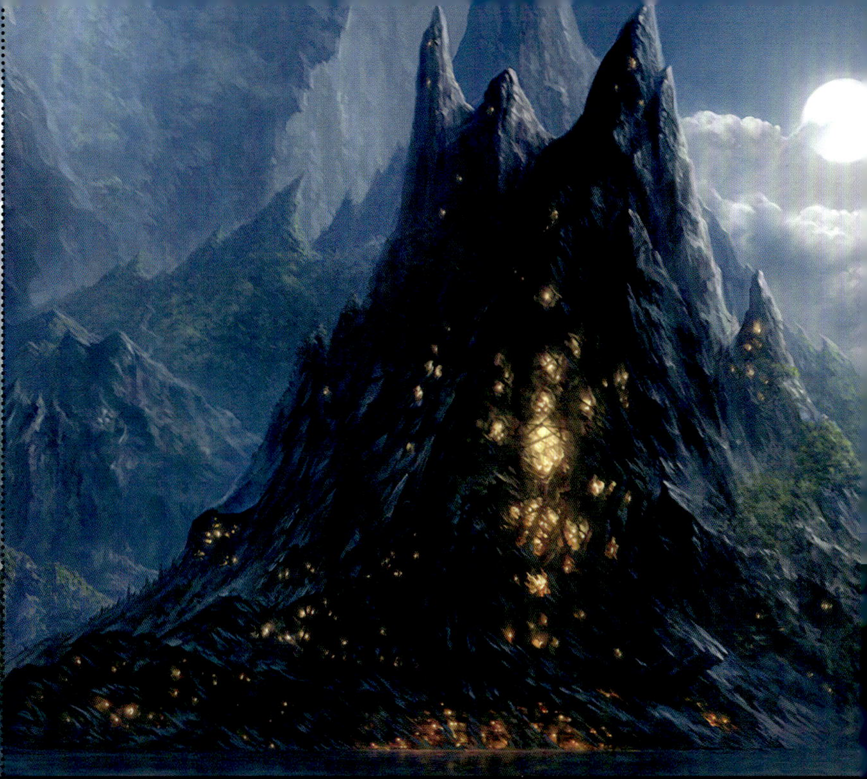

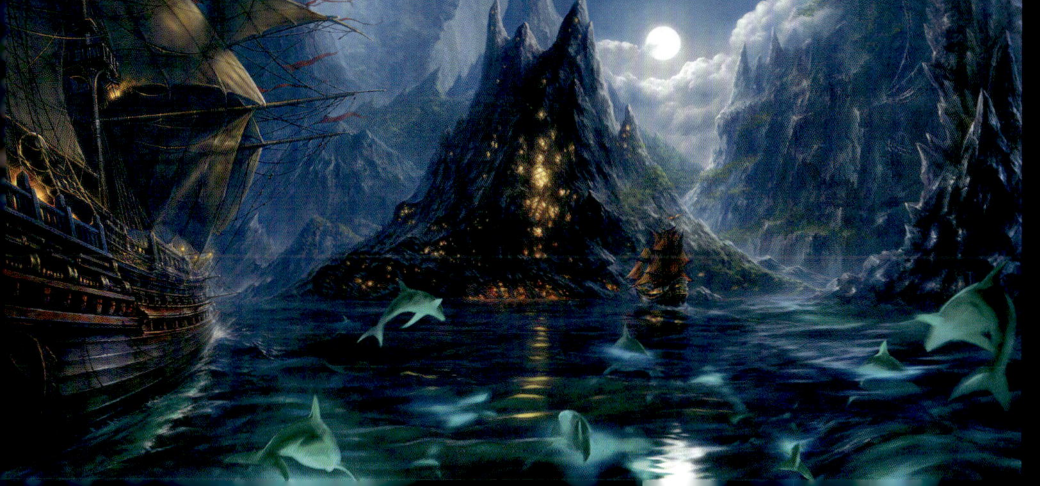

Then, the cliff of the central island's mountain and the lights alon it are depicted. The lights are made brighter and the saturatio turned up. Their colour is changed too from bright yellow to orange yellow, forming a stark contrast to the blueish grey mountain. "hot" scene wrapped in a "cold" pulls the viewer's curiosity towar what might be happening within.

Other objects beside the sea surface and dolphins are then refined t the same degree of precision as the island and warship.

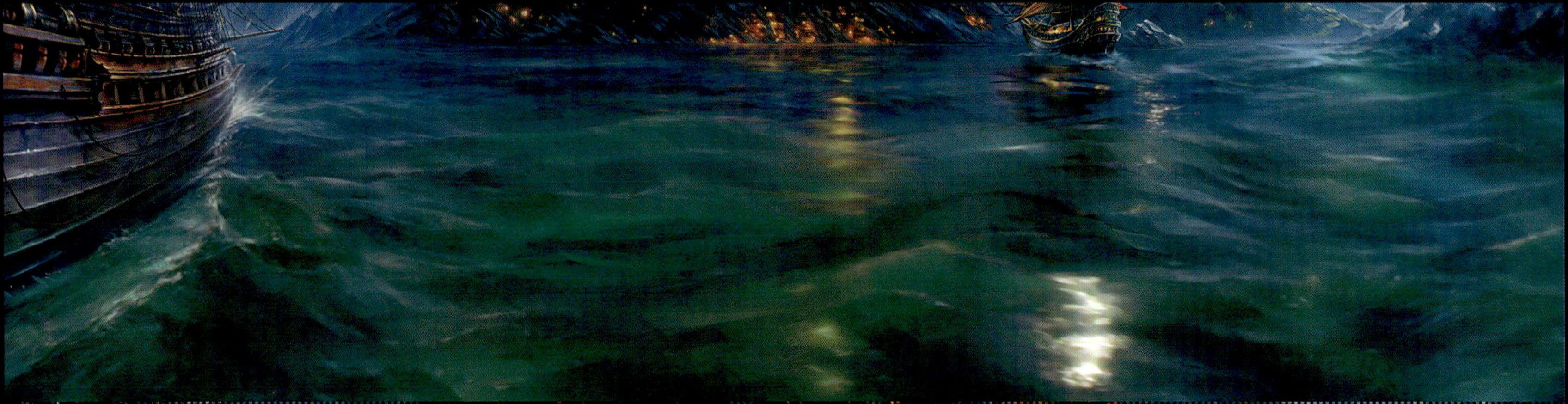

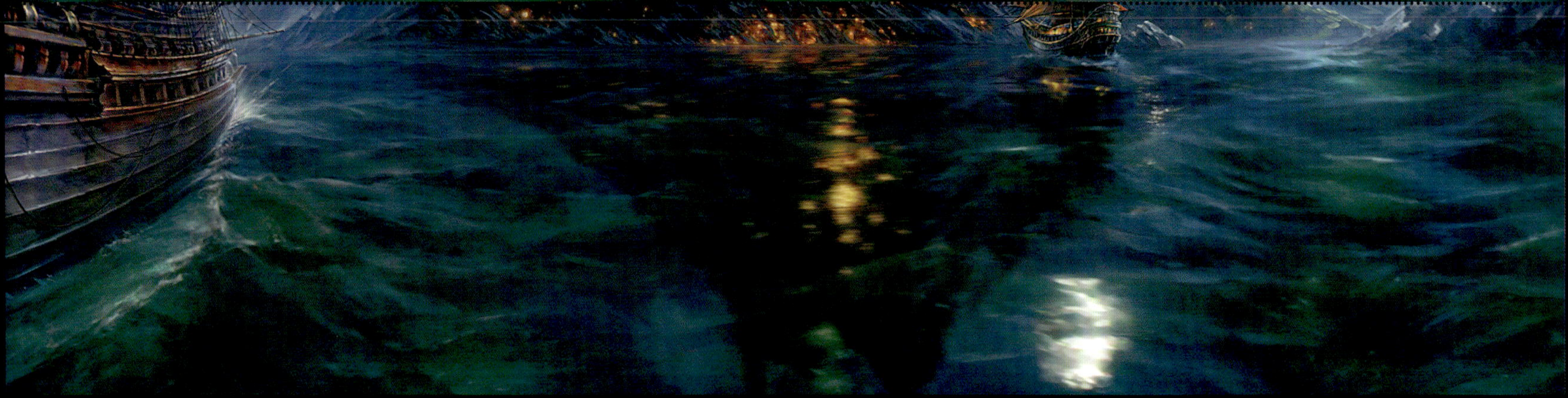

Now, let's begin on the sea surface. The dolphins are temporarily removed to avoid obstruction.

The first step is to bring out the backlighted waves. Without spray yet added, 3S effects make the water appear like jelly. Attention should be paid to the rhythm of wave movement and the way to depict this. The waves' brightness should also be enhanced.

Once reflections from the surrounding objects are added to the sea surface, it is time to adjust the light and shade contrast upon the water under the effects of ambient lighting. This will better integrate the scene as a whole.

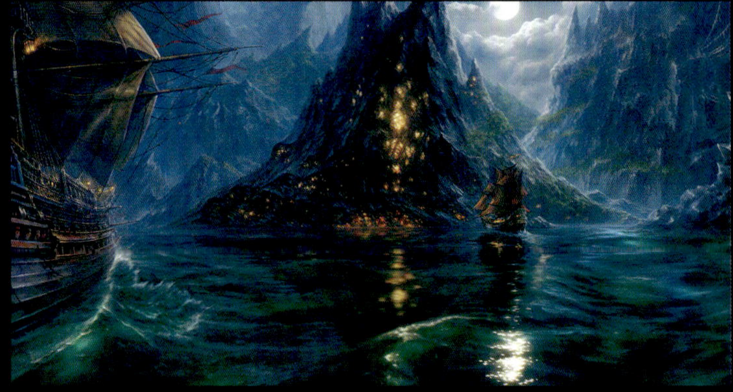

Spray is added to waves. With the rippling of sea waves, the edges of reflections are slightly distorted. The reflection of the moon and the sea waves closest to viewers are also depicted. The glow effect and sparkling flares of light are added to areas where the moonlight is reflected to make it more attractive. A "flare" is a white dot on the sea surface; while "glow" refers to the light-yellow halo around a point.

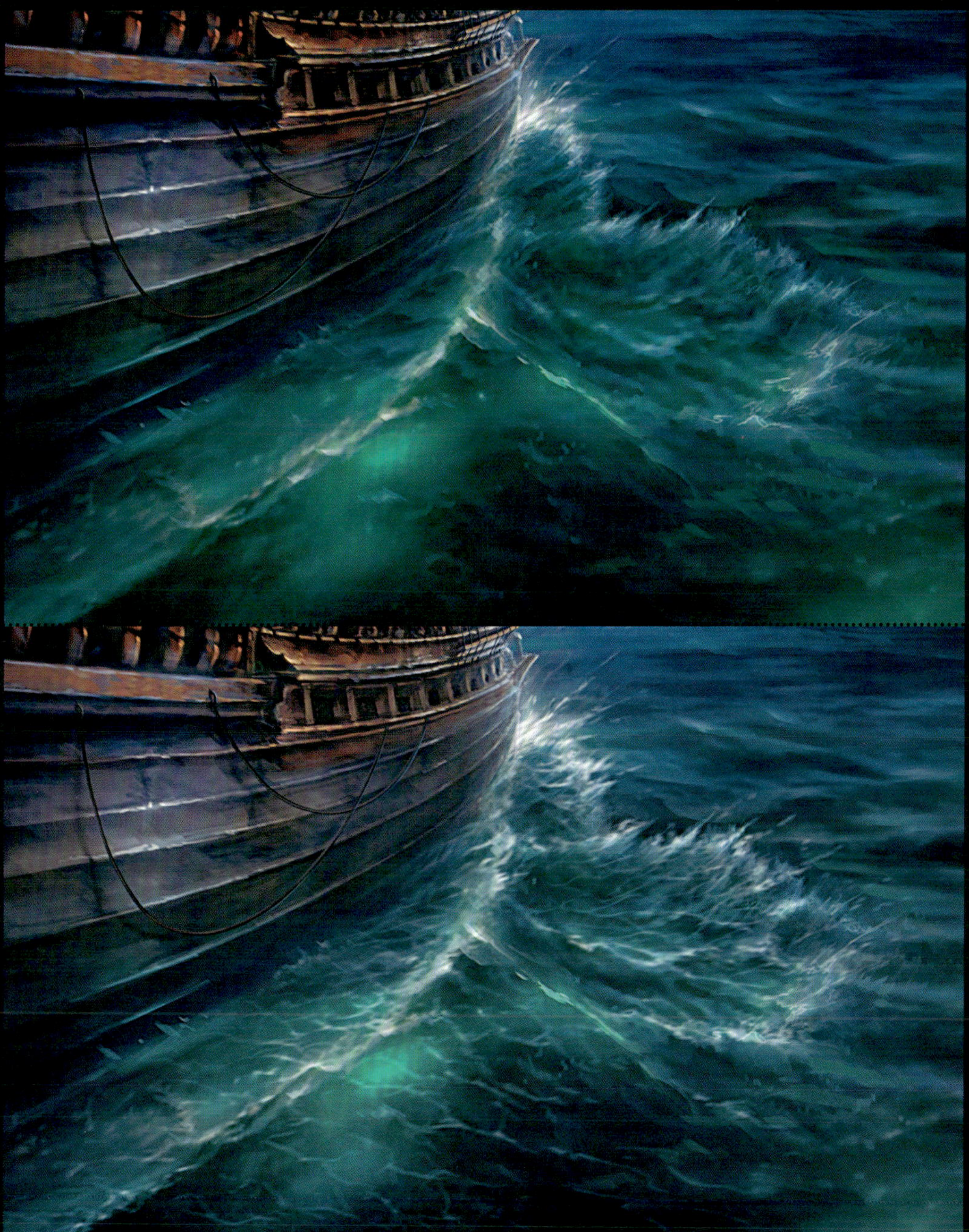

The waves stirred up by the boat in the foreground need more detailed depiction, to the degree of precision already applied to the boat so the elements blend smoothly together.

When a boat sails across water, waves splash outwardly and backwardly. This should be taken into account when deciding on where to insert waves, how to shape them and from what direction the moon light would shine upon them.

More delicate sprays are added to the top of the waves. With the ripples resulting from the water turning over itself, belts of foam would materialize on the wave's surface.

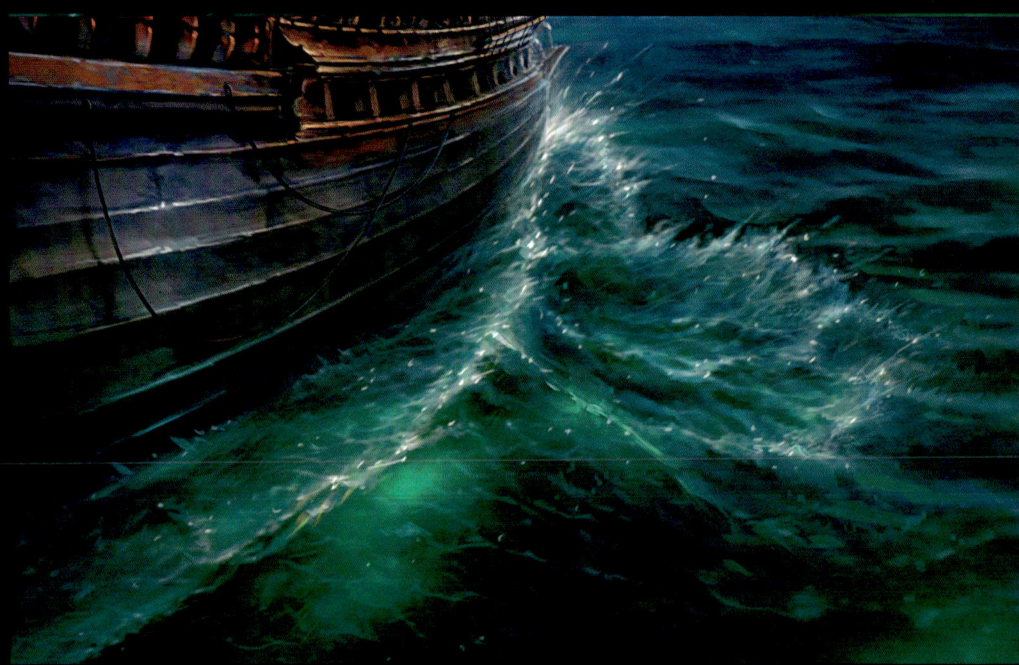

Lastly, the finer details of the waves are adjusted. Highlighted crystal-like droplets are added as decorations and with that the waves stirred up by, the waves' details are completed.

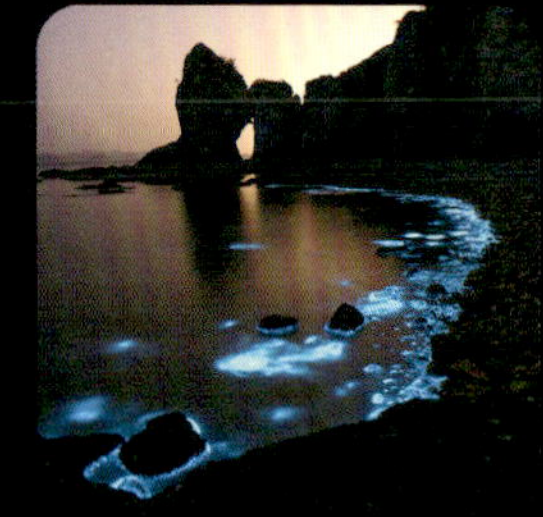

## ▲ BIOLUMINESCENT BEACH

A "bioluminescent beach" is a beach awash with bioluminescent phytoplankton swept onto the beach by sea waves. Against a night sky, the blueish light given out by these beaches sparks a feeling of romance and fantasy. There are only a few bioluminescent beaches across the globe, and the one in Maldives is among them.

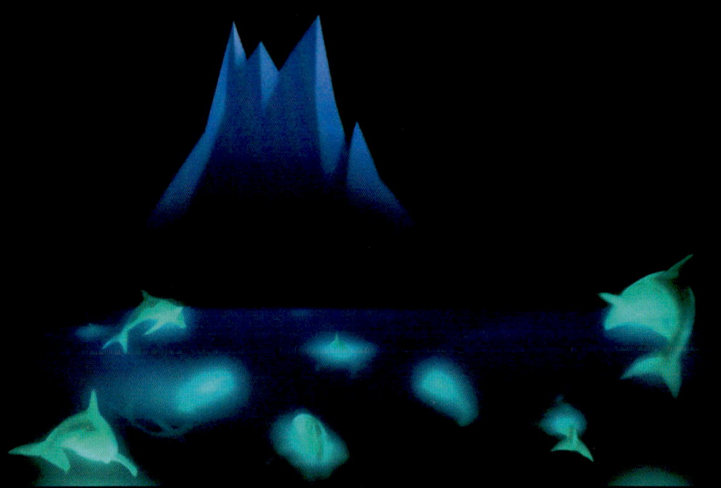

Now, let's add the dolphins into the scene. The size, position, and shape of the previously depicted dolphins should be adjusted to fit the current composition, especially considering the new layout of the waves. The reflections of these dolphins and their glowing must also be included.

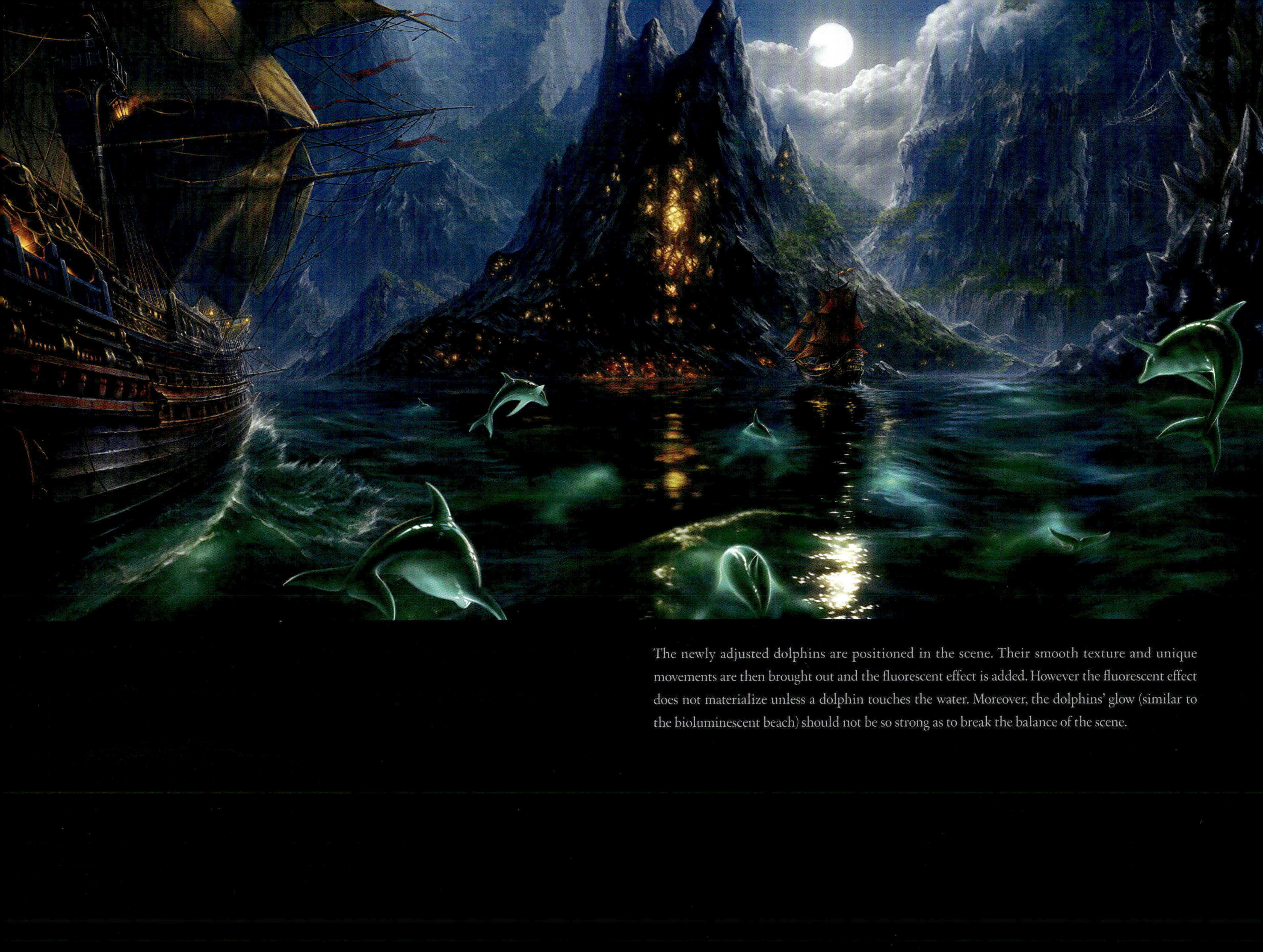

The newly adjusted dolphins are positioned in the scene. Their smooth texture and unique movements are then brought out and the fluorescent effect is added. However the fluorescent effect does not materialize unless a dolphin touches the water. Moreover, the dolphins' glow (similar to the bioluminescent beach) should not be so strong as to break the balance of the scene.

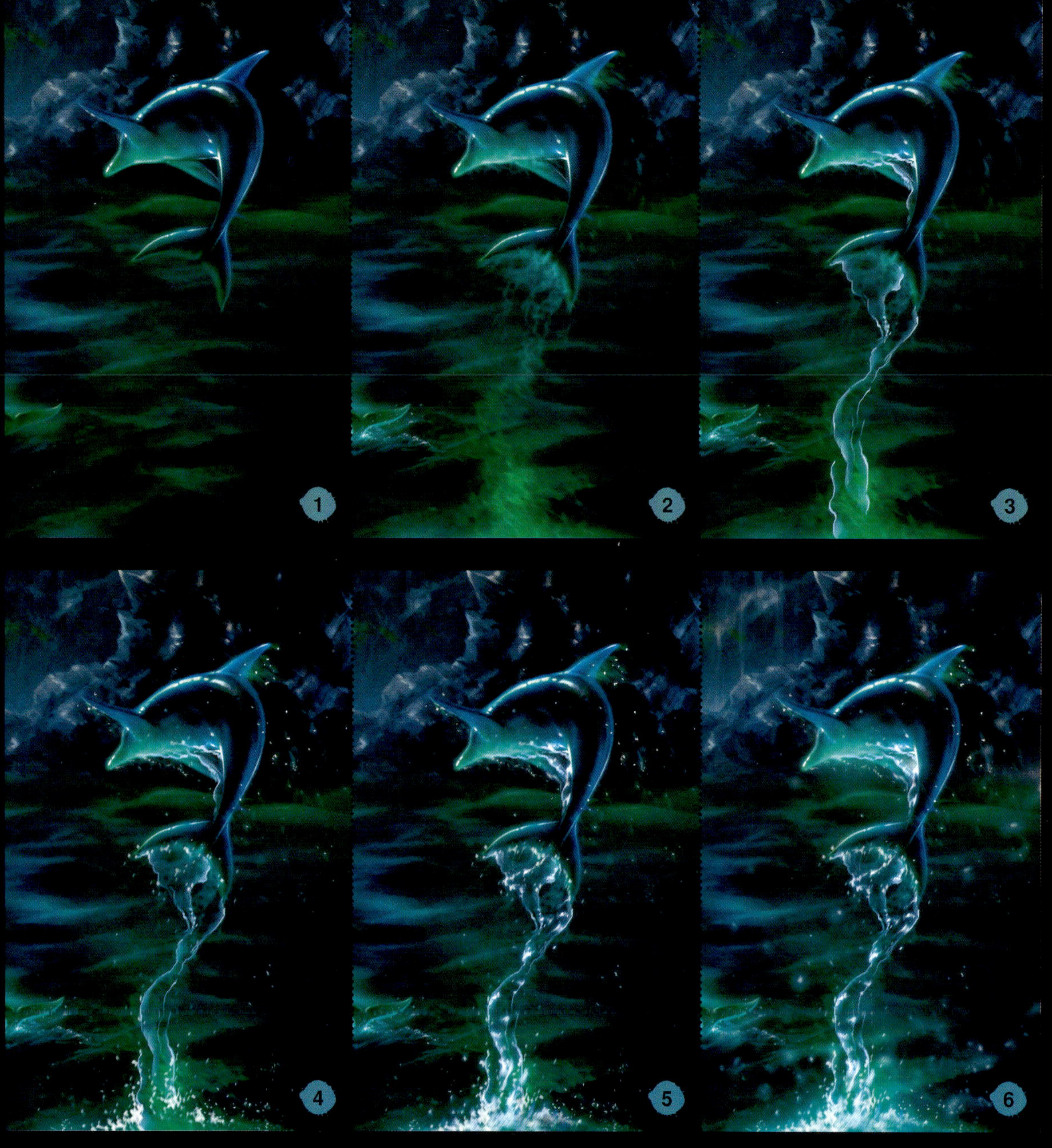


Apart from refining the dolphins, we must remember to include the splash of a dolphin leaving the water.

To better understand the process of depiction, let's consider the dolphin on the right of the scene as an example. We need to distinguish between the "moonlit texture of its dorsal fins" and the "fluorescent effect of its belly".

1. The colour of the dolphins is adjusted to differ from the sea surface.
2. The splash of the water produced by the leap of the dolphins, as well as its trajectory, is depicted in the colour of fluorescent green using void strokes.
3. Along the void movement of the water, a "waterspout" is created. "White" is applied to give form to an empty spout.
4. Highlighted, crystal-like drops of water are added.
5. The point from where the water is splashing upward should be highlighted.The water spout is evenly lit so that it shines with glow.
6. The colour is adjusted. A bluish green glow is added to all highlighted areas.

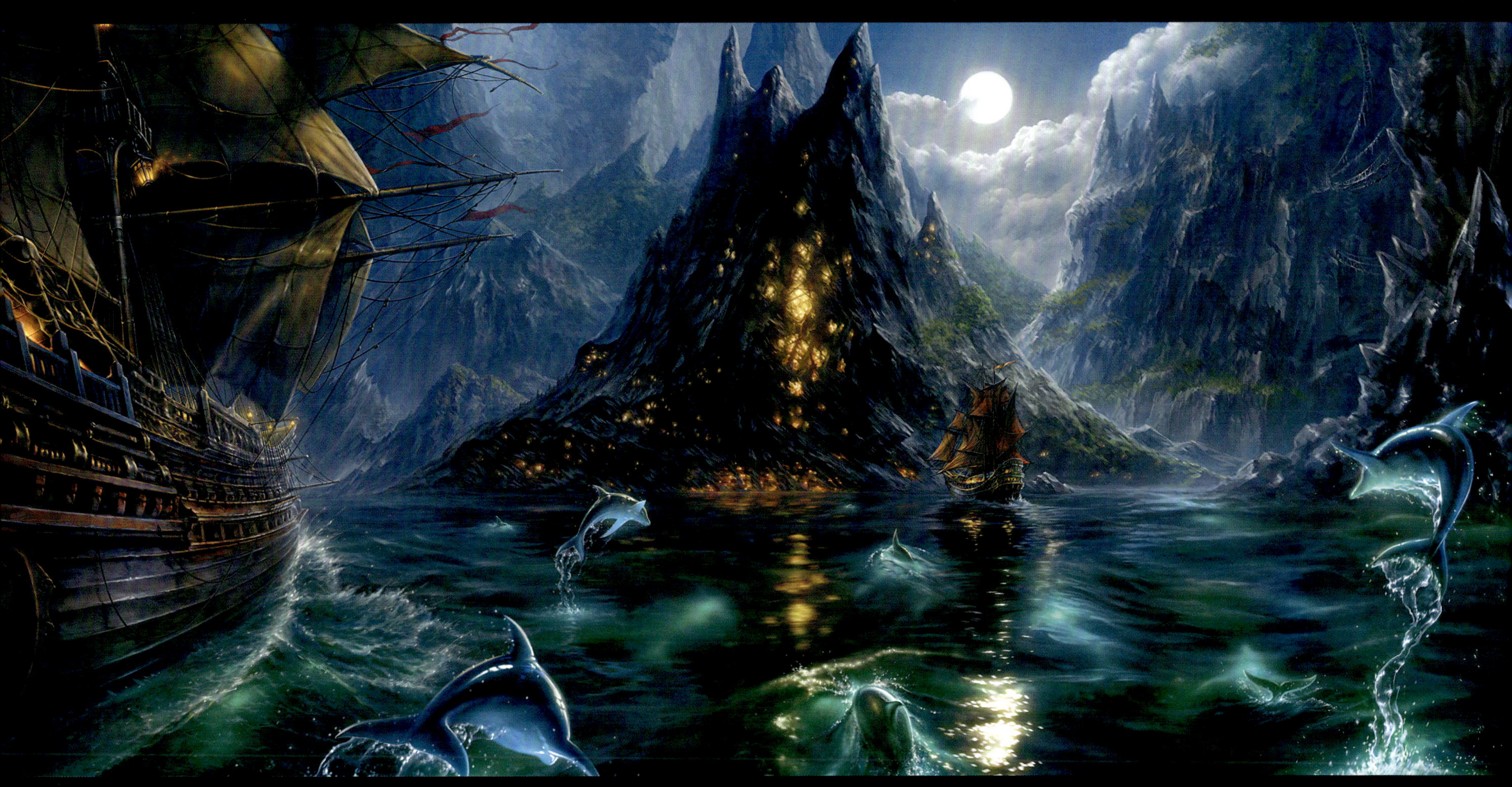

Each of the dolphins is treated in a similar way.

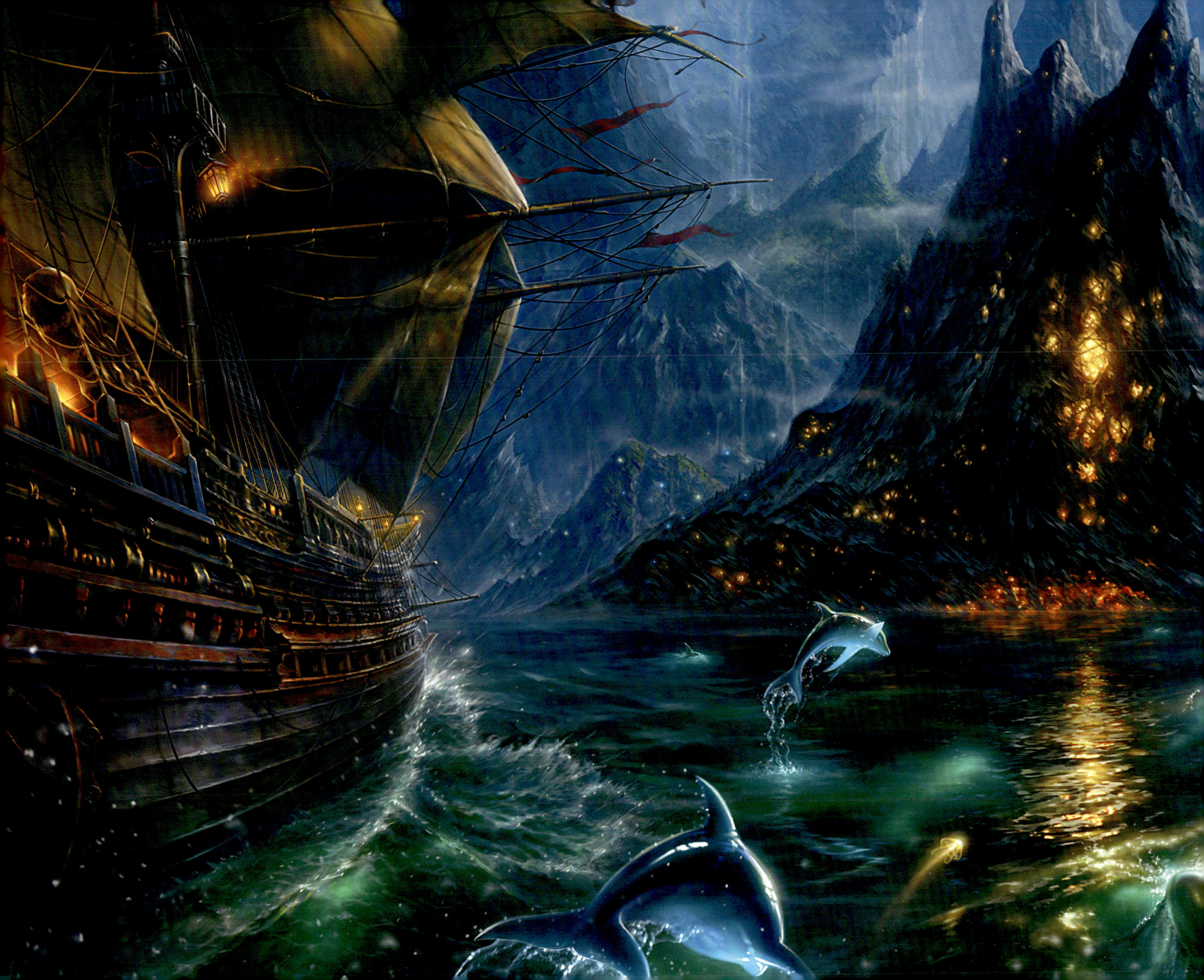

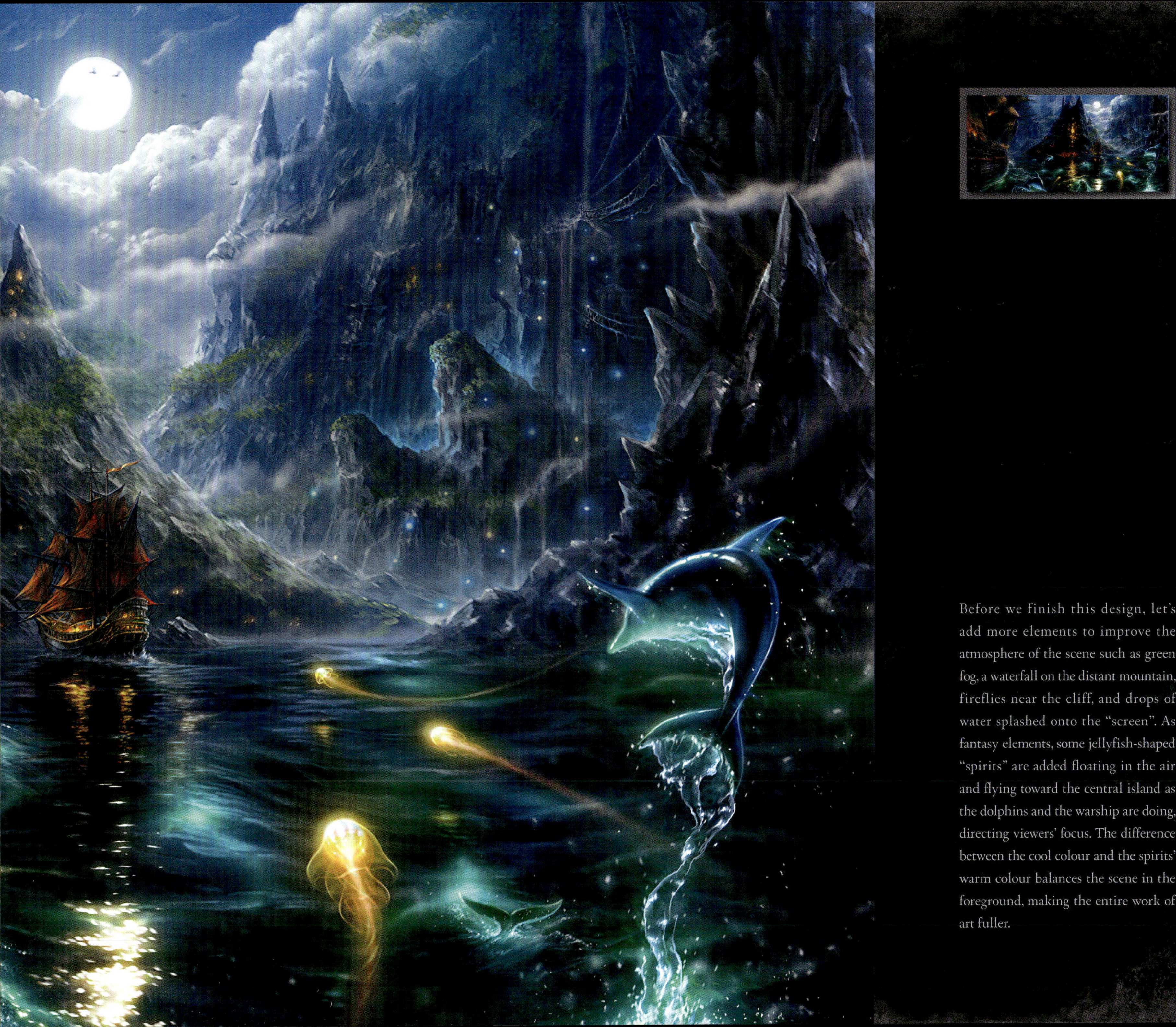

Before we finish this design, let's add more elements to improve the atmosphere of the scene such as green fog, a waterfall on the distant mountain, fireflies near the cliff, and drops of water splashed onto the "screen". As fantasy elements, some jellyfish-shaped "spirits" are added floating in the air and flying toward the central island as the dolphins and the warship are doing, directing viewers' focus. The difference between the cool colour and the spirits' warm colour balances the scene in the foreground, making the entire work of art fuller.

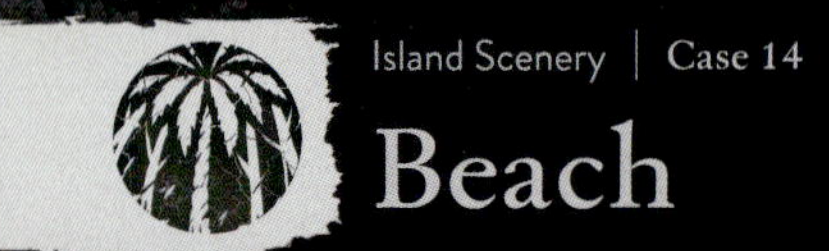

Island Scenery | Case 14

# Beach

In Maldives, I spent most of my time watching the sea. Besides the water house, the beach was best for rest.

The resort island there isn't large. I would roam the beach all around the island's edge when I was free. Nature never failed to impress me – the blue sea, clear sky, and luxuriant trees and plants. Sometimes, even beneath the scorching sun, I chose to cross the beach that was the size of a football field on my walk; other times, I would make a detour through the dense stretches of forests.

The *Beach* depicts my first-hand experience of the beaches in the Maldives. It was sparked from my intent to integrate various elements into one single scene.

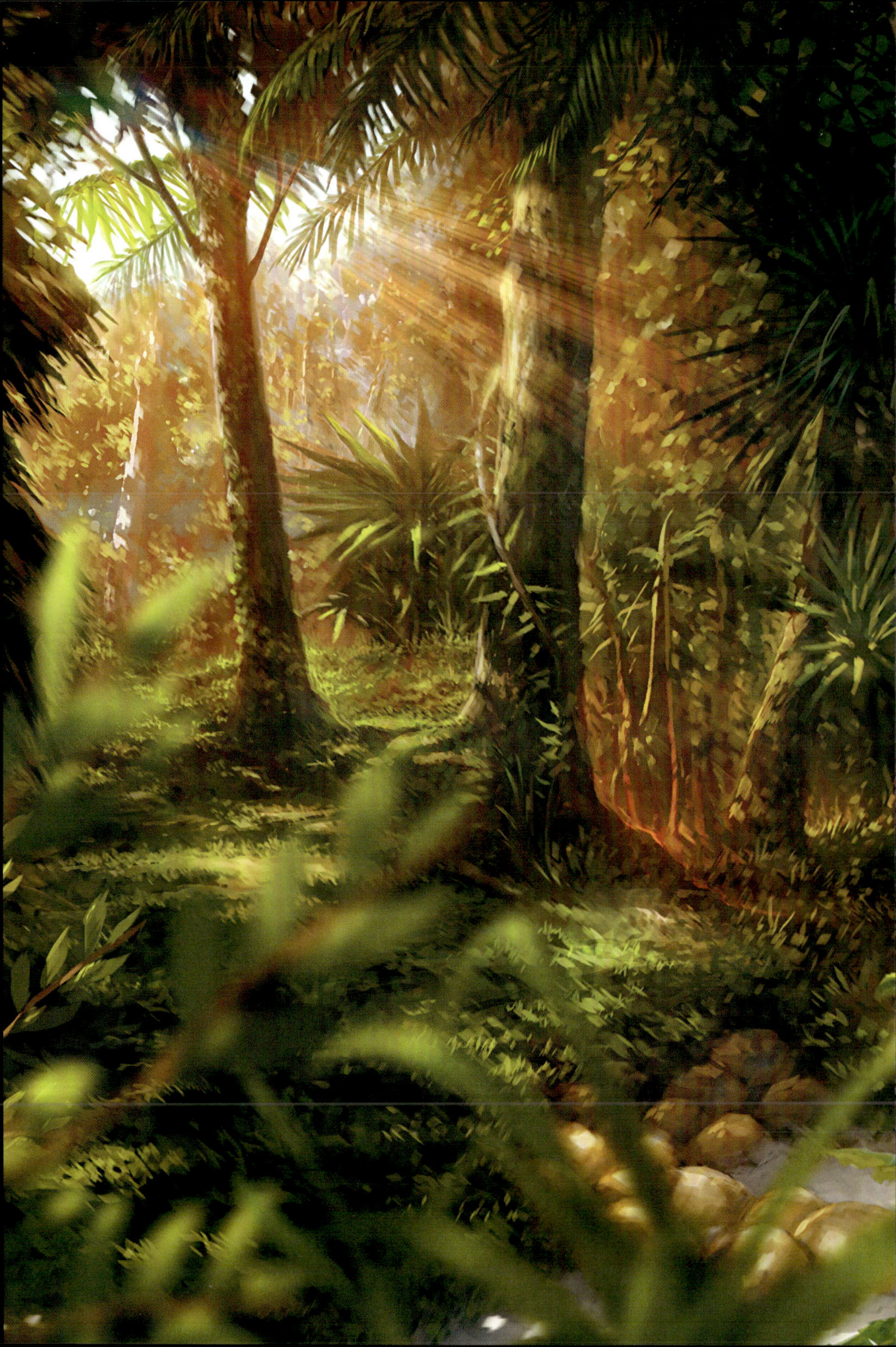

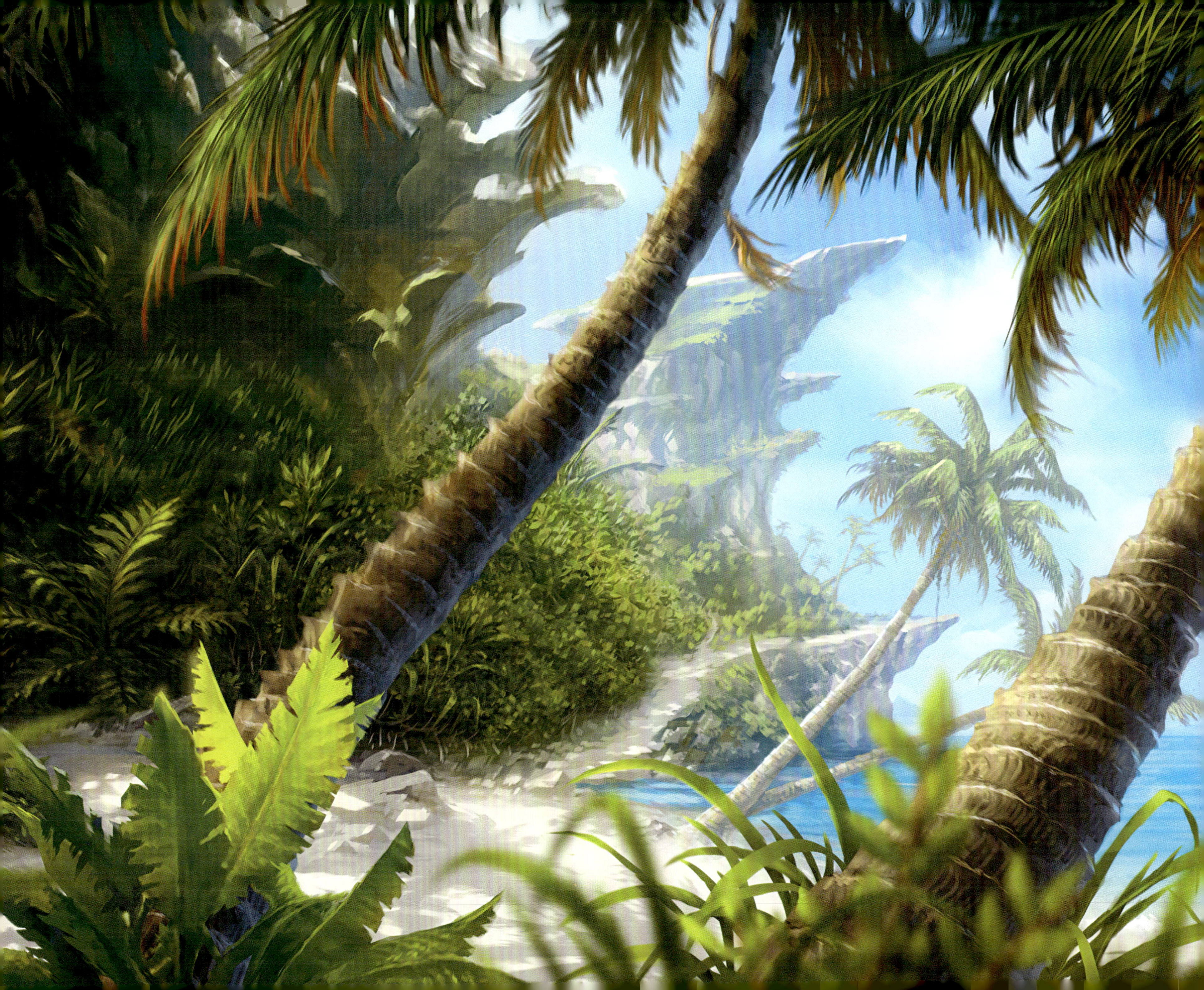

# THOUGHTS ON CREATION

*Seeing azure waves lap around the white and delicate beach, I found myself in a world of purity and peace. If it hadn't been for the tropical heat and the intense ultraviolet rays, I might have stood there all day long, abandoning myself to the transcendent beauty. The island rainforest reaches far along the beach, showcasing its vitality.*

*The Beach depicts my first-hand experience of the beaches in Maldives. It was sparked from my intent to integrate various elements into one single scene.*

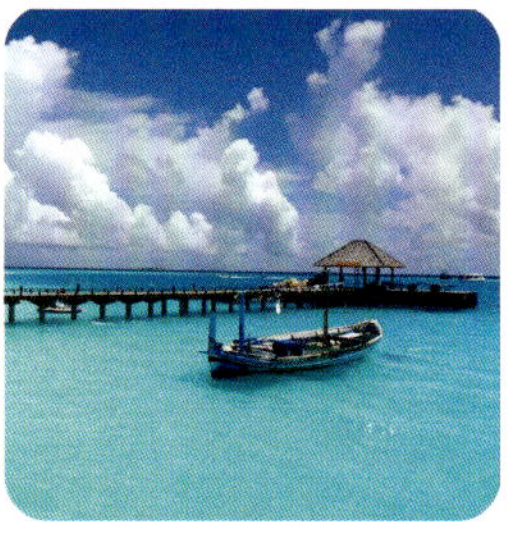

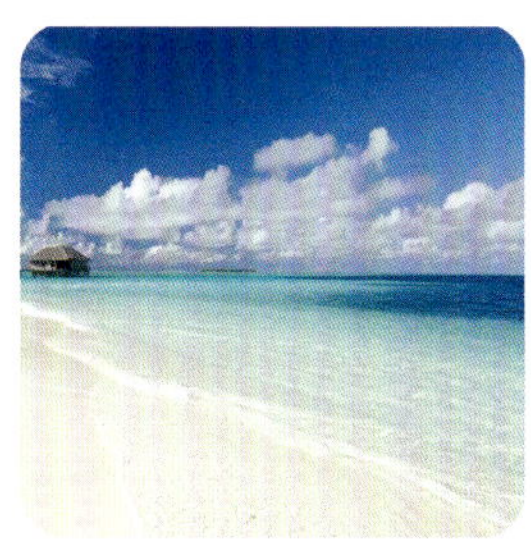

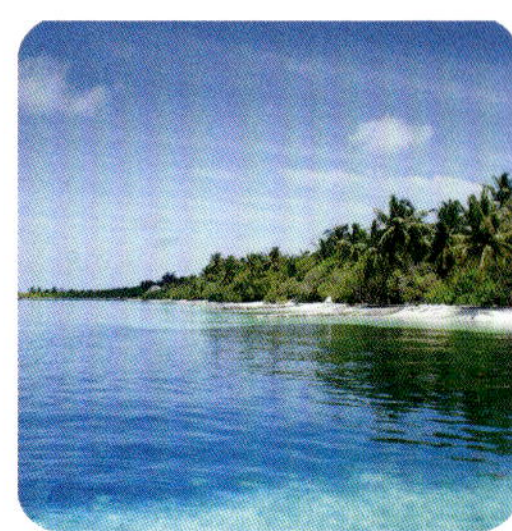

▲ BEACH

On the Maldivian beaches, blue skies and endless sea stretching beneath thick layers of white clouds are common sights.

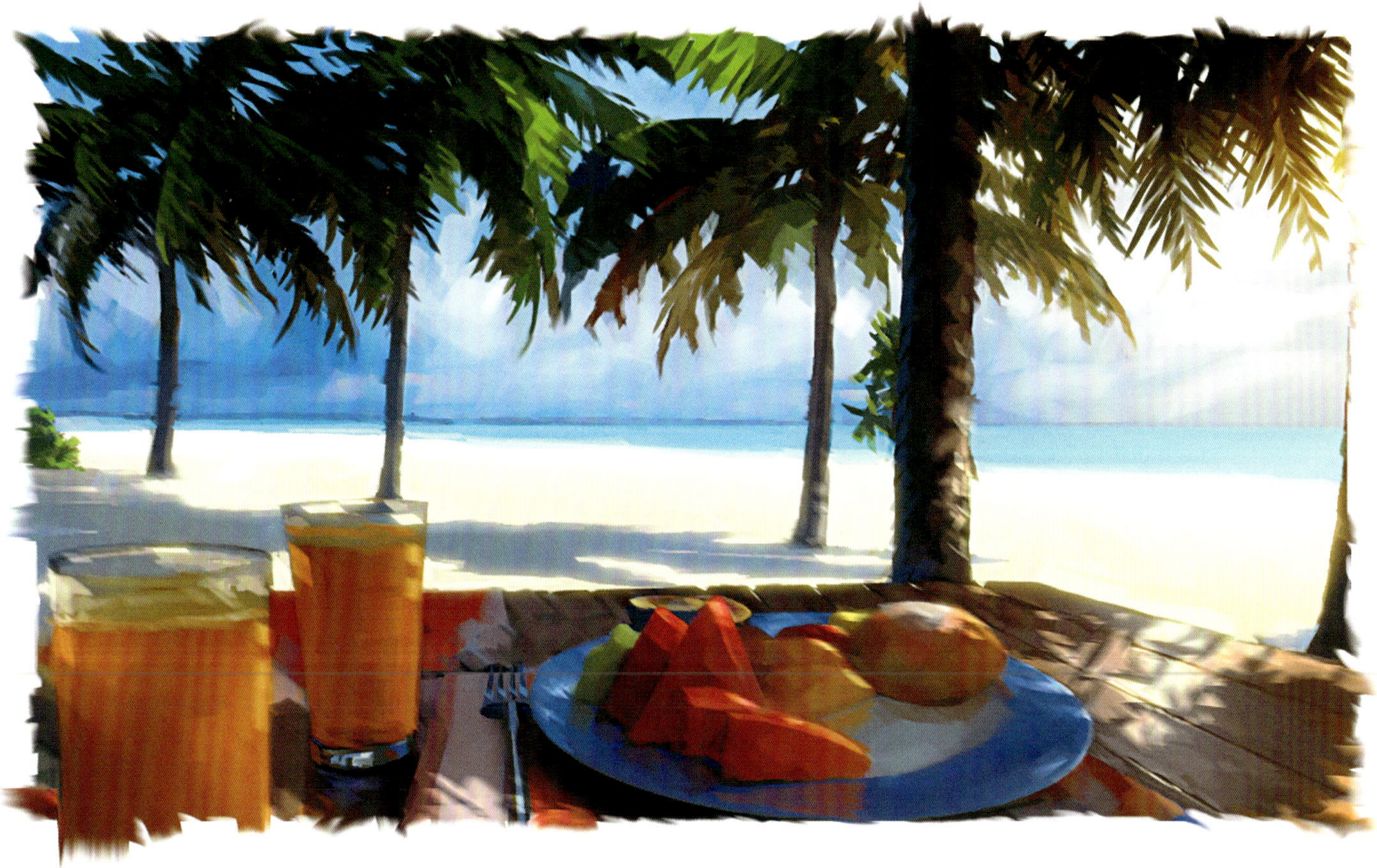

On the resort island, the most leisurely activity is simply to sit watching the blue waters in the sea breeze while eating iced fruit in the shade of lush palm trees to avoid the heat. The picture here captures a scene that people who have travelled to Maldives cherish as one of their best memories.

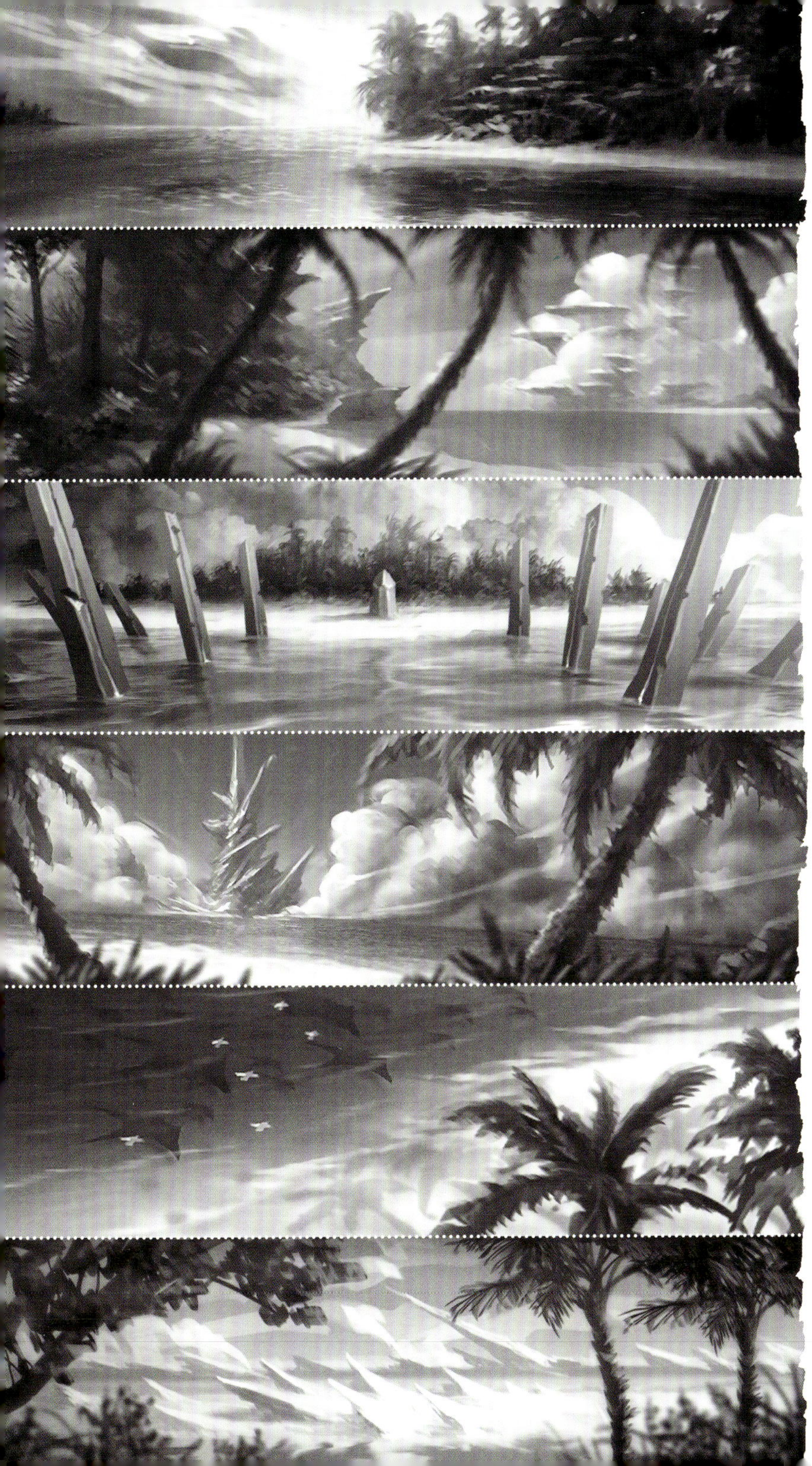

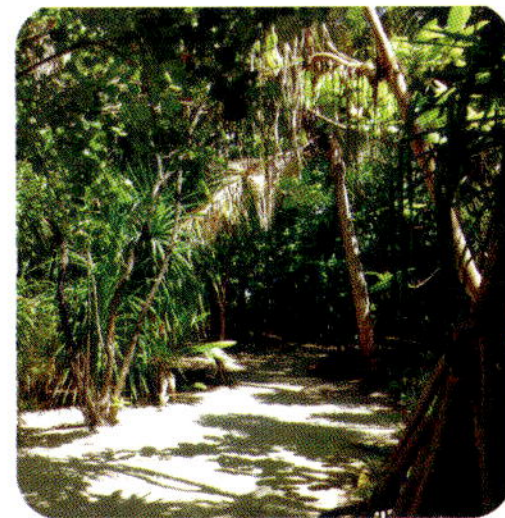

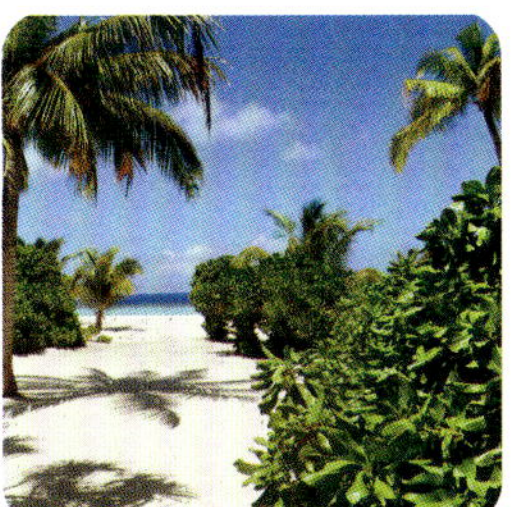

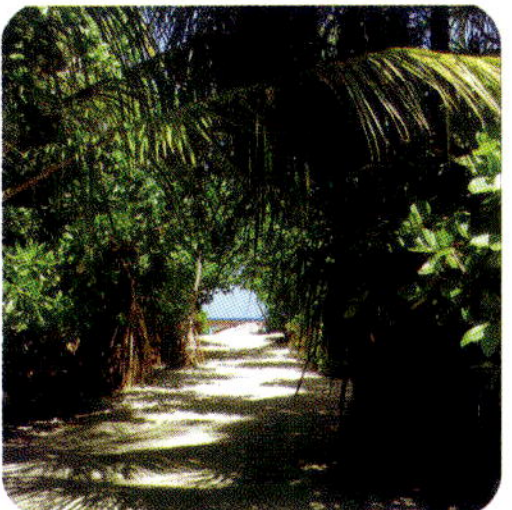

## ▲ RAINFOREST

In the rainforest, I found myself surrounded by swathes of green peppered by bars of sunshine penetrating through the leaves onto the ground. The space between the rainforest floor and palm tree canopy is filled with luxuriant bushes and ferns. But for the water's blue vaguely visible from between the trees, I might have forgotten that I was on an island surrounded by sea.

As this is the book's last example, let's try to work out what such a scene might require before jumping in to the creation.

The most impressive view that comes to mind when I think of Maldives is the "beach seascape". This is adopted as the template for our painting and includes a sea, a blue sky, a beach, luxuriant rainforests and fantasy elements. This is all presented in a horizontal composition, and the aim is to remind viewers of what is unique about Maldives.

Considering that characteristic details can be expressed quickly in a monochrome sketch, several of these sketches are drawn, each depicting the required elements but expressing them differently.

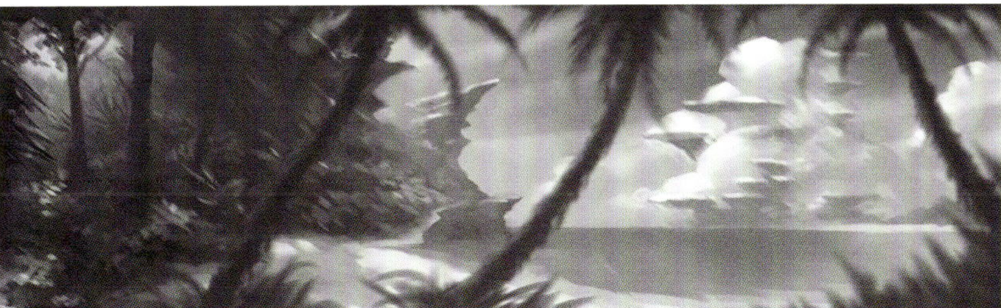

Considering the desire to "give expression to unique local features, depict different objects in different layers, and fit objects into a horizontal composition", this sketch is chosen for further treatment.

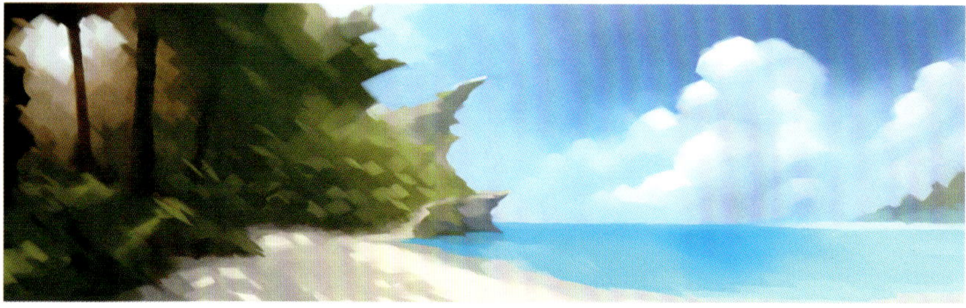

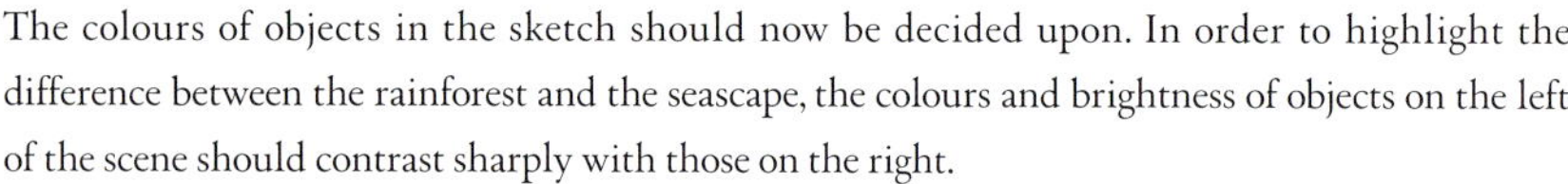

The colours of objects in the sketch should now be decided upon. In order to highlight the difference between the rainforest and the seascape, the colours and brightness of objects on the left of the scene should contrast sharply with those on the right.

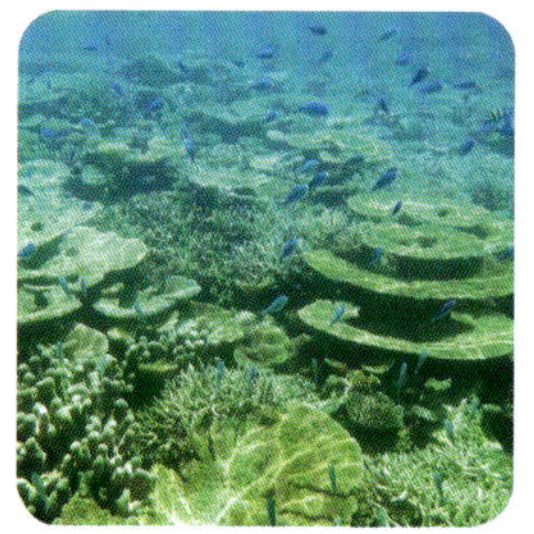

## ◀ CORAL ISLANDS

Maldives is home to coral islands built of tens of thousands of pieces of coral detritus – the dead coral material made of calcium carbonate. These coral islands only form after hundreds or even thousands of years of accumulated growth.

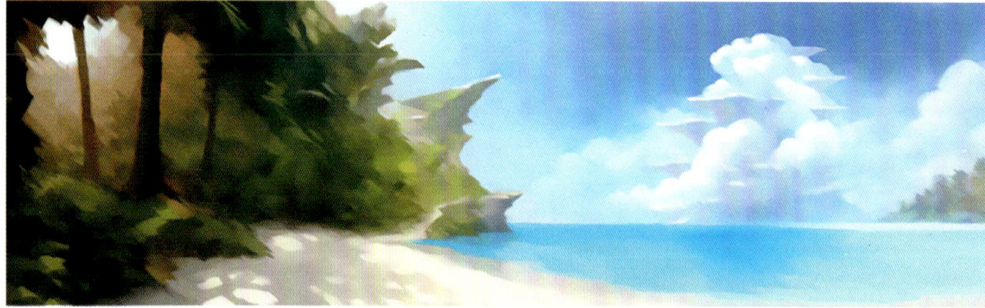

Coral is thus an ideal feature to exaggerate in our fantasy scene. In the distance, a coral-shaped island is inserted, surrounded by a large mass of clouds to allude to its massive size. This slight cover also integrates the colossal structure into its surroundings without being abrupt. In the foreground, coral-shaped rocks are added near the rainforest to match with the coral-shaped island in the distance.

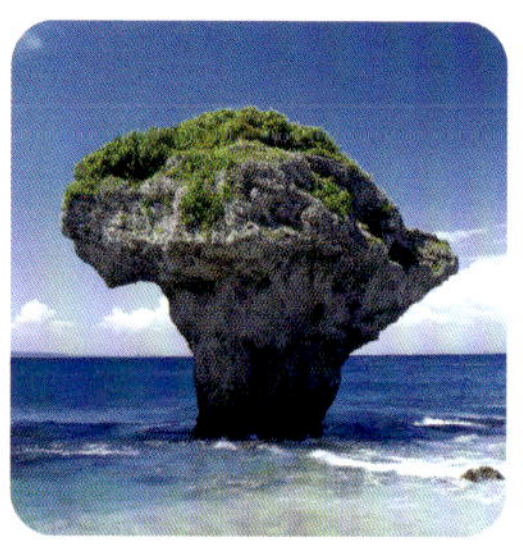

## ◀ CORAL REEF

One colossal coral-shaped coral reef exists in the real world. It is a rock on Liuqiu Island, Taiwan, known as "Vase Rock", named because of its narrow bottom and large top overgrown with plants.

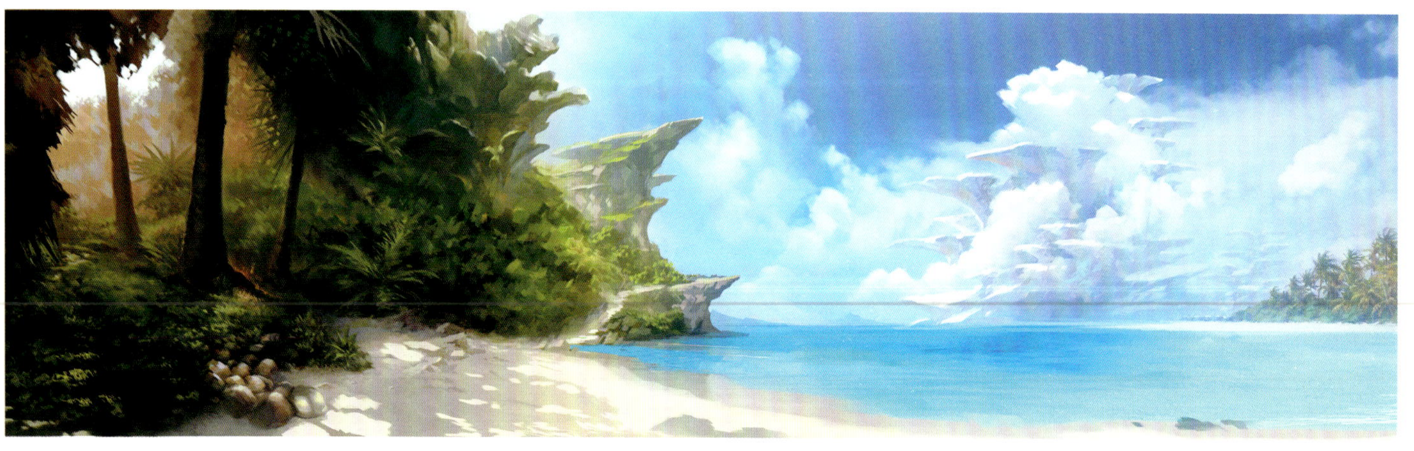

The rainforest in the foreground is refined. The form of the plants and the mountainous structures nearby are purposefully distinct from each other. The colossal coral-shaped island in the distance is improved with reference to relevant materials. The clouds and rainforest are depicted with the same precision as the colossal island.

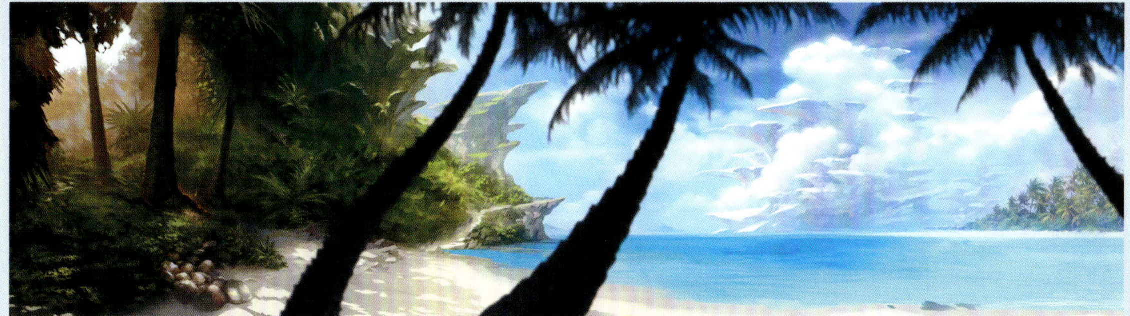

Silhouettes of palm trees are added to the foreground. These palm trees should differ in density and the direction in which they grow to capture the seeming randomness of nature. The original composition should be slightly adjusted to ensure the silhouettes do not block the main objects.

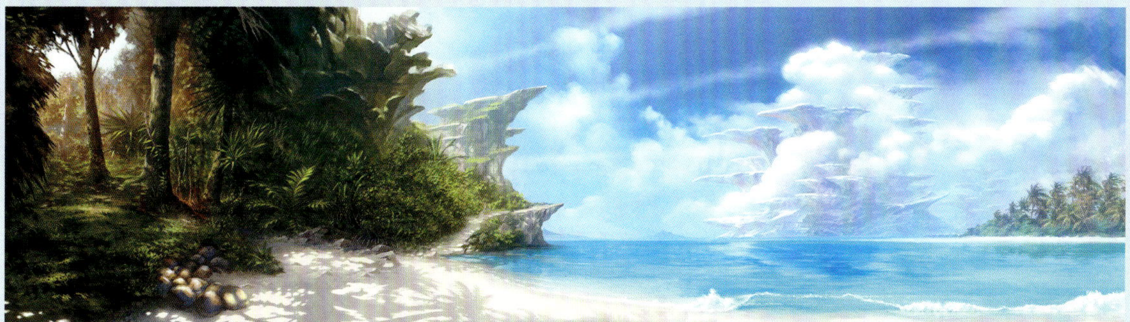

The layer for the silhouettes of the palm trees is closed temporarily, and the elements with a fixed composition are improved. The precision of the "plants", the "beach" and the "distant colossal island" are enhanced. "Shadows from trees" are added to the beach, as well as "sea waves" breaking upon the shore.

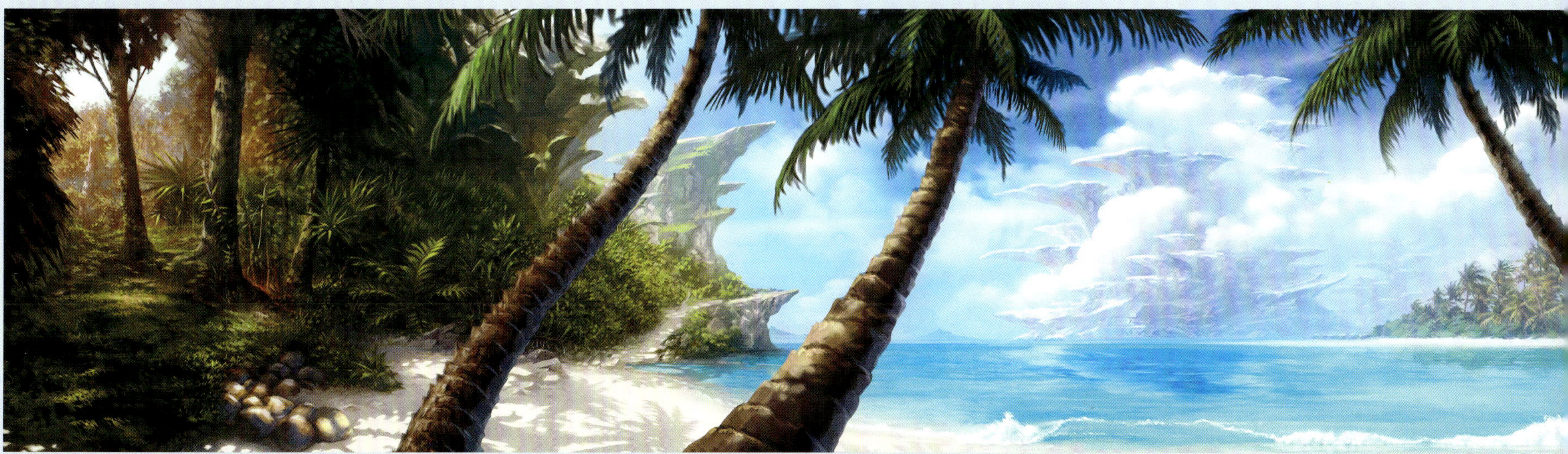

Now that the middle ground and background objects are in place, let's identify an appropriate position for the palm trees according to the shape of their silhouettes and the lighting of the scene.

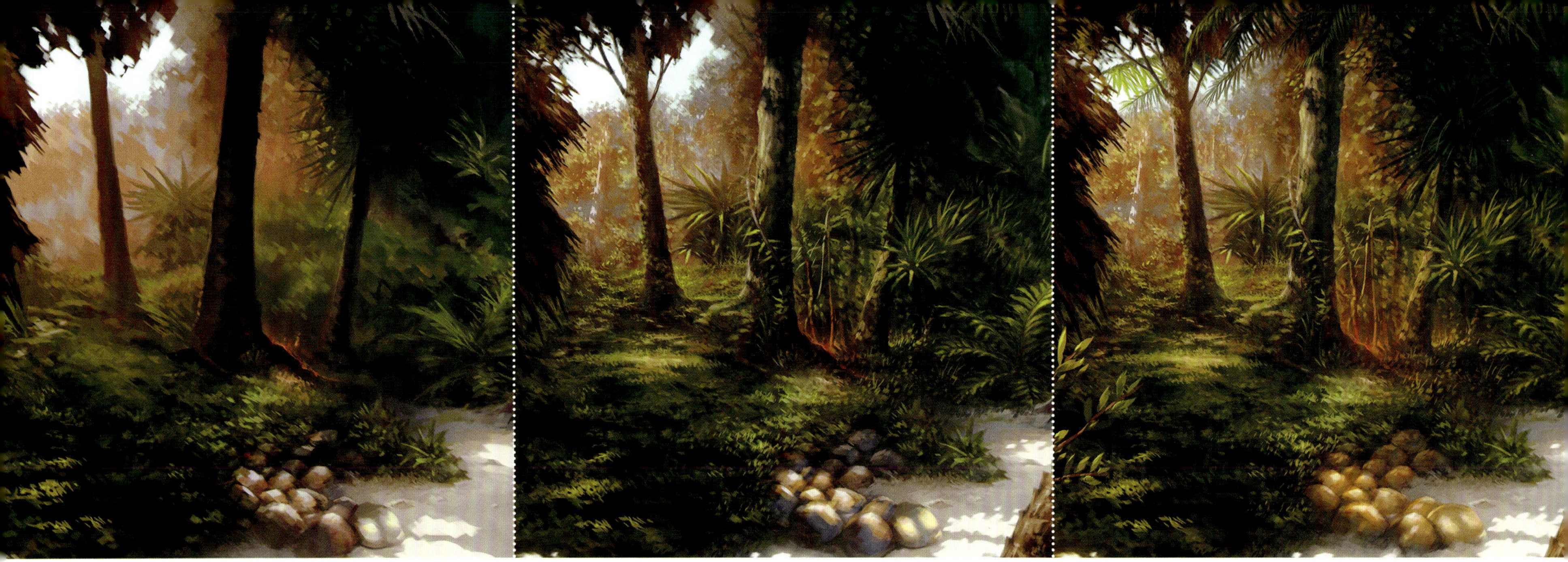

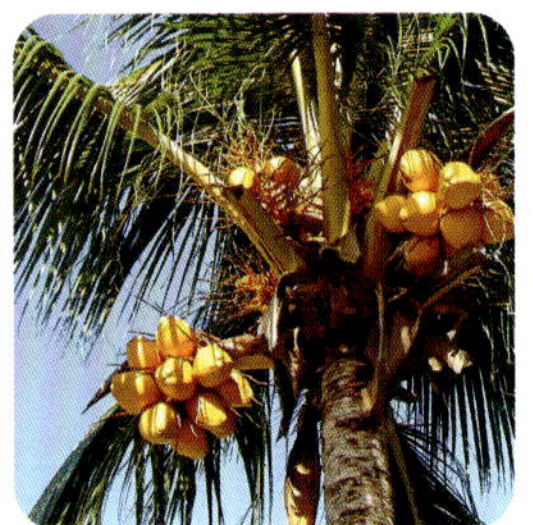

## ◄ PALM TREES

Palm trees usually bear yellow or green fruits at the top of their trunks. The ends of their leaves are usually a withering brown colour. Bringing out these colours makes the whole scene fuller and more expressive.

Depicting the rainforest:

At the current stage, the rainforest takes the shape of a "courtyard" with the sky visible from the upper left of the scene. Organised and intentional decisions about the forest's density ensure the luxuriant rainforest remain bright and well-layered. The light-receiving area is given the colours of "red and purplish grey" to form a stark contrast to the "green" in the shaded areas that receives no light. The rainforests in the distance, middle, and foreground are then refined: the trunks made clearly visible, grass inserted according to the physical features of the land and the sturdy trees interwoven with vines. All these elements pair with the bushes nearby to form the rainforest. Then, "light spots" are added to the ground and the trunks.

As more objects take shape, the colours in different areas are adjusted and smog effects added to bring a stronger structural difference between the objects. In the open area, leaves with 3S effects under backlighting conditions are added to diversify the colour of the scene and mitigate the incompatibility of the sky. Finally, areas of shade and coconuts are added to the beach.

The three foreground palm trees are refined. Bushes and grass are also added to to improve the sense of layering and make the palm trees appear less lonely. Sea waves are adjusted so that they aren't blocked by objects in the foreground. A bright blue is inserted at the foot of the distant colossal island to characterise the scene with a stronger air of the fantasy.

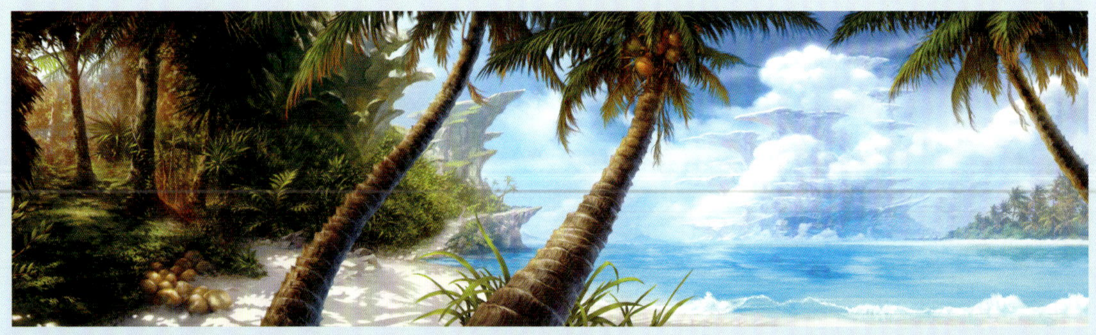

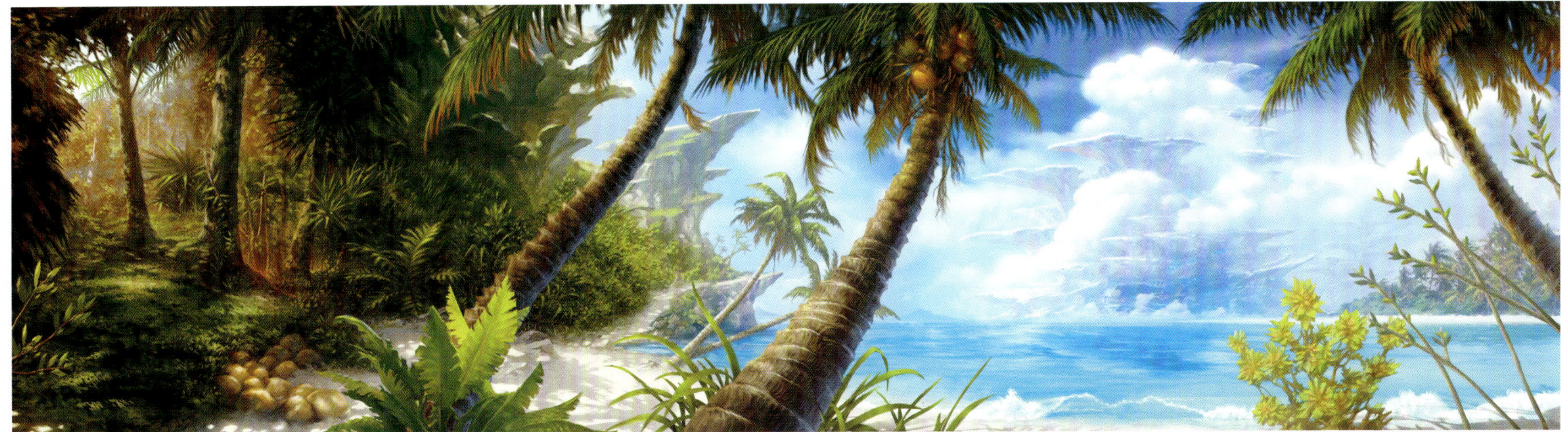

Plants are added to the foreground and palms trees in the distance. The direction in which these plants grow should be based on the existing composition.

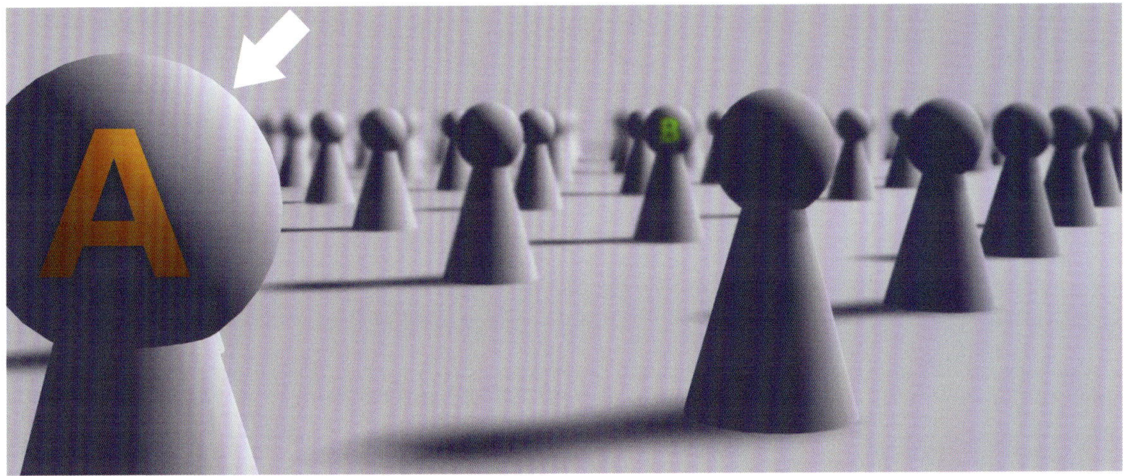


When deciding where to place focus on an image, depth of focus, the distance between the nearest and the furthest objects within the range of a single perspective are important to consider. Take point A and point B as an example: when the focus is on point A in the foreground, point B in the centre plane and other points further away will be blurred, and vice versa. Blurring is a common technique in scene sketching for clearly defining a focus. ("Front depth of focus" is applied to the design of *The Garden* and the *White Mosque* to highlight objects in the middle and in the distance)

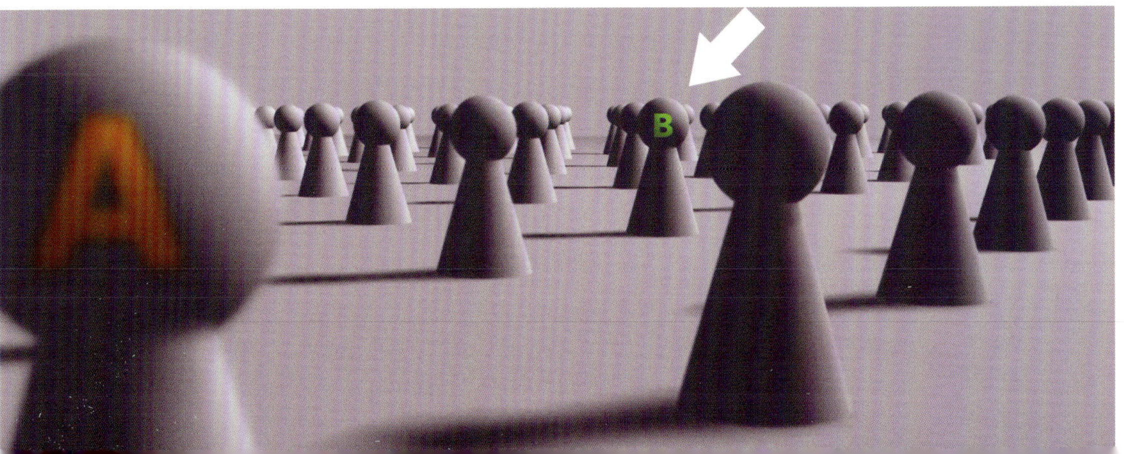

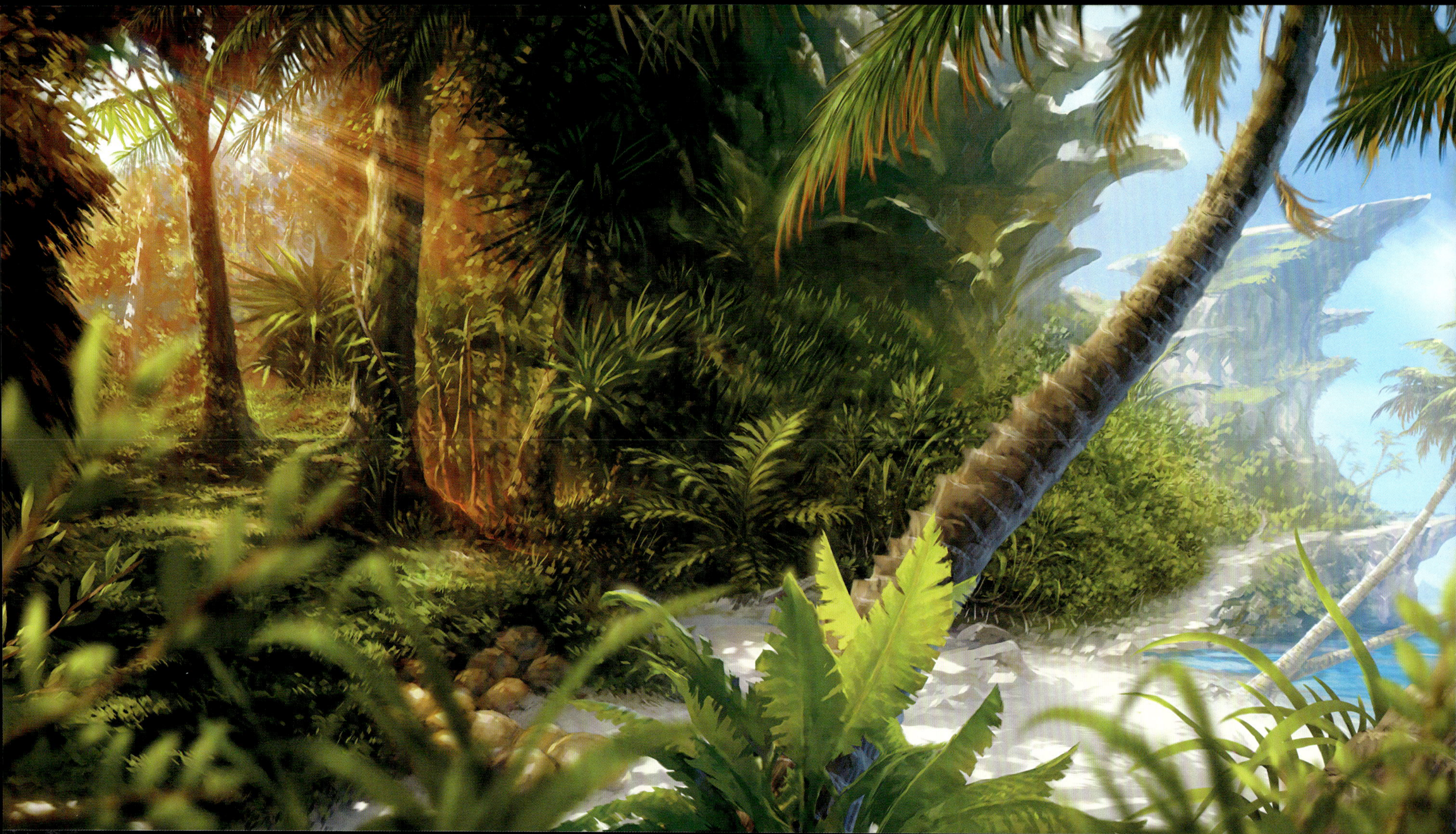

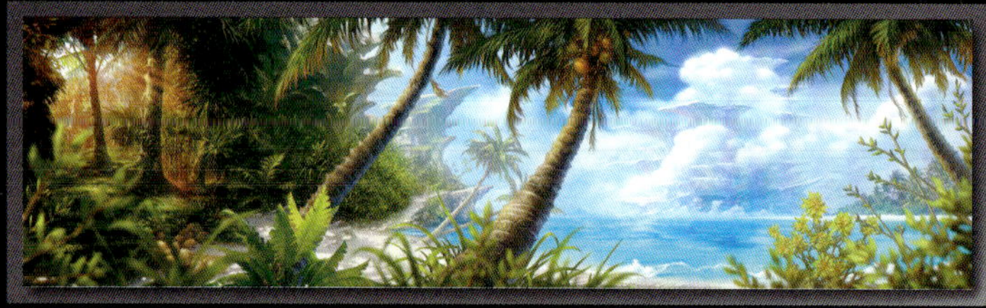

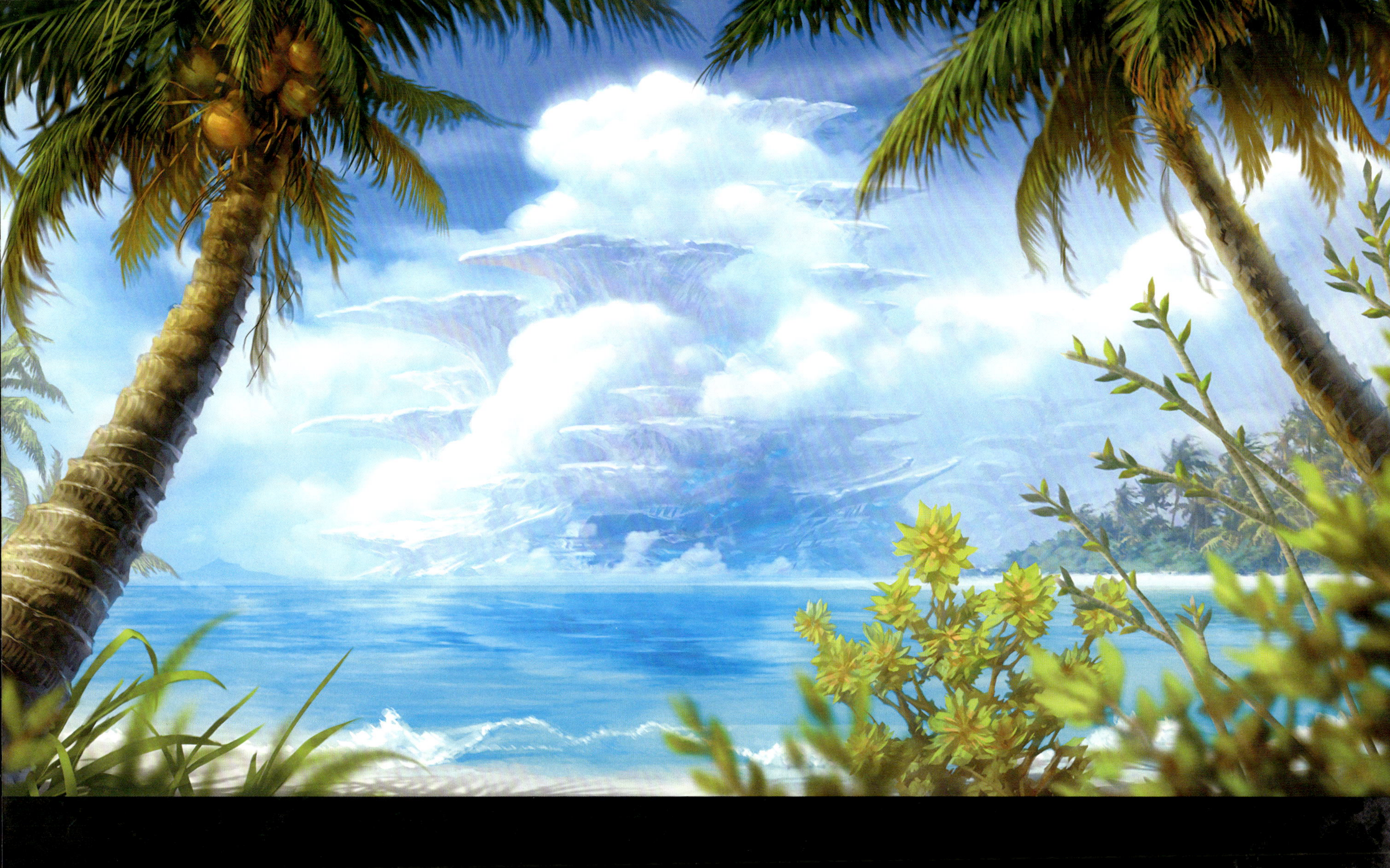

"Front depth of focus" is applied to plants, and the smog effects in the distance are adjusted to improve the sense of layering. "Volume light" is added between leaves; glow effects are added to light-receiving objects in the foreground. The overall atmosphere of the scene is enhanced. Our "fantasy beach" is completed.

As we finish the *Beach*, our journey to the three locations comes to an end. How do you experience this world? From what angle do you see things? How do you express your thoughts or feelings in fantasy? I hope this guide might shed some light in these regards. I also expect to see more excellent artworks from you.

More about the author:

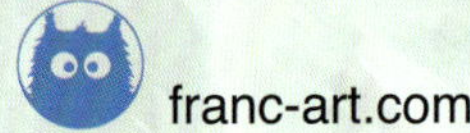
franc-art.com

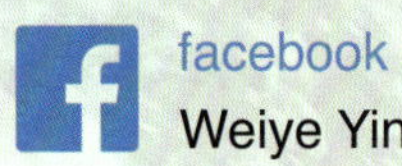
facebook
Weiye Yin

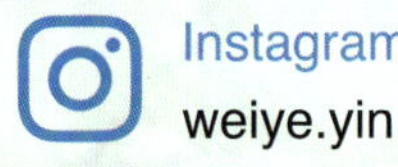
Instagram
weiye.yin

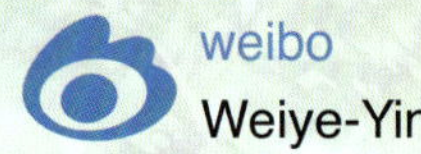
weibo
Weiye-Yin

Acknowledgments:
Zeen Chin, Zhong Mingjuan, Zeng Sheng, Liu Juan

# The World in the Eye of a Fantasy Artist

## — Live from Weiye Yin's Scene Creation

Author: Weiye Yin
Commissioning Editors: Guo Guang, Zeng Sheng
English Editors: Qiu Jinyuan, Si Bin
Translator: Gu Yanping
Copy Editor: Jack Hargreaves
Book Designer: Peng Tao



First published in the United Kingdom in 2019 by CYPI PRESS

Add: Office 102, 85 Tottenham Court Road, London W1T 4TQ
Tel: +44(0)20 7268 3068
E-mail: marketing@cypi.net englisheditor@cypi.net
ISBN: 978-1-913190-28-6

Printed in China